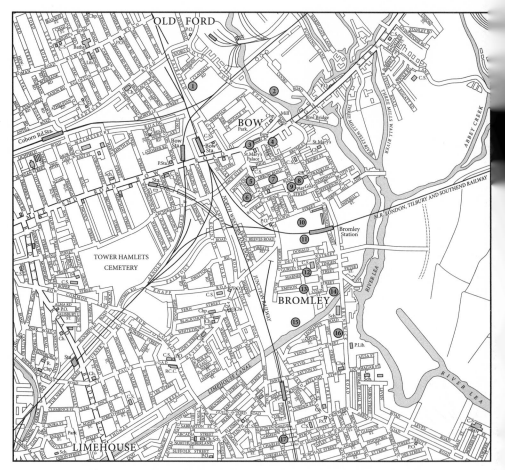

Nellie Dowell and Muriel Lester's East London, c. 1916
Adapted from Kelly's Post Office Directory Map, 1916

① Bryant and May Match Factory, Fairfield Road

② Cook's East London Soap Works

③ Bow Church and Gladstone Statue

④ Factory Girls' Club, Albert Terrace

⑤ Original Kingsley Hall, Botolph and Eagling Road

⑥ Children's House

⑦ Kingsley Rooms, 58–60 Bruce Road

⑧ Bruce Road Congregational Church

⑨ Kingsley Hall, Powis Road

⑩ Stepney Union Workhouse, Bromley, St. Leonard's

⑪ Poplar and Stepney Sick Asylum/Poor Law Infirmary (St. Andrews Hospital)

⑫ Marner Street, school and center of Dowell family life, 1880s to 1900s

⑬ Berger Hall, Regions Beyond Inland Mission and Medical Missionary Center

⑭ R. Bell and Company

⑮ Limehouse Canal (Cut)

⑯ 313 Brunswick Road (Harriet "Granny" Sloan's residence)

⑰ Chrisp Street, Lusitania Riot in Poplar

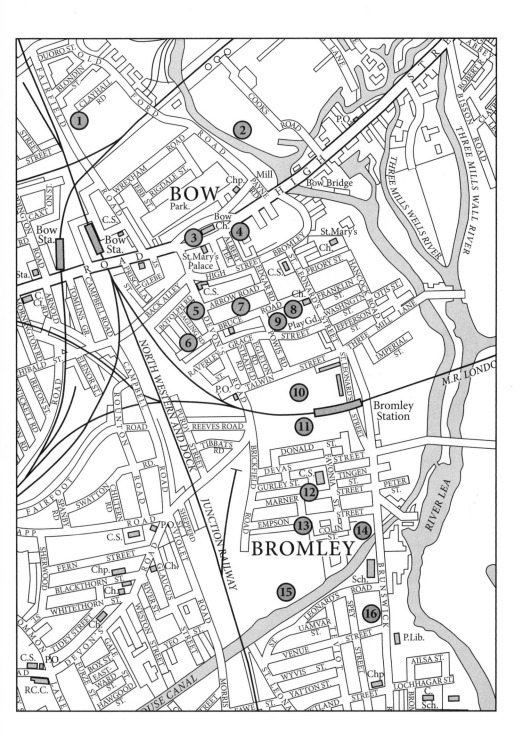

the
Match Girl
and the
Heiress

the
Match Girl
and the
Heiress

Seth Koven

PRINCETON UNIVERSITY PRESS

PRINCETON AND OXFORD

Copyright © 2014 by Princeton University Press
Published by Princeton University Press, 41 William Street, Princeton, New Jersey 08540
In the United Kingdom: Princeton University Press, 6 Oxford Street, Woodstock,
Oxfordshire OX20 1TW

press.princeton.edu

Jacket illustration © Francesco Bongiorni for Marlena Agency. Jacket design by Faceout Studio

Library of Congress Cataloging-in-Publication Data

Koven, Seth, 1958–
    The match girl and the heiress / Seth Koven.
        pages cm
    Includes bibliographical references and index.
    ISBN 978-0-691-15850-1 (hardback)
    1. Dowell, Nellie, 1876–1923. 2. Lester, Muriel, 1883–1968. 3. Women social reformers—
Great Britain—Biography. 4. Feminists—Great Britain—Biography. 5. Great Britain—Social
conditions—20th century. I. Title.
HQ1595.A3K69 2015
305.42092′2–dc23
[B]   2014013276

British Library Cataloging-in-Publication Data is available

This book has been composed in Minion Pro with ITC Benquiat Std display

Printed on acid-free paper. ∞

Printed in the United States of America

1 3 5 7 9 10 8 6 4 2

For Joan, Daniel, Zoe, and Eli—
with love.

Contents

Acknowledgments

THIS BOOK BEARS ONLY my name on its cover and title page. Single authorship is one of the many fictions of the discipline of history. So many have made it possible for me to write this. Endnotes not only point readers to sources, they also begin to tell the story of gladly incurred debts and obligations. That's why I have so many of them.

A year-long fellowship from the National Endowment for the Humanities launched this project and got me into archives. I thank the Department of History at Rutgers University, New Brunswick and the School of Arts and Sciences for generous leave time and research funds. Without this, my scholarship could not happen. Home to a remarkable cohort of scholars in all fields, Rutgers is a bit of heaven for historians of gender, sexuality, women, and culture across time and space. Julie Livingston opened up new possibilities for thinking about the body, pain and medical archives and closely read sections of this book several times. Ann Fabian contributed her artful intellect to honing important arguments. Carla Yanni in Art History has tried her best to teach me how to see and read the built environment and been an invaluable collaborator in institution building through the Rutgers British Studies Center. Many other Rutgers colleagues have contributed insights through conversations they may well not even remember: Indrani Chatterjee, Alice Echols, Kate Flint, Jennifer Jones, Toby Jones, Temma Kaplan, Jennifer Mittelstadt, Barry Qualls, Johanna Schoen, Bonnie Smith, and Judith Surkis. Belinda Davis and Pieter Judson deserve special thanks for homemade delicacies, which sweetened their vigorous critiques of my manuscript as it emerged out of partially formed ideas. I can't imagine a more generous writing group. The brilliant work of Rutgers' graduate students has greatly enriched this book. Some—Allison Miller, Christopher Bischof, Yvette Lane, and Kate Imy among them— also offered cogent critiques of individual chapters.

A research leave at the University of California, Berkeley came at a perfect time as I was writing the first half of this book. Thomas Laqueur has provided years of inspiring friendship and intellectual comradeship. Long ago, he told me that I was writing a history of the ethical subject. At the time, I had no idea what he meant, but his provocation got me going. James Vernon forgave me for asking him to read chapters full of first names and made them better. Other colleagues in Berkeley welcomed me, swapped ideas, and read work: Margaret Anderson, John Connelly, Catherine Gallagher, John Gillis, Carla Hesse, Alan Karras, David Lieberman, Fredric Mintz, Mark Peterson, Ethan Shagan, Jonathan Sheehan, and Yuri Slezkine. Fourteen months as a visiting scholar in residence at the Department of History, University of Pennsylvania provided undisturbed solitude for finishing this book. Lynn Lees, a true model of excellence, made this possible. I kept close at hand her incisive criticisms of the entire manuscript.

Adele Lindenmeyr has been nothing short of a lifesaver. Faster and vastly more intellectually agile than any special delivery service, she read countless drafts and helped bring clarity to my ideas and prose. Paul Steege helped me to think hard about *Alltagsgeschichte*. I presented parts of this project at Johns Hopkins at its inception and much later when it was almost finished. I thank Judith Walkowitz for her astute comments and John Marshall for resisting several key arguments: figuring out why made them stronger. Matt Houlbrook has been part of this from the outset and unstinting in his critical generosity. Sue Morgan and Joy Dixon did their best to guide me through the thickets of Victorian religion, spirituality and theology. Leela Gandhi helped me conceptualize affect and ethics; Martha Vicinus pushed me to sharpen my arguments about female amity and much else while Kali Israel asked good questions about life writing and storytelling. Sally Alexander told me things about what I had written that I could not have seen without her. Sonya Michel brought her unsentimental acumen to bear on several chapters while supporting this work with the great gift of her friendship. For many years, Olivia Dix has made me feel at home in London by opening hers to me.

For conversations about and assistance with this project, I also thank Ross Forman, Anna Davin, Fiona Gibbs, Ellen Ross, Lara Kriegel, Deborah Nord, Helena Michie, Susan Bernstein, Jordanna Bailkin, Charlotte Macdonald, Peter Mandler, Carolyn Steedman, Sybil Oldfield, Susan Pedersen, John Plotz, Diana Maltz, Elizabeth Kolsky, Ramya Sreenivasan, Paula Fass, Graham Mooney, Jane Shaw, Nadia Valman, Emma Francis, and Vivien Dietz. For impeccable transcriptions, I thank Benjamin Dabby. Chris Pond has been a sharp-eyed reader as well as an invaluable intellectual resource about all things related to Loughton, Essex and East London. Chris's labors at the Loughton District Historical Society, like Christopher Lloyd's and the staff of Tower Hamlets Local History Library and Stefan Dickers' at Bishopsgate Institute prove just how crucial deep local knowledge is for producing history. Bishopsgate Institute has been a particularly generous ally in producing images for this book.

Robert Baker opened his Longcot home and gave me access to Mary Hughes' papers. Peter Sander and Biddy Pepin shared Rosa Waugh Hobhouse papers in their respective hands. Niall Hobhouse and Francis Graham put the archival riches of their Hobhouse ancestors at my disposal. I thank archivists, librarians and staff at Tower Hamlets Local History Library, Hackney Archives, Friends House Library (London), the Wellington Municipal Archives, Epping Forest District Museum (Waltham Abbey), Loughton District Historical Society, Bedfordshire and Luton Archives & Records Service, Archives New Zealand, Gonville and Caius (Oxford), Queen Mary, Wellington Library, the National Archives (Kew), the British Library, London Metropolitan Archives, the Peace Collection (Swarthmore College), British Library of Political and Economic Science (LSE), Essex Record Office, Mill Hill School, St. Leonard's School (Scotland), The Modern Record Office (Warwick), Van Pelt Library (University of Pennsylvania), Alexander Library (Rutgers) and its image specialists, and Bancroft Library (UC Berkeley). For help with images, I especially thank Wendy Chmielewski and the staff at Swarthmore's Peace Collection. I owe a particular debt to Tony Lucas at Kingsley Hall, Dagenham for unstinting hospitality; to Alice Mackay and the team of archivists and interviewers who formed the heart and soul of the Heritage Lottery Project to preserve the Lester papers and create a powerful oral history of Kingsley Hall's past.

I benefited immensely from the responses of audiences at many universities and conferences to this work: Kingsley Hall (Dagenham), Rutgers, UC Berkeley, Davidson, Indiana, Columbia, Yale, Princeton, Harvard, Penn State, Johns Hopkins, NYU, Queen Mary (London), Rice, Wisconsin (Madison), Warwick, University of Southern California, Victoria University (Wellington, New Zealand), NAVSA, NACBS, PCCBS,

NECBS, MACBS, and the Delaware Valley British Studies Seminar. Several passages in this book first appeared in my article, "The 'Sticky Sediment' of Daily Life: Radical Domesticity, Revolutionary Christianity and the Problem of Wealth in Britain from the 1880s to the 1930s," *Representations* 120:1 (Fall 2012): 39–82.

It was my great good fortune that Deborah Cohen and Sharon Marcus reviewed the manuscript for Princeton University Press and delivered terrifically smart responses to it. I thank them. Brigitta van Rheinberg is that rare editor who cares deeply about history and knows a lot of it. Her careful reading of each line of the manuscript gave me a critically enthusiastic guide to make it better. What errors of fact and interpretation remain in this book, despite the best efforts of so many, are entirely my own. For editorial assistance, I thank Claudia Acevedo, Christine Retz, Kathleen Cioffi, and Dimitri Karetnikov at Princeton University Press as well as M. Dale Booth, Allison Miller, and especially Rebecca Solnit. My father William Koven and mother-in-law Suzanne Raffel Gruber never tired of hearing and asking questions about Nellie Dowell and Muriel Lester. Their enthusiasm meant the world to me and their deaths taught me that we can become orphans at any age.

This book is dedicated to my family: Joan, who inspires me by making art of daily life, and our wonderful children, Daniel, Zoe, and Eli. Their love makes so much possible.

the
Match Girl
and the
Heiress

Introduction

I CANNOT SAY WITH CERTAINTY how and when they met, but I do know that Muriel Lester and Nellie Dowell loved one another. That they ever met seems improbable, more the stuff of moralizing fiction than history. Muriel was the cherished daughter of a wealthy Baptist shipbuilder, reared in the virtuous abundance of the Lester family's gracious Essex homes.[1] A half-orphaned Cockney toiling in the match industry by age twelve, Nellie spent her earliest years in East London's mean streets and cramped tenements, and her girlhood as a pauper ward of the state confined to Poor Law hospitals and "barrack schools."[2] During the first decades of the twentieth century, they were "loving mates" who shared their fears, cares, and hopes. Their love allowed them to glimpse the possibility of remaking the world according to their own idealistic vision of Christ's teachings. They claimed social rights, not philanthropic doles, for their slum neighbors. They struggled for peace in war-intoxicated communities grieving for brothers, fathers, and husbands lost to the western front. Nellie dreamed of ladies' clean white hands. Muriel yearned to free herself from the burden of wealth. Together, they sought to create a society based on radically egalitarian principles, which knew no divisions based on class, gender, race, or nation.[3] (See fig. I.1.)

I.1. Nellie, her mother Harriet Dowell, and nephew Willie Dellar lived on the first floor of No. 58. Muriel, Doris, and sometimes Kingsley Lester lived at No. 60. By November 1914, they tore down the second floor wall dividing their two homes to create Kingsley Rooms. 58–60 Bruce Road (Photograph taken by author, July 2006.)

This book is about Muriel and Nellie, the worlds of wealth and want into which they were born, the historical forces that brought them together, and the "New Jerusalem" they tried to build in their London slum neighborhood of Bow.[4] Their friendship was one terrain on which they used Christian love to repair their fractured world. The surviving fragments of their relationship disclose an all-but-forgotten project of radical Christian idealism tempered by an acute pragmatism born of the exigencies of slum life. They explored what it meant to be rights-bearing citizens, not subjects, in a democratic polity. Convinced that even the smallest gestures—downcast eyes or a deferential nod of the head—perpetuated the burdened histories of class, race, and gender oppression, Nellie and Muriel believed that they could begin to unmake and remake these formations—and hence the world—through how they lived their own lives.[5] The local and the global, the everyday and the utopian, the private and the public existed in fruitful tension as distinct but connected realms of thought, action, and feeling.

Shadowing Muriel and Nellie are two much-maligned figures of nineteenth-century culture and historical scholarship: Lady Bountiful, who talks sisterhood with the outcast poor in smug tones of condescending sympathy; and the worker-on-the-make, who internalizes capitalist labor discipline, apes her betters, and suffers from an acute case of what Karl Marx called "false consciousness."[6] Just because Muriel vigorously critiqued Lady Bountiful does not exempt her from the charge of (sometimes) resembling her. Nor does it diminish the extent to which some laboring men and women in Bow wanted and expected her to play that part. Likewise, the more deeply that I researched Nellie's life, the clearer it became that I could not cast her as an "organic intellectual"—the term coined by the Italian Marxist Antonio Gramsci in the 1920s to describe workers whose experiences with capitalist exploitation made them into revolutionary critics of it. For the better part of two decades in the match industry, Nellie served her rapacious global capitalist employers on two continents and three countries only too well rather than joining coworkers in the vibrant women's trade union movement. In loving one another and sharing their work in Bow, Nellie and Muriel set out to break—and break free from—these deeply engrained class and gender archetypes that had been so much a part of their upbringing. Their relationship makes it possible to assess just how far it was possible—and impossible—for them to do this. What were the gains from this undertaking? How can we reckon their costs? My answers to these questions foreground the tenacity of Victorian values as well as Nellie and Muriel's recasting of them to serve radical twentieth-century ends.

This book offers an intimate history of very large-scale historical developments and processes—class relations, gender formation, same-sex desire, and ethical subjectivity; war, pacifism, and Christian revolution; shop-floor labor politics and global capitalism; world citizenship and grassroots democracy. It is also a history about intimacy between two women. The "intimate" unlocks the affective economy of their relationship and provides a key to understanding the program they sought to enact.[7] Their story is part of a much broader impulse among thousands of well-to-do women and men in late-nineteenth and early-twentieth-century Europe and the United States to traverse cultural and class boundaries in seeking "friendship" with the outcast. A few like Muriel self-consciously "unclassed" themselves by entering into voluntary poverty to model a society liberated from the constraints and inequalities of class. Nellie could not afford to "unclass" herself. She lived and died a very poor woman. She, like Muriel, crossed borders into a place of their own making, one committed to the unfinished business of reimagining gender, class, and nation by breaking down the hierarchies upholding them.

That place was Kingsley Hall, Britain's first Christian revolutionary "People's House" and the institutional incarnation of Nellie and Muriel's friendship where they tried to translate ideals of fellowship into the stuff of everyday life. Founded in February 1915 in an abandoned hellfire Baptist chapel amid the furies unleashed by the world at war, it was an outpost of pacifism, feminism, and socialism committed to radical social sharing. Muriel and Kingsley Hall's original residents established East London's chapter of the pan-denominational Brethren of the Common Table, whose members satisfied their minimal weekly needs for food, shelter, and clothing and then placed whatever excess remained from their earnings on the Communion table for others to take.[8] They asked no questions and accepted no thanks. A special London correspondent from the United States witnessed the earnest Brethren in conversation at Kingsley Hall. He gleefully reported that the involuntarily poor among them upbraided their well-born friends for excessive self-denial. "It drives me wild to see these people going short of things they want," one widowed mother of four complained. "They ain't used to it. It's going too far."[9] At times comically self-serious, residents of Kingsley Hall decided it was too risky to leave fun to chance: they held temperance "Joy Nights" where men and women could laugh, dance, and socialize.

The Hall also functioned as a vibrant center of community life in East London with its Montessori-inspired nursery school; men's school in civics and Scripture; and restaurant for working women under the auspices of the London Society for Women's Suffrage. Some called it a "settlement house," but Muriel eventually rejected this name, which smacked of missionary uplift incompatible with the Hall's commitment to rights-based democracy. Ardent defenders of human freedom, community members imposed on themselves rules about everything from the proper disposition of toothpaste in washbasins to protocols about gossip. Often mistaken for members of a modern monastery, the residents of Kingsley Hall lived as if each minute detail of their intimately regulated lives resonated through the cosmos. They were so vigilant because the stakes were so high: nothing less than inaugurating a nonviolent Christian revolution in the heart of the world's wealthiest imperial metropolis. They tethered their faith in God's unbounded love to an egalitarian everyday ethics. Muriel declared Kingsley Hall an "overdue act of justice."[10] During the war, jingoistic neighbors suspiciously eyed it as a pacifist refuge for the kaiser's deluded dupes. In the war's immediate aftermath, Marxists (Muriel called them "Communists") belittled their naïve faith that the rich would willingly dispossess themselves of wealth and power.

Kingsley Hall's early history cannot be disentangled from Nellie and Muriel's, but the Hall was never theirs. The language of possession is not quite right. It is at odds with Kingsley Hall's theology and ideology. Residents sought freedom from the tyranny of money and things. Possessions and the desire for them were afflictions of capitalism and its malign handmaiden, imperialism. Many others in the community joined Nellie and Muriel in making Kingsley Hall, foremost among them Muriel's quietly determined younger sister Doris. The two were partners in almost everything they did in East London. Doris was as shy as Muriel

I.2. The two sisters, Muriel Lester (left) and Doris Lester (right), shared their lives and labors as daughters and social workers. The similarity in their modest demeanors, hairstyles, and simple dress belied profound differences between charismatic Muriel and shy but strong-minded Doris. (Left) Muriel Lester, portrait by Paul Swann, 1930. (Courtesy of Bishopsgate Institute.) (Right) Doris Lester, portrait, studio postcard, n.d., Platten Papers, Loughton Library. (Courtesy of Loughton and District Historical Society, Ben Platten Collection.)

was charismatic, but in all sorts of ways she drove their work, especially among children. She moves in and out of Muriel and Nellie's story. (See fig. I.2.)

By the time Muriel Lester died in 1968 in a modest roughcast Loughton cottage, she had become a grande dame of global pacifism and social justice Christianity. Revered and reviled in her lifetime, she hosted her friend Mohandas Gandhi at Kingsley Hall for several months during the 1931 Round Table Conference and marched with him in earthquake-shattered Bihar a few years later. One of the best-known faces of the world-wide peace movement, she circled and recircled the globe as ambassador-at-large for the Fellowship of Reconciliation, the pacifist organization that she and Doris first joined in 1915. She witnessed and exposed the traffic in drugs in Japanese-occupied Manchuria. She rejected war even in the face of Nazi atrocities. She befriended leaders of the United States' civil rights movement, including Bayard Rustin. Along the way, she also inspired an impressive sheaf of scathing confidential reports in the secret files of MI5, MI12, and the India Office chronicling her dangerous anticolonial and antiwar activities.[11] With more than a touch of resentment, at least one relative still remembers her and Doris as the "mad aunts" whose poverty cost the Lester family too much of its fortune.[12] The truly devout in Britain can pilgrimage to Kingsley Hall's branch in Dagenham to see one of her well-preserved modishly simple capes, her signature outerwear. In North America, they can visit the sole surviving Muriel Lester House in the United States: a vegetarian residential cooperative at the University of Michigan in Ann Arbor. All this happened after Nellie's death in January 1923; but it is essential to understanding their history as well as the circumstances that have made it possible to reconstruct their story.

The renown that Muriel courted and accumulated from the 1920s to the 1960s enabled the Kingsley Hall in Bow along with its satellite branch in far eastern Dagenham to survive into the twenty-first century. (It did not hurt that Sir Richard Attenborough made the restoration of Kingsley Hall Bow, so badly treated during R. D. Laing's occupancy of it in the mid-1960s with his community of schizophrenics, part of the filming of *Gandhi*.) It also ensured the preservation of the Lester papers, including Muriel's typescript biographical fragments about Nellie, "From Birth to Death," and Nellie's letters to Muriel. I went to Dagenham looking for Muriel Lester, the once-famous, now-mostly-forgotten Christian revolutionary saint. I found Nellie Dowell.

My first day at Kingsley Hall Dagenham, I read Nellie's witty warm letters to Muriel. I was instantly struck by her humor and intellect as well as her evident discomfort with letter writing and the conventions of Standard English.[13] Full of mundane chat, her longing for Muriel, and events so inconsequential that she probably forgot them the next day, Nellie's letters invite listening to her talk as much as reading what she wrote. They retain the rhythms and freshness of speech as thoughts take flight without regard to formal punctuation. Nellie's letters baffled, delighted, and intrigued me.[14] (See fig. I.3.) Who was Nellie? Why did she write these letters, what did they signify, and why did Muriel save them?

I.3. Nellie wrote this letter to Muriel on Valentine's Day 1912—a token of their loving friendship. Nellie Dowell to Muriel Lester, February 14, 1912, Dowell Letters. (Courtesy of Bishopsgate Institute.)

My training as a social historian brought me to the London Family History Centre of the National Archives with its helpful staff and wonderfully accessible records of births, deaths, marriages, and much else. I had no idea when Nellie died and only a broad range of possible dates for her birth. Her epistolary relationship with Muriel suggested, at least upon initial readings, that Muriel was not only her better but her elder. She must have been born after 1883, I assumed. As I eventually discovered, Nellie had many names and several different dates of birth at various times when she entered institutions and official archives. She was Nellie, Nell, Nella, Ellen, and Eleanor. Nellie can be a nickname for several other first names as well. My initial guesses were all bad ones. By the random accidents that make history and are part of writing history, Kingsley Hall had retained no copies of its own Eighth Annual Report that included Muriel's essay commemorating Nellie's life and death, "The Salt of the Earth." That would have made the task much easier since

Muriel gave the precise date of Nellie's death: January 31, 1923. In any case, I began to believe that I might do something substantial about Muriel and Nellie only when the Bow registrar's office handed me a copy of her death certificate. It told me that Eleanor Dowell was forty-seven and died of mitral valvular disease in 1923 at 58 Bruce Road.

My archival quest and so much of the story that I will tell began with these simple facts. These clues eventually led to census data and to scattered evidence of her movements through London Board schools, Poor Law institutions, public asylums and voluntary hospitals as well as ships' logs to and from New Zealand. Nellie, I came to learn, had a remarkable global life as a proletarian match factory worker and Cockney cosmopolitan *before* she met Muriel. When her father died at sea in 1881, poverty compelled her devoted mother Harriet Dowell—who outlived Nellie by several years—to give her up to Poor Law officials. They classified her as a Poor Law half-orphan and sent her to late-Victorian Britain's most controversial Poor Law school and orphanage, Forest Gate School. Nellie entered the match industry in the year of the world-famous "Match Girls' Strike" of 1888. Labor conflicts dogged her everywhere she went. Her arrival in Wellington in June 1900 was fiercely debated in the New Zealand Parliament and sparked a political crisis for the Liberal ministry. Her labor assignment to Sweden around 1907 was outwardly peaceful, but a time of inward ferment. She began to question truths about God and nation that she had long taken for granted. In the winter of 1909–10, an attack of rheumatic fever abruptly ended her ability to withstand factory labor; it also freed her to devote her time and love to Muriel and their joint ventures in East London. Nellie and her mother Harriett joined Doris and Muriel at the modest row houses 58–60 Bruce Road that served as their headquarters and home.[15]

No sources make it possible to reconstruct how Muriel and Nellie's contemporaries perceived their partnership, besides Nellie's allusion to friendly gossip about them in a single letter. However, depictions of philanthropic ladies and the objects of their benevolence abound in Victorian culture. Scholars have written copiously and critically about what Dickens's indomitable Mrs. Jellyby and her many flesh-and-blood counterparts saw when they looked through their philanthropic telescopes to inspect the "dirtiest little unfortunates" in Britain and its empire.[16] Many others have reconstructed how such unfortunates—so-called objects of private benevolence and public welfare—responded to and resisted the disciplinary imperatives of philanthropists and state bureaucrats to become "heroes of their own lives."[17] It has proved much more elusive to reconstruct and analyze cross-class benevolence and social welfare *in* and *as* a dynamic negotiated relationship between individuals. Nellie's letters offer the possibility of doing that by handing Mrs. Jellyby's telescope to her to find out what Muriel, Kingsley Hall, Bow and public-private welfare looked like through her eyes.

By putting Muriel's and Nellie's stories back together, I reconstruct their Christian revolutionary project as part of their evolving relationship within the broader context of Britain in war and peace during the first three decades of the twentieth century.[18] This book joins unglamorous methods of social history research (turning thousands of pages of different hospital admissions registers in the hope that perhaps Nellie had once been admitted there) with cultural and literary-textual analysis.[19] I combine insights from feminist and queer theory with those of scholars of everyday life and historical geographers' contributions to the interplay between place, space, and self.[20] I track Muriel and Nellie's global itineraries while paying close attention to their day-to-day lives.[21] By approaching large-scale developments as refracted through their relationship, I sustain my focus on class, gender, sexual, and social subjectivity, which can easily fall by the wayside in the exciting new global approaches to modern British history.

I also have written this book because Muriel and Nellie's friendship—its tensions and tenderness, their failures and foibles—moved me. Courage is not a category much used by historians, but it was something that Nellie and Muriel abundantly needed and possessed as they faced the daunting task of changing themselves and their world. Plutarch, the Greco-Roman author of *Parallel Lives*, eloquently distinguished "lives" from "histories" as he grappled with a way to harmonize the Greek past with the demands of the first-century Roman Empire. Lives, he insisted, illuminate moral virtues and vices. They function as didactic mirrors into which we, his readers, gaze as we shape who we are and hope to become. Histories, by contrast, explain what happened in the past as well as how and why it did. Lives capture often entirely private choices indicative of character. Histories revolve around great battles and public matters of governance. I've written this book with the intention of dissolving the boundary between "lives" and "histories." Like Plutarch, I have paired lives. My story, however, is about intersecting, not parallel, lives. Nellie and Muriel were mirrors for one another: each came to understand herself better as they labored with and loved the other. Muriel, in particular, insisted that private choices about apparently trivial matters of quotidian conduct—the stuff of Plutarch's *Lives*—were inextricably entwined with large historical structures. In other words, she rejected the distinction between a private ethical domain and a public political one. Lives made history; history made lives.

Methodologically, this book borrows from both micro- and macrohistories while challenging the distinctions between them.[22] It sometimes mobilizes the slightest shard of evidence such as Nellie's documented arrival in Wellington, New Zealand to move from the very small—her work filling matchboxes for R. Bell and Company—to the very big—British global capitalism and imperial trade policies at the turn of the century. It uses the tools and techniques of biography in reconstituting Nellie and Muriel's lives, apart and together. Its central questions and problems, however, are historical. Shelves groan from the weight of books about women like Muriel Lester—wealthy, well educated, ethically alert, committed to social and political service to humanity.[23] We have none about very poor women like Nellie who spent years in Poor Law institutions and harsh factory settings.[24] *The Match Girl and the Heiress* argues that Nellie and Muriel's historical importance consists both in their achievements as individuals and in what they did—and tried to do—as partners.

Overdetermined serendipity has shaped this book. It explains the utter improbability that Muriel and Nellie would meet *and* the deep structures that made it quite normal for young, well-to-do Nonconformist ladies to befriend factory girls at the turn of the twentieth century. It also captures the predictable frisson of archival discovery that fueled my research: how and why I found traces of Nellie in the records of Marner Street and Forest Gate schools, the Poplar and Stepney Poor Law Infirmary, the Whitechapel Poor Law lunatic ward, London Hospital, and the passenger lists of the *Waiwera* that carried her to Wellington and the *Papanui*, which took her back to London three years later. Working from addresses in the Dowell family census data, I made informed guesses about the educational, medical, and social welfare institutions and agencies to which the Dowell family likely resorted in times of dire need. State policy makers and bureaucrats mapped my path of archival discovery more than a century ago. My job was to think like one of them. This task was made easier by the stability of the British state at all levels—from central government to vestries—and its penchant for keeping close tabs on the poorest of the poor, documenting and preserving each of their encounters. Finding Nellie in the archives felt like the hand of providence, but it was more likely the invisible hand of bureaucratic logic and my own perseverance. Seek and ye shall find.

Nellie's and Muriel's relationship was reciprocal, unequal, and asymmetrical. Muriel had access to wealth, substantial social and cultural capital, and a first-rate education at one of Britain's leading "public schools" for the intellectually agile daughters of the well-to-do. Like every other woman in turn-of-the-century Britain, she suffered the legal disabilities of her sex. She did, however, enjoy a great deal of personal freedom and power. Nellie was poor, perceived as a social problem (first as a Poor Law "orphan" then as a "match girl" and "pauper lunatic") and endured an education that even school officials confessed favored discipline and rote memorization over critical thought and creativity. Like Muriel, she benefitted from a loving and supportive family network to which she was devoted and which proved to be a tremendous asset to both of them in their community-centered work. It was extreme poverty, not a lack of family love that made Nellie Dowell a half-orphan ward of the state in the eyes of Poor Law officials.

As best as I can tell, Muriel and Nellie's love was also reciprocal and asymmetrical. Muriel adored and admired Nellie. She depended heavily upon Nellie's knowledge, wit, tact, and diplomacy in building the networks of human relationships upon which their Christian revolutionary project was founded. Nellie looked to Muriel to guide her political and intellectual development as they studied Tolstoy and other Christian revolutionary texts together. Her letters suggest that she also received material assistance from Muriel, though the precise form and quantity I cannot say. Nellie also longed for a deeper and more exclusive intimacy than Muriel would—and could—give her or anyone else. Love may have animated their vision of radical egalitarianism and Christian revolution, but it forced each of them, in quite different ways, to confront her own emotional and intellectual limits. Love, like the Christian revolution of which it was a part, proved both exhilarating and challenging.

My sources accentuate these asymmetries. Fleeting traces of Nellie's life history are scattered in the archives of Poor Law institutions and other "public" records. For some periods of her life, my account is necessarily speculative. By contrast, Muriel has left behind copious records. She mastered the art of telling her life story in print and in the endless rounds of speeches that she delivered throughout the world from the 1920s to the early '60s. It was part and parcel of the appeal that she made on behalf of the many causes she championed. She published two full-scale autobiographies and drafted several others; she preserved many of her diaries along with the weekly letters she wrote from India—and elsewhere—that she circulated among her friends and followers.[25] We even have a 1931 Pathé film clip that captures her elegant vigorous body movements and precise upper-class diction as she takes viewers on a tour of Kingsley Hall in anticipation of Gandhi's residence there.[26]

As an extension of her religious commitment to truth telling and transparency, Muriel strove to efface the boundary separating her public from her private self. Reflecting on her own shortcomings was part of her daily routine, which in turn provided fodder for her writings and speeches. Pulling back the mask of her public persona—revealing her flaws—was essential to the way she presented herself to the public and to herself. Muriel used candor to acknowledge and disarm her critics. A disgusted agent sent by the United States government to report on one of her Chicago antiwar speeches in December 1939 commented that Muriel had so completely internalized the performance of her own saintliness that even when she thought that she was unobserved, she maintained the same maddening, serene, beatific smile.[27] She could be insensitively self-denying to the point of making others feel uncomfortable about their failure to match her virtue. Nellie's letters and those of other poor Bow friends hint at this by accentuating their sense of unworthiness in comparison to her. Ruth Harris (Comfort), the ill-used wife of the sex guru and a Loughton friend of the Lesters, remembered the day that Muriel came to Folkestone, where she attended boarding school, to take her out to lunch. It was "a great honour and event" marred slightly by the fact that only after she ordered a three-course lunch did Muriel inform her young guest that it was her fast day: "my pleasure will be to see you enjoy [your meal]."[28]

Such stories echo Virginia Woolf's scathing portrait of Miss Kilman in *Mrs. Dalloway* (1925), who starved herself for blockaded Austria's starving millions; lived in a slum and wore the same ugly green mackintosh each day; and reminded everyone about "how poor she was; how rich you were." "She was never in the room five minutes," Clarissa Dalloway mused, "without making you feel her superiority, your inferiority." At the same time, Woolf's belittling, angry dependence on her own Nellie, the housemaid Nellie Boxall, offers a stunning rebuke to Woolf's claims to sisterhood across the class divide. Woolf viciously confided to her diary that Nellie Boxall exists "in a state of nature; untrained; uneducated, to me almost incredibly without the power of analysis or logic; so that one sees a human mind wriggling undressed."[29] I linger over Woolf's relationship with Nellie Boxall because it is an almost too-perfect foil to Muriel and Nellie's partnership. The comparison throws into relief what made Nellie and Muriel's tender reciprocal relationship so extraordinary then and so important now. We know a very great deal about Bloomsbury's loquacious rebellion against Victorianism and far too little about the political, religious, cultural, and gender work of the radical Christian Left.[30]

Because sources by and about Muriel are so superabundant, it is possible to reconstruct where she was and what she thought and did for most of her adult life. The challenge in writing about Muriel is to avoid becoming her authorized biographer, to resist ventriloquizing her self-critical autobiographical prose. By contrast, there are very few sources by and directly about Nellie. Proletarian spinsters don't have literary executors; their family members rarely enjoy material circumstances that would enable them to save letters and papers. If Nellie's papers do exist, I have not found them. The most important sources about her survived *because* Muriel preserved them. Nellie and her letters mattered to Muriel. She made no secret of how much she loved, admired, and depended on Nellie, with her "broad commonsense outlook on life," "staggering generosity" and "genius" for solving problems.[31] In a collection full of missives from major and minor figures in modern history—heads of state, activists and reformers, Nobel laureates—Muriel herself put Nellie's eleven letters in a manila envelope. In the distinctive unsteady hand of her old age, she wrote "Nell" on it. No other documents in her papers bore such indisputable marks of Muriel's self-archiving, at least when I first touched and read her papers. Above and below Muriel's hand is that of another person, possibly Muriel's first biographer, Jill Wallis. She organized the Lester papers into what we call an "archive" by sorting them into folders and numbered boxes. To her, I remain profoundly indebted although she barely mentions Nellie.

After Nellie's death, Muriel coped with the great grief of losing her by writing several biographical essays about her. They provide a basic outline of Nellie's life, without any dates and with almost no names of places, institutions, or people. I have often needed to remind myself to thank Muriel for the clues that she gave me rather than grumble about her many omissions and factual errors. She must have gotten most of her information and misinformation about Nellie from Nellie and her mother Harriet. They function almost as coauthors of these life narratives, which sometimes purport to quote them directly. Muriel celebrated Nellie's life in a two-and-one-half-page printed obituary, "The Salt of the Earth."[32] She drafted but never published a much longer and more detailed biographical narrative about Nellie, "From Birth to Death," which survives in two typescripts of twenty-six and twenty double-spaced typed pages—the first of which Muriel edited extensively. Muriel systematically crossed out the name Dowell each place it appeared in the first draft and wrote the name Short above it—the only name that she used in the second draft.[33] (See fig. I.4.) Presumably, Muriel had considered publishing the story as a socio-fiction (she drafted dozens of such stories drawn from life) while using the name Short to prevent most readers from identifying the Dowells. Contrary to its title, these typescripts are fragments. Both end in midsentence, long before Nellie's death. Neither includes anything about Muriel's life with Nellie or Kingsley Hall. Not a single word. On the basis of Nellie's London Hospital records, I now know that these drafts take Nellie's story up to 1910, the very year of Nellie's earliest surviving letter. Muriel is an emotionally generous narrator of "The Salt of the Earth" and figures in her story about Nellie. By contrast, "From Birth to Death" is mostly narrated through Harriet Dowell's loving maternal eyes. Muriel as author and friend strove to make herself invisible.

I.4. Probably written soon after Nellie's death in January 1923, this oldest surviving draft of "From Birth to Death" shows Muriel's editorial decision to change the name Dowell to Short to preserve's Nellie's semi-anonymity. Muriel never published this story. First typescript page of "From Birth to Death." (Courtesy of Bishopsgate Institute.)

There is a vast amount that I will never know about Nellie and much that must remain speculative. I have often thought of the challenges faced by Thomas Carlyle's fictional narrator of the life of Prof. Diogenes Teufelsdröckh as he followed his world-wandering subject. The "river of his History," traced from "its tiniest fountains" dashes itself over "Lover's Leap" and "flies wholly into tumultuous clouds of spray" before it once again, distantly, collects into a stream. Nellie's history likewise simply disappears for years at a time; she, like the learned protagonist of *Sartor Resartus* (a book that Muriel read at the turn of the century), moved between "the highest and lowest levels," and, in surprising ways, came into "contact with public History itself."[34] We can be certain that Carlyle, consummate chronicler of epoch defining men, would not have viewed her or Muriel as fit subjects of history. The loss, I hope to demonstrate, would have been entirely his.

The Match Girl and the Heiress both draws upon and reorients understanding of several key categories and grand narratives in the making of modern Britain. Scholars have long sought to explain the emergence of collectivist politics and state-directed social welfare in the land of laissez-faire liberal individualism. They have fruitfully debated whether the welfare state arose as an ad hoc response to the pressing demands of circumstances or as an enactment of ideological-philosophical principles. They have "brought the state back in" by emphasizing its internal mechanisms and the workings of civil servants; they have charted the emergence of new forms of expertise about the management and welfare of society like publicly funded school meals. Still others look to society and the impact of social movements, feminist arguments, and working-class political mobilization in demanding an expansion of welfare rights within the framework of shifting conceptions of citizenship.[35] Some, including me, have emphasized the porous boundaries between middle-class women's private voluntary initiatives and the rise of municipal and state maternal and child welfare policies and programs.[36]

This book, like Nellie's life, unfolds within, around, and in the shadow of the New Poor Law (1834), the landmark legislation that shaped public provision of welfare to the poor until 1929.[37] Muriel joined the pre–World War I crusade to abolish the Poor Law altogether and narrated Nellie's life through the prism of her disgust at its inhumanity. Nellie grew up in the Poor Law school and orphanage at Forest Gate that became the flashpoint for acrimonious national debates about the state's obligations to its most vulnerable subjects. She and Muriel lived in the district of East London, Bow and Poplar, that incited metropolitan, national, and international debates in 1921 when its borough councillors defied the state and were jailed for bringing concepts of redistributive justice and economics to bear on welfare and citizenship. As a Poplar Council member heading the borough's Maternity and Child Welfare Committee from 1922 to 1926, Muriel herself played a part in these celebrated controversies. The social, cultural, and political ecology of their slum neighborhood was, I show, an important incubator for their work and social politics. This study looks at the mixed economy of public and private welfare provision for the poor through Nellie's eyes and Muriel's.[38] It analyzes how Poor Law institutions including schools, orphanages, and medical infirmaries shaped not only Nellie's life but constructions of family, childhood, motherhood, work, illness, and the body. Stories like Muriel and Nellie's remind us about the affective, intellectual, political, and cultural work involved in dismantling the apparatus of Victorian benevolence and creating new understandings of rights-based welfare in the twentieth century.

Nellie's participation in the match industry in England, New Zealand, and Sweden elucidates a critical moment in the history of British global capitalism from the vantage point of one of its most essential, easily replaced, and least powerful participants: an unmarried proletarian female worker. Her transnational laboring life played out against a backdrop of massive challenges to British capitalists' economic hegemony from within—by struggles between Labour and capital—and without—by competition with other nations like the United States as well as anti-colonial nationalist movements from Ireland to India.

Histories of capitalism from below invariably emphasize resistance to it and the mobilization of workers through trade unions, socialist, and labor parties. Nellie's history does not. She put job security before worker solidarity. In this respect, she resembled the vast majority of women workers in late-nineteenth- and early-twentieth-century Britain, who were neither trade unionists nor members of labor and socialist political parties. About such women, we know far too little.[39] They are often lumped together into a vast inert body of metropolitan toilers whose supposed passivity Frederick Engels lamented; in Gareth Stedman Jones's influential formulation, such apolitical men and women bartered away class-conscious politics for cultural autonomy from bourgeois meddling.[40] Nor do they have a place in feminist socialist historiography other than as recalcitrant obstacles in the path of gender and economic justice. By *not* resisting capitalist factory disciplines, workers like Nellie are presumed to be the ones who got it wrong; they short-circuit the implicit ethical imperative to root for those who fight against structures of domination. Nellie's history makes it possible to begin to sketch the economic, emotional, and familial logic of such choices and her own. Her laboring life also invites an approach to business history—in this case, the match industry—attentive to family dynamics, class, gender, and cultural analysis.

This book joins efforts by historians to reclaim pre–World War II Britain for Christianity, a salutary historiographical Reconquista. Building on an earlier generation that demonstrated the blurred lines between secular and religious associational activities of local churches in the decades before World War I, scholars have demonstrated that statistical measures such as declining attendance at church and chapel did not herald the "death of Christian Britain." In early-twentieth-century Britain, religion was no mere vestige awaiting respectable burial in history's dustbin.[41] Muriel and Nellie's history underscores the enduring power of religious faith as a resource for those seeking an inclusive vision of social and economic justice in Britain and the world. It has led me to uncover a powerful stream of "practical" or "lived" theology within modern British Protestantism that I call "God is Love" theology. Muriel eclectically drew upon emerging conceptions of "spirituality" and "world religions" as she sought to live as an ethical subject. The Sermon on the Mount provided the scriptural foundations for Muriel and Nellie's vision and practice of Christian revolution. The history of their grassroots labors in East London pushes against the amnesia that clouds just how much Christianity once animated and inspired Left politics in Britain.

I first began to research this book at the peak of President George W. Bush's lavish funding of "faith-based" initiatives at the heart of his "compassionate conservatism" in the opening years of the twenty-first century. For readers in the United States, I hope that this history of Muriel and Nellie's "faith-based" initiatives a century ago suggests the potential for deep religious faith to animate a radical critique and redistribution of power and authority between rich and poor, men and women, white and black, colonizer and colonized.

Influential interpretations of post–World War I Britain emphasize its "conservative modernity," a prevailing mood of escapist despair and decline, and escalating violence against a host of "others," real and imagined.[42] *The Match Girl and the Heiress*, by contrast, highlights an optimistic ethical and religious strand of British political culture in the first half of the twentieth century marked by hospitality to all forms of difference, democratic but authoritarian anti-consumerism, and a commitment to living locally as "world citizens." An immense cottage industry has dissected Bloomsbury's every noisy rebellious gesture in the first decades of the twentieth century. This book tells a much quieter but more politically exigent story about the relationship between High Victorian Christian moral paternalism and twentieth-century rights-based social justice ethics and politics. Like the lifespans of the book's two central figures, Nellie and Muriel, this study bridges the putative divide between Victorians and moderns in showing both surprising continuities and shifts in sensibilities and attitudes from the 1870s to 1920s. "Truth," "reconciliation," and "restitution" were essential to the language and practice of Christian revolution. Nellie's and Muriel's work as peacemakers in wartime Bow prefigured many of the technologies of conflict resolution championed by contemporary human rights activists and global humanitarians. As such, my analysis contributes to an understanding of the early-twentieth-century roots of these developments.

Finally, this study explores the power of love to transform individuals and the world in early-twentieth-century Britain. Love figures centrally in every chapter of this book. Nellie and Muriel's lives, apart and together, demonstrate the capaciousness, variety, and historical specificity of love. Muriel and Nellie's love for one another changed and enriched each of them. Love was the motor of their relationship and their unfinished Christian revolution. I show that it also paradoxically limited and constrained them and their community-based work. Christian revolution was predicated upon effacing the many ways in which differences between people—class, gender, religious, racial—produced oppressive hierarchies. But in all sorts of ways, Muriel and Nellie's love confounded the erasure of difference by insistently demanding and reproducing difference between them. In some chapters love is an indispensable ideological and religious category informing their theology and thinking. Learning to "love thy enemy," Muriel and Nellie believed, was the way to enact Christian revolution in everyday life. In other chapters, I tease out the implications of love for historical understandings of female friendship, same-sex desire, and cross-class eroticism in the early twentieth century. This book, I hope, demonstrates the analytical gains of keeping together the history of affect and politics, feeling and thinking, loving and doing.

Muriel and Nellie's partnership and the institution they nurtured, Kingsley Hall, must be counted among the innumerable early-twentieth-century "small utopias" spawned by European-wide dissatisfaction with the excesses and failures of fin-de-siècle liberalism and the cataclysm of global war.[43] Theirs was a utopian enterprise deeply rooted in the gritty materiality of slum life, not some Arcadian flight into an ideal world of their own making. Utopias, the Austrian-born German sociologist Karl Mannheim famously argued in 1929, are always in dialectical tension with the existing order; for all that they are "incongruous" with and "burst the bounds" of the status quo, they necessarily remain deeply embedded within a "historically specific social life." At least part of why Muriel and Nellie's story matters, I suggest, resides not just in their accomplishments but in their expansion of how people could and did imagine alternative "not yet" futures for themselves, Britain, and the world.[44]

CHAPTER ONE

Victorian Childhoods and Two Victorian Children

HERE IS ONE OF MANY WAYS to tell their story: Muriel Lester had a childhood and Nellie Dowell didn't.

Henry and Rachel Lester doted on their three youngest children Muriel, Doris, and Kingsley. Romping and laughing on the sprawling grounds of Gainsborough Lodge, they bowled on their family green, rowed their full-scale toy boat across imaginary seas, strengthened their limbs in the gymnasium their parents had built for them, and mastered lawn tennis strokes on their well-manicured court. (See fig. 1.1.) Henry Lester even coated the bitter pill of Bible lessons with the irresistible sweetness of his playful paternal devotion. Every Sunday afternoon, the children eagerly awaited "Scripture Characters"—a form of charades Henry invented for them that was sufficiently pious to keep the Sabbath holy.[1]

Nellie briefly enjoyed a secure Cockney life in East London as the daughter of William Dowell, a mariner, and his wife Harriet. That changed when she was five. William Dowell died at sea in 1881, leaving behind five children. There were no safety nets to catch families like the Dowells. Even the most prudent home economist could not possibly save money on a mariner's earnings to protect against future misfortunes in an uncertain world. And so the Dowells fell—slowly at first, then quickly, into the vast residuum of the poorest of the poor. The objects that made a dwelling into a home—pictures, furniture, even beds—disappeared as each made its way to the pawnshop, never to return. Then the family itself was ripped apart. Indifferent Poor Law officials carted off a weeping Nellie and her siblings, first to the workhouse and eventually to Victorian London's most infamous "barrack" school orphanage at Forest Gate. Reared by uncaring strangers, Nellie saw her mother one Sunday each year.[2]

1.1. Muriel, Doris, and Kingsley Lester were born in Gainsborough Lodge in Leytonstone. A comfortable upper-middle-class suburban villa, it sat in a large garden surrounded by fields and playgrounds, which included a full-scale toy boat. Gainsborough Lodge, c. 1964. (Courtesy of Vestry House Museum, London Borough of Waltham Forest.)

Stories like this one abound in Victorian culture. Their implicit argument is simple. Childhood is a phase of life marked by pleasure and play, innocence and imagination.[3] It depends upon financial security and two loving parents, different but complementary in their tutelary roles. Children of the possessing classes get childhood; the poor in general and poor orphans in particular do not.

Muriel's narration of her own childhood and Nellie's reproduced many of these assumptions. It is almost impossible to peek behind the curtain of the Lester family domestic idyll to detect traces of struggle, conflict, and disappointment. By contrast, Nellie's stolen childhood outrages Muriel, all the more because the heroine of Muriel's tale is not Nellie but her devoted, ingenious, loving mother. Harriett Dowell, like Herman Melville's mothership the *Rachel* in *Moby Dick*, goes on her "winding, woeful way" seeking to reclaim her lost children. By telling Nellie's young life in "From Birth to Death" (1923) mostly through Harriet's eyes, Muriel took a strong stance. Contrary to the dominant view of policy makers, Nellie *did* have a family prepared to love and nurture her. Rather than demonize working-class mothers and families, Muriel squarely blames the Poor Law for taking away Nellie's childhood. What Muriel does not seem to question is the conviction that a Cockney half-orphan ward of the state could not, almost by definition, have a childhood.

Can a child *not* have a childhood? Are there many different kinds of childhoods? I approach these twinned questions by exploring Nellie's and Muriel's lives in two ways. I reconstruct their early lives and schooling in rich historical particularity. At the same time, I interpret their histories through the many competing ways in which Victorians told— and historians still do tell—stories about "childhood."[4]

Muriel and Doris Lester wrote copiously about childhood and their own childhoods. Their stories, particularly about working-class childhood, come ready-made with an elaborate political, social, and cultural apparatus.[5] What Nellie thought about growing up mostly remains a mystery. Her views echo faintly in Muriel's stories. Following the few factual crumbs Muriel drops about Nellie's earliest years, I have sought and often found her—or perhaps more aptly, her trace—in the vast archive the British state assembled and preserved as it monitored and provided services for the poorest of its poor citizens. Abject social problems they may well have been, but paupers like Nellie were never invisible in official state records. The Dowell family's decennial census data provides addresses, which in turn allows educated guesses about the most likely School Board of London school she attended. School admission and discharge registers and log books provide more addresses, dates, and curricular and classroom information, which in turn make it possible to guess the Poor Law Union to which Mrs. Dowell most likely turned in her desperate need. Poor Law Unions match closely with Poor Law infirmaries and orphanages, which maintained their own careful records of admissions, discharges, and much else. My archival trajectory in reconstructing Nellie's childhood follows the overlapping networks and logic of the Victorian educational and social welfare system through which she moved as her family's fortunes declined.

THE EDUCATION OF NELLIE DOWELL

A "Very Comfortable" Cockney Childhood

Nellie lived her earliest years among small shopkeepers and skilled artisans with steady employment and good wages. Not poor enough to satisfy journalists' insatiable hunger for spectacles of misery and depravity but not nearly rich enough to govern and guide, such people fit uneasily into broad narratives of modern British history, except perhaps to explain why the late-Victorian proletariat never fulfilled its revolutionary destiny.[6] When the sociologist and social surveyor Charles Booth and his team of investigators sought to measure what remained of the religious life of London in the late 1890s, they all too often found its pulse weak. They did find plenty of "respectable" families like the Dowells hovering somewhere between the "lower middle class" and the "upper working class" "with no very wide divergence amongst them."[7] A doctor attended Harriet Dowell at the birth of her daughter Nellie; a nurse provided home help in its aftermath while a neighbor was paid to clean house and take care of Nellie's three older siblings, Florence, Alice, and William. These were fortunate material circumstances, enjoyed by few East Londoners. Muriel emphasized that the Dowell children basked in their mother's "generous common sense," keen awareness of their health and nutritional needs, "unfailing kindliness," and watchful love.[8]

"From Birth to Death" may be about Nellie, but Mrs. Dowell occupies its moral center. We see Nellie through her mother's eyes. Mrs. Dowell's mother love makes her home but cannot preserve it from misfortunes outside her control. Muriel's opening line foreshadows the family's decline by specifying the temporal limits of the Dowell family's domestic happiness: "For the first few years of her life Nellie was very comfortable."[9] As Muriel's narrative unfolds, the full implications of this sentence become clear. Nellie *had* a childhood before she lost it, or rather, before the Poor Law took it from her.

Public records—census data, marriage, and death certificates—amply support Muriel's account. In 1871, Nellie's father, William Dowell (1844–c.1881), a mariner from Sunderland, Durham, and his wife, Harriet (1846–1931), lived at 9 Granada Terrace, a cluster of seventeen attached houses running along the north side of Commercial Road, one of East London's main commercial arteries.[10] A sprawling public house, the George Tavern, wrapped around the residential dwellings on Granada Terrace. A large patent rope factory and the Roman Catholic chapel St. Mary and St. Michael's, serving the needs of London's growing Irish population, dominated the south side of Commercial Road.[11] From 7:30 a.m. until 11:40 p.m. trams ran every five minutes in both directions along Commercial Road connecting Aldgate—in medieval times the gate marking the easternmost boundary of the walled city of London—to Poplar, the India Docks, and the world's commerce.[12] In the 1840s, Commercial Road had been the notorious haunt of coal whippers who lifted the coal out of the hold of ships; by the time the Dowells moved to Granada Terrace, rambunctious and colorful sailors strolled its length from the docks to the heart of the city of London.[13] "The keen east wind seems to bear a kind of briny flavour" along Commercial Road, observed the writer for Dickens's *All the Year Round* in 1881, and "the men who swarm up to the roof of the tramway-car display a cat-like agility in the process, that suggests the habit of going up aloft." Jammed with cheap clothing marts and big emporia, along with humbler shops catering to nautical clientele, Commercial Road was bordered by "narrow slums and labyrinths of courts and alleys."[14]

William Dowell traveled a well-worn path from the maritime industry of his native Sunderland, a port town dominated by the coastal transportation of Newcastle coal, to London's docklands with its global shipping network.[15] He entered the merchant marine in April 1858 as a "boy," his official rank on the Newcastle-based ship, the *Courier*. At some point during his time as an apprentice from 1859 to 1861, he apparently found either shipboard life intolerable or the attractions of Shanghai irresistible. He temporarily deserted his ship while docked there. It must have been a tense, exciting time to be a young Englishman wandering Shanghai during the final stages of the Second Opium War (1856–60) between Britain and China. William Dowell spent most of the 1860s making his own small contribution to the rapid expansion of Britain's free trade empire in Asia as he regularly sailed between London, Calcutta, and Hong Kong. During these years, he ascended the ranks as assistant bursar, third mate, and second mate. In February 1868, he achieved the rank of first mate in the Merchant Service. By early 1870, he had married Harriet Sloan, moved to Commercial Road in Whitechapel and had their first child, Florence.[16]

A mariner's life was full of dangers and Dowell suffered some sort of mishap aboard the S.S. *Chanonry* in the Gulf of Lyons in 1873 en route from Cardiff to Livorno (Leghorn). He seems to have escaped injury but his first-mate certificate did not survive and he applied for a new copy that year. It was an eventful voyage because newspapers reported that three seamen aboard the SS *Chanonry* had been infected with the "mania" for desertion and faced harsh punishment back in England.[17]

William Dowell must have had colorful stories to tell his wife and young children about the people he had encountered and the places he had seen. No doubt his prolonged absences forced Nellie's mother to rely heavily on her own kin for help raising their five children. Mariners like William Dowell and their families were simultaneously enmeshed in vast global networks of trade as well as intensely local and insular communities of family, friends, and neighbors in East London.

William Dowell earned a very respectable living: first mates received approximately 120 shillings per month in the year 1880 according to average wages published in a House of Commons report.[18] Harriet's kin lived with them: her Irish-born Protestant mother, Harriet Sloan (called "Granny" in Nellie's letters and sometimes spelled Sloane), and two younger siblings, Caroline (Aunt Carry/Carrie in the letters) and David. Caroline (1849–1936), a milliner, and David, a clerk, no doubt contributed a portion of their earnings to the household that allowed the Dowells to occupy the entire Granada Terrace house free from lodgers.

Privacy was a luxury in East London and the Dowells enjoyed more of it than most. The structure of households on Granada Terrace resembled that of the Dowells: multigenerational families whose heads were drawn from that borderland of lower-middle-class clerks and proprietors of small shops and skilled artisans. Several dwellings served as both home and place of business. William Anderson, a bachelor watchmaker and jeweller at No. 11, employed a shopman and an errand boy, both of whom lived with him.

By Nellie's birth on April 17, 1876, the Dowell family had moved to Lucas Street, just off the south side of Commercial Road.[19] A few years later, they migrated to Harding Street, a small side street two blocks further east along Commercial Road. Nellie's family no longer lived with Harriet's adult siblings and hence lost their financial contributions. Nellie's Uncle David married in 1876 and began his own family; Aunt Caroline remained with her mother, Harriet Sloan, after Hugh Sloan's death in 1869. Nellie's family occupied the second floor of a house they shared with a picture frame gilder, his wife, and their two children on still-respectable Harding Street. Unlike those on Granada Terrace, most wives on Harding Street had paid occupations, which suggest that male heads of households did not earn enough to support their families. While the Dowell family fortunes seemed to decline as its numbers grew, Nellie's mother still enjoyed the good fortune of staying home with her children rather than seeking wages in the labor market.[20]

We first glimpse Nellie as a young "child," doubly refracted through Muriel's retelling of Mrs. Dowell's stories. "From Birth to Death" narrates Nellie as exceptional, different not only from her siblings but from neighborhood children. Mrs. Dowell's other children played vigorous games in the surrounding streets. Nellie is too "highly strung, nervous and delicate" for such rough-and-tumble activities. She takes easily to her bed when frightened. She prefers to remain indoors and cut out paper dolls.[21] Like her dolls, Nellie is finely wrought. Muriel's narrative locates Nellie inside the home, the proper place for the cultivation of a girl. It also safely removes her from the unsupervised, contaminating dangers of the street. Few disputed that streets necessarily *were* the playgrounds of most poor children, including Nellie's brother and sisters. Where else could they play given the tight quarters of large families crammed into two- or three-room flats, the lack of neighborhood parks in East London, and the absence of private gardens? It was impossible *not* to see that poor children were remarkably adept at transforming whatever they could find—old boxes, string, and sticks—into toys for their play.[22] But the location of these activities disqualified them from performing what most bourgeois reformers took to be the ethical-moral-imaginative function of "play" in promoting the development of a child.

Nellie's written fluency may well have reflected not only her preference for sedentary activities but also the importance of literacy for the occupational fortunes of her mother's family, the Sloans. Her maternal grandfather, Hugh Augustus Macullough (sometimes spelled Maculloch) Sloan (1810–1869), alternately called himself a "seaman," "mariner," "surveyor of customs," revenue or custom house officer in census, baptismal, and wedding records. His oldest son, Nellie's uncle David (1851–1920) began as a clerk before laboring in a wine distillery and ending his working life as an engine driver. The youngest son, Archibald Henry (1858–1925), was an insurance agent by 1880—a job he pursued for the rest of his life.[23] All three must have been quite literate and numerate. Nellie's grandparents, Hugh and Harriet Sloan, employed a widowed live-in servant in 1851, the same year their children David and Caroline were baptized together at Christ Church, St. George's in the East. Nellie's paternal grandparents, by contrast, were among the illiterate unskilled poor of Yorkshire. Jane Dowell could not sign her name on her son's birth certificate, and her husband James was a common laborer in 1851 who, by the 1861, census listed his occupation as "waterman."[24]

Nellie's native aptitude and the success of Britain's system of universal elementary education (mandated by the 1870 Forster Education Act) in producing a broadly literate urban working class also must have contributed to her gift for expressing ideas in writing.[25] On April 2, 1883, she was received into the infant room of her local London Board school, the Marner Street School.[26] By that time, William Dowell's death had already compelled his wife to move with her five children much farther east to a house on Gurley Street in Bromley-by-Bow, adjacent to Marner Street School.[27] This was a dreary neighborhood of quiet desperate poverty, a "bleak district . . . of treeless streets and miles of small two-storied tenements. Here dwell the workers and the workless, who settle in tens of thousands on the skirts of London's arterial thoroughfares." Marner Street and the surrounding blocks were full of "those who are about to leave it or those who have failed to leave it," interspersed by a few of the "godly and self-respecting poor."[28]

Two months later, Nellie's younger sister Rose, age four, joined her at Marner Street School. The state originally had no intention of providing child care for the poor, but mothers like Mrs. Dowell simply brought underaged children like Rose with them and left them at school along with those old enough to enroll. In response, some schools created reception rooms to provide rudimentary care for pre–school-aged children.[29] The Forster Education Act made schooling mandatory, but it was not free in its first decades. Marner Street School charged two pence per week for each child, unlike nearby schools on Northey Street and Old Castle Street, which served even more impoverished populations and charged the state minimum of one pence per week per child. Even these small sums surpassed the financial ability of parents like Harriet Dowell and the state offered grants to make up the difference.[30]

In the decade after the implementation of the 1870 Act, the enthusiasm of educational reformers, "deluded in their cloudland of hopes and theories," had been tempered by Board school teachers' "hourly contact with ugly, commonplace sordid facts and difficulties."[31] Under pressure of "codes and formulas," Board schools shut out children from "dreamland and poetry," lamented the art critic John Ruskin.[32] Certainly, teachers faced a daunting task as they sought to discipline unruly pupils, satisfy regulations intended to standardize education, and cope with impoverished parents for whom schooling was sometimes less a matter of opportunity than unwanted compulsion.[33] The staff at Marner Street also had to make the most of scarce resources distributed across 1100 pupils, roughly 350 boys, 350 girls, and 450 infants.

Ruskin's dreary assessment did not go unchallenged. Mrs. Westlake, an early member of the School Board of London and former teacher, praised board schoolteachers for enlivening their curriculum with "object lessons" which went beyond rote work of learning the three "R's" by encouraging children to use their senses to observe the world around them. Open to experimental pedagogy, London teachers stimulated their pupils' bodies with newly introduced "Swedish drill" techniques overseen by a "Swedish lady" who was one of the first holders of a diploma in physical education. They awakened students' curiosity about their place in the world through geography lessons that led their charges from knowledge of "their own immediate locality" to London, England, and beyond.[34]

The educational system was its most flexible, creative and gender neutral in the instruction it provided its youngest pupils in the infant rooms, where Nellie and Rose were received. Children at Marner Street School benefited from the pioneering work of the Scottish-born, German-trained Maria J. Lyschinska, who observed Froebel-inspired kindergartens in Berlin and incorporated their methods into the curriculum at Marner Street School in 1883–84.[35] Advanced intellectual exiles and political refugees from Germany's failed "liberal" revolution of 1848 like Johannes and Bertha Von Ronge brought kindergartens with them to Britain in 1851.[36] Marx and Engels may have found their democratic politics "banal, hackneyed, as insipid as water, luke-warm dish water," but there was nothing in the least bit "insipid" about the Ronges' views on the education of young children.[37] Kindergartens cultivated the intellectual and moral self-activity of each individual child and emphasized the educative value of play and self-expression, and the use of "natural phenomenon" as tools of early education. The School Board of London's introduction of kindergarten principles in some schools from the late 1870s onwards marked a considerable opportunity for the movement. The inspector's reports stress the integration of knowledge across disciplines and modes of instruction in Marner Street's infants' room and gave it a coveted ranking of "excellent" based on examination results and personal visits. The surviving records of the school suggest that while it no doubt performed its task of inculcating strict gender and class-specific values, it also provided valuable cultural and vocational resources for poor families and their children.[38] Nellie attended Marner Street at a pedagogically optimistic and experimental moment in its history. It was an increasingly insecure time in her own life.

A Death and Its Consequences

William Dowell's death at sea in 1881 irreparably shattered his family's world.[39] It triggered his family's two-year descent from working-class comfort to abject poverty. Muriel stages the revelation of his death with a simple pathos that highlights Mrs. Dowell's stoic determination to preserve her family and soften the blow to Nellie. Nellie is fundamentally different from her siblings. A "shrewd little girl," she needed special protection because she possessed a finely wrought disposition. The narrator briefly shifts perspective from Nellie's mother to her older brother Will and thus affirms her intimacy with the entire Dowell family.

> even when the letter came which the others always remembered as having made the whole difference to their lives, the letter which Will took from the postman with such pride because the envelope looked abnormally thick and good and had so much grand printing all over one corner of it, the letter whose opening had the astounding dreadful effect of making their mother tremble whose reading had made her cry, even on that never to be forgotten occasion, Nellie was protected.[40]

Will's innocent misreading highlights the grotesque contrast between the letter's outward promise of good things and its devastating contents, between its status as mere words on a page and the inescapable consequences of those words. The narrator piles clause upon clause only to shift the focus of our attention to what really matters for her story, the short declaration that ends it: "Nellie was protected."

What options did Mrs. Dowell have in coping with the financial debacle of widowhood and lone motherhood?[41] First and foremost, she could and did seek full-time paid work while using the infant room at Marner Street School as a form of free childcare for her youngest child Rose. Mrs. Dowell listed no occupation in the 1881 census, completed on April 3, 1881—several weeks before she received news of her husband's distant death. By 1891, she listed her occupation as a match hand taper cutter—a factory job in the manufacture of wooden lucifer matches and wax vestas. Mrs. Dowell may well have migrated east to Bromley-by-Bow in the early 1880s because jobs for women in the match industry were plentiful there. Large firms such as Bryant and May and R. Bell and Co. welcomed widows, who often moved between waged labor in the factory and piecework undertaken at home.

Mrs. Dowell, like her own mother before her, turned to private charity to supplement her earnings. Such women constructed a mixed economy of welfare that strategically combined resources from private charities and local Poor Law authorities with their own waged labor. Harriet Sloan and her daughter, Harriet Dowell secured pensions of 6 shillings per week (Muriel calls them a "pittance") from Trinity House, one of London's most venerable charities founded to support the "decayed masters and commanders of ships" and their widows. Established in the sixteenth century, Trinity House was the official "fraternal" guild entrusted with maintaining lighthouses, granting licenses to watermen plying the Thames, and most crucially and lucratively, regulating the pilotage and navigation of the Thames.[42] Trinity House diverted a portion of its vast funds to its various charitable foundations and trusts. A set of Trinity House's late-seventeenth-century almshouses remains a landmark on Mile End Road today, just across from a statue of the founder of the Salvation Army, General William Booth.[43]

The death of a parent is always a traumatic event in the life of a child. The death of the male breadwinner in a working-class family, even one as seemingly secure as the Dowells, compounded emotional loss with devastating social and economic consequences. In late-Victorian Britain, neither private employers nor the state provided any sort of safety net to preserve the integrity of the family unit. Substantial wage differentials between men and women meant that few lone mothers could keep their households intact without financial contributions from their own children and kin. This was not an option for Harriet Dowell. Left to care for rather than receive earnings from five children, Mrs. Dowell, a thirty-five-year-old-widow with little workplace experience, had no good choices.

Slum Motherhood and the "Hard Face" of the Poor Law

In depicting Mrs. Dowell as a heroic, self-sacrificing and ingenious slum mother, Muriel entered a highly contentious and overtly politicized field of representations. By the turn of the century, motherhood increasingly gave way to the science of mothercraft, whose practitioners claimed expertise and authority in managing family, hygiene, housekeeping, and child nurture. Mothering ceased to be merely a matter of love and good intentions. It demanded discipline, science, education, and training. Confronted by a pan-European crisis of dénatalité as well as fears about empire, race degeneration, and the emergence of cigarette-smoking New Women, many demanded working-class mothers rear fit soldiers and workers for the nation.[44] Some, like Henry Drummond, the best-selling popularizer of Christian altruism, exalted "the kingdom of the mothers" as the apotheosis of the evolutionary process. By virtue of their essentially loving and selfless natures, they were "perfect" biological, social, and ethical creatures.[45] All this attention to mothers exposed poor women to considerable criticism by watchful critics intent on measuring—quite literally—the imperiled health of the nation through the "defective" bodies of working-class children and youth.

Poor mothers putative greed and indifference to their children's well-being were viciously satirized by *Punch*'s contribution in June 1890 to the contentious public debate about amending the Infant Life Protection Act. In December 1889, Parliament debated a "great and growing evil": parents' purchase of life insurance for their ailing and feeble children.[46] *Punch* viciously recast the story of the classical world's most ostentatious exemplar of maternal love and incubator of republican virtue, Cornelia Agrippina, into a parable about the moral turpitude of "mod-

THE MODERN CORNELIA.

[CORNELIA, daughter of SCIPIO AFRICANUS, and wife of SEMPRONIUS GRACCHUS, when a lady displayed her jewels to her, pointed to her two sons, exclaiming, "These are *my* jewels!"]

"THESE ARE *MY* JEWELS."

1.2. *Punch* joined the public debate within and outside Parliament about whether poor mothers sacrificed their children's health to collect burial insurance money. "The Modern Cornelia," *Punch*, June 21, 1890, 299.

ern motherhood." (See fig. 1.2.) A drunken, corpulent harridan starves her listless children to collect burial insurance money for them. Her children, like jewels, have cash value. Her oversized, gloved, outstretched hands mark her violation not just of motherliness but femininity itself. That watchword of scientific charity and conventional moralists— "thrift"—falls on deaf ears in the mother's pursuit of the "devilish gains of Death."[47] Such views corresponded only too well with the unapologetic disdain of Helen Dendy, an influential Charity Organisation Society worker in Shoreditch in the 1890s. Dendy traced the origins and afflictions of the "troops of ragged, dirty stunted little urchins, neglected and crippled in mind and body" to the "ruined lives of their parents. . . ." Without any hint of sympathy for the dire economic circumstances of poor mothers, Dendy acidly asserted that "the mothers are either worn out drudges before they have reached middle-age, or have developed into the careless slatterns who live on the doorstep gossiping with like-minded neighbors."[48]

Poor mothers did have their share of outspoken defenders. A former workhouse boy and journeyman cooper-turned-labor organizer, Will Crooks, blasted the House of Lords committee investigating Infant Life Insurance for daring to suggest that poor mothers put burial insurance money before love for their children. London papers reported that Crooks instructed the Committee that he knew "thousands of families of working people, and was perfectly certain that there was not among them one mother lacking maternal affection."[49] The district nurse, M. Loane, fiercely denounced such cruel calumnies upon the honor of working-class mothers. "It is impossible to show too much respect to a poor woman," Loane insisted, "who has managed to rear her children, fed and clothed them, inspired them with the laments of morality and self-respect, and taught them to love one another and spare a thought for their neighbours. To see such women treated with brusque discourtesy, or condescending patronage, is simply intolerable."[50] The vast majority of nineteenth- and twentieth-century working-class autobiographers, all too aware that so many of their mothers had been beleaguered and belittled by "charity ladies" and "welfare visitors," enveloped them in a protective nostalgic haze.[51]

Muriel infuses her narrative with sympathy and attention to inner psychological states of mind as she describes Mrs. Dowell's household economies and her attempts to cover up the "disappearance" of once-beloved objects, secretly carried to the pawnshop to pay for rent and food. Even Mrs. Dowell's resourcefulness cannot fend off the inevitable dissolution of her family. Strangers arrive with boxes, furniture, and their own "little girls" who quite literally replace Nellie and her siblings. On their final night living together as a family, Mrs. Dowell melodramatically tries to stifle her sobs as she steals into Nellie's room for a candlelit glimpse of her sleeping daughter. Visceral details—sounds and sights—position us as witnesses to the unfolding scene of trauma and loss. We suffer with Mrs. Dowell as she tries to convince herself and her children that good food, nice beds, caring nurses, and gardens await them at the Poor Law school and orphanage to which she must send them.

In fact, many poor women *did* use such Poor Law institutions as temporary stop-gap measures in times of dire need.[52] Some parents—usually mothers—admitted and reclaimed their children dozens of times in a single year. The constant discontinuities of physical care and schooling for such children, so-called "ins and outs," created headaches for Poor Law administrators, doctors, and teaching staff who viewed them as sources of physical and moral contagion.[53] Policy makers interpreted "ins and outs" not as proof of parents' laudable desire to retain custodial control over their children but as evidence of their selfish refusal to do what was best for them.[54] Poor Law officials placed parents in an impossible bind. They condemned them for their supposed indifference to their offspring *and* their determination to remain connected to them. Harriet Dowell was too poor to pursue this strategy. Nellie was admitted and discharged only once from Forest Gate.

No trace of sisterly solidarity softens the female face of the municipal state in the guise of the woman poor law officer sent to collect Nellie and her siblings and squeeze them into the waiting van.

> The street door knocker resounded twice with a smart rap. "Name of Dowell, upstairs," . . . then the footsteps of the Poor Law officer were heard ascending. She tapped at the kitchen door and stood on the threshold, evidently in a hurry. "Name Dowell, four children," announced the hard faced woman . . . "Is this one of them," inquired the woman, pointing to Nellie . . . It was now the mother's turn to cling to the children, but Nellie stumbled to her feet, stood erect, caught hold of her sister's hand and made her way down the stair . . . and started their journey to the unknown.[55]

There is no mistaking Lester's radical—though far from original—critique of the Poor Law: the extreme economic vulnerability of respectable and responsible members of the working class like Mrs. Dowell left them helpless in the face of the cruelly impersonal mechanisms of the marketplace and state poor relief. Mrs. Dowell becomes passively childlike while Nellie literally ceases to be a person: she is merely "one of them." Even Lester's prose quickens ("Name Dowell, four children") as if mimicking officials' indifference to inner psychological torment at the pain of impending separation. Lester's narrative recycled clichéd sentimental idioms of nineteenth-century women's Christian writing about family and home. Abolitionist poems such as Hannah More's "The Sorrows of Yamba" (1797) and industrial problem novels like Elizabeth Gaskell's *Mary Barton* (1848) and *North and South* (1855) showed how systemic violence and injustice—African slavery and the exploitation of white industrial workers in Britain—dismembered families and violated the sacred bonds of parents and children. Such works, like Lester's, compel readers to combine thinking and feeling.

Where did school and Poor Law officials send Nellie and her siblings? Why did they remove them from Mrs. Dowell's loving care? In 1883, the Dowell children, except for the youngest, Rose, transferred out of Marner Street School. She remained with Harriet Dowell for another three years. Nellie's brother William followed in his father's footsteps and apprenticed on the training ship *Exmouth,* a decommissioned flagship from the Baltic fleet.[56] An ambitious scheme developed by East London Poor Law officials, the ship was home, school, and workplace for six hundred boys who received training in basic seamanship as well as room and board. Much like the Marine Society founded by John Fielding and Jonas Hanway in 1756, it tried to solve several problems at once. It removed poor boys from the streets with their criminal temptations; it inexpensively provided for their care while guaranteeing a steady supply of trained labor for the Royal Navy and Mercantile Marine.[57] Seafaring must have agreed with William because by 1898 he had become a petty officer on HMS *Mars.* He was commended at a special meeting of the Royal Humane Society on August 28, 1898 for his bravery in rescuing victims from the waters in a disaster near Blackwall.[58]

Nellie was one of a handful of children that the Poplar guardians sent forty miles out of London to Leighton Buzzard on the northwestern border of Bedfordshire. A parish union town and head of a county court district, Leighton Buzzard had a single wide street with several smaller streets branching off it at the Market Place, then as now dominated by a forty-foot-high fourteenth-century cross; an ancient Church of All Saints; a town hall and corn exchange; and a population—including five

Drawn by W. Alexander F.S.A.   Engraved by Wm Byrne F.S.A. & P. Sparrow

1.3. A medieval cross still dominates the central market square of the provincial town of Leighton Buzzard, where Poor Law officials briefly boarded out Nellie to a foster family. South aspect of the Cross at Leighton Buzzard, Bedfordshire, London. Published 1 November 1803 by W. Byrne, Titchfield Street and T. Cadell & W. Davies Strand. (Courtesy of Bedford and Luton Archive Office.)

nearby villages—of just under 6,000 spread over nearly 9,000 acres.[59] (See fig. 1.3.) By contrast, Nellie's home district, Poplar, had a population of 156,525 in 1881 jammed into 2,334 acres. Reeling from the death of her father and the steady erosion of the material conditions of the Dowell household, she confronted an utterly alien way of life far removed from the tight network of relatives and the familiar landmarks, sounds, sights, and smells of Bow and Bromley's densely congested streets and alleyways. We cannot know how Nellie made sense of her new world. Muriel never mentioned Nellie's time at Leighton Buzzard, perhaps because Nellie herself did not—or chose not to—remember it.

Leighton Buzzard was far beyond the reach of her mother, grandmother, aunts and uncles. The terms of the General Order of the Poor Law Board of November 25, 1870 authorized Boards of Guardians to board out "orphaned" and "deserted" children to certified Boarding Out Committees who coordinated their management with local government and Poor Law officials. Of course, Nellie was neither an "orphan" nor a "deserted child," at least in the eyes of her mother so eager to love and protect her. To borrow Lydia Murdoch's evocative phrase, she had become one of tens of thousands of "imagined orphans" in Victorian Britain removed from their birth families. An Anglican cleric headed Leighton Buzzard's two "Boarding Out" committees charged with placing each Poor Law child in a local family in exchange for a weekly cash payment. Boarding out allowed overburdened Poor Law unions like Stepney and Poplar to subcontract care of particularly vulnerable classes of poor children like Nellie in private families.[60]

This system had several notable advantages in the eyes of its champions. It removed children from two undesirable—and sensationalized—sites within the Victorian imagination: the slum tenement and the pauper family. Like many other late-nineteenth-century schemes designed to reclaim the urban underclass such as Children's Country Holidays and Farm Labour Colonies for out-of-work men, it replaced the diseased environment of the slum with the health-restoring atmosphere of the country. It was cheap and diminished pressure on Poor Law unions and local ratepayers to construct, manage, maintain, and regulate large facilities. It kept children within that most hallowed institution of Victorian life, the family, while removing them from their own. Boarding Out Committees visited, inspected, and supervised "orphans" within their new homes to ensure their well-being, but newspapers regularly reported abuse and exploitation.[61] Some women undoubtedly took in pauper children out of a genuine commitment to their welfare. All needed the income they received. This was a business proposition whose success depended heavily not only on the competence and conscientiousness of the local committees' oversight but the vagaries of placements within specific households.

Neither Harriett Dowell's personal fitness nor the depth of her solicitude for her offspring had anything to do with Nellie's removal to Leighton Buzzard. The mere fact of her destitution constituted prima facie proof of her unsuitability to retain custody of them. This was the judgment that poor families—mothers in particular—desperately sought to avoid even as they devised ways to extract resources from Poor Law institutions to their family's best advantage.[62] Mothers' bitter encounters with the Poor Law provide an essential context for appreciating the politics of Muriel's portrayal of Mrs. Dowell's devotion to her children and her unjust maternal suffering.[63]

Nellie Dowell Becomes a Poor Law Orphan

The guardians did not keep Nellie in Leighton Buzzard long. On July 19, 1883, she was admitted to the Forest Gate Industrial School where her older sister Alice joined her two weeks later. Forest Gate was rate-funded philanthropy on a grand scale—all that was best and worst in mid-Victorian approaches to poverty and children's education. While the residential school was built, funded, and overseen by the Whitechapel Guardians in 1854 at the cost of forty thousand pounds, Poplar Poor Law Union entered into a partnership with the Whitechapel guardians. This guaranteed Poplar's poor children access to over three hundred beds at the school.[64] Nellie occupied one of these beds. Throughout the 1880s, Forest Gate housed, fed, educated, disciplined, and entertained between six and eight hundred children in any given week in its three departments: infants, girls, and boys.

Forest Gate's neoclassical "bare Italianate" style and massive proportions betokened its builders' strong commitment to their own concept of child welfare and pauper childhood.[65] Its construction and management were governed by the logic of aggregation (massing together of paupers) and segregation (separating paupers from their families and dividing them into distinct classes based on age and gender) at the heart of the New Poor Law; and by a vision of efficiency dictated by economies of scale rather than the emotional and psychological needs of children. There was nothing homelike about Forest Gate. To the passerby, it offered an imposing symmetrical civic façade. Its immense sex-segregated dormitories provided its child wards no opportunities to domesticate or personalize the space allotted to them. Metal frame beds must have frustrated most children's attempts to inscribe initials or mark their surfaces with graffiti. There was literally no privacy in these dormitories: the beds were lined up in rows to maximize bodies per cubic foot while making it easy to monitor the children's activities at a panoptic glance. Such schools may have been impersonal, but they undeniably offered their pupils better instruction than the ramshackle educational arrangements of individual poorhouses. Viewing the working-class home as a source of moral pollution, guardians congratulated themselves on placing poor children in "total" institutions that inculcated orderliness, discipline, and compliance with routines.[66]

Not everyone shared this sanguine assessment. In 1873 the President of the Local Government Board, James Stansfield, appointed Jane Nassau Senior Britain's first female civil servant in 1873. She quickly embarked on a public crusade to investigate schools like Forest Gate.[67] Senior's stunning 1874 Report indicted barrack schools, including Forest Gate, for failing to provide pauper girls with love, mothering, a sense of joy and individual worth, life skills and intellectual stimulation. For Senior, such qualities were the essential stuff of childhood. These schools, she contended, left their female wards stunted in mind, body, and spirit, and hence incapable of leading moral, self-supporting lives. Many of these girls quickly disappeared into London's underclass of degraded and fallen women.[68] By denying pauper girls a proper childhood, the state invested in the manufacture of prostitutes. Senior's male colleagues dismissed each of her proposals as sentimental follies: a curriculum that included games and excursions to teach girls how to shop and manage their future households; foster care in families or the creation of a system of small "cottages" each superintended by a matron. They would prove less easy to dismiss twenty years later when one of Senior's most forceful female disciples, Henrietta Barnett, brought them before Parliament and the nation.

Thwarted in her attempt to bring feminine influence to bear on state policy, Senior turned to the private voluntary sector and founded the Metropolitan Association for Befriending Young Servants (MABYS). The talented Senior, a noted opera singer and founder of the British precursor of the Red Cross, died of cancer in 1877 before she could reap the fruits of her benevolent labors. Her niece, Mary (May) Hughes followed in her footsteps in caring for the outcast. She founded rescue homes for Whitechapel prostitutes in the village of Longcot; as the first resident of Kingsley Hall in 1915, she became part of Nellie and Muriel's circle of close friends. MABYS paired each pauper girl with a "lady" volunteer who befriended and advised her.[69] It captured the imagination of middle-class women in the 1870s awakened to their social duties and intellectual powers by the establishment of the first women's colleges and social reform schemes such as Octavia Hill's "lady" rent collectors and Louisa Twining's "lady" workhouse visitors.[70]

For children like Nellie Dowell, accustomed to the cramped dereliction of two- or three-story slum tenements and the freedom of the street and courtyard, Forest Gate must have seemed vast, intimidating, and restrictive, more like the workhouse than a home.[71] Only Nellie herself could have provided Muriel with the detailed description of her reception at Forest Gate. Muriel highlights Nellie's futile resistance to the micro-workings of the school's disciplinary regime as the staff seeks to eradicate her individuality. Nellie uses all the tools of the weak to resist the powerful: tears, inactivity and aggression.[72] This is not a battle that she can win.

> Nellie caused some trouble among the attendants and had even to be taken to the matron during the first month of her stay. She had fallen asleep towards the end of her journey, worn out with her sobbing, and when the train stopped at their destination and the nurse stood her on her feet to awake her, she was glad enough in her dazed state to hold tight to her hand. She sat throughout the tea, pale and dry eyes, but she could eat nothing. . . . It was even found necessary to take her to the matron—an awful and terrifying thing for the inmate of almost any institution. This was because she had pas-

sionately resisted the hair cutter when it came to her turn to be cropped on the first Saturday after her arrival. She had been terrified by the big scissors wielded over her head by a strange person. A strange sense of outrage filled her as she saw herself shorn of her curls.[73]

The inescapable encounter with Forest Gate's barber marked one particularly charged moment in the life of each child sent there. Lice flourished in locks of hair: to control the former required shearing the latter. Nellie's "strange . . . outrage" over her lost curls allows Muriel to convey her own horror at the institutionalized violations of children at Forest Gate. An ardent, independent spirit like Nellie—the sort of person essential to Muriel's vision of a society ordered on radically egalitarian principles of Christian love—was anathema at Forest Gate.

The plainspoken Labour leader George Lansbury knew only too well that decisions about the management of pauper children's bodies could and did erode the fragile boundaries of the child's individuality. In Lansbury's politico-moral calculus, the good intentions of Forest Gate's staff mattered much less than the consequences of their actions. He, like Muriel and Mrs. Dowell, registered his dismay at the sight of the children, "dressed in the old, hideous, Poor Law garb, corduroy and hard blue serge, and the girls with their hair almost shaved off, with nothing at all to make them look attractive in any sort of way." The dehumanization of Forest Gate's children was the logical outgrowth of officials who "looked on the poor as a nuisance" despite getting "their living out of the poor, or because of the poor."[74] It was a "crime," Lansbury contended, for the community to allow the Poor Law to "rob" children of the "pleasures of childhood."[75]

It is hard not to feel grief at just how much we know about what Nellie was supposed to be doing each hour of each day during her years at Forest Gate. Every aspect of life at the school was officially regulated, each thirty-minute block of the day charted with precision. Nellie awakened at 5:45 each morning, washed and bathed, and arrived at morning drill by 6:30, followed by breakfast and prayers between 7:00 and 7:30. (See fig. 1.4.) The Board of Guardians specified what and how much food would be offered to each child each day of the week. Not even the amount and proportions of sugar, flour and water used in the institu-

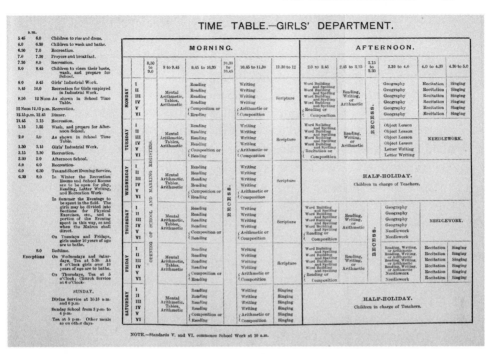

1.4. Like most large residential institutions in nineteenth-century Britain for both rich and poor children, Forest Gate School accounted for every minute of the day and filled it with closely monitored group activities. Forest Gate children enjoyed neither time nor space for privacy. "Timetable for Girls," Annual Report, Forest Gate School, 1888, FGSD/19/A. (Courtesy of London Metropolitan Archives.)

tional suet pudding were left to chance: 10 oz. flour, 3 oz. suet, 1 oz. sugar per pound of pudding.[76]

And what of Nellie's religious life and spiritual development during these early years? Poor Law infirmary creed registers listed Nellie's religion as Church of England. Nellie apparently likened the horror of entering Forest Gate to a frightening illustration from a popular edition of Bunyan's *Pilgrim's Progress,* the epic seventeenth-century narrative retracing the Christian everyman's perilous journey to God's grace. She and all the children at Forest Gate attended Divine Services at 10:15 a.m. and 6 p.m. each Sunday and 6 p.m. every other Thursday. Few poor children in Bow living with their families would have attended services so frequently and regularly. What impact did all this "Poor Law" Christian instruction have on Nellie? According to Mrs. Dowell, not much. Forest Gate taught Nellie a "rude form of religion by people who did not even pretend to believe it themselves."[77] While rivalries between Anglicans and Nonconformists had long dominated parliamentary debates about education, Nellie attended only nondenominational schools controlled by the School Board of London and Poor Law officials. Nellie's schools retained their Christian character, but the content of religious teaching had been hammered out through political wrangling and compromise, not conviction; it aimed to avoid controversy more than inspire faith.

Some officials closest to the provision of religious instruction in the metropolis were not hopeful about its spiritual efficacy. It was no more possible to teach children what truly mattered about God by preparing them for an examination about Scripture facts than it was to quiz them on "brotherly love" and "unselfishness," quipped Edmond Holmes, erstwhile chief inspector of schools. Information about God was altogether different from knowledge of Him, which required "reverence," "devotion," and a capacity to imagine and feel that which could not be seen or touched.[78]

It would be easy to condemn Forest Gate and all those associated with its conception and management as inhumane, intent on stifling a child's creativity and producing a docile class of laborers for the army, navy, servant-keeping households and the capitalist economy. All of these things were at least partly true. Nellie was, in Muriel's telling of her life, an uncooperative victim of—and rebel against—this system, so we have reason to suspect that she found ways to undermine the lockstep severity of the school's regimen. However, this is not the whole story, or rather, there are other stories to tell about Forest Gate. The Superintendent's logbook suggests that the staff worked hard to provide recreation for the children—such as outings to enjoy entertainment at the People's Palace on Mile End Road and swimming lessons. And they likewise struggled to preserve their charges' health by installing the latest sanitary devices in the infants' lavatory on the recommendation of the medical officer Dr. Parker. The head matron and superintendent lobbied the managers to provide holidays for the children and reported the manifest improvement in the children's "general health and appearance."[79] Theirs was an uphill battle against a system predicated on the conviction that pauper children were best served by separating them from their indigent kin. Because Forest Gate was several miles east of Whitechapel and Bow, few parents could even afford the time or the fare to visit their children, except on special occasions.

The institution to which the Dowell children are consigned seeks to mold them into a deferential, patriotic source of labor for the well-to-do. "They were taught," the narrator of "From Birth to Death" bitterly remarks, "to respect the rich and wave Union Jacks ... that one of the really important things in life is that door handles, finger plates, hinges, nozzles to fire hoses, taps and other small brass fittings must be kept in a perennial state of shine."[80] London's chief Inspector of Schools anticipated Muriel's assessment. He acknowledged that "self-expression on the part of the child may be said to have been formally prohibited by all who were responsible for the elementary education of the children of England" in the 1870s, '80s and '90s. School rooms were designed for surveillance and discipline with the children seated in rows ... on long fixed forms."[81] The Inspector of Poor Law Schools for the Metropolitan District, Wyndham Holgate, refused to gloss over the deep structural failings of schools like Forest Gate, which proved competent to teach materials by "fixed rules" "whilst anything that taxes originality of thought is, very often, a lamentable failure."[82] The curriculum reinforced the implicit message conveyed by the organization of space. "Obedience was a recurrent theme in the readers approved for use in the schools, along with diligence, punctuality, patience, tidiness, gratitude and thrift."[83]

The educator Clara Grant headed a London Board school a short distance up Devons Road from Nellie's own school and later assisted Muriel and Doris at Kingsley Hall during World War I. She too recalled with indignation the philosophy undergirding Board school education in the 1880s. "We ought ... to have said, 'What does the child need? What is the best we can give him? He must have it,' but we said none of these things." Board school instruction refused to acknowledge the "common justice" that true education entailed the "fullest development" of each person and instead exacted obedience and cultivated passivity.[84] Grant and Doris Lester championed "self-teaching" along Montessorian lines undertaken by each child at his own pace to develop initiative, "independent judgment" and pleasure in learning.[85] Doris's immersion in the life of Bow and her own friendships with local women, including

Nellie, helped to shape her radical vision of early childhood education as the foundation of citizenship. Her nursery school on Bruce Road (begun around 1912 or 1913) and later Children's House (founded in 1923 as the children-centered part of Kingsley Hall) were antidotes to everything Forest Gate School had come to mean about working-class childhood.

"Robbed" of Her Childhood

Grant's and Lester's values are conspicuously absent from Clara Lucas Balfour's novel about Patience "Patty" Grant, an orphaned and abused "workhouse girl." *Toil and Trust: The Life Story of Patty the Workhouse Girl* was exactly the kind of book children at Forest Gate like Nellie were encouraged to read. It sheds light on the kinds of messages drilled into Nellie as a Poor Law half-orphan. First published as part of a series of shilling morality tales for "Kitchen," Sunday, and Day School libraries in 1860, it remained in print for decades. *Toil and Trust* offered readers heavy-handed moralizing about the rewards of "industry" and "piety," wooden one-dimensional characters, unlikely twists of plot, and a happy ending. Now long forgotten, Balfour was a prolific and popular Christian temperance lecturer and author of exemplary histories and fictions, often about women's achievements and misfortunes.[86] The *Lady's Paper* extolled the "persuasive and attractive eloquence" of this "talented lady" and "friend of humanity;" it likened Mrs. Balfour to Harriet Beecher Stowe, who graciously wrote an introduction for one of her temperance tracts.[87] Balfour insisted that she had drawn Patty's story from real life after making careful inquiries into the fate of workhouse girls who had sought but failed to support themselves as domestic servants. The novel's opening line addressed two readers, one well-born like Muriel who would "think," and the other humbly born like Nellie who would have "felt" what it meant "to be a friendless child . . . to have your bread thrown to you with a grudge, your feeble services repaid with a blow. . . ." Balfour courted both audiences successfully in her lectures at Mechanics Institutes and temperance gatherings. Her tales were explicitly instructive: they provided middle-class and working-class readers with models of right and wrong behavior upon which to base their own actions.

Poor Law orphans in Victorian fiction like Oliver Twist were invariably innocent victims of either unavoidable misfortunes such as their parents' accidental deaths or adults' immoral and imprudent behavior. Patty was both. A workplace accident kills her biological father. Her virtuous mother unwisely remarries a dissolute man with an evil gin-drinking mother who turns Patty into a household "slave" to her own half-siblings. After Patty's mother dies of "hard work" and "heartache," a kindly doctor "rescues" her. Rather than taking her into his own home—the happy fate of Tony, the orphaned street "arab" adopted by an elderly newsagent in Hesba Stretton's *Alone in London*—the doctor sends her to the workhouse as a safe refuge. Balfour is not exactly an apologist for the workhouse but unlike Lester, she does not condemn it. The female ward of the workhouse is a dreary place whose inmates constitute a "promiscuous company" of drunks, deserted wives, and "wretched widows." Patty's moral genius, meek patience and unrelenting toil prevail over all adversities. By the novel's end, we leave her as the proprietress of a snug lodging house.

What is so striking about *Toil and Trust* is just how much it is *not a bildungsroman*. We follow Patty from youth to middle age, but she never grows, changes, and matures as a character because from the moment we first meet her there is nothing childlike about her. She does not play, laugh, get into mischief, act impulsively, or utter an unkind word. As Balfour's narrator explains, Patty's "sufferings and privations, had *robbed* her of her childhood, her present exertions, seemed to put away her girlhood."[88]

What did it mean to be "robbed" of childhood in nineteenth-century Britain and what were its consequences? The Victorians not only fetishized childhood as a time of innocence and purity but manufactured a vast commodity culture around it as well. Novels like *Toil and Trust* and the proliferation of periodicals for and about children such as *Little Folks* participated in the burgeoning print capitalist marketplace in childhood. (We know that Muriel read *Little Folks* because her first publication at age 9½ appeared on its "Our Little Folks' Own Puzzles" page, a feature of each issue.)[89] Children paradoxically became "priceless" treasures even as poor children's exploitation in industrial capitalist workplaces intensified. Julia Luard explained to readers of the *English-*

woman's Review in 1868 that childhood was a time of "open candour and softness of a pure heart and innocent thoughts" sadly incompatible with the daily lives of most young servant girls. An anonymous contributor to the *British Mother's Magazine* in 1845 stressed "the freedom of childhood from the cares and troubles of riper years." Most concurred with the author of the saccharine "Home Without a Mother" that a "mother lost in childhood" meant the loss of childhood's "pleasures." "No mother weeps over the young Ishmaels in the wilderness of the great city," intoned the Reverend James Wells, "these are children robbed of their childhood, whom care and want have made little men and women before they have been boys and girls." Narratives such as *Uncle Tom's Cabin*, hugely popular in Britain, offered readers conspicuous examples of the institutionalized and systematic theft of childhood from slavery's offspring. And when Britons turned their gaze eastward, they were appalled to discover that child marriage in India systematically robbed girls of childhood's freedoms and delights by the age of eight.[90] For such children, childhood was at best fragile and fleeting. Child labor, not childhood, came cheaply in Victorian Britain.

The soft-spoken leader of the Conservative opposition, Sir Stafford Northcote, elaborated the dire consequences for those "robbed" of childhood in an 1881 speech supporting "Preventive Homes" rather than barrack schools for destitute children. His rhetoric is saturated with negations, absences, and lacks.[91] The homes of all poor children, he lamented, possessed "none of the enjoyment, none of the playfulness, none of the cheerfulness . . . none of the innocent prattle" that defined a "real home." This bad situation was only aggravated for those unfortunates whose parents had died or were too poor or too immoral to care for them. He asked his listeners to try to conceive "what a life must be out of which childhood had been taken?" Nothing, he insisted, could ever be done to heal such a wound: "no after advantages can make up for those lost years of childhood."[92]

The children of the poor were doubly disadvantaged in Northcote's formulation. Robbed of childhood, they sustained an irreparable injury, which precluded full adult maturity. Within the deep structure of liberal political thought in Britain from John Locke onward, the educative function of childhood was vital to producing the morally autonomous adult who was capable of exercising the duties and privileges of citizenship. In yet another perverse twist in the developmental logic of child-hood in nineteenth-century culture, those groups robbed of bourgeois childhoods—the poor at home and the "child-like" people of color in the empire—were often rhetorically characterized as permanently child-like in their moral and intellectual limitations. Because they were never truly children, they could not become mature adults and citizens in the political nation.

Northcote made no attempt to reconcile his exaltation of parental love and the family home with his deep suspicion that poor parents could provide neither. It was precisely such views that emboldened so-called child rescuers from the 1860s onwards like Dr. Barnardo and Annie Macpherson to send some poor children to Canada as "appren-tice" farm laborers without the consent of their parents. At such mo-ments, "stolen childhoods" collided violently with poor parents' indig-nant wrath about their "stolen children," all the more so when the rescuers were Protestant and the children Catholic. Rescue and abduc-tion could be and were two names for the same thing.[93]

Muriel's narration of Nellie's childhood does not exactly make this argument. She does make clear that Nellie's removal to Forest Gate ended her childhood, stripped Mrs. Dowell of her right to mother her children, and violated the very laws of nature by frustrating her mater-nal "instinct" to love and serve them. Muriel's choice of the word "in-stinct" carried strong political connotations by 1923. Leading child wel-fare advocates like the eugenicist Caleb Saleeby had enshrined "maternal instinct" as the socio-biological foundation for maternalist arguments to expand social provision for poor mothers while returning them to their rightful places within the home.[94] Muriel's extensive revisions and cross-outs in "From Birth to Death" make visible her struggle to get right this crucial part of her story and argument.

The burden of Her jealousy of the women who were paid to give a perfunc-tory care to her children and hundreds of others became positively painful never lessened became positively painful. She watched the attendants nar-rowly. It seemed monstrous to her that as they glanced round upon the oc-cupants of the visiting room, their eyes never softened when they fell upon her children. The burden of her anguish grew heavier each year. There is no telling what Mrs Dowell suffered in those years.[95]

We can be absolutely certain that she would not have harkened back to the words of the amiable civil service reformer Lord Northcote. Nonetheless, Northcote and Muriel Lester did share one passionate conviction: the education provided by schools like Forest Gate was inimical to the best interests of children and society because it offered neither love nor nurturance. Harriet Dowell acknowledged that Forest Gate cared for the outside of the Dowell children: it fed, clothed, and educated them. But Forest Gate actively discouraged the cultivation of its pupils' spiritual depth and intellectual curiosity.

Forest Gate's endemic failures vexed Henrietta Barnett, the school's most celebrated school manager during Nellie's years there. Henrietta and her husband Reverend Samuel Barnett moved to Whitechapel in 1873 when Samuel became Vicar of St. Jude's. To the dismay of their very poor parishioners, they promptly introduced principles of scientific charity, which eliminated "cash and kind" relief "outside" the doors of the workhouse. To the dismay of traditional Anglicans, they inaugurated an ambitious program of cultural philanthropy with free fine art exhibitions and founded Toynbee Hall university settlement on a nondenominational basis.[96] A disciple of both Jane Nassau Senior and the housing reformer Octavia Hill, Henrietta played a leading role in schemes such as the Metropolitan Association for Befriending Young Servants (MABYS) and the Children's Country Holiday Fund.[97] An outspoken and energetic manager of Forest Gate from 1876 to 1896, she abhorred housing poor children in institutions tainted by association with the Poor Law and pauperism. Committed to a program of "practicable socialism," she accepted the burden and challenge of reforming the barrack school system from within while criticizing its philosophical underpinnings. In her unpublished autobiographical memoir, Barnett took credit for implementing several of Nassau Senior's proposed reforms at Forest Gate during Nellie's time there. She founded a lending library for the school; she organized games and seaside excursions to expose the children to the joys of the world outside Forest Gate and stimulate their imaginations. It marked a considerable triumph in asserting the individual humanity of each child, Barnett believed, when she convinced the inaptly named head matron, Miss Perfect, to address each girl by her Christian name rather than the generic "child." [98]

1.5. Forest Gate School was an immense and imposing institution. The top image underscores it as a well-ordered institution and source of civic pride as men and women promenade on the pathway in front of it. The lower two images highlight the horrific losses caused by the New Year's Eve fire by showing the interiors of the dormitories where "the Children were Suffocated." "Fire at Forest Gate," *Illustrated London News*, January 11, 1890, 56.

Barnett's pleadings had no impact on the broader policies governing barrack school education until disaster struck Forest Gate a year after Nellie's departure. On December 31, 1889, a fire killed twenty-six children in a ward that had been improperly locked shut. The local press condemned mismanagement but ultimately the staff was cleared of any formal charges of negligence. (See fig. 1.5.)

Four years later, Forest Gate once again grabbed headlines and inspired the indignant wrath of East Londoners when several children died of food poisoning. Barnett used these tragedies to mobilize support for and serve on the Departmental Committee on Poor Law Schools (1894–96) chaired by Anthony Mundella. The Committee's well-publicized and controversial findings—based on fifty sessions over two years—reflected Barnett's deep frustration with the impersonality of the school she managed, which lacked utterly the domesticating touch of a mother.[99] The Committee heard over seventy witnesses—Poor Law officials, leaders of child welfare organizations as well as superintendents, matrons and managers of residential schools like Forest Gate. Unlike dozens of similar parliamentary commissions about the lives and labors of the poor from the 1830s onwards, those most affected by the proposed reforms literally had no say in the proceedings. Not a single parent or former inmate of a Poor Law school was called to testify, though witnesses like Maria Poole, longtime secretary of MABYS, spent hours anatomizing their "special failings." Poole produced an ersatz ethnographic guide to London's barrack schoolgirls, all too reminiscent of colonial typologies linking geography, race, and native "character." Poplar girls like Nellie were "dirty, untruthful, frequently dishonest and fond of change," Poole informed the Mundella Committee; St. Pancras girls, by contrast, displayed "restlessness, desire for freedom, and fear to be alone at night." If these girls possessed special virtues, Poole passed over them in silence.[100] (See fig. 1.6.)

The Mundella report marked the triumph of bourgeois expertise over working-class experience. Only one member of the Mundella Committee—the conservative educationist Sir John Gorst—seemed to grasp the illogical cruelty of exalting the family as the cradle of citizenship while refusing to provide resources for loving and able mothers like Harriett Dowell to raise their own children. "Do you think," he asked with considerable pique, "that the treatment of these widows by the State is just? I mean, do you approve of the system by which a widow woman with a large family is made to work day and night, with the impossibility of earning enough to feed and clothe" her children?[101] The Committee refused to consider paying poor widows to raise their own children for fear of pauperizing them and depressing women's already-low wages. The Report called for a root-and-branch overhaul in the education and care of Poor Law children by boarding them with families or establishing small-scale residential units, cottage homes clustered into villages, each with its resident matron.[102] Newspapers as far away as New Zealand joined the chorus of critics who condemned the "disgraceful state of affairs" laid bare by the Mundella report.[103]

Branch.	Special Failings of Local Girls.	Branch.	Special Failings of Local Girls.
Lambeth	Fond of change, untruthful, and unclean in person and work	Camberwell Woolwich	Impertinence, and love of change. Restlessness in their places, no interest in their employers or work, and unwilling to go to work until obliged
Holborn	Not strictly honest in trifles, and untruthful; also a great love of freedom.		
Islington	Deceitful, untruthful, and lazy, with a real dislike to steady work.	Westminster	Impertinence, untruthfulness, and use of bad language
Chelsea	Untruthful, want of punctuality, dirty in person and work. More serious faults are the exception.	Wandsworth	Not so honest as school girls; do not keep their places; dirty and very independent
Marylebone	Untruthful, deceitful, independent, and resentful of interference; great selfishness. A local will fritter all her money on herself. A school girl will spend it in presents (foolishly perhaps) to those from whom she has received kindness	St. Pancras	Restlessness, desire for fredom, and fear to be alone at night.
		Greenwich	Insubordination, restlessness, and expect to do just as they like, and resent being taught.
		Richmond	Want of respect, much given to changing their situations, flighty, and too fond of dress.
Fulham	Self-will and selfishness.	Whitechapel Hampstead	Fond of liberty and change.
Hackney	Ignorance of work, and want of method in it, dirtiness, untidiness, and impatience of control.	Bethnal Green Ealing	——— ———
Deptford	Love of change. A very high opinion of their capabilities, and a proportionate demand for high wages. Much need of a more respectful manner. In some cases a disregard of personal cleanliness.	Poplar	Dirty, untruthful, frequently dishonest, and fond of change.

1.6. Controversial for its harsh condemnation of large impersonal schools like Forest Gate, the so-called Mundella Report was filled with condescending testimony from expert witnesses like Miss Maria Poole from the Metropolitan Association for Befriending Young Servants. This redrawn chart is based on the chart included in Maria Poole's testimony, December 5, 1894, *Report of the Metropolitan Poor Law Schools Committee, Minutes of Evidence*, vol. 2 (London, 1896), 150.

One of the Barnetts' longtime associates at Toynbee Hall, Henry Woodd Nevinson, was an acerbic critic of pauper boarding schools like Forest Gate. His refusal to be bound by bourgeois proprieties in his heterodox private life was matched by his intolerance for injustice: from the mistreatment of London Poor Law orphans to the plight of "slaves" in Portuguese Angola.[104] His 1896 socio-fiction, "Scenes in a Barrack School," reflected his knowledge of the Forest Gate tragedies as well as public policy debates about barrack schools. He narrated the swift cruel descent into poverty of Mrs. Reeve, a respectable East London mother and her four children after the death of her cabinetmaker husband. Like

Lester's "From Birth to Death," "Scenes" told the story of the barrack school from the perspective of a poor mother and her children. As hunger and destitution approach, Mrs. Reeves struggles, as we know Harriet Dowell did, to decide which of her children to keep and which to hand over to Poor Law officials. Like Mrs. Dowell, she tries to diminish the psychological violence of her involuntary choice by focusing on the material security the barrack school promises her children (metal-spring beds, ample food, schooling, the latest hygienic fixtures for bathing and ventilation). Like Lester, Nevinson emphasized the unthinking cruelty of Poor Law officials and staff for whom family tragedies were the invisible backdrop to the mechanical performance of their day-to-day routines. The story ends with Nevinson's assessment of the dreary devastation caused by the school. Mrs. Reeve's son emerges as a "machine-made" man condemned to push an oil truck on the Isle of Dogs; his sister, inept at domestic service, may eventually yield to the insatiable global demand for "pretty girls" like her. Nevinson's conclusions are all the more disturbing because he eschews sensation, moralizing, and melodrama in favor of closely observed detail and irony.[105]

Given the increasingly public character of Barnett's condemnation of Forest Gate, she resigned as school manager in 1896. Two fiery East London Labour leaders, George Lansbury and Will Crooks, immediately joined the Management Committee.[106] Their arrival marked a revolution in the school's history, one in which local working-class residents rather than bourgeois social reformers and shopkeepers assumed leadership. Lansbury continued to serve as a manager of Forest Gate for the next three decades. By the time Muriel, Doris, and Nellie established the first Kingsley Hall in 1915, Lansbury was their most vocal and powerful ally in East London. Dowell and Lansbury must have swapped stories about Forest Gate School.

Frustrated by a system she could not transform from within, Henrietta Barnett devised a system to make up for some of Forest Gate School's egregious failings. She purchased Harrow Cottage, facing the White Stone Pond on Hampstead Heath, where she installed Mrs. Moore, the beloved nurse who had reared her—along with three hand-picked fourteen-year-old girls from Forest Gate School. Each Forest Gate girl stayed at Harrow Cottage for three months (to be replaced by another) to receive training in domestic service along with the love and personal attention of Henrietta and her staff.[107] It was from among these girls that Henrietta recruited servants for Toynbee Hall, the world-renowned outpost of social investigation and welfare that she and Samuel established in Whitechapel in 1884. These servant girls formed a direct bridge between her Poor Law and settlement house work. According to the superintendent's logbook, Mrs. Barnett selected Nellie's older sister Alice to join several other Forest Gate girls at Harrow Cottage on September 12, 1887.[108] Given Henrietta's close relationship with Forest Gate, her deep knowledge of case work methodology from her days as a member of the Charity Organisation Society, and her care in selecting appropriate girls to train at Harrow Cottage, she must have known Alice, Nellie and their family history rather well. Nor was this the first time that the Barnetts' and the Dowells' lives had intersected. Samuel Barnett had officiated at the wedding of Nellie's uncle, Archibald Henry Sloan, on Christmas day 1880.[109]

Henrietta Barnett's ambivalent relationship to Forest Gate School as its leading manager and most outspoken critic captures well just how deeply divided Victorians were about working-class childhood, the state's duties toward poor children and its execution of them. When we view publicly funded institutions like Marner Street School and Forest Gate from the inside—from the perspective of teachers, administrators, school managers and staff—we find ample evidence of devotion, creativity, good intentions, and even some laudable results. As much as Harriet Dowell despised the child welfare system that compelled her to give up her children, she acknowledged that it did provide better material conditions for them than she could. But even those who worked inside these institutions felt constrained by a system that favored efficiency and economies of scale above individuality and initiative. Everyone seemed to concur that it was a great misfortune that so many poor children were "robbed" of their childhoods through no fault of their own. For most, such lost childhoods were unavoidable and acceptable casualties. Better for poor children to lose their childhood than to demoralize their parents and bankrupt ratepayers by providing sufficient "outdoor relief" (cash payments) for mothers like Harriet Dowell to retain custody of their children.

Did Nellie Dowell have a childhood or was she, like the fictional workhouse girl Patty, "robbed" of her childhood? For men and women like Sir Stafford Northcote, the answer seems clear. Nellie did not have a childhood because she did not grow up surrounded by the love of her parents. Those associated with Forest Gate offer a more complicated answer. Henrietta Barnett came to repudiate its impersonality and the lack of family-like relationships among staff and children, which she believed cheated children of childhood. The staff at Forest Gate and in the educational bureaucracy seemed well aware of the school's deficiencies. What is most notable is the extent to which they sought to give children the sorts of pleasures associated with prevailing bourgeois ideas about "childhood" as a time of innocence and play. Forest Gate provided its charges with what might best be called a "Poor Law childhood"—one marked by routines at odds with the cultivation of individuality. Institutions like Forest Gate sought to equip their pupils with low-level occupational skills. Officials' careful tracking of students' working lives reveals a great deal about Poor Law childhood: they measured success by the extent to which their former charges supported themselves without resort to poor relief.

For Muriel, working-class children did, can, and should have childhoods. Nellie's early life before her father's death demonstrated this to her. Mrs. Dowell cultivated Nellie's intellect and nurtured her individuality. The problem, from Muriel's perspective, is that all too often poor children did not have childhoods. Muriel implicitly argues that the proper role of the state and voluntary charities is to support, rather than sever, the bonds connecting family members. The state violates, rather than protects, its most vulnerable wards. In Muriel's telling of Nellie's life, the outrage to Nellie's person betokened by her shorn curls is merely the outward sign of the systemic outrage against the intellectual, moral, spiritual, and social life of the poor. The apparatus of the state, Muriel insists, serves its own deformed imperative by seeking to make working-class children into docile laborers and patriotic foot soldiers for its imperial wars. The state ought to be the guarantor of childhood for all. What exactly does this mean? Muriel's ideas about the sort of childhood girls like Nellie deserved were shaped by how she understood her own childhood. The figure of the slum child haunted middle-class childhood as both its abject outside—everything it was not—and as the object of bourgeois children's benevolent attentions.

THE APPRENTICESHIP OF MURIEL LESTER

Muriel Lester was an expert at telling her life story. No matter what the topic—poverty in East London, economic imperialism and global peace, the struggle for Indian independence, drug traffic in Japanese-occupied Manchuria, Christ's message of universal love, women's rights and wrongs—Muriel's own story leaked into what she said and wrote. This was not a case of rampant narcissism. Her autobiographical impulse had deep roots within the genre of British Protestant spiritual autobiography, which charted the individual Christian's perilous earthly journey to grace. Nineteenth-century Christian philanthropists invariably used life writing to demonstrate not only their path to God but the means by which they discovered their vocation serving the outcast and downtrodden. The fin-de-siècle French sociologist Émile Durkheim imagined a homo-duplex who struggled to reconcile the insatiable egoistic desires of the individual self with the regulative claims of the altruistic social self. Christian do-gooders, including Muriel, resolved this tension by producing narratives in which the making of the "ethical" self hinged upon caring for others.[110]

Childhood played a crucial part in the process of forging—and narrating the formation of—ethical subjects. It was the period in the individual's development that provided the foundation for "proper" moral, intellectual, and spiritual adulthood. When Victorians decried the stolen childhoods of the poor, they also surreptitiously smuggled in justification for excluding the poor from the full rights and privileges of citizenship. Muriel understood this only too well. In her many versions of her childhood, she stressed moments that anticipated and propelled her toward her calling as a pacifist, feminist, Christian revolutionary. She entitled a draft chapter of her first published autobiography, "A nineteenth century child"—suggesting that her story was both her own as well as the story of nineteenth-century childhood itself. Because she devoted her life to educating poor children, Doris Lester was even more keenly aware than Muriel of how her own childhood related to "childhood" writ large as well as to the lives of poor children such as Nellie Dowell, who shadowed—or perhaps more aptly illuminated—Muriel and Doris Lester's prolific writings about childhood and their shared lives as children.

Waifs and Dolls, Sisters and Servants

It would be hard to imagine a more congenial late-Victorian childhood than that of Muriel Lester. By her birth in December 1883, her father, Henry Lester, had long since recovered from a crushing financial debacle in the 1850s as well as the loss of his first two wives in childbirth. He had happily married Muriel's mother, Rachel Goodwin, a widow twenty years his junior. Together they formed what Muriel called a "conglomeration" of families with nine children. Eight of them "owned" father; six "owned" mother; Gertrude, Kathleen, Muriel, Doris, and Kingsley "owned" both parents. We know nothing about how their parents and four oldest siblings coped with grief over their lost spouses and parents. Nor did Muriel and Doris offer even the slightest hint that the Lesters may have faced challenges combining different families into one. No lady visitor came into their home to evaluate their manners, morals, or fitness to care for their children. In *It Occurred to Me* (1937), Muriel conspicuously refused to take up literary modernists' program of anatomizing the hypocrisies, secrets, and subtle psychic terrors of family life.[111] What is clear is that Muriel, Doris, and Kingsley forged an inseparable trio, a kind of nuclear family within their larger family. Apparently several of their siblings impinged so little on their carefree lives that they remain unnamed in Muriel and Doris's autobiographies.

Their father, Henry Lester, was a self-made man. While he never bragged about his achievements or made a show of his wealth, he readily acknowledged his humble origins. He knew that he owed his wealth to his employees' hard labor and tried to repay them as best he could. "Father never for an instant forgot and never let us forget the lot of the Victorian poor," Muriel recalled. One of eleven children of an East London carpenter, Henry made his fortune as a shipwright in the dockland economy. He secured several patents and his firm, Perkins and Lester, flourished in the 1860s. By the 1880s, his years of financial worry and striving were behind him. He had secured all the trappings of an affluent, civic-minded Christian gentleman. He was now a wealthy shipbuilder, prominent member of his Baptist church, and elected member of West Ham's first school board. For Henry Lester, benevolence marked, but did not cloak, his social ascent. A figure of local significance, he chaired the West Ham school board in 1892 and served as President of the Essex Baptist Union. He was part of a steady migration of Cockneys-made-good who built spacious homes in Essex, to the east of East London.[112] Muriel spent her childhood at Gainsborough Lodge in Leytonstone, a prosperous leafy suburb peopled by substantial businessmen and managers of rising fortunes with social aspirations. The Lesters' neighbors included a corn merchant, newspaper proprietor, surgeon, news advertising contractor, and confectionary manufacturer. Several, like Henry, grew up in poor neighborhoods such as St. George's in the East and Spitalfields.[113]

The Lester household combined high spirits with strong moral convictions about godliness and benevolence. Religion and play were woven tightly into the fabric of day-to-day life. Reading a chapter of the Bible before going to sleep each night was as natural as brushing hair and teeth. So too vigorous games and prayer—both in private and as a family—were simply part of the "day's pattern." The Lesters maintained three different charity boxes in their home into which they—along with friends and visitors—were expected to place small-denomination coins each week. Muriel had charge of foreign missions; Kingsley, the book-shaped Bible Society box; and Doris, one for the local poor. These three boxes capture perfectly the domestic and global ambitions of the late-Victorian Nonconformist conscience with its elaborate missionary machinery serving the poor at home and heathens abroad. Undoubtedly, Doris also mentioned these details because they foreshadowed her own and her siblings' future interests. Kingsley would become a clergyman, Muriel would make the world her parish, and Doris would remain deeply attached to the people of Bow as founder and head of her experimental nursery school, Children's House.[114]

Sundays were "red letter days" in the Lester household, full of rituals that celebrated godliness and domestic joys. Their mother Rachel brightened the Sabbath by purchasing chocolates for Henry to distribute to each child. Before eating their ample Sunday roast, Henry insisted that the children bring the first plate of food, hot from the table, to the crossing sweeper stationed nearby. This was a more personal kind of charity than asking the cook or scullery maid to distribute scraps of leftovers to

Our Sunday Text.

Papa
Hold thou me up and I shall be safe.

Mother
Rest in the Lord and wait patiently for him.

Gertrude
The Lord is my light and my salvation.

Kathleen
Bless the Lord O my soul.

Muriel
Looking unto Jesus.

Gertrude Lester June 10
1888

1.7. Muriel's first entry into the Lester Family writing album was "Looking Unto Jesus." Servants shared Sunday morning family prayers with the Lesters but never entered their names or Bible passages into the album. Lester Family Writing Album. (Courtesy of Bishopsgate Institute.)

the local poor, but it still was unmistakably old-fashioned *noblesse oblige*. While Muriel and Doris generally enjoyed the children's sermons delivered by the pastor of Fillebrooke Chapel, Muriel makes clear that she was no spiritual prodigy. She gratefully recalled that her mother allowed the younger children to daydream and play silent games during the interminable adult sermon. Every Sunday, each member of the family selected a line from Scripture, duly entered into a beautiful leather-bound family writing album, and shared a few thoughts about it.[115] (See fig. 1.7.)

In an undated vignette that Muriel scribbled into a red leather diary decades after Henry Lester's death, she recalled that "every morning of the week after 7:30 breakfast the servants would be summoned by a whistle down the tube to the basement and we would all sit quiet while Father read from the Bible. Then we knelt while he gave a short prayer in his own words and we all joined in the 'Our Father.' "[116] Muriel betrays no disapproving irony at the many possible meanings of "Our Father" in the context of a ritual that so powerfully affirmed Henry Lester's patriarchal authority. She narrates a scene of Christian unity and household solidarity that inscribes servants as integral to, but also apart from, the family. Called to ascend from below stairs to join the family in prayer, none entered a Scripture line in the family writing album. This was a privilege reserved exclusively for family and visiting friends. Hierarchy went hand in hand with intimacy in well-to-do households like the Lesters'. Muriel's refusal to criticize her father's class- and gender-based performance as Christian paterfamilias—even long after his death—was a measure of her love and devotion to him. It also required her to set aside the feminist, Christian egalitarian and socialist principles upon which she had based her own life's work.

Henry Lester could not abide by the angry, punishing God of sin and salvation of his devout father who had held Henry's finger above a flame to feel the hellish torments awaiting sinners. Nor did he hew to the narrow sectarianism that divided many Nonconformists from one another. Although Baptists, the Lesters also worshipped at Congregationalist and Methodist chapels and even felt comfortable in the Church of England. No one Protestant denomination had a monopoly on God and godliness. Closely engaged in rearing his youngest children, Henry invented games like "Bible Arithmetic" to hone their knowledge of the Bible.[117] Best of all, Henry fostered his children's love of God by stimulating their imaginations through his weekly "dream" stories in which he and they became characters in Bible stories. In this way, the Bible was much less a record of a distant past than a deeply meaningful story that continued to unfold in the present. God's love was a real presence in their daily lives.[118]

God had plenty of company in the Lester nursery over which their beloved nurse, "Tannie" presided. (Fannie Lilley was her actual name.)[119] Waifs and dolls figured importantly in Muriel and Doris's roseate stories of their nursery world of play and imagination, freedom, and Christian duty. *Just Children,* Doris's privately published set of essays on childhood, explicitly connects these two preoccupations with one another and with her work with poor children in Bow in the first decades of the twentieth century. *Just Children* starts with chapters about "east end youngsters" and concludes with Doris's memories of her own childhood. In her pedagogical politics, all children play, act, think, and make decisions for themselves. There is a subtle note of self-congratulation in her opening vignette: her work as a nursery school educator ensures that no children are "robbed" of their childhood. *Just Children* begins with Bill, "hurtling down the street" toward the big green door of Children's House "with his home-made chariot, an orange box with one creaky wheel and a piece of wood for a pusher;" we watch a "group of little girls . . . undressing, bathing and putting to bed a large unbreakable doll" in Doris's Montessori-inspired nursery school. Doris lightheartedly claimed that she had begun to collect her own "international family" of children long before she opened her nursery school in the cramped back garden of 58–60 Bow Road. Her most beloved "child" was Cosy, a limbless "flat-faced" "plain" Dutch doll who was "part of my very life" and from whom Doris could not bear to be separated.[120]

Muriel's relationship with her favorite doll, the beautiful Iris Riversmere, was no less engrossing and psychologically complex. Fearful that her admiration for Iris, "my beloved companion of the rich brown curls, big eyes, and ever-placid face," had turned into idolatry, a panicked Muriel once literally "knocked" Iris down from her "exalted position" perched on her knees. Doris, in a slyly surreptitious commentary about her sister's lordly demeanor, observed that while Cosy, was "very ordinary," Iris was the daughter of rather grand aristocrats. (Apparently, Iris even enjoyed the comforts of a handmade, inlaid mahogany bed.)[121] This was clearly a case of "our dolls, ourselves." Throughout their lifelong loving partnership as sisters and fellow workers, Doris saw herself as the "plain" and "ordinary" toiler in the shadow of her commanding older sister. Bow people who remembered the sisters frequently echoed this comparison.

Doris's passion for Cosy matched the intensity of her fascination for poor children. Imagination and empathy mingle in her recounting of the literary origins of her awakening to the suffering of waifs, which she attributed to discovering *Little Orphans* among their nursery books. The physical appearance of the orphaned protagonists echoes Doris's descriptions of Cosy and Iris, herself and Muriel.

> [T]he story was of plain Ann, the ordinary orphan, and Ermintrude, the bewitchingly attractive one. Suddenly I awoke to realize there were lots of Anns and Ermintrudes in the world. So I started a pretend boarding school of my own. I invented the children, I chose their names, their ages, their appearances, I clothed them and planned their rooms. Each had her own room decorated in a special colour. I not only housed and fed them, but I educated

them also; the only feature of the scheme that I remember is that all prizes were books bound in rich leather to match the colour scheme of the individual room.[122]

Doris's "imagined orphans" enjoy the privileges of daughters of the well-to-do professional classes. They get sent to a nice boarding school—not Forest Gate School—where each enjoys a room and a color of her own. She rewards their achievements—much as girls like Muriel and Doris were rewarded—with leather-bound prize books.

Late-Victorian school mistresses regularly presented the novels and poems of didactic children's writer Elizabeth Anna Hart as prize books because they so often and so directly addressed the obligations of middle-class girls to their less fortunate sisters. Hart's novel *Clare Linton's Friend* (first serialized in 1884) offers an exemplary guide to the social and moral education of late-Victorian middle-class girls. Books just like it lined the shelves of the Lesters' nursery library. The copy that I own was given to Alice Jackson, a pupil at Christ Church Girls' School in February 1905 in recognition of her "diligence and proficiency." (See fig. 1.8.)

If Balfour's *Toil and Trust* taught poor girls their proper place in the world, *Clare Linton's Friend*, originally serialized in *Little Folks*, instructed middle-class girls how to feel, think, and act toward their downtrodden sisters. Pampered but kind Clare stumbles over orphaned Polly on her snow-covered doorstep and insists on sheltering her for the night. Clare instantly attaches herself to Polly as her benevolent rescuer and petulant owner. Her aggressive affection mimics girls' intense relationships with their dolls as sisters and servants. " 'Papa,' " she cried, 'Hester [the maid] has locked my Polly up, and won't give me the key . . .' '*Your* Polly, Clare! Who gave her to you, I wonder?' "[123]

Indeed: who "gave" girl waifs and orphans to fictional little girls like Clare Linton and her flesh-and-blood counterparts is the question raised and answered by the novel. We know that poor mothers like Harriet Dowell did not voluntarily give away children to become girl waifs for bourgeois children. One answer is that writers like Mrs. Hart did so repeatedly in short stories, novels, poems, and essays published in children's magazines. Take, for example, "A Child's Thought" (1868), one of Hart's popular poems written twenty-five years before *Clare Linton's Friend*. Identification between the bourgeois child narrator and "little

1.8. The prize plate celebrated the recipient's "diligence and proficiency," which mirrored the didactic goals of books like *Clare Linton's Friend* for its schoolgirl readers. Elizabeth Anna Hart, *Clare Linton's Friend* (London, 1900) (In author's possession).

beggar children, with your little ragged dresses" quickly turns into an occasion for refining the child narrator's own moral sensibilities and differentiating her happiness from their misery. The "child" ponders everything beggar children presumably lack: "joys," "caresses," "homes," and "kisses." The vagrant "wanderings" of the beggar children prompt a round of questions about whether "love makes bright your homes at night, your misery to soften; and do you ever, *ever* play, you helpless little creatures . . . and have you any teachers?" Posed as questions, we never doubt that the answer to each is a sad resounding "no."

The final stanza enunciates the ethical action that reading the poem is meant to inspire.

> I think my feelings towards you should
>   be soft and tender,
> And even I might plan, and try some
>   tiny aid to render;
> I'll often give you all I can out of my
>   little treasure,
> And I will pray—yes, every day—that
>   you may have some pleasure![124]

In yet another reminder of the profound difference separating them, the child informs the little beggars that "my life is very pleasant, the past is dear, the future clear, and, best of all, the present; I am a happy child." "A Child's Thought" suggests that poor children get neither happiness nor childhood. Their hardships do, however, enable well-to-do girls like the child narrator to feel good about herself by doing good to them.

Such writings enjoined girls to broaden their moral remit beyond their families to their needy neighbors. Framed as duty, the care of "helpless little creatures" was a privilege crucial to the self-definition of all middle-class females. Clare's relationship with Polly is part of Clare's moral education.[125] She demonstrates genuine affection and trust in Polly—so much so that she herself is briefly "stolen" (actually kidnapped) trying to rescue Polly from the demonic mother "Sal the Sloper." At the same time, *Clare Linton's Friend* repeatedly reduces Polly to Clare's doll-like companion whose fate the Lintons completely control. Hart emphasizes this point when Clare's cocksure cousin Harry ventures gamely into the slums to find Polly. He returns with a half dozen hungry, ragged girls, each professing to be called Polly and more than willing to be Clare's "friend."

> "Have you found Polly?" she [Clare] cried, almost whispering from excitement.
>
> "Polly!" shouted he [Harry], "phoo!- that wouldn't be much—I've found Pollies! Take your choice. Here's half a dozen of them!"
>
> And flinging open the hall door, he displayed on the steps half a dozen ragged children huddled together. . . .
>
> "They all say they're Polly," he cried, with a little wave of the hand toward them. "Pick and choose . . . I couldn't be too particular about measuring," explained Harry; "but they'll about do. . . . I might have had a dozen more, but I couldn't take any except with dark eyes."[126]

Inconveniently, Clare wants only her special Polly—not just any of the Pollies whom Harry has selected from the apparently illimitable supply of them available to any genteel youth willing to shop for them in the slums. Polly—and all slum Pollies—are more animate dolls than persons. Inequality is essential to the love that defines the reciprocities of "friendship" in *Clare Linton's Friend*.

Few girls in late-Victorian Britain actually got a waif of their very own. But their tender, bossy relationships with their dolls taught them powerful lessons about the muddled lines dividing the intimacies of sisterhood from the hierarchies of servanthood.[127] Books like *Clare Linton's Friend* and poems like "A Child's Thought" were part of the Lesters' curriculum in cross-class sisterhood. Muriel and Doris's loving friendship with Nellie Dowell can and ought to be viewed as one legacy of this education, even as both sisters later critiqued its class-based assumptions about power and privilege.

New Girls?

In the late 1880s and '90s, the New Woman burst upon the scene, at once a literary invention and a term describing unmarried, educated middle-class women who boldly claimed for themselves new social rights and duties.[128] Abetted by novelists, journalists discovered that the New Woman made good copy and compelling plots. They eagerly chronicled her dangerous defiance of social conventions as she bicycled along country paths and lanes; went to Girton or Newnham or Somerville to study Greek, maths, and history; smoked cigarettes; ventured into the slums to nurse the poor or live with like-minded women in settlement houses; and dared to earn her own living beyond the authority of husbands, fathers, and brothers. Invariably, fictional New Women and their real-life counterparts paid a high price for their freedoms. Marriage and motherhood were hard to square with their adventurous independence. So too, opposite-sex love often seemed elusive and incompatible with female ambition and personal autonomy.[129]

Writers of juvenile fiction decided that New Women must have emerged from somewhere and invented New Girls who populated a steady stream of novels with titles like *Polly: A New Fashioned Girl* (1889). New Girls tended to be less threatening than their older New Woman counterparts. They were more often high-spirited rather than defiant; enthusiastic rather than zealously dogmatic; unconventional rather than morbid; Christian in their outlook rather than secular or religiously heterodox.[130]

Not many middle-class girls actually lived "New Girl" lives.[131] Muriel and Doris did. What made this possible? Their parents' views about girls, their schooling, and even the posh suburb of Loughton (where the family moved in 1901) contributed to their deeply religious but distinctly "advanced" views about gender and society and their keen sense that they could and should contribute to its betterment. Unlike girls growing up only a generation before them, the Lester sisters never seemed to have doubted that what they thought and did mattered, and that they could and should have their own ideas.

Too godly to be counted among the altruistic aesthetes and cranks of the fin de siècle, Henry Lester embraced some of their distinctly modern ideas. Muriel recalled that her father regularly wore that avant-garde article of hygienic clothing, the Jaeger dressing gown, whose "live wool," unlike "dead vegetable fibres," threw off the body's "malodorous emanations." Lester sartorially identified himself with faddists and Utopian socialists like George Bernard Shaw, Jaeger's most eccentric and famous British champion.[132] Rachel Lester aligned herself with one of late-nineteenth-century London's most politically advanced schemes to improve the lot of the poor. In 1892, she was a founding vice president of the Congregationalist Canning Town Women's Settlement. Canning Town was the all-female branch of Mansfield House begun in 1889 by Balliol graduate Percy Alden—later knighted for his work as Chairman of Save the Children. At both settlements, advanced Liberalism shaded imperceptibly into municipal socialism. Early residents at Canning Town Women's Settlement included West Ham's first alderwoman, the socialist Labour leader Edith Kerrison. The sisters Fanny and Anna Tillyard established a hospital run by women for women. Alden's future wife, Dr. Margaret Pearse, served as its chief consulting physician.[133] Clearly, Rachel supported and appreciated powerful women whose religious convictions propelled them to undertake innovative political and social action in their community. Rachel and Henry allowed their daughters to ride bicycles unchaperoned across the countryside like George Gissing's pretty but unfortunate Monica Madden—a freedom angrily decried by critics as unsexing girls. Doris had no such qualms about the emancipatory consequences of bicycling. She extolled the bicycle for fostering a spirit of independence that "paved the way for the Suffrage Movement!"[134]

Henry and Rachel sent their daughters to a progressive coeducational preparatory school, Wanstead College.[135] Coeducational private schools were unusual in the 1890s and often disdained and dismissed as distinctly "American" and un-English.[136] A 1903 volume of essays seeking to spread the gospel of coeducational secondary schools listed only thirty such establishments in England and Wales.[137] Some of these, including Wanstead College, were mixed sex up to the age of fourteen and single sex for the final two or three years.[138]

The headmaster of Wanstead College, Thomas Beecham Martin, and his wife Emilia were "original, modern and delightful."[139] A former head of an elementary school in Macclesfield before opening his own school in Wanstead, Thomas Martin was the son of a Cornish Wesleyan Methodist minister.[140] In such a small and intimate school environment, Muriel, Doris, and the other students must have been very aware of Mrs. Martin's advanced social, political, and economic commitments as an active member of the Metropolitan Association of Women in Council, which sometimes met at the college. The Council's objects were far-reaching: women's mutual education; support "by every means in our power, measures which will secure to women, the same Parliamentary and other rights as men;" discouraging "class prejudice" while encouraging the "economic independence of women"; and finally, to advance the cause of co-education as a model of "combined action of men and women in all public work."[141]

Mrs. Martin was also a vegetarian. Muriel "caught the habit from her" and kept to it her entire life.[142] Muriel says nothing about how her parents and family responded to and accommodated her radical diet; nor did she elaborate the intellectual and ethical basis for her decision. In the context of the 1890s, vegetarianism nested within a politically and socially heterodox subculture whose boundaries encompassed middle-class socialists, pacifists, Esperantists, anti-vivisectionists, Simple Lifers, and gender-sex bohemians like Henry Salt and his lesbian wife, Kate. London's vegetarian community of restaurants and associations welcomed a young Indian barrister, Mohandas K. Gandhi, who promptly joined the committee of the London Vegetarian Society in 1890.[143]

Turn-of-the-century Loughton proved to be a congenial locale for rearing "new girl" daughters. Despite (or perhaps because of) its social exclusivity, its proximity to Epping Forest's wooded parkland, its direct access via the Great Eastern Railway to East London's philanthropic institutions and the City, Loughton's affluent residents included an un-

1.9. Early twentieth-century Loughton bordered the vast leafy expanse of Epping Forest and was mostly populated by families like the Lesters whose wealth was based in commerce and manufacture. Postcard of Earl's Path, Loughton, c.1908. (Courtesy of Chris Pond, Loughton and District Historical Society.)

usually large number of progressive thinkers interested in social and political questions.[144] (See fig. 1.9.) Arthur Morrison, the "realist" slum novelist and connoisseur of Japanese prints, lived in sprawling Salcombe House, a short stroll down Upper Park Road from the Grange, the Lester's family manse.[145] Aesthetic-minded slum reformers like the chemist Arthur Pillans Laurie, the social statistician and child-welfare champion Hubert Llewellyn Smith, and the radical journalist and economist Vaughan Nash occupied Arts and Crafts homes in Loughton where they established a "colour" (paint) manufactory along Ruskinian lines.[146] Josiah Oldfield, the controversial leader of the vegetarian movement, established Oriolet Hospital, a sanatorium and retreat founded on vegetarian principles located near the Lesters. With more amusement than shock, Loughton's turn-of-the-century chronicler and inveterate recorder of local gossip, William Chapman Waller, commented that Oldfield had abandoned Oriolet and his wife when he ran off with an especially comely nurse employed there.[147] Loughton, much like Hampstead and Bloomsbury, attracted more than its share of "the moneyed and the aesthetic" as well as a radicals, socialists, and advanced Nonconformists.[148] The new ideas percolating in fin-de-siècle Britain found hospitable soil in Loughton among its bohemian intellectuals, civil servants, and reform-minded capitalists like Henry Lester himself. More than railroad tracks connected Loughton to the slums of East London.

Rachel and Henry Lester consistently and intentionally exposed their daughters to some of the most progressive thinking about religion, female education, social problems, and women's roles in society. They were, Doris averred, well ahead of their times when it came to principles and practices of child rearing. Rachel Lester set her heart on sending Muriel to one of Britain's leading girls' "public schools," St. Leonard's in Scotland. England's great public schools for boys—Eton, Harrow, Winchester, and Rugby—enjoyed pride of place for centuries as training grounds for future leaders of church and state. Essential sites for reproducing Britain's ruling elite, they fostered deep institutional loyalty and dense social networks for their privileged male pupils drawn from the aristocracy, landed gentry, clergy, and wealthy professionals. Founded from the 1860s onwards, girls' public schools and "high schools" like St. Leonard's, North London Collegiate, and the Cheltenham Ladies College lacked the pedigreed social cachet of their ancient, richly endowed, all-male counterparts. They drew students largely from the clerical, professional, and business classes. Academic and social hothouses premised on faith in girls' capacity to master heretofore masculine domains of knowledge, these new schools expected girls to think critically, creatively and independently.

St. Leonard's vaulted to the forefront of girls' secondary education when one of its distinguished former students, Agnata Ramsay, placed first in the Classical Tripos at Cambridge in 1887—besting all the men in her mastery of Greek and Latin history and literature. Even Benjamin Jowett, the revered Master of Balliol College, Oxford, lent his enormous prestige by praising St. Leonard's for treating girls as "honourable, responsible beings."[149] The school was a by-product of the movement for women's higher education in Scotland and England that led to granting the Ladies Licentiate in Arts (instituted in 1876) by its illustrious near neighbor, St. Andrews as well as the founding of Girton (as the College for Women in Hitchen in 1869) and Newnham (1871) in Cambridge.[150] For its first three decades, Girton graduates dominated the staff and leadership of St. Leonard's and brought with them their high intellectual standards as well as their intensely homosocial culture of female love and friendship. The first head of St. Leonard's, the Scotswoman Louisa Lumsden, arrived with Constance Maynard, her lover and partner. They served on the staff until their tumultuous relationship deteriorated and both women sought separate venues in which to continue their work of building new institutions for women's intellectual advancement.[151] Schools like St. Leonard's cultivated powerful emotional attachments among students as well as between teachers and students articulated through ritualized, erotically charged relationships called "raves" and "crushes."[152] No evidence suggests that Muriel formed such a relationship, but St. Leonard's offered her ample opportunities to observe them. In her diary, she noted that during a gossipy stroll, her friend Frieda told her all about a fellow student called Joy and "a fuss about a certain girl who liked her."[153]

The *St. Leonard's Gazette* of the 1880s and '90s provides a vivid portrait of a rapidly expanding institution committed to building girls' bodies and characters through strenuous team sports such as lacrosse and hockey, and developing their intellectual faculties through a rigorous curriculum that included Greek and Latin.[154] (See fig. 1.10.) By the time Muriel arrived in 1898, St. Leonard's occupied impressive grounds with ancient buildings and spacious playing fields close by the cathedral and St. Andrews.[155]

In many respects, St. Leonard's was an institutional ideal for the education of female boarding students. It was everything that Forest Gate School was not. Just as Jane Nassau Senior and Henrietta Barnett had demanded the dissolution of Poor Law barrack schools in favor of small cottage households presided over by loving matrons, so too St. Leonard's was divided into Houses, each with its own mistress, dining room, and study, and its own highly cultivated sense of corporate domesticity and identity. No doubt responding to widespread fears that female scholars' devotion to studies jeopardized their health, the girls were not allowed to do work before breakfast or after 8:30 p.m. Academic subjects dominated the morning curriculum from 9:00 to 12:30 p.m. with a range of

1.10. Muriel entered St. Leonard's in 1898 and lived in Bishopshall West, pictured in the background behind the playing fields. She enjoyed success there as scholar, athlete (she played cricket, lacrosse, and field hockey), musician, and leader. She gained the Oxford and Cambridge Higher Certificate before returning home to the Grange. St. Leonard's School, Bishopshall East and West, 1895. (Courtesy of St. Leonard's School, St. Andrews. Fife.)

less strenuous special subjects in the afternoons. The hour and a half after dinner were given over to games and sports each day.[156]

Muriel and Nellie occupied precisely those social and economic locations—the daughter of a progressive, upper-middle-class capitalist and a Poor Law half-orphan—that sanctioned their removal from their families in favor of boarding in an educational institution. If St. Leonard's was a quintessential Victorian heterotopia—a "somewhere" outside the social norms that existed in reality—Forest Gate was its dystopic counterpart. In the eyes of some contemporaries, the independent "new girls" of St. Leonard's and the Poor Law orphans of Forest Gate exemplified disordered family life. They were not harbingers of welcome social change but social problems in themselves.

The expansion of academically and physically rigorous schools for daughters of the well-to-do struck a sensitive nerve in late-Victorian Britain. Medical doctors and social commentators alike alarmed the public with claims that girls were overtaxing their minds with study and their bodies' with bicycling, hockey, and lacrosse at the expense of their emotional and physical well-being. Institutions like St. Leonard's, far from preparing their "old girls" to serve the best interests of the nation, appeared to produce hysterics and mannish spinsters incapable—or worse yet—uninterested in settling into the joys of conjugality and motherhood. They seemed intent on making their "New Girls" into "New Women." The impoverished and orphaned female charges at Forest Gate likewise seemed far removed from Victorian ideals of femininity. Reared without the benefit of mother love and family life, such girls lacked even the rudimentary skills to undertake their domestic obligations as future wives and mothers of the nation's soldiers and workers. Muriel and Nellie's "girlhoods" could not have been more different. But what they shared in common was the expectation that girls like Muriel would befriend girls like Nellie who had been well schooled in deferring to her betters.

Muriel's autobiographical writing offered no commentary on the heated debates surrounding the virtues and vices of her own education. She extolled St. Leonard's for nurturing her gifts as a thinker and leader. Her formidable housemistress of Bishopshall West, the aristocratic Alice de Natorp, taught piano to her girls—one of Muriel's many accomplishments—and nightly read aloud novels by the nineteenth-century's leading women writers: Austen, Gaskell, and Eliot. This was a curriculum designed to encourage girls to ask questions, seek answers for themselves, and lead. On her own, Muriel found time to explore the biographies of two great religious figures, both masters of self-abnegation and spiritual purity: she read the hugely controversial Protestant recasting of St. Francis's story, Paul Sabatier's *Life of St Francis of Assisi* (1893) and Edwin Arnold's poetic rendering of the life of Buddha in *Light of Asia* (1879). Muriel flourished at St. Leonard's. A proficient athlete, she was head girl of Bishopshall West in her final year and her housemistress would remain a generous supporter of the Lesters' work in Bow in the years ahead.

Doris's experience at St. Leonard's could not have been more different. She always felt academically and socially out of her depth and burdened by her teachers' expectation that she would be Muriel's equal. Attuned to the new psychological vocabulary of the interwar period, she retrospectively diagnosed herself as suffering from an "inferiority complex," the term made famous by Austrian psychoanalyst Alfred Adler.

Muriel did little to assuage Doris's self-doubt, perhaps because she was not all that eager to share St. Leonard's with her. In *It Occurred to Me*, she never mentioned how, when, or why Doris joined her at school. Near the end of Muriel's chapter on her school days, Doris simply appears out of nowhere as Muriel's companion.[157] Doris's unpublished autobiography and Muriel's diary fill in the gaps. According to Doris, a place opened unexpectedly at St. Leonard's in midyear and her parents, without much forethought and consultation, trundled her off to Scotland. Muriel noted Doris's arrival in a very short diary entry: "Dor is here with me. pip pip." A short time later, she reflected on her relationship with her younger sister. No doubt signaling heightened anxiety and guilt, Muriel marked these entries in bold capitals, "PRIVATE." "I feel I have a huge field to work in," she opined. "Think of Dor instead of behaving like an absolute dog to Dor as I did yesterday. (I mean in grumpiness)." Doris was the one of many "huge fields" in which Muriel chose to direct her missionary zeal; she was also the first person who required Muriel to reckon with the complexities of negotiating a reciprocal but unequal relationship. Muriel resolved that the sisters should "form each others characters," and assigned Dor the job of ridding Muriel of her "surliness" and her selfish pursuit of popularity.[158]

When Muriel graduated from St. Leonard's, she returned home to the Grange with no certain plan about her future. She and her parents decided against the Cambridge women's college, Girton, though she had passed the entrance examination. A lively, highly educated and attractive young woman from a well-to-do family, she immersed herself in the conventional rituals of day-to-day bourgeois sociability: lawn tennis and teas, parties and foreign travel. The unstated goal of all these activities was to meet and marry an appropriate young man with good prospects and family. What is most remarkable about Muriel's account of this brief period in her life is that apparently no one thought it strange that neither she nor Doris exhibited interest in opposite-sex courtship and romance.[159] In a cryptic diary entry on New Year's Day 1905, Muriel confided her fear for the time when K (presumably her brother Kingsley) "may imagine himself in love. I mt. prevent it, by never imagining myself." Nor did any one appear to question Muriel and Doris's refusal to perform what should have been the paramount task before them: finding a husband. Rachel and Henry Lester put no pressure on their youngest daughters to conform to social expectations about love and marriage. Their older children, married with their own children, had already done the work of reproducing Lester family life.

CONCLUSIONS: THE CHALLENGES OF UNLEARNING

Clara Balfour rightly observed that it was a "great mistake" to assume that schools and schoolmasters monopolized the education of children. "Every place is a school where we learn anything, and every person is a schoolmaster or mistress who teaches us anything."[160] Perhaps the hardest challenge that Muriel Lester and Nellie Dowell faced was unlearning the lessons of and about childhood that so many different teachers—including those who wrote poems and novels, delivered sermons, and produced visual images—had taught them. These teachers urged girls like Muriel to befriend orphans and waifs while expecting poor children like Nellie to express gratitude and deference to their betters. Such lessons constitute one of the deep structures of thought and feeling that eventually brought Muriel and Nellie together. In this respect, the fictional relationship between Clare Linton and Polly, who lost her last name along with her mother, father, and grandmother, is exemplary. When Clare asks her benevolent banker father if Polly can accompany her to "learn lessons," he replies "Certainly not, Clare." "Instead of yes, I say No, most emphatically." Polly's proper schoolroom that day is the kitchen where Papa sends her to keep warm. Nor does Polly aspire to Clare's tuition. She longs for altogether different kinds of lessons. Mrs. Hart puts words into her mouth calculated to gratify the deepest wishes of middle-class readers: " 'May they teach me to be a servant, please, sir? . . . I want to learn to be a servant that I may serve little Miss Clare, sir.' "[161] My point here is *not* that poor girls from the slums of London actually said such words, but that well-to-do girls like Muriel were taught to hope and expect that they would. And Nellie was taught to think and say them.

In all sorts of ways, Muriel enjoyed a heterodox education. It equipped her with potent resources to use as she pondered works like *Clare Linton's Friend*, which consolidated prevailing understandings of class and gender, power and poverty. Not only was she trained to question, critique, and lead, she also read compelling works of literature and Christian thought that acted like solvents upon the cultural, social, and economic foundations of late-industrial capitalism. Muriel's self-directed curriculum at the turn of the century included Olive Schreiner's *Dreams* (1888) with its impassioned analysis of the sins committed by well-intentioned "ladies" whose spotless purity depended upon the existence of an impure class of prostitutes. Schreiner's *Dreams*, Muriel later remarked, had awakened thousands like her to feel "shame rather than pride in possession of riches."[162] According to Schreiner, it was not enough for the altruistic bourgeois narrator of the tenth "dream"—"I Thought I Stood"—to sympathize with her fallen sister. She can only claim genuine moral authority and receive spiritual grace after she lies down in the filthy streets and rises up mud-spattered with the abstracted character Woman. Schreiner calls for a transformation of sympathy, predicated on class distance, into a new and deeper form of identification in which all women join together in the messy struggle against the gender and class formations that produce prostitutes and prostitution. Such an approach to cross-class sisterhood anticipated Muriel's later embrace of the practice of identifying with the dispossessed, to which Rosa Waugh introduced her when Rosa joined May Hughes as Kingsley Hall's first two residents in 1915.[163]

Nellie always faced a much-harder challenge than Muriel. Her experiences at Forest Gate drilled into her the necessity of deference and hard work, while teaching her that remaining free from the Poor Law was the single most important thing she could do. She knew only too well the human costs of becoming a dependent pauper ward of the state. For the next twenty years of her life, Nellie had to find a way to secure her financial independence and help support her mother while mustering the wherewithal to critique the social, economic, political, and gender formations upon which her day-to-day life was built. This proved to be a formidable—and ultimately, unfinished—task in her life. If she retained the rebellious streak of the little girl who initially bucked Forest Gate's regulations, she also became a woman highly adept at accommodating existing power relations to preserve her independence under difficult circumstances.

CHAPTER TWO

Capitalism, from Below and Down Under
THE GLOBAL TRAFFIC IN MATCHES AND MATCH GIRLS

ALICE AND NELLIE DOWELL DID NOT—could not—resume the child-hoods they had so abruptly and involuntarily left behind five years ear-lier when they had been dispatched to Forest Gate School on the east-ernmost outskirts of the metropolis. By the time she left Forest Gate in November 1888, Nellie had spent nearly half her life as a Poor Law ward of the state. Not yet adults but no longer children, the Dowell sisters promptly joined the paid workforce. Alice (identified as "A.D."), "a dear little girl" according to the benevolent lady assigned to look out for her, entered the vast army of female domestics, never to marry or live with her own family.[1] Fair-haired little Nellie followed an altogether different path. Too independent for service, she returned to her devoted mother Harriet Dowell and a dense network of kin in Bromley-by-Bow, includ-ing her maternal grandmother and aunt, Harriet Sloan and Caroline Sloan, and her sisters, Rose and Florence. Nellie and her mother took jobs nearby in the lucifer match and wax vesta industry, one of the larg-est employers of female labor in London. Nellie Dowell, the Poor Law half-orphan, had turned into yet another troubling incarnation of the "social problem": a poor little match girl.

> **A.D.** (Poplar), age in 1888—15; time in School, 4 ½ years.
> *Report*—Very satisfactory. *Particulars*—Sent to service
> from Mrs. Barnett's Cottage Home. A dear little girl.

Match girls mattered to the Victorians. Hans Christian Andersen's popular short morality tale, "The Little Match Girl" (1847), marks the starting point of her career as an iconic figure of urban life and endangered girlhood. The Victorians asked the match girl to perform weighty cultural work for them as she moved across literary genres and cultural venues. Labor conflicts in the match industry in the late 1880s transformed who a match girl was and what she meant. In early July 1888, factory workers at Britain's largest match manufacturer, Bryant and May's in Bow, launched a strike that changed the course of modern British labor history by showing that "unskilled" women workers could discipline themselves into an effective trade union.[2] Nellie and her mother did not participate in the Bryant and May strike, but it radicalized their neighborhood.[3] Bow became a choice destination for philanthropic do-gooders like Muriel Lester, eager to befriend the notoriously rough match factory girls. Overnight, match girls like Nellie turned into the darlings of "new journalists" seeking copy for stories about East London life and labor.[4]

Nellie worked for Bryant and May's chief competitor, R. Bell and Company. Britain's oldest match manufacturer, R. Bell was soon to be embroiled in its own acrimonious strike in 1893–94. The Bell's strike, along with massive restructuring of the global match industry, prompted Nellie's employers to seek new markets and manufacturing sites in Britain's antipodean empire. R. Bell and Co. sent Nellie to its factories in New Zealand and later to Sweden. Nellie remained a minuscule, proletarian cog in the firm's global workforce, but her travels also made her into a Cockney cosmopolitan. Her arrival as an unwelcome "London girl" in Wellington precipitated a major political crisis for the ruling Liberal ministry and provoked New Zealanders to debate the politico-moral economy of the global traffic in matches and match girls.

Nellie's laboring life in the match industry from 1888 to 1909 makes it possible to tell an intimate history of global capitalism from "down under" and "below" from the vantage point of a mobile, poor, unmarried female factory worker. R. Bell and Co. may have been a profit-hungry firm with little regard for workers' rights and workplace justice. For a smart, hardworking young woman like Nellie Dowell, capitalism and global expansion could and did create opportunities for economic independence, greater political power, and fun.

What follows is not the story that I expected—or perhaps wanted—to write about a heroic workingwoman who defied avaricious employers to demand justice for herself and her fellow workers. Such an account would offer a ready-made explanation for why Nellie later joined Muriel in advancing their feminist, socialist, and Christian revolutionary projects in Bow on the eve of World War I. Nellie worked in one of the most politicized female-dominated, class-conscious industries in Victorian Britain, ergo she became a radical. This is not what happened. Nellie, like the silent majority of women workers in late-Victorian and Edwardian Britain, harbored neither trade unionist nor radical political aspirations for most of her working life. Rather than focusing on class consciousness (or its absence), we might learn more by asking why most workers like Nellie put job security before socialism and trade unionism.[5] My account reconstructs the linkages between local and global geographies, between large-scale political economic structures and individual choices, between work and family, between fine-grained attention to the formation of subjectivity and the broad strokes of global history.[6]

THE WORK OF THE MATCH GIRL IN VICTORIAN CULTURE

Pulsing with pedestrians and livestock, cabs and carriages, lorries laden with merchandise and omnibuses crammed with passengers, London's streets were ever-changing marketplaces for the sale of goods, services, and sometimes people.[7] Few figures in this cityscape attracted greater sympathy, while yet generating more cultural anxiety, than poor girls who wandered the streets selling flowers, cress, and matches far from the watchful eyes of their parents. In an 1873 manifesto, Benjamin Waugh, Rosa Waugh Hobhouse's father and founder of the National Society for Prevention of Cruelty to Children, pinpointed what was so troubling about such girls' promiscuously unsupervised access to public space. "[T]he street is the State nursery, to its delinquents she stands *in loco parentis*."[8] Girl vendors necessarily chatted with passing strangers—including adult men—who negotiated for their wares. Such girls caught the eye of the mid-century journalist-cum-street-ethnographer Henry Mayhew, who noted that they often combined trade with begging, commerce with the pursuit of benevolent donations. Some possessed "immoral characters" and their parents sent them to "make out a livelihood by prostitution."[9] (See fig. 2.1.) At once dangerous and en-

2.1. Girl vendors of lucifers who wandered the streets without parental supervision preoccupied Victorian observers; however, Mayhew's written account of the trade focused more on "old men and women out of employ" than the young girl depicted in the illustration. "Lucifer Match Girl" from a daguerreotype by Beard in Henry Mayhew, *London Labour and the London Poor, A Cyclopaedia of the Condition and Earnings of Those That will Work, Those That Cannot Work, And Those that Will Not Work* (London, 1851), verso p. 432.

dangered, innocent and knowing, these girls embodied a host of social problems and preoccupations: urban poverty, child labor, prostitution, and the pathological condition of working-class family life in which parents exploited rather than nurtured their children.[10] It was not always easy to distinguish buying goods *from* such girls from simply buying the girls themselves.

Only a few years before Mayhew's celebrated investigations for the *Morning Chronicle*, the Danish writer Hans Christian Andersen published his short morality tale of child suffering and deliverance from earthly pains about "the little girl with the matchsticks" (1845). Its Anglo-American life began in 1847 with the *Bentley's Miscellany* publication of "The Little Match Girl" as a "Christmas Story."[11] Mary Howitt's translation of Andersen's *The True Story of My Life: A Sketch* (published earlier that same year) as well as Andersen's well-publicized visits to Britain in the 1850s made him into something of a literary celebrity and helped to ensure the ready availability of his tales to English readers. "The Little Match Girl" narrates the final pathetic night of a barefooted, fair-haired young match girl sent by her heartless parents onto the snow-covered streets to sell her bundle of matches on New Year's Eve or return home to face a certain beating from her father. The near-frozen girl, unable to sell a single match, finds solace by striking some of them. Their brilliance momentarily allows her to imagine delights she will never enjoy—a steaming roast goose stuffed with apples and plums, as well as a Christmas tree. The final matches bring her dead grandmother before her. The grandmother lovingly escorts her to God and liberates her from cold and hunger.

The tale provokes acute sympathy for the helpless match girl, whose parents abuse rather than love her. Readers glimpse the cozy pleasures of bourgeois family life through her longing eyes but the tale offers no critique of the economic and social inequalities that produce child poverty. In fact, the narrator deflects such uncomfortable considerations by insisting that those who stumbled upon her corpse the next day could not know "what beautiful things she had seen" and the "splendor and gladness . . . she had entered into New Year's joys."[12] Her Christian death marks the apotheosis of her life—recompense for her innocent suffering, which dissipates the outraged sympathy the tale conjures. Unlike humanitarian narratives so beloved by child rescuers, the story allows readers to feel intense sympathy for the match girl but does not call them to act.[13] Whatever guilt readers may have felt about her death turns into relief that God has rewarded her with eternal salvation. (See fig. 2.2.)

Salvation was neither the most practical nor the only solution to the problem of child labor, although religious conviction motivated politicians like the Tory evangelical Lord Shaftesbury to demand that the state

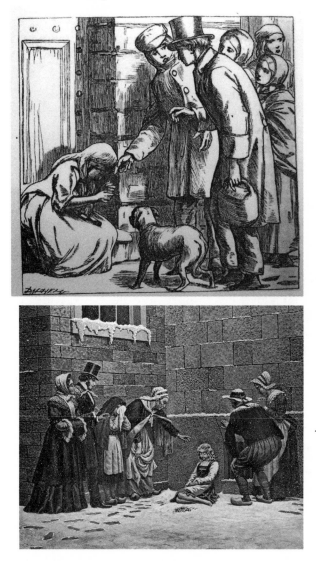

2.2. The dramatic moment when town dwellers first discover the dead body of the little match girl on the snowy street was a favorite subject of illustrators. Andersen's story emphasized the girl's heavenly reward. Illustrations like these compelled readers to confront the emotional impact of Christians' failures to protect her from exploitation. (Top) "The People Find the Little Match Girl," A. W. Bayes, illustrator, Dalziel Brothers, Engravers from H. W. Dulcken, trans., *Hans Christian Andersen's Stories for the Household* (London, 1866), 358. (Bottom) Magic Lantern Slide, "The Little Match Girl," (1905) by Joseph Boggs Beale, Courtesy of Jack Judson Collection, Magic Lantern Castle Museum, San Antonio, Texas; copy of image produced by Ludwig Vogl-Bienek.

shield children from egregious abuses of industrial capitalism. Even ardent defenders of the free market recognized children's special claims to protection, while socialists condemned child labor as symptomatic of the irremediable evils of capitalism. Parliament did pass various forms of protective labor legislation including Factory Acts, which limited children's hours of labor, mandated schooling, and excluded them from workplaces on the grounds of both age and the dangerous character of the employment.[14] The state provided no compensation for children's lost wages to families, so the poor bore the heaviest burden of subsidizing the state's paternalistic interventions. It was a much trickier matter to regulate the labor of child street vendors like match girls since their parents employed them and they had no regular place of work subject to official inspection. At best, truancy officers employed by school boards (and later county councils) from the 1870s onwards could cajole, threaten, fine, and punish parents for failing to comply with school attendance regulations.[15]

From mid-century onward, reformers increasingly differentiated children's rights from the economic interests of their parents: children of the laboring classes, within this social policy framework, required protection from their own parents, whose need for money trumped concern for their offspring's well-being. This perspective undergirded the argument—to the extent that Andersen's story offered one—explaining his Match Girl's fate. Hers was a tale about bad parents, not an immoral political economy. Andersen's tale contributed to the emerging mid-century consensus that poor children needed to be protected not just from avaricious employers but from their own parents. As Marx bitterly observed, humanitarian movements proclaiming the "rights" of the child stemmed from "the capitalistic mode of exploitation which, by sweeping away the economic basis of parental authority, made its exercise degenerate into a mischievous misuse of power."[16]

The instant success of Andersen's tale ensured that visual and literary representations of match girls were as ubiquitous as the girls themselves in the metropolis. Edifying children's fiction such as *Mattie's Home; or, the Little Match-Girl and Her Friends* (1873) and *Little Fan; or, the Life and Fortunes of a London Match-Girl* (1874) amplified Andersen's portrayal of drunken and abusive parents, while providing readers with models of philanthropic action. "Gentlemen" befriend and rescue the eponymous heroines Mattie and Little Fan before placing them in safe "homes."[17] The *Pall Mall Gazette*, ever watchful for injustice and eager for scandal, incited readers to associate ten-year-old Susan Quinn's unlawful abduction in April 1886 with the fate of her fictive counterpart. The story "Only a Little Match-Girl, Not Ten Years Old" detailed the child's kidnapping from the streets where her mother, Mrs. Eunice

Quinn, had sent her to sell matches. Stephen Lawry, a twenty-three-year-old private in the West Yorkshire Regiment, lured her with the promise of a present to a nearby lodging house in one of East London's most notorious streets for a night of debauchery.[18] The *Gazette*'s crusading evangelical editor, W. T. Stead, had good reason to expect readers to connect Susan Quinn's sad story with his own highly publicized abduction and "rescue" of a "white slave" girl less than a year earlier. Stead had by turns horrified and titillated readers by "purchasing" Eliza Armstrong from her mother to expose the "ghastly and infernal traffic" in "maidens" of the poor, sacrificed nightly to satisfy the sexual lusts of men. No amount of wishful glossing could transform Susan Quinn's story into an uplifting tale of Christian suffering and salvation. Sexual danger, not sentiment, animates this recasting of the Match Girl in the service of Stead's controversial campaign to outlaw child prostitution. Stead went to jail for his theatrical antics, but the Criminal Law Amendment Act in August 1885 raised the age of consent from thirteen to sixteen years old.[19]

Little Match Girls like Susan Quinn appeared in many guises and locations in art and literature in the years preceding the strike, and with even greater frequency in its aftermath. The Match Girl circulated widely in popular cheap editions of Andersen's tales adapted for use by school children.[20] She was the subject of fine art in K. M. Skeating's painting, *The Little Match Girl*, exhibited at Liverpool's Walker Art Gallery in September 1886. She entertained and instructed ragged boys at a Christmas gathering of the Ragged School Union in December 1886. Presumably, the match girl's pathetic fate amplified the good fortune of the destitute boys, so recently rescued from the streets themselves, as they feasted on plum puddings.[21] She was the recipient of the unbounded selflessness of Oscar Wilde's eponymous "Happy Prince" (May 1888), who gives the match girl his one remaining sapphire eye—and thus blinds himself—so that "her father will not beat her."[22] The Match Girl was the star of the *tableau vivant* performed at the Anglo-Danish Exhibition staged in May 1888 to raise money for the British Home for Incurables. *The Era* enthusiastically reported that a choir of boy voices, concealed behind the scenes, sang the Christmas carol "Good King Wenceslas" to accentuate the pathos of the Match Girl's lonely death on the snow-covered street.[23] Victorian philanthropists demanded that the match girl, denied Christian benevolence in her own life, reenact her death over and over in fundraising performances on behalf of child rescue agencies while reformers lobbied the state to protect poor children from unscrupulous employers and abusive parents.[24]

HOW MATCH FACTORY WOMEN
BECAME MATCH GIRLS

Performances like the May *tableau vivant* at the Anglo-Danish Exhibition prepared the British public for an even more dramatic spectacle in Bow a few weeks later. Workers at Bryant and May's match factory went out on strike during the first week of July 1888. The strike emerged out of employees' discontent with workplace conditions as well as socialists' and journalists' determination to expose abuses at the firm and turn them into political and print capital. Punitive labor practices exacerbated low wages—ranging from four to thirteen shillings per week—to fuel growing shop floor tensions at Bryant and May in the late spring of 1888: the lack of a separate and safe place for workers to consume meals; inadequate concern for workers' occupational health, especially exposure to poisonous phosphorous; disciplinary fines for inevitable accidents associated with the work. While Bryant and May did nothing to protect workers from phosphorous-laden dust, it penalized them three pence per infraction for dirty feet and untidy workspaces. Management locked out and fined girls who arrived late. Bryant and May pressured employees to remain silent about their afflictions in exchange for company-provided medical and dental care. The introduction of new machinery incited fear that wages would go down while demands for productivity increased.[25]

Trade unionist Clementina Black brought these conditions to the attention of her fellow Fabian Society members, including Annie Besant. On June 23, 1888, Besant published a scathing exposé of Bryant and May, "White Slavery in London," in *The Link*, a weekly penny periodical she edited with W. T. Stead. Subtitled "A Journal for the Servants of Man," *The Link* sought to unite fellow workers across the religious, political, and social spectrum on a platform based upon "great moral ideals" and "common faith in Freedom and in Justice." It championed a wide range of global and local causes, from Irish Home Rule and free speech to the failure of London cardboard manufacturer English and Co. to provide adequate meal breaks for its five overworked boy laborers.[26]

Few could rival Annie Besant's combination of political and journalistic savvy. (See fig. 2.3.) The middle-class wife of a clergyman, Besant burst into notoriety in the 1870s when she joined forces with the leading secularist politician and neo-Malthusian Charles Bradlaugh to provide contraceptive knowledge so that workers could limit family size and control their economic fortunes. The campaign cost Besant her marriage and custody of her children, but it also thrust her into the limelight as one of Victorian Britain's most stirring and controversial platform speakers. By 1888, Besant had migrated toward Fabianism, a middle-class brand of evolutionary socialism. Fabians identified capitalism as the root cause of exploitation but preferred to "permeate" the state (rather than overthrow it) as leading policy makers and civil servants and transform it into an engine for social and economic progress.[27] A self-described atheist in early 1888, Besant had already begun to flirt with Theosophy, a religious philosophy committed to the betterment of humanity that combined teachings from Eastern and Western religious traditions.

"White Slavery" cannily combined sensational journalism with gendered political-economic argument. It juxtaposed Bryant and May's "monstrous" shareholder profits (dividends ranging from twenty-three to thirty-eight percent on investment) with the workers' starvation wages. The firm's treatment of its workers smacked of "tyranny," Besant thundered—a provocative term widely used in the 1880s to denounce all forms of arbitrary un-English subjugation of workers at home and colonial subjects abroad. Besant likened women workers at Bryant and May to "white slaves"—a phrase those seeking repeal of the Contagious Diseases Act had deployed effectively to defend working girls and women from unregulated and exploitative male lust.[28] Besant updated the familiar argument that wage slavery under capitalism was harsher and more profitable than chattel bondage and blasted manufacturer Theodore Bryant's ostensible contributions to civic betterment—erecting "statues" and "parks" in East London—as a flimsy cover for greed. She used neither "match girls" nor "match factory women" but instead called the workers "girls" to underscore their status as youthful innocent

2.3. One of the most forceful and articulate platform speakers in Victorian Britain, Annie Besant attracted substantial media attention as her political, intellectual, and religious commitments shifted in the 1880s from secularism to Fabianism to Theosophy. "Annie Besant, 1889," from *Annie Besant: An Autobiography* (Adyar Deluxe Indian reprint edition, 1939), 441.

victims of capitalist greed.[29] A few weeks later, workers at Bryant and May took matters into their own hands and went on strike. Several newspapers, which fancied themselves righteous defenders of the "people," took up their cause.

From the outset, the Bryant and May strike unfolded on two distinct but connected planes. As historian Louise Raw has shown, match factory women, many daughters of recent Irish immigrants, initiated and led the strike. However, it was also a media event that attracted a glittering cast of middle-class socialists and radical allies, themselves gifted journalists, writers, and self-promoters. The strike marked the convergence of the New Unionism with the New Journalism of the 1880s, with its emphasis on shocking revelations of social abuses.

Who, then, were these factory workers? Press accounts reported that approximately 1,400 workers at Bryant and May went on strike, although only 712 received payments according to the Strike Register. Some were boys and men—ostentatiously not "match girls." The vast majority were young women. Women's work at Bryant and May—like most forms of female manual labor in the nineteenth century—was classified and compensated as "unskilled" regardless of the actual level of dexterity demanded.[30] Women and girls in the match industry performed many different jobs, including minding the machines that turned miles of cotton and jute into the tapers used for wax vestas; filling frames or mechanized coils; cutting tapers (this was Harriet Dowell's job); and putting matches or vestas into boxes (this was Nellie's task). Men always dipped the splints or tapers into trays containing a phosphorous mixture. Dipping was the most dangerous part of the production process because it required sustained and direct exposure to white phosphorous, known to cause phossy jaw, a disfiguring and sometimes fatal necrosis of the bones. All workers were exposed to the poisonous fumes of wet matches and tapers as well as poisonous dust that settled onto their food. No Bryant and May strikers engaged in labor previously associated with "match girls." Not one sold matches like Andersen's Little Match Girl.[31] One might well then ask: by what rhetorical sleight of hand did match factory women come to be known to contemporaries and posterity as "match girls"?

Journalists turned match factory workers into match girls. They initially tested different names for the mostly female strikers, including "wood match girls" and "match factory workers." But within two weeks "match girl," with its suggestion of innocent suffering and passivity, vanquished its rivals because it proved so attractive to the strikers' foes and friends alike.[32] Opponents of the strike depicted the "match girls" as helpless "victims" of "insane" socialist "instigators," "pests of the modern world."[33] The *Star*, under the editorship of the Irish Home Ruler MP, T. P. O'Connor, also represented the "girls" as victims, but not of socialist outsiders. It blasted Bryant and May for exploiting the "girls" and celebrated the heroism of "the match girls' strike" on July 9.[34] In the war of words surrounding the Bryant and May strike, "match girl" was the undisputed victor. During the month of July 1888, "match girls" went from girls selling matches on streets to any female worker associated with the match industry.

Funds poured into the *Link* from across Britain and its empire to support the match girls: the Arts and Crafts bookbinder T. J. Cobden Sanderson donated ten pounds; an "Illiterate House-painter" one shilling.

The names of contributors to the strike fund constitute a "Who's Who" of radical and progressive London. It included Fabians Sidney Webb and Graham Wallas; the Christian socialist founder of the Guild of St. Matthew and defender of music halls, Stewart Headlam; his arch nemesis, the social purity campaigner Mrs. Ormiston Chant; "glorified spinster" New Women Margaret Harkness, Amy Levy, and Clementina Black; leading suffrage campaigners Mr. and Mrs. Pankhurst; socialists William Morris and Edward Carpenter, as well as a panoply of Liberal, Radical, and Socialist clubs and societies.[35] George Bernard Shaw and several fellow Fabians, including Besant, journeyed to Bow to meet the girls and distribute strike funds to them. The match girls' strike at Bryant and May captured the public's imagination and made it into the favorite cause of the great and good of bohemian and radical London in the summer of 1888.

Led by "sturdy respectable" match factory workers, the strike ironically consolidated their public image as "match girls." (See fig. 2.4.) Journalists gave them this name—a kind of fiction that subsequently became its own fact through persistent use. Calling them match girls stimulated sympathy by playing upon deeply embedded cultural perceptions of childhood innocence and vulnerability at the height of Christian evangelical campaigns to gain parliamentary protection for poor children. At the same time, press accounts stressed the self-discipline, comradeship, independence, and determination of the "girls" in the face of their many hardships. Agency and passivity reinforced rather than contradicted one another in this discursive knot.

The Match Girls' Strike was never an end in itself for Besant and her fellow Fabians. It was but one of many ongoing skirmishes—some in workhouses, others in police precincts, still others in School Board schools and sweated workshops—in a much larger struggle to bring justice to the poor and challenge the free market logic of industrial capitalism. For all Besant's social and political radicalism, her views about the incapacity of workers to speak for themselves reflected the prejudices of her middle-class upbringing. As she reminded readers in the chapter she devoted to the "Match-girls Strike" in her 1893 autobiography, she and Stead had founded the *Link* as a mouthpiece to speak for the "dumb and voiceless poor."[36] She began with the assumption that poor workers could neither speak nor act on their own behalf. Who better to play the

2.4. Photographs and graphic images of East London's match factory girls in the 1880s and '90s suggest that most adopted a distinctive style of self-presentation: hair pulled back with fringe or bangs resting above their eyebrows, a tiered hat sometimes dressed with feathers, an overcoat atop a long work apron with a simply tied kerchief at the neck. *Annie Besant: An Autobiography* (London, 1908).

part of the rescued victim than a match girl? Who better to tell her story than a sympathetic middle-class lady, albeit one who whose politics and personal life had led her far from conventional bourgeois domesticity?

Besant and Herbert Burrows served as the first secretary and treasurer of the Matchmakers Union, established as part of the union's victorious settlement with Bryant and May. Besant soon turned from Fabianism and trade unionism to Theosophy and its mystical high priestess,

Madame Blavatsky.[37] She did, however, leave the match girls a parting gift, funded by a large anonymous donation to Blavatsky: a match girls' "drawing room" and club. Located on the north side of Bow Road just across from St. Mary-le-Bow church, the club was an Elizabethan-era structure that had once housed "street arabs" rescued by Dr. Barnardo. "It will want a piano, tables for papers, for games, for light literature," Besant breezily informed readers, "so that it may offer a bright homelike refuge to these girls, who now have no real homes, no playground save the street." While she insisted that the club would not enforce "prim behaviour" and would nurture "cordial comradeship and self-respecting freedom," Besant clearly set out to domesticate the unruly girls—with "no real homes"—whom she had come to admire.[38] Notices about the club appeared in the 1890 volume of *Lucifer*, the too-aptly named "Theosophical Magazine designed to 'bring to light the hidden things of darkness.'" Madame Blavatsky herself graced the club's gala opening on August 16, 1890. Fifty appreciative girls enjoyed tea, singing, dancing, and brief speeches by Besant and Burrows.[39] According to the *Women's Penny Paper*, Besant hailed the union as a "tower of strength," but she could not resist administering a dose of bourgeois moralizing. If the club took the girls off the streets and out of public houses, it would have done its work.[40]

Philanthropists, local clergy, and home mission workers quickly followed suit with their own clubs for Bow's now famous match factory girls, who apparently refused to mix with other groups of factory girls.[41] Bow was already headquarters of the evangelical Regions Beyond Inland Mission with its many clubs for poor mothers, factory girls, and men; its soup kitchens, bands of hope, and medical clinics; and religious services. Its Berger Hall branch on Empsom Street, just across from R. Bell and Company and Nellie's home on Marner Street, sent brass bands roving the streets to recruit match factory girls like Nellie for its factory girls' club on Tuesday and Thursday evenings.[42] Many other philanthropists and Christian missionaries vied with one another to entice London's celebrated match girls to join their clubs and classes. Just to the west of the Dowells' neighborhood, Bow Common was the center of the philanthropic-missionary outreach of the advanced wing of Wesleyan Methodism (called the Forward Movement) under the leadership of Reverend Peter Thompson, "a big burly rough man with a great voice and strong practical way of saying what he has to say."[43] One of his fellow workers, the Rector of Bromley, St. Leonard's, Reverend Parry, was "rather a gassy man: wanting in tact and judgment,"[44] who ran a well-subscribed club for match girls on Albert Terrace.[45] This small side street off the south side of Bow Road was also the location of the "junior girls' club," where Muriel volunteered her time.[46] Perhaps this club, or one of its successors, was Muriel's first philanthropic destination in East London.

Appalled by Bryant and May's cruelty and the roughness of the match girls, Viscountess Clifden and a glittering cast of titled "ladies," including Princess Mary Adelaide, opened Clifden House Institute in the summer of 1890 in three attached cottages directly across from the Fairfield works.[47] (See fig. 2.5.) The institute allied itself with the Young Women's Christian Association Factory Helpers' Union, whose wealthy "lady" helpers claimed to stand between factory girls and "the many hundred difficulties and dangers to which they are exposed."[48] In marked contrast to Besant's Theosophical match girls' club, Clifden House was unabashedly the product of old-fashioned *noblesse oblige*. Its girls were expected to—and apparently did—play the part of deferential objects of benevolence. Its minute book abounds with motions of collective gratitude to various aristocratic ladies who had welcomed the "girls" to their country estates and provided them with meals and warm coats, tea and buns. On Boxing Day 1897, thirty club members played games and feasted on geese sent by Bryant and May for their delectation; meanwhile, the lady managers approvingly noted a "decided improvement in the behaviour of the girls," who were "quieter and less selfish."[49]

At its founding, Bryant and May viewed the Clifden Institute with "indifference, if not with hostility," according to its lady superintendent Miss Nash, who struck Booth's interviewer as not quite a "lady" herself but drawn from the "class from whom come matrons and housekeepers." The girls, for their part, could not say a "good word" about their employers. They had been "a terribly rough lot," Nash informed Charles Booth's interviewer in May 1897. "Decent people scarcely dared to go down the street when they were coming out of work." All that had changed. Club membership apparently had softened and refined the girls and heightened their appreciation for their employers. "The girls have become tractable, decent, and quiet in their dress and behavior,"

2.5. By the 1890s, Bryant and May heavily subsidized Clifden House, a bastion of old-fashioned noblesse oblige charity intended to provide rational recreation and moral uplift for match factory girls."Clifden House," *The Sunday at Home* (1895), 391.

Nash noted with satisfaction at her own civilizing influence; "their relations with the firm are excellent and the firm recognizes that the influence of the girls who attend the Institute, from 300 to 400 in number, has permeated throughout the whole of their female employés [*sic*]."[50] Private benevolence had achieved what the firm's harsh shop floor discipline could not. Miss Nash had made Bryant and May's fiery match girls into docile model workers. Nash's assessment of the Bryant and May match girls suggests that their grassroots radicalism in 1888 had long since dissipated by 1897. It also provides a sobering—and far from heroic—denouement to the Match Girls' Strike notably absent from feminist and labor histories.

The differences between Besant's theosophical club in Bow Lodge and the paternalist Clifden Institute are less striking, however, than the similarities of their services and their underlying assumptions about match girls' "nature." Both offered well-cooked, inexpensive mid-day meals; a library; reading rooms; magic lantern shows and pianos for entertainment and elevation; and excursions to the countryside. Both emphasized match girls' exclusion from and need for the civilizing influence of home. Besant's Bow Lodge may have been founded on radically democratic principles, but there were as many household servants as match girls living there at the time of the 1891 census.[51]

Nash's and Besant's claim that "match girls" had been left outside the civilizing influence of the home became a commonplace by the 1890s. In 1894, the magistrate Montagu Williams published a compassionately critical portrait of the match girls who came before his bench. Williams's description echoed Besant's and encapsulates the post–strike fascination with match girls as convenient archetypes of that exotic species beloved of social commentators: "the factory girl." "Detached from their families" and "not the very best of girls," the girls were, he observed, prone to drunkenness, petty thievery, and had "very lax" ideas about law and order. He attributed their misbehavior to their "squalid and wretched homes" while celebrating their "exuberancy of spirits," kindness, and remarkable solidarity to their "sisters" in times of need. Their inaptitude for domestic tasks such as washing clothes and cooking dinner was matched by their delight in bright colors, large hats, feathers, high-heeled boots, and fringe.[52] (See fig. 2.6.)[53]

2.6

Many observers, including Gilbert Bartholomew, the managing director of Bryant and May, insisted that the girls' love of pleasure compromised labor discipline and time management. They simply stopped working when they had earned enough to pay for a good meal and a penny gaff.[54] The social statistician Clara Collet, no apologist for capitalism, could not conceal her annoyance with the girls' irregular habits.[55] In letters she wrote to Bartholomew in February 1889, she sought his help as she researched her study of working women in East London. Any reliable account of the "industrial conditions of the matchgirls" must refer to Bryant and May, she acknowledged. She assured Bartholomew that Bryant and May was neither worse nor better than "nine tenths" of the firms she had studied and described the "matchgirls" as "unskilled and difficult to manage."[56] In her published essay, Collet suggested that match girls' low wages, so widely condemned in the press, resulted from high levels of absenteeism. Girls got paid very little because they frequently skipped work. Collet blamed the girls' home life and prevailing norms in East London for encouraging the gratification of immediate pleasures at the expense of thrift.[57]

The emerging post-strike consensus about match girls coalesced around a more or less shared set of images and arguments positioning them as embodiments of social problems and promising "raw material."[58] On the one hand, match girls as a class remained "very rough, very wild, very dirty, but not by any means the worst class of factory girls."[59] Distinctly "city girls," their irregularity and restless pursuit of pleasure were symptoms of the deeper psychological disturbances of urban modernity with its "rapidly shifting stimulations of the nerves."[60] On the other hand, their keen sense of solidarity with one another and high spirits had also made them notably susceptible to philanthropic uplift. Besant and Bartholomew may have been the bitterest antagonists during the strike, but in its aftermath they agreed that match girls lacked adequate home lives. The strike alleviated some of the most egregious abuses at Bryant and May and redressed grievances about wages and work conditions. However, the rhetoric surrounding the "match girls" and their strike reinforced late-Victorian reformers' and domestic missionaries' self-serving diagnosis of and proposed solution to the girls' afflictions. At once helpless and ferociously independent, match girls urgently needed the uplifting culture on offer at clubs, home missions, and settlement houses. Only the guidance and friendship of middle-class women, beckoned from their comfortable homes to journey into the slums to serve their outcast sisters, could lead match girls to domestic happiness. This was a path that Nellie and Muriel were only too happy to follow.

MATCH GIRLS' MILITANT: WHY THE BELL'S MATCH FACTORY STRIKE OF 1893/94 FAILED

Nellie's employers R. Bell and Company had good reason to congratulate themselves for escaping the public humiliation endured by their rival, Bryant and May. Employing approximately six hundred workers in Wandsworth and Bromley-by-Bow, R. Bell's owners took pride in their purpose-built factory with its well-ventilated rooftop shed for phosphorous dipping and drying, which inspectors praised for reducing the incidence of necrosis. Nellie and the other box fillers toiled on the second floor.[61] Bell's employees enjoyed a separate well-lit and airy refactory, a further boon to their safety. A writer for the *Sunday Magazine* in 1892 graphically conjured the "incalculable sufferings" of East London's "white slave" match girls while praising R. Bell and Company for its humane protection of its employees from "matchmakers' leprosy."[62]

However, by the summer of 1893, gratitude was in short supply among R. Bell's workers, at least among the 150 who had joined the Matchmakers Union, led by Herbert Burrows.[63] The firm's managing director, Charles R. E. Bell, introduced a larger frame with more matches per row without correspondingly increasing wages. Workers retaliated by sending off empty boxes—sometimes as many as six out of a dozen—for overseas sale.[64] "We are compelled by the severe competition in the trade," Bell explained to Burrows, "to do as our neighbours [Bryant and May] do or we should be shut out of the market." "Is it reasonable to ask us to pay more [wages]" than "our competitors?"[65] The union argued that R. Bell expected its girls to do more work for the same pay. Nor was this its only grievance. R. Bell required the girls to pay for their own medical care and "sweepers" to clean up after them; it illegally compelled them to purchase work materials from their forewoman at inflated prices. Bell's match girls faced excessive fines for petty shop floor offenses and matches that unavoidably caught fire while the girls were working.[66]

Simmering resentments boiled over into a protracted and sometimes violent industrial conflict between R. Bell and Company and its employees in the Matchmakers Union from 1893 until the late summer of 1894. In July 1893, two hundred men and girls hooted, yelled, and "molested" one of the firm's partners, Edwin Bell, as he left the factory—under police escort—en route to Bromley Station.[67] Negotiations between the union and R. Bell remained at an impasse until New Year's Day 1894 when the firm unexpectedly locked the girls out in an attempt to embarrass the union and force them to accept its terms. Members of the Matchmakers' Union Committee asked Charles Bell when they could return to work and he mockingly replied that as Union Committee members "they ought to know." In a transparent attempt to undermine the girls' loyalty to union leadership, Bell disingenuously insisted that their return to work was entirely in the union officers' hands.[68] Local police constables patrolled the intersection of St. Leonard's Street and Bell Road, just north of the Limehouse Cut, leading to the factory's front gates to prevent the factory women from picketing in protest.

The use of police to support industrial capitalists in a labor dispute excited angry comments from MPs when Parliament convened in February. In the years between the Bryant and May strike in 1888 and the Bell's strike of 1894, Parliament had grown more hospitable to the interests of working men and women. Labor leaders with deep roots in East London, Keir Hardie and John Burns, entered Parliament in 1892 and spoke not just for workers but as workers. An advanced Liberal MP who worked closely with his trade union colleagues, J. A. Murray Macdonald represented Bow and Bromley. He rejected the state's constabulary role as defender of industrial capitalists' interests against workers.[69] He questioned Home Secretary H. H. Asquith why Bell's match girls "proceeding peaceably to work," without intention to strike, had been met by police. Making clear his own objections to such intimidation, Macdonald demanded to know if police were to be used in this way at the "instance of private employers?"[70] Eager to enlist Asquith as an ally, Macdonald brought a deputation of Bell's match girls to meet the home secretary and put their case before him.[71]

Three months later, none of the issues dividing R. Bell and its workers had been resolved. R. Bell rebuffed the union's offers to enter into voluntary arbitration. In a gesture calculated to provoke the union, R. Bell dismissed a leading Union Committee member. In solidarity, approximately 150 girls and women promptly went on strike on March 1. Sources offer no clues about the other 450 workers at Bell's; nor is it clear that the strike necessarily closed down production. What is certain is that the union's leaders were once again caught off guard and could not maintain order among the strikers.[72]

The exemplary self-control of the Bryant and May match girls in the face of their hardships had won the public's admiration and lubricated the free flow of contributions to their strike funds. Bell's girls exhibited a great deal more fight and much less discipline. Ellen Conway, one of the strikers, spitefully hurled a rock through the front window of a house inhabited by Bell's forewoman, Kate Hubbard.[73]

Shop floor relations between forewomen and match girls constituted the strike's frontline, where abstract issues about the rights and wrongs of labor and capital turned into small acts of resistance such as lingering in the lavatory and small acts of discipline such as locking its door at the day's end. No social distance separated forewomen like Hubbard from those she supervised. Only a few years earlier, she herself had been a factory hand, packing fusées, a kind of friction match. Hubbard lived not far from the factory in South Bromley along with several other match factory hands. Sharing the same spaces—streets, pubs, music halls—only made it harder to negotiate the gulf in authority dividing forewomen from match girls within the factory. By hurling a rock through Hubbard's window, Conway expanded the arena of conflict into the neighboring streets. Her gesture violently and literally brought the strike into Hubbard's home.

Arrested, held in Holloway Prison, then hauled before the Thames Police Court, Conway denied breaking the window, but the magistrate, Mr. Mead, sentenced her to one month's hard labor for destroying property valued at only one shilling, six pence. Mead justified the extraordinary severity of the sentence by linking the crime to the strike.[74] The union immediately organized the Ellen Conway Defence Fund to cover the costs of appealing the decision to the sessional court, which came before Sir Peter Edlin. Edlin was no friend of organized labor. Only a few years earlier the Holborn Liberal and Radical Association had complained to the London County Council about his unfair sentences in labor disputes and asked for his removal.[75] Even Edlin was appalled by the grotesque disproportion between Conway's crime and her punishment. Conway was, he noted, a "young woman of good character . . . led away by excitement." With considerable understatement, he acknowledged that in halving her sentence to fourteen days' imprisonment, he had "not erred on the side of clemency."[76] Such was the justice meted out to unruly Bell's match girls.

Conway was not the only Bell's match girl of heretofore good character compelled to stand before Mr. Mead and Sir Peter Edlin that spring. The *Pall Mall Gazette* reported on April 10, 1894 that Union Committee member Amelia Gifford (age nineteen) was charged with assaulting two hands recently hired as strike replacements. A month later, Sir Peter Edlin sentenced her to twenty-one days in jail for assaulting a Bell's forewoman, Lily Gardner.[77] Margaret McCarthy (age twenty-five) and Annie Sheehan (twenty-three), like Conway, were the daughters of Irish immigrants. Gossip must have been thick in their—and Nellie's—South Bromley neighborhood not far from the factory as the match girls awaited news about the strike. From the strike's onset in early March until its tepid conclusion in August, R. Bell's directors refused to engage in discussions with the union and demanded total capitulation on their terms. In March, the firm advertised for new hands to replace those on strike. Apparently, McCarthy and Sheehan learned that Emily Cakebread, an unemployed young woman, had responded to R. Bell's advertisement and was offered work there. As Cakebread strolled along the towpath on the south side of the Limehouse Cut—the canal connecting the Thames with Bow Creek and the River Lea—toward the Three Mills Bridge and Bell's factory gates, McCarthy and Sheehan accosted her. "You are not going to Bell's this morning, so go back," they taunted. One of her assailants—dressed in a black crepe hat, striped shawl and white apron—threatened to toss Cakebread into the Cut if she persisted. Cakebread fled to the nearest police officer, who escorted her to work. This was only the first of Cakebread's terrifying encounters with wrathful strikers who stalked her after work. Cakebread required police protection to get home safely each night.[78]

The Bell's strike was a disaster for the Matchmakers Union despite Burrows' best efforts to recycle many of the techniques that had worked so well against Bryant and May in 1888. Perhaps that was the problem. What was novel in 1888 seemed distinctly dated in 1894. Burrows once again took aim at clerical stockholders and held them accountable for the match girls' unchristian sufferings. He renewed his call to the benevolent public to engage in a consumer boycott of Bell's products. He detailed the expenses involved in paying the strikers six shillings each week and solicited funds to replenish the union's empty coffers.[79] But the public remained mostly indifferent. The radical and progressive press covered the strike—*Reynolds*, the *London Dispatch*, *Pall Mall Gazette*—but nothing about it appeared in many leading papers such as the *Times* or the *Daily News*.

In the aftermath of the Bryant and May Match Girls' Strike and the famous Dock Strike the next year, strikes by unskilled workers in East London like tailors and chocolate makers had become so frequent that they hardly qualified as news. The public apparently had exhausted its supply of good will and cash to support strikes. No political celebrities with Annie Besant's charisma and talent for publicity stepped forward to become the face of the Bell's strike. By 1894, Besant cared more for "astral bodies" and "mahatmas" than match girls and committed herself to Theosophy.[80] The Bell's match girls did find some unlikely benefactors at the London May Day celebration in Hyde Park. Six brakes-full of match girls, bearing collecting boxes, arrived to hear speeches by one of the heroes of the Dock Strike, the MP John Burns, the radical Christian socialist slum priest Stewart Headlam, and the Arts and Crafts socialist-poet William Morris.[81] The only speaker who specifically addressed them was a "literary" entertainer costumed in an Ally Sloper top hat and "carrotty wig" who promised to donate half his day's earnings to their cause.[82] This did not bode well for the Bell's match girls.

The fiery actions of Bell's match girls like Conway, Shannon, McCarthy, and Gifford made it difficult to turn their strike into the sort of fairy tale narrative about suffering and redemption so beloved by the British public. This was precisely the way Bryant and May's managing director Gilbert Bartholomew rescripted the Match Girls' Strike in its aftermath. Confronted by the public relations debacle of the 1888 strike, Bartholomew reinvented himself as the preeminent philanthropic supporter of match girls, not their cruel oppressor.[83] By 1895, Bartholomew had charmed and toured so many journalists through the Bow factory that Bryant and May's match girls had apotheosized into the "Cinderellas of our National Household." Lloyd Lester, a reporter for the *Girl's Own Paper*, described the match girls he met at Bryant and May's as "white-aproned dauntless damsel[s] with ... sweeping feathers and 'fringe,' worn Skye terrier fashion, whose nimble fingers manipulate matches with bewildering celerity of motion." Bryant and May's match girls, erstwhile phossy-jawed child victims and rebellious factory hands, had become "bonnie fresh faced girls" doing essential work for the nation.[84]

The Bell's match girls enjoyed no such post–strike rehabilitation. They returned to the anonymity from which they had briefly emerged. A wrenching, protracted, and sometimes violent conflict, the Bell's match girls' strike ended with the union's complete defeat after six costly months. Union Committee members not only lost their jobs, but some suffered the ignominy and trauma of imprisonment for their involvement in the strike. *Reynolds's*, which had provided the most comprehensive reporting about the strike, did not bother to inform readers that it had ended. The Bryant and May strike changed the face—and gender—of British trade unionism. However, it failed to provide a usable template for subsequent generations of match girls. Novelty and what counted as news were so deeply entangled that second acts like the Bell's strike played to empty houses.[85]

How did Nellie respond to the strike and what impact did it have on her life? Let me begin with the one thing that is certain. Nellie made a choice. She either joined the strikers or continued working—and by so doing, weakened the chances for the strike to succeed. She appears no-where in sources about the strike. However, this is hardly surprising, since no strike register has survived and press reports mention by name only a handful of strikers. Muriel suggests that in the first years of Nel-lie's employment, she benefited from match girls' high level of sisterly solidarity, a characteristic universally admired and mentioned by social observers. Fellow workers pooled their scant resources to provide sick money for Nellie in 1890 during the first of her many bouts of rheumatic fever when she was around thirteen years old.[86] They had insisted on sharing food with her and even gave her a waterproof coat (which they pretended was hers) to protect her delicate health. But what is most no-table in Muriel's narrative is that she portrays the foremen and manager as participating in this benevolent conspiracy to take care of Nellie dur-ing her illness: "even the Manager and Foremen made much of her." One foreman affectionately tells Nellie to ask no more questions about the proper ownership of the coat since "it don't do them coats no sort of good to be out of work." "From Birth to Death" erased any hint of the bitter antagonisms dividing workers from their shop floor supervisors at R. Bell and Company.

Muriel's affectionate, not quite critical description of Nellie during these years does not portray a young woman likely to join a trade union and go on strike. Nellie joined the Factory Girls Club connected to the Bow Evening Mission and Night School. "She liked the ladies. Their clothes delighted her; so did their voices and their white hands. Nellie wanted to look as nice as they did." Her encounter with cross-class sis-terly philanthropy left her hungering to be like her social betters. Muriel narrates a moment of social emulation and sanctioned class mimicry, not the awakening of a radicalized class consciousness. According to Muriel, Nellie keenly desired to please her social betters as a way to better herself. She developed close ties with the mission's "slumming" ladies—"Miss Livermore, Miss Cook, Miss Smith, Miss Clarke, Miss

Howard and later, Lady Plender"—that endured over many decades. She mentions several of them in her letters to Muriel written after 1910. Nellie raced home from the factory to present herself to lady workers and fellow members of her Factory Girls Club in a freshly washed blouse. She prized the punctuality mark she received. If such rewards were defining symbols of conformity to bourgeois concepts of time management, they were also emblems of Nellie's commitment to self-discipline and self-improvement. The defiant seven-year-old girl who disrupted routines at Forest Gate Barrack School had grown into an efficient young worker eager for approbation and respectability.

Nellie also had financial responsibilities at home to help support her mother, who lived on a paltry six-shilling weekly pension from Trinity House, supplemented by earnings in the match industry and later as a monthly sick nurse. Such considerations may well have made Nellie reluctant to jeopardize the steady work and wages at R. Bell that kept her out of reach of the Poor Law. As a Poor Law half-orphan, Nellie knew only too well the degradations and indignities of parish relief and the paramount value of financial independence. As one longtime worker among East London's factory girls noted, "they would rather die at their post than receive parish relief."[87]

In 1894, R. Bell and Company took a hard line toward the union. It went on record that it would not rehire strikers and evinced no interest in reconciling with the union. Bryant and May, by contrast, contributed funds to help support Besant's match factory girls club, and its senior managers and their wives—notably Mr. and Mrs. Gilbert Bartholomew— became leading sponsors of Lady Clifden's institute for match factory girls for the next several decades. Nellie's continued employment at R. Bell for another fifteen years—and the firm's decision to send her twice to work in its overseas factories—strongly suggests that she was a trusted and reliable employee, not a trade union member on strike.

The strike must have loomed large in Nellie's day-to-day life for the better part of 1893 and 1894. It spilled out beyond the factory gates into the streets and neighborhoods of Bow, Bromley-by-Bow, and Poplar. Nellie heard her workmates articulate grievances against workplace abuses and witnessed the suffering they endured for a cause they believed was just. She also saw the price they paid individually and collectively in failing to achieve their aims. She must have read or heard about the manifestos circulated by Burrows and others that connected local grievances at Bell's to the broader struggle to secure justice for workers against the machinations of self-serving industrial capitalists. The ongoing labor unrest in the match industry from the moment she entered it in late 1888 constituted the social and intellectual crucible in which she shaped her identity as a worker, a young woman, and a member of her community. The fact that Nellie probably did not play the part of trade union heroine does not diminish its impact on her understanding of her world.

I do not know what lessons Nellie took from the strike because there were—and still are—so many different ways to interpret its meaning. Was she inspired by the bravery of some of her workmates? Did she disdain their intemperate and rash behavior? Did she come to see capitalists like C.R.E. Bell as exploiters of labor or as benevolent providers of stable jobs? Certainly R. Bell and Company, Mr. Mead, and Sir Peter Edlin sent a clear message to the Bell's match girls. Even trifling acts of aggression like breaking a pane of glass would be met by harsh punishment. Nellie might have learned that workers like Amelia Gifford who actively resisted exploitation suffered catastrophic personal consequences; better to maintain job security, work hard, and please forewomen and masters. Given the subtle intellect and sensitivity Nellie revealed in her later letters, she may well have been able both to admire and to distance herself from the strikers.

Nellie's absence from the historical record of the strike is much less surprising than the absence of the strike from Muriel's narratives about Nellie. Muriel inevitably left out information I wished she had included. But I do not think this is a case of omission by authorial design. Given Muriel's skill in framing her narrative to highlight the injuries of class Nellie sustained as a young child and worker, it is improbable that she chose to exclude this dramatic episode in Nellie's life. At the time Muriel wrote her biographical sketches of Nellie, she was a radical Christian socialist, actively engaged in the fight for workplace justice as a member of Britain's most advanced borough council in Poplar. She certainly did not hope to awaken workers to their rights as citizens by encouraging them to emulate ladies with "white hands." Nellie and her family members probably never discussed the strike with Muriel. I suspect that this too was another choice Nellie made.

METROPOLITAN MATCH GIRLS ABROAD: IMMORAL CIRCULATIONS OF MATCHES AND MATCH GIRLS

As tension mounted between match girls and management in the spring of 1894, Charles R. E. Bell left London to seek opportunities to expand his business in Britain's antipodean empire. He saw no reason to stay home and negotiate with the union and the strike committee. The proprietors of R. Bell and Company decided that the firm's survival depended upon acquiring new markets and manufacturing sites for their goods far from the cheap continental matches then flooding Britain.[88] Bell headed to Australia and New Zealand to establish new match factories. After a year of disputes with trade unionists and match girls, criticisms by reporters and MPs, and citations issued by factory inspectors for workplace violations, Bell enjoyed a warm welcome from New Zealand's Liberal prime minister, Richard Seddon, and the colonial treasurer, J. G. Ward. No doubt recalling the troubles he had left behind in London, Bell hoped that "the laboring classes here [in New Zealand] will not drive your Government to passing any measures which will be inimical to the employers of labour."[89]

In Britain, the numbers of match manufacturers shrank each year as the industry consolidated in the face of ferocious competition and ever-smaller profit margins. In New Zealand, newspapers chronicled Bell's efforts to open its first match factory and the public debated its meaning for the country's future. The ministry, eager to help Bell, anticipated the creation of several hundred new jobs for New Zealanders at a time when unemployment had slowly but steadily risen.[90] In the early 1890s, the explosion in the export of meat products to Britain made possible by advances in transoceanic refrigeration drove the New Zealand economy. This did not deter Seddon's government from courting metropolitan capital investors like Bell and promising to protect fledgling home industries from overseas competition. Seddon viewed the match factory as a test case to demonstrate the benefits of his selective use of protective tariffs.[91] When pressed to explain his decision to favor the match industry, Seddon characterized his policy as "fair trade" rather than free trade and claimed that he would only protect industries "naturally" suited for New Zealand.[92] For better and for worse, the political stakes of Seddon's investment in R. Bell and Company were substantial.

Charles Bell flirted with the idea of opening a factory in Auckland but turned his sights three hundred miles south to New Zealand's capital, Wellington.[93] He leased space to begin production in August and acquired property in Newtown—a southern suburb of Wellington—where he erected a purpose-built factory. [94] He sent over several key employees from Bromley-by-Bow—most notably Walter McLay, the foreman in charge of the phosphorous-mixing department, to manage the factory and instruct employees in the art and science of this hazardous industry.[95] Charles Bell also extracted several crucial promises from the government. The precise nature of these commitments became a subject of considerable controversy in the years ahead. Bell testified before the New Zealand Tariff Commission that the Seddon government had verbally promised to maintain preferential tariffs for the match industry "so long as the present government was in power," an open-ended and completely unconstitutional arrangement.[96] During debates about tariffs in 1895, Seddon's parliamentary opposition pounced on this opportunity to denounce Seddon's disregard for principles and his government's usurpation of Parliament's exclusive legal right to make such decisions.[97] Some facts were indisputable. In 1894, the government allowed R. Bell and Company to import duty-free match-making machinery as well as the raw materials necessary for making matches at the lowest possible price. Imported matches made by rivals such as Bryant and May were subject to tariffs, thereby artificially inflating their retail price. The net result was that the "colonial" matches sold for slightly less than their better-established rivals.[98]

What made a "colonial match" a genuine New Zealand product, one worthy of protection from foreign competition? (See fig. 2.7.) New Zealanders asked themselves this question from the moment they first learned of Bell's plan to open a factory. As the *Otago Witness* commented on July 26, 1894, the "expert hands" had been "brought out from England" and "all the ingredients of the wax matches will have to be imported." Charles Bell, perhaps ill-advisedly, made precisely this point at his speech to celebrate the opening of the new factory on July 15, 1895. While the stearine fat was from "New Zealand sheep," gum came from Java, wax from Central America, and potash from Sweden. The seemingly simple wax match, Bell concluded, required materials from "nearly every portion of the globe."[99] Prime Minister Seddon and his wife triumphantly toured the new factory and praised its well-designed interior

2.7. Royal Wax Vesta, early twentieth-century R. Bell and Co. Wellington matchbox. (Object in author's possession.)

and "perfect" ventilation. In remarks calculated to disarm critics, he insisted that Bell's factory posed only an "infinitesimal" danger to the "operatives and neighbourhood" and would soon employ a "large number of girls."[100] The promise of well-paid, safe jobs for New Zealand girls was an essential part of Seddon's justification for the enterprise.

About R. Bell and Company, many in New Zealand knew too much to share Seddon's joy at the opening of the new factory.[101] Charles Bell was badly mistaken if he believed he could escape the problems plaguing his London operation. He failed to grasp that it was not just the matches themselves—as physical objects—that were enmeshed in a vast global network. News about their production and labor relations between R. Bell and its London workers also circulated between metropole and colony via the infrastructure of a global information network in place since the founding of the Press Association and Reuters at mid-century. Advances in telegraphy drastically diminished spatial and temporal distances separating New Zealand and London. New Zealanders had ready access to metropolitan newspapers and, more importantly, to local New Zealand papers containing London news. They were remarkably well informed about the health dangers of the London match industry as well as R. Bell's treatment of its workers.

Rumors that Charles Bell would open his factory in Auckland in July 1894 provoked immediate response. Miss Rees, recently returned from a long trip to London in which she had investigated the economic, social, and philanthropic conditions in East London, concluded her lecture to a women's meeting by condemning R. Bell's treatment of its workers in Bromley-by-Bow. The Auckland Knights of Labour disputed the *Auckland Herald*'s claims that there was nothing "unpleasant, dirty or noxious" about match manufacture. Members discussed two lengthy and damning accounts of the Bell's Match Girls' Strike published by the London *Weekly Dispatch* on May 20 and 27 and resolved to oppose any government subsidies or bonuses to R. Bell and Company. They insisted that the government closely regulate and inspect the factory for occupational health hazards and violations, and they demanded a compulsory living wage for all employees. The *Auckland Star* published a detailed account of the Knights of Labour's resolutions on August 14, 1895, which made its way to London, where Herbert Burrows pasted it into the notebook he assembled to document the union's strike activities. A week later, the *Star* published two long excerpts from an unnamed London newspaper sent to it by the pseudonymous "Lucifer" detailing Messrs. Bell and Company's treatment of its workers. Two of Bell's London match girls, Hettie Michell (age seventeen) and Kate Wright (sixteen), had been caught concealing on their persons a total of three boxes of matches during a "periodical search"—a disciplinary technique used by the firm in the strike's aftermath in which all employees were physically searched for stolen goods.[102]

Such searches indicate an exceptionally high level of mutual distrust and animosity between R. Bell and its workers. The total retail value of the boxes was four pence. Mr. Mead, a veteran of many previous cases involving Bell's match girls, sentenced them to seven days in prison for their crime. "Lucifer" editorialized that "it will be a bad day for this colony when our [New Zealand] girls have to submit to such degradation." The *Star* added its own judgment. It insisted that Charles Bell explain his company's actions to New Zealand's minister of labour and warned the government not to help "perpetuate, on New Zealand soil, the cruelty exhibited in these London prosecutions."[103] News about R. Bell and Company flowed freely between New Zealand and Britain though print and human networks—its impact magnified rather than diminished as it traveled across the vast distance.

The *Star*'s deftly delivered admonition to R. Bell and the government exposed Seddon's calculated political gamble in offering his patronage to the wax vesta manufacturer. As Seddon's biographer James Drummond explained shortly after the minister's unexpected death in 1906, the colony had always "been of an experimental turn of mind" in measures to protect the conditions of daily work for its citizens. "Those who left the Old Country to build up a new nation in the furthermost ends of the earth brought with them new ideas and new conditions," Drummond opined, "and they frankly expressed a hope that the bad features of life in the country they were leaving would not be perpetuated."[104] Was R. Bell and Company a welcome example of New Zealand's modernity, the diversification of its economy, and growing self-sufficiency in meeting demand for manufactured goods? Or had Seddon unwittingly smuggled into New Zealand the worst labor practices that the old world had to offer? What—or whom—had Seddon protected through his protective trade tariffs? These were only some of the questions to which New Zealanders demanded answers in the spring of 1900 when they learned that R. Bell and Company had decided to send a group of London match girls to work in its Wellington factory. Nellie Dowell was one of them.

Before examining the London match girls' part in these larger political, social, and economic debates, it is worth pausing to consider why Nellie accepted R. Bell's invitation to go to New Zealand. It was a momentous decision and one out of character with the intensely parochial nature of her life. Since her involuntary removal from Bromley-by-Bow to Forest Gate School in 1883 and her return five years later, she had moved several times, but always within a fairly short distance from R. Bell and Company. Most of her relatives also lived nearby in their south Bromley neighborhood of Bromley-by-Bow. Nellie's maternal uncle David Sloan, an engine driver, lived around the corner on Empson Street in a complicated ménage with his four sons and a female cousin who had given birth to two of his boys.[105] In the 1880s, Aunt Carrie, a fancy-blouse maker for a well-known West End shop, and her mother, Granny Sloan, had moved five miles north to Islington; but by 1901, they had long since rejoined the family, just south of the Limehouse Cut on Brunswick Road, a major north-south artery leading to the docks. Nellie's sisters Florence and Rose married East Londoners and raised their families in Bromley-by-Bow. Rose married Harry Endersbee, a boot finisher. The newlyweds lived at number two Marner Street, just two doors from Harry's parents, on the same street where both Harry and Rose had grown up as children. Harry's sister, Elizabeth, was Nellie's same age and worked as a match factory girl.[106] Florence married William Dellar, a steel filer. The Dellars moved in with Harriet Dowell at 93 Marner Street and thus relieved Nellie of the responsibility of living with her mother. These household arrangements made it possible for Nellie to leave Bromley-by-Bow for New Zealand in April 1900. All of this underscores just how deeply rooted the Dowell family was in Bromley-by-Bow. They looked for and found spouses within their neighborhood, which in turn bound them ever more closely to a dense network of locally based kin.

The Dowells, like many other families in Bromley-by-Bow, had extensive networks of kin living close to one another. Residents possessed a keen sense of neighborhood territoriality often defined by physical landmarks such as major thoroughfares, train tracks, and canals.[107] Nellie's south Bromley neighborhood was bordered by Devons Road to the west, Bow Road to the north, St. Leonard's to the east, and the Limehouse Cut to the south. Nellie never had to walk much more than fifteen minutes to get to work or to visit members of her extended family. Even a trip to the Epping Forest, the vast expanse of open space and parkland near the Lesters' Essex home, was a costly outing to be savored and remembered. Philanthropic organizations attracted and maintained members by offering them such excursions on an annual basis. Nellie may well have not left Greater London since her short time in Leighton Buzzard as a Poor Law ward in 1883. In going to New Zealand, she grasped an opportunity to drastically expand her horizons.[108]

The Dowells' social and cultural world may have been narrowly circumscribed, but at the same time people and goods from around the globe constantly passed through Bromley-by-Bow. Its proximity to the docks along the Thames and Lea rivers made it a favored home for immigrants, mariners, and dock workers, as well as large-scale industries that relied on easy access to seaborne products such as the pine logs used to make wooden match splints. While almost no immigrants lived in Nellie's immediate south Bromley neighborhood, she worked side by side with the daughters of Irish immigrants who figured prominently in both the Bryant and May and R. Bell strikes.[109] Nor were the Irish the only outsiders infiltrating the surrounding neighborhoods. By the 1890s at least some Jews had drifted eastward from Whitechapel to Bow Road between Mile End Station and Bow Station. The London docks to the south and east of Nellie were home to a small population of colored people: "Lascars," Africans, and Chinese.[110] Nellie then lived in a community that was at once narrowly parochial and integrated into a dynamic global economy, Cockney and yet in some surprising ways also cosmopolitan. Nellie came to embody many of these same qualities by the time she met Muriel.

Twenty-three and unmarried, Nellie embarked from the Royal Albert Docks for Wellington on the *Waiwera*, a 6200-ton cargo ship. (See fig. 2.8.) The voyage stretched from April 11 until June 4, with stops in Cape Town and Hobart. All 141 passengers traveled third class except the imperial soldier and veteran of the Maori Wars, Sir George Whitmore, and one other saloon passenger. They were overwhelmingly young, single, and English; men outnumbered women two to one. Most of the passengers on board the *Waiwera* were "unskilled" workers: laborers, factory hands, box makers, and tailors with a smattering of clerks, butchers, and cabinet makers. Nellie was the oldest of the dozen Bell's match girls at twenty-three; the youngest, Elizabeth Barry, was seventeen.

The dysgenic outflow of healthy English working girls like Nellie and the inflow of undesirable immigrants like Jews infuriated anti-alien xenophobes at the turn of the century.[111] The handful of Jews, Scots, and Irish onboard the *Waiwera* all disembarked in Cape Town. This must have pleased officials in New Zealand who had begun in earnest to regulate who was—and who was not—welcome to settle their island nation. In 1881, 1888, and 1899, New Zealand passed legislation designed to keep out the "yellow peril" of Chinese labor. The 1881 act established a ratio of one Chinese for every ten tons of cargo, later increased to one per one hundred tons; the 1899 act demanded exorbitant payments of a hundred-pound poll tax for each non-British immigrant.[112] Either the acts were extraordinarily effective or the legislature's response wildly disproportionate to the "yellow" peril, because in 1901, there were less than three thousand Chinese in a total population of just over 800,000. Among European settlers, the original imbalance between the sexes had moved closer to parity (405,000 men and 366,000 women), but young, white, single women like Nellie remained desirable immigrants.[113] In the vast global flow of people within the British empire at the dawn of the new century, Nellie and the other Bell's match girls were among the

2.8. New Zealanders and Britons alike celebrated the departure of troops aboard the *Waiwera* from Wellington to fight in South Africa in December 1899 as evidence of increasing closeness between the two nations. A few months later, this same ship carried Nellie to Wellington. *Waiwera, Illustrated London News*, December 9, 1899, 837.

most fortunate. They came to New Zealand seeking a better life: higher wages, cleaner and newer accommodations, and fun.

According to Muriel, Nellie went to an unspecified location in New Zealand for a short time (in the first typescript version of "From Birth to Death" she has crossed out "six months") on something of a lark in search of new experiences. "Everyone agreed that the sea voyage and the fine air would 'suit the littl'un a treat' and a very happy Nellie set out for the Antipodes." Muriel characterized Nellie's job variously as teaching "the girls there how to make matches" or "how to work the machines in a new factory that was just opened." The girls "proved such effective teachers," Muriel breezily explained, "that their job was soon done and they were recalled to Bow to find themselves in a delightful situation." "How Nell loved telling of the joys of that free life, the friendships and the fun. . . ."[114] Muriel's account of Nell's carefree gambols in New Zealand is more than a little rose-tinted, no doubt reflecting how Nellie chose to remember it.

Nellie did go to New Zealand to work in its match industry, but almost all the other facts are not quite right. She lived in Wellington, New Zealand, for over three years, not six months, from early June 1900 through the summer of 1903. Wellington municipal records corroborate the arrival of new machines and R. Bell's applications for building permits to accommodate them between 1895 and 1903. However, Nellie was not sent there to instruct anyone in their use. The factory had been open for five years and many "colonial" girls had worked there for several years before Nellie's arrival. They were old hands, not untrained workers. Bell's New Zealand match girls certainly did not view Nellie as an "effective teacher." She arrived as part of R. Bell's response to ongoing problems with the recruitment, compensation, and disciplining of its female workforce in New Zealand. As Robert "Bob" McKenzie, the leader of the Wellington Match Factory Union, declared, "but for this dispute [between the colonial match girls and R. Bell] the London girls would never have been here."[115] It was "moonshine" to pretend that R. Bell could not find plenty of New Zealand girls to fill its jobs, if only the company treated its workers fairly.[116] I have no reason to believe that Nellie knew anything about these problems when she left London. However, by the time she and the other London girls reported to work the day after their landing, they discovered that they had been newsworthy—and part of the labor dispute—from the moment they had stepped aboard the *Waiwera*.

Rumors that R. Bell intended to "import" girls from its London match factory provoked the ire of Seddon's parliamentary opponents, both within and outside the Liberal Party. Nor did they please Seddon himself. If the purpose of protecting the match industry was to provide jobs for New Zealand girls, then why had R. Bell sent over "slum girls" from London, questioned one MP. Seddon's critics noted that R. Bell and Company had been the only new industry established in New Zealand during the first six years of the Liberal ministry. The cost had been enormous: over 16,000 pounds in tariff revenues had been lost each year while the entire wage packet for those employed in Wellington amounted to less than 5,000 pounds. Protecting R. Bell had cost New Zealanders at least 10,000 pounds per year.[117] Throughout the rancorous debates about the revised tariff schedule raging from June to September 1900, many fumed that it would have been vastly cheaper and more efficient to give each of Bell's workers a one-pound-per-week pension and allow them to do nothing.[118] Such a solution had an added advantage for New Zealanders. They could then enjoy the benefits of duty-free, higher quality imported matches.

The London girls' arrival not only exposed Bell's match girls to critical scrutiny, but opened the floodgates of consumer grumbling about Bell's New Zealand–made matches. Some complained that the heads of the matches broke off when struck and were "apt to light in the eye of the user."[119] One MP, David Buddo, demonstrated the superiority of Bryant and May's imports compared to Bell's New Zealand–made product. He brought with him boxes of each and counted what was inside them. The Bell's box contained 134 vestas, 16 fewer than advertised; the Bryant and May's contained precisely 150. Did this deficit reflect the lack of skill of box fillers at R. Bell's? Or was it indicative of worker resistance to labor discipline, a veiled form of protest reminiscent of the empty boxes packed and sent abroad for export by London girls in 1893–94? Buddo concluded his tirade by pointing out that "however much we may desire protection for healthy industries that pay good wages to workers . . . match-making is not a healthy occupation, and the wages earned are very low."[120]

It was hard to dispute that the "colonial" girls' earnings of fourteen to eighteen shillings per week fell short of a "living wage" (approximately one pound per week for a single woman) and were unworthy of heavy state subsidies through tariff protection. Some members of Parliament insinuated that the Wellington match factory not only endangered workers' health but degraded their morals as well.[121] Revelations that Bryant and May (and specifically Gilbert Bartholomew) had deliberately violated factory regulations and concealed horrendous cases of necrosis fanned the flames of discontent against R. Bell's New Zealand operations.[122] Such shocking behavior incited the "extreme indignation" of a contributor to the *New Zealand Journal of the Department of Labour*. "Here is matter for reflection for the purchaser of the popular wax matches," the author concluded, "these can be made only at the cost of human agony and death." Written for a publication sponsored by Seddon's own ministry, the article unambiguously condemned the manufacture of matches that Seddon himself had done so much to foster.[123] Critics of Seddon's special relationship with R. Bell and Company crossed party lines.

The Wellington Match Factory Employees' Industrial Union of Workers proved even less easy to placate than members of Parliament. Registered as an official union in April 1900, it filed a "reference" against R. Bell with the Conciliation Commission on June 5, 1900, Nellie's first working day in Wellington.[124] During the 1894 strike in London, R. Bell ignored the union's pleas to enter into nonbinding arbitration to settle its grievances. In New Zealand, workers enjoyed vastly more and better protections. The 1894 Industrial Conciliation and Arbitration Act required employers and workers to resolve their differences first through "Councils of conciliation."[125] If this failed to satisfy both parties, they then stood before a Court of Arbitration, whose judgments were legally binding. This compulsory process of resolving labor disputes was a cornerstone of the Liberal ministry's legislative agenda of social and economic reform. The brainchild of the Liberal minister of labour, William Pember Reeves, the act granted legal standing to trade unions to represent workers' interests as elected members of conciliation boards. These boards also included representatives elected by employers' associations. A Supreme Court judge headed each Court of Arbitration along with two assessors, one representing employers and the other workers. New Zealand trade unionists were indispensable partners in bringing together labor and capital, not dangerous troublemakers castigated by the mainstream press in London. This system was designed to ensure industrial peace among the factory population of about 30,000 out of a white population of around 715,000 in 1894.[126]

Several issues divided the Wellington Union and R. Bell—and all of them came to swirl around the arrival of Nellie and her London workmates. Troubles had begun during Christmas 1899, when R. Bell switched how it compensated box fillers. Instead of paying them by the number of frames they emptied, they were paid by the gross of boxes they filled.[127] The Wellington match girls reported that the foreman, George W. Lacey, used intimidation to discourage them from joining the union. He and forewoman Ada Fulton kept close control over the key to the lavatory and locked it at 4:30 p.m. to prevent girls from wasting time at the end of the workday. Girls who arrived late were locked out and lost an entire day's wages. They had to scrub down their own benches and floor space—tasks for which they received no pay. They could not live "respectably" on their wages. Finally, the union argued that R. Bell ought to show "preference" in hiring union members over nonunion workers. Importing the London girls demonstrated R. Bell's determination to circumvent preferential hiring.

R. Bell and Company had its own litany of complaints about the indiscipline of the "colonial girls": they came late, left early, and rarely labored a full week. Insolent and ill mannered, they worked slowly and inaccurately. Corporate coercion went hand in hand with worker resistance. The factory manager Walter McLay, who represented the firm during the first round of conciliation hearings, was a veteran of the 1893–94 strike in London. He vigorously asserted R. Bell's right to import London girls and hire nonunion workers on grounds of "freedom of contract."[128] Here was not only a dispute over work discipline, but fundamental principles about the relationship between labor, capital, and the state.

In the eyes of union leadership, the London match girls had been shipped over to show up the New Zealand girls and weaken the union. It was no accident that all the London girls including Nellie were expert box fillers—precisely the department heretofore most heavily unionized.[129] While New Zealand workers complained that they could not earn a living wage at R. Bell, the London girls had been lured to New Zealand by the prospect of better pay. Charles Bell had emphasized the wage advantage enjoyed by his entire New Zealand workforce. "The girls employed in the Wellington factory were infinitely better off than they were at Home, to the extent of perhaps 50 or 60 percent," Bell had bragged at the factory's opening.[130] This advantage was accentuated by the virtuosic speed at which the London girls performed their tasks. One of Nellie's London workmates earned as much as forty-eight shillings in a single week. R. Bell fired girls at its London factory who did not work quickly and efficiently, a London girl explained to the Conciliation Board during her testimony before it. Such words could not have been welcome to the several dozen trade union members listening to and participating in the proceedings.

The wages of the "exceptionally smart" "energetic and willing" London girls remained newsworthy six years later. In July 1906, one newspaper reported that one of the "London girls" earned forty-one shillings, six pence in a week compared to her "top wages" in London of about "18s for longer hours."[131] In a colonial setting in which a high percentage of white settlers in Wellington (around thirty percent in 1901) were themselves immigrants from Britain or Australia, it is notable that the London match girls continued to be identified as outsiders.[132] They remained "London" girls. R. Bell lost no time in declaring that the "Wellington girls" had only themselves to blame for earning far less than Nellie and the rest of her London mates.

The London girls surely did not endear themselves to their fellow workers by living in a lodging house run (but not owned) by R. Bell's unpopular foreman, George Lacey, not far from the factory.[133] The boardinghouse was, Lacey explained, a private "speculation." The president of the union contended that the London girls "had it drummed into them all the time that they were against the Union" and had been rewarded with the best and most lucrative jobs.[134] Coming from so far and without friends or family in Wellington, the London girls may well have been pleased and relieved to have a safe, respectable place to live together. In any case, they were in no position to refuse Lacey. In "From Birth to Death" Muriel offers Nellie's perspective that "every arrangement for their comfort had been made by the manager of the New Zealand firm." He provided them with board and lodging for ten shillings per week—a bit more than some colonial girls paid but within the range of prevailing rates for Wellington.[135] This left Nellie plenty of money to send home to her mother and to spend on clothing and entertainment. It also meant that Nellie was rarely far from the watchful eye of her foreman who was also her landlord.

In mid-July, the arbitration court handed the Union a complete victory. It mandated substantial increases in pay for each type of work performed in the box-filling and box-making departments; it affirmed the principle of preferential hiring of union members while insisting that all workers be treated equally. The decision did not in fact put an end to the controversies surrounding the arrival of the London match girls. Unable to keep up with demand, R. Bell had imported a large number of matchboxes from its London factory stamped with the misleading label "New Zealand." The commissioner of trade and customs ordered the forfeiture of nearly four hundred cases of these matches, worth over one thousand pounds, on the grounds that the boxes deceived consumers into believing that the London matches had been made in New Zealand.[136]

Seddon, weary of defending R. Bell's business practices, decided to cut his own political losses. He reluctantly accepted that supporting R. Bell and Company was not the best way to demonstrate his increasingly fervent desire to draw "closer the bonds of union" with Britain.[137] He publicly withdrew support for the firm in mid-July 1900 during a parliamentary debate over the London match girls' arrival. "It was true," he confessed, "that Messrs. Bell and Co were getting labour from the old country" and had imported deceptively marked matchboxes. Given the unhappy conditions prevailing in the factory, he did not wonder that "colonial girls" preferred not to work there. Seddon acknowledged that R. Bell had "not kept faith" with the government.[138] He could no longer justify "protecting" a New Zealand match industry that hired "London girls" and imported "London matches." With obvious sarcasm and anger, he observed that the cost of subsidizing the industry had been so great and the benefits so few that it would have been cheaper to provide free matches for the entire colony than continue to support R. Bell. He indicated that he would soon announce a tariff schedule withdrawing protection from the match industry.[139] In the ensuing high-stakes political game of cat and mouse, R. Bell promptly laid off seventy "colonial girl" workers in Wellington in response to the new tariff schedule; others shrieked that the government's sudden reversal of trade policy would scare off much needed capital investors from abroad. In the end, Seddon compromised and reduced protections and R. Bell rehired its workers.

The proprietors of R. Bell and Company had embarrassed their most powerful supporters in the Liberal ministry and infuriated their "colonial girl" employees by seeking to use techniques of labor discipline and factory management out of harmony with ideas prevailing in New Zealand about employers' obligations to their workers. Shop floor bullying and surveillance so effective in Bromley-by-Bow simply did not work in Wellington.

Global capitalism connected people, goods, and services in London and Wellington, but local conditions and national political cultures produced drastically different outcomes for factory workers in the two cities. (See fig. 2.9.) Young women in Wellington refused to accept labor

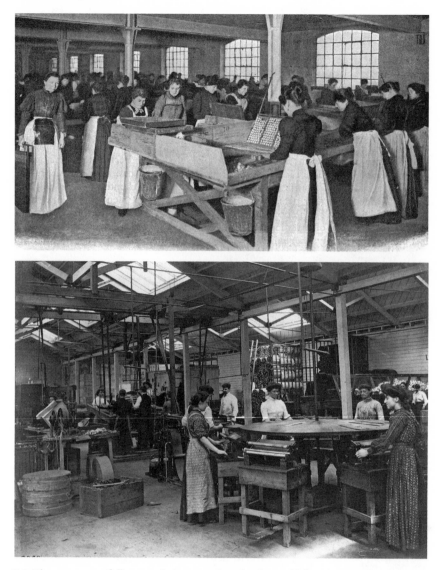

2.9. These two carefully staged photographs of industrial labor on R. Bell's shop floors in London (1901) and Wellington (1906) depict matchbox fillers like Nellie in a modern, clean, and safe work environment that belied the occupational health hazards still posed by phosphorous. (Top) R. Bell and Co. London, c. 1901, from G. R. Sims, ed., *Living London, Its Work and Its Pay, Its Humour and Its Pathos, Its Sight and Its Scenes*, vol. 2 (London, 1901), 330. (Bottom) "People at Work in the R Bell & Co Match Factory, Wellington. New Zealand." Department of Labour: Photograph albums for the International Exhibition, Christchurch, 1906–7. Ref: PA1-o-367–36. (Courtesy of the Alexander Turnbull Library, Wellington, New Zealand.)

conditions and low pay that many of their London counterparts eagerly sought. In London, match girls faced draconian sentences for minor offenses; in New Zealand, the state supported them wholeheartedly. Ironically, R. Bell's defeat in the arbitration court saved the firm from its own worst inclinations by mandating conditions that made it possible to recruit at least some "colonial girls." Nellie and the London girls had been central figures in each of these disputes. Obscure East London factory workers in Bromley-by-Bow, they enjoyed the notoriety of countless newspaper articles about them and major policy debates about the implications of their arrival for New Zealand's global trade policies and its relationship to overseas capital investment.

It is fair to say that Nellie had received a remarkable if unintended education in the political economy of late-industrial global capitalism as a Cockney subaltern in East London and New Zealand. Too young to grasp the lessons of the Bryant and May strike of 1888, she was already an adult during the Bell's strike of 1893–94. Smart, hardworking, and reliable, Nellie almost certainly did not join the union but chose to stick to doing her job well. Schooled in the hostile work environment of East London, a place where those who could not support themselves ended up in Poor Law institutions far from kith and kin, Nellie placed her own and her family's financial security above the claims of solidarity with fellow workers. However, she had no choice but to absorb and think about the issues, large and small, driving the Bell's strike of 1893–94. In New Zealand, she and the eleven other London girls were themselves a key point of contention in these conflicts. MPs' angry rhetoric and journalists' arch commentaries focused on trade policy, relations between labor and capital, and New Zealand national pride. For her part, Nellie had to live with her unwonted celebrity each day she came to work. She worked side by side with "colonial" girls who, unlike Nellie, refused to tolerate R. Bell's managerial practices. It is hard to imagine that these colonial girls offered much of a welcome to Nellie and her London mates.

In spite of her longing for respectability, Nellie had a knack for becoming a "problem" at the heart of major debates in England and New Zealand. Her father's death had made her into a "Poor Law half-orphan" at the metropolis's most notoriously impersonal "barrack" school, which became a lightning rod for national debates about orphans and foster care, working-class family life and education, and the proper role of the British state. Her entry into the wax vesta and lucifer match industry had turned her into a poor little match girl and slum factory worker at the precise moment when the industry became a flashpoint for women's trade union and political activism in East London. In New Zealand, she and her London workmates came to signify the bad faith of R. Bell, the political miscalculations of the Premier, and the manifold sins of the Old World visiting themselves upon the New.

These microdramas between labor and capital at the Newtown factory paled in significance next to the seismic shifts in the global match industry a few months later. The year 1901 was a momentous and portentous one in the British match industry. Liverpool's Diamond Match Company gained a controlling interest in Bryant and May in a complex deal guaranteeing Bryant and May's shareholders a generous fifteen percent return on their investments.[140] This was not merely the triumph of an upstart Liverpool company over a long-established London giant but of American inventiveness over British obduracy and complacency. The Liverpool firm, founded in 1897, was backed and owned by the American Diamond Match Company. In 1896, American Diamond Match introduced self-acting machinery, which eliminated manual labor from the production process: match workers tended machinery rather than made matches.[141] The chief function of its Liverpool firm was to introduce the American company's patented machinery and technologies to Britain and absorb British competitors.

The amalgamation sent shock waves throughout the British business world as a sign of Britain's irreversible economic decline stemming from its adherence to "antediluvian" industrial technologies and business practices. The president of the American Diamond Match Company did little to soften the blow. In a much-quoted speech, he crowed that his company had discarded the machinery currently used by Bryant and May more than fifteen years earlier. His company had invested more than $1,000,000 in research and technology to improve its machinery; it had spent over $250,000 in the last year alone to purchase patents on inventions to advance its productive capacity and efficiency. American business had embraced association of all kinds as a commercial principle, whereas its British counterparts had persisted in aggravating tensions between labor and capital. "You English are too conservative," he explained, "and it is pretty hard work to change you. You Englishmen ought to remember that you cannot stop progress." The *Review of Reviews* put the matter more bluntly: it was time to "Wake Up! John Bull" or face industrial obsolescence.[142]

At least for a few years, R. Bell and Company forestalled the inevitable and maintained its corporate independence from the encroaching monopoly capitalist behemoth, the American Diamond Match Company operating under cover of the Bryant and May name. Just as R. Bell encouraged patriotic consumption through its supposedly "New Zealand–made" matches, so too Bryant and May intensified its public relations campaign—*after* its acquisition by the American Diamond Match Company—to buy its products as a way to "Buy British" and support workers in the British-based match industry.[143] Such campaigns could and did backfire in the increasingly globalized world not just of match production but of political debate. Rabindranath Tagore recalled his own comic attempts to produce "Indian" lucifer matches during the first stirrings of the Swadeshi campaign of 1905 to boycott all British and imperial goods and make everyday consumption a form of Indian nationalism. "The money that was spent in their making," Tagore self-deprecatingly acknowledged, "might have served to light the family hearth for the space of the year." It did not help that his virtuous lucifers ignited only with the help of another light.[144] Unlike Tagore's genuinely "Indian" lucifers, Bryant and May's matches—along with the firm's rhetoric of jingoistic consumer altruism—could not have been farther removed from the reality of its global ownership. The transformation of the global match industry at the dawn of the new century confirmed the wisdom of R. Bell's expansion into the New Zealand market, where even a reduced protective tariff insulated it from direct competition with its vastly more heavily capitalized rivals in Britain and continental Europe.

Labor conflicts in Wellington may have closely resembled those Nellie knew only too well from her years working for R. Bell in Bromley-by-Bow, but the Empire City presented an altogether new world for her. Wellington looked nothing like East London, with its crowded streets, decaying infrastructure, ubiquitous poverty, and environmental degradation. The second most populous city in New Zealand with just under 50,000 people, it was dwarfed by turn of the century Greater London's population which pressed beyond 6,500,000. With its steeply inclined hillsides and shimmering windswept bays and harbors, the city first expanded along the narrow strip of flat land along Oriental Bay. There was plenty of open space and undeveloped land on the outskirts and hills of turn-of-the-century Wellington. Emerging out of the long global agricultural depression, New Zealand entered a phase of increased immigration and economic growth in the early 1900s.

Nellie initially lived in Newtown, a booming suburb set on the hills south of city center. In the early 1890s, few houses hugged the main north-south roads (Adelaide and Revans-Riddiford) connecting Newtown with the city center to the north; but the extension of the tram lines rapidly accelerated suburban development. Aided by gunpowder, dynamite, and skilled excavation, some of Newtown's rocky slopes sprouted modest but attractive cottages, many owned—not rented—by the city's "mechanical" workers. Shops and civic institutions of all kinds from Wellington Hospital and Campbell Oriental Tea Mart to Mrs. Orchard's plush Newtown Academy of Music and Art had followed the new residents. Newtown also welcomed industrial enterprises like R. Bell's factory on Revans Street with its 30 foot by 100 foot curved shed and various outbuildings.[145] The *Cyclopedia of New Zealand* proclaimed the nation's many virtues and proudly displayed the match factory with all its employees assembled before it.[146]

Sometime between her arrival in June 1900 and 1902, Nellie moved out of the foreman's boarding house along with at least one of her London match girl friends, Kate Newman, into a newly built small cottage on Charles Street. (See fig. 2.10.) Was this evidence of disaffection or simply the desire for a different and perhaps more private space? Nellie's new home gave her distance from George Lacey, the factory, and her coworkers. Several of the London girls moved to 8a Rintoul Street, in the bustling heart of Newtown's commercial district. Charles Street lay three quarters of a mile to the south in Berhampore, a working-class district named after the site of a British victory in India during the Seven Years' War. Nellie and Kate lived on a quiet dead end residential block. Between 1898 and 1901, the entrepreneurial pork butcher-turned-real estate developer, Charles Swiney, carved it out of four empty lots off Herald Street and erected around a dozen small cottages.[147] He rented these cottages to local workers—bricklayers, carpenters, journeymen plumbers, a smattering of clerks, and match factory girls.[148] For the first

2.10. Nellie lived on Charles Terrace, a one-block dead-end street with newly erected workmen's cottages including this one in Wellington's Berhampore district. (Photograph taken by author, 2011.)

few years, Wellington city officials tolerated Swiney's self-promoting street naming for the purposes of collecting rates from him; but when they eventually gazetted the street, they refused to humor him any further. They changed its official name from Charles Street to Herald Terrace, the name it still bears. The cottages on Charles Street and those in the surrounding neighborhood remain virtually unchanged since Nellie lived there. Home to successive waves of immigrants, the district remained too poor to attract large-scale redevelopment and capital investment.

It was not just the geography, topography, and climate that differed so dramatically from everything Nellie knew back home. She also encountered a new respect for the dignity of labor and women. Few were rich, but even fewer were poor. New Zealanders had not so much embraced the gospel of equality as much as rejected the inevitability of inequality. Under the leadership of Seddon and the Liberal Party, the New Zealand legislature passed a series of socialistic measures, including old age pensions—what Pember Reeves called "sort of socialism"—without in any sense adopting socialism as a matter of ideological conviction.[149] Theirs was a pragmatic politics designed to secure fair treatment of workers. The electoral bill granting women's suffrage managed to pass the Liberal-controlled Legislative Council (New Zealand's upper house) in the autumn of 1893 without the support of Seddon and his cabinet. It was quickly signed into law—the fruit of nearly two decades of determined organizing by women acting through and in alliance with the transnational Women's Christian Temperance Union.[150] Here too was yet another unanticipated gain for Nellie. She acquired rights of full citizenship two decades before Muriel and almost thirty years before laboring women in Britain.

Nellie returned home to London onboard the *Papanui* in August 1903 with four other "London" girls. While it was unusual for a single white Englishwoman to leave New Zealand, "From Birth to Death" suggests that Nellie never saw herself as an immigrant. She had gone for higher wages and a change of scene, not to make a new life for herself so far from her family. Back in Bow, she apparently regaled her friends and fellow factory club members in Bromley-by-Bow with tales about her New Zealand adventures and encounters with its indigenous Maori people. Muriel included only one of these stories in "From Birth to Death"; it accentuated Nellie's political education as a woman and citizen. It recounted Nellie's experience voting in what must have been the 1902 New Zealand general election: "outwardly they treated it [their right to vote] as a colossal joke but inwardly were very proud and gazed studiously at the photographs of the candidates, drinking in with avidity every detail of their domestic life they could collect." The story highlights Nellie's process of learning about "prohibition" and its centrality to New Zealand electoral politics and women's political culture. Nellie meets a "red-nosed" opponent of prohibition who informs her that prohibition would "kill" joy for and "rob" the workingman of his liquor. Unimpressed, Nellie declares, "That's put the tin 'at on, I guess," and she and the other eleven London girls back the Prohibition candidate. The poll is so close that a revote is necessary and a slick, smooth-talking electoral agent for the anti-prohibition candidate tries to bribe the girls and win their support. The story ends with the girls resolutely rejecting the proffered bribe—one pound each—and mocking the agent for so badly underestimating their political independence and strong moral fiber. Crucially, their block of a dozen votes ensures victory for their candidate. The episode reinforces Nellie's pride in her newfound status in the world and capacity to think and act politically. It is yet another moment when Nellie defines herself in relation to the plebian culture and world around her: she rejects drink, bribery, and corruption in favor of a moralized and feminized politics. She exercises independent political judgment even as her day-to-day labor ensures her own—and her mother's—financial independence. In Muriel's published version of this episode, she offered an explicitly feminist gloss on its meaning: "Thus eighteen years ago the Suffragists' faith was being justified in the lives of quiet, unknown, everyday sort of people."[151]

At least some elements of this story can be corroborated. Nellie and six other London girls (not all twelve of them) were on the electoral roll for 1902, which provided their addresses and occupations along with their names. Most of the London girls, including Nellie, called themselves spinsters. A few, however, registered as "box fillers."[152] Newtown, like Wellington and the rest of New Zealand, had two distinct ballots in 1902, one to elect representatives, the other to determine local drink regulations. It is also possible that Nellie remembered an election of local councilors in Wellington.[153] Nellie's story—and Muriel's recounting of it—may have been accurate, but none of the local newspapers saw fit to report about such a tightly contested race and revote.

I know little about Nellie's life from her return in 1903 until approximately 1906–7 when R. Bell once again sent her to fill match boxes in Sweden. I have not located any record of her arrival in Sweden; nor have I tracked down a branch of R. Bell and Company in Sweden. The Swedish and English match industries had been closely connected from the 1850s when Bryant and May first distributed Swedish-manufactured safety matches by Lundström. Several English firms in the early twentieth century maintained close connections with their Swedish counterparts, occasionally acting as distributors for their goods. Nellie apparently enjoyed the pleasures of village life. But there was nothing bucolic about her workplace environment. Sweden's leading match factories were even larger and more imposing than their London counterparts. This was capitalism on a grand scale.[154]

After Bryant and May's absorption into the Diamond Match empire, it had eyed R. Bell and Company, whose value was enhanced by its strong share of the market in New Zealand and Australia. By 1909, R. Bell and Company had ceased to be an independent corporate entity in New Zealand and had been purchased by Bryant and May. This was im-

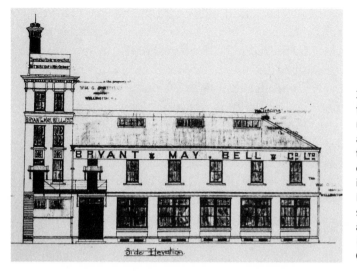

2.11. The architect's plan for the expansion of the match factory shows the addition of a prominent tower as well as the change in name indicating its purchase by Bryant and May. Architectural plans submitted by Bryant, May, and Bell & Co., Ltd., 1910. (Courtesy of Wellington City Archives.)

mediately evident to New Zealanders each time they passed the re-named factory and purchased a box of Bryant, May and Bell matches.[155] (See fig. 2.11.) At approximately the same time Nellie went to Sweden, British match manufacturers formed an association (the British Match Manufacturers' Association) to fend off foreign competition, in particular, Swedish matches. In response, a few British firms forged even closer ties with the Swedish match industry. A parliamentary report from 1920 suggested that these pre–World War I Anglo-Swedish corporations were motivated by the desire "to secure the advantages of the Australian preferential tariff for British goods."[156] My best guess is that Nellie's move to Sweden must have been part of the larger global restructuring of R. Bell, Bryant and May, and Diamond Match.

Muriel's narration of Nellie's time in Sweden captures her at midlife, contemplating fundamental questions about herself, the world, and God. It explores her inner life of thought and feeling at a spiritual and intellectual crossroads. Nellie loved the Swedish countryside, began to learn the language, and forged meaningful relationships there. She "found herself weighing up theories, comparing practice and profession, examining the colossal claims of religion, thinking about God . . . she began to criticize hymns which up until now she had sung with zest merely for the sake of the tunes, she found herself setting one Bible story against another to the obvious discredit of both." Beset by a crisis of faith, Nellie rejected the easy path out of such soul searching: marriage and motherhood. She had a "presentiment that getting married wasn't going to satisfy her." She refused to risk being widowed and left to fend for herself like her mother and grandmother: "you're left without nourishments when you need 'em most, a queer sort of world." Such an explanation sidesteps any questions about Nellie's sexuality and instead emphasizes how gender shaped household resources and married women's economic vulnerability. The so-called Christian world no longer seemed so Christian to her. She questioned the truthfulness of the words of the national anthem she sang at Girls' Guild concerts, which extolled "our just and righteous laws"; she was much less inclined to shout "for our most gracious King at theatres"; she wondered what had happened to "our national sense of fair play."[157] Importantly, Nellie's emerging intellectual critique of patriarchy, empire, and patriotism are the fruit of her own self-reflection stimulated by her global travels. Muriel gave Nellie the last word in this section of "From Birth to Death": "It was all very queer."

Muriel did drop one tantalizing hint about Nellie's personal life after her return from New Zealand indicative of the intellectual milieu that she had entered. Apparently, Harry Snell was one of Nellie's would-be suitors, who continued to press his claims upon her even during her time abroad in Sweden.[158] What part Nellie's relationship with Snell played in provoking her profound disquiet with the verities of dogmatic religion and patriotic nationalism is difficult to judge. Snell was a well-suited interlocutor for her. An eyewitness to the Bryant and May Match Girls' Strike, he had hailed it as a momentous achievement for women workers. He had thought long and hard about right moral action and religion. A quintessential Victorian working-class autodidact, he shared Nellie's zeal for self-improvement and thirst for knowledge. Reared in a culture of radical Nonconformity in Nottinghamshire, he discovered socialism as well as the free thinking Charles Bradlaugh (Annie Besant's erstwhile partner in schemes to promote working-class knowledge of birth control) and the secularist movement while attending evening classes at the University College in Nottingham in the 1880s. He came to

London under the wing of a progressive clergyman who headed the Charity Organisation Society's branch in Woolwich. Snell emerged as a formidable leader in Labour politics and the Ethical Society.[159] The society had a two "churches" in Bow, one on Ford Road and the other close to Nellie in Bow Road.[160]

In many respects puritanical in his moral judgments, Snell helped to outline the principles guiding the Ethical Movement in Britain: "the love of goodness and the love of one's fellows are the true motives for right conduct; and self-reliance and co-operation are the true sources of help." He espoused a "progressive ideal of personal and social righteousness" determined by the individual's "own conscientious and reasoned judgment." He insisted that moral life involved "neither acceptance nor rejection of belief in any deity, personal and impersonal, or in a life after death."[161] We can be certain that Snell responded sympathetically to Nellie's newly articulated discontent with the glib slogans of English jingoistic patriotism. Snell was keenly attuned to problems of race, nation, and nativism. He was on the founding executive council of the first Universal Races Congress in London in 1911 that sought to produce global amity between East and West, North and South.[162] In his 1904 *Tract for the Times*, "The Foreigner in England," Snell defended the rights of Eastern European Jewish immigrants fleeing persecution and blasted British colonial policy for shipping Chinese indentured laborers to South Africa. He astutely observed that "the cry of 'English' necessarily raises the question, 'What constitutes an Englishman?'" The greatness of the English, Snell insisted, depended not upon the reactionary struggle to preserve some imagined purity of race but in the "continuous admixture of different blood."[163]

It was not on account of Harry Snell that Nellie returned to London. She came home because her brother-in-law, William Dellar, had sustained a disabling injury and been consigned as "incurable" to a Poor Law asylum. What Muriel does not say is that the Poplar Board of Guardians eventually sent him to the very same Poor Law complex at Forest Gate that had been Nellie and her sister Alice's home for so many years.[164] The loss of his wages forced her sister Florence to leave Marner Street for even cheaper lodgings on Devas Road. Like her own mother before her, Florence Dellar lacked resources to keep her family together.

She entered domestic service and her mother, Harriet Dowell, adopted her youngest child Willie.

Nellie was determined to support her mother and nephew out of her weekly wages of eighteen shillings. "From Birth to Death" emphasizes her keen sense of gratitude to and economic responsibility for her mother: "She returned to Bow determined by herculean efforts ... to better her position so that her mother should not be the loser through the increase in the family." Nellie moved into 313 Brunswick Road, the three-room flat occupied by her grandmother and Aunt Carrie in 1901, a few blocks south of R. Bell's factory gates. She was heartsick and angry at a social system so cruel that it took a child away from "such a mother" as her sister. Muriel pithily summed up Nellie's growing intellectual ferment and her increasing distance from the core assumptions of late-Victorian philanthropic benevolence and cross-class relations: "The Evening Club [with its philanthropic ladies] didn't seem to Nellie so satisfactory in her new mood."[165]

Nor did R. Bell and Company seem so satisfactory to her. On May 19, 1909, a "Miss Lester, The Grange, Loughton," filed a complaint with a women's watch guard committee, the Industrial Law Committee, founded in 1898 to promote the enforcement of laws protecting industrial women workers. Muriel Lester had learned from an unnamed worker that R. Bell and Company had continued to use the now-banned form of yellow phosphorus that caused necrosis.[166] I suspect that Nellie was Muriel's whistleblowing informant. Sometime that same year, Nellie ended two decades of employment at R. Bell's and took a job at Cook's East London Soap Works.

Cook's was an immense industrial enterprise just across Bow Bridge to the north and east of Bromley-by-Bow. (See fig. 2.12.) The noisome odors produced by soap manufacture saturated the atmosphere and had shocked Muriel's sensitive nostrils when she opened her window as her first-class carriage sped from her Loughton home through Bow en route to West London. Always delicate, Nellie suffered another bout of rheumatic fever in 1908. A few weeks before Christmas 1909, the fever returned and Nellie had to give up her job at Cook's. This time its consequences were devastating and changed the course of Nellie and Muriel's lives.

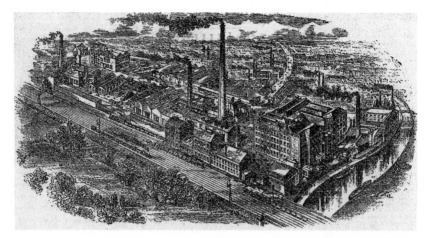

2.12. Cook's East London Soap Works was a vast industrial complex that dominated the east side of the River Lea north of Bow Bridge. It was Nellie's last employer of her industrial waged labor. Its owner served as chairman of the managing committee of Forest Gate School during Nellie's time there. "East London Industries," *East End News*, June 5, 1906, clipping collection. (Courtesy of Tower Hamlets Local History Library.)

CONCLUSIONS

Britain's global capitalist economy teetered at its precarious height during Nellie's working life in the match industry. The accelerating integration of the world economy—enhanced communication and transportation networks, well-organized London-based capital markets as well as an "unprecedented increase in inter-continental migration"—strengthened Britain's ties with much of its empire while fueling anti-colonial nationalist movements.[167] Such developments encouraged providential imperialists like W.T. Stead to foretell a Union of English-Speaking peoples (a "great Federation of English-speaking commonwealths") that would usher the poor and outcast of all races into a new Kingdom of Heaven on Earth.[168] They also provided the macro-economic conditions that encouraged New Zealand's Prime Minister John Seddon to entice R. Bell and Company with tariff protections and led Nellie Dowell from Bromley-by-Bow to Bell's Wellington wax vesta factory. Thickening political and economic ties between Britain and New Zealand did not—and could not—efface the profoundly different ways in which each state defined citizenship and understood its role in regulating relations between labor and capital. Match factory girls in New Zealand had vastly more rights than their London counterparts that extended from the polling booth to the shop floor.

It was pure coincidence that the SS *Waiwera*, the ship that brought Nellie from London to New Zealand, had transported New Zealanders several months earlier to fight on behalf of their mother country against the Boers in southern Africa.[169] For political economist J. A. Hobson, these global flows were intimately connected. He insisted that the grotesque maldistribution of wealth—the under-consumption of the ill-paid laboring poor and the subsequent flight of capital to the far reaches of empire—would hasten Britain's geopolitical and moral exhaustion. In Hobson's classic marriage of Ruskin's ethics and Marx's economics, *Imperialism: A Study* (1902), imperialism subjugated Britons to profit-mongering financiers and jingoistic media moguls while exploiting the white working class at home and non-white races globally. The Boer War, he admitted, had temporarily and artificially produced greater solidarity between white Australasians and Britons. Nellie unobtrusively slipped into Hobson's grand narrative under cover of aggregate anonymity in one of his many statistical charts. She was one of the 14,922 outward-bound passengers from the United Kingdom to Australasia in 1900.[170] Nellie's story and Muriel's retelling of it don't align with Hobson's. White proletarian factory girls have no place in his account. And Nellie apparently did not experience either empire or global capitalism as a malign system of exploitation. No doubt this reflects both her personality and the privileges of whiteness in the British empire. It is possible to read against the grain of "From Birth to Death" and speculate that Nellie must have contemplated her whiteness in New Zealand. Muriel mentioned in passing that Nellie returned home from New Zealand with tales of the Maori people she had encountered there.[171]

Nellie's global circulations provide one set of answers to the question: what did capitalism look like from below and down under? Britain's global match industry from the 1880s to 1920s was ferociously competitive, compelled to adapt to market forces and new technologies, characterized by draconian labor discipline while subjecting its low-paid workers to severe occupational health hazards. Firms like R. Bell and Bryant and May developed entire advertising campaigns, which intentionally made virtues of their vices. They trumpeted the safety of their production process while concealing documented incidents of phossy jaw caused by the continued use of dangerous (and eventually banned) substances. They urged customers to engage in everyday consumer patriotism by purchasing so-called British or New Zealand matches even as they knew full well that no such thing existed: matches were truly global products.

Nellie's arrival in Wellington prompted New Zealanders to look long and hard at British industrial capitalism in the guise of R. Bell and Company. They did not like what they saw. They condemned R. Bell and closely regulated its labor and commercial practices. As best as I can tell, the story Nellie told Muriel about her laboring life emphasized opportunity and adventure, not constraint; workplace solidarity, not trade union strife; financial security, not exploitation. In so many ways, the intimate story of Nellie's laboring life in the match industry does not square with the political-economic one that I have assembled. Nor does her story betray traces of deep inner conflicts about her choices. The black internationalist and sociologist of race W.E.B. Du Bois asked, "how does it feel to be a problem?" His answer was that for African Americans it meant bearing the burden of double consciousness, forever aware of being part of and excluded from what it meant to be American.[172] A different answer emerges from my examination of Nellie's life. As a white proletarian worker in Britain and its empire, Nellie, it seems, never saw herself as a problem.

Nellie Dowell toiled in what was arguably the most radical sector of late-Victorian Britain's female workforce: the match industry. She lived in one of London's most class-conscious political districts, in which workers gained a substantial voice in local government and Poor Law administration by the 1890s: Bow, Bromley-by-Bow, and Poplar. And yet, the more deeply I researched Nellie's working life in the match industry, the less evidence I found that she was radicalized by it. Nellie chose not to participate in the industrial strife that literally followed in her footsteps during her global travels in the match industry. In light of the profound insecurity of her childhood experiences as a Poor Law half-orphan ward of the state, Nellie used her keen intellect and strong work ethic to ensure economic security for herself and her family. Her choices, rooted in the logic of family life and pride in her own labor, require no apology, although they certainly invite explanation and analysis.

The ties of family trumped solidarity with fellow workers. Nellie's story underscores a point that defies the statistical impulse at the heart of social welfare policy. The trauma of incarceration in Poor Law institutions cannot be reckoned exclusively in terms of numbers of individual men, women, and children within the walls of Poor Law schools, casual wards, asylums, and unions. Their experiences must be understood as something kept vivid through stories and memories like the ones Nellie and Harriet told Muriel, that were coextensive with the kinship networks at the heart of neighborhood and community in East London. Preserving her independence—defined as freedom from the clutches of the New Poor Law and supporting herself and her mother without resort to charity—remained Nellie's highest priority. In Muriel's story about her, Nellie and her mother refused to be victims of the Poor Law while acknowledging its horrors.

Nellie was an exemplary company girl, not a proletarian radical, for the better part of her working life in the match industry. As a nonunion worker in a unionized workplace in Wellington, she abetted R. Bell's global capitalist business strategies as well as its ongoing attempts to weaken the union, discipline its female workforce, and squeeze profits out of its labor. Seen through the interpretive lens of historians of late-industrial capitalism and labor, Nellie was a proletarianized and exploited worker. This seems indisputable, except that this is not how she saw herself or how Muriel told her story. Muriel suggests that Nellie had an extraordinary ability to find pleasure and humor in even the most difficult circumstances. She may well have been grateful for steady work and the opportunity her employer extended her to explore the world. If her choices strike me as necessarily political—the refusal to become a trade union member—they probably did not for her.

Thanks to R. Bell and Company, Nellie enjoyed an extraordinary expansion in political and social freedoms as a fully enfranchised white woman. She saw for herself that leading politicians and state actors could be and were committed to a "sort of socialism" favorable to workers. While her antipodean travels enhanced her status at her factory girls' club in Bow, she must also have realized just how much less she counted in British society and politics as a disenfranchised, propertyless wage laborer. Her time in Sweden, Muriel suggests, marked the beginning of deep shifts in her worldview. As she adapted to a new language and an altogether different culture and way of life in Sweden, Nellie reflected upon and began to recast her previous experiences in ways that challenged truths she heretofore had taken for granted. Her brother-in-law's disablement and the breakup of the Dellar family touched chords deep within her about the traumas of her own youth and made only too clear the inadequacy of metropolitan poor relief and charity. While Muriel does not specify the character of Nellie's growing dissatisfaction with her philanthropic "lady" friends, she hints that Nellie came to see more clearly how such "friendships" were predicated on the reproduction of class differences, not their erasure. Nellie may have been a company girl, but she became a Cockney cosmopolitan with an unusual breadth of outlook and experiences. Her literal border crossings as a "match girl" anticipated—without foreshadowing—the social, cultural, and class crossings at the heart of her love and friendship with Muriel.

Sometime between 1903 and 1909, Muriel and Nellie met each other. When Nellie first encountered Muriel she would have rightly recognized her as yet another well-intentioned slumming lady. Muriel, for her part, must have seen in Nellie that exemplary figure much beloved by journalists and coveted by philanthropists, the Cockney match girl. Because "From Birth to Death" simply ends midsentence on the bottom of the typed page, I had long assumed that Muriel must have narrated the circumstances of their meeting in the now lost pages. With the aid of Nellie's hospital records and the dating of her earliest surviving letter, I know that "From Birth to Death" narrates events *after* Muriel and Nellie had already become "loving mates." Muriel simply chose not to mention when, where, or how they met. She never becomes a character in "From Birth to Death" but remains its invisible narrator.

The lost pages of "From Birth to Death" have loomed large in my own imagination as the source that would answer my most pressing questions. Archival fragments invite such optimistic fantasies. They incite but also frustrate "an urge for plenitude" and "more and more linkages to work into the torn fabric of the past."[173] These lost pages also remind us that archives, like the life stories we make from them, are always fragments. The historian's work of mending the torn fabric of the past is necessarily—and perhaps happily—unfinished business.

CHAPTER THREE

"Being a Christian" in Edwardian Britain

THE SECOND ANGLO-BOER WAR (1899–1902) in South Africa had not gone smoothly for the world's paramount military power. Britain had suffered a series of humiliating defeats at the hands of a ragtag force of Dutch-descended farmers determined to protect their Boer republics from annexation by the British imperial behemoth. When Lord Roberts's relief forces lifted the Boers' seven-month siege of the small border town of Mafeking on May 17th, 1900, Britons raucously took to the streets. Muriel Lester scribbled the joyous news into her schoolgirl diary.[1] A vocal minority, including the future Great War prime minister Lloyd George, hazarded their good names by denouncing British military aggression in South Africa as immoral imperialism actuated by gold and diamonds, not God and civilization.[2] Seventeen-year-old Muriel disdained such dissenting voices for their unseemly "pratings" after peace.[3] Twinning militant Christianity with militarism, she joined the struggle for British supremacy in South Africa with the true Christian's "spiritual fight." Britain's empire was God's will. The war had made her "fearfully proud of anything English" and "glad and proud to be one of Christs' [sic] followers." She even filled a khaki-covered album with pictures displaying "British prowess and native infidelity—any sort of native."[4] At the dawn of the new century, Muriel Lester was smug about the superiority of all things British and no less pleased with herself.

A decade later, Muriel was a committed pacifist feminist enmeshed in the overlapping worlds of religious modernism and ethical socialism. Although she never renounced her deep attachment to Britishness, she embraced internationalist perspectives and criticized British global aggression. Christianity animated her devotion to brotherhood and sisterhood across divisions of class, race, religion, gender, and nation. She threw herself into various benevolent projects in the slums of Bow, a hotbed of labor and socialist politics in the metropolis. The British empire had retained little of its luster and even less of its romance. A supporter of the humanitarian Congo Reform Association, Muriel knew that unspeakable cruelty and violence lurked just beneath the thin veneer of civilizing missions like King Leopold's in the Congo.

In the years before World War I, Muriel Lester, along with so many Edwardian seekers, forged a new sense of herself as an ethical subject and a Christian obliged to act justly to others, near and far. How she did this and its consequences are the subject of this chapter. This was an ongoing process for Muriel, a lifelong pilgrimage animated by God's love. It meant balancing—and connecting—two different parts of her life, two competing geographies of self: the verdant upper-middle-class comfort of Loughton with its private demands to care for her aging parents; and the dull dirty streets of Bow with her growing public commitments to its people. As she traveled by first-class rail between these two locales, she reckoned with what it meant to be a dutiful Victorian spinster daughter *and* an Edwardian New Woman in the slums.

Even in her schoolgirl diary entries of 1899–1900, the stakes of openly "being a Christian" were high for Muriel: "to let everyone want to copy me." It's hard not to smile—or wince—at her immodest ambition. "Being a Christian" meant becoming a person whom others would emulate. It was self- and other-directed, inward and outward, solitary and social. Muriel's commitment to being a Christian had its own internal history, a developmental logic rooted in the idiosyncrasies of her psychosocial and spiritual autobiography. But it was also shaped by shifting and expanding possibilities available to an educated single woman in the fin-de-siècle metropolis. Her journey from her parents' Victorian progressive Nonconformity to Edwardian Christian radicalism was not a lonely one. She had plenty of inquisitive and self-critical fellow travelers.

Essential to Muriel's ethical remaking was her engagement with a broad range of theological ideas and social reform initiatives from the 1880s to World War I that revolved around "God is Love" as the central fact of Christianity. Muriel's writings offer many clues about the people, ideas, and movements that challenged and transformed her. Some, like Tolstoy's radical Christian ethics and R. J. Campbell's New Theology movement, she fully acknowledged. Others, like Theosophy and the

Brotherhood Church, she never named but bear striking affinities with her emerging theological and social convictions.[5] Fin-de-siècle commentators were undoubtedly preoccupied by fears of race degeneration and cultural decadence, but these years also spawned a bewilderingly lush array of countercultural critiques of imperialism, materialism, and economic inequality. The excesses of Britain's liberal bourgeois culture of possessive individualism called forth a deep yearning for new forms of social sharing, community, and spirituality. These opposing tendencies were part of the heterogeneous cultural formation within which Muriel made choices about her own life.[6]

Muriel's romance with the slums of Bow and her friendships with men, women, and children living there allowed her to test out theories and decide which to keep and which to discard. Her lived "theology of love" and her loving labors among her Bow friends were always—and necessarily—entwined endeavors. Somewhere along this path, she met Nellie Dowell and they embarked on their bold venture to remake themselves and their world on Christian revolutionary principles.

"GOD IS LOVE"

The years between the 1890s and World War I witnessed a robust, experimental, and transnational engagement with what I am loosely calling "God is Love" theology. J. R. Seeley, author of the best selling and controversial history of Jesus as merely a "young man of promise" (*Ecce Homo*, 1865), lamented the "ethical famine" of the 1890s while recognizing the "immense opportunity" this presented to those able to satisfy the collective hunger for moral guidance.[7] It was during these years that Muriel Lester elaborated her understanding of God's love as the galvanizing force of private and public life and the foundation of her socioreligious concept of reconciliation.

Muriel thought long and hard about God as she crossed the threshold from youth into young adulthood. Worship and church-related activities increasingly animated her daily life. However, like most women, she had no opportunity to study or develop a systematic theology. During these years, she delivered no sermons, wrote no theological tracts. Muriel's ideas about religion—what scholars call "women's theology"—

must be found in sources far outside the usual purview of historians of theology in her private letters, autobiographical writings, and unpublished diaries. This means that I often simply don't know where Muriel stood on particular questions of doctrine and scriptural interpretation.

Muriel knit together her theological thinking—her lived theology—out of an eclectic range of Christian traditions, some radical and others mainstream, emphasizing God's inclusive love rather than His suffering on behalf of a fallen humanity.[8] God's love was central to nineteenth-century Christians across denominational divides, from love-feasting Methodists and sober Broad Church Anglicans to hellfire evangelicals. It's hard to make sense of the profound significance of the Atonement for Victorians without God's redemptive love for humanity.[9] In the tradition that sustained Muriel and to which she contributed, God was more like an encouraging albeit divine friend than a stern father.[10] Sin and suffering were no longer the Janus-face of God's love.

Muriel's father, Henry Lester, encouraged his daughters to think deeply and critically about God and religion. He rejected the notion that theology was an exalted intellectual endeavor reserved only for clerics and the learned. He opened his Presidential Address to the Essex Baptist Union in 1904 with the democratic assertion that all who loved God also loved to discourse about Him. In so doing, every person could and did produce something worthy of the name "theology." His own theology celebrated God's love and the joys of loving God. "My simple conception of theology," he proclaimed, "is almost enough for me. 'God in Christ—reconciling the world unto Himself.'"

Understanding the mystery of reconciliation and living by it was no simple matter. "Shall I ever master that?" he modestly asked.[11] It took Muriel the better part of five decades to elaborate the implications of this passage from 2 Corinthians as the scriptural bedrock of her revolutionary Christianity and global ministry of peace for the Fellowship of Reconciliation.

Muriel's reading list at the turn of the new century, dutifully inscribed in her diary, provides one way to retrace her religious, spiritual, and intellectual itinerary. Who Muriel was cannot be conjured out of the sum of the books that she read. They do, however, provide insight into her evolving religious and ethical sensibility. While her diary includes responses to major historical events ("our Queen is dead") and soul searching about faith and friendship, it also served as a commonplace book. She copied favorite passages from Browning, Tennyson, Pater, Milton, Browne's *Religio Medici,* and the Gospel, which quite explicitly spoke to her own questions and hopes. Her reading was purposeful, pleasurable, and self-reflexive.[12] She veered from her steady diet of novels (Dickens, Eliot, Austen, Gaskell, Kingsley, and Mrs. Ward) to social criticism and practical theology. After a double dose of Darwin and Drummond (*The Descent of Man, The Ascent of Man*), she turned to *The Heart of the Empire,* C.F.G. Masterman's overheated essays by leading New Liberals demanding publicly funded social services to address the problems of modern city life. Arthur Balfour's coolly reasonable disquisition, *The Foundations of Belief,* insisted that "Nature" was "indifferent" to both human happiness and morality. Humans cultivated disinterested virtue and "ethical sentiments," Balfour argued, "merely because they were crucial to "our survival."[13]

Muriel was keen to feel God's love, not understand nature's indifference as the foundation of her own belief. She found ample doses of it when she read Charles Wagner's *The Simple Life* (English translation, 1901). A burly Alsatian Protestant pastor and minister to the poor in Faubourg St. Antoine in Paris, Wagner enjoyed growing celebrity in Anglo-America with his lyrical anodyne pleas to cast off the tyrannical "inner anarchy of desire" for material goods in exchange for spiritual goodness itself.[14] He warned his followers to avoid the dangers of excess introspection, "this dissecting of oneself," which led to self-centered inaction. Wagner distilled the essence of his practical theology in his explanation of why "the invisible God came to dwell among us, in the form of a man:" "*Love.*"[15]

It was Muriel's encounter with Tolstoy's "primly-bound" *Kingdom of God Is Within You* that most profoundly transformed her ideas about God and society. It stands between Matthew Arnold's *Culture and Anarchy* and *Anna Karenina* on her reading list. Tolstoy's ethical and Christian writings had begun to attract an ardent following in Britain spurred by his well-publicized open letter to Czar Nicholas and the first Hague Convention of 1899, which sought to limit arms and encourage the creation of international bodies to arbitrate disputes between nations.[16] (See fig. 3.1.) A handful of Tolstoyan communities dotted the Cotswolds and Essex countryside by 1900. Members wore homespun loose-fitting

3.1. Photographed in simple peasant garb, Count Tolstoy enthralled a large British audience, including Muriel, in the first years of the twentieth century. The headline informed readers that Tolstoy was "THE REFORMER WHOSE BIRTHDAY IT WAS FORBIDDEN TO CELEBRATE." *Illustrated London News*, September 19, 1908, 412.

frocks, engaged in strenuous physical labor as craftsmen and farmers, and scrubbed their whitewashed dwellings—sparely furnished with hand-carved tables and chairs. Some followed Tolstoy in striving for a purified fellowship between men and women, which banished altogether the messiness of sexual desire and sex. Others experimented with "free love" and freedom from private property, to the amused horror of their many critics.[17] High-minded ethics often mingled with affected aesthetics. There was nothing simple about their commitment to the Simple Life. Tending to the communal good demanded constant self-regulation and a good deal of self-reflection.[18] The pugnacious Anglo-Catholic G. K. Chesterton found Tolstoyan Simple Lifers irresistible targets and quipped that there was "more simplicity in the man who eats caviar on impulse than in the man who eats grape-nuts on principle."[19] (See fig. 3.2.)

Tolstoy's renunciation of copyright made possible the widespread availability of his radical Christian writings in English translation and

"THE SIMPLE LIFE."

Charwoman. "IF YER PLEASE, SIR, TH' LANDLORD SAYS AS 'OW 'E CAN'T DO NOTHIN', 'COS THE THATCHER'S BUSY WITH THE RICKS."

3.2. *Punch* mocked male Simple Lifers, whose inept attempts to rusticate themselves signaled their failure to perform their husbandly duties. "The Simple Life," William Gunning King, illustrator, *Punch's Almanack for 1906* (Courtesy of Punch, Ltd.).

expanded the ranks of British Tolstoyans.[20] At the turn of the century, booksellers flooded the market with three-pence editions of Tolstoy. When Muriel's friend Stephen Hobhouse casually purchased and read a cheap edition of Tolstoy's brooding *Confession* at the Oxford train station in January 1902, he experienced a conversion so powerful and sudden it left him physically sickened by the prospect of inheriting Hadspen, one of England's loveliest gentry estates.[21] Broken in mind and body, he fled Oxford for a German health resort, where he endured milk diets, fasting, and rest cures. For Stephen, embracing Tolstoy meant rejecting not just his patrimony but distancing himself from his civic-minded parents, the right honorable Henry Hobhouse and his able wife, Margaret Potter Hobhouse. "It is not the least of my troubles," he wrote his father, "that I cannot shape my hopes after those of my parents," which has "led me in spite of my better self into a want of affection and coldness. . . ."[22] Tolstoy not only opened up new spiritual vistas for him, but also brought him close to an emotional, psychological, and ethical abyss. "I cannot make up my mind just how far to compromise in accepting things as they are, and striving after them as they ought to be," he confided to his sympathetic aunt, the pro-Boer Kate Courtney. His own class privilege blocked his path to the "unity and brotherhood of man" that he so earnestly sought, but he could not think or take action or feel his way out of his ethical conundrum.[23]

Muriel did not have a conversion experience akin to Hobhouse's; nor did her deepening commitment to living by Tolstoy's principles estrange her from Henry and Rachel Lester. Reading Tolstoy, however, did mark a decisive moment in her thinking and left her a convinced pacifist and apostle of non-violent resistance. "It changed the very quality of life for me," she recalled.[24] We can find in Tolstoy's religious, spiritual, and social writings the seeds of many concepts that Muriel later adopted and adapted. Tolstoy and his far-flung army of disciples, including Muriel, sought to regenerate the world from within. Change began with the self, not with social, economic, and political institutions. Muriel, like Tolstoy, turned away from the great and powerful and immersed herself in the "life lived by unconsidered millions."[25] Muriel accepted Tolstoy's "law of non-resistance" and his "law of Love" forbidding all forms of violence, especially violence against evildoers who themselves used force to harm others.[26] In *What Do I Believe* (1884), Tolstoy insisted that geopolitical boundaries separating nations—"frontier lines"—had no impact on moral obligations to others and the essential unity of all people across borders. His public denunciation of militarism and the "coarse fraud" of patriotism made him *persona non grata* with secular authorities in Czarist Russia and forced some followers into exile. He revered Christ's teachings and perfect life, but his unapologetic disdain for Church dogma and organized religion prompted the Orthodox Church to excommunicate him. Tolstoy cultivated the persona of an angry Old Testament prophet, denouncing the sins of materialism in favor of simplicity of life. His critics belittled him as a latter-day Quixote, battling the windmills of modernity.

Tolstoy's disciples, committed to their master's injunction to speak the truth fearlessly and wholly, proved unflattering biographers. The publication of Aylmer Maude's candidly critical *Life of Tolstoy* (1910–11) revealed to British readers the narcissism of Tolstoy's self-denial and the lengths to which others went to subsidize his asceticism. (Maude was among the first speakers Muriel invited to address workers at her Sunday evening services at Kingsley Hall in 1915.) Tolstoy's striving for ethical perfection could—and did—look a lot like lunacy to others. Maude's *Life* convinced Bernard Shaw, one of Britain's most eccentric connoisseurs of eccentricity, that Tolstoy and the Tolstoyans had gone too far. Shaw concluded that the public Tolstoy was a man of genius, but the private Tolstoy an insensitive sham, capable of "inhuman callousness": "in the ordinary affairs of life he shirked every uncongenial responsibility whilst availing himself of every luxury he really cared for." "We are amazed," Shaw lamented, "at the extent to which a man who was boundlessly sympathetic on paper with imaginary beings could be so outrageously inconsiderate to real people at his own home."[27] Muriel, unlike Shaw and Maude, seems to have turned a blind eye to Tolstoy's peccadillos. She cared only for his ideas.

The British Tolstoyans whose social and theological views most closely anticipated Muriel's own clustered around the first Brotherhood Church in Croydon in 1894. Muriel was well acquainted with the church by World War I, when angry patriotic mobs vandalized it as an unpatriotic pacifist outpost. One of its founders, John Coleman Kenworthy, believed that the truths of the Kingdom of God resided within each person.[28] They would be revealed through an un-heroic revolution of "small things" enacted according to principles of everyday brotherliness. An ardent anti-colonialist, he condemned Britain's "robberies and oppressions in Ireland, India, South Africa and the world over" as a modern version of ancient Rome's tyrannical moral turpitude. The fiction of Pax Britannica was sustained by the reality of endemic violence to human dignity. Living as Jesus lived would "revolutionise the conduct of individual life" and create a "new and fraternal order outside the capitalistic system"—a "voluntary cooperative commonwealth." It would hasten a "new social order right through the old one" with "the mildness and gentleness of the sunrise which shines away the night and ushers in the day."[29] God's love, not the combined forces of a revolutionary proletariat, would cleanse Church and State. The true Christian forgave injuries rather than demanded reparation for them.[30] To a remarkable extent,

Kenworthy prefigured Muriel's vision of conflict resolution and the means by which God's love would precipitate Christian revolution.

Fellow Brotherhood Church leader William Jupp, like Henry Lester and Muriel, put "reconciliation" at the heart of his theology and social philosophy. A former Congregationalist minister heavily influenced by Whitmanic ideas of manly comradeship and a member of the socialist Fellowship of the New Life, Jupp anticipated Muriel's formulation of the relationship between an all-loving Christ and the "law of reconciliation."[31] He proposed a Darwinian meta-narrative of religious evolution marked by stages, the last of which he called "the light of reconciliation and great peace." "It was not pardon for wrong things done," he explained, "but reconciliation with the righteousness yet to be attained that alone could save or satisfy the upward reaching soul." Reconciliation entailed yielding to Jesus's ideal of goodness. It was a process of becoming that invited imperfect men and women to bask in the "restoring power of love and friendship."[32]

Restorative love and friendship also animated the Anglo-Canadian Lily Dougall's Christian mysticism and provided yet another model for Muriel's emerging theological thinking. For Dougall, neither wrath nor suffering had any place in God's nature and activity: "only love and good are infinite, eternal, and omnipotent." In place of punishment and retribution for wrongdoing, she extolled the "recreative power of friendship"—in which individual and corporate meld together, warmed by God's loving friendship.[33] Where Muriel always yoked her vision of God's loving friendship to doing in and for the world, Underhill cared much more for the perfecting of the inner life.

One stream of thought conspicuously—and surprisingly—absent from Muriel's writings about her ethico-religious education was Theosophy. The London Theosophical Society, at the urging of Annie Besant, had founded a club for match factory girls in its "Bow Lodge" at 193 Bow Road in the aftermath of the Match Girls' strike of 1888.[34] Officers of Bow Lodge were connected to some of East London's most prominent philanthropic organizations: its Treasurer, the school teacher Harry Banbery, resided at Toynbee Hall's bohemian student hostel, Balliol House, in the 1890s and tried to improve conditions for inmates of the Whitechapel Poor Law casual ward and infirmary.[35] When Muriel began visiting Bow around 1902, Bow Lodge had a thriving Boys' Brotherhood Club devoted to "the great work of the Universal Brotherhood."[36] Men and women affiliated with Theosophy figured prominently in Muriel's life. George Lansbury, the Lester sisters' chief guide and political patron in Bow and Poplar, served on the Building Committee of the Theosophical Society in 1911. He offered a lengthy justification for his support of Theosophy's fraternal principles in *My Life* (1928). The Society's supporters included feminist luminaries Charlotte Despard and Emmeline Pethick-Lawrence, both part of Muriel's broad circle of "advanced" women engaged in suffrage, antiwar, and social welfare work.[37] All of this strongly suggests that Muriel must have been familiar with Theosophy, its teaching, and its socio-political outreach in Bow in the decade before World War I.

Theosophy's hospitality to the feminine aspects of the Divine, its close alliance with anti-colonial movements in India in the first decades of the twentieth century, and its spiritualization of everyday life harmonized with Muriel's vision of women's potential as religious leaders and her growing receptivity to non-Western challenges to empire. Theosophists shared Muriel and Doris's admiration for Tolstoy's "Unecclesiastical Christianity" with its soul-centered critique of materialism.[38] The Lesters would certainly have had no cause to disagree with the principle uniting Theosophists across their differences: their devotion to fostering the "Universal Brotherhood of Humanity without distinction of race, creed, sex, caste or color." Unconditional love for all creation, animate and inanimate, buttressed the "Universal Divine Principle" elucidated by Theosophy's charismatic Russian leader, Madame Helena Blavatsky. HPB, as she was called, developed a syncretic anti-dogmatic fusion of Eastern and Western philosophical, scientific, and religious teachings based on divine messages from Tibetan Mahatmas that she faithfully recorded. Moses and Jesus offered profound wisdom, Blavatsky acknowledged, but they mattered a good deal less to her than Buddhist and Hindu teachings.

This was undoubtedly the rub for Muriel and Doris. They remained unapologetically certain that Jesus and Christianity had a monopoly on religious truth. Neither she nor Doris flirted with anything like religious relativism.[39] Nor were they initially drawn to the various mystical impulses then coursing through Christian spiritual questers like Evelyn Underhill in prewar Britain.[40] Years later, Muriel confessed to Gandhi that she was startled by the depth of his grasp of the Sermon on the Mount and Christianity and embarrassed by her own aversion to Hinduism. No matter how hard she tried to understand Hinduism, she "never found anything in it" and disliked its institutions.[41] Her respect for human difference fell short of reverence for religious diversity. If Muriel had once joined the Theosophical match girls' club in Bow in 1902 (as her only biographer believes), she went out of her way to conceal this association with a religion whose occult and esoteric mysteries were incompatible with how she understood her Christian faith.

Heterodox champions of God's Law of Love powerfully influenced Muriel's ideas about being a Christian. But so too did several mainstream strands of religious thought and action that increasingly overlapped by the outset of the new century. Pan-denominational "social gospel" Christianity joined gospel preaching with outreach to the urban poor. Incarnational theology, with its sacramental reverence for the body, increasingly made common cause with Christian socialism. Liberal Protestant theological emphasis on God's immanence and growing interest in the humanity and divinity of the historical Jesus encouraged people of faith to solve earthly problems. What all these theological developments shared in common was intense focus on Jesus's embodied life on earth, which in turn justified growing concern for the material and economic hardships faced by the poor. The most influential mid-century advocate of social Christianity was Reverend F. D. Maurice. He forged a path between the sin-centered theology of evangelicals and the incense, vestments, and rituals of High Churchmen. His Christian socialism emphasized that the "Fatherhood of God" necessitated the "brotherhood of mankind." Rejecting the doctrine of eternal punishment, he offered a domesticated language of Christian fraternity to Britons frightened by Chartists' and continental socialists' strident language of class.

By the 1890s and 1900s, High, Low, and Broad churchmen alike claimed Maurice as their common theological forbear. His Christian socialist heirs numbered gadfly radical outsiders like the feminist anti-imperialist Fabian socialist, the Reverend Stewart Headlam.[42] They also included powerful leaders *within* the established Church like Charles Gore, who held the bishoprics of Worcester, Birmingham, and Oxford. Love, divine and human, was at the heart of Bishop Gore's moderate— and influential—Christian socialist theology. In *Lux Mundi* (1889), he combined sacramentalism, evidence about the historical Jesus, and a plea for workers' rights with the conviction that the Incarnation was a "self-emptying of God." God had chosen to reveal Himself "under conditions of human nature and from the human point of view."[43] By taking human form as His son Jesus Christ, God accepted the limits of what Jesus, as man, knew at that particular moment in history. Science was no threat to faith because there was no need to make Jesus's teachings match the findings of modern inquiry. His Bampton Lectures (1891) detailed the implications of his view of the Incarnation. Because God chose to "express" *and* "limit" Himself in "true manhood," He contains "the prototype of human self-sacrifice . . . for God is love." Men and women returned God's love for humanity through loving "self-effacement." [44] Forgetting the claims of self was the path to God and an expression of the divine within each person. Well-to-do Christians like Muriel demonstrated "self-effacement" by caring for others, especially the poor. This required a profound sympathy of thinking, seeing, and feeling *with* another. It was also a call to action based on love, not struggle, between rich and poor.

The historical Jesus led some to doubt, deism, and the religion of humanity. For others like Muriel, Jesus's earthly life strengthened their sense of the importance of His doctrine of love for modern life. With the English translation of *What is Christianity?* (1901), the Lutheran Church historian and practical theologian Adolf von Harnack brought his understanding of the historical Jesus to a large British audience, including the Lester sisters. Doris used Harnack to develop a series of lessons for the boys in her Loughton Sunday school class.[45] Harnack balanced a critical historical approach to the Bible with faith and a keen sense of obligation to the poor. He abhorred extremism in all its forms and discounted miracles and mysticism. He meticulously applied historical methods to the Gospels, but he did so to understand—rather than permanently fix—their contextual meaning. It was an essential high privilege of Christianity "to adapt its shape to the course of history," to interpret the Gospel in light of modern needs. He dismissed Franciscan-style ascetic renunciation, then gaining a small number of adherents in the 1890s across Europe, as sentimental coquetting with misery. So too he argued that the Gospel provided no blueprints for the economic reorganization of society along socialist lines. Christianity did offer a powerful model of the right relationship between individuals and society that rejected class conflict in favor of solidarity between rich and poor within "a community . . . as wide as human life itself and as deep as human need." This Christian community would transform the socialism of "conflicting interests" into one resting on "spiritual unity."[46] Christians otherwise divided by national, political, and religious commitments shared Harnack's longing for an alternative to the proletariat's war against capital. Spurred by the godless mischief of socialists, even the reactionary Holy Father, Leo XIII, awakened to the "utter poverty of the masses" and enjoined "brotherly love and friendship" as an antidote to class conflict in *Rerum Novarum* (1891).

For Muriel, Doris, and their pupils, Harnack challenged them to imagine their own world reorganized according to the laws of the Kingdom of Heaven, and to imagine living their own lives following Christ. Like so many other Christians in late-nineteenth and early-twentieth-century Europe and America, the Lester sisters demanded that religious devotion ally itself with "social enthusiasm" in finding answers to urgent industrial questions.[47] Individual salvation and the regeneration of society went hand in hand. The evangelical founders of the Salvation Army, Catherine and William Booth, had come to this conclusion as Catherine faced her fatal cancer. William launched his comprehensive scheme *In Darkest England and the Way Out* (1890) with its vast apparatus of physical, social, and moral redemption: slum lassies for the infirm, farm labor colonies for the unemployed, soup kitchens for the hungry, marching bands for the masses, even a lucifer match factory. In return for such largesse, the poor were expected to sit through an hour or two of religious services.[48] Muriel disliked the fevered emotions unleashed by evangelicals like the Booths, whose belief in fallen humanity starkly divided the damned and the saved. The Salvation Army loved and forgave sinners, the better to convert and save them. This was not how Muriel understood God's work or her own.

The roots of Muriel's abhorrence of sin-focused religion must be found in Henry Lester's determination to liberate his children from the psychic horrors of the hellfire religion to which his own father had subjected him.[49] Even as Henry Lester assumed ever more prominent public duties as President of the Essex Baptist Union, first in 1887–88 and once again in 1903–4, he and his family never felt bound to a single church or denomination.[50] In the 1900s, Muriel and Doris worshiped in the family's Loughton Baptist Union church along with Anglican churches, Congregationalist and Wesleyan Methodist chapels, and Quaker meetings. At her mother's urging, Doris regularly took tea at the

3.3. Reverend Reginald John Campbell's dramatic good looks were part of his theatrical public persona as Edwardian London's most celebrated preacher. Charles T. Bateman, *R. J. Campbell, M. A., Pastor of the City Temple, London*, photograph by E. H. Mills (London, 1903), frontispiece.

rectory with the Anglican rector of Bow, Reverend Kitcat, and his wife. It pleased Rachel Lester to know that the Kitcats were keeping an eye on her youngest daughter during her lengthening sojourns into the surrounding slum streets.

Sometime between 1905 and 1910, Muriel finally found a preacher, a theology, and a movement that spoke to her deepest needs to combine outward action bringing citizenship to the poor with inward contemplation drawing her close to God. Various streams of "God is Love" theology, progressive politics, and social activism converged in a controversial religious movement cleverly packaged under the vague but catchy name, The New Theology. The New Theology electrified the Lester sisters and a broad swath of the British public. It owed much of its success to its flamboyantly ascetic white-haired high priest, the Congregationalist minister R. J. Campbell. (See fig. 3.3.) For a few brief years before World War I, Campbell made theology matter to men and women across the religious and social spectrum. "The man in the street began talking about immanence and transcendence," one disaffected disciple recalled, "with the same familiarity with which he discussed free trade and protection." The Lester sisters joined thousands who crowded into the City Temple, "the Mecca of theological rebels," to hear his pan-denominational sermons.[51] Eloquence and passion more than made up for theological inconsistencies, at least until Campbell subjected his own teachings to critical scrutiny and abandoned them in favor of more orthodox Anglicanism during World War I.

Campbell staked out a theological middle ground between divine immanence and transcendence. God was immanent—present throughout the entire universe; He revealed himself everywhere in and through His finite creation. However, the finite universe could not and did not exhaust God's transcendent infinitude.[52] Campbell's dialectical formulation of God's simultaneous immanence *and* transcendence appealed to those committed to changing their world while seeking spiritual solace through faith in a transcendent God. The demands of modern life and the teachings of Jesus were wholly compatible, he insisted.

The New Theology provided a path into pacifism, internationalism, socialism, and religious modernism for the Lesters and many other spiritual seekers.[53] Its humanism, faith in reason, and commitment to social reform captured perfectly the aspirations of progressive Liberalism at the high tide of its moral and political authority. Campbell's alliance with one of East London's beloved politicians and leader of the Independent Labour Party, Keir Hardie, only deepened its appeal to radical Christians, intent to bring justice to the outcast at home and abroad. Campbell imagined that if Christ came to East London, he would "strike straight" at the root causes of poverty, degradation, and class division.[54] His best-known follower, Reverend William Orchard, remained closely allied with the Lesters and their work for the next several decades. He aptly summarized the message of the New Theology: "following Jesus consisted in practicing the truths He taught, copying the character He displayed, and living the life He lived, which was much more urgent than holding theories of the Atonement. . . ."[55] Here was a Christianity unfettered from dogma, miracles, and doctrines, a theology of everyday life that invited believers to enact their faith through the most banal tasks.

Muriel's desire to follow Christ impelled her to chastise her elders in the family's Union Church in Loughton for their unchristian behavior.[56] How could they hope to convert the "masses," she wondered, when they failed to heed God's call to brotherhood. In the name of brotherly love, she claimed religious and spiritual authority as a young woman.[57] In an undated diary entry probably from around 1904 she recorded a scene that she either imagined or reconstructed from actual events.

> I know I hardly ought to be standing up now. It is unusual for such as I to speak because I am not a man, and I am young. . . . I have been listening to my elders and betters speaking for some time, and it seems they have forgotten some things that seem very fresh in my memory and I cannot forget. . . . "Let Brotherly love continue converting the Soul." I've heard you talk of conversion of the masses but I've never heard any of you exhort each other by repeating Christ's plans for converting souls –, It is "Let Brotherly love continue."[58]

The present tense lends urgency and immediacy to the unfolding scene. She speaks and writes; the reader of her diary, like her "elders and betters," hears and witnesses. Muriel provides no context to explain what events may have triggered her dramatic public rebuke of male "betters."

Muriel then turns from accusation to a non-conflictual way to reckon with differences in this extended diary entry. She criticizes her elders while refusing to separate herself from them. She shifts from "I" and "you" to an inclusive "we." I quote this diary passage in its entirety because it articulates the core precepts that guided Muriel's love-based theological thinking and her social work for the rest of her life, one that she came to call "reconciliation."

> I think some of us are very eager to pick wholes in each other, we do not hear & forbear, give & take, nor bear each other's burdens. It seems when a question is raised, we go out of our way to disagree, whereas if we could take our stands on the broad basis, which we all acknowledge, we could forget the differences, rub off the corners, & agreeing to differ in accidentals, we could agree on essentials, & cultivate the habit of seeking what we all agree on & ignoring particular dangerous ground

The cultivation of common ground makes it possible to avoid "dangerous" disagreements over "accidentals" and "particulars." She acknowledges difference ("agreeing to differ") while overcoming its tendency to divide. In the years ahead, reconciliation offered Muriel—as it had Brotherhood Church leaders Jupp and Kenworthy before her—a way to do God's work and challenge social hierarchies. It promised to produce mutual understanding across social, ethnic, geopolitical, religious, gender, and economic divides. God's love guided her, but friendship was how she chose to enact these border crossings.

Espousing brotherliness proved easier than living it. Muriel struggled to banish egoism, pettiness, and her craving for popularity. Echoing Charles Gore's call for "self-effacement," she tried to "forget myself a bit" rather than thinking about "who likes me." On New Year's Day 1905 Muriel resolved to leave behind "malice, envy, & horrible sensations." She yearned to master the "habit of thinking of other's good" and get "nearer to Jesus," so near that she would "crucify" herself with Christ.[59] She outlined a clear plan to achieve her goal of self-loss: be "pure" from "foolish thoughts," "egoism," and "insincerity;" abandon the desire for admiration; refuse to think "much of things of this world." By Easter, she ecstatically recorded the "marvelous finding" of her "newly discovered" Faith, her rebirth in Christ.

> In Services of joy at Chapel this morning the little worrying doubt came—unbidden. I longed for it never to recur to sting me, yet have always shrunk from probing deep down in my soul. I have been lazy too & the lazy desire not to be worried began to paralyse me I feared. Then someone prayed.

> 'Let nothing come between us and a Vision of Thee.' Significant. I realized the difficulty of & the need to realize God is—& Christ is here & nothing else matters.

Proofs of her new "Faith" crowded in. She found them everywhere. In the quiet of her room as she prayed, her Bible fell open to John 3: "marvelous miracle. How good that God heard my Prayer." The Gospel of Mark was no less comforting. Each verse spoke to her with newly profound meanings. Mark 8:34 ("Whosoever will come after Me, let him deny himself, take up His Cross and follow Me") fortified her devotion to "think[ing] of others." "This precious Faith that has come is beautiful and comforting" and she prayed to "keep it forever." If God's immanence ("Christ is here") made possible an utter loss of self, it also heightened her powers. "It enables me to do all things & may enable me to turn others to goodness. Christ is my God & no one can rob me of Him."[60] This was a momentous spiritual experience, which she explored only in the safe precincts of her diary. She expunged it entirely from her public utterances and published autobiographical writings. Perhaps she found it too painful to recall the rapture of Easter 1905 in light of the subsequent spiritual disquiet that troubled her later that year.

Despite Muriel's quest to construct her own "God is Love" theology around the loving doctrine of reconciliation, she could not always banish the sin-centered theology of Atonement. On Sunday, July 30, 1905, she confessed a "horrid thought—messenger from Satan?" "People are so wicked and ignore things so largely" that she "cd not trust myself to keep up heart and stake all on the certainty that I must conquer." Her diary entries for this period burst with the rhetoric of sin and salvation that she had tried to reject as incompatible with God's love. Doubts now confronted Muriel, she confessed to her diary, like "snares" and "tricks," a vocabulary more redolent of John Bunyan than Leo Tolstoy. She longed for the wildfire spirit of Renewal, which had quickly gathered 100,000 Methodist converts in Wales that year, to light up England. (The Welsh Revival received substantial attention in the newspaper of the family's Loughton Union Church and from its leaders.) Muriel's public silence about this spiritual struggle may have reflected her inability to square her optimistic, love-saturated theology with dark anxieties about Satanic messages. There is no reason to ask or expect Muriel's lived theology—or anyone else's—to achieve logical consistency. Her "lived theology" was bound up in the unruliness of feelings and her struggle to become a young woman and an ethical subject.

By New Year's Day 1906, Muriel found herself exhausted and dispirited. Doris remained maddeningly dependent on her. When Muriel dared to suggest that she wanted to sleep apart from her younger sister, Doris brooded all week and Muriel vowed to "cherish her" even more. Daily reminders to "adore Him first of all" had not stifled her need to please herself. She welcomed the New Year with a painful headache.[61] It would take her the better part of the next decade, punctuated by several complete breakdowns, to regain the serenity of mind, body, and spirit that she had so briefly enjoyed during Easter 1905.

FOUNDATIONAL FABLES, ETHICAL AWAKENING

It was not only the strains of securing her "precious faith" that gave Muriel a headache. By late autumn 1905, her social and religious work in Bow had also run into difficulties. She had spoken against a fellow worker, Louie (Louisa Emily) Harris, a family friend through Loughton Union Church and the daughter of soap manufacturer Booth Harris. Muriel feared that she had "spoilt a friendship" along with her "enjoyment" of the "Bow Mission." I'm not certain which of the many Nonconformist strongholds Muriel's "Bow Mission" was. Was it a satellite of Peter Thompson's Wesleyan East End Mission or William Lax's Poplar and Bow Mission; or Reverend John Parry's on Albert Terrace; or one of the many Night schools and girls' clubs in Bow attached to the Factory Girls' Helpers Union set up by the evangelical Lucy Guinness?[62] Muriel never said. Some, like Peter Thompson's "ministry of love" based upon "real fellowship with the people," certainly harmonized with many of Muriel's views.[63] What's remarkable is just how many there were, all cheek by jowl within a few blocks of one another. Reflecting on unspecified troubles at the Mission, Muriel upbraided herself for insufficient sympathy for weakness (presumably an unnamed friend's) and prescribed more prayer for herself. Imlac's wisdom in Samuel Johnson's *Rasselas* consoled her: "a new day succeeded to the night and sorrow is never long without a dawn of ease." On top of all this, there was the daily challenge of balancing the claims of Bow with home duties at the Grange.[64]

If Muriel kept absolutely quiet about her spiritual travails (except in her diaries), she never tired of talking about how she first fell in love with Bow and its people in 1902. On something of a lark, she accepted an invitation to a party at a factory girls' club near Bow Church. (See fig. 3.4.) Her description verges on parody as she invokes one journalistic cliché after another about slums and slumming. She offers herself as the idle rich girl in search of "new sensations," who finds fundamental truths about her life's work and her world in the least likely of places. It is a fairy tale in reverse, a foundational fable of moral transformation whose heroine happily goes from riches to rags.[65]

Muriel's story chronologically bridges her pampered late-Victorian youth and her young womanhood as an Edwardian Christian radical. A

BOW CHURCH

3.4. Bow Church sits on an island in the middle of Bow Road along with the controversial statue of William Gladstone erected by the owners of Bryant and May Match Factory. It was a major hub of Muriel's political and philanthropic work. Bow Church, "Sunday in East London," *The Sunday at Home* (1895), 388.

story of social awakening, it is meant to explain her ethical transformation. In the version that she published in *It Occurred to Me* (1937), she "threads" her way down "narrow turnings" and through "murky streets" "ill lit by occasional gas lamps." Muriel reminds her readers that everything she initially sees, thinks, smells, and feels in Bow is filtered through dense layers of images of the slums—remembered conversations, newspaper stories, pictures, and novels. With more than a slight hint of ironic disavowal, she introduces "the famous East End, in the public eye the disreputable haunt of thieves, drunks, and hooligans."[66] Read my story, she seems to say, if you want to get behind these superficial commonplaces to find deeper human truths.

It Occurred to Me attributes her earliest impressions of East London to disparaging comments made by Lester family household servants when she was a child entrusted to their care. As Muriel's train passes on the tracks above Bow, her nostrils are assaulted by the dense acrid smell of the factory where bone manure was transformed into "sweet scented soap." (This factory, Cook's, would be Nellie's last employers for whom she engaged in waged factory labor in 1909.) From the safety of her carriage, she "stared down at the rabbit-warren of unsavoury dwelling-houses, gardenless, sordid.... I could not believe they were human habitations." She turns to the nurse accompanying her and inquires, "Do people live down there?" The nurse's reply is "clear-sounding in my ears still: 'Oh yes. Plenty of people live down there but you needn't worry about them. They don't mind it. They're not like you. They enjoy it.'"[67] Well into the twentieth century, some domestics did derive their sense of status and prestige from those they served, which allowed them to sharply differentiate themselves from the laboring poor.[68]

Muriel's version of this moment in her childhood echoed Victorian novelists' depiction of servants as vigilant defenders of their masters' and mistresses' superior status and proxy for their own.[69] Her story conscripts servants to do the dirty work of perpetuating racialized class prejudices. The nurse, *not* her parents, imagines the poor as an undifferentiated dehumanized collectivity inhabiting their own separate affective and sensory world. "They don't mind it" means "they" are not "us." They don't even smell and feel the same things that we, who travel in first-class train carriages, smell and feel. Such claims short-circuit the power of empathy and identification, which propelled men and women of wealth to see the poor as their brothers and sisters. "They" flattens the social micro-geographies and status hierarchies within East London's myriad neighborhoods and streets. The urban poor were acutely aware of the differences between the side of the street whose houses had bay windows and lace curtains and those less respectable households across the street that did not.[70] They were never simply "they."

Lester's vignette contrasts sharply with Virginia Woolf's "utopian longing" for the servant-filled world of the nursery as a site of aboriginal freedom and creativity.[71] The nursery may have functioned as a lost Eden in Woolf's imagination—"in the beginning, there was the nursery" (*The Waves*)—but Muriel casts it as a site of the original sin of capitalism. Servants' presence in the nursery insinuated wage relations and social inequality into the home. For all that Muriel came to reject domestic service as a socioeconomic institution, she did retain deep affection for the Lester family's household servants. *It Occurred to Me* opens with an extended homage to Fanny Lilley, her nurse "of the old school" who lovingly sang and told stories to her. On some nights when Muriel was too tired to make the journey all the way back to Loughton, she stayed with Fanny, who in retirement apparently took her own flat in Stratford. If other upper-middle-class young "ladies" did this in Edwardian Britain, I have not found them.

Of course, servants were never Muriel's only source of knowledge about slums and slum dwellers. Serious and popular literature offered her a vast cultural repository of anxious prejudices. In "A Street" (first published in *Macmillan's*, 1891), the Lesters' near neighbor in Loughton, Arthur Morrison, satirized the many different "notions" of the East End circulating at the fin de siècle. For some, it was an "evil growth" hiding "human creeping things . . . where every citizen wears a black eye." For others it was populated by a race of clay pipe-smoking, soap-despising unemployed; for still others, it was simply the place from which begging letters and unending appeals for charity emanated. For Morrison, it was an unlaughing place of daily struggles with croupy infants, grimy flowerpots, and bloaters. Cut off from the "outer world," Morrison's East Enders remained oblivious to the "rise and fall of nations."[72] They were all too aware of the material forces of hunger and deprivation. During the freezing cold winter of 1903 when Muriel first began to visit Bow regularly and unemployment spiked in East London, Morrison appealed to readers of the *Daily Chronicle* on behalf of honest poor women like Harriet and Nellie Dowell. "Looking 50 before they are 30," they refused to clamor for relief or make a sensational spectacle of their suffering. "It is their pride to keep their trouble a secret." Their bitter ironic reward for such self-reliant stoicism, Morrison declared, is to "go unrecognized" by those eager to help them.[73]

A writer for *All the Year Round* distilled the late-Victorian dialectic of knowing and not knowing East London that Muriel strategically recycled in her autobiography. It was *terra incognita* for "multitudes who know nothing of that uttermost east which lies beyond the east of the City proper" and yet "we all have an idea of it, and, directly or indirectly, we all have business relations with it." "Those of a better class who have lingered last and longest in the east," the writer temptingly advised readers, enjoy "great compensations of a somewhat peculiar kind" in its "moral Sahara." In this concatenation of orientalist tropes, East London is an empty desert whose occupants are implicitly likened to anti-domestic nomadic peoples. For this very reason, it promises unnamable "peculiar" pleasures for the well-to-do hardy enough to venture beyond the "City proper." The writer coyly suggests that there is something "improper" about this city outside the City while gesturing at the entwined economies—"business relations"—that link East London with the rest of the metropolis. He concludes by contrasting two different ways to narrate East London. While the "abnormal and exaggerated yields the readiest and most picturesque material for the writer, yet perhaps deeper and more intense interest belongs to the simple annals of the poor, their constant struggle for existence. . . ."[74] Surface spectacle jostles with the anthropology of the ordinary as competing approaches to narrating the slum. If Muriel first came to East London in pursuit of "picturesque material" she soon threw herself into the distinctly mundane struggles of getting by in Bow.

What she finds at the factory girls' party that first evening around 1902 overturns her preconceptions about slums and slum dwellers. In an unpublished draft of *It Occurred to Me*, she described herself as falling in love with the girls and their world. "I went, they conquered," she pithily summarized. The girls are both more and less like her than she expected.

> The party marked an epoch for me. These girls, who danced with me, entertained me, made conversation to set me at my ease and plied me with refreshments, were just like myself some of them, the same age, nineteen years old. Yet how experienced they seemed! How assured! What natural dignity! They were much more mature and independent than I. Why were some of them pale, others thin, with bent shoulders? Compared with them, I was a pampered, sheltered, ignorant idler. Why should they go on working, producing pleasure and ease for such as I?[75]

For the next decade, she sought to answer this question. Dutiful daughter of the bourgeoisie, Muriel had long been trained to shape herself in relation to helpless poor girls. Muriel inverts the patron-client relationship: the capable benevolent factory girls bestow upon her—rather than receive from her—kindness and wisdom. Their pale bent bodies bear the burden of their labor and Muriel's pleasures. She is their dependent, a member of a dangerous social class, the undeserving rich.

At the turn of the century, there was nothing unusual about a young lady visiting the London slums. Armies of philanthropic women descended on poor districts throughout Europe and the United States as parish workers for the local vicar, health and friendly visitors, rent collectors for progressive housing schemes, settlement house residents, school care committee members, and social workers. It was almost *de rigueur* for a New Woman to test her mettle by venturing into a London slum, at least in the countless novels about her dangerous exploits.[76] During Muriel's time at St. Leonard's, a woman settlement house worker from South London had urged the privileged female scholars to see for themselves how the poor lived and to better the lives of poor girls.[77] Many, like Muriel and Doris, answered this call to personal service.[78]

Lady visitors were encouraged to extend their relationships beyond the clubroom and penetrate the private domestic interiors of girls' slum dwellings. The Hon. S. Lyttleton exhorted the girls' club worker to "try and get to know her girls in every relation of life, and for this a sympathetic plan of visiting their homes will be found most useful. The girls will probably be out at work, but there will be an opportunity for a talk with the mother and the other sisters at any rate."[79] This was just what Muriel intended to do.

With the eagerness of an anthropologist gone slumming, Muriel recalled how "avid" she was "to find out about these people." She set out to learn their "etiquette," the "syntax" of their speech, and the "secret" of their "perfect unhurried manners." Immersion in the culture of Bow would, she hoped, give her access to residents' ideas, feelings, and homes. Muriel's opportunity came soon enough, when a "dear old woman in a long-skirted black dress with a white crocheted collar told her daughter to 'bring the new young lady in for a nice cup of cocoa before she sets on that long journey to Loughton, being as 'ow this 'ouse is close to the club, and it's that cold in them trains.'"[80]

Her hostess that memorable evening in 1902 was Eliza Pryke, whose daughter Beatrice (1877–1911) was Muriel's first beloved friend in Bow. Eliza and her husband, Walter, a smith and farrier from Sudbury in Suffolk, lived in Bow on Albert Terrace, a small one-block street just off the south side of Bow Road next to the factory girls' club that Muriel first visited. They shared the house with a German butcher and his English wife. The Prykes, with their five children and a lodger, occupied the second floor. By the time Muriel met them Walter had died. Mrs. Pryke paid the rent with help from boarders, like the milk carrier Alfred Wood, and the earnings of her nephew, Alfred, a machinist, along with contributions from two of her children, Walter and Beatrice. Walter and Beatrice worked at the Berger Patented Rice Starch works just a short distance away founded by one of East London's most philanthropic evangelicals, William Thomas Berger.

Beatrice (whom Muriel called by her nickname Beattie) was a revelation for Muriel and, in so many ways Nellie's precursor in Muriel's affections and imagination. With bent shoulders, spectacles, and a "bronchitic wheezing" that rattled in her throat, the gaunt Beattie Pryke had "not beauty of feature or garment to make her desirable." All the same, Muriel likened her to G. B. Shaw's charismatic maiden warrior, St. Joan, beatified by the Catholic church in 1909. "She had delicate consideration for others, integrity, fineness of judgment, courage." Muriel also marveled at the Pryke home, its "triumph of home economics not only in marketing, cooking and serving, but in the disposal of human bodies." Muriel knew only too well how often Ladies Bountiful and friendly visitors had recorded their shocked views of East Londoners' unmade beds and slovenly housekeeping. She would have none of their condescension.[81]

The Prykes enraptured Muriel. But what did they think about their young, wealthy, inquisitive visitor, so intent to befriend them? Only one of Beatrice's letters to Muriel, written the year before her death in 1911, has survived. It suggests both genuine trust and intimate inequality between them. Beattie's letter to "Dear Miss Lester" mingled profound gratitude for Muriel's faith in her goodness with a keen sense of her unworthiness: "you do prais [sic] me in letter much more than im worth." "I have God to thank for you that Sunday night some time ago when your farther [sic] came up in the [Albert] terrace from that time I tried to lead a different life but often done wrong." (See fig. 3.5.) Beattie adds an important detail omitted from Muriel's story. Apparently, Henry Lester was by her side as she threaded her way through Bow's dark streets.

Beattie's letter shows how Muriel went about "being" a Christian by making "everyone want to copy me"—the goal she had set for herself

BOW.

Bow Road.   1910

Dear Miss Lestie

      having recieved your letter this morning I dont know how to thank you it's to good of you and you do prais me in letter much more than I am worth was so sorry to hear that you were upset on monday night but never mind it wont happen no more

I have God to thank for you that Sunday night some time ago when your father came in the terrace from that time I tryed to lead a different life but often done wrong. I made up my mind to leave off my bad habits drinking beer I got so that I would go and have a glass in the public house and thought nothing of it have you to thank for it all please dont let any one see this letter it makes one ashame of them selfs thank you for coming in it cheer mother up hopeing your brother is improveing with best love

      from Beatrice Pryke

3.5. Beatrice Pryke to Muriel Lester, 1910, Lester 2/5/, Lester Papers. (Courtesy of the Bishopsgate Institute.)

nearly ten years earlier. She remains Beattie's moral guide and superior, who implicitly condemns her for enjoying a beer at the pub. "I made up my mind to leave off my bad habits drinking beer," she confesses. "I got so that I would go and have a glass in the public house and thought nothing of it have you to thank for it all" Beattie uses extra blank space on the page instead of periods to signal the end of one thought or sentence and the beginning of the next. She rhetorically enacts and deflects her shame, confusion, and self-consciousness at the boldness of her own admission: "please don't let any one see this letter it makes one ashame of them selfs." Shame betrays the strain of bettering herself by securing Muriel's approval. She concludes on much safer territory: their mutual care and concern for one another's family members. "thank you for coming in it cheer mother up hopeing your brother is improveing with best love from Beatrice Pryke."

Beattie constructs a dynamic of praise and shame in which Muriel's encouragement metamorphoses into a subtle form of discipline, a reminder to Beattie of the need for vigilant moral self-regulation. Beattie equates the gift of Muriel's praise with "worth": too much praise leads to excess or false valuation. Under the force of new ideas unleashed by her reading of Tolstoy, Muriel had embarked on the long process of rejecting the "gift" relationship as a Victorian vestige of social and economic inequalities. Beattie, like most poor East Londoners, had no other way to understand Muriel's "friendship" except as a form of charity. The gift of Muriel's love cannot be separated from the psychological burdens it exacted on the laboring men and women who apparently were eager to receive it.[82] Beattie wanted approval and friendship, not equality, with Muriel. Muriel used praise to push Beattie to internalize Muriel's own values—in this case, temperance. Intimacy, didacticism, and inequality coexist within this epistolary trace of Muriel's pursuit of radical Christian egalitarianism.

Beattie Pryke's affectionate, self-critical letter strikes a recurring theme in Muriel's relations with her closest working-class friends. East Londoners insisted on Muriel's fundamental difference—and apartness—from them. To emulate Muriel, Beattie had insisted in her letter, was to "lead a different life." Muriel's friends in Bow had far too much at stake to allow her to become one of them. After all, the status derived from their association with her depended upon her *not* being one of them. In assuming the right to praise and judge women like Beattie, she reproduced class-based prerogatives in the very act of rejecting them. Beattie's letter crystallizes an ethical dilemma Muriel faced throughout her life: Would it be possible to convince the poor and the powerless with whom she sought solidarity to rethink their own ideas about who she was and what she represented? Could she uproot her own assumptions about the poor and relinquish her deeply engrained bourgeois privileges?

The burden of Muriel's encouragement also weighed heavily on George Bowtle (1892–1931). A bricklayer's son, George and his lifelong friend Ben Platten (1893–1941) were members of Doris Lester's Loughton Sunday school primary class and later Muriel's junior class. For the next three decades, the two men remained stalwart supporters of Doris and Muriel's joint ventures in Loughton and Bow. Ben eventually served

3.6. The impressive neoclassical facade of the Loughton Union Church signified the wealth and self-confidence of its members' recent social ascent into the ranks of the comfortable upper middle class. The small building in the foreground, the Lodge, served as Sunday school where Muriel and Doris taught. Loughton District Historical Society Photographic Collection (Courtesy of Chris Pond and LDHS).

as a leading Trustee of Kingsley Hall. The Bowtles lived on Smarts Lane, Loughton's poorest quarter of dilapidated ancient cottages. One turn-of-the-century resident recalled that it seemed "transplanted from a London East End street" overrun with "drunks, wife-beaters and barefooted urchins."[83] George apprenticed to a maker of tennis bats and hockey sticks; Ben was studying to become a teacher and eventually worked as an accountant. The two friends joined Muriel and Doris as teachers on the Sunday School Committee in 1911.[84]

In the summer of 1914, Muriel invited George to become leader of the Junior Club at the Loughton Sunday school. (See fig. 3.6.) Bowtle felt overwhelmed by his unworthiness of this sacred trust. Apparently, he had done something that he considered profoundly sinful, which, in his own eyes, disqualified him from teaching innocent students. To Muriel, he explained that he appreciated her "earnest spirit" and confidence in him. She had commended him for striving "nobly." She had assured him that "we are all unworthy" and that it was "good" to be "dissatisfied with ourselves." He was not convinced. Her praise pained him. He wanted her to understand his real position. Two years ago, he had failed in his duty as a Christian and it "loom[ed]" and "darken[ed]" his life. She saw only his "polished side," not his true "everyday life." It wasn't just that he lacked "courage to figure in Christ's work." He "shudder[ed]" when he "imagine[d] myself sitting in Junior [Sunday School], amongst those innocent children as an example of Christ." Overwhelmed by his own unnamed sins, he could not bear to become a "Stumbling Block to God's little ones."

In an extended postscript, George demonstrated how much he had—and had not—learned from the Lesters' Sunday school lessons. He took as his text Luke 12:1–5 when Jesus warns his disciples and the "innumerable multitude" around him about the dangers of hypocrisy. All-hearing God knows even those secrets we have "spoken in darkness [and] in the ear in closets." Jesus admonishes his listeners to fear only him who "hath power to cast into hell." To accept Muriel's offer would be hypocrisy. God knew George's "everyday" sins even if Muriel did not. Like Muriel in 1905, he found Bible passages that spoke directly to his disturbed spiritual condition. He found no comfort in them. There was a "real living Satan within each of us," George lamented, against whom he had to remain perpetually vigilant. Did Muriel ever share with George her own fears about Satan's "snares" and "tricks"? His letter suggests that she had spoken in generalities rather than specifics. She had told him, "we are all unworthy;" she had not said, "I too am unworthy but still do God's work." Muriel's friendship with George empowered him and expanded his sense of possibilities. At this particular moment in his spiritual life, it also stymied him. He could not achieve the goodness that Muriel seemed to embody and to which she entreated him to aspire. Like Beattie, he had tried to lead a Christian life. He too had "often done wrong."

George Bowtle's sin-saturated Christianity was utterly at odds with the instruction on offer in the Lesters' Sunday school classroom and Doris's evening club.[85] Their teaching increasingly revolved around Matthew 5 (the "Sermon on the Mount") not Luke 12. Doris had banished Satan from her Sunday school curriculum in favor of Tolstoy's loving God of justice. Under Doris's tutelage, George and Ben and the other boys had studied Tolstoy's critique of Kaiser Wilhelm's 1890 speech to military recruits. Doris had worked hard to make her classroom into a laboratory for exploring ideas and practices of democratic freedom. She had thrown her weight against traditional teaching methods to "get out of the blasphemous S[unday] S[chool] routine by which [the boys] kept an exemplary silence during the Saintly old Superintendent's ten-minutes-long prayer." Play, touch, movement, and imagination animated her lessons with the goal of encouraging students to engage in critical independent thought. George Bowtle's exegesis of Luke 12 demonstrates that he had certainly learned how to think for himself. He had found the devil within, not Tolstoy's Kingdom of Heaven. This could not have pleased Muriel or Doris.

The Lesters' Sunday school teaching in Loughton left them ample time for lawn tennis and garden parties while extending their philanthropic work in Bow. They followed well-established networks of Nonconformist benevolence linking families like theirs in posh Essex suburbs with the slums of Bow. For example, the minister of the Lesters' former Baptist chapel on Fillebrook Road in Leytonstone, Reverend W. Knight Chaplin, also served as pastor of the Poplar and Bromley Tabernacle on Brunswick Road, not far from Nellie's grandmother Harriet Sloan.[86] The family of soap manufacturer Booth Harris was very involved in the Loughton Union Church; one daughter, Louisa, volunteered at the Bow Mission along with the Lester sisters; another, Mildred Harris, was among the first "workers" at Kingsley Hall in 1915. Suburban grandees like Henry Lester (born in Poplar) and Booth Harris (born in Bethnal Green) gave back to the communities they had left behind as their businesses prospered.

Around 1907–8, Doris convinced Muriel to accept an invitation to lead a women's meeting connected to the Bruce Road Congregational Church in Bromley-by-Bow under the leadership of its new minister, John Earle Morrell. (See fig. 3.7.) The Welsh-born Morrell had started life as an "artistic decorator," and became a "portrait painter" by the time he moved with his parents to Marylebone in London in the mid-1890s. A lifelong bachelor, he "lived a solitary life in lodgings" with two middle-aged widows and their children in Bow.[87] Muriel was struck by his "passionate devotion" and "complete sincerity of spirit." So too were nearby residents. Widowed Mrs. Richardson confidentially informed Muriel, in tones of admiration mingled with surprise, "'D'you know, I

3.7. By 1900, Bruce Road Congregational Church was surrounded by densely packed two- story slum houses, a far cry from the open suburban landscape depicted in this 1860s' image. Bruce Road Congregational Church, 1867. (Courtesy of Tower Hamlet's Local History Library.)

believe he's [Rev. Morrell] a Christian.' "[88] This was Muriel's fondest hope for herself.

By Bow standards, Bruce Road was distinctly respectable: the Congregational Church flanked the southeastern corner of the block, a Methodist church occupied the southwestern corner, with a smattering of regular wage earners and even a doctor inhabiting the two-story terraced houses on the north side of the street. Working-class respectability did not translate into religious vitality, however. Bruce Road was spiritually moribund in the years before Morrell's arrival. The deep comfortable galleries of Bruce Road Congregational Church swallowed up the fifty odd middle-class women and girls, none from the neighborhood, attending Sunday services and left the church "very bare." A mere dozen adults graced the services at Bruce Road Methodist church, which looked "perfectly dead and deserted."[89] Bruce Road Congregational had failed to keep up with most slum churches, which sponsored soup kitchens, girls' and boys' clubs, crèches, teetotal recreation for adults, mothers' meetings, and penny savings clubs. Church-connected programs constituted a faith-based system of welfare, free from the stigma of the Poor Law, that East Londoners, including Nellie, used as best they could. "The churches of those days [the early 1900s]," recalled one lifelong resident of Poplar, "were doing exactly the same as Social Security today. The Methodist Church would have bread tickets, boot tickets, coal tickets, meat, milk."[90] Morrell's invitation to Muriel signaled his commitment to reinvigorating his church and expanding its outreach to the working-class men, women, and children living in its shadow.[91]

It's not clear whether it was Reverend Morrell or Muriel who called the group on Bruce Road a "Women's Meeting" rather than the more traditional name for such gatherings, "Mothers' Meetings." Clubs for adult women like Muriel's were strategically essential to the success of churches, settlement houses, and home missions as they faced the challenges of the new century. The first suffragan Bishop of East London gushed that their "astonishingly rapid rise and progress" in the early 1880s was proof enough of their value.[92] They anchored social and religious institutions because poor mothers controlled access to children, husbands, and families. As the Superintendent of the Bow Methodist Mission readily acknowledged, "we could hope to do little until the women were our allies."[93] The Daily News's religious census of 1902–3 noted that women vastly outnumbered men, "conspicuous by their absence," at church services in London's poorest neighborhoods including Bow and Poplar. Only churches engaged in "active, aggressive social work" predicated on the "universal brotherhood of man" would contribute to national life.[94]

Mothers' meetings gave members a break from domestic duties albeit to make them better homemakers through friendly chats on health, nutrition, mothercraft, housekeeping, and hygiene. Some even hired an elderly widow to mind the children during meetings. All offered cake and abundant cups of hot tea, a chance to socialize with neighbors, and the "friendship" of "lady" managers like Muriel. Those run by chapels and churches included Bible study or short services and prayer.[95] Satirists found them an irresistible target. Violet Myers lampooned the formality of printed invitations, stilted conversations, and sentimental songs about married love. In Myers's witty sketch, a poor widow wonders why husbands in these songs never grow old, get drunk, and lose their jobs like her own unlamented late spouse. The well-meaning befuddled ladies sing off-key, run out of stale cake, and serve tea that's "no better nor ditchwater." Norman Maclean's illustrations mock the vague gospel of brotherly love meant to ennoble the proceedings. A framed banner declaring "Love One Another" tilts precariously behind two earthbound mothers who complain about the tea while appearing indifferent to the child sitting on the floor at their feet.[96] In another satirical illustration, even the other philanthropic ladies can hardly stifle their yawns as one of them feebly attempts to give the bored mothers a dose of musical uplift. (See fig. 3.8.)

By her own account, Muriel took this quintessentially Victorian institution of feminine noblesse oblige—the Mothers' Meeting—and turned it into a distinctly modern Women's Meeting. Inept at most household tasks, Muriel readily acknowledged that she was unqualified to instruct Bow's matrons in how to sew, cook, clean, and take care of their babies and children. Instead, she invited speakers to teach them about industrial laws designed to protect workers from occupational hazards; they enjoyed "good music" and joined the thriving women's suffrage movement in Bow. They held window-garden competitions and used religion and prayer to make sense of their day-to-day lives.[97] At a time when women had few opportunities to preach, the mothers' meeting at Bruce Road Congregational Church gave Muriel a space in which to develop her skills as public speaker on social, civic, and religious topics. More importantly, Muriel's relationships with the women of Bruce Road grew into lifelong friendships with their entire families. By 1912, the Lesters and the Dowells had moved there and made it the hub of their community-based activities.

Before settling into the small terraced house at Sixty Bruce Road, the Lester sisters rented rooms in several different parts of Bow for several years. Doris, not Muriel, inaugurated this new phase in their relationship with the local community and one another. She convinced her parents to allow her to stay behind while they, accompanied by Muriel, vacationed in Italy amid "mimosa and orange groves."[98] Doris boarded

"Call this *tea*?"   *Norman.*

3.8. Norman Mac-
lean's cartoons and
satirical captions, "Call
this tea?" (top) and
"In the music-room"
(bottom) captured
Cockney mothers'
skeptical reception of
the watered-down tea
and boring entertain-
ment on offer at phil-
anthropic mothers'
meetings. Violet
Myers, "A 'Mothers'
Meeting' in the East
End," *The Idler* 17 (July
1900): 569–74.

with two elderly spinster parishioners of the Rector of Bow, Reverend Kitcat.

> "Why," I asked, "need the house [the Grange] be kept going just for me? Why can't I spend my nights as well as days in Bow?" This was indeed in those days a revolutionary suggestion! However, I persisted in pressing the point. . . .

Basking in her independence, Doris, with Nellie's help, "carr[ied] on Muriel's jobs as well as my own" at the Factory Girls' Club on Albert Terrace and Mothers' Meetings at Bruce Road Congregational Church. In one draft of her unpublished autobiography, she confessed that she "felt quite heartbroken at the thought of giving up my independence and my room in Bow."[99]

When Muriel returned from Italy, the sisters worked out a new arrangement that allowed each the independence she craved from the luxurious life at the Grange. "The idea was that Muriel and I should fulfil [sic] our functions as Box and Cox, when one was in Bow the other would be home at Loughton! So our new and adventurous life began."[100] This arrangement ensured that Rachel and Henry Lester always had one of their unmarried daughters tending to them at home. It also gave Doris a chance to get out from under Muriel's shadow since they were rarely in Bow or Loughton at the same time. It was a neat and sometimes precarious balancing act. They simultaneously fulfilled traditional daughterly obligations in Loughton while enjoying the freedoms of New Women in Bow. As pacifist feminist Emmeline Pethick-Lawrence recalled, drawing on her own experiences of living among the people, "the very idea that women should leave their homes and live in the comparative freedom of a community, in order to carry out rather subversive principles of social sharing, was a bombshell to the large mass of conservative low-church and Nonconformist opinion."[101]

Because of and despite its noise, dirt and deprivation, Bow brought Doris and Muriel "a serenity and selflessness almost beyond imagination."[102] They described themselves as inhabiting "two worlds." Sometimes the distances between these worlds uncomfortably collapsed. At a party in Loughton, Muriel carelessly chatted about work-related grievances that one of her factory girl friends had shared with her in confidence. She was unnerved when her story traveled to the ears of the factory manager, who pressed Muriel to reveal her informant's name.[103] For all that Muriel imagined Bow and Loughton as two separate worlds, they were also always connected for her. That was, after all, her self-chosen task.

GOD'S EMPIRE

Did God love Britain's empire? In 1900, Muriel and the vast majority of Britons across the political spectrum were absolutely sure that He did. By 1910, revelations of horrific cruelty in the Congo perpetrated by King Leopold of Belgium under cover of Christian humanitarianism had severely tested confidence in this alliance. The first place that Muriel and Doris rented in Bow sometime around 1910 put them close to the domestic epicenter of debates over Britain's and evangelical Christianity's culpability for the carnage in the Congo. Only the year before, Muriel had publicly joined the campaign to bring some measure of justice to the Congo. Her involvement in this movement, the Congo Reform Association, marked a crucial turning point in her emerging global consciousness and her growing antipathy to colonialism and imperialism. As is so often the case, Muriel was not an entirely reliable guide to her life story. Tales of Protestant missionary endeavors in the Congo had been part of her religious upbringing in Leytonstone and Loughton as well as her work in Bow from the turn of the century.

An attic room in Doric Lodge (founded in 1884), the women's residence of a training college for home and overseas missionaries, was Muriel and Doris's first shared residence in Bow.[104] In their writings, the sisters made very little of Doric Lodge and the larger organization of which it was a part. Muriel called it a "severe-looking appendage of a missionary-training college." Doris dismissed it as a relic from a bygone era.[105] In this judgment, they were badly mistaken or willfully disingenuous. Doric Lodge was part of the East London Training Institute for Home and Foreign Missions, one of Britain's most ambitious—and modern—global evangelical ventures.[106] Henry and Fanny Grattan

3.9. Saving souls and global benevolence was a family business for Dr. Harry Grattan Guinness, his wife Fanny Grattan Guinness, their children and grandchildren. Dr. Harry Guinness, *Not Unto Us, A Record of 21 Years Missionary Service* (London, 1908), frontispiece.

Guinness, Anglo-Irish evangelicals and relatives of the brewery moguls, founded the mission in Bromley-by-Bow in 1873 in partnership with Dr. Thomas John Barnardo. The entire missionary complex was renamed the Regions Beyond Missionary Union (RBMU) in 1899—and, to add to confusion, was better known as the Regions Beyond Inland Mission.

RBMU's headquarters in Bow included Harley House for men and Doric Lodge for women. The enterprise was nondenominational, red-hot premillenarian, and global in its reach.[107] In the 1860s, Henry ("Harry") Grattan Guinness was among Britain's best known revivalist preachers before he turned his gaze south and east to save heathen souls in Congo, Peru, India, and China. (See fig. 3.9.) This was urgent business as he and Fanny prepared for the Second Coming. His eschatology, with its elaborate charts of the relationship between Biblical prophecy and "soli-lunar" cycles, was as abstruse and hermetic as anything Madame Blavatsky ever penned.[108] Christians needed God's punishing judgment, he insisted. He devoted an entire book to refuting the dangerous heresy of fellow Baptist Revivalist G. O. Barnes, who dared to preach "God is Love and nothing else." For Barnes, love was God's domain, punishment the devil's.[109] Not for Grattan Guinness.

Fanny and Harry Grattan Guinness's theology could not have been farther from Muriel's "God is Love" theology and Campbell's religious "modernism"; but their understanding of the global flows of empire and their techniques for selling their godly labors to their well-healed supporters and to the heathen masses were distinctly modern. In the service of Christianity, they mastered new information and visual technologies of photography and magic lanterns. The RBMU was remarkably cosmopolitan in personnel and outlook.[110] Students came from across Britain and over twenty different countries. Their curriculum included study of "world religions": Islam, Hinduism, Buddhism, Confucianism, Taoism, Shintoism, and Roman Catholicism. They engaged in sustained comparisons of each religion's founders, revealed texts, and doctrines of God and man, albeit through their own evangelical Christocentric lens. Harley College and Doric Lodge gave its graduates a vastly deeper grasp of culture and religion around the world than the Lesters' demanding curriculum at St. Leonard's.[111] Muriel and Doris would certainly have stood to learn a great deal from the other women they encountered at Doric Lodge as they climbed to their attic room.

RBMU missionaries occupied the front lines of encounters between rich and poor in London as well as white Britons and people of color in Africa, Asia, and South America. They served apprenticeships in East London by succoring the poor in Nellie's neighborhood before their overseas postings. They figured prominently on the lists of Christian "martyrs" slaughtered in the Boxer Rebellion in China during the bloody summer of 1900. Two of the slain missionaries, the Nathan sisters, were members of the Lesters' Loughton Union Church; commemorating their deaths preoccupied the congregation at the time Doris and Muriel first assumed responsibilities and leadership there.[112]

For their education, many students at Harley House and Doric Lodge paid no fees: the enterprise was funded entirely by donations from the faithful. Some of Doric Lodge's students worked as trained nurses at

Bromley House Institute on Brunswick Road across from Granny and Caroline Sloan, where they ran a modern maternity and child welfare clinic in an ancient Tudor manor house that still stands. Others served as staff at Berger Hall with its medical clinic, Evening Night School and Girls' Evening Home for Factory Girls. Nellie and most of her family lived within a block or two of Berger Hall. I suspect it housed the Factory Girls' Club and Night School where Nellie formed some of her most enduring friendships with various "lady" helpers including Lady Marion Plender (the daughter of a suburban Essex "upper division" customs officer). We know that Nellie turned to Berger Hall for medical services after 1910.[113]

Henry Stanley's 1877 best-selling account of his expedition into darkest Africa inspired evangelicals including the Grattan Guinnesses to take godly action. Harley College provided the first recruits for the Livingstone Inland Mission (1880) to bring Christian truths to the Belgian Congo. Nine years later, the mission sent its missionaries upriver to establish the Congo Balolo Mission. For the next twenty years, the Grattan Guinness family and students from their East London headquarters took pride in their leading role in civilizing and converting the Congo.

All that changed around 1903 just as Doris and Muriel deepened their bonds to Bow. Dr. Henry Grattan Guinness, Fanny and Harry's son, publicly acknowledged the cataclysmic deformation of the RBMU's Christian labors in the Congo, where he himself had once served. King Leopold II of Belgium, masquerading as a benevolent Christian monarch, had imposed a regime of terror on the quasi-enslaved African population compelled to harvest rubber to satisfy the insatiable demand of bicycle-crazed Europeans and Americans. Leopold's overseers executed or maimed the bodies of conscripted Congolese workers who failed to meet their rubber quotas. Overseers literally needed a severed human body part to account for each bullet they had discharged, lest they be punished for wasting precious ammunition in hunting for food.[114] The death toll must be reckoned in tens of thousands. The dismembered bodies of survivors offered irrefutable "proof" of atrocity. The Regions Beyond monthly periodical published articles illustrated by graphic photographs of limbless men, women, and children taken by its own missionaries. Victims wrapped white clothes around their dark torsos, the better to highlight their gruesome injuries.[115] (See fig. 3.10.) Skeptics wondered why the Grattan Guinness's missionary empire had been so slow to bring their case to a broader public. After all, Henry Jr. had first received reports about such horrors as early as 1895 when he had importuned King Leopold to make changes. Had evangelicals like Grattan Guinness implicitly come to terms with Leopold's murderous minions and entered into a "conspiracy of silence" in exchange for the right to extend their work of saving souls?[116]

As the Lesters strengthened their ties to Bow at the turn of the century, Henry Jr. launched a determined public relations campaign to identify RBMU with the humanitarian response to the Congo catastrophe rather than with its origins in the 1880s and '90s.[117] Along with the radical journalist Edmund Morel and the British consul Roger Casement, Henry Grattan Guinness helped found the Congo Reform Association in 1904 to demand an end to the

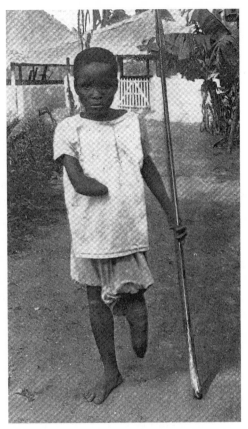

3.10. Photographs played a crucial role in the Congo Reform Association's campaign to end King Leopold's reign of terror. This frequently reproduced photograph of Impongi, a boy victim of Congo "misrule," accentuated his atrocious mutilation as well as missionaries' success at rehabilitating him. "Impongi," from Dr. Harry Guinness, *Not Unto Us, A Record of 21 Years Missionary Service* (London, 1908).

systematic violence and dissolve King Leopold's personal rule over the Congo Free State. From 1906 to 1908, Regions Beyond missionaries including Guinness, acting on behalf of the Congo Reform Association, fanned out across England with their magic lantern slides to soften the hearts, awaken the consciences, and open the pocketbooks of Nonconformity. Savoring its stunning success in the 1906 parliamentary elections under the banner of the Liberal Party, Nonconformity—both its evangelical and progressive wings—flexed its muscles once again and pushed the Liberal government to demand an end to Leopold's rule. In 1908, Leopold yielded to international pressure and reluctantly handed over his private fiefdom to the state of Belgium.[118]

Critics of empire's evils like the pro-Boers and supporters of the Congo Reform Association should not be equated with enemies of imperialism, although some were. Muriel reckoned with Leopold's atrocities—and their implications for Europe's relationship with Africa and the "white man's burden—as part of a political-religious crusade waged by the forces of evangelical Nonconformity at the height of its early-twentieth-century power and influence. The Congo Reform Association's most secular spokesman, Edmund Morel, sought to make empire virtuous, not condemn and dismantle it. Morel called for Africans to be granted the economic benefits of free labor and free trade while replacing an exploitative and murderous imperialist regime with a benevolent and paternalist one.[119] These were radical demands to be sure, but still a far cry from the platform of the first Pan-African Conference that met in London in the summer of 1900. The cosmopolitan American sociologist of race, W.E.B. Du Bois helped craft the "Address to the Nations of the World" calling for African self-government as part of the worldwide struggle against racism.[120]

In April 1909, Muriel was a founding member of the Women's Branch of the Congo Reform Association.[121] She was no stranger to Congo triumphs and troubles. Stories of missionary heartbreak and success were deeply interwoven in her childhood and young adulthood. Congo missionaries from Harley College and Doric Lodge spoke frequently at the Loughton Union Church in the early 1900s.[122] Muriel attributed her embrace of the Congo Reform Association to the heartfelt testimony of Berger Hall's evangelical pastor in Bow, whose words haunted her. He had seen "a sackful of human hands" during his time in the Congo. This unnamed preacher could only have been Pastor Daniel Hayes. Trained at Harley College and sent as a missionary to the Congo, Hayes had returned to Regions Beyond's headquarters in Bow to lead its Berger Hall branch. Hayes had "that ineradicable Congo fever in his blood."[123] Preacher and pastor, politician and philanthropist, he joined the Poplar

Borough council. "Day and night," Muriel could not get Hayes's words out of her head.

> I wanted all parsons to perform their proper function, to be prophets, to speak out the truth so that no one could go on contentedly talking about Europe as though it were Christian, and honouring crowned heads as though some were not murderers, and priding themselves on carrying the white man's burden of civilization when we were torturing Africa with our callousness and greed.[124]

In Muriel's account of her ethical growth, this was a key turning point. The bodies of Congo's victims exposed Europe's civilizing and Christianizing claims as hypocritical fictions. God emphatically no longer loved empire.

Muriel took herself from Pastor Hayes in Bow to suburban Enfield where she went to R. J. Campbell's home to implore him to use his bully pulpit on behalf of the Congo's innocent victims.[125] Her journey makes visible links, forged on the common ground of global humanitarianism, between two theologically warring groups within Edwardian Nonconformity: religious modernism and missionary evangelicalism. When they set aside their differences, they could—and did—help give the Liberal Party a mandate to enact an ambitious social reform program including the Feeding of Necessitous School Children (free school meals for poor children) and Old Age Pensions. Muriel's journey also makes visible unresolved tensions within her own theological thinking between missionary and modernist impulses.

FROM PAUPERS TO CITIZENS

Muriel did not need to look as far as Africa to find systematic injustice against blameless men, women and children. Bitter personal experience convinced many in Bow and Poplar that the Poor Law sanctioned state violence against the most sacred and important human institution: the family. Stories like Nellie's abounded in East London: young families ripped apart by the state because the male breadwinner's untimely disablement or death left his survivors impoverished. What infused these stories with explosive political and emotional capital in the early twentieth century was the fact that once helpless children, erstwhile Poor Law wards of the state, were now in positions to shape policy and make laws as members of Parliament, Borough Councils, and Boards of Guardians. One such man was Will Crooks, Poplar's genial MP. He could neither forget nor forgive the Poor Law officials who had sent him and his siblings off to the Poor Law Barrack School at Sutton after their father, a ship's stoker, lost his arm at work. Like Harriet Dowell, Mrs. Crooks had wept over her sleeping children as she worked late into the night in an unsuccessful effort to hold her family together. Separated from his terrified and confused younger brother once they arrived at the school, Crooks still seethed with indignation decades later.[126]

Loathed by the poor since its passage in 1834, the New Poor Law's punitive principles remained intact despite dozens of amendments and administrative modifications over the decades.[127] On the eve of their electoral trouncing by the Liberals in January 1906, the Conservative government of the urbane philosopher-turned-politician A. J. Balfour convened a Royal Commission on the Poor Laws and Relief of Distress. The commissioners' task was to investigate the Poor Law and offer recommendations about how best to modify it in light of twentieth-century conditions. After years of deliberation, the majority report affirmed key elements of the status quo, condemned outdoor relief, and revived Victorian rhetoric identifying poverty with moral failing. The 716-page minority report, penned mostly by Fabian sociologist Beatrice Potter Webb with help from her husband Sidney, demanded that the state ensure a "national minimum of civilized life" for its citizens. It emphasized the deep structural causes of poverty and sought the wholesale reorganization of poor relief. It called for the abolition of Poor Law schools like Forest Gate and the absorption of their students into local schools. It demanded a unified medical service to care for all citizens, regardless of their ability to pay.[128] By May, the Webbs had launched a national out-of-doors campaign to gather popular support for the minority report, the National Committee for the Break-up of the Poor Law. The Committee had 300 members in June 1909; by November 1910, it numbered over 30,000.[129] Muriel was among them. She was so enamored by the minority report and the National Committee's educational campaign that she secured a private interview with Beatrice Webb.

One of the four signatories of the controversial and much discussed minority report of the Royal Commission on the Poor Laws was Bow's favorite son and Muriel's inspirational mentor in local politics, George Lansbury. In allying themselves with Lansbury, the Lester sisters gained a formidable backer as well as ready-made group of enemies. Highly critical of bourgeois philanthropy as self-serving and condescending, Lansbury praised "Muriel Lester and her sister" as among the handful of great women like Annie Besant and Karl Marx's daughter Eleanor "who treated the workers as equals and worked to ensure not mere acquiescence in their Socialist teaching but active intelligent co-operation."[130] (His homage to and erasure of Doris is symptomatic of just how much Muriel overshadowed her sister.)

Few combined Lansbury's gift of ready laughter and warm common-sense with adamantine hatred of the Poor Law. "A hefty rough-looking handful," he joined the Marxist Social Democratic Federation (SDF) in 1892 and quickly made a name for himself with his feisty plainspoken eloquence.[131] In the 1890s, his rhetoric was uncompromising in its economic materialism: Liberals and Conservatives were much the same, he argued, because both consigned "my class" to be "the wage slaves of those who own the means and instruments of production, distribution, and exchange."[132] Even during this most secular phase of his career, he likened his SDF branch meetings—held in Annie Besant's Theosophical Match Girls club in Bow—to "revivalist gatherings." The SDF left room in its ranks for those who could not and would not cast off either belief in some kind of Christian God or the forms and structures of organized religious life.[133] The former domestic servant and SDF activist in South London, Mary Gray, established Socialist Sunday schools in Battersea in the 1890s that flourished in the early twentieth century.[134]

When Muriel first met Lansbury in Bow, he had recently returned to the Church (in 1904), after long detours among secularists and several years sending his own children to be educated by the Ethical Society of East London.[135] His language, like that of Keir Hardie and so many members of the Independent Labour Party, was deeply and sincerely Christian.[136] West Indian writer and radical Claude McKay was not convinced: Lansbury was "symbolic of all that was simon-pure, pious and self-righteous in the British Labour movement."[137] Lansbury was determined to do nothing less than "Smash up the Poor Law." He sought to replace it with a humane system of state welfare that preserved, rather than dismantled, families by providing weekly cash payments (called "outdoor relief") to poor widows like Nellie's grandmother and mother, Harriet Sloan and Harriet Dowell. Men in Poplar wanted work, not doles. Lansbury aimed to give it to them. In the 1890s, he and Crooks had used their positions on the Poplar Board of Guardians and the Management Committee of Nellie's Poor Law orphanage at Forest Gate to shift the terms of poor relief in Poplar. (See fig. 3.11.) They banished the ugly coarse blue serge workhouse uniforms that Nellie had been forced to wear and replaced them with regular clothing at the same cost to ratepayers. They improved and varied the food; they offered unemployed men paid agricultural work in Labour colonies as an alternative to incarceration in Poor Houses.[138]

3.11. Religion played a crucial role in the early twentieth-century Labour movement and in the lives of two of East London's most beloved politicians, Will Crooks and George Lansbury. (Left) "Mr. Will Crooks on Piety at Home," and (right) "Mr. George Lansbury, L.C.C., on The Power that Remakes Men" from *Labour and Religion by Ten Labour Members* (London, 1910), 56, 68.

In response to Crooks and Lansbury's efforts, local businessmen formed the Poplar Municipal Alliance. The Alliance lambasted them for skyrocketing rates of poor relief, accused them of maladministration, and impugned their integrity as public servants before the 1906 Parliamentary Committee of Inquiry convened by J. S. Davy, the Chief Inspector for the Local Government Board to investigate the Poplar Board of Guardians. A respected Committee member on the Royal Commission (1905–9), Lansbury was also chief witness and whipping boy of Davy's inquiry. No detail of Poplar's supposed maladministration of the Poor Law proved too minute for Inspector Davy. Did Lansbury and Crooks know that Guardians had supposedly consumed beer in the workhouse cellar while "hobnobbing with the paupers over salmon and oysters"?[139] Why had they sanctioned the purchase of Irish cambric handkerchiefs at 3d a piece? Had Guardians purchased them for their own delicate noses? With rising indignation, Lansbury explained that the Guardians placed six handkerchiefs in the box of each Poor Law girl going out to domestic service. Crooks wondered whether the chief inspector thought it would be more economical for the girls to use their cuffs.[140]

The point that stuck for the Lesters was this: nothing less than the best was good enough for the poor children of Bow and Poplar and their parents. In this regard, the Lesters demanded much more for their neighbors than the Webbs and the Fabian Society, who more pragmatically hoped that the state would satisfy its citizens' minimum needs. Human dignity always trumped economy for Crooks, Lansbury, and the Lesters. These were crucial lessons that the various Edwardian controversies over Poor Law reform and relief along with their growing networks of friends in Bow and Poplar like Beatrice Pryke taught Muriel. It was part of a process of beginning to see the world through the eyes of her poor friends and neighbors. It meant seeing the poor not as downtrodden subjects with duties, but as rights-bearing citizens.

CONCLUSIONS

"Religious ideas have the fate of melodies," George Eliot's narrator observed in *Scenes of Clerical Life* (1858), "which, once set afloat in the world, are taken up by all sorts of instruments. . . ."[141] Muriel was eager to be such an instrument, not just of religious ideas but of God's loving will. Her self-directed reading of Christian thinkers such as Tolstoy and Harnack, her social work in Bow, her friendships with poor women and men, and her encounters with dynamic religious leaders including R. J. Campbell and Pastor Hayes in Bow did not suddenly turn her into a Christian revolutionary. There was, in fact, no single moment of transformation. These ideas and experiences were part of her "road of personal development" toward free religion in the name of human freedom.[142] They wore away her inherited Liberalism and pushed her toward a new social justice gospel founded on God's love. They were part of a process of ethical remaking that heightened her sensitivity to how structural inequalities in power and resources between people across the globe produced day-to-day violence incompatible with her "God is Love" theological thinking. A good life, Muriel increasingly recognized by 1910, meant subordinating the enjoyment of worldly goods to fostering the social good. This was the key to "being a Christian" in Edwardian Britain.

Scholars of Victorian and Edwardian religion have not written about "God is Love" as the cornerstone of a discrete theology or theological position or even a theological tendency in the early twentieth century. When we shift focus from systematic theology to "lived theology," to Henry Lester's democratic understanding of theology as the discourse that flows from the everyday thinking, writing, and talking of men and women about God—we find "God is Love" theology broadcast widely across late-Victorian and Edwardian culture. Its distinctly unsystematic basis gave it broad purchase and versatility among a range of progressive Christians at the turn of the 20th century who, like Muriel, were intent to live ethically.

It's no surprise that Muriel was appalled by Congo atrocities and aligned with The New Theology by 1910. However, I was not prepared to find her dutifully in charge of the Baptist Zenana Mission's sweet stall at the Loughton Union Church in 1908–9 raising money to help "oppressed" Indian women held "captive" in the zenana—the exclusively female quarters within South Asian households.[143] Established by Baptist women in the mid-nineteenth century to uplift their benighted dark sisters in India, the Baptist Zenana Mission was an old-fashioned evangelical Christian charity, the sort rightly associated with missionary imperialism.[144] It's not where a vegetarian, Tolstoyan, New Woman-in-the-slums, religious modernist ought to be. Or at least, so I thought. But Muriel was. Why?

Let me offer two possible explanations. First, her sweet stall work speaks to the persistence of her divided life, her two worlds. She may have been an independent woman in Bow, but, in Loughton, she remained the dutiful spinster daughter doing what such women did. She helped at charity bazaars; taught Sunday school; and accompanied her wealthy parents on elegant holidays to fancy Riviera hotels. She does not appear to have participated in the broader networks of bohemian sociability that so often sustained Edwardians who shared her religious and social commitments. If she dined at London's vegetarian restaurants and mingled with their crankish sandal-wearing patrons, she has left no record of these outings.

Second, despite the profound theological and doctrinal differences separating Campbell's religious modernism from the evangelical Christianity of the Grattan Guinness missionary empire and the Zenana Mission, these groups sometimes could and did make common cause. To an extent that Muriel never acknowledged, she remained immersed in both evangelical and modernist Christianity—in Loughton as well as in Bow. Despite its cultural condescension, the Baptist Zenana Mission was part of a century-old Baptist missionary project that believed fervently in the spiritual equality of all people, black and white, before God.[145] New Theology *and* evangelical global benevolence encouraged Muriel to act on her understanding that being a Christian meant caring for the souls and bodies of the outcast poor at home and abroad.[146] Between 1902 and 1910, Muriel had repeatedly asked herself the question: could she live ethically in a world riddled with inequality and injustice? "God is Love" theology affirmed for her that she could.

CHAPTER FOUR

Body Biographies in War and Peace

NELLIE AND MURIEL FORGED THEIR PARTNERSHIP through illness. Each endured incapacitating pain during the years of their deepest collaboration from 1910 until Nellie's death on January 31, 1923. In March 1910, a disastrous bout of rheumatic fever left Nellie in a catatonic stupor. It forced her out of industrial waged labor while freeing her to devote herself to her work with Muriel and Doris in Bow. For the next decade, Nellie's physical world contracted as her political and intellectual horizons expanded. Her breathing and movements grew increasingly labored until she could no longer leave her small row home next door to the Lesters on Bruce Road.[1] From approximately 1910 to 1917, Muriel's physical and mental health was so precarious that she often broke down and required Nellie's care. Tending to her aging parents in Loughton as well as her public work as a pacifist, socialist, and feminist during World War I proved a daunting debilitating task. In 1916–17, Muriel too experienced a complete collapse. It clarified her understanding of the vital links between mind and body so crucial to her religious, spiritual, and somatic life for the next five decades.

Nellie and Muriel shared illness. It was one ground on which they produced their intimacy. In caring for one another's broken bodies, Nellie and Muriel fashioned a set of practices and a language of love between women. Muriel's "God is Love" theology and social politics had led her first to Bow and then to Nellie. Drawn to morally uplifting Christian organizations like Night Schools and church-sponsored factory girls' clubs, Nellie had a long history of friendships with philanthropic ladies before she met Muriel. Their infirmities, however, cemented and transformed their relationship.

Profound illness broke down their self-sufficient bodies along with the boundaries guarding them from the hands of others. It led them to probe their innermost selves. It also opened up emotional space for them to love one another while touching, writing, and talking about their two bodies in ways that were acceptable to their families, friends, neighbors, and most of all, to them. Each inhabited her body through what medical anthropologists call "the lived experience of the body-self." They also always had "social bodies" constituted through and by representation. The quite different medical and caring resources available to rich and poor in the early twentieth century shaped Nellie and Muriel's body biographies.[2] Their bodies, in sickness and in health, provide sites where the "latent socioeconomic, physical, cultural, and moral planes" of their society explicitly intersected.[3] In reconstructing the histories of their two bodies, I move across scales of analysis, from the minutiae of Nellie's body temperature on a given day to the structure of the modern scientific research hospital and global concepts of spirituality.

The first decades of the new century gave rise to new understandings of human interiority as well as unprecedented levels of state-sanctioned violence against bodies.[4] These two developments conspicuously came together in the rehabilitation of some white British soldiers whose bodies were put back together by orthopedists and whose minds were probed by psychiatrists.[5] Such fractured men often stand in for the "shock" of modernity and its traumatic birth.[6] Muriel and Nellie's body biographies offer a way to reorient the histories of these epochal developments from men to women, from the western front to the home front, from the violence of guns and bombs to the traumas of industrial capitalism and oppositional politics. Muriel and Nellie's embodied life histories unfolded against the backdrop of a wide range of fragile male and female bodies in the early twentieth century including suffragettes, conscientious objectors, Christian Scientists, and disabled soldiers.

Nellie and Muriel's loving friendship and their embodied histories throw into relief several central concerns about modernity—from the supposed triumph of science and bureaucratic efficiency to the trauma of world war and the healing balm of psychology. Religion and science vied with another in their claims to cure the sick body by knowing its workings from the inside out and the outside in. Nellie's and Muriel's bodies in war and peace provide a way to explore how the entangled global histories of religion and spirituality, the human and medical sciences, produced competing and overlapping understandings of human insideness. Illness and love came before and enabled the full development of their Christian revolutionary politics, labors, and institution building in Bow. That comes next.

TAKING NELLIE'S TEMPERATURE

Let me begin with a story about Nellie's suffering body.

In December 1909, Nellie Dowell recognized the steady advance of her old enemy, rheumatic fever. Her ankles, fingers, jaws and, "chest bones" ached. Her breathing was labored; her mobility impaired. She was no stranger to illness. Not long after leaving Forest Gate Industrial School, fever had wracked her small body and her limbs had jerked involuntarily to the dance of St. Vitus. Her mother Harriet brought her to the Poplar and Stepney Poor Law asylum hospital where she remained five weeks recovering from chorea, a common streptococcal infection.[7] (See fig. 4.1.)

Victorian doctors could do little to prevent the chorea's inevitable sequelae: rheumatic fever and mitral valvular degeneration.[8] Widely perceived as a pathological by-product of urban poverty, rheumatic fever struck Nellie in 1901 and returned in 1906 and 1908.[9] During the cata-

4.1. "Poplar and Stepney Sick Asylum," *Illustrated London News*, December 2, 1871, 299.

strophic attack of 1909–10, she initially responded well to bed rest over the Christmas holidays. However, eight weeks later, her condition worsened and her doctor insisted her survival depended upon rushing her to the great hospital of East London. She "hovered between life and death" and slipped into incoherence and semi-consciousness. Sometimes she raved; but at other times she was as "quiet as a tomb."[10]

At least this last part was how Muriel told the story after Nellie's death in 1923. Nellie's hospitalization figures prominently in Muriel's two typescript biographical fragments, "From Birth to Death" and her published homage to Nellie, "The Salt of the Earth." London Hospital, East London's world-renowned voluntary teaching hospital and medical school, is approximately two miles—the distance Muriel specified in her story—from Nellie's South Bromley home. Its Admission and Discharge register confirmed that she went there. Nellie spent eight days in London Hospital from March 3 to March 11, 1910 when orderlies transported her to the lunatic ward of the Whitechapel Poor Law Infirmary.[11] The staff of London Hospital generated an impressive array of documents detailing her past and present condition, her outside and inside, as well as their efforts to treat and represent her disease. They measured the output of her urine and observed its color; they mapped the sounds of her chest and logged the rate and strength of her pulse. Twice daily, Nellie's nurses took her temperature and recorded it on a graph—with a dotted line indicating "normal" at 98.6 degrees.[12] (See fig. 4.2.)

Nothing about Muriel's accounts of Nellie's hospitalization prepared me for the seemingly incontestable "facts" of her vital signs. Her body temperature never went above 99 degrees at any point during her hospitalization. She never had a fever (the nurse entered "T. normal" on her chart).  Of course, very sick people often don't have fevers. But none of the other measures of her bodily functions suggests that she was in the throes of a life-and-death crisis when she arrived at London Hospital. In fact, at least one doctor's note suggests that her condition was improving and that she was not even suffering from an acute case of rheumatic fever at the time of her admission. (When a historian of British medicine, Dr. Fredric Mintz, himself a former cardiologist, reviewed Nellie's medical file for me, he could not understand

4.2. "Temperature and Urine chart" from Dr. F. J. Smith, Medical female patients' case notes, 1910, RLHLH/M/14/65. (Copyright of The Royal London Hospital Archives.)

why she had been admitted in the first place.) Only on the day before her transfer to the lunatic asylum did she spiral into an acute morbid condition: her body temperature plummeted, she vomited twice and she became "restless." Muriel's narratives and Nellie's London Hospital case records—and the stories about Nellie Dowell and London Hospital, health and disease, the body and interiority they so tersely summarize and enable—form an essential part of my analysis.

Nellie Dowell's hospital case report is very ordinary. Nothing distinguishes it from hundreds of others filed under the name of her attending physician, F. J. Smith.[13] What makes them extraordinary to me is that they are Nellie's. Much like the significance of an old photograph of people we have never met, the value of Nellie's medical case report derives from knowing it is hers. Nellie Dowell's medical case record moves effortlessly across registers as it folds the singular into the general, the idiosyncratic into the exemplary.[14] It straightforwardly documents a "case" of rheumatic fever—an abstractable set of physiological measurements (person X evacuated Y urine on Z day) and formulaic observations ("skin moist") disciplined into categories, charts, and codes ready for London Hospital's doctors to transform into data for their medico-scientific studies.

Nellie's London Hospital medical file is so brazenly invasive in reporting the condition of her interiors that my exhilaration at finding it was tempered by discomfort at reading it. Had Nellie Dowell, that perpetually obscured object of my historical sleuthing, come too sharply into focus? Nellie's letters to Muriel are arguably more private and intimate than her medical records. And yet in reading them, I felt no sense of violating an imagined ethical boundary protecting the defenseless dead's encounter with the historian. Why? Let me gesture at a key difference. Archives bear the embedded histories of social and institutional relations that enable and haunt their production and preservation. Nellie wrote her letters as an affirmation of self, an act of will; Muriel kept them as tokens of their love. Produced by the hospital, her medical case file chronicled the breaking down of her personhood and makes no apology for its profoundly non-consensual denouement. The hospital kept her file and tens of thousands of others like it for use in medical research.

The tensions between abstraction and embodiment, the impersonal and the too-personal animate my attempt to reconstruct Nellie's medical crisis in 1910 and explore its historical and methodological significance. Muriel's stories about Nellie and the supposedly scientific facts of her medical record are densely sedimented sources, which contain the perspectives of many different people. "From Birth to Death" is narrated mostly through Harriet Dowell's eyes and includes "direct quotations" of Nellie and her mother in Muriel's improvised Cockney vernacular. Muriel based much of what she wrote about Nellie's hospitalization on information she could have learned only from Harriet and Nellie themselves. Harriet and Nellie were also her physicians' chief informants about her past medical history. The medical case report includes notes by various ward nurses as well as five different doctors—the admitting physician, her attending physician, and specialists in vascular, rheumatic, and nervous disorders.[15] All of these texts are not only multivoiced, but in some ways they are also multi-authored, albeit in not quite the same way.

"From Birth to Death" informs us that Nellie's hospitalization and involuntary confinement left her in a catatonic state for several months. Only after discovering Nellie's hospital records did I realize that she penned the first of her loving letters to Muriel in November 1910 just as she began slowly to recover from the trauma of her hospitalization. Nellie's illness and its immediate aftermath allowed Muriel and Nellie physical and emotional proximity that redefined the nature of their relationship. If illness precipitated their intimacy, it also gave Nellie a recurring topic in her letters as well as a language of love with which to address "Dear Miss Lester."

NARRATING NELLIE

Muriel wrote all three of her stories about Nellie in 1923, sometime after Nellie's death in late January 1923. By that time, she had become a vocal critic of modern allopathic biomedicine, with its drugs, invasive technologies and body disciplines. She also had assumed a seat on the Poplar Borough council in 1922, which had grabbed headlines across the English-speaking world in 1921 by defying a court order to pay compulsory rates to defray administration costs of metropolitan government. Led by Muriel's friend George Lansbury, the Poplar Rate Strike of 1921 was part and parcel of the borough council's adoption of a radical program of economic and social justice. Its planks included equal pay for men and women; a generous minimum wage for municipal workers;

and a call for equalization of "rates" across London to relieve the tax burden of poor districts like Poplar. The government's decision to send the councilors to prison backfired: their physical sufferings only added a glow of martyrdom to their principled stance. The death of George Lansbury's daughter-in-law, the Labour councilor Minnie Lansbury, a short time after her release from prison, accentuated awareness of state violence against those seeking justice for workers and the poor at home and abroad. Prison had broken Minnie Lansbury's body, not her mind or spirit.[16] Muriel replaced Minnie Lansbury on the Poplar Council. She headed its Maternity and Child Welfare committee, which demanded extensive publicly funded services for mothers and their children.

Given Muriel's political commitments in 1923, it is hardly surprising that she cast Nellie's story as an example of the failure of private philanthropy and institutionalized allopathic medicine to address the root cause of Nellie's infirmities: her poverty. Nellie's doctor repeatedly warns her mother to give her daughter something more nourishing than tea and something warmer than a mesh cotton blanket. The doctor grows more frustrated as Mrs. Dowell appears to ignore his pleading. Like so many other well-intentioned outsiders, the doctor perceives Mrs. Dowell through deeply embedded assumptions about working-class mothers' feckless domestic economy. Muriel shifts to Mrs. Dowell's perspective and by so doing blasts those who would implicitly blame East London's poor mothers for failing to care for their children. "But always Mrs. Dowell's pride forbade her to tell him it was not only rheumatic fever that Nellie was suffering from, but also, and just as acutely, poverty. He might have put two and two together and guessed that, she [Mrs. Dowell] thought." Muriel characterized such blinkered responses to poverty (the inability to "put two and two together") as a form of "economic imperialism" that deformed bourgeois perceptions, including her own, of the stark economic choices confronting the poor.[17] Elsewhere, she called this "the foolish innocence," which is subsidized by wealth and ease.[18]

Deploying tropes of depth and surface, Harriet Dowell critiques modern medicine with its new technologies of interiority such as radiograms and Rontgen rays that purport to reveal truths secreted within the body. "But there people who could look into a locked up box as it were and describe to your face what was going on inside your chest, you couldn't expec' them to see the things that were right under their noses." So too, Nellie's philanthropic lady friends who run her evening night school and factory girls' club "didn't see wot was staring 'em in the face so to speak."[19] They bring Nellie grapes and flowers, rather than milk and woolen blankets. Muriel's message—as articulated by and through Harriet Dowell—is unmistakable. The poverty of the respectable poor like the Dowells is not legible by their self-presentation. It cannot be read on their surfaces; they do not flamboyantly perform their poverty to elicit charity. Nutritious food and warmth count more than sympathy in the fight against disease. Muriel implicitly argues that only a system of health care that empowers the poor will meet their needs. Health care ought to be a social right, not a philanthropic gift.

Muriel's account of Nellie's time in London Hospital demonstrates a surprisingly detailed knowledge of its institutional apparatus and hierarchies. (See fig. 4.3.) "From Birth to Death" explains the circumstances that led to the supreme indignity of Nellie's confinement in the Poor Law "mad ward" while critiquing London Hospital's claims to balance care for individuals with managerial efficiency and bureaucratic rationality. As the reader follows Mrs. Dowell's journey, we see the breakdown in the hospital's complex circuitry controlling the flow of information and the disposition of bodies. When Harriet Dowell visits Nellie on Wednesday in Gurney Ward, Nellie no longer recognizes her and stares at the ceiling with "unseeing eyes." (See fig. 4.4.) The kindly Sister in charge of the ward promises to telegraph Mrs. Dowell if Nellie's condition worsens, but Mrs. Dowell returns on Sunday to an empty bed and understandably fears the worst. "Her head swam, her knees seemed to give way, she swayed where she stood. She felt someone collide with her and heard the matter of fact, stern voice of the nurse, 'Steady there, Mother. Look where you're going to please.'" This is a collision not just of bodies, but of incompatible modes of feeling and being. The nurse, "irritated by the interruption of routine which Visiting Day always caused," demands that Mrs. Dowell not "make a scene." But make a scene she does. She races from the officious junior nurse (presumably a probationer) to her supervisor, the regular ward nurse, whose "brisk cheery" voice "lacerates the nerves of patients;" to the Porter, who re-

4.3. London Hospital had many ways of gathering information about and representing the bodily interiors of patients like Nellie Dowell. Understanding their psychological needs was not part of the hospital's brief. Dr. F. J. Smith, Medical female patients case notes, 1910, RLHLH/M/14/65. (Copyright of The Royal London Hospital Archives.)

4.4. This photograph (c. 1923) documented the well-ordered modernity of Gurney Ward and created the false impression that staff members outnumbered patients. According to Muriel, Nellie occupied the bed in the far left corner of the ward during her catastrophic hospitalization in 1910. Gurney Ward, 1923. (Copyright of The Royal London Hospital Archives.)

fuses to disclose any information about Nellie because to do so would violate hospital regulations.[20]

Only the Sister treats Mrs. Dowell with dignity, but she too has singularly failed to live up to the panoptic demands of London Hospital's Head Matron Eva Luckes, who expected her Sisters to know "all that goes on in a large ward."[21] Nor did any trace of the egregious breakdown in communication make its way into Luckes' notes for the week, though she did express unhappiness with one of the nurse probationers on Nellie's ward, Miss Elsie Marvin, who was "not satisfactory . . . not thorough."[22] The Sister in charge of Nellie's ward explains that Nellie had grown so restless and violent that the nurses "had felt themselves unable to cope with her resistance" and transferred her to the "mental ward" of the workhouse.[23]

Muriel's word choice is significant: Nellie is not mad, she enacts "resistance"—although precisely what Nellie resists is never clarified. Sister apologizes for the "extraordinary error" of not telegraphing, but Mrs.

Dowell cannot be comforted: "The mad ward! My Nellie, gentle as a babe! Oh, if you'd only called me to sit with her." "Sitting" with Nellie was out of the question within the highly regulated space of the late-Victorian hospital. Nurses positioned family visitors like Mrs. Dowell as sources of "hygienic and moral contamination"—not allies and partners in healing their loved ones.[24]

Mrs. Dowell finds Nellie in the lunatic ward, broken in body and spirit, "with her forehead pressed against the window panes, gazing out into the world of freedom, counting the bars which emphasized her captivity and with tears streaming down her cheeks." At this point in "From Birth to Death," the narrative voice subtly modulates. Where previously the omniscient narrator relied upon the testimony of Mrs. Dowell and Nellie, now the narrator seems to speak from her own direct knowledge. Mrs. Dowell somehow extracts Nellie from the "mad ward," despite the fact that it is a Sunday and no magistrate is available to sign the necessary papers. No doubt Mrs. Dowell went to heroic lengths to release Nellie from "captivity." However, the Admission Register of Whitechapel Infirmary contradicts at least one detail of Muriel's story. Nellie was admitted on Friday morning, March 11, as a "homeless" or "destitute" "mental" patient. She was discharged to her mother on Monday March 14, not Sunday March 13.[25] "For months afterwards," the narrator of "From Birth to Death" explains, "Nellie's friends feared for her reason. She seemed obsessed by the idea fact that for two days she had been a pauper lunatic. Almost every moment of her incarceration was relived each day. Her memories haunted her."[26]

Muriel's narrative emphasizes the extraordinary power of classification and naming on Nellie's sense of herself. Called a pauper lunatic, she becomes one. As a seven-year-old who had suffered the trauma of involuntary removal from her mother to a Poor Law orphanage from 1883 until 1888, Nellie had spent a lifetime ensuring that she would never again be subjected to the degradation of the Poor Law. She had stood apart from her friends and fellow workers in London and Wellington, New Zealand when they had gone on strike to protest her ruthless employer's imposition of unjust wages and work conditions. She had used her exceptional skills as a match factory worker to earn steady wages and secure her economic independence and personal freedom. Keeping her job and supporting herself and her mother mattered more to Nellie

4.5. London Hospital was a grand private voluntary hospital serving East London's impoverished and diverse population. "The London Hospital from Whitechapel Road," E. W. Morris, *A History of the London Hospital* (London, 1910), 234.

than workplace solidarity. Muriel's narrative emphasizes that Nellie was helpless to prevent the hospital and the Whitechapel Infirmary from reducing her to a condition of abject dependence. The last extant page of "From Birth to Death" literally ends mid-sentence with Nellie "inert and passive" as the Charity Organisation Society denies Mrs. Dowell relief to help pay her rent. In Muriel's narrative, Nellie and her mother repeatedly encounter institutions and organizations—public and private—intended to succor the poor in their time of need that singularly fail to do so. "From Birth to Death" narrates Nellie's health crisis of 1910 in a register of moral outrage, which documents the soul-destroying machinery of a not-yet-repealed Poor Law.

Muriel's stories about Nellie's hospitalization offer an alternative to the self-congratulatory way in which officers of London Hospital characterized their institution. E. W. Morris, London Hospital's longtime Secretary and Governor, published his *History of the London Hospital* at the time of Nellie's hospitalization in 1910. (See fig. 4.5.) He affectionately chronicled its past and present achievements with an eye to stimulating philanthropic bequests. He paid homage to London Hospital's modernity as both an instrument of bureaucratic rationality and a car-

ing institution that refused to reduce patients like Nellie to mere "cases."
Morris introduced readers to the Hospital through the gratefully ador-
ing eyes of one of its impoverished patients "coaxed back to health and
happiness" whose "love" for the Hospital "is often mingled with a tenderness most touching." He celebrated the well-oiled modern machinery of the hospital with its up-to-date systems of communication, its
dazzling therapeutic technologies such as Finsen lamps and Tyrnauer
baths, and its efficiency in delivering 1,200 hot dinners across eight
acres of buildings. Morris extolled the "very full and careful notes . . . of
every case treated." "Classified and bound," these individual case reports formed "one of the most useful medical and surgical reference
libraries in the world."[27] They also document how hospital staff represented patients—including Nellie—in fulfilling their scientific and therapeutic mandates.

Much like Nellie's body temperature, her "case" file is disconcertingly
cool compared to the heat of Muriel's rhetoric. It presents Nellie as stable
and in relatively good health at the time of her admission and for the
first six days in hospital. Far from hovering near death, Nellie's doctor
observed "she has been better since in Hospital." Her once disabling
pain had dissipated; her digestion and appetite were good, her urine
normal. Over and over again, doctors and nurses commented on the
normality of her inward and outward signs. With utter detachment, the
file preserves her doctors' evaluation of the condition of her body surfaces and orifices. Her teeth are dirty and she has two stumps in the back
of her mouth; her tongue is "pink little furred;" her menstrual cycle
("catamenia") is "always regular" but she has "slight leucorrhoea" or vag-
inal discharge "present" during the doctor's physical examination. Only
the report of the vascular specialist indicated conspicuous evidence of
the long-term effects of rheumatic fever on her heart valves.[28]

The ideology of London Hospital permeated all its record keeping. In
Nellie's medical case file, she *almost* becomes the disease that afflicts
her. She is "case no. 624, Gurney Ward, S [single]; 30 (she was nearly
34)." She presented as a classic case of rheumatic fever but she is "becoming," her doctor notes, "Rheumatoid Arthritis type." "Chorea when
aet 12; sore throat at times. 9 yrs ago—1st attack ankles; 3 yrs ago and
last year—2nd and 3rd attacks. Ankles, knees, fingers. Treated at home.
6 weeks in bed last time. 4th and present attack: 11 wks ago—in ankles,

'chest bones', knees, fingers, jaws, much better now." Her P(resent) C(ondition): Knees and elbows only stiff; skin moist, Fingers wasted; Pulse, reg[ular], small." Her case file demonstrates the Hospital's aspiration to reduce disease—and hence Nellie as its bearer—to its scientific management. Nellie is quite literally all— and only—a diseased body.

And yet there are many moments when the case file cannot quite contain Nellie who spills out and beyond its carefully ordered pages. Nowhere is this more apparent than in the reports filed by the specialist in neurological and mental disorders. He initially described Nellie as a "somewhat nervous woman; lies quietly in bed and appears to be comfortable." The word "nervous" appears in the notes of nearly each of the nurses and doctors who observed her; it was also the word Muriel herself used to describe Nellie as a child. On her seventh day in hospital, her doctor added an ominous new entry: "Pt very noisy now. Suffers from delusions." The specialist in Mental Diseases decided she had become of "unsound mind": "morose, suspicious, & delirious." Invariably, these words signaled a patient's removal from London Hospital to the Lunatic Ward of the Whitechapel Infirmary.[29]

Why was Nellie sent to the lunatic ward? It is tempting to retrospectively diagnose her condition by offering a pharmacological explanation for Nellie's apparent change in behavior. She did receive a potent cocktail of different kinds of painkillers and narcotics including morphine; tincture of belladonna; tincture of opium; as well as a narcotic sedative and depressant, hyoscine, used at the turn of the century to relieve rheumatic pain and hysteria in women. Any one of these drugs might have induced the kind of behavior Muriel and her doctors described. She may have become disoriented by the experience of being in a hospital ward, so different from her slum flat on Brunswick Road.

We might also explain Nellie's transfer as an outcome of the indifference of London Hospital staff except that surviving evidence strongly contradicts such a claim. Her physician, F. J. Smith—a prominent Harley St. doctor and graduate of Christ's, Balliol, and London Hospital's

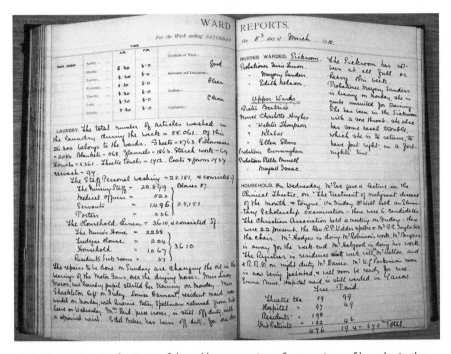

4.6. Matron Eva Luckes's careful weekly accounting of every piece of laundry in the entire hospital reflected the institution's commitment to economies of scale and accountability. Eva Luckes, Ward Notes, March 3–8, 1910, Matron's Log Book, LH/N/6/13. (Copyright of The Royal London Hospital Archives.)

own medical school—was renowned for his work on diseases of the chest and forensic medicine as well as his passionate commitment to serving the needs of his poor patients as individuals. Smith and other medical men used their unpaid affiliations with leading research hospitals to establish lucrative private practices and collect data for publications, but by 1910 he was already a wealthy man and highly respected clinician.[30] If the drugs administered to her triggered Nellie's removal to the lunatic asylum, it was also a function of how the hospital allocated its scarce resources and managed its patients' bodies. Within the medico-administrative logic of London Hospital, which tabulated the precise number of articles washed each week—55,061 for the week ending March 8, 1910—restless patients simply demanded too much time and attention from busy ward nurses and orderlies.[31] (See fig. 4.6.) They needed to be sent away.

Nellie's doctors and nurses at London Hospital were capable of distinguishing a delirium induced by fever or temporary incoherence caused by drugs from severe mental illness; but they lacked the resources to care for patients suffering from any of these conditions. The Hospital had no mental disorders ward. Nellie entered the Hospital as a case of rheumatic fever. She exited it—against her will but perhaps also because she exercised her will—when the medical staff described her as a case of mental disorder.

Nellie's removal to the Whitechapel Lunatic Asylum was much more than a shift from one therapeutic-disciplinary institution to another. It meant her reclassification from a charity patient at a private voluntary hospital to an involuntary inmate as a pauper lunatic ward of the state.[32] Poor Law infirmaries and asylums emerged from the 1860s onwards out of sheer necessity. Crusading medical journalists like Dr. Ernest Hart (Samuel and Henrietta Barnett's brother-in-law) had shamed workhouse officials by publicizing egregious cases in which sick paupers had died because they had failed to receive medical attention.[33] These institutions remained notoriously underfunded and understaffed even as they emerged as the *de facto* system of hospitals for most poor people in England. Admission to the lunatic ward was itself a complicated process, which must have left little time for medical staff to provide care for their patients. The admitting Poor Law medical doctor interviewed each patient, assessed her physical and mental condition, and communicated directly with a nurse from the medical ward who had recommended transfer.

The certification forms of the Whitechapel lunatic ward tersely summarize the results of these interviews. They chronicle the 23-year-old Jewish man who was absolutely certain he was going to marry Baron Rothschild's daughter and the Indian immigrant who claimed that he was a Bengal prince, come to Britain to demand that Queen Victoria (dead for several years) return his kingdom to him.[34] They constitute a remarkable archive not just of profound mental illness but collective cultural fantasies and reparative longings of the outcast poor. Admission to the Whitechapel lunatic ward generally required speaking with family members—clearly something that did not happen in Nellie's case. Perhaps this explains why the form certifying Nellie's admission as a lunatic has not been preserved. The staff at London Hospital and the

Whitechapel Infirmary may well have decided it was best to destroy the records chronicling the consequences of Nellie's "captivity."

Nellie's physical collapse in March 1910 marked the end of her two decades as an independent wage-earning factory worker. It left her economically insecure and vulnerable. It required her to rethink who she had once been even as it also allowed her to imagine in altogether new ways who she might become. For all their profound differences in tone and intent, "From Birth to Death" and Nellie's medical case file can both be read as narratives of exhaustion. Just as Nellie's doctors noted her "wasted" left hand, so too she was spent, used up. In an almost shockingly literal way, Nellie, the factory hand, had lost full use of her hand. Much like a piece of obsolete equipment, she had imparted a minute fraction of the total value of her hand into each of the millions of matches she had stuffed into matchboxes—exactly one hundred fifty at a time—twelve hours a day for twenty years for her employers, R. Bell and Company. Her value dispersed into commodities, she retained none for herself. Nellie could no longer support and understand herself through the labor she had performed so well for so long. She grasped an opportunity to redefine who she was by deepening her ties with Muriel and her ambitious schemes in Bromley-by-Bow.

"YOU DON'T LOOK NEAR SO WELL REALLY"

In the summer of 1916, Muriel suffered a debilitating breakdown of body, mind, and spirit. Her breathing was jerky, her heart missed beats and then raced furiously. It was an unpropitious time for her to be laid up at the Grange, her parents' lovely Loughton home. Kingsley Hall, the Christian revolutionary people's house and community center that she, Doris, and Nellie had founded in wartime Bow in February 1915, was still in its infancy. Hostile neighbors suspected that the Hall's pacifist-feminist residents loved their German enemies better than their countrymen. Who would tend to Muriel's evening clubs and classes, the women's suffrage kitchen serving cheap nutritious meals, her public ministry, and her various antiwar campaigns? For eight tedious months, she consigned herself to her doctors' care in the expectation that swallowing their medicines and obeying their orders would cure her. The family doctor, no doubt intent to curtail her activities in Bow, prescribed rest at home in Loughton supplemented by long solitary walks—"four hours if possible"—in Epping Forest.[35] An expensive masseuse came twice weekly to relax her tense muscles and nerves. Nothing worked and she fretfully contemplated a circumscribed life of semi-invalidism. If Nellie's "wasted" hand signaled her exhaustion as useable manual labor in the industrial workplace, Muriel, it seems, had likewise depleted her psychological and physical reserves. Much like "riding the rims" of a bicycle with flat tires, she had "liv[ed] on my nerves" and worn them jagged and raw.[36]

It dawned on her one afternoon in 1917—or so she claimed—that "there could be no respite from my struggle until I had somehow discovered how to harness my own puny, unreliable spirit to the Eternal Spirit." She came to see her illness as rooted in her disharmony with God's love, in her cultivation of pride, scorn and anger rather than opening herself to God's re-creative spirit.[37] The spiritual technology she devised for healing herself she called her "Prayer of Relaxation." It required a full hour each day of complete solitude and uninterrupted silence.

Muriel's Prayer eclectically combined physiology and psychology with Christian prayer, yoga-inspired meditative practices, and auto-suggestive techniques.

> I stretched myself out on my back concentrated on the nerve plexus at the back of the waist. Then I relaxed my muscles. This was no easy task, for I certainly had been seriously ill. I loosened my finger muscles and spread out my hand as though it were the model for an artist; made the whole arm relaxed, loosened, so that when it was raised, it fell heavy and inert . . . then the same with the toes and the feet . . . and the face muscles . . . I would listen to my own breathing, noticing it, how regular it had become, and as I listened it became slower . . . now the artificial stimulus [of daily life] was withdrawn and the nerves were recovering their tone. The tiredness was gradually transformed into deep restfulness, until I could say to myself, not in words, but in my mind, "With every breath I draw, I am breathing in the very breath of God." These life-giving exercises I continued indefinitely until my whole being seemed to be enveloped by a great sense of peace. . . .[38]

What precipitated Muriel's breakdown? Why did she find her way out of allopathic medicine with its biomedical "cures" for "disease" to the power of God's restorative Spirit with its promise of transformative "healing" in the name of "health"?[39]

Muriel is my chief informant about her own breakdown. In a type-script account of her illness, which Muriel entitled "1916- Very Early a/c of finding the Prayer of Relaxation," she linked her collapse to Bow and Kingsley Hall.[40] She began to feel "funny," she recalled, eighteen months after the Hall's founding in February 1915. In the margins, she made this connection even more explicit. "I was just over 33. Work at K.[ingsley] H.[all] kept expanding. Trustees, lawyers, accountants & banking ac-counts and a lot of voluntary help and public life—were all new to me and I became pale and wan looking."[41] Muriel recycled an explanation that had served well several generations of high-strung public men in Victorian Britain like the great Free Trade Liberal John Bright; she had worked too hard doing "men's" work for the public good.[42] The cause of her affliction *was* her affliction: selfless overwork.

No sources survive showing Muriel through the eyes of her doctors and nurses, friends and family members, with one important exception. Nellie had a great deal to say about Muriel's body and health. It was among her favorite topics. Her letters indicate that Muriel battled vari-ous health woes almost continuously from 1910 until her breakdown in 1916–17. Muriel's collapse had been long in coming and fulfilled Nellie's worst fears about her "closest friend on earth." On Valentine's Day 1912, Nellie enjoined Muriel to "ly on your back & scribble it [a letter to Nel-lie] & then I shall know you are resting your back."[43] Six months later, Muriel's back troubles still worried Nellie. Directly addressing Muriel and then responding to her own question, she "wondered if you were all quite well . . . how is your back I hope it is better."[44] In an undated letter probably written in December 1912 as Muriel and her brother Kingsley escaped the London damp and cold, Nellie seemed to endorse one of Muriel's favored explanations for her ill health: "don't work to[o] hard you are losing all your flesh you don't look near so well really." Nellie believed that Muriel's labors "tramping" around "dirty old Bow" weak-ened her. If dirt is matter out of order, Muriel, by virtue of her ladylike cleanliness, was a body out of place in Bow. It was also where Nellie most wanted her to be.[45]

Muriel refused to see herself as that familiar fin-de-siècle figure of degeneration, the morbid hysterical feminist spinster.[46] She must have known that she fit the bill down to its particulars. She was a feminist; she was unmarried; she was highly educated; she suffered from "nerves;" and she spent her time in the insalubrious slums of London rather than its perfumed drawing rooms. The political battle to control such women, their bodies as well as their representation, was waged at fever pitch in the decade before World War I. Through hunger strikes and public marches, feminists strategically used their bodies as weapons in their citizenship campaigns. The militant suffragette Emily Wilding Davison famously sacrificed hers for "The Cause" by throwing herself to her death under the King's horse during the Epsom Derby of 1913. Their critics as well as the British state likewise recognized feminists' bodies as sites for articulating and enacting their own gender and social politics. Anti-suffrage artists depicted them as anorectic unwomanly witches and lunatics while the state violated their bodily insides through forced feedings in prison.[47]

Muriel retrospectively tried her best to foreclose such interpretations of her breakdown by advancing her own. Mind, body, and spirit were intertwined just as nerves and the heart muscle were physiologically connected. Her illness, she insisted, stemmed from her failure to keep them in proper balance.[48] She eschewed allopathic medicine's diagnostic-disease model to which London Hospital subjected Nellie. Nellie's symptoms and case history, supplemented by clinical observations and test results, authorized medical staff to diagnose, name, and treat her disease. The structure of the hospital and the absence of a mental ward materialized its separation of mental from physical illness. Healing mind and spirit had no place in its delivery of up-to-the-minute allopathic medical services to the London poor.

The span 1916–17 undoubtedly marked a period of acute crisis in Muriel's life, a slough of despond worthy of a modern pilgrim's impeded progress. However, her own testimony—published and unpublished—suggests that neither her breakdown nor her ideas about the healing power of God's love simply "dawn[ed]" on her in February 1917. As with so much of Muriel's writing about turning points in her life, she produced many versions of this story, each with different details, each suggesting slightly different chronologies.

The origins of Muriel's shift from allopathic medicine toward spiritual healing can be traced to the previous decade. Her Prayer of Relaxation eclectically drew upon early twentieth-century transnational con-versations about spirituality, the body, health, and disease. During the interwar years, Muriel importantly contributed to these exchanges as a celebrated lay preacher, pacifist lecturer, and social worker. Before and during the war, she remained an eavesdropper—listening, observing, and borrowing from others as she saw fit.

It's not possible to reconstruct precisely Muriel's movements in 1910 when Nellie fell into a catatonic stupor. However, it's hard not to ask: where was she when Nellie needed her the most? Muriel probably knew nothing about Nellie's troubles that March because she spent so much of the year far from London. She and her parents made pilgrimage via Egypt to the Holy Land, where Muriel witnessed the "shameful" degra-dation of Christendom's holiest sites under the "scornful" supervision of bayonet-wielding Ottoman guards and bickering Christians paralyzed by sectarian rivalry. In Nellie's first surviving letter to Muriel, she looked forward to hearing tales about Muriel's adventures in "Egypt." The Les-ters then enjoyed several months in Mentone, a favorite destination of sun-seeking English tourists perched high above the Mediterranean in the Alpes Maritimes.[49] Doris, ever dutiful, stayed behind in a rented room in Bow to look after their many joint enterprises: the Mothers' Meeting at Bruce Road Congregational Church, the nonsectarian Fac-tory Girls' Club, and their Graded Sunday school classes in Bow and Loughton.

En route home from the continent, Muriel met a Christian Scientist "lady" who extolled the restorative powers of ten quiet minutes of daily meditative prayer and urged her to read "Mrs. Eddy's book," presumably her best seller *Science and Health with the Key to Scriptures* first pub-lished in 1875. (In an unpublished draft, she specifies that the meeting took place in April—placing her on the continent during Nellie's hospi-talization.)[50] The lady Christian Scientist deeply impressed upon Muriel that "Christians had no business to be weary, weak or miserable." "As though to test me," Muriel recalled years later, "a noxious germ settled in my throat on arrival in Paris. I wrestled with myself, refusing to give it even the hospitality of buying gargle or lozenges. It was hard work for a day and half, and then all was well. . . . Jesus relied with confidence upon God's cooperation in overcoming disease. This is a law of nature that we haven't yet learnt."[51] Here, Muriel offers a version of "hard work" depen-

dent on inward discipline and stillness. It functions as an antidote to the
ravages caused by the hard work of external doings even as it allows her,
as a Christian, to engage the world more vigorously and efficaciously.

What "law of nature" had she learned from Christian Science? The
flamboyantly prim, much-married Mrs. Mary Baker Eddy had cut a
large path across Victorian America. In language soaked in Manichean
imagery of light and dark, she promised to free men and women from
the fetters of their physical bodies and the crude dominion of matter
over spirit. There was a lot about Eddy's theological idiom to attract Muriel. First of all, it was woman friendly. Eddy paraphrased and rewrote
the Lord's Prayer to acknowledge God's male *and* female qualities: "Our
Father which art in Heaven" in her hands became "Our Father-Mother,
all-harmonious."[52] (Her critics cynically suggested that this revision encouraged her followers to worship her as the mother-god.)[53] Second,
Eddy promulgated her own version of "God is Love" theology. In her
chapter on "Prayer," she emphasized the fullness and perfection of God's
love: "Jesus aided in reconciling man to God by giving man a truer sense
of Love, the divine Principle of Jesus's teachings, and this truer sense of
Love redeems man from the law of matter, sin, and death by the law of
Spirit,—the law of divine Love."[54] She also challenged the entire apparatus of allopathic medicine, then consolidating its authority over a range
of alternative practices, including homeopathy. Faith and prayer, not
drugs, provided all that was necessary to heal the sick. Illness was merely
a construct of human consciousness that had failed properly to welcome
God's love: "Everything is as real as you make it," Eddy explained. "By
knowing the unreality of disease, sin and death you demonstrate the all-
ness of God."[55]

The same year that Muriel met her lady Christian Scientist on board
the Mentone-to-Paris train, Oxford's Regius Professor of Medicine Sir
William Osler offered an astute analysis of Mrs. Eddy's claims and cures.
Christian Science expressed the revolt against materialism and the
drug-saturated bodies of modern life. Its protest was a welcome sign of
youthful vitality. But it was also a "chaotic mass of rubbish." Mrs. Eddy's
denial of the reality of disease and pain was "monstrously puerile" and
more than a bit "comic." As another acerbic critic remarked, Christian
Science recommended that the best way to treat a "severed artery" was
to "argu[e] with it like a congressman."[56] It posed real dangers to credu-

lous seekers after its spiritual pabulum. Cynical detractors suggested that Christian Science owed its success in America and, to a lesser extent in Britain, to the surfeit of dyspeptics and neurasthenics for whom its spiritual healing was just the right sort of medicine. Its votaries were "idle women with money to spend" suffering from the overpressured, overstimulated "mental life" of the modern metropolis.[57] Sir William Osler acknowledged that Christian Science did in fact sometimes work wonders for those afflicted by "functional disorders" such as shattered nerves rather than "organic ones" like cancer. It gave them generous doses of optimism and freedom from the unrest of their daily rounds. Psychology, not physiology, subsidized the success of this new and dangerous "cult" among bourgeois women negotiating the challenges of modern life.[58]

Christian Science had established a beachhead in Britain in 1896, when Mrs. Eddy sent her disciple, Pastor Julia King-Field, to lead its first London congregation. By the time its impressive Byzantine-styled Portland stone building on fashionable Sloan Terrace had opened its doors in 1909, the movement had already splintered. Spiritual questers often don't make obedient followers. Many bridled against Mrs. Eddy's demands for complete doctrinal conformity. One offshoot of Christian Science was the Higher Thought Centre near High Street, Kensington, under the "inspired espionage" and "selfless service" of Mrs. Alice Callow.[59] Its guiding principles took self-help and positive thinking to one logical endpoint: "Man controls circumstances, instead of being controlled by them" because of the "absolute oneness" joining Creator and Creation.[60] Its roster of speakers suggests its hospitality to religious, gender, and sexual heterodoxy: it included Brotherhood Church leader J. Bruce Wallace, founding member of the Fellowship of the New Life, Edith Lees Ellis, and the homosexual Simple Life socialist, Edward Carpenter. It was these same activists whose ideals informed Muriel's "God is Love" theology and daily life at Kingsley Hall. By 1910, the Higher Thought Centre had formed its own suffrage organization that used "silence" as its main weapon. Here was one suffrage organization whose members could not easily be caricatured as shrieking hysterics.

Muriel seems to have extracted from Christian Science its axiomatic belief that allopathic medicine more often than not produced illness rather than cured it. She equated "lozenges and gargle" with the spiritually bankrupt and physically harmful world of commodified medicine.[61] Soon after returning home, she used prayer to call upon what she called "the Creative Spirit" to "put to route" a disease afflicting a small boy whom she knew. God was a source of "confidence" and "positive 'certain-sureness'" for Muriel; she would not see the boy's illness as God's "will."[62]

It wasn't just an isolated sore throat or an unnamed boy's illness that made Muriel pay attention to Mrs. Eddy's message. Muriel's precarious health and that of the people around her whom she most loved opened her up to new ideas about the body, illness, and God. Muriel no longer inhabited her body with the self-confident ease of the robust hockey-playing graduate of St. Leonard's. The balancing act between the two worlds of Loughton and Bow, of socialite and social worker, took a much heavier toll on Muriel than Doris. Doris, shy and uncomfortable with the limelight, never felt the tug and attractions of upper-middle-class sociability. Muriel did. Disgusted equally with herself and the glassy-eyed gamblers she met in Monte Carlo's casinos in 1913, Muriel lectured fellow guests at her Riviera hotel about the lives of "her" Bow factory girls.[63] (Nellie must have been the heroine of her story that evening; by that time, Nellie and her mother Harriet had moved next door to the Lesters on Bruce Road.) Muriel's tone is hard to gauge. Did she in hindsight recognize just how overwrought and absurd it was for her to scold the selfish rich and preach solidarity with London factory girls amid the cosseted luxury of their—and her own—Riviera hotel? Perhaps that was her point. In any case, the vignette hints at her growing instability of mind and body and her need to clarify her priorities.

The conspicuous failure of allopathic medicine to heal Nellie and her brother Kingsley must have further accentuated her growing doubts about its efficacy. When she returned from the Continent in the spring of 1910, she immediately faced the aftermath of Nellie's devastating en-counter with London Hospital's pharmacopeia of pain-relieving, mind-altering drugs. The next year, Kingsley suffered a severe medical crisis. After graduating in 1909 with a First in Chemistry Part II from Caius College, Cambridge, he and Muriel briefly shared a flat in Hampstead. [64] (See fig. 4.7.) While training for the Baptist ministry in 1910–11, he un-derwent surgery for appendicitis. It left him prone to debilitating illness. The Lesters organized their family life around finding resorts and sani-taria—in the English countryside and on the Continent—to prop him up. When he was well, Kingsley regularly joined Doris, Muriel, and Nellie in Bow. His easy humor and love of pranks charmed their friends on Bruce Road, including Nellie. She fretted about Kingsley's health because she liked him and because his illnesses so often took her beloved Muriel away from her and Bow. "I can't help sitting thinking of you going so far at away from me," Nellie confessed as Muriel and Kingsley fled dreary London in late 1912. Adopting a stoic stance, she continued, "but never mind its all for a good purpose bring Mr. Kingsley home quite well & strong. . . ." This proved an elusive goal.[65]

Muriel's anxieties about Kingsley's health exacerbated her own "nerves." His death in September 1914 was one of the defining traumas of his sisters' lives despite—and perhaps because of—the family's decision to cast aside the outward conventions of black crepe and darkened windows. With steadfast good cheer, the Lesters were determined to celebrate his life rather than mourn his loss.[66] Whether this gave Muriel or Doris sufficient scope to grieve is hard to say. His death triggered an exponential increase in his sisters' activities and obligations in Bow, as if they could transform his loss into their good works. Muriel invested his short life with a youthful aura of sweetness, generosity, and promise.[67] The family created an elaborate mythology about discovering a note among Kingsley's papers, which left all of his money to Doris and Muriel in support of their philanthropic work. The magazine of his old public school, Mill Hill, suggests this was not entirely true. The December 1914 number of *Mill Hill Magazine* reported that a paper was found among Kingsley effects "expressing his wish that 100 guineas be left to the Mill Hill games committee."[68] Nellie, their neighborhood friends, along with "boys" from the Loughton Union Sunday school, Ben Platten and George Bowtle, helped the Lesters tear down the upper-story wall separating their small home at 60 Bruce Road from Nellie's next door at 58. They christened the new space "Kingsley Rooms" to commemorate the memory of Kingsley's "altruistic" life. It was also a constant reminder of his death.

By late December, Muriel and Doris accepted their father's challenge to refurbish an abandoned hellfire Baptist Chapel around the corner from Bruce Road and turn it into the first Kingsley Hall—a triumph of a loving God over a punishing one. Muriel immediately threw herself into thorny negotiations with the London Society for Women's Suffrage about who would cover the costs of launching a suffrage restaurant for wives of soldiers and sailors and women war workers from nearby Pearse's Army Factory and Anderson's Water-proof Factory. By January 9, 1915, Muriel had succumbed to the pressure. Her correspondence with the Society continued unabated, but she had checked herself into Huntley's Health and Pleasure Resort.

Huntley's was an elegant hydropathic retreat in Bishop's Teignton, Devon long favored by progressive Nonconformists, including the Lesters.[69] (See fig. 4.8.) Muriel had spent many months there with Kingsley between 1912 and 1914 during his frequent illnesses and had thrown herself into religiously based charitable work in the community.[70] Muriel must have overcome her growing scruples about the booming commercial health economy of spas, mineral waters, and curative baths. Huntley's menu of services included Turkish, hot and cold baths; massages; galvanic stimulation; and a simple "restorative" diet consumed in a stunning setting overlooking the Teign estuary.[71] This pampering failed to reinvigorate Muriel. By January 23, with Kingsley Hall's opening less than three weeks away, she moved to another hotel, Erin Hall in Torquay, a haven for invalids and semi-invalids seeking restorative sea breezes.[72] Remarkably, neither Muriel nor Doris ever wrote a single word about Muriel's deteriorating health, much less her absence from Bow during the crucial weeks before the opening of Kingsley Hall. Not for the first or last time, Doris along with Nellie and their circle of friends must have taken over many of Muriel's jobs.

Muriel's divided life, Nellie's hospitalization, Kingsley's illness and death, and the pressure of her growing public obligations in Bow contributed to her deteriorating mental and physical condition in the years between 1910 and her breakdown in 1916–17. To add to Muriel's woes, her father survived a serious illness while her mother's angina worsened in 1915. One calamity seemed to follow another. Her socialist, pacifist, and feminist politics in wartime Britain, examined much more fully in the next chapter, provoked suspicion, anger, and sometimes violent assaults on her person and her reputation. These tense years severely tested her commitment—and Nellie's—to loving neighbors who did not love them.

Muriel's "God is Love" theology, along with her engagement with Tolstoyans and vegetarians in the first decade of the twentieth century had already brought her into close contact with a range of religious and ethi-

4.7. Kingsley Lester's precarious health preoccupied the entire Lester family. After his death in 1914, his sisters opened Kingsley Rooms and Kingsley Hall to commemorate his altruistic life and their love of him. (Courtesy of Bishopsgate Institute.)

4.8. The Bishop's Teignton Hydropathic resort was a well-appointed sanatorium favored by the Lesters and many other wealthy Nonconformists. Huntley's, Bishop's Teignton Hydropathic. (Postcard in author's possession.)

cal traditions far outside mainstream Nonconformity. All of these factors encouraged her to explore early-twentieth-century Britain's flourishing pluralistic culture of medical, spiritual, and healing practices. This was a contentious domain. Allopathic doctors, hospitals, and medical schools discredited and disparaged their many rivals. And devotees of various forms of divine healing overlooked what they shared in common, the better to viciously attack one another.[73] At the same time, it was a moment of great fluidity that made it easy for Muriel to borrow from many different traditions in forging her own approach to faith, spirituality, the body, and health.

MURIEL LESTER'S SPIRITUAL THERAPEUTICS

If religious modernism and evangelical missionary Protestantism framed Muriel's religious life in the first decade of the twentieth century, Christian mysticism and faith-healing traditions in dialogue with Eastern "spirituality" and German naturopathy shaped how she cared for her mind, body, and spirit during the next several decades. The powerful currents of late-nineteenth-century secular modernity strengthened the movement toward a world characterized by disenchantment, bureaucratic efficiency, and scientific rationality. But this is only part of the story. The new century also gave abundant signs of a spiritual renaissance buoyed by revived interest in magic and mysticism, faith and feeling.[74] Muriel borrowed the phrase "The Renascence of Wonder" to characterize moments of childlike joy that she believed were essential antidotes to the soul-deadening mechanized routines of adult life in the modern world.[75] World War I's industrialized mass violence heightened the ostensibly anti-modern tendencies of modernity by fueling interest in paranormal religious-psychic phenomena.[76] To cope with the irrationality of the war's indiscriminate carnage and the loss of his own soldier-son Kingsley, Britain's beloved master of ratiocination, Sir Arthur Conan Doyle publicly affirmed his longstanding attraction to Spiritualism. So too did many others. Theirs was a grief that refused to accept the finality of death. The unquiet war dead seemed only too happy to converse with the living.[77]

Christian Science and its eccentric offshoots were only one among many sources of Muriel's evolving spiritual therapeutics. The more complicated her own life felt, the more she was drawn to Christian apostles of simplicity. She turned to Robert Hugh Benson's queer novel, *Richard Raynal, The Solitary* (1904) about an androgynously beautiful fifteenth-century mystic and ascetic contemplative, who espouses simplicity and silence in making himself a vessel for God's message.[78] The seventeenth-century lay Carmelite kitchen worker from Lorraine, Brother Lawrence, helped Muriel reconceptualize the relationship between the body, illness, prayer, and spirituality.[79] His Catholicism proved no impediment to his popularity in early twentieth-century Britain. Perhaps it was his emphasis on the disciplined hard work involved in opening one's heart to God's presence, in disavowing worldliness, that paradoxically appealed to the Protestant strivings of women and men like Muriel. His maxims as well as his conversations and letters (published as *The Practice of the Presence of God*) circulated widely in cheap editions like the 6d "New Heart and Life Booklets" published in "artistic wrappers" by H. R. Allenson and available in English and Esperanto. Lawrence offered homely advice about how he brought God's loving presence into every moment of his life by emptying his heart so God could fill and possess it. His was emphatically a lived, felt, embodied theology of the everyday. Being with God required neither church nor chapel since God could be found from within.

Lawrence sacramentalized everyday life: he felt more united to God in the conduct of his humble quotidian occupations than when he retired to pray and meditate. Feeling and doing, not thinking, paved Lawrence's path to God's love. Pain and sickness were favors from God, whom he called "the only Physician of all our ills . . . the FATHER of the afflicted, ever ready to succor us." It was much better to endure bodily pain for love of God than to poison the body with doctors' remedies. Diseases of the body created opportunities to cure diseases of the soul. "Can a soul truly with God feel pain?" Lawrence asked.[80]

Many in early-twentieth-century Britain, including Muriel, answered Lawrence's question, but none did so with more lyrical power than Evelyn Underhill. Instinct and intuition counted more than reason, stillness more than motion for Underhill, Britain's most eloquent twentieth-century student of mysticism and Christian psychology. Contemplation was the fruit of rigorous self-discipline achieved through meditative mental calisthenics. The mind learned to shut out the false reality of stock exchanges and barristers' briefs, of surface appearances and the confining logic of classifications in favor of "fluid facts which have no label." The most intense love and purified desire, abetted by an iron strong will—emphatically not "sentimental aestheticism or emotional piety"—guided the quest for the sensory paradise of union with God. At least this was how Underhill interpreted the signs of her restless times during that fool's paradise summer of 1914. Nor did Underhill retreat from this position amidst the din of guns on the western front and the ceaseless hum of munitions factories at home.[81] War made mysticism more necessary, not less, she argued.

On long prewar rambles in Cornwall, Doris introduced Muriel to Underhill's ideas.[82] Characteristically, it was Muriel who did the most with them in her private life and, later, in her public ministry from the 1920s to 1950s. Underhill and Lester were active members of the Guild of Health and contributed to its publications. Left-wing Anglican ministers like Percy Dearmer and Francis Boyd, eager to reconcile their faith with the latest discoveries of modern science, founded the Guild of Health in 1904.[83] They refused to give the psychologist and psychoanalyst a monopoly over tending to the inner lives of men and women. Jesus, Guild members insisted, was "the Divine Psychologist."[84] Silence was the way to welcome God's indwelling. It cleansed the "subconscious" of its neurotic "complexes" far better than then the noise of psychoanalytic talk. The Guild harmonized God and Nature by arousing the Church to a "fresh recognition of the place due to the healing of the mind and body in the Gospel message of Salvation." Individual and corporate health was indivisible. Its members, like Underhill and Lester, refused to accept a "mutilated gospel that disconnects body from the soul."[85] The Guild provided a forum to exchange ideas about mind, body, and spirit, many deeply influenced by South Asian religious beliefs and body disciplines.[86] The body was nothing less than a school for faith for Lester and Underhill. Mysticism and modernity, faith and science, happily sustained one another. Unlike Christian Scientists, Guild members insisted that the body, its pains and sufferings, were as real as the Incarnation itself.[87] Like Mrs. Eddy, they insisted that faith had everything to do with achieving good health.

Underhill's *Practical Mysticism: A Little Book For Normal People* (1914) translated for a broad lay audience the arguments and spiritual message contained in her erudite best seller, *Mysticism: A Study in the Nature and Development of Man's Spiritual Consciousness* (1911). *Practical Mysticism* was an early-twentieth-century "how to" and "self-help" book for the everyman and everywoman. "Normal People" may have been Underhill's intended readers, but *Practical Mysticism* advanced its argument by inventing and invoking a queer genealogy of Western poets and mystics, saints and sensualists like Walt Whitman and Joan of Arc,

Florence Nightingale and General Gordon.[88] Underhill deftly negotiated the fine line separating her celebration of the joyful physicality of mystical union with God from explicit eroticism.[89] *Practical Mysticism* had plenty of competitors on bookshelves overflowing with guides to living a good life. Practitioners of the booming business in physical culture and life reform such as the muscular vegetarian yoga-loving Eustace Miles also promised to rescue beleaguered souls from the enervation of modern urban life.[90]

Underhill's Christian psychological understanding of interiority spoke directly to people like Muriel struggling to harmonize conformity to the demands of surface sociability (the temporal flux of "becoming" for Underhill) with pursuit of a spiritual vocation (the eternal permanence of "being"). For those whose "worried consciousness" had become a "restless and complicated thing," Underhill offered words of comfort. There was, she assured her readers, a "stillness" at the "centre . . . [at] one with the rhythm of the Universal Life." This was an insideness utterly at odds with London Hospital's technologies that allowed doctors to see the inner workings of the body while remaining blind to the needs—and souls—of patients like Nellie. It also differed from what Underhill called "psychoanalysis," which accounted for the strife and contradictory impulses of mental life without providing a way into the truest self.[91]

To explain the communion of the purified self with God, Underhill, like Muriel, directed her gaze East to the poetry of Kabîr, the fifteenth-century Muslim weaver-turned-disciple of the Hindu guru Ramananda. The version of Kabîr to whom she turned was one Underhill had helped to invent for the English-speaking world.[92] *One Hundred Poems of Kabîr* was the outcome of her collaboration with the Bengali poet Rabindranath Tagore, who visited England in 1912–13. Tagore and Underhill depicted a Kabîr who exalted a loving God and a God of love. He reconciled Islam and Hinduism, the everyday homespun pleasures of married life with divinely transcendent delights. Underhill likened him to Paul, "the tentmaker," and Bunyan, "the tinkerer." Most scholars now concur that Tagore-Underhill's representation of Kabîr bore at best a hazy resemblance to the historical one. By the time *One Hundred Poems* was published for the London-based India Society in 1914, Tagore had become a literary sensation. He was awarded the 1913 Nobel

Prize for Literature for his English-language poems, *Gitanjali*, the fruit of his engagement with the Irish poet W. B. Yeats.

Tagore's literary partnerships suggest that Kipling's oft-quoted line that "East is East, and West is West, and never the twain shall meet" could not have been less true in early-twentieth-century Britain.[93] As Kipling readily acknowledged, the "twain" met every day in all sorts of exciting ways and unexpected places. Fitness guru Eustace Miles opened his popular *Avenues of Health* (1902) with a long quote from that champion of a revivified virile Hinduism, Swami Vivekananda, whose teaching had inspired Tagore.[94] Vivekananda's 1895 platform appearances in England, like Tagore's in 1913, electrified audiences. Clothed in long "orange-coloured robes of the Buddhist priest" with a "monk-like girdle" around his waist and a massive turban on his head, he preached and embodied a universal "spirituality" based upon the renunciation of gross material things in exchange for perfect union with the "supreme and absolute self."(See fig. 4.9.) Far from asserting the essential and exclusively Oriental origins of his teachings, Vivikananda acknowledged his debts to European Romanticism and the writings of a German weaver's son, Johann Fichte.[95] As Peter Van der Veer persuasively argues, the point of such genealogical excavations is not to identify the true origins of "spirituality" with Christian mystics or German romantics or Indian gurus. Rather, he shows that the very concept of "spirituality" developed in tandem with the idea of the "secular" as twin facets of modernity. Both emerged out of the global circulation of people and ideas between East and West. Spirituality was so attractive to women like Underhill and Muriel Lester because it "enabled the inclusion of a variety of traditions under the rubric of universal morality without the baggage of competing religious institutions and their authoritative boundary maintenance."[96] In the first decades of the twentieth century, Underhill distrusted institutional religion altogether. Lester simply felt free to move between churches and institutions as she saw fit.

Underhill's fusion of Indian philosophical and religious traditions with mystical Christianity prefigured and influenced Muriel's own spiritual therapeutics. Muriel frequently drew upon Tagore in her writings and lay religious services, long before they met and became friends in 1926. A borrowed line from *Gitanjali* helped Muriel practice Brother's Lawrence's "Presence of God" among the crowd of commuters she en-

4.9. Swathed in orange turban and robes, the Swami Vivikananda captured a wide following in Britain and the United States in the 1890s with celebrated appearances at major international congresses and gatherings. Swami Vivekananda, December 1896, London, image courtesy Wikimedia Commons.

countered riding the London underground. As she prayed for passing strangers, she silently quoted Tagore's words to herself, "Thou hast pressed the signet of eternity upon many a fleeting moment of my life." To readers of the *Evening Standard* in 1921, she casually mentioned that she included selections from Tagore and Edward Carpenter, Britain's foremost poet of democracy and same-sex love between men, along with the Bible in her religious services.[97] Such "religious" readings signaled Muriel's commitment to all sorts of transgressive border crossings.

Through prayer, Muriel learned how to heal her sick body while loving all of God's creation. To think like God meant ignoring "barriers of class, race, and nation" and "dropping all labels."[98] In her Christian therapeutics, the quest for individual health necessitated the pursuit of global social justice. A world without labels was one free from oppressive hierarchies. In Underhill's terms, this promised fluidity without flux. For Muriel, the body was the most intimate locale from which humans embarked on the task of building up the Kingdom of God on earth. Her own body functioned as a fine-tuned barometer, registering not only her own struggle to achieve health-giving balance but the world's. Spiritual practices such as her Prayer of Relaxation restored Muriel to health. Health was itself spiritual.

The actual techniques of breathing and posture Muriel used in her Prayer of Relaxation were heavily indebted to those of Henry Lindlahr. Lindlahr popularized the science of German naturopaths, Louis Kuhne and Adolph Just, as well French psychologist Émile Coué's work on the power of autosuggestion.[99] Kuhne and Just taught modern men and women how to lay claim to their most primitive life forces through contact with water, light, earth, and air. Coué championed the power of self-spoken words to shape each person's physical and psychic reality.[100] In Lindlahr's *Practice of Nature Cure* (first published in 1901 and often reprinted), he outlined a daily regimen for health that anticipated Muriel's. "When you awake in the morning from sleep, lie flat on your back in a completely relaxed position. For a few minutes let a feeling of rest, peace and good will permeate your whole being. Then in a prayerful attitude of mind . . . say . . . I am thankful for being alive and for all the privileges and responsibilities which life confers upon me. . . . By the power of the divine will within me I WILL BE WHAT I WILL TO BE."[101]

Here was a democratic system of self-help calculated to empower every man and woman. Achieving good health lay largely in the hands of the afflicted, not in expert knowledge controlled by institutional allopathic medicine.[102] Disease, far from manifesting either the will of God or the invasion of germs from outside the body, stemmed from the individual's failure to live in harmony with God and Nature. "We are what we say and believe we are," might be one way to summarize Lindlahr's lowbrow scientific teaching. The dark side of this relentless do-it-yourself optimism was its implication that the sick were responsible for their own infirmities.

Muriel's Christian therapeutics, consolidated in her 1917 Prayer of Relaxation, gave her a portable healing technique combining solitude and contemplation with action. Derived from a wide range of global sources, it reflected her syncretic approach to faith and spirituality. It made literal her rejection of the opposition between mind and body, reason and feeling, science and faith. The Prayer of Relaxation was a ritualistic practice and a highly disciplined performance of bodily postures and utterances that Muriel enacted with sacramental devotion. Her health problems from 1910 to 1917 are a powerful reminder that Muriel struggled to achieve the persona of inward and outward serenity that she later came to project so effortlessly. Through habitual repetition, Muriel and those around her must have found it hard to differentiate the performance of self from the self. This was Muriel's paradoxical goal: to produce an inside so filled with God's love that there was no agonistic self to be anatomized, psychoanalyzed, or pathologized.

BODIES AT WAR

Muriel's catastrophic collapse must be set against the extraordinary traumas war exacted on human bodies at the homefront and the warfront. Praying oneself back to health with "autosuggestive" messages about God's loving "breath" may have done wonders for Muriel in 1917. But what could it do for millions of women and children suffering hunger and the shattered bodies of soldiers returning home from the War's far-flung fronts?[103] As Muriel convalesced at the Grange in 1916–17, this thought must have crossed her mind. Every day, she had no choice but to see the injured soldiers in the fifteen-bed Voluntary Aid Detachment (VAD) Hospital, Braeside, established two hundred yards from the Grange in a "gabled Victorian villa" in its own garden.[104] (See fig. 4.10.) Braeside was a satellite institution attached to the Colchester Military Hospital. Such hospitals were staffed by doctors and nurses, many, like Muriel, daughters of the well-to-do who volunteered to do their part for the nation at war. Wounded soldiers were sent there to convalesce, some to return to military service, others to civilian life with pensions based

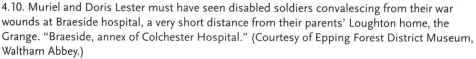

4.10. Muriel and Doris Lester must have seen disabled soldiers convalescing from their war wounds at Braeside hospital, a very short distance from their parents' Loughton home, the Grange. "Braeside, annex of Colchester Hospital." (Courtesy of Epping Forest District Museum, Waltham Abbey.)

on the extent and nature of their disablement.[105] Muriel positioned such men as neither blameworthy perpetrators of war's horrors nor as soldier-heroes, but as instruments and victims of mechanized mass violence. Like the soldiers' wives and women war workers fed at Kingsley Hall's suffrage kitchen, they too needed to be counted among the victims of an industrial capitalist imperial state.

The men's bodies with whom Muriel had the most reason to identify were those of her many friends who refused to serve the warfare state. It was one of the few compensations of Kingsley's death, Muriel admitted, that he had been spared the social opprobrium, pain, and suffering that awaited conscientious objectors in World War I Britain.[106] In its exaltation of the right and need of the individual to exercise free moral will, the prewar liberal state affirmed two principles incompatible with its war effort: an all-volunteer army and the legal category of conscientious objector. In theory, the volunteer army ensured that only men of the highest caliber would be sent into battle because they had chosen to serve their country. This form of recruitment was meant to demonstrate the superiority of the British state and its respect for the freedoms of its citizens compared to its continental counterparts. It proved a dysgenic nightmare as the opening months of war disproportionately claimed the lives of highly educated, physically fit well-to-do men.

Suffering for the sake of conscience has a long history in modern Britain. However, the individual's right to claim conscience as the grounds for exemption from complying with a law had been codified only recently around parents' refusal of compulsory vaccination of their children. Parliament included a "conscience clause" in the 1898 Vaccination Act (amended and made simpler in 1907).[107] Muriel had also seen the power and limits of "passive resistance" at the turn of the century when leading Nonconformists led by Reverend Clifford invoked religious conscience and refused to pay taxes to protest the new Education Act's funding allocation for Church of England schools. Henry Lester had joined Clifford's movement and some of the family's property had been placed under an order of distraint.[108] H. H. Asquith's Liberal government established a set of procedures and institutions (Local Tribunals, Appeals Tribunal and a Central Tribunal) by which men could prove the *bona fides* of their conscientious objection to war and be offered a range of alternative forms of non-combatant service or absolute exemption. Put another way, the Liberal government invented the conscientious objector to wartime service who then confronted the State as an intractable problem. Britain's manpower needs far outstripped its ability to attract recruits at home and in its empire—which contributed hundreds of thousands of colored men from India, Africa, and the Caribbean. As Asquith's government teetered on the brink of dissolution, an illiberal wartime coalition gathered strength; compulsion in the name of militarist patriotism was inevitable. Muriel's breakdown more or less coincided with the state's introduction of conscription in 1916—a process set in motion by the National Registration Act of 1915 followed by conscription of unmarried and finally married men in June 1916.

What impact did this have on Muriel? Many in Muriel's close circle of friends and fellow workers, including Ben Platten and Stephen Hobhouse, claimed conscientious objection and went to prison for their convictions.[109] She spent her days "accompanying friends to tribunals, attending the subsequent proceedings, and visiting them in jail."[110] Ben Platten had been one of Doris and Muriel's first students in their Loughton Sunday school in 1902. His family was part of a small number of artisans and laborers living in their well-to-do suburb. Platten and his best friend George Bowtle had volunteered their services for each of the Lester sisters' schemes in Loughton and Bow. They had been part of the original group of men and women who created Kingsley Rooms on Bruce Road and refurbished the first Kingsley Hall. Platten wrote to Muriel on behalf of her Bruce Road men's group to console her after Kingsley's death in September 1914. By that time, he had taken a post as an elementary school teacher at Buckhurst Hill Boys' School near Loughton. His application for exemption from military service on grounds of conscientious objection was thus a matter for more than usual public concern and discussion. After all, he was charged with instructing and guiding boys and young men. A well-known town elder publicly declared that he would rather his son dead than endure exposure to Platten's despicable teachings on Christian conscience.

Muriel must have felt proud of Platten and terribly responsible for him. As he informed the Appeal Tribunal in Loughton, "before the war he had learned the Sermon on the Mount so well that when the war started he had no hesitation in taking such an attitude."[111] In his original application for complete exemption from military service, he outlined his reasoning. War was inconsistent with Christ's principles. He could undertake no labor that would bolster the warfare state. War, he explained, could only be eradicated by the recognition of the "Brotherhood of Man." To the Secretary of the Committee on Employment of Conscientious Objectors, he later elaborated "the only sure basis on which society can be built is Love as expressed in the life and death of Jesus Christ."[112] These were the core lessons Muriel and Doris had taught him.

A local Essex newspaper hints at just how accountable Muriel and Doris must have felt for Platten. It reported that Platten submitted a letter vouching for his conscientious objections to war from none other than Henry Lester along with the new minister of Loughton Union Church, Dr. Wicks. Nor was Muriel immune from the sting of local gossip about who had led young Loughton men like Platten to lose their "souls," "honour" and "manhood." The "Loughtoniana" column of a local newspaper provocatively asked, "Who is behind these Loughton conscientious objectors, teaching them their new gospel? If what we hear be true, someone is doing a grave disservice to the country." [113]

What part such vicious insinuations played in Muriel's collapse is impossible to say, but they surely exacerbated her frayed nerves.

Platten, like most conscientious objectors, kept vigilant tabs on his own body and wrote a detailed manuscript about his three months in Maidstone prison and Wormwood Scrubs prison. (He published a short version of this in 1920 for Kingsley Hall's periodical *The Gleam*.) Producing such narratives were a form a resistance and part of conscientious objectors' collective strategy to cultivate public sympathy. Young and healthy, Platten apparently had no problem adjusting to the scant diet and harsh discipline of prison life before his release to undertake civilian work building roads in Scotland for the duration of the war. By his own reckoning, he managed rather well. Platten's ease in withstanding the state's bodily work demonstrated the efficacy of his ethics and his manly fortitude.

Such was not the case for conscientious objector Stephen Hobhouse, scion of a great Somerset landed gentry family. Hobhouse had married Muriel's friend and co-worker at Kingsley Hall, Rosa Waugh, in the late spring of 1915. This was a union of "Eminent Victorian" families in the name of Christian social justice. Rosa's father Benjamin was the founder of the Society for Prevention to Cruelty to Children and her brother-in-law, Sir William Clarke Hall, the leading force behind the Children's Charter of 1908. Hobhouses—from John Cam to Emily and L. T.—had dotted the landscape of radical political culture for the better part of a century. Doris and Muriel Lester and Rosa and Stephen Hobhouse supported one another's daring experiments in Christian ethics for the rest of their long lives.

Muriel had known about Stephen for years. Mutual friends had even urged him to court Muriel. High-strung, often depressed and inclined to excessive introspection, he had a long history of nervous breakdowns since his Tolstoy-inspired renunciation of his family estate more than a decade earlier. He, like Muriel, had also moved into a small slum flat in East London, the better to do God's work. Successive imprisonments as a conscientious objector in 1916–17 left him badly weakened in mind and body. Surviving his ordeal endowed Stephen with an aura of moral purity, but it was far from a masculine victory.

Stephen Hobhouse's prison letters to his wife Rosa excruciatingly detailed his bodily functions and deprivations as well as his own self-imposed mortifications.[114] Rosa, one of Kingsley Hall's first two residents, was Nellie and Muriel's close comrade and interlocutor during these years. She circulated Stephen's letters widely and even published sections of them. Stephen's able exceptionally well-connected mother Margaret Potter Hobhouse (Beatrice Webb's sister) shared a distilled version of them with the entire world in her best-selling chronicle of the unjust treatment of conscientious objectors, *I Appeal unto Caesar*. Mrs. Hobhouse also broadcast news about Stephen's afflictions at the hands of the state in hundreds of private letters to leaders of church and state, many of whom were family friends.[115] By 1917, Stephen Hobhouse was Britain's best known and most controversial conscientious objector. His selfless labors on behalf of the outcast poor *before* the war challenged public perceptions of conscientious objectors as selfish shirkers. This did not please leaders of the war effort like his godfather, Lord Alfred Milner, and the Prime Minister Lloyd George.[116]

Reports about conscientious objectors' bodily sufferings—their beatings and abuse by soldiers and prison guards, the horrendous conditions of their incarceration and restricted diets—were a staple of pacifist papers like the *Tribunal* and the *New Crusader*. (See fig. 4.11.) They were the stuff of daily conversation among Muriel's friends and fellow travelers. Such tales produced an updated Protestant martyrology of suffering in the name of Christ, which abetted conscientious objectors' claims to the moral authority of victims of state violence. They had two other crucial functions. For the British state, conscientious objectors' suffering in prison after an initial refusal of exemption became the only acceptable proof that an objector's conscience was genuine. Denial of conscience and subsequent willingness to endure repeated punishments perversely proved that a man had always—already—possessed one. Second, objectors' bodily disablement in the name of conscience functioned as a de facto rebuttal of those who frequently contrasted conscientious objectors' selfish desire for comfort with their soldier-hero brothers' unspeakable hardships and deprivations.

Did Muriel think about her breakdown as a somatic, psychological, and distinctly female response to her principled stance as a pacifist? Was it the only way she—as a woman—could participate in the War's masculine moral economy of embodied suffering? She does not say but I suspect that she did. While Muriel's health troubles predated the war, her nervous breakdown in 1916–17 made manifest the war raging within

4.11. This cartoon reflects the centrality of body politics to debates around conscientious objectors, their popular representation, and their experience of imprisonment."What a CO Feels Like," *The News Sheet* 13 (1917): 8. (Courtesy of Swarthmore College, Peace Collection.)

her. Nellie was determined to do her part to get Muriel better even as she longed for Muriel to return to Kingsley Hall, to Bow, and above all, to her.

GRAMMARS OF DIFFERENCE, EROTICS OF ILLNESS IN NELLIE'S LETTERS TO MURIEL

Muriel's many illnesses from 1910 to 1917 ensured that she was often convalescing far from Bow and Nellie. Her physical absence from Bow instigated Nellie's letter writing and Muriel's. Letter writing gave Nellie a way—physically, intellectually, and psychologically—to connect with Muriel, to collapse the distances between them. Nellie's letters were one means by which she articulated who she was in relation to Muriel. They convey words, ideas, and feelings. They are also objects, literally ink on paper. Muriel held, read, reread, and ultimately archived them for herself and posterity. They bear Nellie's trace as their author and Muriel's as their recipient.

Nellie's letters enunciate and constrain several sets of intertwined dynamics between distance and desire, presence and absence, hierarchy and equality. They are full of chatty details about mutual friends and neighbors, Muriel and Nellie's efforts to live by their own rigorously ethical creed, the ravages of war on the homefront, and Nellie's unsatisfiable longing to be close to Muriel. Throughout all the letters, Nellie discusses her health and Muriel's. Love and illness are the master tropes of her letters. Their rhythms and patterns approximate spoken rather than standard written English. Written in "informal" prose with little regard to rules of grammar and syntax, they burst with conviction and freshness.[117] Their immediacy is one rhetorical effect of her writing, a way that Nellie demanded Muriel's attention and affection. The speaker implied by a pronoun, the "I" or "you," shifts without warning in midsentence. Thoughts sometimes follow a logic of feeling and association rather than sequential argument.

Nellie's letters bear striking resemblance to Gertrude Stein's daring World War I modernist texts. Comparing them challenges entrenched hierarchies of literary value: Stein's writing is literature, Nellie's letters aren't. It also encourages the kind of careful analysis of form and language that we take for granted in reading Stein. Listen to these snippets of dialogue from Stein's wartime "Do Let Us Go Away, A Play" (1918) and then to a passage from one of Nellie's wartime letters to Muriel:

> (The lawyer.) I went often to see you and every day I said I love you better I do love you better. That's it.
> They were together and they said John are you going. He said something.
> They were altogether. I often think about it.

And this second passage:

> (Paul) Thunder. It will not rain yet. It usually does not at this season. I hope that a war will come. I would like to be interpreter.

Here is Nellie's description of an early winter evening in wartime Bow (see fig. 4.12):

I think now the
nights are drawing in more
will come Kingsley Hall
will look like your lovely
Hall at Loughton but how
can it, that looks to clean
only fit for Sunday clothes
don' touch but ours is
come in don't go home &
change come & be happy
(nice cup of tea a) Dough
Nut or a cocanut Bar
ask Miss Harris
about a nice cup of tea
lovely. two bites & the
Dough Nuts gone
its pouring of rain & our
lodger is coming home to
tea I think she is happy[118]

4.12. Nellie Dowell to Muriel Lester, n.d., Nellie Dowell Letters. (Courtesy of Bishopsgate Institute.)

Nellie wittily evokes the upper-middle-class tidiness and scolding formality of the Grange ("your lovely Hall at Loughton") as "only fit for Sunday clothes don' touch." She captures without judgment and without benefit of the ponderous compound verb—"are gone"—just how quickly hungry people eat free doughnuts: "two bites & the Dough Nuts gone." Her use of the present tense makes her palpable—as if she were standing directly before Muriel. There is a delightful disconnection in the successive clauses "its pouring of rain and our lodger is coming home to tea I think she is happy" that creates the effect of taking us into her mind, almost as each thought enters it. Nellie does not explain that perhaps her lodger will come home *because* it is raining outside and she needs the comfort of tea and Nellie's company. Nor does Paul in Stein's text explain that the sound of thunder prompts him to think about the arrival of rain, which leads him to anticipate the coming of war; and with war, the part he hopes to play in it as an interpreter. With remarkable compressed economy, both women convey meaning without needing to fill up the spaces between each clause.

Stein critics call her use of such techniques "auditory consciousness" and laud her daring attempt to reproduce the mind's "associational paths" as part of her representation of human interiority.[119] Stein herself characterized it as writing "the movement of the words spoken by someone who lately I have been hearing sound like my writing feels to me as I am writing."[120] Nellie, unlike Stein, did not set out to revolutionize literary forms and conventions. She wrote letters to engage and manipulate Muriel's feelings, not intervene in the domain of "literature." There is, however, more than a morphological resemblance between Nellie's and Stein's prose. The speech patterns of working-class moderns like Nellie provided the audible archive upon which Stein, the literary modernist, drew in her writings. How Nellie used language—not just the information contained in her letters—is historically significant. Her language, like Stein's, cannily represented inner feelings, desires, and longings. Her literary practices must be counted among the many border crossings that motivated and sustained her relationship with Muriel.

To read Nellie's letters is to imagine hearing her clear strong voice. However, they emphatically do not offer direct access to some authentic naïve proletarian. They are deceptively candid epistolary performances. Nellie calls attention to the moment and scene of her writing as well as the impact of her prose on Muriel. She sought Muriel's approval for her literary efforts even as she excused her grammatical shortcomings by reminding Muriel that she lacked a room of her own in which to write. In the midst of her nephew Will's disruptive antics—he "dressed the cat up and bandaged his paw"—Nellie averred that

> this is a funny
> letter all I can hear is Aunt
> Nell so how do you think I
> am writing to you with these
> monkey's round me[121]

The letter leaps from critical self-reflection about her compositional abilities to the social conditions of her writing to direct conversation with Muriel.

Nellie knew that her own grammar rhetorically enacted difference even as she reflected on how difference structured her relationship with Muriel. At the end of a letter about Muriel's role as her teacher and moral guide, Nellie imagines Muriel as a critical reader of her letter. The letter metamorphoses into a schoolgirl exercise, scrutinized by the teacher for "mistakes."

> You will see my mistakes you
> know you are going to give me
> lessons in writing letters some
> day, I hope for you are my teacher
> in every thing so please tell me
> my mistakes & if you have time
> & not catch cold later on give
> me some more chapters[122]

Such expressions remind us that Nellie toiled over these letters and recognized their significance. Her eloquence redounds to Muriel's credit. Her "mistakes" create opportunities for more private "lessons," which included reading and discussing chapters of books together such as a volume of Tolstoy's Christian writings.

Nellie's non-conforming prose underscored her status as that elusively desirable object of bourgeois benevolence, the Cockney factory girl. She invites Muriel to spend more time with her by appealing to

Muriel's pedagogical and missionary impulse to improve her skills as a writer. If Muriel lovingly encouraged Nellie to want to be more like her, Nellie mastered the art of reminding Muriel of her obligations to Bow and to Nellie. Nellie's letters show her using difference to serve her own needs. As with so many of Nellie's expressions of love, illness hovers close on the horizon. Her request for "more chapters" is accompanied by the caveat that Muriel "not catch cold later."

Letter writing was an expression of love and a form of labor, which required Nellie to draw upon the cultural and intellectual resources available to her. Health and illness are recurring themes in them. For example, she informed Muriel that her mother, Harriet Dowell, was too sick to leave the house and her nephew Willie had broken his leg and was hopping around her tiny flat. Nellie also frequently discussed her own precarious health. After her hospitalization and confinement, she understandably distrusted doctors even as her broken body required ever more vigilant care. Instead of returning either to London Hospital or the Poplar and Stepney Poor Law Asylum hospital, she decided to take advantage of her close proximity to the Christian evangelical medical mission, Berger Hall, established by the Grattan Guinness's Regions Beyond Inland Mission in South Bromley. (See fig. 4.13.) Nellie confided to Muriel that "Mother [Harriet Dowell] and I are both going under Dr. Macrae at Bergar Hall he has done the Scout [Harriet] a lot of good I have lost all faith in Drs but I ll give him a trial."[123]

Nellie and Muriel played the part of nurse and patient for one another. These roles created opportunities for substantial physical and emotional intimacy between them even as it allowed them to negotiate—and renegotiate—relations of power and authority across their differences. This is evident in an early letter Nellie wrote soon after she returned home after spending a month recuperating with Muriel and her parents. Nellie recalls a scene of great intimacy with Muriel that is all the more stunning when contextualized. Henry and Rachel Lester must have invited Nellie to join them—and share a bedroom with Muriel—on a family holiday in pursuit of good health. It's hard to imagine what their servants thought about this witty Cockney ex-factory worker sharing such close quarters with the elegant educated Miss Lester. "I hope I shall always know you for you don't know how I love you, for all you have

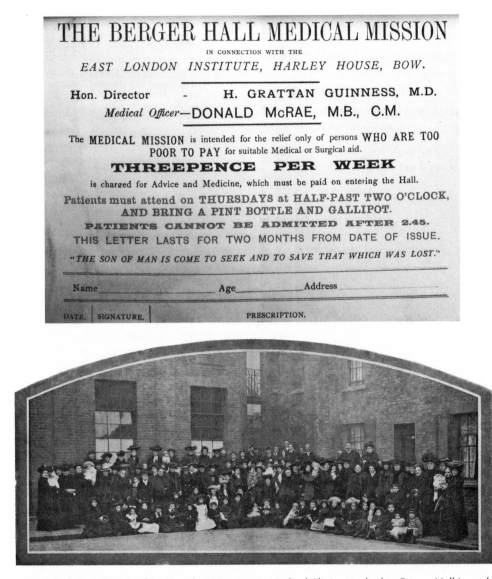

THE BERGER HALL MEDICAL MISSION

IN CONNECTION WITH THE

EAST LONDON INSTITUTE, HARLEY HOUSE, BOW.

Hon. Director   -   H. GRATTAN GUINNESS, M.D.

Medical Officer—DONALD McRAE, M.B., C.M.

The MEDICAL MISSION is intended for the relief only of persons WHO ARE TOO POOR TO PAY for suitable Medical or Surgical aid.

THREEPENCE PER WEEK

is charged for Advice and Medicine, which must be paid on entering the Hall.

Patients must attend on THURSDAYS at HALF-PAST TWO O'CLOCK, AND BRING A PINT BOTTLE AND GALLIPOT.

PATIENTS CANNOT BE ADMITTED AFTER 2.45.

THIS LETTER LASTS FOR TWO MONTHS FROM DATE OF ISSUE.

"THE SON OF MAN IS COME TO SEEK AND TO SAVE THAT WHICH WAS LOST."

Name_____ Age_____ Address _____

| DATE. | SIGNATURE. | PRESCRIPTION. |

4.13. Called the "Church of the People," MacKenzie Medical Clinic attached to Berger Hall issued tickets to poor men and women like Nellie granting them access to low-cost medical care outside the Poor Law asylum and hospital. Large numbers of people from Nellie's South Bromley neighborhood, including Dowell family members, came to see Dr. McRae and his staff on clinic days. *Sources*: (Top) Charles Booth Papers, B/176. (Courtesy of the Library of the London School of Economics and Political Science.) (Bottom) People outside Berger Hall's MacKenzie Clinic, Dr. Harry Guinness Clinic, *Not Unto Us, A Record of 21 Years Missionary Service* (London, 1908), 60–61.

done for me I can never repay you, but if I ever stop with you again I'll brush your hair off for it was a pleasure I don't often get and sleeping in your room and keeping you awake to talk to me."[124] (See fig. 4.14.) Nellie invokes tropes of exchange, debt, and delight.[125] She claims she can "never repay" Muriel but then immediately suggests that brushing Muriel's hair is one way she already has. This form of repayment produces intense pleasure for Muriel and Nellie. Gratitude for Muriel's part in restoring Nellie's health cannot be separated from the pleasures of their shared bedroom.

Nellie captured the importance of illness to their relationship in a letter she wrote to Muriel in 1916:

I have not gone off
I will when you get better
for I feel I have got
something to do with your
illness[126]

Nellie's phrase that she had "something to do with [Muriel's] illness," did not mean that she had caused Muriel to be sick but rather that Muriel's illness gave her something to do. Her self-chosen job was to make "my patient" Muriel strong so that they could do their joint work of waging peace in war-mad East London.[127]

On Valentine's Day 1912, Nellie diagnosed Muriel's work for their Bow neighbors as the root cause of Muriel's illness: she toiled too hard on behalf of others.[128] This was a diagnosis that Muriel herself came to endorse. Nellie conceived of her labor to care for Muriel as vital to Muriel's efforts on behalf of Bow. Muriel's physical exhaustion leveled the playing field between them by giving Nellie a chance to "beat" Muriel at her own game of nurturing others:

are you really better I have
thought about you, & was so
sorry for I know you won't
give in & rest & look after
every one else I think I
can beat you, now you always
think you are strong, but I

4.14. Nellie Dowell to Muriel Lester, 1916, Nellie Dowell Letters. (Courtesy of Bishopsgate Institute).

> know now & when you come
> home & do your Tramping
> round Bow, I shall have to
> look after you[129]

As Muriel's nurse, Nellie claims to know her patient better than she knows herself. Her phrase, "but I know now" implies that she possesses insights that Muriel lacks. After all, Muriel "thinks" she is strong but Nellie "knows" that she is not. Muriel needs Nellie to "look after" her. From Nellie's perspective, Muriel equates "rest" with a kind of submission, a "giv[ing] in." Nellie's admiration for Muriel's devotion to Bow vies with her faint disapproval of Muriel's "tramping round Bow." Nursing Muriel bolstered Nellie's sense of her own authority but it also risked repositioning her as the bourgeois invalid's servant.[130]

Christian prayer was no substitute for Nellie's ministrations during Muriel's catastrophic breakdown. As Nellie explained in an undated letter probably written in the autumn of 1916, when zeppelin attacks and gunfire were fairly common over Bow:

I am so glad you are better
I don't want you to go away now
you have got me well to look after
you, I know what you have gone
through with ear ache poor little
Arthur has been laid up a week
with it & he looks so frail and white
I hope you don't look like that[131]

Illness bound them together in a complex web of reciprocity ("now you have got me well to look after you") even as discussing their neighbors infirmities (Arthur's ear ache) affirmed their shared world of interests and community-based labors. The word "now" functions as a syntactically ambiguous bridge between two separate but linked thoughts. Nellie does not want Muriel to go away "now"; at the same time, Nellie is "now" well and thus able to take care of Muriel. As this letter makes clear, Muriel's ill health gave Nellie permission to write and talk about Muriel's body even as she imagines Muriel's physical condition by describing "poor little Arthur's" frailty. Illness offered Nellie and Muriel a socially legible and acceptable explanation for their deepening physical and emotional intimacy.

Nellie's letters chronicled her physical ailments and Muriel's decisive role in taking care of her. Nellie believed that Muriel's interventions had literally saved her life: "You have been a true friend to us & I shall never forget you for it, I might have been with poor Annie by now if you had not looked after me & told me things for my own good."[132] On March 24, 1912 she was

thankful to say I feel
alright so you see that my
change with you done me
a lot of good & built me
up for the rest of the
winter[133]

Illness let Nellie integrate herself into the Lester family. Nellie closed virtually all her letters to Muriel by sending her best wishes and affection to Henry and Rachel Lester. Muriel reciprocated by writing her prose narrative "From Birth to Death" through Harriet Dowell's eyes. Loving one another's families affirmed their own love. It also permitted them to see one another as family members—a form of fictive kinship with one another.

Nellie's preoccupation with health—her own and Muriel's—needs interpreting against the backdrop of her traumatic incapacity to engage in traditional waged labor and her identification of illness with the workhouse and its humiliating loss of independence. She daily witnessed the devastating impact of sickness on working-class families and households. In a rare moment of self-pity, she lamented to Muriel that she "got sacked" from everything she did—everything, that is, except from her "work" with Muriel. Aware of her own physical and economic vulnerability, Nellie fretted and thought of "all sorts of things, I ought not to worry over my future but I thought I had to go & earn something you did not tell me anything before you went & I got worried I hope never to live on my Mother or anyone."

I suspect that Muriel left Nellie money without seeking or receiving Nellie's assent. Nellie's gratitude does not alter the fact that Muriel may well have acted within a philanthropic gift economy predicated upon class and economic inequality. It also hints at how essential Muriel and Doris were for Nellie's economic survival. Did they regularly help pay the rent of Nellie and Harriet Dowell's flat directly next door to them on Bruce Road? My guess is that they did. Nellie devoted her days and nights to sustaining the sisters' many projects in Bow. She could not have had time to do much else, besides taking care of her many nieces and nephews who move in and out of her letters. If the Lesters gave Nellie money, she certainly did more than her share of community-centered labor to earn it. Such an interpretation gestures at the possibility that Nellie and Muriel created an economy that rewarded care giving as ethically and socially valuable work.

However much Nellie wished to be with Muriel, she also protectively wanted Muriel to be away from the health-endangering demands and dirtiness of life in Bow. Nellie enacted her ambivalence on the level of syntax, which literally mimics the free associative rhythm of spoken English as conflicted feelings flow into one another:

> Just a little note to you
> so glad you are having a
> lazy time & out of dirty
> bow at present, but I wish
> you were here so many
> would be glad to see you
> poor little Emma West
> is so very ill with Rheumatic
> fever, but I am pleased to
> say she is a little better[134]

The end of the line of writing on the page sometimes substituted for punctuation and suggests that her literary production was partially shaped by a visual spatial relationship of words on the page rather than the regulatory abstractions of formal grammar.

On the level of content, Nellie transmuted her individual longing to be with Muriel—her "wish you were here"—into a collective desire for her return—"so many would be glad to see you." This gladness functioned as a subtle reminder, one that does not quite rise to the level of rebuke, that Muriel is having a "lazy time" and *not* doing the work of caring for their mutual friends and neighbors in Bow. Nellie literally did Muriel's work for her by devoting her attentions to Emma West: "today I go round and sit with her to give her Mother a little time downstairs to look after the rest of her family I know she [Emma West] is a favourite of yours." She concluded this train of thought by claiming that she does not "want to write and tell you any troubles" though this is precisely what she has just done by informing Muriel that one of her favorites is "so very ill with Rheumatic fever." This sentence carried powerful resonance since Muriel knew only too well that her foremost favorite, Nellie, had almost lost her life and sanity to rheumatic fever. Nellie's phrase, "she is *a* favourite of yours," [my italics] suggests that Nellie may have seen herself as one of many especially beloved girls and women in Bow vying for Muriel's love.

Nellie used illness and bodily infirmity to produce an intimate argot, her own language of love. In caring for Muriel's sick body and being cared for by Muriel, Nellie found a way to rhetorically enact mobile relations of reciprocity across the vast class divide that separated them. She also produced a version of herself as an embodied desiring proletarian subject, albeit one whose desire to have and "belong to" Muriel could never be satisfied; and whose body was unfit for factory labor. In a rare moment of witty self-affirmation in 1922, Nellie allowed herself to acknowledge just how much she meant to Muriel: "bless your old gums you do love your old fashion Nell sometimes not so clever, but such a warm spot for such friends."[135]

Nellie never confused reciprocity for equality. Nor did she want to be Muriel's equal. Muriel's clean white hands were always part of what made her so attractive to Nellie. As she poignantly explained to Muriel, "I do hope some time I can do something for you you see if you was one of us & wanted help it is easier for us to give help but you of course are different." Nellie cherished Muriel's "difference" even as she struggled within herself to allow Muriel to be like her and tramp through the dirty streets of East London as they engaged in social, religious, and political work.[136] Nellie was acutely aware of her nonconforming grammar. She liked to imagine Muriel looking over her shoulder as she engaged in her epistolary exercises, commenting, correcting, applauding her efforts. Nellie enacted and thematized a grammar of difference that playfully recognized difference itself.

"WHY IT IS I DON'T KNOW"

What sort of friendship was Muriel and Nellie's? A body of brilliant feminist and queer scholarship on women's friendships provides a broad range of interpretive strategies by which to make sense of the surviving fragments of their remarkable partnership. Scholars now recognize the social and cultural centrality of white middle-class women's "romantic friendships" to nineteenth- and early twentieth-century Anglo-American domesticity. Spanning a continuum from chaste to fully sexual relationships, such friendships nested comfortably within and complemented marriages to men.[137] Other women forged "erotically charged" "intimate friendships" that were much less congenial to patriarchy even as they borrowed the spousal language of opposite-sex conjugality. Martha Vicinus's nuanced cultural anthropology of such partnerships emphasizes "the intricate interplay between the spirit and the body" in women's language of amity and exchanges of Bibles, prayers, and locks of hair. Some preferred the "erotic pleasure of unfulfilled, idealized love" to physical consummation; others, like Mary Benson, wife of the Archbishop of Canterbury, enjoyed sexual relationships with her female spiritual soulmates. For Benson, religion and erotic love between women were "inextricably twined cords."[138] Vicinus ushers "intimate friends" into the ranks of lesbians. Such an approach presumes rather than asks whether these women *had* a sexual identity at all. It is far from clear that either Muriel or Nellie understood herself through and with her sexuality. What happens when we shift focus from sexual identity (was she a lesbian?) to explore the conceptual space between "the sexual" and "the erotic"?

Cogently critiquing the blurry inclusivity of the continuum paradigm, Sharon Marcus defines "the sexual" as "genital arousal" while situating "the erotic" in the expansive and labile domain of desire and pleasure. Armed with this distinction, she offers precise historically informed procedures by which to differentiate friendship, erotic obsession, and sexual partnership while acknowledging that sometimes extant evidence makes this impossible. "We can distinguish female friends from female lovers," she avers, "only by situating [their] words in the fullest possible context." "In iterated, cumulative, private language and mutual dependence, we can locate a tipping point that separated Victorian women's ardent friendships from the sexual relationships they also formed with one another."[139]

Can such a "tipping point" be found in Nellie's "private language" of love? In what ways did Muriel and Nellie's cross-class loving partnership reproduce or part ways with the well-delineated rituals of middle-class women's friendships? We know a great deal about how elite men like Oscar Wilde eroticized working-class men, the "rough trade" with whom they had sex. About how class difference may—or may not—have structured female same-sex desire and sex, we know far too little. Nellie's and Muriel's partnership promises a way to open up this field of inquiry.

As Nellie struggled to reclaim her personhood after her release from Whitechapel's Poor Law lunatic ward, she and Muriel turned to God to

heal her psychic wounds and bind them closer together. Sometime in
November 1910, Muriel left Nellie a Bible. Nellie

> wondered where it [the Bible] came from
> & looking inside saw your name
> dated the 21 that is our special
> date to remember our first
> loving each other
> but I am ashamed to say it is
> new & put away it will be the
> only one I shall use now[140]

Nellie narrated a moment in which Christian faith and love cross, overlap, and merge. Muriel introduced Nellie to a well-established ritual in
which the gift of a Bible betokened God's love as well as Christian love
between giver and receiver. (See fig. 4.15.)

Guiding a beloved friend to God was a well-trodden pathway by
which women heightened their intimacy with one another. In the seven-
teenth century, "seraphic friendships" untainted by sexual desire helped
women (and even some men and women) lead one another toward
mystical union with God. Letters served as ideal vehicles for such friendships by reducing the temptations of fleshly pollution. Physical presence
mattered less than spiritual intimacy.[141] Eighteenth-century female
Methodists sustained an "erotics of friendship" in which "romantic gestures and emotions . . . were consciously cultivated as an aid to spiritual
progress."[142] For middle-class women like Muriel, Bibles, along with
locks of hair and rings, were among the most important objects of exchange within a female gift economy of Christian love. Not so for Cockney factory women in early twentieth-century Bow like Nellie who
could not afford such gifts. Laboring women pooled their money to help
out their "mates" in times of crisis. Those in steady employment sometimes "clubbed" funds to help each other make specific purchases. But I
suspect that none of Nellie's relatives or friends in Bow had ever received
the gift of a Bible, much less one from a woman as fine as Muriel. Nellie
and Muriel began with vastly different cultural frames by which to interpret the meaning of Muriel's gift and love. What was familiar to Muriel
was probably quite unfamiliar and extraordinary for Nellie.

4.15. Nellie Dowell to Muriel Lester, 1910, Nellie Dowell Letters. (Courtesy of Bishopsgate Institute.)

Nellie's Bible, like the declaration of their feelings, remained "new." Her delight in finding it mingled with shame. Syntactically, her confession of shame follows directly after "our first loving each other." She has disappointed Muriel, or so Nellie imagined, because she has not immediately begun to study, read, and handle the Bible. She has kept it too new. This will change, she promises: "it will be the only one I shall use now." Nellie expressed her desire to have and be with Muriel by desiring to be like Muriel and gain her approval. By inscribing Nellie's Bible with her name and the date of their "first loving each other," Muriel sacralized and commemorated their loving partnership. Nellie's Bible must have been the most precious thing that she ever owned: God's word literally touched by her beloved friend's hand.

We will never know what Muriel and Nellie said on the twenty-first but it marked one of the many transformations of love that Muriel hoped would flow from her "God is Love" theology. The year 1910 was a pivotal moment in Nellie and Muriel's lives. From Muriel's perspective, "our special date to remember our first loving each other" may well have inaugurated a new phase in her lifelong project to use God's love to re-make the world, one soul at a time. From 1910 until her death in 1923, Nellie joined Doris as Muriel's indispensable partner in bringing Christian revolution to Bow. Love was the engine and goal of this revolution in everyday life. It proved exhilarating, confusing, and challenging for Nellie and Muriel.

Nellie's letters consistently lament Muriel's many absences from Bow and express her longing for a greater and more exclusive intimacy than Muriel seemed willing to sanction. Muriel seems to have understood the power of absence. She did not physically hand Nellie her Bible but left if for her to discover on her own. Perhaps she felt too shy to witness Nellie reading her loving inscription. When Nellie was with Muriel, she suffered the pangs of a schoolgirl crush and found herself shy and tongue-tied.

> I do miss you
> why it is I don't know
> every time is worse to me but
> I always feel shy of you when
> you come home
> so don't take notice of me
> & think I don't love you.[143]

Nellie acknowledged that letter writing allowed her to be closer and more expansive with Muriel than their actual time together. In a gesture that Muriel could not have overlooked, Nellie penned this undated

The Grange,
Loughton
Essex.

Dear Miss Lester
Just a little note to you
so glad you are having a
lazy time & out of dirty
how at present, but I wish
you were here so many
would be glad to see you
poor little Emraa West
is very ill with Rheumatic
fever, but I am pleased to
say she is a little better
today I go round & sit
with her to give her Mother

4.16. Nellie Dowell to Muriel Lester, n.d., Nellie Dowell Letters. (Courtesy of Bishopsgate Institute.)

letter on stationery with the printed return address crossed out: ~~The Grange, Loughton, Essex~~. (See fig. 4.16.) By so doing, Nellie implicitly invited Muriel to remember their shared intimacies and confidences at the Grange. She had been welcomed there as a beloved friend and family member. The crossed out words underscored her removal from this cherished scene: the Grange was not her home, the Lesters, not her family.

Distance inflamed desire while liberating Nellie to articulate her feelings.[144] She enacted this dynamic by moving from the emphatic assertion, "I do miss you," to the unanswered question, "why it is I don't know" which culminated in a complex double negative: "don't . . . think I don't love you." This rhetorical structure recurs throughout the letters and did important psychological work for Nellie. She asked Muriel to "take notice" of her by giving her permission to ignore her and "don't take notice of me." She laid a strong claim to her feelings for Muriel only to soften and deflect them through questions and negatives. A process of thwarted self-discovery sustained their epistolary relationship. Nellie did not know and could not name why she missed Muriel so much, why each separation only intensified and made "worse" her longing for her. Rather than posthumously presuming to know what Nellie did not, we may be better served considering the implications of her "not knowing."

Knowing and not knowing, naming and not naming same-sex desire have preoccupied scholars for at least four decades. Knowing and naming same-sex sexual desires marked, we are told, the simultaneous birth of homosexual identities and communities as well as the emergence of harsher forms of surveillance and punishment of them.[145] Assertions of sexual self-knowledge recapitulate the metanarrative of "coming out." They function as signs of empowerment for the individual and the community into which the sexually knowing self is ushered.[146]

Nothing suggests that Nellie had access to sexological categories, even if Muriel may have. Those who have examined most closely who did—and did not—have knowledge of "lesbianism" across British society in the early twentieth century have found no evidence that proletarian laboring women like Nellie would have even heard the word.[147] We can chart with much greater precision the Mediterranean voyages of F. R. Leyland's SS *Lesbian* in the late nineteenth century than the youthful life history of its sexological namesake during this same time period.[148] Nellie would have been much more familiar with "mateship"—a form of mutually supportive, loving friendships between laboring women.[149]

For the past two decades, "queerness" has emerged as an analytical category detached from categories of identity and their twofold politics of self and community. Queer offers an alternative to gay and lesbian that encompasses a broad range of nonconforming desires and practices, imaginings and actions. Refusing fixity, queerness disrupts normative categories of identity that produce insiders and outsiders, those who belong and those who do not.[150] Some argue that its purchase depends upon its mystifications, illegibility, and refusal of identity. That which cannot be fixed cannot be held hostage to the imperatives of

norms themselves. Such an account dismantles a gay and lesbian pan-
theon of foremothers and forefathers in favor of those who evaded or
refused to name their sexuality.[151]

What intellectual work can queer do in thinking about Muriel, Nellie,
and their relationship? Muriel's rejection of all "labels" as constitutive of
oppressive hierarchies and norms might be construed as a kind of queer
politics *avant la lettre*. Characterizing Nellie's feelings for Muriel as
queer rather than homoerotic or lesbian forecloses the need to make
claims about her sexual identity and underscores the likelihood that neither Nellie nor Muriel felt the need to invoke languages of sexual self-
hood.[152] In any case, it's not possible to parse the boundaries between
non-sexual caring labor and the erotic pleasure that Nellie and Muriel
may—or may not—have felt when Nellie brushed Muriel's hair and they
chatted late into the night.[153] What is extraordinary is that they managed
to create for themselves a world in which a wealthy shipbuilder's daughter and a half-orphaned match factory girl could share such intimacies
and revel in such pleasures with the blessings of their families.

Nellie's language of love is entirely untouched by sexology or what
Laura Doan calls "Sapphic modernity." She sometimes playfully used
terms such as "Old Maid" and "widower" to denote sexual and marital
status. On Valentine's Day 1912, she coped with Muriel's long absence by
asking Muriel to find her a "proper widower" but only "one that will let
me go with you or he will not suit." Had they joked with one another
about the respective demands of "proper" and "improper" widowers? As
if to deflect the danger of masculine intrusion upon their intimacy, she
immediately reassured Muriel that "I am longing for the time to see you
again it seems Months instead of weeks since I saw you & then I did have
you all to myself sometimes." "Having" Muriel all to herself was a pleasure Nellie craved but rarely enjoyed. She accompanied her declaration
of unwavering love for Muriel—"nothing will turn me what if you do"—
by purporting to be "a miserable Old Maid." Her capital letters imply
irony, a recycling of a stock phrase that she does not quite accept for
herself. Nellie loves Muriel and enjoys herself far too much to be either
"miserable" or an "Old Maid."

Nellie's lighthearted substitution of Muriel for a hypothetical "proper
widower" hints at a language of same-sex domestic partnership; but it
does so without any trace of gender "trouble." Nellie invokes neither

husband-wife relations nor an eroticized sisterliness so typical of wom-
en's "intimate friendships." In "From Birth to Death," Muriel quoted
Nellie's own explanation for why she never married. Marriage provided
no security for working-class mothers like her beloved grandmother
(Harriet Sloan), mother (Harriet Dowell), and older sister (Florence
Dellar). Their loss of male breadwinner spouses through death or disablement had impoverished them and their children. Nellie, so Muriel
tells us, was determined to avoid the gendered violence of poverty on
families, especially its material, affective, and psychological costs to
women as wives and mothers. Class, economics, and gender—not sex,
sexology, and identity—explain Nellie's choice to remain single.

What about Muriel's love for Nellie and her own status as an unmarried woman? Not a single word or phrase in Muriel's three biographical
sketches of Nellie suggest that she harbored erotic feelings for her. She
conveys admiration, gratitude, tenderness, empathy, and love for her.
But longing? Or possessiveness? Or desire? None. This may be a function of when she wrote these narratives and deeply asymmetrical
sources. Muriel drafted her homages to Nellie in 1923, nearly thirteen
years after their "first loving" one another. Nellie had been an invalid for
several years, rarely venturing out of her house next door to the Lesters
on Bruce Road. The years of their most intense partnership were over.
Several other single women had joined what Muriel called her "synthetic family" in Bow and claimed their share of her affections.[154] Nellie's
letters are without doubt the most erotically charged documents in Muriel's emotionally cool archive. Muriel's letters to Nellie have not survived, although Nellie alludes to them in her own. The libidinal asymmetries in their friendship may well be accentuated by archival
asymmetries. There is no Nellie Dowell archive apart from Muriel's
where we might find Muriel's loving letters to Nellie written as their relationship unfolded and deepened after 1910.

In her prolific body of published life writing, Muriel never discussed
singleness and sexuality, her own or others.[155] In response to a challenge
posed c. 1925 by an "intellectual brother in law" about why she lived at
Kingsley Hall, Muriel explained one benefit of the Hall to the young
people in the local community: "Sex relationships can develope [sic] nor-
mally in Kingsley Hall instead of being either fiercely repressed or fur-
tively experienced in the semi shadow of a street door." Here, she articu-

lated a sense that there is such thing as normal sex relationships but that they require suitable environmental conditions in which to flourish. Rather than reflecting on her own sex feelings, she shifted ground by declaring that Kingsley Hall allowed her to "spend my life in the midst of one of the jolliest biggest families I've ever known." [156] There is no evidence that Muriel experienced romantic attraction to any person. Nor did anyone feel the need to invoke a youthful "disappointment" in love to explain why she never married—a tactic used by the biographer of the famous bachelor bishop of London, Arthur Foley Winnington Ingram. Her friend, the pacifist memoirist Vera Brittain, mourned a fallen soldier sweetheart while forming an intimate companionship with Winifred Holtby and marrying.[157] Perhaps Muriel was untouched by sexual desire or celibacy was what she wanted.[158]

Contemporaries did not share Muriel's reluctance to talk about sex and singleness. In the late nineteenth and early twentieth century, defenders and critics of spinster do-gooders proffered psychosexual accounts of them. Some, like sexologist Havelock Ellis and homosexual rights advocate Edward Carpenter, praised single women for turning their "inverted" or "uranian" same-sex desires into social good. Altruism, they argued, expressed their homosexuality. For William Dampier Whetham and his wife Catherine (Stephen Hobhouse's first cousin), single women like Muriel lacked the "wholesome instinct of the family." They were social menaces disguised in the sheep's clothing of disinterested virtue. As part of their jeremiad against the "caravanserie" of restaurants, hotels, and modern consumer culture, the Whethams joined Muriel in calling for "simplicity of life." At the same time, they pathologized unmarried women whose "social, political, philanthropic, and educational work" grew out of their selfish quest to gratify their own desires for influence in public life.[159] Selfishness, not selflessness, actuated their apparent benevolence.

Muriel's fellow traveler, the pacifist socialist Maude Royden, readily borrowed continental psychoanalytic frameworks in discussing her own unmarried life of Christian social action. Royden talked fearlessly and wrote prolifically about sex. She took a leading role in shaping a Christian psychology and sexology in the interwar years.[160] In 1916, she detailed the social, economic, and gendered circumstances that siphoned poor women into the sex trade as prostitutes. Her defense of the power, dignity, and beauty of sexuality, *Sex and Common-Sense* (1921) rescued sex from "furtive whisper[s] and silly jokes." "The great impulse of sex is part of our very being," and, she declared, "it is not base." It was ennobling, a reflection of the divine impulse of creation in humanity. She even dared to imagine the young man Jesus in his "agony of long-ing" and fleshly temptation. The greatest lovers of the outcast—Jesus, St. Francis, St. Catherine, and St. Theresa—suffered the torments of unsat-isfied sexual desires. They refused to "repress" or "dissipate" their sex drive "but so used it for the service of man that there is in all the history of man, no life so rich, more human, more full of love, more full of cre-ation, or more full of power than the lives of these celibate men and women, who learned from Christ how they could live and love."[161]

Royden anticipated Freud's much more celebrated and influential analysis of St. Francis and other ascetic saints in *Civilization and Its Dis-contents* (first published in 1930). Freud argued that Francis and his ilk protected themselves from the "uncertainties and disappointments of genital love by turning away from its sexual aims" and instead loving "all men alike." "Inhibited" sexual aims manifest themselves in "evenly sus-pended, steadfast, affectionate feeling."[162] For Royden, the satisfactions of such altruism were emphatically not protection from disappointment or the redirection of a sex impulse that somehow had gone astray.[163] With unflinching honesty, Royden confronted the imperative to liberate single celibate women from the constraints of social conventions, which compelled them to "repress" their natural and healthy hunger for inti-macy.[164] Royden's response to the explosion in psychology and sexology during the first three decades of the twentieth century was to embed these "sciences" within her radical Christian theology of social justice.

This was just what Muriel would not do. She never went to the "dark places of psychology" where Virginia Woolf believed the truths of the self and modern life were secreted.[165] Muriel was not evasive or out of date or repressed. She was every bit as modern and vastly more progres-sive in her social and personal politics than Woolf. Her breakdown in 1916–17 had led her to find another place where truth resided. And it was brilliantly illuminated by God's love. The Prayer of Relaxation healed her mind and body. Practicing the Presence of God was the ther-apy she chose to discover the Divine deep within her. Like fellow Guild of Health members, she was well informed about the latest books and articles in psychology and psychoanalysis, which were regularly reviewed in the Guild's publications. For Muriel, Jesus was the master psychologist of the modern world and God's love its most potent resource. In place of a psychosexual identity, Muriel trained herself to find God's love within her. Filling herself with God's love may well have left no room inside Muriel for sexual desire and romantic love.

In Nellie's most incisive, complex, and candid assessment of her relationship with Muriel and their shared labors at Kingsley Hall, she represents Muriel both as a daughter of the pristine luxury of the Grange, and as "Mother" of "dear old Kingsley Hall" in "dirty old Bow." The letter probably dates from 1916 when a "zep" bombed Kingsley Hall in the early morning of September 24.

> Your Nell did want to be
> with you longer. you always
> push me off lately if I had
> have known I was not going
> to see you again I would
> not have gone for that ride
> & I would not come at all
> but I wanted to see you
> that was better than all.
> but you did try to be jolly
> with the women & got to
> excited. you did not let
> me show you Kent Hills on
> Bromley Bridge
> you don't know how I
> have taken your many kindness
> to me. You have been my best
> friend on this earth & I
> always feel I belong to you
> somehow, you have held me
> back so I ought to love
> you & do anything for you[166]

This letter verges on but never quite turns into a disappointed lover's lament. (See fig. 4.17.) It is a queerly powerful missive. It conveys Nellie's hurt that Muriel refused her the exclusive intimacy she craves. The

look so lovely in your
own home & your Mother
looked much better than
she did when she came on
that Monday. every one feels
ill over this war. I don't
worry over the Zeps but I
don't want to see people
killed around me I sit &
star gaze & half the night
I was jolly glad you were
not here Miss Doris was'nt
a bit afraid. I don't know
weather I looked after them
or they me. I must have
got the hint for I only just
shut the door. they are more
frightened of my Tile than
Zeps.
I am so glad you are going
to try & see Will he is
digging trenches he seems

have taken your many kind
to me. you have been my best
friend on this earth & I
always feel I belong to you
somehow; you have held me
back so I ought to love
you. I do anything for you
I keep getting back from
every thing & I feel I don't
do for you all now. to old
I even hold the light for
the germans to come but
I did look after them.
I like Miss Harris very
much & I miss them both
to day. for I went to bed
unhappy. for I do want
you to get well & strong
& come back but you

4.17. Nellie Dowell to Muriel Lester, n.d. (1916), Nellie Dowell Letters. (Courtesy of Bishopsgate Institute.)

opening, "Your Nell," ostensibly confirms Nellie's deepest desire to "belong" to Muriel. The phrases that follow in quick succession make clear Muriel's unwillingness to possess Nellie as fully as she wishes: "you always push me off lately." Nellie softens the rebuke of "always" with "lately," implicitly recalling a time when Muriel did not push her off. The word "somehow" is syntactically ambiguous. It ends the thought "I always feel I belong to you somehow;" but it also begins a new one, "somehow you have held me back." "Somehow" disrupts the logic of Nellie's wishful claim to belong to Muriel by registering Nellie's disappointment in Muriel's demand for distance. Nellie invokes the powerful obligations binding the giver and receiver of kindness. She "always" feels she "belongs" to Muriel, her "best friend on this earth."

While Nellie states that she "ought to love you [Muriel]," the letter asserts Nellie's insistence that Muriel "ought" to return her love. She concludes with an expression of love for Muriel and the dirty world they share. "I can't be happy till you come home to dirty old Bow and dear old Kingsley Hall with all its dirt it shows its use for the purpose its got for, it only wants its Mother." It was an act of supreme generosity for the erstwhile match girl who coveted a lady's clean white hands to sanction the immersion of her own best beloved lady, Muriel Lester, in "dirty old Bow" to serve its people. To do its Christian revolutionary work of cleansing Bow, Kingsley Hall, like its Mother, had to get dirty. Nellie knew and accepted this.

Nellie's description of Muriel as "Mother" of Kingsley Hall suggests that she may have seen herself as one of the Hall's—and Muriel's—many daughters in their radical reconfiguration of family as an elastic public and private unit. During Kingsley Hall's first decade, its residents were unmarried women committed to self-denying lives advancing the social good. By the early 1920s, the press dubbed Kingsley Hall a "modern monastery."[167] Perhaps Nellie, by naming Muriel the Hall's "Mother," articulated her sense of belonging to a quasi-monastic community of women, bound to one another by deep ties of affection and mutual obligation. Muriel, the charismatic "Mother" of this sacred and secular family, was its spiritual leader; and, at least for Nellie, the elusive object of her desires.[168] If Kingsley Hall "wanted" Muriel, so too did Nellie.

Reconstructing their friendship through their own writings is inescapably claustrophobic. No evidence makes it possible to see Nellie and Muriel as others saw them. Nellie does offer one mediated glimpse of a neighbor's impression of them in her earliest surviving letter. On a rainy Sunday night in mid-November 1910 Nellie reported to Muriel that she and "Miss Doris" were getting along "splendidly" without her: "but I do miss you ever so much no one can take your place now." After recounting all her hard work "visiting" neighbors and organizing a charity bazaar, Nellie urges Muriel to "enjoy yourself & don't come home & say I have got some news I am going away again or I shall follow you." With evident delight, she informed Muriel that a poor neighbor in Bow, Mrs. Starling, had asked her "if I missed you."

> fancy asking that question they
> all ask me that, you are well

asked for round Bromley I think
they really do love you for yourself
so make haste home & don't
stay there[169]

Nellie's retelling of this story is playful and coy, as if "all" their neighbors are acknowledging something about the women's relationship in a way that neither of them could. She implies that Mrs. Starling's question is an odd impertinence—"fancy asking that question"—but then immediately makes it normal by noting, "they all ask me that." Rather than declaring her own love, Nellie deflects attention away from the subject of gossip, their relationship, to the much safer topic of their neighbors' esteem for Muriel: "they really do love you for yourself."

Nellie began each of her letters to Muriel with the same formal opening: "Dear Miss Lester." She adhered to the well-established naming conventions of her time. The older sibling, Muriel, was always "Miss Lester" and her younger sister was always "Miss Doris." (Muriel's older sister, Kathleen was married so Nellie called her "Mrs. Hogg.") At first glance, such formality seems to betoken *only* class difference and emotional distance hard to square with Nellie's full-bodied passionate closings: "Your Nellikens" and "Your loving Mate Nell xxx accept these." How could they have remained on such seemingly formal terms and yet also have been loving partners? Are there other possible interpretations of "Dear Miss Lester"?

When Nellie addressed Muriel as "Dear Miss Lester" she underscored something they knew and cherished: they had found a way to love one another across a vast social and class divide. Difference produced desire even as Nellie and Muriel desired difference.[170] Nellie frequently repeated "Dear Miss Lester" in the middle of her letters, sometimes when she resumed writing after a break. Each repeated direct address invited Muriel to conjure Nellie physically before her. Each reminded Nellie about what she found so achingly attractive about Muriel: her difference. Iteration intensifies intimacy by eroticizing difference.

Formal salutations were compatible with the most sensual sexual relationships between women. The devoutly pious Anglican Constance Maynard (1849–1935) and her agnostic lover Louisa Lumsden (1840–1935) founded Muriel's public school, St. Leonard's in Scotland.[171] Maynard's stunningly frank diaries and manuscript autobiographies record her struggle to reconcile her fleshly delight in other women ("the abandonment of enthusiastic love") with her exalted spiritual and pedagogical vocation.[172] In the midst of a particularly stormy exchange with her bedmate in 1877, she confided, "for all my griefs I could not keep my hands off Miss Lumsden, and begged her to come home with me."[173] In the privacy of her diary, Louisa remains "Miss Lumsden" even as Constance has her hands all over her—a reminder to Maynard that Miss Lumsden was her senior as well as her Head Mistress at St. Leonard's.

The point is *not* that Nellie and Muriel enjoyed the physical "abandonment of enthusiastic love" like Maynard and Lumsden. I think they did not. Rather, I have suggested that "Dear Miss Lester" conveyed a wide range of meanings, at once conventionally formal and heterodoxically intimate. There is little to be gained in pinning down Nellie and Muriel's loving friendship with a name. Vera Brittain had come to a similar conclusion in 1963 as she finished writing her history of the "rebel passion" animating Muriel Lester and her fellow Christian revolutionaries. Brittain had tried "to define the difference between Agape, Eros, and Philo," but found she could not do it. "It is really too subtle for English to explain," she confessed, "except through poetry."[174] Nellie's letters to Muriel incite and frustrate the impulse to define the nature of their love. Muriel and Nellie transacted their transformative love and

revolutionary Christianity in the literal, affective, imaginative, and intellectual *space between* "Dear Miss Lester" and "Your loving Mate Nell xxx accept these."

CONCLUSIONS: DIALECTS FOR THE HEART

Few rivaled the author of *Aurora Leigh* in her mastery of the languages of love. By turns plaintive and disarming, Elizabeth Barrett spoke "comfortable details" to restore friendship's frayed ties in a letter to a girlhood friend. There were, she averred, as many "different dialects for the heart" as there were "tongues." Far from conjuring the Babel of mutual incomprehension, the poet invited her friend to contemplate the plenitude and variety of "tongues" that speak from and to the heart, while offering her letter as one exquisite example.[175] In her letters to Muriel, Nellie invented her own "dialect for the heart."

Nellie's heart dialect mobilized a grammar of difference through tropes about caring for the sick body, hers and Muriel's. Her epistolary erotics enact double gestures of reciprocity and inequality, sameness and difference, knowing and not knowing, having and wanting. These unresolved tensions fill the pages of her letters and allow us to glimpse how she used language to express her own embodied subjectivity. Canny rhetorical performances intended to produce quite specific effects on Muriel, her letters are a remarkable archive of affect. They retain a sense of freshness and spontaneity a century after she penned them. This too is an effect of her use of language—as palpable, playful, and, in its own way as skillful as Gertrude Stein's wartime experiments.

Against the reductive bureaucratic logic of London Hospital that first defined Nellie as a disease-bearing body and then handed her over to be reclassified as a pauper lunatic, she used her letters to Muriel to express wit, hurt, delight, and tenderness. They convey ephemeral information about their shared interests, remind Muriel how much Nellie longed for her, and prod Muriel to write back to her. Like Claude in Arthur Hugh Clough's epistolary verse novel about *not* "exactly" being in love, *Amours de Voyage* (1849), Nellie wrote to her beloved so that "you may write me an answer."[176] Nellie, like Muriel, understood the affectionately coercive powers and implicit obligations of friendship and letter writing. Her letters to Muriel were one way she reclaimed her personhood in the aftermath of her soul-shattering horror of being a "pauper lunatic." They were as much a technology of interiority as London Hospital's twice daily thermometer measurements and Rontgen rays. Using her letters, she reassembled a self in relation to Muriel as well as to the world they inhabited and the one they sought to make.[177]

Muriel's breakdown in 1916–17 and her health struggles during the preceding six years made her distrust allopathic medicine. During her long period of doctor-mandated "rest" in Loughton in 1916–17, she grew weary of her own "morbid" absorption in monitoring her body, in listening to the rush of blood and the beating of her heart. She came to recognize her illness as a problem of her inner moral and spiritual life. Her Prayer of Relaxation was her solution. It offered an alternative path inward whose destination was self-knowledge achieved through joyous union with a loving God. The Prayer was simple, but its genealogical antecedents spanned centuries, religious traditions, and continents. It was an eclectic global spiritual formation that performed its healing work within that most intimate of locales, Muriel's innermost being.

Muriel's spiritual therapeutics were just as modern as Freudian psychoanalytic approaches to mental health, but vastly more portable, democratic, and economical. They required no professional "expertise" in the human sciences, with their investment in extending their authority into the most private recesses of humanity.[178] In place of Freud's model of the self as modernity's secreted battleground of competing forces of ego, id, and superego, Muriel offered the prospect of inward stillness and harmony. Her psycho-spiritual techniques participated in and contributed to the proliferation of vernacular psychologies in the early twentieth century that bridged religion and science, Eastern and Western understandings of body and soul.[179]

Prayer worked for Muriel. For the next five decades after the resolution of her crisis of 1916–17, it sustained her exceptionally robust life as she crisscrossed the globe as an ambassador of peace and reconciliation. Muriel was one of those people who seemed perpetually spry and youthful. Regally erect in her bearing, she exuded that peculiar mix of vigor and serenity, confidence and humility that we associate with saintliness. It drew many to her; it repelled some. She had not always possessed this embodied persona, I have argued. It was the result of deliberate spiritual labor in the aftermath of her 1916–17 breakdown. Prayer did not, could not, "cure" Nellie's mitral valve degeneration; nor could it compensate for nutritional deficiencies in her diet caused by poverty that made her so susceptible to recurrent illness. While Muriel's sphere of activity expanded, Nellie's physical world grew ever more circumscribed. At forty, she had an old woman's body even though her intellect, wit, and spirit remained fully intact.

Despite Muriel's devotion to exploring her inner life, she paradoxically has left behind very little of it. The titles of Muriel's two major autobiographies, *It Occurred To Me* and *It So Happened* suggest that she casually offered readers ideas just as they "occurred" or "happened" to her—something more than afterthoughts but much less than program-matic Confessions in the tradition of Augustine and Rousseau. The sur-viving drafts of these books show this was not true. They were carefully crafted texts, much like the archival remains of Muriel's interiority. De-spite the relative paucity of archival sources by and about Nellie, we know more about her physical and psychological insides than Muriel's.

Muriel's decision to preserve Nellie's letters indicates just how pre-cious they were to her. Nellie's letters mattered. They documented the remarkable success of their utopian project to use Christian love to break down the barriers separating half-orphaned Cockney match fac-tory workers like Nellie and wealthy educated daughters of the urban bourgeoisie like Muriel. Nellie's letters also disclose the limits of their love and the ways in which Nellie and Muriel, in quite different ways, powerfully resisted their own project. For all their determination to transcend hierarchies and efface boundaries of difference, Nellie and Muriel kept finding ways to reproduce them. Nellie pushed back against Muriel's egalitarian project by loving Muriel partly *because* Muriel was her social better. Nellie delighted in reminding Muriel to love her be-cause she was not her equal. Muriel invited Nellie to enter into sacred intimacy while fleeing from its implications. Muriel found it easier to love ever-widening communities of people in need—in Bow, East Lon-don and the world—than to love any one person. The letters show Mu-riel and Nellie constructing boundaries even as they sought to obliterate them, unmaking and remaking their worlds.

CHAPTER FIVE

Love and Christian Revolution

"Loving means making experiments all the time."
—Henry Hodgkin, *Lay Religion* (1918)

ON FEBRUARY 13, 1915, East Londoners greeted the latest of a long line
of institutions founded for their betterment, Kingsley Hall. This was an
unpromising time for Muriel and Doris Lester to launch a scheme along
pacifist, feminist, and socialist principles of social sharing. Turkey had
just initiated the mass deportation of Armenians while German U-boats
began to trawl the waters surrounding Britain. War, H. G. Wells assured
Britons, not God's love, was the only way to end all war.[1] In the eyes of
many of their "Hun"-hating neighbors, the sisters and their friends had
set themselves apart from the community to which they claimed to belong. They cared far too much for the civil rights of German "enemy
aliens" and too little for the state's insatiable appetite for men to fill the
ranks of Britain's all-volunteer army and navy. Nor was it clear precisely
what kind of institution it was. Muriel cultivated this ambiguity. Eighteen years after its founding, she published a pamphlet, "What IS Kingsley Hall?" celebrating its definitional uncertainty as an institution while
proclaiming its unequivocal principles. (See fig. 5.1.) "A Settlement? An
East End University? A Church? OR WHAT?" None seemed to fit. "It is
a difficult place to stick a label on, because its members ignore barriers
of race, creed, nation and class." She offered "People's House" as the best,
albeit provisional, name for it.[2]

About Nellie's centrality to creating and sustaining this "people's
house," Muriel had no doubts. "Never has there been a better friend to
Kingsley Hall than Nellie," she readily acknowledged in the Hall's report
for 1923. Nellie, who always had so little, had given more than anyone.

What IS Kingsley Hall?

A Settlement? An East End University? A Church? OR WHAT?

It is a difficult place to stick a label on, because its members ignore barriers of race, creed, nation and class. Perhaps the best way to describe it is to call it a People's House. Its aim is no less than to set up the Kingdom of Heaven in Bow.

And Anyone Can Belong to It.

It was founded, thought out and paid for by lovers of Christ who were working under His direction when they opened the place and when they started the Clubs and Concerts, Services and Socials, and all its other activities.

Year by year, hundreds of pounds have been needed to keep it going. This money has been prayed for and worked for, and received. Month by month, valuable voluntary service has been freely given by people of all creeds, classes and character who wanted to contribute something to the building up of the Kingdom of Heaven on earth.

In our last syllabus these words were printed :—

Kingsley Hall :—

1. Honours all men.
2. Breaks down barriers of sect, nation and race.
3. Gives service voluntarily.
4. Depends for Peace and Safety, not on Army or Navy, but on goodwill and understanding.
5. Was dedicated to God, every room of it, bricks, mortar and underlying earth—for the purpose of spreading the Kingdom of Heaven on earth, here and now. "He dwells here : whoever enters is the guest of God "

3

5.1. *What IS Kingsley Hall?* (London, 1933), Lester/7/2/12, Lester Papers. (Courtesy of Bishopsgate Institute.)

Her intellectual, spiritual and affective labor had been vital to the Hall's founding and development.

> She cherished [the idea of the Hall], helped it to grow, made it seem real. Whenever the dream began to grow hazy she would discuss it in terms of flesh and blood and by fitting actual people into its imagined framework, she increased one's faith. After its birth, it was Nell one turned to in every crisis.[3]

What Muriel never quite said was that for her Kingsley Hall was the bricks-and-mortar incarnation of their loving friendship. It was also the instrument that she, Doris, Nellie, and their neighbors used to enact their vision of a Christian revolution in everyday life.

Muriel's close colleague Henry Hodgkin, the Quaker Christian revolutionary founder of the Fellowship of Reconciliation (FoR), believed that "loving" meant "making experiments all the time."[4] This was certainly true for Nellie and Muriel. Their love was incubator and testing ground of their Christian revolutionary social politics. Their "aim" was no less than to set up the Kingdom of Heaven in Bow.[5] Hubris uneasily rubbed up against humility in their self-effacing project to use the power of love—God's and their own—to remake themselves and the world.

Bringing God's revolutionary message of love to the world required prayer, which in turn demanded unwavering discipline of mind, body, and spirit. Individual meditative prayer was far too important for Muriel's very survival to leave to happenstance. She reserved space for it in Kingsley Hall and set aside particular times each day for it. She likewise expected and demanded members of Kingsley Hall's community—at the Hall itself, at 58–60 Bruce Road, and later at Children's House (founded in 1923)—to weave prayer into the warp and woof of their daily lives.

The path to freedom in Bow, England and the world was no less dependent on order and discipline. During Kingsley Hall's eventful first decade, Muriel elaborated exceptionally detailed rules of daily life for community members, which proscribed what she called "anti-social" behaviors incompatible with God's earthly Kingdom. It was anti-social and "may even smack of egotism" to leave the dregs of toothpaste in the washbasin; it was anti-social to clear away tea things and "leave sticky sediment un-noticed on the table;" it was "positively dangerous to other people's health" to leave the sugar jar uncovered. Muriel echoed wartime restrictions on gossip imposed by the Defense of the Realm Act (DORA, 1914) in the name of national security when she dictated a precise script for community members to use when confronted by comments and complaints about an absent third person: "I can't listen unless so-and-so is here."[6] She likened the dangers of such talk to "secret diplomacy," a term widely used by contemporaries to account for the insidious origins of World War I.[7]

Order and discipline were Muriel's antidotes to the flabby excesses and illusory freedoms of early twentieth-century bourgeois liberal individualism.[8] Strict daily routines at peace-loving Kingsley Hall paradoxically mirrored the militarization of civilian life and soldiers' regimented disciplines. Perhaps this should not be surprising: the militant Christian has often been figured as a zealous foot soldier in God's army.[9]

In modern British history, Christianity and revolution have frequently seemed fundamentally incompatible at least since the French Jewish historian Élie Halévy argued (as early as 1906) that Methodism saved Britain from the violent social and political upheavals that bedeviled its cross-Channel rival.[10] In the mid-nineteenth century, Karl Marx's invectives against religion as an opiate of the masses solidified the identification of the revolutionary Left with irreligion set in motion by the Jacobins.[11] To be sure, the link between citizenship and membership in the established Church of England generated political dissent and constitutional change during Catholic and Nonconformist campaigns of the 1820s and '30s to remove their legal disabilities. The phalanx of "church and state" also encouraged the growth of exuberant oppositional variants of Nonconformity upon which, I have argued, Muriel drew in forging her "God is Love" theology.

The roots of British Labour and socialism in religious Nonconformity in the late nineteenth and early twentieth century have long been acknowledged, but usually to explain their reformist and evolutionary bent. By this reckoning, religion contains and diverts revolutionary impulses even when it is allied to progressive social and political programs.[12] This was not so for Muriel and Nellie. Their faith animated and demanded a revolution in moral values *and* socioeconomic structures.

Kingsley Hall's pacifist principles only further compound the case against its claim to be genuinely revolutionary. As Liberal protestant theologian Reinhold Niebuhr pointed out to Muriel Lester when they shared a platform in 1934, pacifism was a weapon only the privileged could afford.[13] It domesticated and defanged popular revolution by taking away the most effective weapon of the dispossessed: their potential to enact violence in pursuit of justice and equality.[14] In the aftermath of the Bolshevik Revolution (1917), some found it difficult to take seriously Kingsley Hall's brand of revolution. Were the rich simply going to hand over their wealth to the poor because their consciences told them to "follow" Jesus?[15] For Muriel, the answer was "yes." To revolutionize her own life, she undertook ever more daring "experiments in personal economics" culminating in her much-publicized transfer of her inheritance to a restitution fund controlled by and for the people of Bow in 1927.[16]

These are powerful arguments against regarding Muriel and Nellie's project as revolutionary. They were too cogent for Muriel to sweep aside. They remain too cogent for me to ignore. However, rather than starting from the premise that Christian revolutionaries were the unwitting dupes of bourgeois capitalism, I take seriously—and on their own terms—both the idea of Christian revolution and their attempts to enact it. Muriel's "God is Love" theology, especially her interpretation of the Sermon on the Mount, inspired her understanding of Christian revolution, which in turn produced her social politics. Transformations of mind, heart, and soul, Muriel believed, went hand in hand with the fundamental restructuring of the economy and politics. The individual self and the social self were indivisible in her understanding of Christian revolution. Disciplined governance of the embodied self could not be separated from the practices of participatory self-government at the heart of democratic citizenship in the modern world.

The precise mechanisms by which a purifying worldwide Christian revolution would unfold Muriel never specified. Paradoxically, the Great War that she so vehemently condemned did a great deal of cleansing work for her. Even as she decried war's destructive violence as contrary to God's love, it refined and radicalized her ideas and practices. In its devastating wake, the war made millions in Britain and Europe eager to find peaceable alternatives to resolving conflicts between states.[17] Kingsley Hall and Muriel came of age amid the tidal wave of revolutionary energies unleashed by war and its immediate aftermath—that "Indian summer of nineteenth century radical visions."[18] These visions galvanized men and women across Europe to undertake intense socioeconomic, cultural, and political experiments, ranging from small-scale Simple Life communes to soviets predicated on worker control over industrial shop floors. Muriel shared the Canon of Hereford's optimism that "we have good reason to be confident that God intends to build up a better Europe, a New Jerusalem on the ruins of the old" just as He had sent Jesus to proclaim His healing gospel at a much earlier period of "World-crisis."[19]

For the likes of Virginia Woolf, George Orwell, and John Maynard Keynes, interwar Britain may well have been a "morbid age" on the verge of a catastrophic implosion.[20] It was full of promise and possibilities for the Lesters, Nellie, and their band of fellow workers at Kingsley Hall. They devoted themselves to the joyful exacting labor of building the New Jerusalem, soul by soul, in their corner of Bromley-by-Bow. They developed ideas and practices about the dynamics of power in interpersonal, social, and national life that continue to inform the aspirational endeavors of global humanitarians and advocates of restorative justice. Muriel believed deeply that Kingsley Hall was one place where Christian revolution could and would begin. My analysis of Muriel and Nellie's pacifist Christian revolutionary partnership also begins there with its founding and evolution during an epoch of unprecedented violence and revolution in Europe.

HENRY LESTER'S GIFT

Muriel never tired of telling the story about the precise moment that Kingsley Hall was born. It went like this. Soon after their brother's death on September 14, 1914, Doris and Muriel used the money that Kingsley had left for them to expand their small slum dwelling at 60 Bruce Road. With their Bow friends, they knocked down the second-story wall between their home and Nellie's next door at number 58. (Nellie's family occupied the first floor.) This created an upstairs space big enough to hold their clubs and classes. They called it Kingsley Rooms. But the sisters were not content. They kept criticizing "established things" and talking about how much they wanted an even larger space to match their ambitions. Henry Lester had heard enough of this talk. Then and there, he offered to purchase and renovate a suitable property for them. Henry pressed them to answer. Would they accept his challenge? Muriel hesitated. "'It struck me dumb' . . . I was appalled, terrified."[21] A few days later, members of Muriel's Bruce Road Men's Adult School found just the right place, a disused Strict and Particular Zion Baptist chapel, one block west and one block north of 60 Bruce Road at the corner of Eagling and Botolph Road.[22] Where once Hell's fires had scorched sinners' souls, God's healing love would now envelop all who entered Kingsley Hall, regardless of class, race, religion, and nation. Unlike tales that Bloomsbury "moderns" told about their rebellion against their

Victorian forbears, Muriel gives pride of place to eighty-year-old Henry Lester. He is the prime mover and benevolent Victorian paterfamilias, nothing like one of Lytton Strachey's neurotic "eminent" Victorians.[23] Henry boldly pushes his daughters to turn disaffection into joyful action.

The day before the Hall's opening, rubbish still littered the refurbished former chapel. The Lesters had belatedly discovered that rats had gnawed through parts of the foundation, compelling them to replace the rotten wood with sturdy new beams. With their band of working-class friends from Loughton and Bow, they toiled through the night cleaning up the mess. Illness prevented Henry Lester from making the journey from Loughton to Bow for the opening ceremony, so his letter of welcome was read out loud. Few Essex men-made-good were more forthright about their Cockney roots than Henry Lester. The labors of the people of Bow and Poplar, among whom Henry had been born in the 1830s, had allowed his shipbuilding business to prosper. Kingsley Hall was his gift of thanks to the people of Bow. The pastor of Bloomsbury Chapel for whom Kingsley Lester had last worked, Reverend Thomas Phillips, spoke fondly of their dead brother's altruism and likened Muriel to Jane Addams of Chicago.[24] George Lansbury beseeched everyone to demand better lives for themselves. God loved saint and sinner, virtuous and vicious, rich and poor, so why should men harshly judge anyone in need? (See fig. 5.2.) He traced Kingsley Hall's origins to the Christian socialists of the 1840s and the famous university settlement, Toynbee Hall, founded by the Barnetts in Whitechapel in 1884. This was a lineage that Muriel later came to disavow.[25] But that winter evening in early 1915, she was content to bask in George Lansbury's praise. He urged his listeners to "rally round Miss Lester and her work, not to leave it all for her to do" but to "take hold of the place and manage it and organize it themselves." Then "Miss Lester" herself spoke. Kingsley Hall would "rub the sharp corners" off everyone, she hoped, and "break down the prickly barriers" separating people, nations, and churches.[26]

Two laboring men from the Bruce Road Adult School gave the last short speeches, proof that they did not need Lansbury to tell them to make the work their own. They already had. This was essential to Muriel's ideas about participatory democratic citizenship, which depended upon working-class men, women, and children making decisions and

5.2. George Lansbury helped celebrate all of Kingsley Hall's landmark events. He is photographed, with a smiling Muriel wearing a hat behind him, at a tree-planting ceremony. "George Lansbury planting tree at Kingsley Hall, Bow, November 1929," Lester/6/10, Lester Papers. (Courtesy of Bishopsgate Institute.)

speaking for themselves. George Mortimer, a worker at Spratt's dog biscuit factory along the Limehouse Cut, invited the men in the audience to come around on Sunday mornings and join the lively debates at the Men's Adult School.[27]

Mortimer was an obvious choice to speak for Bromley-by-Bow's workingmen. He, his wife, and daughters had long been attached to the Lester sisters and Nellie. His daughter Lily, a dog biscuit packer at Spratt's, was an early member of Muriel's Sunday Bible class at Bruce Road Congregational Church and a special favorite of Nellie's. After Kingsley Lester spoke to Muriel's Bible class in November 1910, Lily had impressed Nellie by "giving right out" in front of all the other girls that she hoped to be "ready to meet God." This was, Nellie thought, "very plucky of Lilly [*sic*] for it wants doing among her work girls." As a former work girl herself, Nellie knew from firsthand experience that such public declarations of Christian convictions in an institutional setting—a Bible class—pushed against rather than conformed to prevailing norms in Bromley-by-Bow. Poor women in London like Nellie were more often than not "conduits of belief in working-class families," but these beliefs tended to mix "religious sentiment" with popular folk wisdom disconnected from church teachings and formal structures.[28]

Long-term friendships with families like the Mortimers and the Dowells allowed the Lesters to cross generations and sexes in building up dense networks of fellow workers and followers. These men, women, and children constituted the core of what Muriel called "Kingsley Hall people." Without them, Kingsley Hall might never have opened, much less flourished. They filled the hall on its inaugural evening and joined its clubs and classes. Doris and Muriel had cultivated these friendships since their arrival in Bow at the turn of the century. After the sisters moved into 60 Bruce Road in 1912, Doris announced that they would systematically survey their neighborhood. "Doris decided," Muriel recalled, that "every house in the nieghbourhood [*sic*] had to be visited by her or me. Accompanied by one of our local friends it was a serious job. Doris made me do it, but I enjoyed it as much as she did once we had got started."

Two things distinguish the Lesters' "visits" from those undertaken by generations of Ladies Bountiful before them: the presence of a "local friend" and Muriel's growing awareness that neither wealth nor good intentions gave her the right to intrude on her neighbors' privacy.[29] In one typescript account of the origins of Kingsley Hall, Muriel recalled the impact of a "visit" on her understanding of how to break down "prickly barriers" dividing rich and poor. A master of self-critical auto-biographical reflection, she berated herself for knocking on her neighbor's door on washing day in Bromley-by-Bow. Only someone like her who never had to wash her own clothes would be so insensitive, she confessed.[30] This gaffe taught Muriel that friendship and mutual aid, not surveillance and superiority, opened doors and hearts in Bromley-by-Bow. Muriel's vignette shows her transforming the meaning and purpose of Victorian charitable visiting to serve her emerging Christian revolutionary program at Kingsley Hall. Visiting exposes for critical scrutiny, rather than reproduces, class privilege.

Who was the Lesters' unnamed "friend" and what part did she play in the "serious job" of visiting? Was she their partner or their Cockney Sherpa whose local knowledge smoothed the sisters' way? Nellie's letters strongly suggest that she was this "local friend," who guided the Lesters *and* was their partner. As early as 1910, she reported to Muriel that "I have been trying all the week to do some visiting but my mother is still very poorly so I have to do everything but I have managed Monday's for Miss Doris & I think we all get along splendid together but I do miss you. . . ." Reminding them to remain loyal to their beloved Miss Lester, Nellie regularly visited members of the Women's Meeting when Muriel was away from Bow.

> they say Oh no
> they have not left Miss Lester
> meeting they mean to come
> so we are hoping to get a good
> number by the time you come
> home

Nellie's use of the pronoun "we" indicates the depth of her investment in this enterprise. It was hers as well as Muriel's.[31]

Doris, Kingsley, and Muriel opened the doors of their home at No. 60 to the neighbors they had so recently "visited" in 1912. Doris fondly recalled that "Nella" (her nickname for Nellie) brought along several friends to the housewarming party, who had been terrified and then delighted by Kingsley's elaborate masquerade as a ghost.[32] The sum total of these visits had helped to produce the bonds of friendship and trust between the Lesters and their Bromley-by-Bow neighbors that emboldened them to accept their father's challenge and open Kingsley Hall in 1915.

George Lansbury brought Kingsley Hall's opening celebration to a rousing conclusion singing "God Save the People" by the Corn Law rhymer Ebenezer Elliott.[33] Elliott's stirring words were beloved by the working poor: "the people," "not thrones and crowns but men," were God's children, on whom "man's clouded sun shall brightly rise, and songs be heard instead of sighs." Elliott's "People's Anthem" may have originated in early Victorian political and economic debates about People's Charters and Corn Laws of the 1830s and '40s, but it accrued new meanings as a song of protest and hope in early twentieth-century transatlantic struggles for social justice. For Lansbury and the Lesters, Elliott's refrain "God save the people" was a call to action, not passive consolation in the face of earthly suffering. Muriel insisted that Kingsley Hall was a tool for the people of Bow to use in working out their own salvation.[34] My hunch is that this finishing touch was Lansbury's impromptu flourish, not Muriel's.[35]

Doris did not speak that evening. Nor had anyone mentioned her, at least in the surviving transcripts and press reports of speeches.[36] Did it rankle her to hear Lansbury implore the audience not to leave Muriel— "Miss Lester"—to do all the work alone? Perhaps not, for Doris shunned attention. Unlike Muriel, she seemed indifferent to public acclaim and adulation. Lansbury must not have known that Muriel had convalesced in posh Devon health resorts for much of January. This left Doris, Nellie, George Bowtle, Ben Platten, the Mortimers, and many others to carry on the work without her.

Muriel was blessed with charismatic charm and a rare talent for inspiring others; but it was Doris and Nellie who often found themselves thrown together to keep things going at Kingsley Hall. Acting as Muriel's surrogate, Nellie gushed

> You [Muriel] ought to have seen
> your little sister go out to
> the wedding she looked
> beautiful I was proud to
> walk beside her to the
> Station & now tonight she
> is far happier with her
> Demonstration [a task performed for graded Sunday school teaching]
>   & then Nell
> is going to see her safe for
> the night I know she will
> be tired

Nellie's letter allows us to glimpse her own warm and independent friendship with Doris. Helping and looking after Doris gave Nellie another way to claim Muriel's gratitude.

What is most striking about the opening ceremony in February 1915 is *not* the speakers' or Muriel's enunciation of a revolutionary program, but their respectful invocation of the past. There were many models upon which the Lesters could draw as they consolidated their activities in Bow—Doris's Montessori nursery school and graded Sunday school and Muriel's Men's Adult School, Women's meeting, Factory girls' club and Sunday Bible class—into a single institution under their own control. From the Barnetts' university settlement, Toynbee Hall, the Lesters adopted cross-class hospitality, bringing together all sorts and conditions of people. With its Elizabethan revival architecture, sculptures, and carpeted public rooms, Toynbee Hall was an elegant place, especially compared to the cramped simplicity of Kingsley Rooms and the first Kingsley Hall. The poor invited to attend Toynbee Hall's teas and "at-homes" were not meant to emulate the domestic arrangements enjoyed by their benevolent betters. Contact with cultured minds and tasteful interiors would fill their "emptier" minds with elevating ideals and thoughts.[37] Recent graduates of Oxford and Cambridge, Toynbee men lived in well-appointed rooms with Delft-tile fireplaces. The only laboring people admitted to their inner sanctums were the female servants whom Henrietta Barnett recruited from among the fourteen-year-old Poor Law girls leaving Nellie's orphanage at Forest Gate. Their invisible labors carrying, washing, scrubbing, and sweeping subsidized elite male settlers experiments in cross-class fraternal sociability.[38]

These trappings of bourgeois ease were what the Lesters emphatically did not want. Nor would the first two residents of Kingsley Hall, Mary (May) Hughes and Rosa Waugh (Hobhouse), tolerate a servant tidying up after them. Each woman had already started on a journey of renunciation of worldly comforts as she sought to achieve what Rosa called identification with the oppressed. Rosa's work at an East London Summer Vacation Play Centre in 1913 had opened her eyes to the "intolerable cruelties" of poverty, including the endless barrage of nosy questions that social workers smugly inflicted on the poor.[39] It diminished the humanity of the poor, she insisted, to think of them "exclusively in relation to their hardships."[40] Rosa's principled repudiation of bourgeois values challenged Muriel intellectually and provided excellent copy for journalists. With photographers in tow, they reported that the daughter of the revered Benjamin Waugh and daughter-in-law of a former cabinet member, the Right Honorable Henry Hobhouse, insisted on doing her own heavy work scrubbing stairs and windows in her slum flat. Hughes called herself "Comrade" to express her solidarity with the people. It took convincing to get her to use the modest bathroom at Kingsley Hall since it was an amenity that very few in East London enjoyed. On its door, she posted a note explaining "This luxury was not necessary but due to the great kindness of Mr. H. E. Lester who gave this Hall to the people of Bow."[41] From the outset, the Lesters connected their faith in God's illimitable love to their everyday ethics: the commandment that people take full personal responsibility for cleaning up their own dirt.

Self-disciplined acceptance of responsibility for managing dirt was a corollary of their understanding of self-government. The Lesters expected members of Kingsley Hall's mixed-sex social club to elect stewards to manage the club and keep it spotless. It was the stewards, not the Lesters, who issued the handsome invitations to community members to join them for the first anniversary gala celebration of *their* club. (See fig. 5.3.) At the same time, club regulations reflected Muriel's priorities. Members dusted chairs every Thursday and Sunday. They sprinkled that "magical disinfectant"—Sanitas sawdust—and swept it up at the end of each club night.[42] Muriel's sincere desire to inspire her neighbors to make decisions for themselves ran up against her profound aversion to untidiness—physical, interpersonal, social, and psychological. The elaboration and imposition of rules about cleanliness diminished the risk that those she empowered would mess things up. She elevated hygienic household management to a first principle of citizenship and Christian communitarianism.

Kingsley Hall's insistence that its residents and members perform their own housekeeping labors had several notable precedents among Nonconformist women's "settlements" as well as communal experiments undertaken by sandal-wearing, socialist, vegetarian iconoclasts of the 1890s.[43] A member of the Fellowship of the New Life, Edith Lees (Ellis) urged men and women to "join hands with all classes" and live "unluxurious" lives among workers, "not as patrons and philanthropists."[44] Badly underpaid and overworked, domestic servants were an "ethical litmus test" whose fair treatment was essential to democracy. However Ellis, unlike the Lesters, did not see the performance of menial tasks of physical labor as essential to the moral betterment of the individual.[45]

THE KINGSLEY HALL STEWARDS
request the pleasure of your company at the

First Anniversary Meeting

to be held

at 8 o'clock p.m., on Monday, March 6th.   *1916.*

The Chair will be taken by
Councillor THOMAS GOODWAY.

Speakers :
GEORGE LANSBURY and MURIEL LESTER.

Mrs. Le MARE, A.R.C.M., will play the Violin.
The KINGSLEY HALL CHORAL CLASS will sing.

Light Refreshments will be served at 60, Bruce Road,
6—8 p.m., when the Kingsley Rooms, the Montessori
Apparatus and Scouts work will be on view.

R.S.V.P. to the Secretary,
Kingsley Hall,
Botolph Road, Bow, E.

[P.T.O.

5.3. The Kingsley Hall Stewards' invitation, March 1916. Lester Papers. (Courtesy of Bishopsgate Institute.)

Living as the poor lived, "doing their own 'chores,' even their own scrubbing," was an essential part of daily life in the radical experiments in communal living championed by the astronomer-nurse-novelist Honnor Morten in East London and later at Tolstoi Settlement in the Sussex village of Rotherfield.[46] Workers at Tolstoi Settlement (called "Sisters") paid one guinea a week for the privilege of tending to the health needs of poor children sent from the London slums to recuperate. They reserved an hour each day for silent reflection or meditation. Dressed in very plain dresses, the nursing Sisters rotated through and performed the tasks essential to running the settlement: kitchen labor, including cooking; housekeeping and cleaning; and caring for the children. Taxing labor alternated with periods devoted to mandatory recreation and rest. The Rotherfield settlement's strict discipline promised freedom to settlers exhausted by their pursuit of "pleasure or strenuous endeavour." Its democratic domesticity ensured that all members rotated through each form of labor necessary to sustain the community.[47]

Morten's settlement with its highly ordered schedule anticipated routines at Kingsley Hall. Quiet meditative prayer—three times each day—structured residents' lives at Kingsley Hall. Each person undertook some form of manual labor at the Hall to contribute to its maintenance. After residents prepared, served, consumed, and cleaned up a simple communal breakfast, local children poured into the Hall for Montessori classes from 10–12:30 p.m., Monday through Friday. Doris, the trained teachers, and the children put away the toys and pedagogical objects into cupboards to make way for the women workers who flocked to the Hall at midday for nutritious meals and sociability. Mid-afternoons were no less hectic. The Hall hosted a baby clinic run by doctors and nurses from the Royal College of St. Katharine's. Muriel's women's meetings and various work groups dedicated to humanitarian causes filled in the rest of the afternoons. At dinner, residents ate either a vegetarian or meat dish, but never both. Nights and weekends, the Hall was jammed with neighbors. The Kingsley Hall Club for men and women offered an alcohol-free public house six nights a week for mixed-sex sociability and discussion of pressing industrial and political topics. From early morning until 10 p.m. on Sunday, Muriel led various groups in religious services, discussions, and lectures by outside speakers.[48]

Many social welfare centers—secular and religious alike—in London were just as busy as Kingsley Hall. What made all this into the Lesters' homespun brand of revolutionary Christianity was how they arranged these activities and the way they distributed power and authority. Take, for example, the Kingsley Hall Club. At 7:50 p.m., club stewards, elected by their peers, stoked the furnace, set out games, leveled up billiard and bagatelle tables, prepared food for the bar, and opened the doors. Members decided that if roughs, atheists, or communists knocked on their door, they too would be welcomed. Some people came for games and refreshments; others, straight from factories, were eager to debate conditions of industrial life with their peers. "Our 'intelligentsia,'" Ben Platten reported, engaged in a "heated controversy on the virtues and faults of Karl Marx and a much-abused social system." With evident pleasure, Muriel noted "One little group of girls is now writing a chapter for a book on 'Women and Factory Life,' which is to be published by some

Social Students later." Still others studied the history of workers' protest movements from John Ball to the present under the tutelage of Oxford-trained Miss Cicely Craven—later distinguished for her publications about the reform of the penal system.[49] Each club night ended with the same rituals: joyful dancing for fifteen minutes followed by cleaning the space. Members then invited those who chose to remain, Muriel explained, to come together in prayer.

> 'Time, please!' calls the Steward, and most of the members flock out; after the sweeping all the lights are turned out but one, and in the semi-darkness those who are working and longing for the new day, those who feel a bond of unity drawing men together, and breaking down the barriers of sex, class and race, gather in a circle for silent prayer. A mighty force seems to bind us together, radiating from the centre of the group.

Enacting their solidarity with one another and welcoming God's inclusive love, members concluded the evening by singing Anglican theologian Edwin Hatch's hymn, "Breathe on us, breath of God: Fill us with life anew, That we may love what Thou dost love, and do what Thou wouldst do."[50]

Most of the initial leaders of the Kingsley Hall Club had been members of Muriel's Bruce Road Men's Adult School. Muriel always traced the origins of Kingsley Hall not to daring experiments in social service and democratic communitarianism pioneered by women like Honnor Morten and Edith Lees Ellis but to laboring men in her Adult School. As brass finisher Jack Rollason explained, the Men's Adult School "was the first Kingsley Hall Club" and the precursor to Kingsley Hall itself.[51] The hallmark of Adult Schools since their inception in Nottingham in 1843 was informality, brotherliness, scripture study, and open debate. They attracted "the independent minds of our artizans," who refused to be patronized by their social superiors while also welcoming the ragged and the illiterate. All members had votes in the management of the social club attached to each school.[52] They demanded no profession of conversion, no test of temperance.[53]

When Muriel established the Men's Adult School in the early summer of 1914, she was exhilarated to engage directly with men. They were, she believed, less prone to petty squabbles and backstabbing than all-female groups. [54] After a dozen years of independent work in the slums, Muriel, at thirty-one, finally felt prepared for the challenge of being the lone woman—and leader—among working men. The scarcity of men in wartime Britain more than a commitment to single-sex communities of women explains why residents of Kingsley Hall were overwhelmingly female during its first years.

With members of the Men's Adult School, Muriel first tested out several of her most significant ideas about community, neighborhood, and politics. In her own account of the origins of Kingsley Hall, she figured the Men's Adult School as a laboratory for and a prototype of Kingsley Hall. (See fig. 5.4.) She invited her harshest critics to scrutinize the Adult School's activities from the inside. The Minute Book for the first meeting on June 21, 1914, laid out its principles. "The Basis of an Adult School is the practical teaching of JESUS CHRIST;—therefore it follows that there are no limits to its power. Roman Catholics, Protestants, and Atheists

5.4. Henry and Rachel Lester regularly entertained their daughters' Bow friends, including members of Muriel's Bruce Road Men's Adult School. They are pictured in the garden of their Loughton home, the Grange. Muriel is third from front on the right; the family's servants stand behind a seated Rachel Lester. Source: *First Year's Report*, Kingsley Hall (London, 1916), 5. (Courtesy of Bishopsgate Institute.)

are equally welcome. . . . In an Adult School we recognize that Life and Religion are one. Try how we may, we cannot separate ourselves from the love of God, for He is our Father, and all men are brothers."[55]

God's love implied radical inclusivity. It joined all in universal brotherhood, even Atheists who wanted no part in it. Respect jostles with superiority in Lester's practical theology as God makes room in His capacious imperium for those who deny His very existence. For Muriel, inclusion within God's beloved community was compulsory. Outside no longer defined inside because she would not imagine—or allow—an outside. Muriel, a master of oppositional politics, knew how to use her status as troublesome "outsider" to draw attention to her critique of militarist and bourgeois capitalist values. Her refusal to allow atheists to be outside of God's love mirrored her determination to love those who called themselves her enemies. Love was a potent weapon in Muriel's peacemaking arsenal.

From the initial meeting, Muriel pushed Adult School men to imagine great things for themselves and their community.[56] She envisioned their collective future.

> There was a beautiful castle floating in the air this morning a dream of taking 2 shops in St. Leonard's [a major north-south thoroughfare in Bow just to the east of Bruce Road] and turning them into a Public House, which should excel all others in its cleanliness, & cheerfulness, where billiard tables should be good, where clubs could be held, & concerts take place, where Friendly Societies could hire rooms for their Meetings; a Public House which was not 'tied,' out of which no brewer could make a farthing, which needed no license, a P.H. without beer, a great jolly well Club, whose doors should never be shut till the very last licensed House had closed for the night.

With a combination of idealistic naïveté and hardheaded practicality, Adult School members leapt from discussing the best way to construct bed frames by recycling metal poles to defining Heaven. Was Heaven a place in the future or a state of mind to enjoy in the present? They resolved that each of them needed to set up the Kingdom of Heaven "here and now" because "Jesus is in our midst today, strengthening us just as really as he ever was." They blithely collapsed the distances separating them from the biblical past. God was not only within them but He and they were agents of change in the world.[57]

The Lesters drew upon many sources—and resources—when they accepted Henry Lester's gift and opened Kingsley Hall. With Nellie's help, they mobilized networks of human capital and bonds of friendship among their neighbors upon whose labors Kingsley Hall relied and for whom it existed. The founding of Kingsley Hall makes visible both deep continuities as well as significant shifts in the history of benevolence and social welfare from the 1880s until 1915. Comparing Kingsley Hall in 1915 to Toynbee Hall in 1884 highlights radical changes in the philosophy and practice of philanthropy. No Toynbee Hall man cleaned soot from his own fire grate or established an intimate working friendship with a member of the local community anything like Muriel and Nellie's partnership. However, such a comparison obscures the extent to which in the intervening decades Edith Lees, Honnor Morten, and others had undertaken innovative experiments that paved the way for the Lesters' utopian project to connect the gritty quotidian realities of life in Bow with their vision of Christian revolution.

In Muriel's oft-told tale of Kingsley Hall's founding, it was always—and only—to Bruce Road Men's Adult School that she first turned for help. This was, in fact, not true. She also sought support from another much better known organization. In mid-December 1914, Muriel paid a visit to the London Society for Women's Suffrage near Victoria Station in Westminster. Muriel never wrote about her own and Kingsley Hall's entanglement with the organized suffrage movement in late 1914 and early 1915. Nor did she preserve any archival traces of this fiasco. Thankfully, the London Society did.

FEMINISMS AT WAR

Muriel was a lifelong feminist and supporter of women's suffrage. Throughout her six-decade career as a global humanitarian, she remained keenly attuned to the relationship of gender (she called it "sex") to forms of oppression rooted in race, class, religion, and nation.[58] Nonetheless, references to women's suffrage and feminism were conspicuously absent from the speeches delivered at Kingsley Hall's opening ceremony. Muriel was the sole woman to address the crowd. She publicly acknowledged the crucial contributions of Bruce Road Men's Adult School. She said nothing about the support she got from Doris, Nellie, and members of their Women's Meeting.

Muriel's silences are all the more puzzling because the period from December 1914 to April 1915 was the first and only time that she put feminist politics and organizations at the center of her life. In December 1914, she agreed to serve as founding Secretary for the Bow Branch of the highly regarded London Society for Women's Suffrage in exchange for allying Kingsley Hall with it. On the very day Kingsley Hall opened in mid-February, the *East London Observer* ran a short notice that made it seem as if Kingsley Hall were the London Society's newest branch.[59]

Behind the scenes, an altogether different story unfolded. Muriel was mired in debilitating negotiations with leaders of the increasingly prowar London Society, in particular the formidable Philippa ("Pippa") Strachey, about the nature and future of Kingsley Hall. Two years later, Muriel and Nellie publically allied themselves with the London Society's archrivals and political enemies within the feminist movement. They joined Britain and Bow's leading pacifist feminists—Maude Royden, Sylvia Pankhurst, Charlotte Despard, Julia Scurr, and Nellie Cressall— in an ill-fated march across East London to demand a negotiated peace settlement. What initially led Muriel to the London Society? Why did she erase this episode from the early history of Kingsley Hall? What did Nellie think about women's rights? How did both women find their way to feminist pacifist activism in wartime Britain?

Nellie and Muriel have left behind few clues about their stances on the urgent issues that divided women's suffrage campaigners before and during World War I: the role of working women in the movement; the place of militant tactics and violence in politics; and the relationship of feminism to pacifism and the wartime state. In the years before the founding of Kingsley Hall, Nellie and Muriel had quite different experiences with women's politics. Nellie had exercised full citizenship rights long before Muriel when she voted in national elections in Wellington, New Zealand at the turn of the century. However, no direct evidence survives indicating her thoughts about suffrage and feminism. Sketching the paths into politics available to poor laboring women like Nellie in early twentieth-century Bow makes it possible to elucidate some of her political choices.

To make sense of Muriel's disastrous decision to ally herself with the London Society, I consider the particularities of suffrage politics in Bromley-by-Bow as well as internecine conflicts among national leaders of the suffrage campaign. Key figures in the national and metropolitan suffrage movement altered their views and shifted alliances as the broader political landscape in Britain changed in response to challenges ranging from Irish nationalism and Labour Party politics to the onset of world war.[60] As the suffrage movement fractured, new organizations proliferated, some overlapping and others mutually antagonistic. The point to keep in mind is this: Muriel found herself caught in the crossfires of these battles and was fortunate to extricate herself from them relatively unscathed.

Nellie Dowell and Women's Political Culture in Bow and Poplar

Only Battersea and West Ham rivaled Bow and Bromley as hotbeds of radical politics in the metropolis with a long history of support for the rights of women as workers, mothers, and citizens. The Matchgirls' Strike at Bryant and May's in 1888 thrust Bow's "unskilled" women workers, many of them daughters of Irish immigrants, into the center of debates about women's work and the New Unionism. By continuing to work for R. Bell and Company during the bitter strike of 1893–94, Nellie explicitly rejected this route into women's trade unionism and socialist politics. Soon after the strike at Bryant and May's, residents of Bow and Bromley chose Liberal women's suffrage campaigner Jane Cobden (daughter of the leader of the Anti-Corn Law League Richard Cobden) to represent them in the first London County Council elections of January 1889.[61]

By the early twentieth century, a new generation of working-class feminists rose to prominence in Bow and Poplar. The erstwhile laundress and future Mayor of Poplar Nellie Cressall (1882–1973) and Poor Law Guardian Julia Scurr (1871–1927) championed working women's rights as socialist members of the Labour Party. (See Fig. 5.5.) Both later worked closely with the Lesters, but in the decade before World War I,

5.5. Socialist feminist leaders in Bow like Councillor (and eventually Poplar Mayor) Nellie Cressall recognized that women's concerns as housewives and mothers were political. "Mrs. Cressall At the Stove." (Courtesy of the Press Association.)

the sisters remained far too tame for fiery figures like Scurr and Cressall.[62] They joined forces with oft-imprisoned militant suffragette Sylvia Pankhurst after she moved to Bow in 1912.[63] For the next dozen years, Scurr and Cressall supported Sylvia Pankhurst's various initiatives, including the East London Federation of Suffragettes and the Mother's Arms, a former pub that served as headquarters for Pankhurst's social welfare activities.[64]

Cressall's and Scurr's paths into and styles of working-class feminist politics throw into relief the very different choices that Nellie made as she dipped her toes into East London's turbulent political waters just before and during World War I. Unmarried and apolitical, Nellie had put job security and the economic needs of her mother and kin before worker solidarity and female trade unionism during her two decades in the match industry. She served her apprenticeship in Bow's social politics as a beneficiary of elite "ladies" religiously based philanthropy, not as a member of one of Bow's thriving socialist organizations such as the Social Democratic Federation and the Independent Labour Party.

Cressall and Scurr, unlike Nellie, were schooled in a robustly anti-deferential style of political protest and direct action. Each married a prominent leader in prewar Labour politics in Bow and Poplar: Cressall's husband was George Lansbury's political agent and Scurr's husband a leader of the Dock, Wharf, Riverside and General Labourers' Union. For them, marriage was a conduit to socialist and feminist politics. Motherhood gave them authority to speak about the pressing economic hardships women faced as they tried to feed and clothe their families. Scurr helped organize a delegation of unemployed women who met with Conservative prime minister Arthur Balfour in 1905 to demand steady jobs and wages. In June 1914, she lectured Liberal prime minister Asquith about the "murderous" effects of "modern industrialism" on poor families and the way women experienced poverty more acutely than men at work and home. When Asquith pushed Scurr to renounce militant tactics, she refused to back down. She tartly reminded him that men used "all sort of methods" to achieve their aims, so why shouldn't women?[65]

Nellie clearly chose not to follow these powerful and outspoken Cockney women into feminist politics after her return to Bow from New Zealand in 1903. When she did enter political life at several critical junctures after May 1915, it was always, literally, by Muriel's side in public demonstrations on behalf of peace. For all Muriel's zeal to empower the poor, not one of her close circle of working-class women friends at Kingsley Hall, including Nellie, ever emerged as an independent political leader in her own right like Scurr and Cressall.

In light of Bromley-by-Bow's hospitality to socialism and feminism, it's no surprise that in 1910 George Lansbury was elected to represent the district in Parliament. No man in pre–World War I Britain was more closely identified with socialist politics and women's suffrage than Lansbury. He was also the Lesters' chief mentor and friend in local politics. Not long after the Lesters and the Dowells moved next door to one another on Bruce Road in 1912, Lansbury shocked his rank-and-file Labour Party supporters in Bow and Poplar by vacating his seat in Parliament to seek reelection under the banner of women's suffrage. His aim was to force the hand of his own party and the Liberals to enfranchise women.

At a time when Labour MPs of all stripes—socialist and trade unionist—numbered only forty-two, Lansbury's decision was a high-stakes gamble. It infuriated Labour Party leaders, who saw no reason for Lansbury to jeopardize his own—and the party's—control of an important seat in Parliament. It electrified his Conservative opponents who saw Lansbury's single-issue focus on women's suffrage as an opportunity to push him out of Parliament.[66] Lansbury insisted that Labour vote "constantly and relentlessly" against all measures put forward by Asquith's Liberal ministry until they had either "driven" Liberals from office or "compelled them to introduce and carry a proposal to give votes to women on equal terms with men."[67]

Lansbury's extreme position pleased almost no one. It asked Labour leaders to oppose government measures in support of their Irish nationalist brethren who had entered into a parliamentary alliance with the ruling Liberals in pursuit of Irish Home Rule. It compromised pro-suffrage Liberals' efforts to work with their own party's leadership. It badly divided the Labour Party, many of whom had supported the Liberal government's social welfare initiatives such as Lloyd George's scheme for unemployment insurance.[68] Nor did Lansbury succeed in uniting feminists and Labour Party activists in Bow, who failed miserably to coordinate their efforts and resources in registering and transporting voters to polling places in Bow and Bromley. Militant suffragettes, embarking on the most violent phase of their sex war against male domination in public and private life, simply would not take orders from Lansbury's male political agents in Bow.[69] In short, Lansbury's reelection campaign was a fiasco that mirrored only too well the confusion into which he had thrown his feminist and Labour supporters. The Guild Socialist periodical, *The New Age,* snidely editorialized that "little as Mr. Lansbury knew himself what were the motives of his adventure, the public and his own constituency knew less."[70]

The national and metropolitan press recognized a good story when they saw it. They joined the hordes of socialists, Conservatives, feminists and anti-feminists who turned Bow and Bromley's drab roads into colorful street theaters and vivid print copy in November 1912. "The purple, green and white of the Women's Social and Political Union and the green, yellow and white of the Women's Freedom League" floated from "motor-cars and vans all over Bow and Bromley" in an attempt to rally voters to Lansbury's cause.[71] The election made Lansbury into the lion of feminism. Nonetheless, when the final vote was tallied in late November, he had lost by 731. The 1912 parliamentary election in Bow and Bromley marked a flamboyant convergence of local and national politics in Muriel and Nellie's neighborhood. It was also part of their political education.

Muriel Lester and Feminist Politics

Lansbury's by-election campaign coincided with several momentous developments in the history of women's suffrage. Emmeline Pethick-Lawrence and her husband Frederick, notable figures in the militant Women's Social and Political Union (WSPU), joined their leader Emmeline Pankhurst in jail in the spring of 1912. All three were convicted for conspiring to incite felony. Upon her release, Mrs. Pankhurst dedicated herself to all-out sex war and escalating levels of violence against property, including arson. After their release, the Pethick-Lawrences migrated toward "militancy without violence."[72] This independent stance Mrs. Pankhurst would not tolerate and, by Ocotober, the Pethick-Lawrences left the WSPU.[73] To the delight of *Punch*, feminists were now forced to ask themselves, "are you a Peth or a Pank?"[74] (See fig. 5.6.) According to Doris, Muriel declared herself a "Peth." This is the only extant clue about Muriel's position in the tangled web of feminist and suffrage politics on the eve of World War I.[75] But it is an important one.

What did it mean to be a "Peth" and why did Muriel become one? Like Muriel, Emmeline Pethick-Lawrence came to feminism through her long apprenticeship serving the poor, first as a "sister" at the Methodist West London Mission and later as founder of a girls' club and social settlement. In 1901, she married an equally high-minded and idealistic fellow social worker, Frederick Lawrence. Together, they embarked

5.6. "The Split: Are you a Peth or a Pank?" *Punch*, October 30, 1912, 349.

on their life partnership as the Pethick-Lawrences.[76] "Self-consecrated from girlhood to social service," Emmeline Pethick-Lawrence mingled feminist politics with Christian faith to produce a distinctively spiritual idiom of protest.[77] "The Woman's Movement means a new religion," she informed readers in the January 1908 number of *Votes for Women*, the periodical that she and her husband financed and co-edited for the Women's Social and Political Union.[78] She linked suffrage to the spontaneous and vital "awakening at last" of working women whom she urged to join her "army of the spirit."[79] For "Peths," militancy meant a willingness to endure violent assaults on their bodies such as force feeding in prison in the name of their great cause. Crucially for Muriel, Peths refused to mirror state violence by perpetrating their own.

Peths were hard to differentiate from members of the Women's Freedom League, led by the venerable Charlotte Despard since 1907. Freedom League members engaged in nonviolent militancy such as tax resistance and boycotting the 1911 census.[80] By 1914, many former members of the WSPU including the Pethick-Lawrences, Julia and John

Scurr, Charlotte Despard, and George Lansbury joined forces to found yet another organization, the United Suffragists.[81] The bewildering proliferation of organizations, each with its own acronym, demanding women's suffrage on the eve of World War I points to growing tensions within an unruly movement divided over tactics and goals.[82] The onset of war in August 1914 only deepened these divisions. The best-known leaders of the suffrage movement, Mrs. Pankhurst and Mrs. Millicent Fawcett, set aside their differences and mobilized women to serve the warfare needs of the state. For them, opposition to the war was a species of pro-Germanism.[83]

What was the position of the London Society for Women's Suffrage in these debates and what initially made Muriel ally herself and Kingsley Hall with it? The London Society proudly traced its roots to the earliest days of the organized campaign for the parliamentary suffrage of the 1860s. It was the largest constituent branch of the National Union of Women's Suffrage Societies (NUWSS), whose president was the Constitutional Suffragist Millicent Fawcett. Key leaders of the London Society in 1915, in particular members of the powerful Anglo-Indian Strachey clan (Oliver, his sister Pippa, his wife Ray, and their mother Lady Strachey) were red-hot for war. In December 1914, the Stracheys had not yet engineered the expulsion of their antiwar and pacifist rivals in the London Society and the National Union. But they made no secret of their disdain for pacifists. If Muriel did not know this when she first joined forces with the London Society, she quickly came to regret her misalliance with it.

Through its "Women's Service," the London Society poured its energies and resources into a clearing house for women workers, volunteer and paid, as well as women's social clubs across London.[84] As soon as Britain declared war, male breadwinners flocked to the armed services and left their wives and children to fend for themselves. Payments from the War Office to military families began more slowly.[85] This gap tipped precarious working-class family budgets into crisis exacerbated by devastating increases in the cost of everyday staples. From August 4 to August 15, the price of white sugar tripled and rice doubled in local shops in Nellie and Muriel's neighborhood. Wives endured long humiliating waits to receive paltry doles from underfunded and ill-prepared charities like the Soldiers' and Sailors' Wives Fund.[86] Clubs like those run by the London Society alleviated distress by providing essential goods and services for poor women. In joining forces with the London Society, Muriel presumably wished to draw on its experience running women's clubs. The London Society must have seen Muriel as a godsend. She combined deep local knowledge of Bow with apparent eagerness to manage and pay for their East London branch.

Muriel left her December 1914 meeting with the London Society with the mistaken conviction that it had agreed to take on all of Kingsley Hall's bookkeeping functions including the receipt of donations and the disbursement of funds. She was only too happy to leave this sort of business work, so far outside her own and Doris's competence, in able experienced hands. Muriel was a completely unknown East London social welfare worker with few connections in the suffrage movement and even fewer among the great and good of the metropolis. Her sphere of influence had heretofore been confined mostly to the axis connecting Loughton's wealthy Nonconformists with religious philanthropic networks in Bow. She may have been a grand lady in Nellie's eyes, but for prominent people like the Stracheys she remained indistinguishable from hundreds of other do-gooders in East London. Muriel may well have been flattered by Pippa Strachey's enthusiasm to enlist her services and dazzled by the cachet of the London Society's list of supporters. Its vice-presidents on the eve of World War I included leading married "ladies" in women's suffrage, philanthropy, and education such as Mrs. S. A. Barnett, Mrs. Henry Sidgwick, and Mrs. Henry Fawcett.[87]

The months during which Muriel worked most closely with the London Society and its secretary Pippa Strachey were among the most acrimonious in the Society's history. Profoundly undemocratic in their vision of Britain and its empire, the Stracheys liked power and knew how to wield it. For several years, they had battled against those seeking to democratize the suffrage movement by broadening its geographic and class basis.[88] The Stracheys were determined to purge the London Society and the National Union of Women's Suffrage Societies of antiwar and pacifist leaders, most notably Catherine Marshall and Kate Courtney. Marshall and Courtney threw all their political and intellectual weight behind an effort to convince the National Union and the London Society to send official delegates to the Women's Peace Conference in The Hague in April 1915.[89]

Organizers of the Hague Conference originally had hoped to harness the optimism of pre–war women's pacifist internationalism to prevent the outbreak of hostilities. Events, of course, had overtaken their plans. Instead of preventing war, the Conference hoped to lobby for its peaceful and speedy resolution.[90] In February 1915, The National Union (NUWSS) Executive voted against sending representatives to The Hague. To do so, the victorious majority within the National Union believed, would be tantamount to consorting with the enemy, not affirming global sisterhood. Marshall and Courtney's defeat was the Stracheys' triumph. It left antiwar feminists and their supporters no choice but to resign en masse from leadership within the London Society and National Union.

With undisguised glee, Pippa Strachey reported that she had been kept busy in the spring of 1915 "sweeping away pacifists" out of the London Society and the National Union. A few weeks earlier, her sister-in-law Ray confessed that she had enjoyed being "swallowed up . . . in the effort to beat the pacifists out of the suffrage society." The pacifists' "vague and visionary propaganda" on behalf of a "just" settlement after the war threatened to be the "ruin of [women's] suffrage."[91] Muriel may not have followed closely these bitter internal struggles within the London Society and National Union, but she was well aware of the broader public debate about the appropriateness of British feminists' participation in peace talks with women from belligerent and neutral nations. Among the British delegates whom the government blocked from attending The Hague Women's Peace Conference that spring was one of Kingsley Hall's first two residents, Rosa Waugh.

It was, however, not fundamental principles about democracy, war, and peace so much as concerns about administration, finance, and leadership that first came between Muriel and the London Society. A storm of protest from the London Society greeted Muriel's first modest promotional pamphlet of December 1914 announcing the creation of Kingsley Hall with its East End Working Women's Club. The rub was Muriel's request that donations for Kingsley Hall *and* the Working Women's Club be sent to the London Society's treasurer, serving as Kingsley Hall's Honorary Treasurer. For Muriel, this arrangement guaranteed the bona fides of her fledgling scheme at Kingsley Hall.[92] The London Society informed Muriel that she had acted under "a misapprehension": the Society never took responsibility for the finances of any "outside undertaking."[93] Only the East End Working Women's Club was attached to the London Society. The rest of Kingsley Hall's financial affairs did not concern them. This placed Muriel in a very difficult position. She could hardly withdraw the two hundred copies of the pamphlet already circulating among prospective supporters, she explained to Miss Strachey.[94]

To make matters worse, it was clear that the London Society arrogated to itself—and not Muriel or Doris—the right to dictate what services Kingsley Hall's Women's Club would and would not provide the people of Bow. The Executive Committee had seen no reason to invite Muriel and Doris to explain their vision for Kingsley Hall. Hiding behind the passive voice of collective corporate authority, the London Society organizer informed Muriel that the Executive Committee already had made major decisions about Kingsley Hall's future. "It was decided at the last Committee that the idea of opening a Day Nursery and Training Home at Bow should be postponed indefinitely."[95] The Lesters could not "postpone" a program that already existed. Doris had been running a flourishing day nursery along Montessori-inspired lines on Bruce Road since 1913. She had every intention of bringing it to Kingsley Hall. Educating Bow's youngest to become able and energetic decision-making citizens was essential to the Lesters' Christian revolutionary program.

Muriel evidently knew very little about the London Society and the Society next to nothing about Muriel. Why else would Pippa Strachey, busy inoculating the London Society and the National Union from the pestilence of pacifism, have been so eager to enlist Muriel as head of its Women's Service in Bow? And why would Muriel, committed to advancing democracy across the class divide, ally herself with a group of pro-war elite women who had done their best to keep power tightly within their own grasp? It is a sign of Muriel's political ineptitude and naïveté that she proudly told Strachey about the impressive lineup of pacifist feminists—Charlotte Despard, Maude Royden and George Lansbury—whom she had enlisted as Kingsley Hall's Sunday evening speakers for 1915.[96] Miss Strachey could not have been pleased.

Muriel's unfortunate entanglement of Kingsley Hall with the London Society came to an end, more or less, by April 1915. Without ever mentioning the Christian revolutionary principles on which Kingsley Hall had been founded, Muriel wrote to Strachey that the daily demands of work made it impossible for her to chair the London Society's Bow branch. A London Society member in Bow and wife of the pioneering leader of the Methodist Forward movement in East London, Rosalie Thompson, fretted that the Women's Service scheme at Kingsley Hall would soon collapse for lack of adequate funds. This is where the archival trail of the London Society's relationship with Muriel and Kingsley Hall ends.[97] Kingsley Hall's Report for the Second Year makes no mention of the London Society. Muriel and the London Society had gone their separate ways. A heavy financial liability for the Lesters, the cost-price restaurant and club at Kingsley Hall continued to enjoy the enthusiastic support of the women workers who dined there.[98]

Muriel's original promotional pamphlet for Kingsley Hall that had so alarmed Strachey and the London Society reveals just how inchoate her ideas were about Kingsley Hall. The top of the pamphlet was dominated by the heading "SUPPORTED BY," which listed thirteen of the London Society's most prominent members including Mrs. Henry Fawcett, Lady Frances Balfour, Viscountess Gladstone, Lady Strachey, and the Marchioness of Salisbury. Muriel assured prospective donors that a "lady" would always be present at the Hall to oversee its work. This was not the best way to launch a democratic, bottom-up "people's house" for enacting Christian revolution along socialist lines. Muriel's connection to the London Society and bourgeois women's philanthropy may well have made Sylvia Pankhurst wary of Kingsley Hall and the doings of its leading "lady." Notices about speeches and events at Kingsley Hall did not begin to appear regularly in Pankhurst's paper the *Woman's Dreadnought* until August 1916, nearly a year and a half after its founding.[99] By that time, Nellie, Doris and Muriel had more than proved their willingness to suffer opprobrium for bearing public witness to their radical Christian pacifism and socialism.

Muriel's unsuccessful negotiations with the London Society clarified her priorities. Power struggles among members of the Executive Committee of the National Union and fighting among fellow feminists and suffrage campaigners in 1914–15 helped to make the erstwhile social investigator and Liverpool social worker, Eleanor Rathbone, into a savvy political operator. Rathbone learned "never to let an impossible ideal get in the way of an achievable good."[100] Based on the actions she took, Muriel seems to have taken away quite different lessons from her experience with feminist and suffrage politics in 1914–15. She deepened her commitment to the "impossible ideal" of bringing the Kingdom of Heaven to earth. In the future, she sought alliances with people, organizations and movements that squarely shared her pacifist Christian ideals.

If the prestige of the London Society's glittering list of supporters and its experience with women's clubs had initially lured Muriel, these assets had come at far too high a price. The impeccable philanthropic pedigrees of Kingsley Hall's first two residents, May Hughes and Rosa Waugh Hobhouse, offered more than enough cachet to assure the benevolent public that the Lesters' new scheme was trustworthy. Hughes and Waugh Hobhouse, like the Lesters, were fervent pacifists, socialists, and feminists. The daughter of the great public school reformer and novelist of muscular Christianity Thomas Hughes, May Hughes was a beloved figure in East London by the time she moved into her tiny room above Kingsley Hall in February 1915. The renown of her goodness and love for the people was so great that her offer to help, Muriel acknowledged, "set us free from every pang of anxiety."[101] Hughes literally took the clothes off her back and swapped them for the rags of her poor neighbors, to the consternation and sensitive nostrils of her closest friends. Rosa Waugh occupied the room just across the hallway from Hughes. Rosa may have been a penurious art educator attached to one of the London County Council's evening recreation schools for poor children but her father Benjamin Waugh and brother-in-law William Clarke Hall were world-famous leaders of the child welfare movement. Muriel's early speeches and press reports about Kingsley Hall invariably mentioned the distinguished lineage of the Hall's first two residents. Such references signaled continuities between their Victorian philanthropic fathers and their daughters' gentle but radical recasting of their paternal inheritances.

Emmeline Pethick-Lawrence believed that the early-twentieth-century women's movement marked the birth of a new religion. Not so for Muriel. Feminism was too riddled with internal conflicts, its leaders too willing to wage war against one another, to offer Muriel and Kingsley Hall a safe spiritual and political home. Nor had Muriel come to feminism seeking a new religion. She remained quite happy with the faith that she had never lost.

RECONCILIATION AND CHRISTIAN REVOLUTION

During World War I, pacifism occupied the center of Muriel's faith while her faith served as the foundation of her pacifism.[102] In the fraught summer of 1914, Muriel and Men's Adult School members discussed and debated, line by line, the Sermon on the Mount. "It took us months to get through those three chapters [Matthew 5–7]," Muriel recalled, "so modern and revolutionary did they prove to be."[103] After August 4, Muriel defiantly refused to pronounce "a moratorium" on the Sermon on the Mount even as she witnessed, seemingly overnight, the disappearance of Britain's vibrant culture of antiwar internationalism.[104]

The Sermon on the Mount had immense implications for Muriel's thinking about relations between men and women, rich and poor, white and black, metropole and colony, state and society, the community and the individual. Part of what made her such an effective platform speaker and leader was her sincere refusal to separate theory and practice, love and politics, stories about her life and stories about changing the world. Her experiences in wartime Bow propelled her toward increasingly radical ideas about revolutionary Christianity. At the same time, her exposure to and contact with Christian revolutionary thinkers associated with the Fellowship of Reconciliation (FoR)—Henry Hodgkin, Theodora Wilson Wilson, Wilfred Wellock and Bernard Walke—reshaped her daily life and Nellie's at Kingsley Hall. What Muriel put together, her ideas about Christian revolution and her quotidian practices, I prize apart by analyzing Muriel's immersion in Christian revolutionary ideas during and immediately after World War I. No doubt Nellie had her own ideas about Christian revolution, but the absence of surviving sources precludes analysis of them. The next section puts these ideas back into conversation with Nellie and Muriel's activism and partnership in Bromley-by-Bow.

The Sermon on the Mount, from its injunction that "whosoever shall smite thee on thy right cheek, turn to him the other also" to its admonition that "Ye cannot serve God and mammon," had long provided radicals with powerful arguments against the market-based logic of industrial capitalism in nineteenth- and twentieth-century Britain.[105] John Ruskin, denouncer of mammon's soul-destroying impact on modern workers, knew every word of it by heart because, he explained, it contained "the things that Christ thought necessary for all men to understand."[106] Tolstoy took the Sermon's "Law of Love" as the basis for his entire religious and social program of redistributive economics, his rejection of war and militarism, and his doctrine of non-resistance in the face of evil. The Anglo-Catholic social critic G. K. Chesterton quipped that the Sermon was "sanity preached to a planet of lunatics," a view Muriel enthusiastically endorsed.[107] For both of them, the Sermon on the Mount was an ethical ideal *and* a guide to living in the world. Charles Gore, the influential Bishop of Birmingham and founder of the Christian Social Union, argued that the Sermon announced a "new social order," which encapsulated the whole of the "moral law of the Kingdom of Heaven."[108] The Right Reverend Charles Stubbs, Liverpool's clerical champion of democracy, imagined reorganizing his beloved city according to the Sermon's lessons. Where Jesus told his followers to "Love your enemies," political economists instructed theirs to "undersell your friends;" where Jesus enjoined, "resist not evil," political economists advised striking first, "lest ye be struck or locked out."[109] (See fig. 5.7.)

Like Stubbs, Muriel anticipated the day when political economy and "the philanthropical finance" of the Charity Organisation Society [COS] would give way to "humanitarian enthusiasms."[110] The last extant sentence of "From Birth to Death" bitterly recounts the COS's heartless rejection of Harriet Dowell's plea for help in the aftermath of Nellie's cata-

CHRIST SAYS—	POLITICAL ECONOMY SAYS—
Love your enemies.	Undersell your friends.
Resist not evil.	Strike, lest ye be struck or locked out.
Thou shalt love thy neighbour as thyself.	Every man for himself, and the Devil take the hindmost.
Blessed are the peacemakers.	*Laissez-faire, laissez-passer.*
Blessed are the meek, for they shall inherit the earth.	Property in land is for the most part the result of State grants for military service.
Give to him that asketh thee.	Indiscriminate charity is a frightful evil.

5.7. Charles Williams Stubbs, *Christ and Economics, In the Light of the Sermon on the Mount* (London, 1894), 64–65.

strophic hospitalization in 1910. Its "philanthropical finances" were anathema to Muriel. There would be neither Poor Law nor Charity Organizers nor paupers in the world that Muriel and Nellie toiled to create.

No group of men and women thought more deeply about the implications of the Sermon on the Mount in wartime Britain or exerted a more powerful influence over the Lesters' ideas about Christian revolution than the pan-denominational Fellowship of Reconciliation (FoR). Doris and Muriel joined FoR committees in October 1915. Doris appeared as a founding member of the Educational Subcommittee of the FoR in the Minutes of Council for October 11–12, 1915 but she seems to have done very little with the group.[111] Muriel joined Tom Attlee (brother of the future Labour prime minister, Clement Attlee) and Henry Hodgkin among others on the Social Service Committee. She tackled key tasks such as preparing leaflets about the labor conditions of wartime women's work, which earned her a place on the General Committee by 1917.[112] By the early 1920s, the London Union of the FoR was so closely connected to Muriel that its General Committee sometimes met at 60 Bruce Road or Kingsley Hall.[113] From the 1930s through the '50s, Muriel was the FoR's global spokeswoman and "traveling Secretary." By the time she retired to her modest cottage in Loughton on the edge of Epping Forest, she was, Vera Brittain asserted, the FoR's "best known woman evangelist" who "habitually repudiated convention" while speaking in her soothing musical voice.[114]

The Fellowship, founded in Cambridge in late December 1914, traced its origins to feverish attempts by liberal Protestants to affirm their commitment to friendship, peace, and brotherhood in the summer of 1914.[115] From August 1 to 3, a group of Christians from across Europe had met on the German-Swiss border in Konstanz for the World Churches Conference. Before boarding their trains to return to their respective homes, the Quaker leader of the Christian Student Movement in Britain, Henry Hodgkin, embraced Lutheran pastor and secretary of the Church Committee for Friendly Relations between Great Britain and Germany (*Kirchliches Komitee zur Pflege freundschaftlicher Beziehungen zwischen Großbritannien und Deutschland*), Friedrich Siegmund-Schultze. They declared their indivisible "oneness in Christ." This gesture of manly amity was vital to how the Fellowship narrated its beginnings. It signaled the centrality of love in the Fellowship's radical Christian politics and its defiance of the bellicose patriotism that demanded Germans and Britons face one another as enemies.[116]

From the outset, the FoR proclaimed its goal "to establish a world-order based on love . . . and to take the risks involved in doing so in a world which does not as yet accept it."[117] Alienated by mainstream Protestant churches' uncritical enthusiasm for war, the FoR's founders felt called to "a life of service for the Enthronement of Love in personal, social, and national life."[118] Hodgkin, Richard Roberts and Lucy Gardner led members in prayer to forge a community, which shared their conviction that true Christianity was irreconcilable with war in all forms: the violence of everyday life in capitalist societies; the exploitation of native peoples in empire; and armed struggles on the battlefronts of World War I. Karl Marx, J. A. Hobson, Karl Liebknecht, Rosa Luxemburg, and Vladimir Lenin among many others had connected the exploitation of workers at home to the extraction of resources and violence of imperial domination abroad.[119] What was distinctive about the FoR as avatar of "The Christian International" was its attention to the micro-workings of power in daily life, its insistence on the religious foundations of revolution, and the rejection of force as a means to achieve its aims.

Henry Hodgkin brilliantly analyzed the deforming dynamics of unequal power in everyday life, where it stealthily operated in the interstices of social relations. He admired the passionate energy of Christian idealists like Muriel but cautioned that it was unethical for them—and for him—to allow charisma and intellect to overawe others, even for their own good. "The type of forceful personality that makes the best propagandist" was, Hodgkin warned, "the very one which is most liable to fall into this cardinal error." "Even if we avoid the more obvious danger of domination," he continued, "we may convey a sense of superiority in our tones and gestures."[120] The risk of such acute reflexivity was that it would foster both self-critical awareness of the unintended effects of power and paralysis. Being a Christian revolutionary was hard work. It demanded striking a balance between monitoring one's words and body language with the capacity to act decisively. The project of dismantling deference, Hodgkin knew, was always a two-way affair that required the consent of all parties involved. The rich and powerful could not simply divest themselves of their privileges because they wanted to. Nor would their good intentions bring about a Christian revolution. This required the active equal partnership and will of the poor and outcast.

Muriel never acknowledged the dangers of such subtle, unintentional forms of "domination" as she reflected upon her relationship with Nellie and their mutual friends in Bow. Nellie did—though not in Hodgkin's abstract language. She refused to be Muriel's equal, I have argued, because she did not want to be. She loved Muriel at least partly because Muriel was so different from her.[121] Muriel's upper-class accent, word choices, and gestures always marked her social superiority in Bow, though this too she never acknowledged.

From the moment she stepped onto Indian soil in 1926 en route to visit Rabindranath Tagore and Mohandas Gandhi in their respective ashrams, she was oppressively aware of how her status as a well-to-do white Englishwoman trapped her within a matrix of colonial inequality. Muriel echoed Hodgkin in recognizing that even minutely small gestures contained within them and reproduced the whole bitter legacy of empire. The "low bow of the grave faced Hindu" was the Janus face of the "imperious snatch—a quick, jerky action that is quite unmistakable—of the English master without a word of thanks."[122] Indians' reverential devotion to their English masters was little more than a mask, a survival strategy to avoid hard swift kicks. "I tried to explain to them [Indians] that I was not their master—but [the village headman] insisted I was, and was right." In one of those many moments when Muriel ruthlessly dissected her own ideas and actions, she confessed to Doris, "I am [their master], so are you and we are responsible—it is awful."[123] Race in India made painfully visible to Muriel what class in Bow did not. Even the most zealous commitment to Christian revolutionary principles in her personal dealings with others could not undo deep histories of exploitation.

Coming from a wide range of religious and political positions, FoR members never attempted to paper over their disagreements. Instead, they sought common ground that celebrated difference while allowing them to work corporately to achieve their goals. "Undifferentiated cosmopolitanism" aspired to an unhealthy universalism that obliterated the "treasures" of difference, Hodgkin contended. The FoR's approach to difference lay at the heart of "reconciliation" as a tool for resolving conflicts between individuals, peoples, and nations alike. Reconciliation was, Hodgkin explained, rooted in a "passion for harmony."[124] It was, like Christian Revolution, a method as well as a way of thinking, living, and feeling. It was never a fixed destination. Retribution, reparations, and retaliation between individuals and warring nations had no place in this method of peacemaking. Muriel and other FoR leaders decoupled the process of reconciliation from acceptance of blame and apology: one freely forgave perpetrators before and without their acknowledgment of their wrongdoing. For the Welsh Methodist minister Richard Roberts, who came up with the name Fellowship of Reconciliation, reconciliation was nothing less than the art and practice of turning enemies into friends.[125]

The FoR posed big and truly important questions about God, humanity, and the world. It also allowed itself to get bogged down in arcane fine points that got in the way of effective action. Even practical thinkers like FoR members Lilian Stevenson and Maude Royden found themselves caught up debating whether "moral indignation" fostered an "attitude of condemning others" rather than openness to working with others to overcome disagreements. Meetings regularly stretched over several days with Quakerly silences occasionally interrupting the intense flow of animated talk. It's hardly surprising that the General Committee failed to recruit even one "working class member" to join its ranks.[126] What laboring man or woman could afford to give up two days of work to ponder (as the future Archbishop of Canterbury, William Temple, did in March 1915) whether something could be called a "compromise" if it had been "involuntarily" imposed?[127] The atmosphere at FoR meetings was so rarified that one of its most heterodox members, Reverend Stanley James, longed for the appearance among them of "a sweaty, mud-stained and foul-mouthed soldier from the Front."[128] Such a man would not have ruffled Muriel. Plenty of them lived around her, Doris and Nellie in Bromley-by-Bow. It's hard to imagine how Muriel summoned the patience—and found the time—for these gatherings. We know that she did, even during her protracted nervous breakdown of 1916–17.

Muriel's work with the FoR brought her into close contact with everwidening circles of thinkers who critiqued and reconceptualized Europe's and Britain's place in the world. Hodgkin's writings about Christian revolution, for example, generously cited past and present poets and religious leaders from around the globe. By so doing, he textually enacted his plea to transcend the borders dividing people from one another. *Lay Religion* (1918) opened with Hodgkin's homage to the "great sages" of China; it moved deftly from Evelyn Underhill's "regulative principle of love" to Rabindranath Tagore's image of "white robed simplicity" in his poem, "Nationalism," to Keshab Chandra Sen, leader of the Brahma Samaj, on Christ's combination of supreme meekness, truth telling and fearlessness in the face of death.[129] In Hodgkin's hands, quotation performed global fellowship. This was a technique Muriel often borrowed in her programs and services at Kingsley Hall, which liberally included writings from many different traditions.

The global dimensions of the war spurred some of its keenest opponents, including Muriel, to conceptualize "world citizenship" as a stimulus to and necessary corollary of Christian revolution. The group of men and women associated with the publication of the radical pacifist paper the *New Crusader*—renamed the *Crusader* when its first editor was jailed—offered Muriel a far-reaching analysis of global war, global capitalism, and imperialism. (See fig. 5.8.) There were substantial overlaps in personnel and ideas between Britain's various pacifist, antiwar, and anti-conscription groups.[130] The restless former cowboy and Welsh Methodist minister Stanley James worked very closely with Muriel on the Social Service Committee of the FoR. At the same time, he wrote regular columns for the *New Crusader* and supported Kingsley Hall.[131]

The founding editor of *The New Crusader* and interwar Britain's "most remarkable Christian socialist pacifist," Wilfred Wellock, spent his youth as a laborer in the textile mills of the Lancashire town of Nelson before improbably making his way to the University of Edinburgh.[132] His understanding of the world had been shaped by his immersion in Ruskin's moral economics, Tolstoy's Christianity, and anarchist Peter Kropotkin's politics.[133] At the war's outset, he joined the No-Conscription Fellowship to protect the rights of men of conscience against the un-English imposition of military conscription. He refused to take exemption on grounds of his status as a Methodist lay minister, preferring to defy the warfare state and accept imprisonment at Wormwood Scrubs as a conscientious objector. He looked forward to the "next phase in the

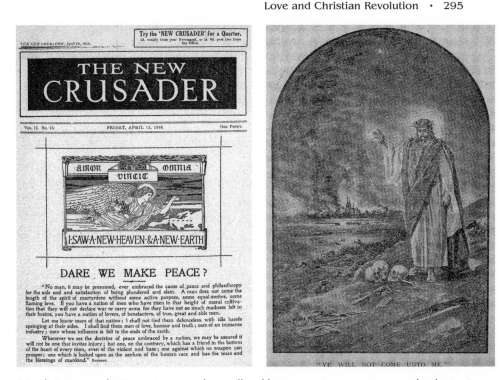

5.8. Christian revolutionary iconography oscillated between extremes: at once ardently utopian about the prospects that love would conquer all and hard hitting about the gruesome human costs of war and violence. (Left) "AMOR VINCIT OMNIA," *New Crusader*, April 12, 1918, p. 1. (Right) "Ye Will Not Come Unto Me," *New Crusader*, May 3, 1917, 4. (Courtesy of Swarthmore College Peace Collection.)

history of human development . . . the realization of world-citizenship, the creation of international consciousness." This consciousness, in marked contrast to Marx's account of the birth of world history and class consciousness in volume one of *Capital*, depended upon "spiritual relationships" and "fellowship" between individuals, peoples, and nations. The "crusade" of modern times was a "worldwide spiritual movement" to liberate all people to love one another. Reconciliation, not class conflict, was the route to this new heightened consciousness.[134]

The money behind the *Crusader* as well as many of its most original ideas came from Muriel's FoR colleague, the novelist Theodora Wilson Wilson.[135] The flamboyant Wilson was an early friend of Kingsley Hall.[136] Like the Lesters, she grew up in the virtuous ease of the Nonconformist bourgeoisie and had engaged in conventional sorts of philanthropy like setting up a Sunday school and Evening Home for working girls in her native Westmoreland. She also played a prominent role in Liberal women's suffrage organizations in the 1880s and '90s. By the eve of World War I she had abandoned Liberalism, embraced socialism and suffrage militancy, and become a Quaker.[137] A gadfly within the FoR, Wilson chastised members for their preference for talk over action. She traced networks of human exploitation and unfair labor practices fostered by global capitalist corporations and mobilized shareholders to demand that companies pay their employees enough to "live a full and free life." She directly connected the dividends of the British bourgeoisie with their distant human costs worlds away. Wilson sought to stir up a shareholders' revolt as part of the "reorganization of the present Industrial system" to benefit the "highest good of the workers and the best interests of the community."[138]

For some quietist members of the FoR, Wilson's aggressive methods flirted unacceptably with tactics of domination. Could a Christian revolution be achieved without resort to force? This was a question that Muriel's colleagues asked themselves over and over as they tried to balance ethical thought with necessary action. Wilfred Wellock, like Muriel, emphatically rejected violence and relied upon the overwhelming "force" of God's Love to bring about Christian revolution. "Bloody revolutions" accomplished nothing; he preferred to kill "the lies that are mutilating" mankind rather than wage armed battles against German militarism. The pacifist was the true "knight errant" and adventurer of modern times, who "faced a hostile world," armed only with "truth."[139] "You cannot kill hatred and violence," Maude Royden explained, "by means of hatred and violence."[140] Revolution began by convincing individuals, one by one, who collectively would then express their will as "the people." For radical Christians like Muriel, revolution took place in seemingly inconsequential everyday interactions and behaviors, rather than in moments of dramatic conversion and political upheaval. "We are what we do, just as civilizations are what people make them by their everyday conduct," Wellock insisted.[141]

In April 1917, the *New Crusader* reminded readers about the tools in their "everyday" Christian revolutionary arsenal as they pursued peace. "Pray. Sacrifice. Pay. Talk. Think. Study. Get Going."[142] Such ideas about revolution had already been challenged by actual revolution in Russia the month before. Words notably missing from the FoR's lexicon included "liberate," "overthrow," "emancipate"—key concepts under discussion at the Council of Workers and Soldiers Delegates that met in Leeds six weeks later to welcome the Russian Revolution. The first letter read out loud there was from George Lansbury, who extended heartfelt solidarity "with our brothers of the proletariat in Russia, in France, in Germany—(cheers) in Austria, in Italy, in the United States—one with all the world's workers, who have been deluded, coerced, exploited by their Governments in this war." In phrases meant to provoke fear among vested political-economic interests, Lansbury spoke of Lloyd George's wartime ruling coalition as a "provisional government." [143]

Russia's two-phased revolution in 1917—moderate and constitutionalist in February, radical and Bolshevik in October—heartened and perplexed champions of "world citizenship" in Britain like Muriel. It widened existing fissures among Christian revolutionaries and socialist pacifists. In 1915, Henry Hodgkin's rejection of a colleague's contention that force could be used "redemptively" was mostly a matter for theoretical consideration.[144] Such distinctions had become deeply consequential in 1917.

Early accounts of the Bolshevik seizure of power only compounded confusion. On November 8, 1917, the *Times* described Lenin as a "pacifist" and said the coup d'état was "accomplished without bloodshed." In loosest contemporary usage, Lenin was a "pacifist" in that he urged negotiation, rather than armed force, to bring about the immediate end of war between nations.[145] Christian revolutionary pacifists also shared Lenin's view (though it is very unlikely they had read any of his works) that World War I was itself a capitalist imperialist conflict. However, this same *Times* article published the "proclamation" of the Bolshevik Military Revolutionary Committee that promised the use of "force without mercy" against those who defied its demands.[146] Such language flatly contradicted the FoR's core principles.[147]

Muriel has left no record of her own thoughts about these great world historical events in Tolstoy's native land. As a voting member of the FoR's General Committee, she endorsed the Resolution that it sent to the people of Russia in January 1918. Even allowing for the Committee's imprecise knowledge of events in Russia, the document is in equal measure naïve, idealistic, and wishful. It opened with thanks and praise for the

> service which the Russian nation has done to the cause of humanity and of reconciliation . . . by striving to bring about a speedy and universal peace. . . . We, too, desire to see the government of the world based upon justice and human brotherhood both in international and social life.

With disregard for Bolshevik views on God, the priesthood, class war ("crushing the resistance of the bourgeoisie" in Lenin's words) and the virtues of violence, the Resolution continued,

> we believe that as followers of Jesus Christ we are bound to seek to establish His perfect law of Love among men and that the present order is a denial of the power of His life and teaching. We believe . . . that methods of violence and bloodshed can never establish righteousness and justice, but that these will dawn upon the world as men are ready to manifest the qualities of enduring faith, courageous devotion and utter self-sacrifice, qualities which have always been characteristic of the Russian people.

Revolutionary Russia and later the Soviet Union remained an object of intense fascination and fear for the British Left—Christian and secular—throughout the interwar period. The FoR's proclamation makes clear that when many radicals in Britain looked at the Russian revolution in 1917–18, they saw reflected back their hopes and dreams for themselves and their nation.[148]

To prepare for the "dawning" of "righteousness and justice" in Britain, the Fellowship's Social Service Subcommittee asked members to reply to a questionnaire whose profundity teetered on absurdity and self-parody. Muriel sat on this committee and its questions and conclusions closely mirrored her own.

> Did Christ lay stress on a life of poverty? Was this poverty to be of a material or a spiritual character? What does the acceptance of such poverty imply? Is it concerned with things other than material possessions, e.g. the use of force, knowledge, eloquence, privilege, etc.? Is there an intrinsic spiritual value in poverty whether voluntary or compulsory?

A month later, the committee summarized responses and distilled from them a set of practical guidelines about the ethical conduct of daily life.

They exhorted members to buy cooperatively rather than competitively; to undertake each day some task of manual labor; to find the minimum sum on which to live satisfactorily; to understand the habits of thought of some section of society to which by their upbringing they did not naturally belong.[149] This was precisely how the residents of Kingsley Hall and 60 Bruce Road had chosen to live their daily lives.

The FoR's endorsement of such altruistic quotidian routines attracted the High Church Anglican clergyman Bernard Walke, already experimenting in anti-materialistic Christian living in Cornwall.[150] Walke became a celebrity in interwar Britain for two things: his Christmas nativity play annually broadcast by the BBC and the sacking of his gorgeously decorated parish church, St. Hilary's, by ultra-Protestants enraged by his Catholic ritualism.[151] Muriel was deeply drawn to Walke's ideas. She made an odd match with the ascetic aesthete priest with a fondness for dandiacal silk stockings, who preached unorthodox ideas about divine love, voluntary poverty, and the Christian sacraments. The two had met by 1918 when Walke approached the FoR for help "propagating" the Brethren of the Common Table among the FoR's members and branches. He soon joined Muriel on the FoR's General Committee.

Walke insisted that the Communion table was the foundational site for enacting community and a primitive form of communism. Love, he explained, was the "sole basis of human society." The table at which Jesus and his disciples partook of the last supper of bread and wine "stands as token of the Divine Brotherhood and brings to view the overflowing life and riches of God given to the world in Jesus Christ." He fused God's superabundant economy of love with a love-based political economy governing relationships among Brethren. Just as Jesus freely shared and sacrificed his life to enrich humankind, so too Brethren literally put their wealth on the Communion table for others to take according to their own needs. Need was emphatically not based on calculations of family budgets and earnings and external surveillance by charity visitors. Rather, it was entirely a matter of individual conscience. Members "frankly" disclosed their "needs" and "means;" their Brethren, "in the Spirit of Christ," supplied those needs. The first Brethren who joined Walke at St. Hilary's were, he recalled, "a queer company with little in common beyond a dissatisfaction with our social system" which included a Marxist named Ernest, a London tramp, and a Scottish Presbyterian minister.[152] In dramatic contrast to Muriel's interpretation of his message at Kingsley Hall, Walke insisted that rules be kept to an absolute minimum. "I believe the end we seek will be achieved not by rules & standards," he explained to Rosa Waugh Hobhouse, "but by an infection of spirit."[153]

The onset of World War I eviscerated much of the vibrant pre–war culture of pacifist internationalism and Christian radicalism.[154] For those few like Muriel, Lansbury, Hodgkin, Wellock, Wilson, and Walke, who held fast to their abhorrence of force and violence as fundamentally contrary to God's love, World War I intensified their Christian revolutionary faith and sharpened their critique of capitalism, imperialism, and colonialism. It deepened Muriel's understanding of the connections between global forces and the local lives of laboring men, women, and children in Bromley-by-Bow. The war also turned those who espoused "God is Love" theology from fringe figures in the landscape of theological modernism and progressive social politics into national dangers and enemies. *After* it was sacked and partially burned in October 1917, the pacifist socialist Brotherhood Church in Croydon received more sympathetic national publicity from papers like the *Daily News* than it ever had during its previous two decades of public ministry.[155] Stephen Hobhouse, Rosa's husband and Muriel's friend, went from an obscure albeit exceptionally well-connected social worker and peace activist to a household name among Britain's leaders of church and state because the government insisted on jailing him repeatedly for his convictions.[156]

The weakest link in this program of Christian revolutionary love was translating it from a creed of personal transformation into one that could change the world around them. What did Walke mean by "infection of spirit"? By what means would such moral "infections" revolutionize the state and the economy, structures that most socialists placed at the very core of their analysis? While mechanisms of mass killing efficiently mowed down tens of thousands, sometimes in a single day, the FoR expected justice and righteousness to "dawn" upon the world when men were ready. All of this depended upon those who possessed power and wealth voluntarily relinquishing it so that they could share in the benefits of bringing God's Kingdom of Heaven to earth.[157]

"LOVE YOUR ENEMIES, BLESS THEM THAT CURSE YOU"

Muriel and Nellie waited for neither an "infection of spirit" nor a "dawn-ing" of righteousness to begin the work of changing themselves and Bromley-by-Bow. War created innumerable opportunities for them to put into practice Matthew 5:44: "love your enemies [and] bless them that curse you." Outspoken opponents of war, including Muriel, faced daily threats and insults; like conscientious objectors, they were persons "to be rebuked, bullied, and condemned."[158] Protecting Muriel and Kingsley Hall from such dangers was a task Nellie relished. With her deep roots in Bromley-by-Bow and extensive network of family, friends, and workmates, Nellie saw and heard about practically everything that happened in their neighborhood. At home all day, this became her new job, which she conducted on or near the doorstep of No. 58 Bruce Road with wit, tact, and diplomacy. "In the days of Kingsley Hall's unpopular-ity," Muriel recalled, "woe be to the idle gossiper who chanced to say a word against it within her hearing."[159] Almost from the moment Kings-ley Hall opened, Muriel and Nellie's commitment to living the Sermon on the Mount was severely tested. Their friendship sustained them through these ordeals and was in turn nourished by them.

Pacifism and militarist patriotism split apart families, great and hum-ble. John French, Lord Ypres, was Commander-in-Chief on the western front. His sister, Charlotte Despard, led Nellie and Muriel on peace marches and corresponded with Muriel about whether wartime Prime Minister Lloyd George possessed a "spiritual element" susceptible to ethical awakening. (Despard was not optimistic, Muriel was.)[160] War also would soon divide the Dowells of 58 Bruce Road. After Nellie's brother-in-law, the gun filer William Joseph Dellar sustained a disabling injury, her sister Florence could not afford to feed, shelter, and clothe her children. Rather than allowing Florence's children to be shipped off to a Poor Law orphanage, Harriet Dowell and Nellie took in Florence's oldest son, Willie (William Henry Dellar). By 1911, Willie was living with Nellie, her mother, and her milliner aunt Caroline on 313 Bruns-wick Road, the busy corridor leading from the Limehouse Cut to the entrance of the Blackwall tunnel. Nellie, her mother, and Willie soon moved next door to the Lesters while Caroline occupied a room two doors away at 64 Bruce Road.[161]

Nellie adored her nephew. Tales of his endearing silly antics enlivened her letters. While recovering from a leg injury in February 1912, Willie, "a perfect monkey," delighted in his crutches. "A funny boy but a loving little Chap," he had made all the nurses at the hospital laugh. He also knew how to "press" his Aunt Nell's "button" with "tricks" like bandaging their cat's paw.[162]

By 1915, Nellie's laughter had turned to worries about her nephew. In an undated letter probably written in 1916, Nellie was pleased that Muriel intended to visit Willie, then stationed with his regiment in the Essex village of Ongar.

> he is digging trenches he seems
> rather unhappy I want to
> go one Sunday or some
> day to see him it's a long
> time now since we saw
> him I hope they don't send
> him out to France for all
> the poor lads are gone[163]

Willie had enlisted in the army in July 1915, following in the footsteps of his father, who must have recovered sufficiently from his injuries to pass the Army's physical examination. Nellie's letters do not say why Willie did this. It must have hit everyone at 58–60 Bruce Road quite hard.

Here was an opening to love a person whose decision to join the army contradicted Muriel and Nellie's deepest convictions. Nellie reflected on the implications of Willie's wartime service and that of the other "lads" from Bromley-by-Bow. Like Muriel, she differentiated opposition to the war from her tender regard for its soldiers. War had made responsible men of mischievous boys. She pondered a "beautiful letter" explaining "excately [sic] what the war was like" written by a soldier who once had been a troublemaker in Muriel's Sunday school class. War had brought home to him and the other "young ones" the lessons that Muriel had taught them. These soldiers, Nellie concluded, were now "quite good different to what they were." The experience of war,

Nellie suggests, had made Muriel's teachings more powerful, not less, for her former students.

Muriel penned a vignette in her antiwar book *Kill or Cure* (1937) about an unnamed young man whose story closely resembles Willie Dellar's down to its details. I suspect she based it on Willie's. Muriel used the story to explore why young men like Willie enlisted in the army. England had not given the boy a "very good start in life" after his father was taken to an incurables hospital and the family thrown into poverty. William Joseph Dellar was sent to just such a hospital around 1906–7, hastening Nellie's return from Sweden. He still remained confined within London's medico-Poor Law complex at the time of the 1911 census as a workhouse inmate in Nellie's former orphanage at Forest Gate.[164] His incarceration there must have been an especially bitter blow for all the Dowells, a reminder that too many punitive elements of the Poor Law still darkened the lives of working people.

In Muriel's story, the boy's "old granny" took him to her home and "denied herself a good deal to feed and clothe him." With Nellie's support, this was precisely what Harriet Dowell had done for her grandson Willie. Nellie had made Willie and Harriet Dowell's maintenance the highest priority of her laboring life in the match industry. Propaganda about the Allies' "high ideals" in their fight against "coarse German militarism" and patriotic sermons from pulpits, Muriel explained, convinced the boy in her story that war "was being waged for the sake of the Kingdom of God." "He went to the recruiting office," Muriel noted without trace of condemnation, "gave in his name with a false age, and became a soldier."[165] This too is what Willie Dellar had done. A year shy of the legal age of enlistment, he went to Shaftesbury Street in Shoreditch on July 2, 1915 and joined the Army as a private.[166] In Muriel's vignette, the boy survives gassing but his militarist ideals do not. The recipient of a medal for his service, Willie Dellar returned to Bruce Road after the war and remained there long after his Aunt Nellie and grandmother Harriet died.[167]

Willie's enlistment came on the heels of the so-called Lusitania Riots of May 1915, one of the most traumatic episodes in Muriel, Nellie, and Kingsley Hall's history. Kingsley Hall won few friends in Bromley-by-Bow when Nellie, Muriel, and Kingsley Hall's Montessori teacher E. A.

Hargrove interposed their bodies between angry mobs and German resident aliens during London's anti-German rioting following the sinking of the Cunard's luxury ocean liner, the *Lusitania,* on May 7, 1915. Almost twelve hundred perished off the southern coast of Ireland. Kingsley Hall had closely identified itself with Quakers and pacifists led by Stephen Hobhouse, who, in the name of English liberty, sought to defend the property, persons, and civil rights of resident German and Austrian "enemy aliens."[168] Most of the Lesters' East London neighbors were in no mood to differentiate good Germans from bad. They were only too happy to lump together anyone whose name smacked of German ancestry, no matter how many decades a family had lived in and served the neighborhood.

The First Year's Report of Kingsley Hall (1915) included a harrowing account of the mob's frenzied rage. (See fig. 5.9.) "The Anti-German Riots" was written by "E. A.", presumably Kingsley Hall's Montessori teacher Ethelburga A. Hargrove. The story deftly mingled the utter banality of everyday life—the arrival of fat letters in the afternoon post— with its violent extraordinary interruption. "The street seemed to hold its breath" as "ominous" tramping sounds of a "big body of determined men" drew neighbors out of their homes to witness vigilante justice. The men would show "their patriotism" and give the "Government a good example in the treatment of alien enemies." The author of "Anti-German Riots" refused to blame the rioters for their behavior. She characterized the riot as a response to their own social and economic marginality as dehumanized cogs: "they were powerful individual personalities this afternoon—glorious change after having merely been a part of a machine since they left school at 14."[169] The national and local press also refused to condemn the rioters, but for quite different reasons. East Londoners were retaliating against the inhumanity and brutality of the enemy Hun. The caption for a *Daily Sketch* photograph of East London women absconding with a chair from a ransacked German home approvingly noted that it was "their only chance to show their hatred of German brutality."[170]

From the first German naval assaults on the southern coastal towns of Hartlepool and Scarborough in December 1914, Britons had grown accustomed to newspaper stories about scenes of devastation and destruction against civilians, especially women and children. Air raids in

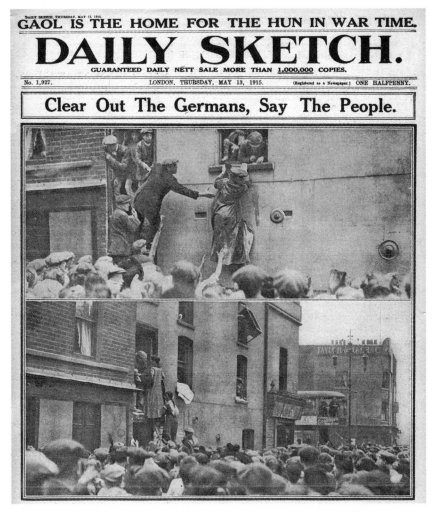

GAOL IS THE HOME FOR THE HUN IN WAR TIME.

DAILY SKETCH.

GUARANTEED DAILY NETT SALE MORE THAN 1,000,000 COPIES.

No. 1,927.   LONDON, THURSDAY, MAY 13, 1915.   (Registered as a Newspaper.) ONE HALFPENNY.

Clear Out The Germans, Say The People.

5.9. The local and national press ran extensive stories, accompanied by photographs, illustrating and defending popular violence toward so-called "enemy aliens" in Bow and Poplar during the riots after the sinking of the *Lusitania* in May 1915. "Clear Out the Germans Say the People," May 13, 1915, *Daily Sketch*, 1. (Courtesy of John Frost Newspapers/Mary Evans Picture Library.)

January 1915 prompted the *Times* to lament the "inhuman destruction of the weak and helpless" and condemn the "recrudescence of brutality such as the world has not witnessed for a thousand years."[171] The British state highlighted German attacks against blameless innocents as part of its ongoing campaign to muster recruits to its volunteer army.[172] The

5.10. Bernard Partridge, "Take up the sword of justice," printed by David Allen & Sons Ltd., Harrow, Middlesex (London, 1915). (Courtesy of the Library of Congress Prints and Photographs Division Washington, D.C.)

Parliamentary Recruiting Committee's *Take Up the Sword of Justice* (1915) depicted an unbowed martial Britannia who looks heavenward as she walks Christlike upon the water clutching her sword of justice. (See fig. 5.10.) In the background, the *Lusitania* remains afloat while its civilian victims sink to their deaths. Their outstretched hands in the turbulent waters echo J.M.W. Turner's famous painting *Slavers Throwing Overboard the Dead and Dying* (1840) and beseech the viewer to rescue them from such wanton injustice. It is a measure of the malleability of the rhetoric of outrage that the press construed East Londoners' assault on the English wife of a German-born baker as a justifiable response to German atrocities. In written and photographic press imagery of the

Lusitania Riots, British women ceased to be victims of "Hun" brutality and became agents of justifiable revenge. They had taken up Britannia's sword of justice.

"Anti-German Riots" offers a bittersweet celebration of the value of the local knowledge earned by dint of sharing in neighbors' lives. The local is not only a location, but a way of knowing predicated on a sense of affinity and sympathy. The author forestalls the rioters with her insider knowledge about the generosity and patriotism of the targeted Anglo-German victims, Mr. and Mrs. Paul, whose son is fighting on the Western Front. "They are splendid people who live here. Many's the pound of tea they have given away; always ready to do anybody a good turn." She contrasts the Pauls' devotion to their community with the ignorance of the rioters as outsiders, who have come from another part of Poplar. "You don't live here, do you? You see, all of us who live so close must know them best." The day-to-day bonds of neighborhood and neighborliness—produced through countless unrecorded acts of mutual aid and friendship—eventually prove no match for the more fleeting but also much more powerful bonds of patriotic nationalism that crudely made "neighbours" into "aliens" and enemies. The rioters move next door to a butcher's shop and loot its entire contents: "Soon wild shouts of triumph issued from the doors as, one by one, great strong women came running out carrying mattresses, pictures, chairs, sheets, and blankets." The entire story unfolds under the passively watchful eyes of the local police, who sanction the violence by their refusal to prevent it.[173] For Sylvia Pankhurst, the looting was sheer barbarism: cowardice masquerading as patriotism.[174]

Muriel also narrated the Lusitania Riots in *It Occurred to Me*. She too did not blame her neighbors and instead pointed to the influence of a jingoistic newspaper that incited a "gang of roughs" led by a "stranger" to maraud through Bow and Poplar. A scene of terrifying atavism unfolds as a "welter of maddened people" tosses beds and wardrobes from upper story windows onto a storefront canvas awning and run off with fifty pound bags of flour.[175]

Muriel left out one very important detail: Nellie never once left her side during this ordeal. In "The Salt of the Earth" (1923), Muriel told the story of the Lusitania Riots as a notable moment in the history of their loving friendship.

> In the anti-German riots, when the mob in Bow went mad over looting and
> some of us had to intervene to protect life, there was Nell, who had been
> standing pale as death beside me, suddenly flinging her arms round my
> waist to hold me back from facing the fury of the throng. Nell's arms proved
> too weak to hold one, but her forethoughtful love was a protection by day
> and by night.[176]

No doubt, Nellie clung to Muriel because she was terrified for her own
safety and Muriel's.

In Muriel's telling, the affective and the political press up against one
another, much like their two bodies.[177] Muriel allows her readers to
glimpse Nellie's language of love for Muriel and for their shared project
of enacting Christian revolution in Bromley-by-Bow. Nellie's embodied
gesture performs politics as love and love as politics. It would be hard to
imagine a story that more fully illustrated Muriel's most cherished ideas
about love and Christian revolution as a lived enterprise.

The unbounded nature of community at Kingsley Hall, which excluded none and welcomed all, the poetics of cross-class friendship, and
the politics of possession and dispossession coalesce in "Stolen Goods,"
a story printed in the Second Year's Report for 1916. The author was
"N.D."—Nellie Dowell.[178] Kingsley Hall's annual reports are filled with
similar essays written by the women and men of Bromley-by-Bow about
their lives and experiences at the Hall. The Hall's reports are multivoiced texts whose individual contributions were sometimes signed,
sometimes marked by the semi-anonymity of initials, and sometimes
attributed simply to a "club member." One contributor wittily remarked
that the Lesters had found a clever way to have others bear the literary
burden of writing their reports for them. The sisters' commitment to
making Kingsley Hall "common property" extended to its representations in print. Dispersed authorship enacted shared authority.[179]

Zeppelin raids over East London in 1916–17 provide the backdrop to
Nellie's story, most notably the bombing of one of Bow's main north-
south thoroughfares and Kingsley Hall in the early morning of September 24, 1916. East Londoners had initially greeted zeppelins as curiosities to be gawked at. They had crowded the streets to see the immense
humming flying machines filling the sky above them. They learned
quickly enough to fear them and seek safety in air raid shelters in secure

cellars. The raids gave Kingsley Hall opportunities to serve their neighbors. Muriel and Doris offered the local Watch Patrol free use of the Hall from 10 p.m. to 5 a.m. every night. At the first indication of a raid, volunteers in the Kingsley Watch Patrol (KWP) fanned out across the streets and knocked on every door to warn residents to find shelter. Helpers at Kingsley Hall (Misses Archer, Butcher, and Ogden) organized evacuation drills as part of civilian defense preparation.[180]

Nellie managed to find humor in every situation including the spectacle of watching fellow pacifists assume unaccustomed quasi-military roles. "I have thought of you these nights of danger," she wrote to Muriel, safe at the Grange.

we had such heavy fireing
your sister said you did not have it
much. The first night Miss Archer &
Miss Ogden Mother Aunt & Miss Butcher
you would have laughed Miss Butcher
is a good sport I call her Corporel
Jhonstone Miss Archer putting her
through the drill & the rest joined

Nellie took comfort—physical, spiritual, and psychological—holding tokens from Muriel of their partnership: a volume of Tolstoy they had studied together and small statues of St. Christopher, protector of travelers from dangers, and St. Timothy, hands clasped in prayer. "Last night was worse than all," she confessed, "but I felt better and quite jolly with my face to the wall every time the gun went off."

& then I had a
good look around. I took our a little
blue bird of happiness* off the
wall & put him in my chest & then
I looked at my old friend in front
of me Tolstoy, on the mantle shelf
was our dear boy, & Christopher in
the middle Aspiration [a short prayer] dear little
Timothy, & those strong hands

---

*The bluebird of happiness was a popular symbol of domestic, household-centered happiness.

clasped in prayer. I said it to them
jokeing after digging the cane in
All that was trying to sleep[181]

We glimpse Nellie's increasing physical disablement. She now kept a cane close to her, though she apparently used it for comic effect rather than mobility during the raid.

The zeppelin attack of September 24, 1916 seriously damaged Kingsley Hall and dramatically collapsed the distance separating home front from warfront. Recounted in several different essays published in the *Second Year's Report* for 1916, the bombing raid laid bare the Hall's interior. The "outside wall was blown across the street, windows shattered, and roof a wild medley of broken tiles," reported one of Kingsley Hall's helpers.[182]

The global forces sustaining the war implicitly frame Nellie's micronarrative about the unfolding of small-scale events at Kingsley Hall in the raid's aftermath. Her narration of "Stolen Goods" demonstrated acute awareness of the efficacy of "small gestures" as well as her skill in translating the lessons she had learned about techniques of "reconciliation" through reading and studying Tolstoy with Muriel.[183] The story shows her working as an intermediary between the Hall and its neighbors—even as she occupies both positions simultaneously. While scouring her front steps, she contemplates the loss of several cherished gifts donated by Kingsley Lester and stolen by local boys in the confusion after the zeppelin raid. Can she restore these precious objects without casting blame upon—and thereby alienating—the thieves? This was the challenge she faced as a Christian revolutionary peacemaker.

For much of the story, Nellie is literally at the threshold, neither inside nor quite outside. She engages various passersby and extracts information from them about the missing objects, including a dulcitone and several emblazoned school shields. Much like Nellie's letters, "Stolen Goods" reproduces the easy flow of her thoughts. Nellie values the "stolen goods" because of the meanings and feelings they bear for her, for the Lesters, and their community. She narrates a history of the many benevolent uses to which the stolen "dulcetone piano" had been put to brighten the lives of her neighbors. "They take it round the courts and alleys every Christmas, singing carols, and also to the infirmary where they carry a Christmas tree, and give the little sick children toys," Nellie wistfully recalled. "Now it is gone."

> I was cleaning the front door step and thinking so much about the piano and the shields being carried about the streets by people who did not think what it meant to the two sisters, and how unhappy they were about them; I was hurrying to get done, to get them back somehow, when a woman passed; I gave her a cheery word, and said, "Hello! what's up with you?" Then she started telling me all her troubles; she had her little boy with her—one of the lads of the rough brigade. 'Now, Dicky,' I said, 'you know who has got the piano and shields, tell me; they belong to friends that have been very kind to you' (meaning the mother).[184]

As a Cockney insider, Nellie knows exactly how to get her neighbors to tell her where the "stolen goods" are. They, in turn, can rely on her to use the information in a way that will not violate the community's norms and stir up conflict. Nellie is only too happy to comply with the poor boy's request, "don't split on me." Rather than accusing anyone of stealing the objects, Nellie writes a letter to the mother of "our rough boys, poor but tricky" who had made off with them. Her pronoun choice "our" shuts down the space between an imagined virtuous "us" and a criminal "them." She opens by assuming that the mother is the benevolent custodian of the objects rather than an accomplice to petty theft. She circumvents conflict and creates common ground between them by insisting that the woman, like Nellie, wishes to help out and make happy the "Miss Lesters."

> I hear you have got the shields, taking care of them for Miss Lester. Will you let me have them? I am sure you will, they belong to her. I have known the Miss Lesters for years and their brother. They leave their home and do all they can to help people and make them happy. I want to make her happy . . . to-morrow by having the shields here.

Here is Tolstoyan "reconciliation," not as an abstraction, but as a lived social process that itself cannot be divorced from Nellie's affective investment in Muriel's happiness. Nellie's version of the story ends well for everyone, a too tidy moral fable, perhaps. The mother returns the objects "with pleasure." Nellie pleases herself by pleasing the Lesters. And the boys, "quite happy and chatty now," return to their club at Kingsley Hall where Nellie rewards them with a good book and a warm fire.[185]

The bombing raid, much like the anti-German riots a year earlier, marked a turning point in Kingsley Hall's history. Both events brought the violence of global war home to Bromley-by-Bow. Both underscored Nellie's affective and political labor in loving Muriel and sustaining Kingsley Hall. The effects of these two events on the Hall's relationships with local people differed quite dramatically. In the eyes of their neighbors, the bombing proved that Kingsley Hall people were neither the Kaiser's spies nor his allies. The Hall's supporters now claimed the moral authority of innocent victims. Over and over, they demonstrated their hatred of the war *and* their solicitude for its foot soldiers. Kingsley Hall proudly displayed an Honor Roll near its front entrance that listed each local man serving the nation in the armed forces.

Two months later, in November 1916, Muriel, Nellie and fellow pacifists received encouragement from a most unlikely quarter, the Fifth Marquess of Lansdowne—former Viceroy of India, Secretary of State for War, and Foreign Secretary under Lord Balfour's conservative government.[186] A cabinet minister without portfolio in 1916, Lansdowne circulated a memorandum suggesting that the time had come for a negotiated settlement. A few weeks later, he reiterated his stance in a letter to the *Daily Telegraph* that stunned and disgusted the patriotic public. Prolongation of the war, he argued, "will spell ruin for the civilised world, and an infinite addition to the load of human suffering which already weighs upon it. . . ."[187] Mr. Punch ridiculed Lord Lansdowne's "grievous disservice to his country" as an old man's inexcusable lapse in judgment undertaken in a "fit of war-weariness."[188] The government did its best to hush up the matter. In April 1917 Sylvia Pankhurst decided to reinvigorate debate about the Landsdowne letter. She mobilized the FoR, the Independent Labour Party, her own East London Suffragettes, and various other feminist pacifists, including Charlotte Despard and Maude Royden, to march across East London from Canning Town to Victoria Park via Poplar and Bow to stage a large demonstration in support of a swift negotiated peace settlement.[189]

The march began inconspicuously enough at Barking Road in Canning Town with a small group of men and women bearing their slogans "nailed to broom sticks." As they crossed into Poplar, Bromley, and Bow, the contingent from Kingsley Hall led by Muriel, Nellie, May Hughes, and Rosa Hobhouse joined them carrying a large black cross. These were well-chosen symbols. The marchers transformed tools of humble household labor—broomsticks—into instruments of protest while proclaiming the Christian basis for their demand to end the war. Men from Bow's numerous pubs emptied onto the streets to enjoy the show and lightheartedly mock the demonstrators with sardonic shouts: "Three cheers for the Kaiser." As the protestors, now swollen to nearly a thousand strong, approached the park and crossed Ducketts Canal, the mood changed. Frank Hancock, one of the marchers, recalled

> The throng pressed us closer; instead of four abreast, we got down to two, then single file, and then isolated individuals. Over heads I could see the banners falling into the hands of rough crowds. . . . Then the Cross went down, and still we staggered on. Then it was impossible to move forward or backward. There was a solid howling mass of 'patriots.' None of us reached the Park Gates—some of the demonstrators were roughly handled, men's and women's clothing torn, hats and caps thrown away. . . .[190]

Maude Royden's compassion for the attackers—which included white dominion troops on leave and local roughs—did not diminish her revulsion at the naked bestiality of such intimate proximity to those "with the lust to hurt and destroy."[191]

The assault caught many of the peace marchers unawares. It came as no surprise to Muriel. "My ~~precious~~ dearest friend and neighbor, Nell Dowell, had scented trouble days before," Muriel recalled. Nellie played St. Christopher and St. Timothy to Muriel—supporting and protecting her from harm on their Christian revolutionary travels. Anticipating arrest, Nellie had packed Muriel a little bag with "tooth brush, night things and some food." Successive bouts of rheumatic fever had taken their toll on Nellie's body and left her increasingly disabled in body, though undiminished in mental and spiritual vigor.

> I hated to see her labored breathing as she kept pace with our marching step. When the storm broke she called to me to keep still and let things take their course. There was nothing else to do. I can't remember exactly what hap-

THE NEW CRUSADER.

PEACE DEMONSTRATION, VICTORIA
(SUNDAY, APRIL 15th)
"SMASHED UP" BUT—TRIUMPHANT!

5.11. "Peace Demonstration, Victoria Park," *New Crusader*, April 19, 1917, 4. (Courtesy of Swarthmore College Peace Collection.)

pened. . . . Little by little members of our party collected together. 'Where's Mary Hughes?' asked someone anxiously. Another replied that Rosa Waugh Hobhouse was looking after that frail and stalwart saint.[192]

For Christian revolutionaries like Muriel and Nellie, such apparent defeats were always spiritual victories. This was the beauty of the Sermon on the Mount's logic: struck by their enemies, Christians turned the other cheek. To give love for hatred was a precious chance to live by Jesus's exalted beatitudes and show the world the power of God's love. It's hardly surprising, then, that the *New Crusader* published an ecstatic headline about the "peace demonstration": "'SMASHED UP' BUT—TRIUMPHANT!" (See fig. 5.11.) While the *New Crusader* honored Sylvia Pankhurst for "scattering the seed of Christ's Peace, Goodwill and Brotherhood," she was not easily consoled. Embittered by East Londoners' failure to protect her and the marchers, she warned them not to publicly "spurn and revile those who have comforted you, whom you respect and to whom you will turn again in time of anxiety and trouble."[193] The Lusitania Riots, the bombing of Kingsley Hall, and the violent disruption of the Victoria Park "Peace Demonstration" were personal triumphs of Christian revolutionary love for Nellie and Muriel, moments of acute sociopolitical crisis in which the "prickly barriers" separating love, activism, and politics collapsed.

Muriel was a nobody when she first ventured to the London Society for Women's Suffrage in December 1914. By 1918, she had fully recovered the vigorous health of mind, body, and spirit that sustained her grueling global ministry of peace until her partial retirement at age seventy-five. She had also become a somebody—a leader in her own right, a person to be reckoned with not only in Bromley-by-Bow and London but among Britain's pacifist feminist community.

TELLING THE TRUTH, BECOMING AN HEIRESS

Muriel's experiences with her Bow neighbors during these years of wartime trauma and Christian witness opened her eyes to the everyday ethical dilemmas of being poor. They pushed her to ask new questions about the relationship between Christianity, truth telling, and poverty. In a probing essay she published in the *Christian World* in August 1918, Muriel asked herself and her readers whether it was possible to reconcile "East End life and Christianity." "Ought One to Speak the Truth?" she wondered.

This should not have been a hard question. The "deceit and untruth" of war accentuated pacifists' absolute commitment to truth as a precondition for the pursuit of reconciliation.[194] As she confronted the material and economic facts of her neighbors' lives, such certainty seemed to be yet another privilege that the poor could ill afford. Jesus's precept in the Sermon on the Mount (Matthew 5:8), "Blessed are the pure in heart, for they shall see God" was a cruel mockery under conditions in which husbands and wives had no choice but to share the same room, sometimes the same bed, with their children. "As a result of overcrowding," she explained, "the children's minds are often saturated with such sordid and degrading ideas . . . you will be haunted ever afterwards by the lewd and stunted ugliness of their conversation." Even when the working poor had the money to move their families into less cramped apartments, landlords routinely rejected tenants with large families and those coming from unrespectable streets. This troubled a member of the Kingsley Hall Club, who asked Muriel whether he should truthfully fill out the landlord's questionnaire. Muriel advised him to be a Christian, tell the truth, and risk rejection. Later that evening, she reflected on her answer. "I became disturbingly aware that preaching from a clean and pleasant house had no dire effect on myself, but only on my hearers." How could she spark a Christian revolution if she remained trapped in the "foolish innocence which is engendered by comfort and money?"[195] The obvious answer was to eschew comfort and seek poverty. Muriel did just that. To do so most effectively with maximum publicity, she decided that she also had to become an heiress.

The literal collapse of one of the Hall's outer walls in the 1916 zeppelin raid suggested a strategy that Kingsley Hall's residents and helpers took to heart: the value of making all that they did completely transparent to those around them. Determined to conceal nothing from their neighbors, Kingsley Hall's residents at the Hall and Bruce Road in practice reserved no space for their exclusive use—although at the outset, the living room was meant to be their own. If the front door to No. 60 was closed, neighbors went through Nellie's house at No. 58 and entered through the back garden. In an undated letter Muriel wrote to residents of 60 Bruce Road sometime after Nellie's death in 1923, she explained that "we have hostile and friendly eyes on us all the time as well as those which are neutral at present but watching, reserving their opinion, weighing up the pros and cons of our lives before they decide whether to copy us or to show us up." Nellie had always intervened on their behalf with their neighbors, deploying her diplomatic gifts, humor, and common sense to solve every problem they created for themselves. Without Nellie, they were now on their own, she explained. They would have to figure out how to live openly beyond their neighbors' reproach.[196]

Residents' lives remained on display—blurring the boundaries between inside and outside, public and private. Privacy, private life, and private property seemed at odds with their vision of a community bound by the desire not to possess but to share. In a letter to Muriel, Nellie playfully captured the joyful openness of Kingsley Hall, which she contrasted with the stiff "only fit for Sunday clothes" formality of the Lester family home in Loughton. Kingsley Hall beckoned all who passed to "come in don't go home & change, come & be happy (nice cup of tea a) Dough Nut or a cocanut bar. . . ."[197]

Daily life at Kingsley Hall and its nearby satellites was never just "cocanut" bars and "nice cups of tea." In their imaginations, the Lesters and the residents of Kingsley Hall broke down the walls separating peoples, races, churches, nations, and sexes.[198] But quotidian practices constantly reminded them of their ongoing struggle to eradicate the class privileges and blinkered assumptions so deeply engrained within many of them. Muriel gently chided Tom Smith, a fine craftsman who mended furniture at Kingsley Hall, for not sharing his thoughts at meetings. She was abashed when his wife pulled her aside and explained that he was silent because he could not afford dentures and was too embarrassed to reveal his empty gums. Muriel's story refuses readerly sympathy for Tom Smith's toothlessness. His silence is a measure of laudable self-pride and stoic independence, not quiet suffering that entreats Lady Bountiful to rescue yet another victim through her benevolent offices. Muriel dramatized the blind spots produced by her own bourgeois background that insulated and distanced her from the day-to-day realities of her neighbors' lives.[199]

Some of the Lesters' neighbors subjected them to cruel criticism, which they accepted and publicized in their quest for personal transparency. In January 1920, Muriel published a scathing letter by a self-proclaimed communist and "friendly comrade" in Bow that blasted her soft white hands and accused her of being a "rich middle class woman 'preaching platitudes to Eastenders, while living myself on a bloody stew composed of the blood, bones, and sweat of the workers.'" His hard-hitting rhetoric reflected workers' increasingly strident demands for the overthrow of capitalism fueled by militant socialists from Red Clydeside in Glasgow to the Third International in Moscow.[200] Muriel's genteel hands become bodily proof of her complicity with capitalist exploitation. Rather than rebut her "comrade's" factual errors or take offense at his familiar charge of the humanitarian-as-hypocrite, she "intensified and broadened [his criticisms]" and entreated workers "to work harder still for the overthrow of the present system."[201] Precisely what form this would take, Muriel never explained. No doubt Lester infuriated her "comrade" by making his criticisms her own. Her self-critical performance magnified her virtue.

Workers did not need Muriel to remind them of the failures of the "present system" as they confronted a severe economic slump in the early spring of 1921.[202] Many came to see the immense financial and social costs of winning the war. For socialist-pacifists like the Lesters, the years between Armistice in November 1918 and the spring of 1921 were scarred by the naked brutality of the British state in Ireland and India, which merely extended the industrial capitalist, militarist, and imperialist logic of the war itself. While some Britons defended the massacre of peaceful Indian protesters at Amritsar and the "dirty war" against Sinn Fein in Ireland, many did not.[203] Muriel and Kingsley Hall hosted Hannah Sheehy-Skeffington, whose martyred pacifist husband was an innocent victim of the British military suppression of the Irish "Rising" during Easter 1916.[204] Humanitarian organizations including *Save the Children Fund* bombarded the British public with graphic images of Austria's starving children in ways that made only too evident the human devastation and immorality of the continued Allied blockade of central Europe after the Armistice on November 11, 1918.[205] The Kingsley Hall community adopted an Austrian war orphan, Marie, who lived with Nellie and Muriel's friends, the Mortimers, and went to school at the Hall's Montessori kindergarten. Marie embodied the renewal of internationalism that was such a marked feature of interwar British political culture, which subsidized the creation of the League of Nations. Drawing on a long political tradition linking women with the politics of hunger, a black-clad Muriel led a march of East London mothers from Bow to Westminster to demand immediate relief for Europe's innocent postwar victims.[206]

Such factors—economic failure, humanitarian crises, and violent reprisals against nationalist movements in the Empire—encouraged Britons to rethink their views about the war and its opponents. This rapid shift in public opinion in the three years following the war enabled Kingsley Hall's supporters such as George Lansbury to reenter Parliament in 1922. Even New Crusader Wilfred Wellock managed to gain a seat in Parliament in a 1927 by-election and once again in the 1929 general election.[207] By 1921, the keenest proponents of war and the militarization of civil society "had been banished to the margins of political life" as Britons reinvented themselves as defenders of a "peaceable kingdom."[208] In the postwar battle to determine the future of Britain and save the soul of Europe from its own self-destructive barbarism, Kingsley Hall's ethics and politics of reconciliation increasingly seemed like a legitimate political and economic strategy, not the contemptible idealism of an eccentric pacifist fringe.

The original residents of Kingsley Hall—Rosa Waugh Hobhouse, May Hughes, and Muriel, along with Muriel's FoR colleague Stanley James—seized this moment to renounce their wealth altogether in their widely circulated manifesto of March 15, 1921 inviting the British public to join them in "voluntary poverty." All four were founding members of Bow's chapter of the Brethren of the Common Table.[209] The manifesto affirmed their Christian obligation to meet "the needs of others, whether in our country or abroad" as a way to share God's love through the "sacrament of fellowship." They sought the blessing "derived from intimate contact with the sorrows of the oppressed." The Bow Brethren's meetings began with silent prayer, followed by welcoming the Presence of God, "then we become severely practical, and individually declare our incomes, earnings and doles." "It isn't enough to give away money," Muriel explained, "we feel we have no right to possess it."[210]

The manifesto made clear just how far Muriel was willing to go to unmake the Victorian philanthropic gift economy. By her reckoning, the Brethren could not give away wealth that they never rightfully possessed. Members placed food, clothing, and excess earnings on the table for others to take freely. They short-circuited the mutual obligations binding the giver and recipient of a gift by refusing to offer or accept thanks. The Brethren repudiated all tests of financial worthiness and moral judgments about what constituted need. Need was left entirely to the conscience of each person. Nor did they care if rascals and scoundrels took advantage of them because this permitted the Brethren to show them God's love.

What made the voluntary poverty story so compelling was who the signatories were and what, at least in the public's imagination, several of them had personally sacrificed on behalf of their noble Christian revolutionary principles. Newspaper coverage of the manifesto in Britain and the English-speaking world was extensive and suggests a well-orchestrated public relations campaign. The *Evening Standard* declared that the Brethren consisted of "an heiress or two, a curate, a writer, a teacher, a dog biscuit packer, an out of work carpenter, a dock labourer, a young widow on relief and a journeymen printer."[211] The headline of Salt Lake City's *Deseret News* on July 1, 1921 screamed in large-font letters, "Millionaires And Paupers Join in Self Denial." The story, widely reprinted, included a photograph of Rosa ironing her wash in her dreary Hoxton tenement along with a portrait of a smiling, distinctly modern Muriel.

The reporter, Hayden Church, had expected to interview Muriel at Kingsley Hall in Bow, but she had been called to the Grange to care for Henry Lester. Church made the most of the contrast between Muriel's apparently sincere embrace of austere poverty and the splendor of her life at the Grange, "a perfect gem of a country mansion, surrounded by velvety lawns, flower gardens a riot with color, a tennis court." "I look rather a hypocrite, don't I," Muriel confessed, before explaining that her Bow neighbors, frequent guests at the Grange, had "more right to it [the Grange] than we have."[212] Daughterly duty, she insists, not a desire for ease compelled her to live part of each week at the Grange. Such stories gave the distinct but not strictly accurate impression that Muriel was herself among the Brethren's "heiress or two."

Rosa Hobhouse underscored the profound difference between *choosing* voluntary poverty—a willing desired renunciation—and *being* poor: "it was impossible to claim that our sharing in their outward circumstances even approached the inner reality of our neighbors' experience." The poor, she argued, endured immoral and unjust "compulsory want"; "voluntary poverty" was itself a privilege. She knew only too well that she retained her cultural capital and resources of wealthy friends and family members.[213] The manifesto signatories' self-dispossession was part of their ongoing effort to free themselves from the burdens of private property and achieve complete transparency in relation to their neighbors.

All four signatories, in quite different ways, never entirely reshaped their lives to conform fully to their vow of poverty. Doris had conspicuously not entered voluntary poverty and Muriel often relied on her for financial support after Rachel and Henry Lester's death. While Stephen Hobhouse had renounced his claims to his family's Somerset estate, he and Rosa had consented to the creation of a Hobhouse family trust upon which they drew to pay for costly treatments for Stephen's debilitating physical and psychological ailments. (Both Muriel and Rosa made public these financial safety nets that insulated them from the full burden of their vows.)[214] The most self-denying of the four was May Hughes. She also retained the most direct control over her inheritance, which included several substantial properties in the lovely Berkshire village of Longcot. She converted one building into a sanctuary for rough lads from Whitechapel and another into a home for fallen women. She agonized for almost a decade over the sale of a third property, fancifully called Bareppa, to the family of her uncle's devoted groom. In the end, she finally agreed to the sale on the condition that the purchasers promised to be beacons of Christian revolutionary light and love in their small village. For May Hughes, voluntary poverty went hand in hand with her own brand of benevolent paternalism.[215]

The signatory who most egregiously violated the spirit of their Christian revolutionary vow was Stanley James. A man of roving ways and unsettled religious convictions, he had been a cowboy in the Canadian Rockies and a rail-riding hobo in the American West. When he returned to Britain, he assumed his father's Methodist pulpit in Wales, married, and started a family. He eventually drifted to London, apparently without his wife and children, where he worked for the FoR, sometimes edited *The Crusader* and delivered stirring pacifist socialist sermons to his Nonconformist Walthamstow congregation. He also grotesquely abused his ministerial authority to seduce idealistic vulnerable female congregants.

The diaries and letters of three lower-middle-class women, Ruth Slate, Eva Slawson, and Minna Simmons, record in painful graphic detail how James preached from his pulpit the "religion of love which must unite all" while using a small private room in the church to have sex with some of them. "He [Stanley James] came to see me. We had a most lovely talk. We had been to Maude Royden's meeting and it had been the means of one of those soul talks," Minna Simmons confided to Ruth Slater in July 1916. Had Maude Royden's lecture combined discussion of pacifist feminist antiwar work along with one of her frank chats about women's healthy sexual desire when expressed in monogamous marriage? Perhaps, but Minna did not say. In any case, Stanley James used this opening to turn discussion of God's love into his own lovemaking with her.

> Well dear we went into the front room alone and he kissed me, opened my dress and kissed my breasts too, and he said how he felt I was his. He was just going away when he came back and pleaded with me dear to give him everything a woman can give a man. I told him I was sure we should regret it but no dear anything that would make me his. 'Well dear, I did.' The tears I have shed have quite washed away any wrong I did.

Tragically, Minna felt no rage at James, whom she eventually dismissed as an incorrigible "serial dipper." Instead, she directed her fury at herself for loving James while she sought to shift the terms of their relationship to a higher non-physical spiritual plane. James apparently expressed no remorse for what he had done to her. He had more than lived up to one of his favorite pen names, "The Tramp."[216] Completely unaware of James's despicable behavior, Muriel publicly extolled his "great work" to reporters eager to learn more about each of the signatories.[217]

The 1921 Voluntary Poverty manifesto set the stage for Muriel's even better-publicized refusal to accept her share of Henry Lester's wealth at the time of his death in 1927. (Henry left an estate worth £62,000, a considerable fortune; he may well have spent at least that much keeping Muriel and Doris in poverty and supporting their various causes.) This was the moment that Muriel most fully colluded with the press to make herself appear to be an heiress, albeit for the sole purpose of drawing attention to her critique of capitalist wealth.

The October 17, 1927 headline of the *Daily Chronicle* trumpeted "Rejected Legacy," which told a romantic story about the daughter of a wealthy shipbuilder, Muriel Lester, who had "rejected" the £400 per annum inheritance her father had left her. (See fig. 5.12.) Muriel spoke before a crowd of Bow people whom she had gathered by circulating an open notice to the women of Bow that she intended to return *their* money by creating a "Restitution Fund." She deftly played the part of anti-celebrity media darling who performed her own selflessness for the good of Poplar.

> 'You know that my father made most of his money in East London,' she said. 'He got on very well with the workmen, but as they made the money I felt that the annuity of £400 a year which he left me ought to go back to the workpeople. However, I cannot find the people who made the money. So I decided that it should go to the people of Poplar and you have to decide what is to be done with it.'[218]

With the advice of the Christian socialist author of *The Acquisitive Society* (1920) R. H. Tawney, Muriel handed over her money to a trust run by and for her neighbors.[219] A group of local residents, mostly women, decided to subsidize "home helps" to mothers before and after childbirth.[220] Inherited wealth was "outworn, cumbersome, unsporting and unchristian," Muriel jauntily informed an interviewer.

Her gesture was political argument and action. It was a deft ethical maneuver that allowed her to negotiate the tensions between her roles as

5.12. This double portrait photograph captures Henry and Muriel's mutually supportive and loving relationship. Dressed like a 1920s' anti-flapper in monastic sackcloth fabric with a simple belt, Muriel looks reverentially at Henry Lester who reads an illustrated daily newspaper. "Henry Edward Lester and daughter Muriel," Lester/6/6, Lester Papers. (Courtesy of Bishopsgate Institute.)

loving late-Victorian daughter and twentieth-century Christian revolutionary modern woman. The *Daily Chronicle* summed it pithily: "Refused £400 a year legacy and now scrubs floors."[221] It also allowed Muriel to articulate a version of what today we might call "restorative justice" as a supplement to her commitment to the radical redistribution of resources. She was not giving money to anyone: she was returning it to those who had produced it in the first place. It is also an early example of creating a "restitution" fund as a way to rectify past injustices in the absence of a clearly identifiable injured party.[222] Because Muriel could not find the individual men and women whose labors had created her father's fortune, she returned to their community that which should have been theirs.

Muriel's "rejected legacy" became part of an enduring mythology about her as the selfless English heiress who by the 1930s had become a "saint, a modern Joan of Arc" crusading around the world "for the Sermon on the Mount."[223] The *Los Angeles Times*'s church editor James Warnack contemplated history's highest exemplars of moral virtue and spiritual leadership, the sources of "the real power and progress of civilization." "The Nazarene was such a man and so was St. Paul, St. Francis and Spinoza—and, further back, Gautama Buddha, Krishna, Confucius and other sages." These were predictable, perhaps even inevitable, choices. When he turned to the modern world, he found several "great ones" worthy of their predecessors: Gandhi, Kagawa, and Albert Schweitzer—"yes, and Muriel Lester and Evangeline Booth."[224] This was the extraordinary company that Muriel Lester kept in 1936, at least for her far-flung admirers.

Nellie did not live to see Muriel disinherit herself or attain global renown. By war's end, the physical boundaries of Nellie's world grew smaller as her health worsened. She played no part in Muriel's marches and protests from 1918 onward; nor did she contribute any more articles for Kingsley Hall's annual reports. In one undated Christmas letter to Muriel, she asked her to "excuse this scribble & shaky hand its heart is on its hook"—a humorous expression she used to describe the chest pains that dogged her footsteps and kept her close to 58–60 Bruce Road. "During these constant and terrible attacks one could not sit up with her, hour after hour," Muriel recalled, "without realising that in Nell one saw a type of the dispossessed, suffering their age long oppression at the hands of an acquisitive society."[225]

This was not how Nellie saw herself, Muriel acknowledged. Even at such times, Nellie's wit remained as expansive as ever. She was amused by the postman's struggle to decipher May Hughes's funny handwriting as he delivered a letter addressed to "Nellikin." "Miss Hughes" was, Nellie decided, "one of the best true as steel, never mind." Nellie even made light of wartime food shortages that tested her ingenuity to produce good meals: "Good bye God bless you all my old friends have a lobster for a change."[226]

In December 1922, Nellie sent Muriel her last letter, a Christmas greeting. (See fig. 5.13.) Despite its brevity, Nellie's note is a rhetorically and emotionally complex piece of writing. It opened with her usual wit

5.13. Nellie Dowell to Muriel Lester, Christmas 1922, Nellie Dowell Letters, Lester Papers. (Courtesy of Bishopsgate Institute.)

and dexterity. "A real live gentleman sent me 3£ to do what I like," she told Muriel, "so I hand you one to do what you like." Nellie's humor quickly gave way to an uncharacteristic air of exhaustion and sadness at her uselessness. It wasn't just that she felt unworthy of such a large gift, "I don't deserve & I know it." She also felt "I am no good for anything in your line." Physically incapable of withstanding the rigors of factory labor after leaving London Hospital and the Whitechapel Lunatic Ward in March 1910, Nellie had become Muriel's partner in the everyday work of Christian revolution. Twelve years later, that too she could do no longer. "Even you only love me and keep me it's quite enough to know that. Nell." The blotted overwriting on the page suggests that Nellie struggled with the word "love." It appears that she also wrote the word "like"—uncertain which sentiment most accurately captured Muriel's feelings for her in her diminished condition. Her terse closing indicated unusual reserve, nothing like the long effusive final salutations of her previous letters.

Muriel publicly offered the Kingsley Hall community a highly edited rosy version of this letter that erased the psychological demands it made on her.

> Nell was superlatively human, and steel strong in her likes and dislikes. She had a genius for always being on the spot when needed, an instinct for knowing how to make people comfortable even in the presence of her mortal pain. Her generosity was staggering. One Christmas, a pound note arrived for the children's work; a pound note from Nell—it was like the gift of a thousand pounds from another.

Muriel needed Nellie, or perhaps more aptly, her final memories of her, to be a source of light, humor, wisdom, and courage as she faced the world without her. As with her brother Kingsley's death, Muriel did not mourn because Nellie had "entered into fuller life."[227]

A few weeks after penning her Christmas message, Nellie was admitted to the very same hospital—the Poplar and Stepney Poor Law Sick Asylum renamed St. Andrews—to which Harriet Dowell had taken her when chorea first struck her in 1890. She stayed nine days before returning home to 58 Bruce Road on January 26.[228] She died there on January 31, 1923.

No medical case files survive for St. Andrews from this period. Muriel could not bear to narrate Nellie's final encounter with the medical establishment that had so singularly failed her. She used words to articulate feelings beyond the power of words themselves. All she would say was that Nellie's final experience of institutionalization was so bad that "it is recorded in another place," by which Muriel presumably meant in Heaven. It was not lost on Muriel that the Poor Law had outlived Nellie Dowell, her "dearest friend and neighbor," so cruelly buffeted by its inhumanity. Much had changed in the provision of poor relief, medical

THE SALT OF THE EARTH.

In Memoriam, NELLIE DOWELL, *who entered into fuller life, January 31st, 1923.*

NEVER has there been a better friend to Kingsley Hall than Nellie, though for years she has not often had the strength even to walk the few hundred yards from her house to visit it, but there is probably no man or woman living who has given more to us all than Nellie gave.

She was standing by in the Spring of 1914 when the idea of the Hall was conceived. She cherished it, helped it to grow, made it seem real. Whenever the dream began to grow hazy she would discuss it in terms of flesh and blood, and by fitting actual people into its imagined framework, she increased one's faith.

After its birth, it was Nell one turned to in every crisis. Always she had some constructive suggestion to give, and over and over again, when one seemed to be baulked at every turn and no way out was visible in any direction, one would go in next door hopelessly, as a last resort "just to tell Nell." One

— 15 —

5.14. Muriel Lester, "The Salt of the Earth," 8th Annual Report, Kingsley Hall (1923), 15.

care, and social welfare since the early 1880s, in no small measure because of the political and affective labors of men and women like George Lansbury, Muriel Lester, and Nellie Dowell. But not enough.

Muriel probably sat down to draft her biographical sketch of Nellie, "From Birth to Death," soon after Nellie's death. She incorporated many passages of "From Birth to Death" into her only published account of Nellie's life, "The Salt of the Earth." (See fig. 5.14.) This was a very well-chosen title. For Christian revolutionaries, *to be* the Salt of the Earth was to live the exalted ideals of the Sermon on the Mount: "Ye are the salt of the earth: but if the salt have lost his savour, wherewith shall it be salted? It is thenceforth good for nothing, but to be cast out, and to be trodden under foot of men." (Matthew 5:13). Reverend Richard Roberts, Muriel's FoR friend and colleague, glossed the meaning of this famous phrase. "Men who are salt" have "achieved a definite Christian personality," he argued. "The business of the Church in the world is the manufacture of salt, the creation of moral personality." Only such people had the "grace and the power" to "arrest and destroy the principle of self-regard and degeneration. . . ."[229] Muriel inscribed Nellie as the embodiment of the Sermon on the Mount, God's words made flesh.

For so much of Nellie's life, Poor Law officials and medical doctors made her into a "case," to be helped, studied, disciplined, and managed. This Muriel would not do. She drew upon a much older literary genre, the exempla, which served religious writers as an "example" and "an illustrative story."[230] If Nellie's letters are the most full-bodied loving documents in Muriel's vast archive, "The Salt of the Earth" is the most full-bodied loving essay Muriel ever wrote. In offering these judgments, I can't pretend to hide behind the mask of historical objectivity. In telling their story, I have argued that part of what makes their entwined histories so compelling is how they always connected politics and feelings; head and heart; mind, body, and spirit.

CONCLUSIONS

The Great War must be counted among the most decisive and dramatic ruptures in British history. For many, it was no less than the midwife of modernity and its aftermath merely a continuation of war-by-other-means. In imagining what a reconstructed postwar Britain might become, Muriel, Doris, Nellie, and their Kingsley Hall friends used mundane practices to unmake and remake the late-Victorian and Edwardian philanthropic legacy they inherited. Violence, trauma, fragmentation, loss are the familiar keywords in how men and women in the 1920s and '30s—and subsequent historians—have characterized the shift from so-called Victorian to modern values. Since 1924, Virginia Woolf has trained us to listen for the sound of "breaking and falling, crashing and destruction" "in or about December 1910" when, she insists, "character changed."[231] Others use no less violent language but insist that the Great War extinguished Victorian liberalism. War's carnage, we are told, produced a decade of escapist long weekends and violent "aftershocks." Britain demonized and brutalized outsiders—Jews, women, Indian nationalists, trade unionists—as impediments to making whole the fragmented national body.[232]

Without disputing the cogency of such interpretations, I have elucidated their dialectical alter ego.[233] Muriel and Nellie's friendship and their shared labors at Kingsley Hall underscore the gradual evolution of and continuity in social action from the 1880s to the 1930s, a sensibility of inclusive hospitality to outsiders, and the emergence of a "peaceable" postwar consensus animated by Christian values and politics.[234]

Religion at Christian revolutionary Kingsley Hall admitted no division between the damned and the saved, the true convert and the false witness. Muriel articulated the far-reaching inclusivity that flowed from her understanding of God's love in a moment of piqued annoyance at her own—and others'—failure to live a fully Christian life. "If there is one person in Number Sixty [Bruce Road] whom we feel we can't love," she admonished, "to that extent Christ is failing. He is reviled, neglected, forsaken, unloved, rejected of men and crucified again every time we let one person remain outside the circle of our heart's love."[235] Secreted in the very heart of Muriel's revolutionary Christianity was a God so loving that He embraced and loved everyone: Catholic and Protestant, Jew, Muslim, and Hindu; rich and poor; black and white; and even those who questioned or denied His existence. What Muriel did not and could not see is that the refusal to exclude was—and is—not the same as compelling everyone to be included. This distinction eluded her self-critical field of vision.

For Muriel, Nellie's life enacted the Sermon on the Mount's revolutionary message of love. Nellie's last written words in her final letter to Muriel testify to the transformative power of this love while subtly asking Muriel to accept its limits. "You only love me and keep me it's quite enough to know that. Nell." The phrase that jolts is "keep me," and all that it implied about Nellie's deepest desire to be Muriel's and, perhaps, her economic dependence on Muriel. During the last years of Nellie's life, Muriel had done everything she could to free herself from possessions and possessiveness as a way to enact Christian revolution in her personal life. Determined to distance herself from the philanthropic gift economy of the Victorian Lady Bountiful, Muriel wanted to believe that it was possible to separate altogether loving and keeping. Nellie, the match factory girl who never stopped yearning for a lady's clean white hands, comforted herself knowing that Muriel both loved her *and* kept her. This was Nellie's truth and it was "quite enough" for her.

Afterlives

⁂

MURIEL ADDRESSED THE FESTIVE CROWD assembled in September 1928 to celebrate the opening of the new Kingsley Hall on Powis Road, a block from 58–60 Bruce Road. (See fig. A.1.) In the fourteen years since founding Kingsley Rooms, much had happened in Muriel's life and much more in the world. Rachel Lester's death in 1918, followed by Nellie's in 1923 and Henry Lester's in 1927, had loosened the ties binding her to Loughton and East London. After years of intense engagement with the affairs of household, street, neighborhood, and borough, she had begun to apply the techniques of reconciliation that she and Nellie had developed in Bromley-by-Bow to the British Empire. By the time she returned in 1927 from extended sojourns to the ashrams of India's best-known anti-colonial nationalists, Rabindranath Tagore and Mohandas Gandhi, Muriel had embraced fully the concept of "world citizenship" as part and parcel of her ethics and politics of Christian revolution. She made herself into a member of Gandhi's corps of white western women engaged in informal diplomacy on behalf of his and India's great cause.[1] If Nellie had served as intermediary between Muriel and their Bow neighbors, Muriel now took on this role for Indians and Britons. As she explained to Tagore in 1934, she saw herself as "a sort of safety-valve, a message taker, from side to side, an interpreter in a small way—longing for our two races each to bring the best out of the other—instead of continually annoying and misunderstanding the other."[2]

Despite and because of her commitment to securing global justice for "the least among you," Muriel increasingly found herself talking and writing to the greatest and most powerful in Britain and the empire. During the interwar years, she corresponded and met with viceroys, secretaries of state, prime ministers, famous humanitarians, and peace campaigners from Japan to South America. She preached before United States presidents and met privately with Eleanor Roosevelt. The new Kingsley Hall reflected the growing international stature of its charis-

A.1. "Kingsley Hall, Bow," *Architect's Journal*, July 16, 1930, 79.

matic leader while materializing the Christian revolutionary principles upon which it had been founded in 1915.

Designed by Charles Cowles Voysey in close consultation with Muriel, the Hall announced its founders' reverence for simplicity, transparency, and God's love.[3] In light of Muriel's exceptionally detailed rules of residents' lives at Kingsley Hall (down to procedures for cleaning mahogany table surfaces), it should come as no surprise that she attended to every architectural feature of the new building. The flat rooftop boasted a garden donated by A. A. Milne along with austere monastic cells with tall doors and waist-high casement windows that offered minimal privacy and even less comfort for their occupants. Weather permitting, male and female residents were encouraged to sleep on cots on the sex-segregated rooftop loggias to gain the health benefits of fresh air and sunlight. Voysey had already tested out the design of rooftop sleeping at Children's House, which he had built in 1923 to accommodate the Lesters' child welfare activities in the same Bromley-by-Bow neighborhood.

The visibility of Kingsley Hall residents' mundane daily activities was meant to reassure their East London neighbors that the Hall and its members had nothing to hide from them. A small "sanctuary" chamber, suited for "practicing the presence of God" through silent meditative prayer, greeted those who entered through the hall's plain oak doors just to the right off the front vestibule. Most community members went straight into the spacious unadorned ground floor hall with its semicircular oak-paneled chancel punctuated by an echoing arched window in the center. (See fig. A.2.) Muriel made a point of noting that the honey-hued oak had been harvested from the forests of Britain's erstwhile enemy, Austria. Here was yet another way to show the power of reconciliation to turn hatred into love and beauty. The circular vaults created the illusion of height despite the fact that the ceiling was flat and the ground floor hall bore the heavy burden of holding up the club rooms, kitchens, bathrooms, library, office, and sleeping spaces of the upper stories. Worship, Muriel explained, was the foundation upon which everything else depended. Unlike the first Kingsley Hall, no one donated physical labor to help build it. However, members and residents did keep it spotlessly clean. They prepared and served all the meals, washed the community's linens and clothing through closely regulated, rotating housekeeping duties. While some residents shared the Lesters' well-to-do socioeconomic backgrounds, others, like their unemployed neighbor Alf Butcher, were no strangers to the rigors of such manual labor.[4]

The dedication ceremony and its varied cast of participants reflected Muriel's attempt to balance competing demands and ideals, to link the Hall's past with its future. Determined to liberate herself from cash and commodities, Muriel necessarily courted and depended upon men and women of wealth to pay for and maintain the new building. This disturbed Rosa Hobhouse, who felt keenly that the institutional expansion

A.2. Circular Chancel with Gandhi bust, Kingsley Hall Bow. (Photograph by author.)

of Kingsley Hall came at an ethically perilous cost.[5] Perhaps this also explains why King Edward VII's godson, Lord Knebworth, Edward Antony James Bulwer-Lytton, presided over the dramatic opening ceremony. A man wielding an impeccable Conservative aristocratic pedigree, he had absolutely no credentials to herald the latest phase of Muriel's Christian revolutionary project.[6] Bulwer-Lytton emphasized that Kingsley Hall supplied what skeptical Britons so badly needed: "big ideals." Kingsley Hall and Muriel had done "magnificent" work putting their ideas into action, he observed. Tom McCarthy, a longtime Kingsley Hall Club member, carried the old Hall's simple wooden cross as he led the people of Bow, eight hundred strong, into their new Hall. This cross, two sticks held together by string, had become the Hall's symbol of protest against social injustice since Muriel carried it during her 1919 march from Bow to Westminster to demand an end to the allied blockade of Germany and Austria.

Muriel began her speech by recalling a handful of "absent friends" whose labors had made this great day possible. Nellie, dead for five and a half years, was among them. This was the last recorded time that Muriel spoke or wrote explicitly about Nellie Dowell.[7] For the next forty years, Nellie simply disappeared from Muriel's public and print utterances. Muriel could not have forgotten her. Nellie's mother, Harriet Dowell, and her nephew Willie Dellar and his family continued to live at 58 Bruce Road for at least another decade and remained involved with Kingsley Hall.[8] And she must have reread Nellie's letters sometime in old age when she put them into a wrinkled manila envelope and wrote "Nell" on it. (See fig. A.3.)

In 1937, Muriel decided to publish her first autobiography, *It Occurred to Me*. By then, she had become a global celebrity with a knack

A.3. Muriel collected and put Nellie's letters into this envelope at some point in old age, probably in the last few years of her life. Envelope for Nellie Dowell Letters, Lester Papers ML/4, Kingsley Hall, Dagenham.

for publicity. "Publicity is the only thing some people fear," she explained and "telling the truth is perhaps the pacifist's only weapon."[9] She had successfully negotiated for her friend Mohandas Gandhi to stay at Kingsley Hall in the autumn of 1931 during the Second Round Table Conference in London to discuss constitutional reform in India. Reporters the world over flocked to the Hall and interviewed its saintly founder, the woman who had rejected an inheritance to serve the poor. Doris, it seems, stuck ever more closely to her work for children and escaped their notice altogether. To the delight of journalists, Muriel helped to broker the famous meeting of the great-souled Mahatma with the world's most beloved champion of the underdog, Charlie Chaplin.[10] In 1934, she marched with Gandhi in earthquake-devastated Bihar. By 1937, Nazi Germany was mobilizing to exact what it saw as justifiable retribution for the victorious allies' vindictive treatment of the Fatherland after World War I. Even absolutist pacifists and conscientious objectors during World War I began to countenance the use of military force to stop Hitler. Now, more than ever, Muriel believed that the world needed stories like hers about the lives of peacemakers.

Muriel told that story on the pages of *It Occurred to Me*. It teems with persons and personalities of East Londoners. Muriel mentioned by name the starch factory worker Beattie and her mother Mrs. Pryke, her first hostess in Bromley-by-Bow. They had invited the naïve society girl to join them for a cup of hot cocoa before traveling home to Loughton after Muriel's unforgettable night at the factory girls' club on Albert Terrace in 1902. She recalled Edith, the lovely single mother whose early death meant tragedy for her three orphaned children. But no Nellie Dowell. There is one passage in Muriel's entire published autobiographical oeuvre that unambiguously but anonymously alludes to Nellie as "our ex-factory girl helper." It concerns Muriel's sense of responsibility during World War I for running three kitchens: her parents' in Loughton, the Dinner Club for factory girls at Kingsley Hall, and the one at No. 60 Bruce Road. At Bruce Road,

> our ex-factory-girl helper could always be depended on to work miracles. We became so accustomed to her genius that, I'm afraid, we took it for granted. How mean and poor-spirited an attitude that is! And how one longs to rectify it when the benefactor is gone beyond reach![11]

This admiring passage makes painful reading for me. It seems so paltry compared to Muriel's heartfelt published appreciation in "The Salt of the Earth" (1923) and in one of her early undated typescript histories of Kingsley Hall that elaborated Nellie's crucial part in their public work at moments of crisis. Nellie's letters do make clear that she enjoyed preparing good meals for her family and the Lester sisters despite wartime food shortages. No doubt, as Nellie's disabilities restricted her physical mobility, she made herself useful by taking on more household duties at 58–60 Bruce Road. Muriel's phrase "ex-factory-girl helper," however, seems such an inadequate way to characterize Nellie and their tender partnership, so intimate yet so demanding. It erases Nellie's contributions to the political and religious dimensions of their Christian revolutionary project and consigns her to a wholly class-based female domestic sphere. Why did Muriel decide *not* to name Nellie if the impulse behind her writing this compensatory homage was to properly acknowledge her "genius" in a way that Muriel had failed to do while she was alive?

I can't definitively answer these questions, though I will return to them. They compel me to reconsider the document that figured so crucially at the outset of my research, Nellie's death certificate. (See fig. A.4.) It was the first document that I found that gave me the basic "facts" about her: her proper name, Eleanor, along with her age and date of death. This information led me to so many other archival discoveries about Nellie. As Nellie was dying, her younger sister Rose Dowell Endersbee was with her. Muriel's terse description of Nellie's death in "The Salt of the Earth" makes clear that she too sat up with Nellie and comforted her in her mortal pain. Rose must have filled in the bureaucratic forms for Nellie's death certificate as the official "informant." The sisters had remained close although Rose, like so many others East Londoners, had been upwardly and eastwardly mobile. She had long since left Bromley-by-Bow. In 1923, she lived in the eastern suburb of Barking with her children and her husband, Harry, who worked in the insurance industry. What startled and disturbed me was Nellie's listed occupation: "spinster domestic housekeeper." The designation "spinster" had a very long life in official record keeping, many decades after the term itself had fallen into disfavor. Spinster seemed to me discordant with the languages and categories by which Muriel and Nellie had composed their independent adventurous lives, but at least it was not hard to explain.

FC 698256

| | | CERTIFIED COPY | | | of an ENTRY | | | | |
| Pursuant to the Births and | | | | | Deaths Registration Act 1953 | | | | |

			Registration District		poplar				
1923.	Death in the Sub-district of Bromley					in the County of London			
Columns:-	1	2	3	4	5	6	7	8	9
No.	When and where died	Name and surname	Sex	Age	Occupation	Cause of death	Signature, description and residence of informant	When registered	Signature of registrar
379	Thirty First January 1923 58 Bruce Road	Eleanor DOWELL	Female	47 Years	Spinster Domestic Housekeeper	(1) Valvular disease of heart (mitral) Certified by E C de M Morgan MRCS	Rose Endersbee Sister Present at the death 1 Aldersey Gardens Barking	Thirty First January 1923	F Butler Registrar

A.4. Copy of Nellie Dowell's death certificate. (Copy in author's possession.)

But "housekeeper?" In light of Muriel's and Kingsley Hall's radical critique of domestic service as incompatible with Christian revolutionary democracy, this struck me as a cruel irony, an injustice.

How and why had this happened? Was this Rose's misperception—or perception—of her sister? A local registrar may have asked Rose what Nellie did and interpreted Rose's words in this conventional way. Or was it just possible that this was how Nellie saw herself? Perhaps Nellie, a woman so committed to and good at hard work, needed and liked this perfectly honorable category, "domestic housekeeper," to justify why Muriel still "kept" her. If Nellie and Muriel's friendship had instantiated their Christian revolution, Nellie had also—always—asserted her right to place limits upon it. It was Nellie who reminded Muriel that she loved her partly because Muriel was "different." "You of course are different" she had written matter-of-factly to Muriel. It was Nellie who always sought to protect Muriel from the dirty dangers of slum life. It was Nellie—and all the poor men and women who joined forces with the Lester sisters—who paradoxically may have had just as much to lose as to gain in imagining a radically egalitarian world, without distinctions of class and caste and free from private property. Perhaps it was asking too much of those who had next to nothing to give up their dreams of having something.

A year before Nellie's death, Muriel held political office for the first and only time as a socialist feminist member of the Poplar Borough Council from 1922 to 1926. Her new responsibilities meant that she had less time for Kingsley Hall, Nellie and their neighbors on Bruce Road. Poplar Borough council, however, did provide an ideal platform from which to extend woman-centered values of love and care into the arena of public policy and local politics. As chair of Poplar's Maternity and Child Welfare Committee, she combined Christian revolutionary principles with maternalist politics.[12] In August 1923 the Ministry of Health summoned her to Whitehall for failing to follow its orders to cut spending for child welfare services in Poplar. In uncompromising terms, Muriel chastised the officials she met for their outrageous request, which could only harm Poplar's children. To reduce the children's allotment of milk by even one half pint contradicted Christian conscience and the laws of health; she would have none of it. "We women enjoyed the struggle," she gleefully recalled.[13] Her tactics in Poplar politics were a continuation of Victorian domestic ideology, with its injunction for proper ladies to bring moral values out of their homes into their local communities. These were also the years during which Muriel earnestly strove to diminish the realm of private life and her own attachment to things and private property. She intentionally structured "home" life at Kingsley Hall to unmake Victorian domesticity and critique its class and gender bases. In place of privacy, she strove to live transparently and communally. In place of private property, she embraced voluntary poverty. In place of separate spheres, she expected men and women to share equally in Kingsley Hall's domestic routines and duties. Evacuating private life altogether was the logical, albeit unsustainable, end point of Muriel's effort to reimagine domesticity and invent a new kind of "public house."

Muriel's discontent with her own Christian revolutionary critique of private life simmered for several years before she finally expressed her feelings in words. "Living in Kingsley Hall," she admitted, "was like living in public. We were never free from inspection and interruption."[14] Even the space within the Hall that was supposed to be private—what Muriel tellingly called "the home of the household"—was overrun with other people. Kingsley Hall was permanently in a state of "open house." "Neighbours known and unknown, friends new and old, strangers from abroad and from the next street, know that our door is never shut and they take full advantage of the fact."[15] Sylvia Parrott Bishopp, who lived across the street from the Lesters on Bruce Road in the 1920s and '30s, fondly remembered that she and others came and went as they pleased "into the household part of the hall." Yet the hall's poor neighbors did not emulate its erasure of private life and property. Muriel, worn out by the rigors of living transparently at Kingsley Hall for so many years, noticed that the laboring poor of Bow increasingly invited the residents of Kingsley Hall to have tea in *their* private homes, in *their* "tiny gay kitchens," on *their* "best China" (my emphasis). "There was a good deal to say," she concluded, for "'living private,' though we were supremely proud of Kingsley Hall."[16]

Muriel's observation repays careful analysis, both for what it suggests about the utopian aims of Christian revolution at Kingsley Hall as well as the needs and aspirations of some working-class men and women in post–World War I Britain. Economic depression hit East Londoners particularly hard by the spring of 1921. At the same time, some were able to take advantage of interwar Britain's consumer revolution that enabled them to purchase more household goods and labor saving devices. Expansion in London County Council housing in the 1920s also brought domestic amenities—private kitchens, toilets, and bathrooms—within reach of more working-class households. Members of Kingsley Hall's household tried to liberate themselves from private homes and "best" China. These were precisely the things that most people in Bow wanted.

Moreover, the local men and women who joined the "people's house" sometimes did so as a means of separating themselves from their slum neighbors' lives, not immersing themselves in their sordid realities. Kingsley Hall and Children's House were beacons of peace, beauty, and refinement in a part of London that "stank to high heaven" of boiling bones from the nearby Cook's soap factory, Nellie's last factory employers. As Grace Neary (born in 1918) recalled, she always washed her hands and said a little prayer upon entering Kingsley Hall—a sacramental gesture mingling personal hygiene and spirituality, which separated the unclean, dirty life outside Kingsley Hall from the purer, higher one within its walls.[17]

Opening the doors of Kingsley Hall to all never meant that everyone chose to walk through them. The testimonies of working people who loved the Hall illustrate how their desires sometimes did not harmonize with the inclusive ideals of the Hall's founders. They needed and wanted the Hall to be an oasis in Bow even as they wove their engagement with it into their daily lives. Sylvia Parrott and her sister literally grew up at Kingsley Hall and Children's House. Their mother kept them apart from other children in Bromley-by-Bow and sent them to the People's House to "live more like Kingsley Hall precepts," including vegetarianism. For poor people like Nellie Dowell and the Parrotts, Kingsley Hall offered an alternative to some of the prevailing cultural norms of working-class life in Bow. With a tinge of embarrassment and regret, Parrott admitted that "we were brought up to be quite snobs. . . . I think my mother was probably wrong to keep us so, so far apart, but the biggest threat she could ever give to us was 'You don't want to be like them. You don't want to work behind the counter in Woolworth's, do you?'"

For Sylvia's mother, trapped by her own life circumstances, Kingsley Hall promised an escape route out of Bow and the working class altogether ("being like them"), not a means to transform their neighborhood into a heaven on earth for all to enjoy and share. "It was a cultured life [at Kingsley Hall]," Sylvia recalled. "It was a life of the spirit you might say, or of the mind whereas . . . Bromley-by-Bow was a pretty grotty place it was. . . . it was very slummy and sleazy and men, many of the men were very feckless and drank all their money and so forth, you know just what you think of as a slum dwelling, but Kingsley Hall was not like that." Sylvia was only too aware that she, like her mother before her, reproduced high-Victorian bourgeois stereotypes about the depravity and degradation of "slum" life that Kingsley Hall's founders so vigorously denounced. Sylvia and her sister did in fact leave Bow and the working class. With the guidance and inspiration of their parents, along with Kingsley Hall's household and teachers, they earned places at an ancient endowed grammar school in Bow and eventually at university. For Sylvia, Kingsley Hall "wasn't a Bow life at all."[18]

Idealistic working-class families like the Parrotts did not necessarily accept Muriel's aspiration to create an inclusive community without borders free from social hierarchies. Muriel appealed to her neighbors' dreams for a better life and a more just world, but for at least some, their participation in the Hall betokened their apartness from and superiority to the very community they helped to create. Kingsley Hall offered a path of upward social mobility into bourgeois domesticity, not the erasure of class difference. Sylvia Parrott and many others of her generation were inspired by the Lesters' and Kingsley Hall's ideals. Nonetheless, they chose not to set up the Kingdom of Heaven "here and now"—the original dream of members of the Bruce Road Adult School in 1914. For the Parrotts and so many working-class Britons, staying where they were in the slums was too high a price to pay—even for Heaven.

Nor was there anything unusual about their desire to leave Bow and Poplar. For generations, it was what ambitious East Londoners like Henry Lester himself had done. A 1924 pamphlet, *Poplarism: The Truth about the Poplar Scale of Relief and the Action of the Ministry of Health*, succinctly declared, "Nobody stays in Poplar by choice."[19] Mrs. Parrott's disparaging admonition about Woolworth counter girls recalls Nellie's longing for a lady's clean white hands. Both breathed new life into Victorian class and gender discourses drilled into them by their childhoods of material deprivation even as the Lesters helped them forge new social and political subjectivities.[20] Nellie's and Mrs. Parrott's stories underscore how resistance and accommodation to bourgeois capitalist and consumer modernity overlapped and coexisted as each shaped the other.

Muriel had her own reasons for questioning the viability of the Christian revolutionary project that she and Nellie had done so much to nurture. She grasped the irony of her longing for the material comforts and privacy of "home" within the "public household" she had labored so hard to create. From the 1930s onwards, she chose not to live permanently in the Hall or any of its satellites. When she was in Britain, she sought the privacy of either her sister's modest cottage on Baldwin's Hill abutting Epping Forest or a small flat a few blocks from Kingsley Hall. Muriel, like the Parrotts, did not stay in Bow to bring the Kingdom of Heaven to it. She increasingly spent most of her time far from East London. She made the world her home and used the tools of reconciliation and Christian revolution to battle nonviolently against colonial oppression and the exploitation of women and workers.[21] In coming face-to-face with the psychic and affective impossibility of giving up entirely the "private" and "private life," Muriel necessarily gestured toward the limits of revolutionary Christianity and her own pursuit of moral "perfectionism."[22]

Kingsley Hall promised salvation by small steps. Its rules sought to instruct residents in how to live with complete honesty and integrity with one another and in accordance with a prosaic ethics of daily life that people clean up the "sticky sediment" they left behind in encounters with one another and the world. But everyday life and its objects—"best china" and "gay kitchens"—proved to be one rock upon which its utopian project foundered. So too did Muriel's insistence that nurturing the psychic and material well-being of the morally self-sufficient individual—the essential actor in the inherited liberalism she ostensibly rejected—ought not be sacrificed for the collective good. Perhaps Muriel's recognition that the principled perfection she sought at Kingsley Hall could not—and should not—be achieved must be counted among the most redemptive and powerful lessons that she had learned.[23]

Unlike Muriel, Nellie had to stay in Bromley-by-Bow. Poverty and later ill health combined to keep her close to Bruce Road and its microworld of front steps, side streets, and acrid odors. When she did escape Bow to be with Muriel, she experienced acutely the psychological strains and physical disorientation of travelling across borders. On July 1, 1912, she thanked Muriel for taking her on holiday. "When I got to Paddington [rail station], I wished I was going back instead of going home, it seemed so close & stuffy everywhere I went." Her trip made her look "much better," but it had also deeply unsettled her. "I am afraid going away like that makes me feel dissatisfied at home. . . ." This was—and was not—what Muriel had hoped to achieve. Muriel intended to stir up discontent with unjust social and economic relations as a way to prod her neighbors to make and demand better lives for themselves. Dissatisfaction with home life was never part of Muriel's plan. Bow's "close & stuffy" atmosphere proved an even more intractable problem. It ensured a steady migration, usually farther east, of many Bow residents to less crowded, more salubrious suburbs.

Doris, like Nellie, kept Bromley-by-Bow, Kingsley Hall, and Children's House at the center of her everyday life. Unlike Nellie, this was entirely her choice. After her return to India and Gandhi in 1933–34, Muriel could no longer sustain the fiction that she was still head of Kingsley Hall. She sent Doris a short cable announcing her resignation, followed by a long letter that was by turns exuberant, plaintive, apologetic, disarmingly manipulative, and sincerely self-effacing. It captured

Muriel at a painfully vulnerable moment, in which she seemed unable to claim any part in Kingsley Hall's success. "Please tell Sonie [a fellow worker at Kingsley Hall] she is right. I have been very poor in my behaviour at K.H. with awful muddles I have left for her and you! I knew I was no organizer and I've created havoc. . . . But I daresay we've done some good too. . . . But of course we have—you have—anyhow. (Even Gandhi's Ashrams are rotten shows in lots of ways. lots and lots of ways.)" Having diminished her own accomplishments, she then immediately reasserted her position as Doris's wiser older sister and advised her "precious child" to work with the trustees to "get hold of a man to take on and run the place."[24]

Doris's reply has not survived. In her unpublished autobiography, she reflected on this unwelcome, but not unexpected, sequence of events. "As there was no possible successor in the offing, and as everybody realized that whoever took over after her would have an unenviably thankless job, the Trustees asked me to hold the fort temporarily until a successor could be found. It was obviously impossible for me to refuse. . . ."[25] To her American friends, Alan and Elizabeth Hunter, Muriel rationalized the burden she had thrust upon Doris and her resignation. "I've written her [Doris] and the other trustees," she explained, "that they must not count on me, and had better look round for a man, a minister, who would come in and take on the flock I have neglected. And the more I thought of it, the more I saw how urgent was Bow's need. I am always dashing away and leaving them bereft. And the work suffers, tho' of course they are lovely in letting me go."

No one had let Muriel go. She had. Her insistence that a male minister replace her could not have bolstered Doris's confidence. Nor did Muriel explain why she believed that only a man ought to succeed her. There were plenty of women in interwar Britain, well trained in schools of social work, lay preaching, and local politics, to take on such a leadership role. Perhaps Muriel wanted to counterbalance the all-female staff of Children's House. She may also have believed that a male head would find it easier to recruit male residents to the Hall.

Muriel made no effort to contain her joy at releasing herself from the burden of Kingsley Hall and constant negotiations with Doris. "It's like a new relationship thinking of you, with no Bow bones of contention. I am so thrilled." Then, as a guilty afterthought, she asked Doris, "D'you mind? You could come out to me? Could you, darling? Will it stop you going to Berlin. I hope not."[26] In light of the tremendous increase in work and responsibility Muriel had just heaped on Doris, Muriel must have known that Doris could neither "come out" to India to see her nor go to Berlin to attend her conference on teaching methods. Muriel came close to acknowledging Doris's role in subsidizing her newfound freedom. "So I've been feeling a bit oppressed about my beloved Bow," she told the Hunters, "knowing God would look after them but feeling every now and then that I was putting too heavy a load on Doris." She concluded her letter with the postscript urging the Hunters to "write to Doris as naturally as you would to me—we are as alike as 2 peas."[27]

But in so many respects Doris and Muriel were not "as alike as 2 peas." Their pronounced differences in thought, temper, and interests generated the creative tensions that nourished and strained their relationship. In the weeks after Doris assumed leadership of Kingsley Hall, Muriel self-servingly wrote to "Dorrie" that she "must be a saint now." "Your letters have the veritable unconscious glow. Shall I ever be able to live up to you?"[28] No discernible saintly glow illuminated Doris description of the drastic changes in her life following Muriel's resignation. The next twelve months, she wrote in her unpublished autobiography, were "the most devastatingly difficult ~~and thankless unproductive~~ of my life." Not for the first time, Doris found herself cleaning up Muriel's messes. In the midst of describing her "good experiences" at Kingsley Hall—the all-night-long candle lit "peace" vigils, meetings with people interested in the idea of "community," conferences of graded schoolteachers— Doris cut short her story. "However, the doings of Kingsley Hall are mainly chronicled elsewhere*, so of them I will write no more." The asterisk took her readers to the bottom of the page: "*It Occurred to Me by Muriel Lester." This is where her extant manuscript autobiography abruptly ends—as if Muriel's published autobiography made it unnecessary for her to write anything more about her story and theirs.[29]

The two sisters' archives have had afterlives as complex as their own relationship. My work in their rich, extensive, and deep collection of papers happily coincided with a period of intense community interest in them. The Heritage Lottery Fund awarded a grant to preserve and conserve the archive and "make [Muriel Lester's] legacy more widely known."[30] Preserving and reorganizing an archive necessarily changes it.

Few things seemed more important to me than coming across the well-worn envelope in which Muriel had placed Nellie Dowell's letters. It told me something significant about the high value of Nellie's letters to Muriel. In the process of being re-archived several times since I began this project, this envelope appears to have been lost or destroyed. It is nowhere to be found at Bishopsgate Institute, the gateway between the City and East London, where the entire collection of Kingsley Hall and Lester papers moved in the spring of 2013. The envelope had already gone missing the last time I looked for it at Kingsley Hall's branch in Dagenham. The letters are now separated from Muriel's container for them, divorced from one element that signaled their significance and endowed them with meaning for me. I don't fault the able and dedicated team of workers on this preservation project. Their labors have ensured that many others can and will read Nellie's letters to Muriel and so much else about Kingsley Hall and Christian revolution in early-twentieth- century Britain. They created a brilliant new archive of oral history interviews of friends, workers and neighbors of Kingsley Hall from the 1920s onwards whose stories powerfully enriched and challenged my thinking. But archives *do* change just as what we see and find in them changes as we ask new questions of them and of ourselves.

There is one more afterlife to consider: the landscape of memory in Bromley-by-Bow. The Blitz, slum clearance, and urban planning transformed the area and most of East London during Muriel's lifetime. German bombs destroyed the south side of Bruce Road while sparing the entire north side, including Kingsley Rooms, the Lesters' and the Dowells' houses at 58–60. Five-story concrete-frame, brick-veneered council flats with external hallways now loom over most of Bruce Road, whose west end culminates in a tall concrete tower block. On the southeast end of Bruce Road near the Bruce Road United Reformed Church is a much less imposing set of three-story yellow brick flats. The small sign on these flats reads "Lester Court," inconspicuously linking the sisters with the place and community that they had served so ardently.

The same cannot be said of the actual buildings and institutions that they themselves had founded: Children's House and Kingsley Hall. Children's House remains a center of early childhood education but it has long since been absorbed into London's public school system. A sturdy brick wall topped by a high chain-link fence protects and separates the school, its grounds, and its pupils, from its surroundings. The London County Council blue plaque on its façade commemorates the one day H. G. Wells stopped by to open the building. It says nothing about Doris's lifelong visionary leadership of it. In 1954, the London County Council agreed to acknowledge Kingsley Hall's historical significance with its own blue plaque. (In 1973, the structure received recognition as a Grade II-listed building.) The plaque harkened back to the moment when the world's gaze had turned to Bromley-by-Bow and its most famous visitor had walked its streets in the half darkness of the pre–dawn hour. The plaque reads quite simply: "Mahatma Gandhi, 1869–1948 stayed here in 1931." (See fig. A.5.) No paperwork survives documenting who submitted the necessary nomination forms. My strong hunch is that Muriel engineered the plaque's erection and wording.[31]

Gandhi's stay at Kingsley Hall in 1931 was a coup for Muriel. It secured for her and the Hall an enduring afterlife in the footnotes of the Mahatma's world-historical struggle. It also made her an accessory to her own disappearance from the commemorative landscape of Bromley-by-Bow. A newspaper called Kingsley Hall's plaque "a memorial to the hall's past."[32] It would be more apt to say that the plaque subsumed and erased Muriel, Doris, Nellie, and all the rest of Kingsley Hall's history into an episode that satisfied the press's craving for dramatic headlines and Muriel's desire to support Gandhi while publicizing Kingsley Hall. In a letter to the left-wing publisher of affordable good books as engines of democracy, Victor Gollancz, Muriel offered her own assessment of the blue plaque's significance. The work at Kingsley Hall "seems nothing much at present [June 1963]," she confessed without bitterness, "but the LCC plaque reminds passers-by that Gandhiji spent 10 weeks here during the Round Table Conference. His fellow Indians in Delhi are eager for us to keep his room on the roof as an open Memorial to his stay." Would Gollancz consent, she wondered, to replace the tree in front of the Hall, planted by Gandhi in 1931, and long since destroyed by Hitler's bombs?[33]

Blue plaques leave little room for nuance in narrating the afterlives of the people and events they memorialize. Muriel's interpretation of Kingsley Hall's plaque shows her at peace with retirement while still enacting Christian revolutionary ideals. The tree-planting ceremony that No-

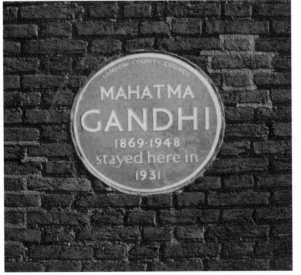

A.5. Muriel succeeded in so closely identifying Gandhi with Kingsley Hall that she participated in her own and Doris's erasure from the landscape of public memory in Bromley-by-Bow.
(Top) "Mr. Gandhi at Kingsley Hall, Becontree," *Grays and Tilbury Gazette*, November 28, 1931, (Courtesy of Bishopsgate Institute.)
(Bottom) Photograph of blue plaque, Kingsley Hall Bow. (Photograph by author.)

vember had all the hallmarks of one of Muriel's carefully choreographed symbol-laden performances. Invited speakers, she insisted, should not expect to be "segregated" from the people of Bow. She sought out representatives of the world's faiths—Sikhs, Muslims, Christians, Hindus, Jews—to join together in a gesture affirming global brotherhood and sisterhood.

The idea to invite Gollancz had not been Muriel's, but Alice Whipps' (1911–93). Alice, who kept her hair short clipped and preferred to go by the masculine nickname Al, had first mentioned Gollancz to Muriel. Like Nellie, Al was a poor girl from Bromley-by-Bow who had turned up at Kingsley Hall's Youth Club. In 1933, Al moved into Kingsley Hall as a resident.[34] (See fig. A.6.) At some point, Muriel drafted a short pen portrait of Al entitled "Our Al"—nothing as detailed and extensive as "From Birth to Death," but full of warm appreciation for Al's many gifts.[35] Even during Nellie's lifetime, there had always been other Cockney women and girls like Al who laid claim to Muriel's friendship. Try as she did, Nellie never succeeded in monopolizing Muriel's affections. Muriel was constantly creating and renewing what she called her "synthetic family" of beloved unmarried female friends, who like Nellie and Al, she integrated into her vast network of kin. Al, Doris, and Muriel's ménage in the cottage on Baldwin's Hill was the last of many such households that Muriel had formed since her first at 58–60 Bruce Road in Bromley-by-Bow.

Muriel and Doris had changed Al's life altogether. They had opened up for her new vistas of possibility. Al and so many working-class children of her generation had opportunities that Nellie never did. After a successful career as a trained nurse while tending to her own parents, the unmarried Al had decided to devote herself to Doris and Muriel as they faced the infirmities of old age. So great was her love for them that she refused to take days off. Nor would she accept anything like fair wages for her labors. She cleaned and cooked for Muriel and Doris and tended to their bodies. To call Al their "spinster domestic housekeeper" would not be altogether wrong. Except that it is not quite right. She was also their intellectual and social partner, a collaborator and comrade whose ideas mattered. Muriel must have told Gollancz that Al deserved all the credit for suggesting his name. Gollancz wrote Al to thank her. Her reply captures the mingling of thinking and feeling, of loving and

A.6. Muriel (left) had a genius for creating what she called "synthetic families" with other unmarried female friends like Al (Alice) Whipps (center) and Mu or M. J. (Alice Muriel) Pullen (right), a longtime fellow worker at Children's House. "Muriel Lester, Alice 'M. J.' Pullen, and Alice Whipps in garden," Lester/6/8, Lester Papers. (Courtesy of Bishopsgate Institute.)

caring that had also profoundly marked Muriel's partnership with Nellie. "Your name," Al told Gollancz, "and all you stand for and your books, have always given me great inspiration and pleasure." "It is indeed a great priviledge [*sic*]," she continued, "to help Muriel Lester in the care of her sister Doris. Both these remarkable women did much for us Bow folk."[36]

On January 20, 1968, Muriel sat down to write her last will. For a woman who had lived in great simplicity, she had somehow managed to accumulate a lot of things: some from her parents; others from Doris; and still others, gifts from her admirers the world over. She carefully matched each object, saturated with history and meaning, with each of her many beloved friends and relations. To her niece, Margaret, Lady Bemrose, she left her "favourite possession," her mother's cracked Japanese bowl and lid, which had once graced the corner cupboard of Gainsborough Lodge's drawing room. To Garry Lester Hogg, she left a teapot stand tile that Doris had purchased in Jerusalem in early 1939. To Al, she left a full page of lovingly chosen items—Pakistani silver spoons and a brooch and a red easy chair among them. (See fig. A.7.) She also penned a remarkable tribute celebrating Al's generosity and their shared life of fellowship. At the top of p.102 in the humble notebook that served as Muriel's unofficial will, she wrote "Al & I." "We have for so long a time, shared our joys & sorrows, & the Ups & Downs of running a house &, at the same time keeping up the old fellowship with Bow &

A.7. Muriel used a small notebook to include instructions to her executors about the disposition of her property to her many friends and relatives. "Al and I," Notebook (1968) with handwritten directions to her executors disposing of her possessions, Lester/1/2/12, Lester Papers. (Courtesy of Bishopsgate Institute.)

Dagenham folks that it is difficult to even try to separate my belongings from hers."[37]

When Muriel wrote these words, had she forgotten Nellie? I don't think so. Nellie's disappearance from Muriel's stories about herself, her neighbors, and revolutionary Christianity reflected a life in which love and friendship were the foundation of theology, ethics, social politics, and world peace. Nellie always mattered to Muriel. After her death in 1923, Muriel had moved on. As she had made clear after her brother Kingsley's death in 1914, Muriel believed that continuing the legacy of the dead, not mourning them, was the only way to honor their memory. Muriel had done just that. She forged new relationships with many others like Al Whipps, who became her partners in bringing the Kingdom of Heaven to earth. Their stories had mingled with and become hers. Like Muriel and Al's "belongings," it was difficult to "even try to separate" them.

Fair-haired little Nellie Dowell was a match girl only according to the logic and language used by the press in the late 1880s to describe both girls who sold matches on the streets and the female factory workers who made them. Muriel Lester became an heiress only long enough to publicly disinherit herself and set up the Restitution Fund. Theirs was a reciprocal, unequal, intimate, and emotionally charged relationship across a vast socioeconomic and cultural divide. This history of a match girl and an heiress, however, was no fairy tale friendship admitting of a simple moral fable. In place of flamboyantly disruptive acts of rebellion, we find in their story earnest self-scrutiny and a willingness to confront uncomfortable truths joined with reverence for Victorian predecessors; in short, the peaceful adaptation of Victorian philanthropy to radical twentieth-century goals. Far from mounting a rearguard defense of "Victorian values," Nellie and Muriel campaigned for an expansive and inclusive vision of citizenship grounded in Christian revolutionary principles of restorative social and economic justice. The history of Muriel, Nellie, Doris, and their "people's house" challenges the trajectory of putative "de-moralization" from "Victorian virtues" to "modern" doubts so eloquently but unconvincingly traced by Gertrude Himmelfarb.[38] Muriel's preoccupation with a democratic but hyper-regulated management of dirt—sticky sediment in its infinite variety—betokened her refusal to create a sanitized domain of ethics apart from politics, of private life apart from public duty. Far from rejecting the relevance of values to social politics, Muriel and Nellie strove to make themselves—and modern life—moral.

Nellie and Muriel's love and friendship took place at the fault lines between needs and dreams, between the messiness of day-to-day life and the pristine perfection of the not-yet realm of utopian aspirations, between the litter-strewn streets of Bromley-by-Bow and the precincts of the Kingdom of Heaven on Earth. Their relationship, like the Christian revolution it signaled and advanced, was a process, a way of living in the world, an unfinished work-in-progress. Christian revolutionary love may have brought them together, but there were some wounds of poverty that even this mighty force could never heal.

Manuscripts and Archival Collections

Archives New Zealand
    Register of Unions and Employers Organisations
    Seddon Family Papers
Bishopsgate Institute
    The Lester Papers
        Doris Lester Papers
        Nellie Dowell Letters
        Muriel Lester Papers
        Kingsley Hall, Papers and Reports
        Children's House, Papers and Reports
British Library of Politics, Economics, and Sociology
    Charles Booth Papers:
        Poverty Notebooks
        Religious Survey Notebooks
    Fellowship of Reconciliation Papers
        London Union
        England
    Leonard and Kate Courtney Papers
    George Lansbury Papers
Essex Record Office
    Annual Reports of the Essex Baptist Union
    Loughton Union Chapel Magazine
    Loughton Union Church
        Deacons' Minute Books
        Minutes of Sunday School
Hackney Local History Archives
    Minute Book, The Club for Working Girls, Clifden Institute
    Records of Bryant and May Limited
Hadspen, Somerset
    Hobhouse Family Papers (Margaret Potter Hobhouse; Rosa Waugh Hobhouse; Stephen Hobhouse)
India Office, British Library
    Files on Muriel Lester
Imperial War Museum (Gage Cengage)
    Women at Work Collection
Library of the Society of Friends, London
    Rosa Waugh Hobhouse, unpublished typescript autobiography
    Stephen Hobhouse Papers, typescript edited by Rosa Hobhouse

London Metropolitan Archives
    Forest Gate School District
        Superintendent's Reports and Journals
        Minutes of the Forest Gate School Managers Committee
        Register of Children, Poplar Board of Guardians
    Henrietta Barnett Papers
        Unpublished Autobiography
    Building Inspections and Approvals: Kingsley Hall Correspondence
    Marner Street School
        Admission and Discharge Registers
        Log Book, Marner Street Evening Continuation Class for Males
    Oriolet Hospital Reports
    Stepney Board of Guardians
        Whitechapel Infirmary, Admission and Discharge Register
        Whitechapel Infirmary, Porters Admission and Discharge Registers, Lunatic Certifications
    Blue Plaques
    Family Welfare Association
Longcot
    Mary Hughes Papers, in private hands
Loughton
    Loughton District Historical Society
        Photograph Collection
    Loughton Library
    Benjamin Platten Papers
        Photographs
        New Clippings about Conscientious Objection
        School Notebooks
        Letters, Diaries
Modern Record Centre, University of Warwick, Coventry, UK
    Clara Collet Papers
    Victor Gollancz Papers
    YWCA Archives
Queen Mary University, Mile End, London
    Constance Maynard Papers
Royal London Hospital Archives
    Records of St. Andrew's (Poplar and Stepney Infirmary) Hospital
    Records of London Hospital
        Medical Index
        Patients Case Notes
        Admission and Discharge Registers
        Official Ward Books
Swarthmore College
    Muriel Lester Papers
Tower Hamlets Local History Library
    Clippings Collection

Rosa Hobhouse, manuscript materials collected for Mary Hughes
  biography
Poplar Borough Council, Minutes
Trades Union Congress History Archives On-Line
  Match Girls' Strikes: strike register, correspondence concerning Bryant
    and May and R.Bell and Company
Wellington
  Wellington City Archives
    Wellington City Council Rate Books
    Architectural Plans
  Alexander Turnbull Library
    Photograph Collection
Women's Library (now transferred to BLPES)
  Agnes Maude Royden Papers
  London Society for Women's Suffrage
    Kingsley Hall Committee

Notes

Introduction

1. The essential starting point for work on Muriel Lester is Jill Wallis's *Muriel Lester: Mother of World Peace* (Middlesex, 1993); see also Richard Deats, ed., *Ambassador of Reconciliation. A Muriel Lester Reader* (Santa Cruz, 1991); Vera Brittain, *The Rebel Passion: A Short History of Some Pioneer Peacemakers* (London, 1964). The family briefly did live at Hindhead in Surrey (c.1898–1901). Caroline Moorehead vividly describes Muriel Lester as "a tall, stately, cheerful and occasionally scatty woman with wispy fair hair wound in Catherine wheels over her ears and rather long teeth" as well as an "extraordinary figure in the history of European pacifism." See Caroline Moorehead, *Troublesome People: Enemies of War, 1916–1986* (London, 1987), 97.

2. On the idea of the "Cockney," see Gareth Stedman Jones, "'The Cockney' and the Nation," in *Metropolis: Histories and Representations since 1800*, ed. D. Feldman and G. Stedman Jones, (London, 1989), 272–324. On Cockney as identity and form of linguistic representation, see Patrick Joyce, *Visions of the People: Industrial England and the Question of Class, 1848–1914* (Cambridge, 1991), esp. Part Four. Muriel, like most middle-class writers, offered her own version of Nellie's Cockney speech in her writings about her.

3. On the place and power of friendship as a form of politics, ethics and countercultural performance, see Leela Gandhi, *Affective Communities: Anti-colonial Thought, Fin-de-Siècle Radicalism and the Politics of Friendship* (Durham, 2006); on the "expressive power of friendship," see Patricia Hill Collins, *Black Sexual Politics: African Americans, Gender and the New Racism* (New York, 2004), 271. For essential work on the meaning of female amity in modern Britain, see Martha Vicinus, *Intimate Friends: Women Who Loved Women 1778–1928* (Chicago, 2004); and Sharon Marcus, *Between Women: Friendship, Desire, and Marriage in Victorian England* (Princeton, 2007).

4. My work on "neighborhood" and "community" in Bow has been shaped in conversation with the immensely influential sociological study by Michael Young and Peter Willmott, *Family and Kinship in East London* (London, 1957). I have also borrowed Jerry White's remarkable attention to the microworkings of space, place, and persons developed in his two landmark studies, *Rothschild Buildings: Life in an East-End Tenement Block* (London, 1980); *The Worst Street in North London: A Social History of Campbell Bunk, Islington between the Wars* (London, 1986).

5. Muriel explored the global historical implications of small gestures such as the imperious "snatch" of the English in India in her chapter "Manners," in *My Host the Hindu* (London, 1931). See also her account of the ways in which white Europeans fight against but ultimately capitulate to the deforming day-to-day imperatives of colonialism and empire in India, "December, 1926, Letter 14, Correspondence and Form Letters Written from India," Box 1, Lester Papers, Swarthmore College.

6. Important work on bourgeois women's philanthropy and social welfare activism in Britain includes Frank Prochaska, *Women and Philanthropy in Nineteenth-Century England* (Oxford, 1980); Anne Summers, "A Home from Home: Women's Philanthropic Work in the Nineteenth Century," in Sandra Burman, ed., *Fit Work for Women* (New York, 1979); Jane Lewis, *Women and Social Action in Victorian and Edwardian England* (Aldershot, 1991); Martha Vicinus, *Independent Women: Work and Community for Single Women, 1850–1920* (Chicago, 1985); Deborah Nord, *The Apprenticeship of Beatrice Webb* (Ithaca, 1989); Judith R. Walkowitz, *City of Dreadful Delight: Narratives of Sexual Danger in Late-Victorian London* (Chicago, 1992) and *Nights Out: Life in Cosmopolitan London* (London, 2012), chap. 2. See also Seth Koven, *Slumming: Sexual and Social Politics in Victorian London* (Princeton, 2004), chaps. 3 and 4. On the representation of middle-class women's philanthropy in literature, see Dorice Williams Elliott, *The Angel Out of the House: Philanthropy and Gender in Nineteenth-Century England* (Charlottesville, 2002).

7. On the "domains" of the intimate, affect, and politics, see Ann Laura Stoler, *Carnal Knowledge and Imperial Power: Race and the Intimate in Colonial Rule* (Berkeley, 2002), 12.

8. Rev. Bernard Walke founded the first chapter in Cornwall in 1918. See Bernard Walke, *Twenty Years at St. Hilary* (London, 1935)

9. Hayden Church, "Millionaires and Paupers Join in Self Denial," *Deseret News* [Salt Lake City, Utah], July 2, 1921, sec. 3, 1.

10. See Muriel Lester, *It Occurred to Me* (London 1937), 59.

11. See Public and Judicial Department, Subject: Miss MURIEL LESTER, IOR (India Office Records), l/P&J/12/445, British Library.

12. Private communication, Alice Mackay to Seth Koven, June 19, 2012.

13. Muriel collected these letters and put them into an envelope. When I first read them, they were listed under ML/4, Muriel Lester Papers, Box 4, Kingsley Hall, Dagenham. They have subsequently been rearchived and catalogued as "Letters from Eleanor "Nellie" Dowell, 2/5, Muriel Lester Papers, Bishopsgate Institute. On working-class writing and literacy, see Carolyn Steedman, *The Radical Soldier's Tale: John Pearman, 1819–1908* (London, 1988). On letters as sources for reconstructing female friendship, see Carroll Smith-Rosenberg, "The Female World of Love and Ritual: Relations between Women in Nineteenth-Century America," *Signs* 1:1 (August 1975).

14. Hereafter, I refer to these letters as Nellie Dowell Letters, Bishopsgate. Nellie's eleven surviving letters consist of fifty pages of writing (I count each side of the stationery as one page). Nellie dated only three of them, all from 1912. She used several different return addresses, indicating her residence at the time of writing. I use a broad range of internal evidence to offer likely dates for all the letters—varying from specific events in London history such as zeppelin raids over Bromley-by-Bow; events in Nellie's and Muriel's lives such as Muriel's trip to Palestine and Egypt in 1910 or Nellie's last illness and hospitalization from December 1922 to her death in January 1923; census and voting registers that give Nellie's addresses; and passing remarks within letters such as the day of the week (i.e., raining on Sunday night) combined with the date and month (but no year). Imprecise and imperfect as these techniques are, they provide a reasonable approximation of chronology essential to my interpretation and analysis of the letters. In the body of this book, I indicate when I have made an educated case about the date of a

letter. When I quote from the letters that Nellie herself dated, I indicate that in my text and endnote.

15. The two side-by-side houses were so closely connected that one worker recalled that she usually entered through Number 58 (Nellie's house), walked through it to the back garden and then into the unlocked back door of Number 60. See Gwen Morley, "Timothy & the Angel," *Adventures in Fellowship, Being the Eight Annual Report of Kingsley Hall* (London, 1923), 11.

16. The phrase comes from chapter four of Charles Dickens's novel, *Bleak House* (1853). The landmark analysis of socioeconomic relations between rich and poor in Victorian London remains Gareth Stedman Jones, *Outcast London: A Study in the Relationship Between Classes in Victorian Society* (Oxford, 1971).

17. For the United States, Linda Gordon has pioneered work that accentuates the role of poor women across racial divides in shaping social welfare in relationship to policy makers and middle-class female reformers. See *Pitied but Not Entitled: Single Mothers and the History of Welfare, 1890–1935* (New York, 1994). For a more heavily "client-centered" approach, see Linda Gordon's influential study, *Heroes of Their Own Lives: The Politics and History of Family Violence* (NY, 1988). For Britain, Lynn Hollen Lees's *Solidarities of Strangers: The English Poor Laws and the People, 1700–1948* (Cambridge, 1998) notably demonstrates how the poor instrumentally used Poor Law policies and institutions to serve their own ends. In her hands, social policy operates at the intersection of the needs of policy makers, politics, and the poor themselves. Other major works that narrate and analyze social welfare from the perspective of its ostensible objects include Ellen Ross, *Love and Toil: Motherhood in Outcast London, 1870–1918* (Oxford, 1993) and Anna Davin, *Growing Up: Home, School and Street in London, 1870–1914* (London, 1996).

18. There are many notable examples of "double biographies" that use paired lives to advances important historical arguments. Two that have particularly influenced my own approach include Sybil Oldfield's beautiful *Spinsters of This Parish: The Life and Times of F.M. Major and Mary Sheepshanks* (London, 1984) and Patrick Joyce, *Democratic Subjects: The Self and the Social in Nineteenth-Century England* (Cambridge, 1994).

19. See Geoff Eley's meditation on the relationship between 1960s' social history and cultural historical approaches of the 1980s and '90s, *A Crooked Line: From Cultural History to a History of Society* (Ann Arbor, MI, 2005).

20. See feminist historical geographer Gillian Rose's work on Doris Lester, Children's House and Bromley-by-Bow, "The Struggle for Political Democracy: Emancipation, Gender, and Geography," *Environment and Planning D: Society and Space* 8:4 (1990): 395–408.

21. Historians have increasingly turned to biography in analyzing "transnational" and global lives. For compelling examples, see Linda Colley, *The Ordeal of Elizabeth Marsh: A Woman in World History* (New York, 2007) and Martha Hodes, *The Sea Captain's Wife: A True Story of Love, Race, and War in the Nineteenth Century* (New York, 2006); see also Angela Woollacott, Desley Deacon, and Penny Russell, eds., *Transnational Lives: Biographies of Global Modernity, 1700-Present* (New York, 2010) and Clare Anderson, *Subaltern Lives: Biographies of Colonialism in the Indian Ocean World, 1790–1920* (Cambridge, 2012). See also Antoinette Burton's exemplary use of "lives" to illumi-

nate global itineraries and large scale developments, *At the Heart of the Empire: Indians, and the Colonial Encounter in Late-Victorian Britain* (Berkeley, 1998) and *Dwelling in the Archive: Women Writing House, Home, and History in Late Colonial India* (New York, 2003), and *The Postcolonial Careers of Santha Rama Rau* (Durham, 2007).

22. For a witty probing analysis of these methodological issues, see Jill Lepore, "Historians Who Love too Much: Reflections on Microhistory and Biography," *Journal of American History* 88:1 (June 2001).

23. See, for example, useful biographies about Muriel's contemporary and founder of Save the Children, Eglantyne Jebb: Clare Mulley, *The Woman Who Saved the Children: A Biography of Eglantyne Jebb, Founder of Save the Children* (Oxford, 2009) and Linda Mahood's explicitly feminist theoretical interpretation, "Eglantyne Jebb: Remembering, Representing, and Writing a Rebel Daughter," *Women's History Review* 17:1 (February 2008): 1–20 and *Feminism and Voluntary Action: Eglantyne Jebb and Save the Children, 1876–1928* (Basingstoke, 2009). Microhistories centered on the life of the humble and obscure have mostly remained in the province of early modern historians, who accentuate the deep gulf separating their readers from the mentalité of their historical actors while also offering lessons for the present. Notable masters of this form of historical writing include Carlo Ginzburg, Natalie Davis, and Laurel Thatcher Ulrich. Historians of modern Europe have largely not undertaken similar full-scale reconstructions of the mental, social, economic, affective, and political lives of the very poor.

24. By the turn of the century, there was demand for "lives" of poor workingwomen, but it was filled mostly by writers of sociofictions. See *Autobiography of a Charwoman as Chronicled by Annie Wakeman* (London, 1900).

25. Muriel published two full-scale autobiographies, *It Occurred to Me* (London, 1937) and *It So Happened* (New York, 1947). Several other books are largely autobiographical and include *My Host the Hindu* (London, 1931), *Entertaining Gandhi* (London, 1932) and *Kill or Cure* (Nashville, 1937).

26. This film clip is freely available on the World Wide Web through several locations including Youtube.com.

27. See Muriel Lester Files, India Office Records and Private Papers, IOR/LPJ/12/445, File 214/32, British Library.

28. Ruth Harris Comfort to Christopher Pond, October 3, 1997, letter in private hands. Alex Comfort married his mistress, who was also his wife's close friend, soon after the publication of his best-selling *Joy of Sex*.

29. See A. O. Bell and A. McNeillie, eds., *The Diary of Virginia Woolf, Volume 3, 1925–1930* (London, 1981), 241. On Miss Kilman, see Virginia Woolf, *Mrs. Dalloway* (London, 1925, 2012), 13.

30. For a brilliant analysis of Woolf's relationship with Boxall, see Alison Light, *Mrs. Woolf and the Servants: An Intimate History of Domestic Life in Bloomsbury* (London, 2008).

31. See Muriel Lester, "The Salt of the Earth," *Adventures in Fellowship, Being the Eighth Annual Report of Kingsley Hall* (London, 1923), 15–17, hereafter cited as Lester, "The Salt of the Earth," (1923).

32. Ibid.

33. The two drafts of "From Birth to Death" are key sources, which I cite frequently. I refer to the first draft, with the name Dowell crossed out, as Lester, "From Birth to

Death, 1." It is now catalogued under "Early Correspondence, From Birth to Death: Life of Nellie Dowell, Lester/2/5, Lester Papers, Bishopsgate Institute. I refer to the second draft, which uses only the name Short, as Lester, "From Birth to Death, 2." It is now catalogued under "Published and unpublished articles," Lester/2/15, Lester Papers, Bishopsgate Institute.

34. Thomas Carlyle, *Sartor Resartus, The Life and Opinions of Herr Teufelsdröckh* (London, 1831), 108.

35. Examples of this vast influential literature include David Roberts, *The Victorian Origins of the British Welfare State* (New Haven, 1960); Peter Mandler, 'The Making of the New Poor Law *Redivivus*", *Past and Present*: 117 (1987): 131–57; Hugh Heclo, *Modern Social Politics in Britain and Sweden* (New Haven, 1974); and James Vernon, "The Ethics of Hunger and the Assembly of Society: The Techno-Politics of the School Meal in Modern Britain," *American Historical Review* 110:3 (2005). Indispensable accounts of the intellectual and political arguments buttressing state welfare development include José Harris, "Political Thought and the Welfare State, 1870–1940: An Intellectual Framework for British Social Policy," *Past and Present* 135 (May 1992); on working-class pressure and political mobilization, see Pat Thane, "The Working Class and State 'Welfare' in Britain, 1880–1914," *Historical Journal* 27:4 (1984). On the impact of feminist politics on welfare policy development, see Susan Pedersen, *Family, Dependence and the Origins of the Welfare State: Britain and France, 1914–1945* (Cambridge, 1993).

36. See "Borderlands: Women, Voluntary Action and Child Welfare in Great Britain 1840–1914," in Seth Koven and Sonya Michel, eds., *Mothers of a New World: Maternalist Politics and the Origins of Welfare States* (New York, 1993).

37. See Michael Katz's landmark *In the Shadow of the Poor House: A Social History of Welfare in America* (New York, 1986).

38. On these boundaries, see Geoffrey Finlayson, "A Moving Frontier: Voluntarism and the State in British Social Welfare," *Twentieth Century British History* I:2 (1990): 183–206. See also Jane Lewis, *The Voluntary Sector, the State and Social Work in Britain* (Aldershot, 1995) and Elizabeth Macadam, *The New Philanthropy: A Study of the Relations between Statutory and Voluntary Services* (London, 1934). See also Michael Katz and Christoph Sachsse, eds., *The Mixed Economy of Social Welfare* (Baden-Baden, 1996). For work demonstrating the variety and vitality of interwar voluntary social action, see Kate Bradley, *Poverty, Philanthropy and the State: Charities and the Working Classes in London 1918–79* (Manchester, 2008) and Frank Prochaska's many books, including *The Voluntary Impulse: Philanthropy in Modern Britain* (London, 1988), and *Christianity and Social Service in Modern Britain* (Oxford, 2008).

39. For a path-breaking analysis of laboring women who mobilized in their neighborhoods around "female consciousness" and a commitment to the existing sexual division of productive and caring labor, see Temma Kaplan, "Female Consciousness and Collective Action: The Case of Barcelona, 1910–1918," *Signs* 7:3 (Spring 1982). Like Kaplan's, my analysis emphasizes everyday life and neighborhood as a site for women's revolutionary activities and ideas.

40. Gareth Stedman Jones, "Working Class Culture, Working Class Politics in London, 1870–1900: Notes on the Remaking of a Working Class," *Journal of Social History* 7:4 (Summer 1974).

41. For an excellent starting point for the debate on the historical boundaries be-

tween secular and religious activity in churches, see Jeffrey Cox, *The English Churches in a Secular Society: Lambeth, 1870–1930* (Oxford, 1982) and Hugh McLeod's sweeping, *Secularisation in Western Europe, 1848–1914* (New York, 2000). For a recasting and re-periodization of the debate, which emphasizes women's roles, see Callum G. Brown, *The Death of Christian Britain: Understanding Secularisation 1800–2000* (London, 2001). For summaries of these debates, see J.C.D. Clark, "Secularization and Modernization: The Failure of a 'Grand Narrative,'" *The Historical Journal* 55:1 (2012): 161–94; and Jeremy Morris, "Secularization and Religious Experience: Arguments in the Historiography of Modern British Religion," *The Historical Journal* 55:1 (2012): 195–219.

42. See Alison Light, *Forever England: Femininity, Literature and Conservatism between the Wars* (London, 1991); Richard Overy, *The Morbid Age: Britain between the Wars* (London, 2009); Susan Kingsley Kent, *After Shocks: Politics and Trauma in Britain, 1918–1931* (Basingstoke, 2009); and Robert Graves and Alan Hodge, *The Long Weekend: A Social History of Great Britain, 1918–1939* (London, 1940). For a synthetic account that balances new forms of leisure such as motoring, the pursuit of domestic pleasures, and the impact of economic reorganization with politics, see Martin Pugh's optimistic assessment of the interwar years, *We Danced All Night: A Social History of Britain Between the Wars* (London, 2008).

43. Jay Winter, *Dreams of Peace and Freedom: Utopian Moments in the Twentieth Century* (New Haven, 2008).

44. See Karl Mannheim, *Ideology and Utopia, An Introduction to the Sociology of Knowledge*, trans. Louis Wirth and Edward Shils (New York, 1936), 192, 199, 210. Mannheim's model cannot accommodate the distinctly Christian and spiritual basis of Kingsley Hall's socialism.

Chapter One. Victorian Childhoods and Two Victorian Children

1. "Victorian Sunday," interview with Kathleen Lester Hogg by Jean Yorke, BBC Radio Broadcast, June 5, 1960. Lester/2/1, Lester Papers, Bishopsgate.

2. See Lester, "From Birth to Death, 1." Bishopsgate.

3. On the emergence of the cult of childhood innocence, see Viviana Zelizer's hugely influential *Pricing the Priceless Child: The Changing Social Value of Children* (New York, 1985).

4. On lives and names, stories and biography, see Kali Israel, *Names and Stories: Emilia Dilke and Victorian Culture* (Oxford, 1999); see also Carolyn Steedman, *Strange Dislocations: Childhood and the Idea of Human Interiority, 1780–1930* (Cambridge, MA, 1995); and *Landscape for a Good Woman: A Story of Two Lives* (New Brunswick, NJ, 1987). On working-class childhood embedded within a Marxist interpretive frame intent to valorize the agency of poor children, see Steve Humphries, *Hooligans or Rebels? Oral History of Working-Class Childhood and Youth, 1889–1939* (London, 1981). Humphries's account emphasizes children's multivalent forms of resistance to the practices of everyday bourgeois capitalist values and the disciplining force of adults.

5. Doris studied at Britain's most advanced colleges and centers of early childhood education, including a degree course at Westhill College under Archibald Hamilton Brown and Emily Huntley that combined progressive politics, paternalist racism, and

pedagogy with training in the emerging fields of psychology and child life. Westhill also put Doris in touch with many Quaker leaders of the student movement in prewar Britain with whom Muriel worked closely. On the early history of Westhill College, see Jack Priestly, "The Lumber Merchant and the Chocolate King: The Contributions of George Hamilton Archibald and George Cadbury to the Sunday School Movement in England and Wales," in Stephen Orchard and J.HY. Briggs, eds., *The Sunday School Movement: Studies in the Growth and Decline of Sunday Schools* (Milton Keynes, 2007). For an example of paternalist racism, see Emily Huntley, *The Book of Little Black Brother* (London, 1911).

6. Scholars in the 1960s and '70s paid considerable attention to the so-called "labour aristocracy" as they sought to explain why Britain, the first industrial capitalist nation, failed to produce a revolutionary working class. See R. Q. Gray, *The Labour Aristocracy in Victorian Edinburgh* (Oxford, 1976); Eric Hobsbawm, *Labouring Men* (London, 1964). However, such scholars saw a clear and strong line separating labor aristocrats from the lowest ranks of the middle class.

7. Charles Booth, "Sunday Walk to Visit churches, Poplar, Bromley." January 26, 1902, B385, pp.191. Booth papers, BLPES. "Respectability" was a keyword in Victorian Britain—one of whose meanings derived from its opposition to the "unrespectable" even as the precise socioeconomic conditions it described varied. On flexible and overlapping definitions of respectability, see F.M.L. Thompson, *The Rise of Respectable Society: A Social History of Victorian Britain* (Cambridge, MA, 1988).

8. Lester, "From Birth to Death, 1." Bishopsgate.

9. Ibid.

10. Nellie's parents may well have chosen to live in Granada Terrace because their next-door neighbor, Rebecca Middleton, like William Dowell, had migrated to London from Sunderland. My thanks to Christopher Lloyd, the learned and generous local history librarian, Tower Hamlets Local History Library, for figuring out the precise location of Granada Terrace; it does not exist in most maps because it was not a street per se.

11. According to the Kelly's Post Office Directory for 1875, there were several fancy drapers on Granada Terrace along with a nearby bank. On the history of Commercial Road, see Sydney Maddocks, "Commercial Road," *The Copartnership Herald* 2:21 (November 1932). There is a long line of authors who evoke the sounds and sights of East London including Walter Besant, *East London* (London, 1899); William Fishman, *East End 1888: A Year in a London Borough Among the Labouring Poor* (London, 1988), and John Marriott, *Beyond the Tower: A History of East London* (London, 2011).

12. See *Cook's Handbook for London* (London, 1878), 18.

13. See J. Ewing Ritchie, *Here and There in London* (London, 1859), chap. 12.

14. "Sunday with the Sailors," *All the Year Round* (June 18, 1881): 273.

15. In the 1871 census, all of the male Dowells living in Sunderland are listed as "seamen."

16. I have reconstructed William Dowell's seafaring life using his extant "Masters Certificates" of 1868 and 1873 for achieving the rank of First Mate. Issued by the Lords of the Committee of Privy Council For Trade and authorized by the Board of Trade, these forms document the applicant's rank, dates of service on each ship, name of ship, and its point of origin. It also includes a list of testimonials, a column for special notations as well as date and place of birth, current residence, description of voyage, and reason for applying for a replacement copy of the certificate. Dowell's First Mates' certifi-

cates are Number 87677 for 1868 and Number 97748 for 1873. The originals are housed in the National Maritime Museum but I accessed them via Ancestry.com. Harriet and William married in early 1870 and their first child, Florence, was born later that year.

17. On the misfortunes of the S.S. *Chanonry*, see "District Intelligence," *Western Mail*, January 28, 1873, 3. I have reconstructed William Dowell's working life through two of his surviving certificate applications for qualifying as first mate.

18. See Mates and Petty Officers' Wages, table 24, *Parliamentary Papers, House of Commons and Command*, vol. 87, 1895, C. 306, p. 42.

19. This is the dwelling in which Eleanor Dowell was born according to her birth certificate.

20. On these sorts of gender-based household choices and economies, see Jan DeVries, *Industrious Revolution: Consumer Behavior and the Household Economy, 1650 to the present* (New York, 2008).

21. Lester, "From Birth to Death, 1." Bishopsgate.

22. See Anna Davin, *Growing Up Poor: Home, School and Street in London, 1870–1914* (London, 1996).

23. All of this information is derived from documents readily available on Ancestry. com. See birth certificate of Harriet Sloan (later Dowell). Archibald Henry Sloan was married to Elizabeth Morris by Rev. Samuel Barnett, Vicar of St. Judes, Whitechapel and future Warden of Toynbee Hall on Christmas Day, 1880. See marriage records, St. Judes, Whitechapel, December 1880.

24. Harriet Sloan (Dowell) was baptized at St. Mary, Whitechapel on January 28, 1846, accessed via Ancestry.com.

25. On working-class reading and cultures of literacy, see Jonathan Rose's panoramic *The Intellectual Life of the British Working Classes* (New Haven, CT, 2001). See also David Mitch, *The Rise of Popular Literacy in Victorian England: The Influence of Private Choice and Public Policy* (Philadelphia, 1992).

26. April 2, 1883, Admission Register, Infants, Marner Street School, Bow, 1882–1888, LCC/EO/Div5/MAR1/AD/7, London Metropolitan Archive. Somewhat surprisingly, her deceased father William is still listed as her guardian, though Harriet is listed as guardian for her sister in another admission record. Perhaps this is because the form allows for either the father or the guardian. She transferred out of the school on June 23, 1884. Her birth date is listed as April 16, 1877 rather than her actual date of birth, April 17, 1876. It hardly seems possible that her mother had forgotten her age; perhaps Harriet Dowell sought to extend Nellie's schooling.

27. Their house could not have been more than six years old, since the Metropolitan Board of Works only approved the cutting and laying of the street in 1877 and noted that the name of the street needed to be fixed on posts until the construction of houses on the street. See MBW/BA-24451, London Metropolitan Archives. The streets around Marner Street School (Marner, Empson, and Gurley Streets) remained an important center of Nellie's family life for the next three decades.

28. "Sunday in East London. Bow and Bromley," *Sunday At Home* (1895): 389, 391.

29. See Davin, *Growing Up Poor*. As Davin explains, the provision of any form of infant care was hotly contested by those who rightly feared the transformation of public education into a form of publicly funded childcare. Children were admitted to the infants' room by age 4.

30. Lone motherhood was, from the outset, a key criterion for remission of school fees by the London School Board. In 1883, requests for fee remission by poor widowed women like Mrs. Dowell were handled by the Charity Organisation, working in concert with the school board. See Gretchen Galbraith, *Reading Lives: Reconstructing Childhood, Books, and Schools in Britain, 1870–1920* (New York, 1997), 92. School fees ranged from one pence in the poorest districts to six pence per week in the most well-to-do. See "Report of the School Management Committee for the Half-Year Ended on the 22 March, 1883," *School Board for London*, (London, 1883). By 1892, the SBL largely eliminated school fees altogether—thus avoiding the time-consuming process of certifying each individual application for fee remission. On the history of single motherhood in the late-nineteenth and twentieth centuries, see Pat Thane and Tanya Evans, *Sinners? Scroungers? Saints?: Unmarried Motherhood in Twentieth-Century England* (Oxford, 2012), especially chap.1.

31. James Runciman, "The New Departure in Education," *Contemporary Review* 54 (1888): 33.

32. On Ruskin's efforts to encourage pupil teachers to bring imagination to their instruction, see Christopher R. Bischof, "Making Good: British Elementary Teachers and the Social Landscape, 1846–1902," PhD diss., Rutgers University, 2014, chapter 2.

33. On school attendance, see David Rubenstein, *School Attendance in London, 1870–1904: A Social History* (Hull, 1969).

34. Mrs. Westlake, "The London School Board," *Macmillan's Magazine* 41 (1879–80): 85. On board school and LCC geography lessons, see Christopher M. Bischof, "Making Good," chapters 2 and 3.

35. On Lyschinska, see "Preface," *The Kindergarten Principle, Its Educational Value and Chief Applications* (London, 1880). For a detailed account of the infants' room curriculum and its implementation, see M. J. Lyschinska's "Report of the Superintendent of Method in Infants' School, for the Half Year Ended 24th March 1882," in "Report of the School Management Committee for the Half-Year Ended on the 24th March, 1882," *School Board for London* (London, 1883), 173–77. See also Sarah Tooley, "According to Froebel, an Interview with Miss Mary Lyschinska," *The Woman's Signal* 69 (April 25, 1895): 258–59.

36. On the history of the British kindergarten movement, see Kevin Brehony, "The Kindergarten in England, 1851 to 1918" in Roberta Wollons, ed., *Kindergartens and Cultures*, (New Haven, CT, 2000), 59–86. Kindergartens in continental Europe, especially Wilhelmine, Germany, had played important roles as centers of progressive social and political thought as well as key venues for women's expanding roles in civil society. See Ann Taylor Allen's path-breaking work on kindergartens and women's politics, *Feminism and Motherhood in Germany, 1800–1914* (New Brunswick, NJ, 1991). While Margaret McMillan, a prominent early childhood educational reformer connected her pioneering Deptford nursery with her work for the Independent Labour Party and her socialist politics, the British kindergarten movement as a whole was never identified with politics. See Carolyn Steedman, *Childhood, Culture and Class in Britain Margaret McMillan, 1860–1931:* (New Brunswick, NJ, 1990). On the work, aspirations, struggles, and achievements of London's women's schoolteachers, see Dina Copelman's excellent *Class Acts: London's Women Schoolteachers, 1870–1930* (London, 1996).

37. On Marx, the Ronges, and London kindergartens, see Rosemary Ashton, *Victorian Bloomsbury* (London, 2010), 274–80. See also Karl Marx, *Heroes of the Exile* (written in 1852, first published in 1930) for his comments on Ronge.

38. See Logbook, Marner Street Evening Continuation Class for Males, LCC/EO/DIV05/MAR1/LB, London Metropolitan Archives. The surviving logbook details the rich array of educational and social activities of the class and the fortunes and successes of its students. There was overlap between the staff of the regular school and the continuation class. When the history of education of London is viewed from the vantage point of individual schools and staff, it is possible to see the limitations and constraints of both social control and Foucauldian models. While the educational system was certainly disciplinary and sought to reinforce values shaped by the needs of a bourgeois capitalist society, these institutions also genuinely strove to accommodate students' needs and did provide means of gaining skills that offered students socioeconomic mobility.

39. I should explain some of the problems surrounding my documentation of William Dowell's death. Only one William Dowell died at sea in the 1880s, at least according to the official records of maritime deaths. Such deaths were recorded and preserved separately from the rest of the population. William Dowell's death certificate indicates that he was a sailmaker who died of consumption on board the *Rialto* in the spring of 1881. There were two major ships called the *Rialto* in the 1880s: one was a Wilson Line steamer that carried passengers between Hull and New York. The other, operated by Albion Shipping Company, disembarked from the South West Docks in London on a global circuit. Given the family's location nearby in East London, I feel certain that he worked on the ship operated by the Albion Shipping Company. (This information is based on the "Shipping News" columns of the *London Times* for the 1870s and '80s.) I cannot square the information on this death certificate (which also has his age wrong) with the incontrovertible evidence that Nellie's father had been a certified first mate since 1868. In "From Birth to Death," Muriel even called Nellie's father a ship captain. This is probably how Nellie remembered what she had been told about her father but it almost certainly was not true. Extant records for ship's captains are quite complete; and captains' names appear in all sorts of maritime publications indicating routes taken by ships. Muriel's narrative describes the receipt of the letter from his employers, which informed his family that he had died at sea, but Muriel's dates are wrong. She claims that Nellie enjoyed nine secure years with her family but we know that Poor Law officials sent Nellie to Forest Gate School when she was age seven.

40. Lester, "From Birth to Death, 1," Bishopsgate.

41. On discourses of "lone motherhood" in nineteenth-century Britain, see Jean Carabine, "Constituting Sexuality through Social Policy: The Case of Lone Motherhood 1834 and Today," *Social Legal Studies* 10, no. 3 (September 2001): 291–314; on the economics and job fortunes of widows like Mrs. Dowell, see Andrew August, *Poor Women's Lives: Gender, Work and Poverty in Late-Victorian London* (Madison, NJ, 1999); for an overview of widowhood, see Joan Perkin, *Victorian Women* (London, 1993), chap. 7; on the diversity of forms of partnership and parenting arrangements outside strictly conjugal units, see John Gillis's magisterial *For Better and For Worse: British Marriages, 1600 to the Present* (Oxford, 1985).

42. On the history of Trinity House, see "The Trinity House," *The Penny Magazine*

(January 21, 1843): 22–24. See also, Ernest W. Low, "Trinity House: Its Origins and Its Work," *The Windsor Magazine* (July-December 1895): 675–86.

43. Unfortunately, the minutes and records of Trinity House's charitable operations for the 1860s through 1890s were destroyed in the Blitz so I cannot reconstruct the conditions under which Harriet Dowell and her mother received their widows' pensions.

44. On motherhood and mothercraft, see Ellen Ross, *Love and Toil: Motherhood in Outcast London* (New York, 1993), chap. 7; on the convergence of discourses of empire and mothering, see Anna Davin, "Imperialism and Motherhood," *History Workshop Journal* (Spring 1978): 9–65. Among the many important contributions to this scholarship are Sylvia Schafer, *Children in Moral Danger and the Problem of Government in Third Republic France* (Princeton, 1997); Edward Ross Dickinson, *The Politics of Child Welfare from the Empire to the Federal Republic* (Cambridge, MA, 1996), chap.1–3.

45. Henry Drummond, *Ascent of Man* (New York, 1894), 336. On Drummond, see Thomas Dixon, *The Invention of Altruism: Making Moral Meanings in Victorian Britain* (Oxford, 2008), chap. 7.

46. See *House of Commons Papers, Reports from Committees*, vol. 11 (February 11, 1890–August 18, 1890), *Children's Life Insurance*, Appendix D (London, 1890), 230.

47. See "The Modern Cornelia," *Punch* (June 21, 1890): 299.

48. Dendy, as reprinted in Ellen Ross, *Slum Travelers: Ladies and London Poverty, 1860–1920* (Los Angeles, 2007), 70. For a sensitive analysis of poor mothers as both historical subjects and objects of policy makers, see Ross, *Love and Toil*.

49. George Haw, *From Workhouse to Westminster: The Life Story of Will Crooks, M.P.* (London, 1907), 71.

50. On the figure of the working-class mother in middle-class accounts of slum life, see Ross, *Love and Toil*. See also M. Loane, *The Next Street But One* (London: 1907), 67. The author M. Loane was probably an authorial composite of two sisters, one of whom was a nurse. See Susan Cohen and Clive Fleahy, introduction to M. Loane, *The Queen's Poor* (London, 1905, reprint 1998).

51. For two examples of homages to working-class motherhood in autobiographical writing, see Joe Williamson, *Father Joe: The Autobiography of Joseph Williamson* (London, 1963); Kingsley Royden, "A Friend in My Retreat: Family Life in Bromley St. Leonard between the Wars," *East London Record* 1 (1978). See also David Vincent, *Bread, Knowledge and Freedom* (London, 1981).

52. For analysis of the poor's instrumental use of Poor Law institutions and services, see Lynn Hollen Lees, *The Solidarities of Strangers: the English Poor Laws and the People, 1700–1948* (Cambridge, 1998).

53. For this and many other details of the administration of the so called poor law barrack schools in London, see Lydia Murdoch's persuasive account and analysis in *Imagined Orphans: Poor Families, Child Welfare and Contested Citizenship in London* (New Brunswick, NJ, 2006).

54. On "ins and outs," see findings of Mundella Report, *The Education and Maintenance of Pauper Children in the Metropolis*, vol. 2 (1896).

55. Lester, "From Birth to Death, 1." Bishopsgate.

56. William Dowell, born in 1872, was discharged from the *Exmouth* on April 30, 1887 to the ship *James Eleanor* at 15s/ month. For records of the *Exmouth*, see Poplar

Training School, Forest Gate: Register of Children, Poplar Board of Guardians, POBG/214/1, London Metropolitan Archives.

57. On the Marine Society, see James Stephen Taylor, *Jonas Hanway, Founder of the Marine Society: Charity and Policy in Eighteenth-Century Britain* (London, 1985).

58. "The Blackwall Disaster, A List of Gallant Deeds," *Reynolds's Newspaper*, August 28, 1898, 5. The article indicates that Dowell was twenty-six in 1898; Nellie's brother was born in 1872 and hence also twenty-six. It seems very likely that the William Dowell commended was her brother.

59. My description of Leighton Buzzard at the time Nellie was sent there is based on the entry for the town in *Kelly's Directory of Bedfordshire, Hunts, and Northamptonshire* (London, 1885), 70–75.

60. See C. S. Loch, introduction to *The Charities Register and Digest* (London, 1890), 304.

61. There is a large and excellent literature on child protection and abuse in Victorian England. See George K. Behlmer, *The Child Protection Movement in England, 1860–1890* (Palo Alto, 1977); *Child Abuse and Moral Reform in England, 1870–1908* (Palo Alto, 1982); Louise Jackson, *Child Sexual Abuse in Victorian England* (London, 2000); Roger Cooter, ed., *In the Name of the Child* (London, 1992); see also Harry Hendricks, *Child Welfare: England 1872–1989* (London, 2003) for a compact and persuasive account of competing agendas of reformers and their perceptions of the dangers of childhood.

62. Lylie Valentine lived in Bromley-by-Bow just around the corner from Kingsley Hall. She recalled that when her father died, Poor Law officials suggested her removal from her destitute mother who responded, "Over my dead body." See Lylie Valentine, *Two Sisters and the Cockney Kids* (London, n.d.), 2. On poor families' extraction of resources from and use of Poor Law institutions, see Lynn Hollen Lees, *The Solidarities of Strangers: the English Poor Laws and the People, 1700–1948* (Cambridge, 1998).

63. George Lansbury, *My Life* (London, 1931), 132.

64. Because it combined children from several different Poor Law unions, it was called a "district" school. For an excellent summary of its administrative history, see Walter Monnington and Frederick Lampard, *Our London Poor Law Schools: Comprising Descriptive Sketches of the Schools* (London, 1898), 36–41.

65. See Bridget Cherry, Charles O'Brien, and Nikolaus Pevsner, *London 5, East: Buildings of England* (London, 2005), 67.

66. See Lydia Murdoch, "From Barrack Schools to Family Cottages: Creating Domestic Space for Late-Victorian Poor Children," in *Child Welfare and Social Action in the Nineteenth and Twentieth Centuries*, ed. Jon Lawrence and Pat Starkey (Liverpool, 2001).

67. Jane Nassau Senior was the sister of Tom Hughes of *Tom Brown's Schooldays* and daughter-in-law of the wealthy political economist Nassau Senior.

68. See *Third Annual Report of the Local Government Board, 1873–1874* (London, 1874).

69. See Sybil Oldfield, "The Government Inspector," "Mrs. Senior's Report," "The Reception: 1874," in *Jeanie, an 'Army of One': Mrs Nassau Senior, 1828–1877, the First Woman in Whitehall* (Sussex, 2008). On the relationship between women, social policy, and the private sector, see Seth Koven, "Borderlands," in Seth Koven and Sonya Michel, eds., *Mothers of a New World* (London, 1993).

70. The Young Women's Christian Association organized similar schemes including the Factory Helpers' Union and Girls' Friendly Society by which "ladies" instructed and protected "our working sisters" from the dangers of a "nineteenth century spirit of restlessness and passion for liberty." See Lady Laura Riding, "The Guardianship of Working Girls," in *The Official Report of the Church Congress, Held at Exeter, On October 9th, 10th, 11th, and 12th*, ed. Rev. C. Dunkley (London, 1894), 257–64. See also Louisa Twining, *Recollections of Workhouse Visiting and Management during Twenty Years* (London, 1880); Octavia Hill, *Homes of the London Poor* (London, 1875).

71. The school, its surrounding buildings, and grounds, occupied twelve acres of land.

72. On the disciplinary dynamics of poorhouses, see Felix Driver, *Power and Pauperism: The Workhouse System, 1834–1884* (Cambridge, 1993). This account, unlike Driver's, does seek to examine these dynamics from the perspective of one of its poorest and most vulnerable inmates, Nellie Dowell, as well as officials, teachers, and parents.

73. Lester, "From Birth to Death, 1." Bishopsgate.

74. George Lansbury, *My Life* (London, 1928), 149. For a breezy journalistic defense of Forest Gate School with its happy girls clothed in "neat blue-serge dresses and white aprons" see "Forest Gate School," *All the Year Round*, vol. 3 (1890), 204.

75. Lansbury made this argument about workhouse diets for poor children in Cardiff in 1907. See Jonathan Schneer, *George Lansbury* (Manchester, 1990), 47.

76. See Annual Reports for Forest Gate School, 1883–1888, FGSD/1, London Metropolitan Archives.

77. Lester, "From Birth to Death,1" Bishopsgate.

78. Edmond Holmes, *What is and What Might Be: A Study of Education in General and Elementary Education in Particular* (London, 1911), 92–94.

79. Superintendent's Report and Journal, August 3, 1888, Forest Gate School District, 1887–1888, PoB.G.215/5, London Metropolitan Archives.

80. Lester, "From Birth to Death,1" Lester Papers, Bishopsgate. On this system of education, see Stephen Heathorn, *For Home, Country, and Race: Constructing Gender, Class, and Englishness in the Elementary School, 1880–1914* (Toronto, 2000).

81. Edmond Holmes, *What Is and What Might Be*, 116

82. Wyndham Holgate, "Report for the Year 1885," *Fifteenth Annual Report of the Local Government Board* (1885), 46.

83. See Anna Davin, *Growing Up Poor: Home, School and Street in London 1870–1914* (London, 1996), 118, 114, 124–25.

84. Clara E. Grant, *Farthing Bundles* (London, 1929, 1st ed.; 1933), 33.

85. Grant also saw a useful place for the more economical and traditional method of collective classroom work done in unison under the direction of the teacher. Such exercises were cost-effective, demanded "communal activity," and hence promoted "the social sense." In detailing her own innovative methods of teaching and curriculum, Grant also effectively summarized the older methods of instructions used by Board School teachers when Nell was a student in the 1880s and 90s. See Clara Grant, *The Teachers Book of Individual Occupations, with Occupations Based on the Montessori Ideal of Individual Work* (London, n.d.), 5, 12.

86. On Balfour, see Dawson Burns, *Pen-Pictures of Some Temperance Notables* (London, 1895), 96–103 and "The Band of Hope Jubilee," *Wings*, March 1, 1897, 31. An 1883

article in the *Englishwoman's Review* characterized her as "the first woman it was our lot to hear from a platform, and her quiet feminine manner, equally removed from insipidity or extravagance, her simple, well-chosen words, and her earnest purpose doubtless did much to reconcile the general public to the idea of a lady lecturer." See "A Pioneer in Temperance Work," *The Englishwoman's Review* (February 15, 1883): 62. She gave a lecture on the "Influence of Women" at the Whittington club according to "Table Talk," *The Lady's Newspaper*, May 6, 1848, 363. Some of her work was wholly admonitory such as the "Victim" or an "Evening's Amusement at the Vulture," which showed the disastrous consequences of a woman's misspent night at a gin palace. Others reclaimed the lives of admirable women such as Anna Barbault and Mary Somerville as examples of women's ability to make important intellectual, social, and moral contributions to society. For scholarly assessment of Balfour, see Kristin Doern, "Equal Questions: the 'Woman Question' and the 'Drink Question' in the Writing of Clara Lucas Balfour, 1808–1878," in Sue Morgan, ed., *Women, Religion and Feminism in Britain, 1750–1900* (Basingstoke, 2002).

87. See the review of Balfour's *Morning Dew Drops* in *The Lady's Newspaper*, September 3, 1853,134. John Maw Darton turned Balfour's own life story, like those of her fictional heroines, into an example for young women to follow who wished to combine womanliness with commitment to bettering society. See John Darton, *Famous Girls Who Have Become Illustrious Women of Our Time Forming Models of Imitation for the Young Women of England* (London, 1880), 313–23.

88. Clara Lucas Balfour, *Toil and Trust: The Life Story of Patty the Workhouse Girl* (London, 1860), 1, 14, 15, and 40.

89. See Muriel Lester, (Aged 9 ½) Gainsborough Lodge, Leytonstone, Essex, "Metagrams," *Little Folks* (1894).

90. See Julia Luard, "On the Education of Young Servants," *Englishwoman's Review* (April 1, 1868): 407; James Wells, "The Outcast," *The Children's Treasury and Advocate of the Homeless and Destitute* (November 8, 1879): 220; "Home Without a Mother," *Liverpool Mercury* (April 19, 1859). On the lost childhood of Tamil children, see "A Missionary's Wife," "Under the Palm Trees," *At Home and Abroad: A Wesleyan Missionary Magazine for Young Helpers in the Work* (April 1, 1895): 64; on child marriage and childhood, see Annette Beveridge, "The Hindu Mahila Bidyalaya," *Englishwoman's Review* (February 1, 1876): 49. On stolen childhood and slave narratives, see Wilma King, *Stolen Childhood: Slave Youth in Nineteenth-Century America* (Bloomington, IN, 2011).

91. On discourses defining poor children by what they lack, see Shurlees Swain and Margo Hillel, *Child, Nation, Race and Empire: Child Rescue Discourse, England, Canada and Australia, 1850–1915* (Manchester, 2010), 43.

92. See Sir Stafford Northcote, "Preventive Homes," *Night and Day: A Monthly Record of Christian Missions and Practical Philanthropy* (May 1, 1881): 119–20.

93. For two excellent explorations of philanthropic "abduction" revolving around race, religion, and poverty, see Linda Gordon, *The Great Arizona Orphan Abduction* (Cambridge, MA, 1999); and the "Save the Dublin Kiddies" Campaign of 1913, see Lucy McDiarmid, *The Irish Art of Controversy* (Ithaca, NY, 2005), chap. 4. On Barnardo's role in sending slum children to Canada as indentured apprentices, see Joy Parr, *Labouring Children: British Immigrant Apprentices to Canada, 1869–1924* (Montreal, 1980).

94. See Caleb Saleeby, *Woman and Womanhood: A Search for Principles* (New York,

1911), chap. 12. On the intersection of eugenics, child welfare, and maternalism, see Seth Koven and Sonya Michel, "Womanly Duties: Maternalist Politics and the Origins of Welfare States in France, Germany, Great Britain, and the United States, 1880–1920," *The American Historical Review* 95:4 (October 1990): 1076–1108.

95. Lester, "From Birth to Death, 1." Bishopsgate.

96. See Seth Koven, "The Whitechapel Picture Exhibitions and the Politics of Seeing," in Daniel Sherman and Irit Rogit, eds., *Museum Culture: Histories, Discourses, Spectacles* (Minnesota, 1994). On art as philanthropy, see Diana Maltz, *British Aestheticism and the Urban Working Classes: Beauty for the People* (Basingstoke, 2006).

97. See Seth Koven, "Henrietta Barnett: The (Auto)biography of a Late-Victorian Marriage," in Susan Pedersen and Peter Mandler, *After the Victorians* (New York, 1994). See also Micky Watkins, *Henrietta Barnett in Whitechapel: Her First Fifty Years* (London, 2005).

98. Henrietta Barnett, "Be-friending the Friendless," *Autobiography*, chap. 5, LMA/4063/006, Henrietta Barnett Papers, London Metropolitan Archives.

99. Henrietta published extensively about Forest Gate and left a detailed account of her work there in her two-volume biography of her husband. See Henrietta Rowland Barnett, *Canon Barnett, His Life, Work and Friends*, vol. 1, (Boston, 1919), chap. 11.

100. See Maria Poole's testimony, December 5, 1894, *Report of the Metropolitan Poor Law Schools Committee, Minutes of Evidence*, vol. 2 (London, 1896), 150.

101. See John Gorst, Question to Miss Baker, November 23, 1894, *Report of the Metropolitan Poor Law Schools Committee, Minutes of Evidence*, vol. 2 (London, 1896), 95–96.

102. The relative costs and advantages of small-scale cottages versus large-scale barrack schools remained a subject of debate throughout this period. In 1897, the Sheffield Guardians undertook a comparative cost analysis and concluded that they could provide cottages and small homes for pauper children at a weekly cost of 7s 10 1/2d versus 12s 2 1/2d at Forest Gate. See "Poor Law Experiments," *Times* (London), December 25, 1897, 10. The report was subjected to withering criticisms and accusations of partiality and bias by workhouse officials. See *Poor Law Schools: A Criticism of the Report of the Departmental Committee Ordered to be made by a Conference of Managers Representative of all the Metropolitan Board of Guardians, May 1896* (London, 1897). For an ardent defense of Poor Law boarding schools, see W. Chance, *Children Under the Poor Law, Their Education and After-Care Together with A Criticism of the Departmental Committee on Metropolitan Poor Law Schools* (London, 1897). The Whitechapel Union terminated its arrangement with Poplar—and ceased to send children to Forest Gate—in 1897 in favor of a cottage system. See Henrietta Barnett, *Matters that Matter*, (London, 1933), 152–55. No doubt it was this publicity that led Crooks and Lansbury to join its managing committee.

103. "LONDON POOR LAW SCHOOLS," *Wanganui Herald*, May 30, 1896, 3.

104. See Angela John, *The Life and Times of Henry W. Nevinson* (New York, 2006); Angela John, *Evelyn Sharp: Rebel Woman, 1869–1955* (Manchester, 2009). Nevinson penned many autobiographies including his three-volume autobiography *Changes and Chances, More Changes More Chances*, and *Last Changes Last Chances*, which Ellis Roberts abridged as *Fire of Life* (London, 1935).

105. Henry Woodd Nevinson, "Scenes in a Barrack School," *Nineteenth Century*

(March 1896), 493–94. Nevinson incorporated many details, in particular a deadly fire soon after Christmas, to signal that Forest Gate was his model. One aspect of Nevinson's story must have irritated Mrs. Barnett. He belittled the benevolent labors of "thoughtful and energetic" ladies, including Barnett, to protect pauper-girls-made-servants by befriending them. Catherine Scott, the secretary of MABYS, denounced Nevinson's insinuation that workhouse girls were destined to become "white slaves." She claimed to preserve the honor of workhouse girls who could not speak for themselves by citing published statistics proving that the vast majority led self-respecting and self-supporting lives. Apparently, it never occurred to Scott that former workhouse girls could speak for themselves. See Catherine Scott, "A Note on 'Scenes in a Barrack School,'" *Nineteenth Century* (May 1896), 871–72.

106. See *Minutes of the Forest Gate School Visiting Committee*, vol. 1 (1897), POBG/83/1, London Metropolitan Archives. Lansbury narrowly defeated Crooks to serve as chair of the committee in October 1897. Surprisingly, the two often had different views about the school's management. In many ways, it is possible to trace the roots of Lansbury's world-famous grassroots Poplarism to his work on this committee.

107. When Henrietta Barnett led a deputation to the Local Government Board in 1894 to demand an inquiry into the education of pauper children in barrack schools, she noted that during the previous fifteen years, she had taken 135 girls directly from Forest Gate into her home "under my personal observation." See "The Barrack Life of Pauper Children," *The Englishwoman's Review* (October 15, 1894).

108. See Poplar Training School, Forest Gate, Register of Children, 1887, POBG/214/02 and Superintendent's Report Book and Journal, 1887, POBG/215/05, London Metropolitan Archives.

109. See December 25, 1880, Parish Register, St. Jude's, Whitechapel, accessed via Ancestry.com

110. Durkheim famously developed this argument in his *Division of Labor in Society* (1893, English translation, 1933).

111. For such self-lacerating analysis, see *Stephen Hobhouse: Reformer, Pacifist, Christian. An Autobiography* (Boston, 1952). See also Deborah Cohen, *Family Secrets: Shame and Privacy in Modern Britain* (New York, 2013). chap. 6.

112. See Muriel's substantial typescript biographical sketch of her father, "My Father," Lester/2/1, Lester Papers, Bishopsgate.

113. This is based on census data of their Leytonstone neighborhood. The Lesters briefly left Essex for Hindhead in Surrey around 1898 only to return to Loughton in Essex around three years later.

114. Doris Lester, "Notes for an Autobiography," Lester/3/1, Lester Papers, Bishopsgate.

115. This remarkable album has survived and includes Muriel and Doris's first entries. Lester Family Writing Album, Lester/1/1/1, Lester Papers, Bishopsgate.

116. See Red Leather Diary, Lester Papers, Lester/1/2, Lester Papers, Bishopsgate. See also her typescript account of these prayers, Lester Papers, 2/1a, Lester Papers, Bishopsgate Institute.

117. "Victorian Sunday," interview with Kathleen Lester Hogg by Jean Yorke, BBC Radio Broadcast, June 5, 1960. See Lester/2/1, Bishopsgate.

118. See Verona Doris Lester, "A Victorian Sunday," in *Just Children* (privately printed), 28.

119. Lilley was a local girl, born in Buckhurst Hill, Essex in 1872. See Census data for 1891 accessed via Ancestry.com.

120. Verona Doris Lester, *Just Children* (n.d., privately printed), 5–6, 23–25, Lester/ 3/4, Lester Papers, Bishopsgate.

121. Muriel noted this detail in her last typescript autobiographical fragment, written in 1965. See "At 80, from 1883," Lester/2/1a, Lester Papers, Bishopsgate.

122. Verona Doris Lester, *Just Children* (privately printed), 24 in Lester Papers, 3 /4, Bishopsgate Institute.

123. Elizabeth Anna Hart, *Clare Linton's Friend* (London, 1900), 41. The novel was serialized in the *Frank Leslie's Sunday Magazine*, vol.16, 1884.

124. Anna Elizabeth Hart, "A Child's Thought," in *Poems Written for a Child* (London, 1868), 45–47.

125. The novel participates in a long literary tradition in which spoiled, well-to-do children learn to become moral, strong self-sufficient selves through their relationships with a poor child. Thomas Day's *Sanford and Merton* (1783) chronicles the way in which a creolized indolent child of white Jamaican planters comes to Britain and befriends a poor boy who teaches him how to be a proper boy. In this novel, issues of race and social status intersect to show that cross-class friendship between children is essential to educating the well-to-do child in his proper duties.

126. Hart, *Clare Linton's Friend*, 116–17.

127. On girls' passionate and erotically charged relationships with their dolls, see Sharon Marcus, *Between Women: Friendship, Desire, and Marriage in Victorian England* (Princeton, 2007), chap.3.

128. For a precise reconstruction of her literary genealogy in the periodical press between 1893 and 1897, see Michelle Tusan, "Inventing the New Woman: Print Culture and Identity Politics During the Fin-de-siècle," *Victorian Periodicals Review* 31 (Summer, 1998).

129. Muriel read the best-selling novel *Marcella* (1894) chronicling its headstrong idealistic New Woman heroine who abandons her independence for conjugal love. *Marcella*'s famous author, the social reformer and child-welfare advocate Mrs. Humphry Ward, confessed with some bitterness that her own mid-century education had been all too typical in its deficiencies. "Poor teaching, poor school-books" and "indifferent food" ensured that she learned "nothing thoroughly or accurately." See Mrs. Humphry Ward, *A Writer's Recollections* (London, 1918), 129–34.

130. See Sally Mitchell's marvelous *The New Girl: Girls' Culture in England, 1880–1915* (New York, 1995).

131. See Carole Dyhouse, *Girls Growing Up in Late Victorian and Edwardian England* (London, 1981).

132. Muriel Lester, *It Occurred to Me* (New York, 1937), 3. On Shaw and Jaeger clothing, see Ruth Livesey, *Socialism, Sex, and the Culture of Aestheticism in Britain, 1880–1914* (Oxford, 2007), 122–23.

133. On this hospital run by women for women and the settlement, see Anna Tillyard, "Nursing Branch, Report of Work," *Second Annual Report of Women-Workers in Canning Town, East London* (London, 1893), 16–19 and Margaret Pearse, M.D., Resi-

dent Physician, "Medical and Nursing Report," *Third Annual Report of Women-Workers in Canning Town, East London* (London, 1894), 22–27.

134. Doris Lester, "Notes for an Autobiography," Lester/2/1, Lester Papers, Bishopsgate. See Patricia Marks, *Bicycles, Bangs and Bloomers: The New Woman in the Popular Press* (Lexington, KY, 1990). Hilary Marland demonstrates the broad range of responses among doctors and women themselves to the health and social implications of bicycles on girls' and young women's lives. Moderation, Marland argues, was the keynote of this debate as with so many others surrounding girls' sports, physical culture, and intellectual development. See Hilary Marland, *Health and Girlhood in Britain, 1874–1920* (Basingstoke, 2013), esp. chap. 3.

135. The 1901 Census lists the school as "Woodlands" rather than Wanstead College on 74 Woodford Road, directly next door to another small private school, Gowan Lea, into which it was eventually incorporated. See W. R. Powell, ed., *Victoria County History: A History of the County of Essex*, vol. 6 (London, 1973), 337.

136. On this debate, see "Co-Education," *The Speaker*, August 29, 1896, 220. See also the debate about co-education and American values conducted in the pages of the *Times* in 1896.

137. Alice Woods, ed., *Co-Education, A Series of Essays by Various Authors* (London, 1903), 143–44.

138. See Michael Sadler, *Report on Secondary and Higher Education in Essex* (Chelmsford, 1906), 150.

139. See Doris Lester, Typescript autobiography, III, "School Days and Holidays," Lester/3/1, Lester Papers, Bishopsgate.

140. This information comes from census data for the Martins from 1861 onward, accessed via Ancestry.com.

141. See "Signal From Our Watch Tower," *The Woman's Signal*, August 4, 1898, 72–73.

142. Muriel Lester, *It Occurred to Me* (New York, 1937), 6.

143. On the connections between these radical "domestic" ideas with anticolonial activism, see Leela Gandhi, *Affective Communities: Anticolonial Thought, Fin-de-Siècle Radicalism and the Politics of Friendship* (Durham, NC, 2006).

144. On the attractions of Loughton to "radicals," see Chris Pond, *A Walk Round Loughton* (Loughton, 2002), 5.

145. The child of a haberdasher, Morrison, like Henry Lester, had been born in very humble circumstances in Poplar. Unlike Henry, he went to great lengths to conceal his social origins and styled himself a "man of letters" born in Blackheath in his 1901 census return.

146. Other prominent Toynbee Hall men who moved to Loughton included G. L. Bruce and Cyril Jackson, both distinguished educationists and reformers.

147. Printed materials and annual reports for Oriolet Hospital are in the large Charity Organisation Society file investigating Oldfield. See A/FWA/C/D330/1, London Metropolitan Archives. These reports include an interview with his estranged wife about his conjugal irregularities and infidelity. See also Richard Morris and Chris Pond, eds., *Loughton a Hundred Years Ago, Being the Text of Itinerary of Loughton 1905–1912 by William Chapman Waller* (Loughton, 2006).

148. Chris Pond, *The Buildings of Loughton and Notable People of the Town* (Loughton, 2003), 4.

149. Illness compelled Jowett to cancel his plan to visit St. Leonard's in 1891. See notice of speech by Prof. Lewis Campbell about Jowett's interest in the school in *The Woman's Herald*, October 26, 1893, 574.

150. On the history and culture of these "public" schools for girls, see Carol Dyhouse, *Girls Growing Up in Late Victorian and Edwardian England* (London, 1981), chap. 2.

151. See Elizabeth Edwards, "Homoerotic Friendship and College Principals, 1880–1960," *Women's History Review* 4:2 (June 1995): 149–63. On Maynard and Lumsden's relationship, see Naomi Lloyd's fine study, "Evangelicalism and the Making of Same-Sex Desire: the Life and Writings of Constance Maynard," PhD diss., University of British Columbia, 2011. See also Pauline Phipps, "Faith, Desire and Sexual Identity: Constance Maynard's Atonement," *Journal of the History of Sexuality* 18:2 (2009): 265–86.

152. Martha Vicinus, "Distance and Desire: English Boarding School Friendships," *Signs* 9:4 (Summer 1984): 600–622.

153. See Muriel Lester Diary, June 4, n.d. [c.1899], Lester/1 /1, Lester Papers, Bishopsgate Institute.

154. On the centrality of sport to the curriculum at St. Leonard's, see Kathleen McCrone, *Playing the Game: Sport and the Physical Emancipation of English Women, 1870–1914* (London, 1988), chap. 3, Former headmistress of St. Leonard's, Miss Dove, insisted that "I do not speak too strongly when I say that games, i.e., active games in the open air, are essential to a healthy existence, and that most of the qualities, if not all, that conduce to the supremacy of our country in so many quarters of the globe, are fostered, if not solely developed, by means of games." See Jane Frances Dove, "Cultivation of the Body," in Dorothea Beale, Lucy H. M. Soulsby, and Jane Frances Dove, *Work and Play in Girls' Schools* (London, 1901), 398.

155. According to the *St. Leonard's Gazette*, Muriel was one of fifty-seven new girls to arrive in the autumn of 1898. See *St. Leonard's Gazette* 5:3 (October 1898): 336.

156. For a detailed adulatory account of daily life at St. Leonard's and its system of instruction in academics and sport, see Alice Zimmern, *The Renaissance of Girls' Education in England, A Record of Fifty Years' Progress* (London, 1898), 153–57. On the house system at St. Leonard's see the volume celebrating its 50th anniversary in Julia Grant, Katharine McCutcheon, and Ethel Sanders, eds., *St. Leonard's School, 1877–1927* (London, 1927), chap. 4. On the use of furnishings and design to cultivate domesticity within female public schools, see Jane Hamlett, *At Home in the Institution: Material Life in Asylums, Lodging Houses, and Schools in Victorian and Edwardian England* (Basingstoke, 2014), chap. 4.

157. Muriel Lester, *It Occurred to Me* (New York, 1937), 10.

158. See Muriel Lester Diary, entries from c. 1899, c. 1900, and January 1, 1905, Lester/1 /1, Lester Papers, Bishopsgate Institute.

159. At least one of the children who attended Doris's first nursery school and kindergarten at Kingsley Hall in 1915 did wonder about Doris's marital status. Lylie Valentine recalled asking Doris why she had never married and had her own children. Lylie recalled Doris's answer to her: "I am married to Bow and you are all my children." "That

was true and she loved us all," was Lylie's comment. See Lylie Valentine, *Two Sisters and the Cockney Kids* (London, 1978), chap. 2.

160. Mrs. C. L. Balfour, *Toil and Trust* (London, 1860), 19.

161. Hart, *Clare Linton's Friend* (London, 1900).

162. Muriel Lester, *Kill or Cure* (Nashville, TN, 1937), 12–13.

163. On Rosa's influence on her thinking about wealth and poverty, see *It Occurred to Me*, 86–87; on Rosa's commitment to and experiments with a "deepening understanding" of the lives of her poor neighbors, see Rosa Hobhouse, *The Interplay of Life and Art* (1958), unpublished typescript autobiography, pp.110–26, Friends House Library, London.

Chapter Two. Capitalism, from Below and Down Under: The Global Traffic in Matches and Match Girls

1. The Metropolitan Association for Befriending Young Servants (MABYS), an organization championed by Mrs. Barnett, produced an annual report about the status of the Forest Gate girls under its care. The purpose of the report was to document the association's successes and failures. The report made no attempt to exaggerate the efficacy of its benevolent labors. It is full of damning summations of reckless, bad, and sometimes even illegal behavior by the girls. The report also reflected MABYS's belief in its right—in fact obligation—to offer moral judgments about its girls as well as the assumption that only middle-class readers would ever have access to its reports. It used a system of partial anonymity: it identified each girl by her initials as well as a host of particular details about her, rather than her given name and surname. This partial anonymity has made it possible for me to deduce that Alice Dowell is "A.D.," who entered Forest Gate as a ward of Poplar and then went to "Mrs. Barnett's Cottage Home." Maria Poole, MABYS secretary, gave Alice the highest possible evaluation of her behavior and progress as a servant: "very satisfactory." In the eyes of MABYS, she was "a dear little girl." See *Report of the Metropolitan Association for Befriending Young Servants, for the Year Ended 31st March, 1888*, which is itself part of the Forest Gate School District *Annual Report, 1888* (London, 1888), 26. The MABYS report for the following year actually named A.D. as "Alice" in its "particulars" and noted that she was still doing well in her "first place." See *Forest Gate School District, Annual Report, 1889* (London, 1889), 24.

2. Contemporaries called this expansion of trade unionism to unskilled workers the New Unionism. Articles about New Unionism and its putative defeat of "Old Unionism" appeared with increasing frequency in 1890. See, for example, "The Revolt of the Breechless," *Scots Observer* 4:95 (September 13, 1890): 425; and Frederic Harrison, "The Old and New Unionism," *The Speaker* 2 (September 13, 1890): 288. Both articles reported on the 1890 meeting of the Trades Union Congress in Liverpool.

3. Their names do not appear in the well-preserved Strike Register at the digitized Trades Union Congress History archives. Several of their immediate neighbors on Marner Street did go on strike. See http://www.unionhistory.info/matchworkers/registercontents.php. Hereafter cited as TUC online archive.

4. There is a vast and excellent literature on New Journalism. On New Journalism in relation to sexual and gender dissidence and fin-de-siècle culture, see John Stokes, *In the Nineties* (Chicago, 1989), esp. chap.1, and Laurel Brake, "Endgames: The Politics of The

Yellow Book, Decadence, Gender and the New Journalism," in Laurel Brake, ed., *The Ending of Epochs* (Cambridge, 1995). Useful general starting points include Joel Wiener, *Papers for the Millions: The New Journalism in Britain, 1850s to 1914* (Westport, CT, 1985); for "New Journalism" within the broader context of Victorian press, see Mark Hampton, *Visions of the Press in Britain, 1850–1950* (Champaign-Urbana, IL, 2004); and for excerpted examples, see Stephen Donovan and Matthew Rubery, *Secret Commissions: An Anthology of Victorian Investigative Journalism* (Peterborough, Ontario, 2012).

5. My analysis does not reject the salience of class as an analytic category or as a way to characterize social relations so much as use it as one of many factors important in understanding Nellie's working life in the match industry. Many scholars have pointed to the insufficiency of class to explain working-class thoughts, actions, feelings, and behavior. For particularly influential critiques of Marxist approaches to class and class consciousness, see Patrick Joyce, *Democratic Subjects: The Self and the Social in Nineteenth-Century England* (Cambridge, 1994) and *Visions of the People: Industrial England and the Question of Class 1848–1914* (Cambridge, 1991); Carolyn Kay Steedman, *Landscape for a Good Woman: A Story of Two Lives* (New Brunswick, NJ, 1987).

6. This chapter joins a body of work that seeks to combine global history with cultural and gender analysis by using an individual "life" as one site where these histories overlap. See Desley Deacon, Penny Russell, and Angela Wollacott, eds., *Transnational Lives: Biographies of Global Modernity* (New York, 2010). It also heeds Michael Roper's call to integrate analysis of cultural discourses and forms with emotion and subjectivity. See Michael Roper, "Slipping Out of View: Subjectivity and Emotion in Gender History," *History Workshop Journal*, 59 (Spring 2005): 57–72.

7. See James Winter, *London's Teeming Streets* (London, 1993), for a brilliant analysis of the dynamic dialectical tensions of streets as places of constant flows and obstructions.

8. Benjamin Waugh, *The Gaol Cradle, Who Rocks It?* (London, 1873), 78.

9. Henry Mayhew, *London Labour and the London Poor: The Condition and Earnings of Those That Will Work, Cannot Work and Will Not Work, Vol.1, London Street-Folk* (London, n.d), 142.

10. On girl flower sellers as social problems, see Yvette Florio Lane, "Flowering Trades: Work, Charity, and Consumption in 19th and early 20th Century Britain," Unpublished doctoral dissertation (in progress), Rutgers University.

11. The tale actually unfolds on New Year's Eve. See H. C. Andersen, "The Little Match Girl," trans. Charles Beckwith, *Bentley's Miscellany*, 21 (1847): 105–6. It was immediately reprinted in the March 1847 number of the American Christian periodical *The Universalist*, devoted to the doctrine of "universal benevolence." See *The Universalist* 12 (March 6, 1847): 271.

12. Ibid., 106.

13. See Thomas Laqueur, "Bodies, Details, and the Humanitarian Narrative," in *The New Cultural History*, ed. Lynn Hunt (Berkeley, 1989).

14. These included the 1802 Health and Morals of Apprentices Act; the 1819 and 1825 Cotton Mills and Factories Acts; the 1833 Mills and Factories Act; the 1842 Mines and Collieries Act; and the 1847 Hours of Labour of Young Persons and Females in Factories Act (Ten Hours Act). While schooling became universally mandatory in 1879, the state did not make it free until the early 1890s.

15. See David Rubinstein, *School Attendance in London, 1870–1904: A Social History* (Hull, 1969).

16. Karl Marx, *Capital*, vol. I, trans. Samuel Moore and Edward Aveling (London, 1887), 489.

17. M.C.T., *Mattie's Home; or, the Little Match-Girl and Her Friends* (London, 1873); G. Todd, *Little Fan or the Life and Fortunes of a London Match-Girl* (Edinburgh, 1874). Not all "match girl" stories blamed parents, and writers freely adapted Andersen's tale. For example, "Mother's Story" makes no mention of the match girl's parents. When the kindly grandmother dies, the match girl is left to fend for herself on the streets before her own frozen death. See "Mother's Story," *The Child's Companion*, June 1, 1881.

18. See *Pall Mall Gazette*, April 1, 1886, 14.

19. See Judith Walkowitz, *City of Dreadful Delight: Narratives of Sexual Danger in Late-Victorian London* (Chicago, 1992); Deborah Gorham, "The 'Maiden Tribute of Modern Babylon' Re-examined: Child Prostitution and the Idea of Childhood in Late-Victorian England, " *Victorian Studies* 21:3 (Spring 1978): 353–79.

20. See *Glasgow Herald*, May 1, 1890, for a review of one such school edition edited by Alfonzo Gardiner for John Heywood's *Literary Reader*. Some images of the match girl, including Mary Ellen Edwards's ("MEE") widely circulated illustration from the children's magazine *Little Folks*, accentuated her utter isolation and the inhospitable urban environment. Edwards depicted the barefoot little match girl in the midst of a blizzard clasping her ragged shawl in a huddled position. Her outstretched hand holds matches, but she is the sole person in the image. Her vacant stare underscores her passivity and helplessness. Edwards's image accompanied W. E. Fowler's poem "The Little Match Girl."

21. "Dinner and Entertainments to the Poor," *Daily News* (London), December 27, 1886, 3.

22. Oscar Wilde, *The Happy Prince and Other Tales* (London, 1888).

23. The exhibition was widely covered by the press. See "Anglo-Danish Exhibition," *Era*, May 19, 1888, 17 and May 26, 1888, 15. See also *Daily News* (London), May 11, 1888, 5. Given the ubiquity of match girls and heiresses in Victorian popular literature, it is hardly surprising that a playwright eventually combined both figures in a single character. The play *Matches* (1899) starred a poor match girl discovered to be the heiress daughter of a military officer. Transformed into a proper lady, she eventually falls in love with her wealthy guardian. *Country Life Illustrated* blasted it as a "tawdry stage novelette of the most mediocre and namby-pamby kind." See "Matches," *Country Life Illustrated*, January 28, 1899, 122. See also Man. [pseud.], "An Exquisite Matinée," *The Saturday Review*, January 21, 1899, 76–77.

24. On the protection of children through the "policing of parents," see George Behlmer, *Friends of the Family: The English Home and Its Guardians, 1850–1940* (Stanford, 1998), chap. 2.

25. See Louise Raw, *Striking A Light: The Bryant and May Watchwomen and their Place in History* (London, 2009) for a detailed analysis of the history and historiography of the strike.

26. See Annie Besant and W. T. Stead, "To Our Fellow Servants," *The Link, A Journal for the Servants of Man* (February 4, 1888): 1; and "The People's Pillory," *The Link* (February 4, 1888): 3.

27. On Besant and birth control, see Walter Arnstein, *The Bradlaugh Case: Atheism, Sex and Politics Among the Late Victorians* (Columbia, MO, 1983); on Besant's remarkable career, see A. H. Nethcot's two-volume biography, *The First Five Lives of Annie Besant* (Chicago, 1960) and *The Last Four Lives of Annie Besant* (Chicago, 1963). For a reliable starting point on Fabianism, see Norman and Jeanne MacKenzie, *The Fabians* (New York, 1978).

28. See Judith R. Walkowitz, *Prostitution and Victorian Society: Women, Class and the State* (New York, 1980).

29. See Annie Besant, "White Slavery in London," *The Link* (June 23, 1888): 2. Besant based her article on interviews with match factory women at Bryant and May. The firm was determined to ferret out Besant's informants and coerce them into signing a statement contradicting her allegations. When the match workers refused, Bryant and May dismissed a "trouble maker" at the Victoria factory for defying her foreman on July 2 or 3. Her fellow workers promptly went out on strike in solidarity.

30. Designating women's work as unskilled sustained a wage gap between men and women, a point of broad agreement among employers and most male trade unionists and workers as well as a point of considerable conflict between men and women. For employers, women's low wages meant higher profits. Laboring men sought to preserve "property in skill" as their exclusive domain and demanded a breadwinner wage sufficient to support their families. On gender conflicts in the workplace, see Sonya Rose, *Limited Livelihoods: Gender and Class in Nineteenth-Century England* (London, 1992). In fact, few men in East London received a family wage and female work in the match industry required considerable skill: speed, dexterity, and concentration. These were skills best learned by children trained to perform rapid, repetitive hand movements as their bodies matured into adulthood. Up to the early 1880s, match manufacturers such as Bryant and May and R. Bell's regularly hired children as young as seven or eight to work half shifts. While many contemporaries were dazzled by the dexterity and speed required by match factory work, Mrs. Fenwick Miller dissented. She argued that "any girl" could obtain the necessary skill in a few months. Such girls needed only the "very slightest degree of natural ability." Florence Fenwick Miller, "Ladies Column," *Illustrated London News*, July 21, 1888, 74.

31. Louise Raw persuasively argues that former Bryant and May match factory women sometimes did produce matchboxes for the company in their homes to accommodate the demands of marriage and motherhood. There was considerable fluidity between women employed by Bryant and May in the factory and those who worked at home to supply the company with matchboxes. See Louise Raw, *Striking A Light: The Bryant and May Watchwomen and Their Place in History* (London, 2009). Raw importantly recasts the strike as the work of the match factory women themselves rather than viewing them as following the lead of Besant and Burrows.

32. See "The Press and the Match Girls," *The Link* (July 28, 1888): 4.

33. On July 7, 1888, the *East London Advertiser*, defender of conservative business interests, published an unsympathetic account of the strikers under the heading "Bryant and May's Match Girls on Strike," blaming outsiders for fanning the "flames" of unrest. The match girls had come to curse "loud and deep the advice of socialist outsiders." *East London Advertiser*, July 7, 1888. The *Advertiser* ultimately altered its position in the aftermath of Bryant and May's acknowledgment that some of the girls' grievances were

true. However, it shifted the weight of blame to the failures of foremen and women rather than the "gentleman" capitalist owners of the firm. See *East London Advertiser*, July 21, 1888, 6. The *Times*, no friend to radical causes, wholeheartedly concurred. It adopted the term "match girls" in the first of several articles condemning "Social Democrats" as "pests of the modern industrial world" for fomenting disharmony at Bryant and May. See the editorial on "the strike of the match girls," *Times* (London), July 14, 1888, 11. The article provided a detailed narrative of the strike with harsh condemnation for the instigators, "agitators who make it the business of their lives to sow discord between employers and employed." The *Times*, in exonerating the match girls of blame for their ill-advised actions, also stripped them of any trace of agency. It insisted "the course they have followed has not been of their own choice."

34. *Reynolds* ran a short article on the strike of Bryant and May's match girls on July 8, 1888. The *Star* provided both the most in-depth and sympathetic coverage of the strike, which in turn helped establish the fledgling paper's reputation for hard-hitting news coverage. Bryant and May's labor practices remained one of its favorite targets for the next decade. On the *Star's* later campaigns against "phossy jaw" at Bryant and May, see Carolyn Malone, "Sensational Stories, Endangered Bodies: Women's Work and the New Journalism in England in the 1890s," *Albion* 31:1 (Spring 1999): 49–71.

Albion. On July 13, 1888, the *Daily News* ran a story on the strike of "matchmakers" at Bryant and May.

35. See "The Strike Fund," *The Link* (July 21, 1888): 4–5.

36. Annie Besant, *An Autobiography* (London, 1893), 331–32.

37. Burrows shared Besant's interest in Theosophy and was a very active member of the British Section of the movement.

38. Besant, *Annie Besant: An Autobiography*, 331–38.

39. See notices about activities in "England," *Lucifer* 6 (March 1890): 68 and "Opening of the East London Working Women's Club," under "Theosophical Activities," *Lucifer* 7 (September 1890): 79–80. My thanks to the archivist of the Henry S. Olcott Memorial Library of the Theosophical Society in America for sending me copies of the relevant issues of *Lucifer*.

40. "Women Out of Work, An East End Club," *Women's Penny Paper*, August 23, 1890.

41. "Interview with Rev. J. T. Hazzard, Baptist Minister, The Lighthouse and Blackthorn Street Chapel, Devons Road, Bromley by Bow," n.d., B176, p. 11, Charles Booth Papers, British Library of Politics, Economics, and Sociology (BLPES).

42. See "A walk among the following churches: Dr Thacker's Church; St Mary Bow; St Leonard's; Congregational Church Bruce Road; Methodist Church; Strict Baptist Church; Bow Road Baptist Church; Wesleyan Church; Harley Street Congregational Church; Holy Trinity Stepney; Presbyterian Church Bow Road; Berger Hall; St Andrews Mission Church," January 22, 1899, B385, p. 91, Charles Booth Papers, BLPES. W. Hayward, the minister in charge of Berger Hall, informed Charles Booth that most members of Berger Hall came from the surrounding five or six streets and included dock laborers, railway men, brick layers, and matchmakers from Bryant and May's and Bell's, the latter of whom filled up the ranks of Berger Hall's Sunday school and church. See "Interview with W. Hayward, Harley House, Bow Road and Berger Hall, Empson Street, Bromley, Baptist," n.d., B176, pp. 24–47, Charles Booth Papers, BLPES.

43. Charles Booth, "Walk among the following churches: St Annes Limehouse; Salvation Army Citadel; Coverdale Congregational Church; Father Higley's Church; St Matthews; St James the Less; Wesleyan Mission; St Dunsta's Stepney Green; Congregational Meeting House," February 27, 1898, B385, p. 11, Charles Booth Papers, BLPES. On Thompson and the Forward Movement, see "God's Work, and His Workers. Wesleyan East-End Mission," *Wesleyan-Methodist Magazine*, April 1890, 312. The article notes Thompson's particular success in attaching "ladies" from "better-class Circuits" with the Girls' Home. For a contemporary history of the Forward Movement, see James E. McCulloch, *The Open Church for the Unchurched or How to Reach the Masses* (London, 1905).

44. On Parry see, "Report of visit to St Friedeswide, Christ Church Mission," May 24, 1898, B385, p. 27 Charles Booth Papers, BLPES.

45. "Interview with C.J.O. Sanders, honorary superintendent of Wesleyan Mission Devons Road," n.d., B176, p. 205, Charles Booth Papers, BLPES.

46. The Hon. Superintendent of the Wesleyan Mission on Devon's Road, Bow, C.J.O. Sanders had founded the Albert Terrace mission soon after the strike, around 1890. See "Interview with C.J.O. Sanders, honorary superintendent of Wesleyan Mission Devons Road," n.d., B176, pp. 203–4, Charles Booth Papers, BLPES.

47. For notice of its opening, see the *Morning Post* (London), June 27, 1890, 5 and July 5, 1890, 2.

48. Marguerite, "The World of Women," *The Penny Illustrated Paper and Illustrated Times*, May 31, 1890, 345.

49. Minute Book, The Club for Working Girls, Clifden Institute, entry for December 27, 1897, D/B/BRY/!/2/540, Hackney Local History Archives.

50. "Interview with Miss Nash, superintendent Clifden House Institute," May 19, 1897, B178, pp. 62–69, Charles Booth Papers, BLPES.

51. At the 1891 census, three matchmakers lived with Bow Lodge's matron, Ann Catherine Lloyd along with three household servants. Bow Lodge closed for renovations in the late 1890s and reopened in the early 1900s. Lloyd left Bow for India to serve as matron of the girls' residence of the Central Hindu College in Benares.

52. Montagu Williams, *Round London: Down East and Up West* (London, 1894), chap. 2.

53. Images like this one of tea-drinking factory girls satirized attempts to domesticate her. "The Story of a London Factory Girls' Club," *Girl's Own Paper*, January 5, 1895, 222.

54. "Interview with Mr. Gilbert Bartholomew, managing director of Bryant and May's match factory," June 8, 1897, B178, pp.132–45, Booth Papers, BLPES.

55. For a good analysis of Collet's views on factory girls, see Emma Liggins, "Women of True Respectability?' Investigating the London Work-girl, 1880–1900," in *Women and Work Culture: Britain c. 1850–1950*, ed. Louise Jackson and Krista Cowman (Burlington, VT, 2005), 89–103.

56. Clara E. Collet to Gilbert Bartholomew, February 8, 1889, and February 11, 1889, D/B/Bry/1/2/563, Records of Bryant and May Limited, Hackney Archives.

57. A hint of anti-Irish disdain slipped into Collet's account, albeit surreptitiously. The strike originated at the Victoria factory branch of Bryant and May, whose female hands were well known for their Irish backgrounds. On the Irishness of all the workers

at Bryant and May's Victoria Works, see Lloyd Lester, "The Matchmakers of East London: A Visit to Bryant and May's," *The Girl's Own Paper* 17 (1895): 148. See also *East London Advertiser*, July 7, 1888, which described the first group of "match girls" to go on strike as girls aged fifteen to twenty of "Irish extraction." For Collet's published essay, see Clara E. Collet, "Women's Work," in *Life and Labour of the People in London*, vol. 4, *Trades of East London*, ed. Charles Booth (London, 1893), 323–24.

58. Millicent Fawcett Garrett, "East-End Match Girls," London *Standard*, July 23, 1898, 4.

59. This was how Miss Smith, head deaconess at the Bromley House Institute on Brunswick Road (just across from Granny Sloan and Aunt Carrie), characterized the match girls who used the medical and maternity clinic services provided by Bromley House. See "Interview with Miss Smith, deaconness in charge of Bromley Training Institute of mission nurses in connection with Harley House (Dr Grattan's Guinness Institute)," June 8, 1897, B173, p. 213, Charles Booth Papers, BLPES.

60. The phrase comes from Georg Simmel, "The Metropolis and Mental Life" (1903) reprinted in Gary Bridge and Sophie Watson, eds., *The Blackwell City Reader* (Oxford, 2002), 14. Representations of match girls do not conform to some key elements of Simmel's formulation, with its emphasis on rational calculation.

61. See Dr. Cunningham's report, "Visit to Messrs. R. Bell and Co., Limited, Match Factory, Bow," in Professor T. E. Thorpe, Professor Thomas Oliver, and Dr. George Cunningham, *Reports to the Secretary of State for the Home Department on the Use of Phosphorus in the Manufacture of Lucifer Matches* (London, 1899), 141–44.

62. William Preston, "'Darkest England' Matches," *Sunday Magazine* (1892): 448–49.

63. Mrs. Thornton Smith replaced Annie Besant as secretary.

64. C.R.E. Bell to Herbert Burrows, Dec. 29, 1893, TUC online archive.

65. C.R.E. Bell to Herbert Burrows, January 5, 1894; January 2, 1894. TUC online archive.

66. Such matches were called "burnts." Burrows detailed these complaints in a circular, "Strike of Match Girls at Bell's Factory, Bromley, London" (May 1894), TUC online archive.

67. The commissioner of police reported to Home Secretary H. H. Asquith that his officers had faced difficulties protecting Mr. Bell from "molestation." No one could have confused Bell's match girls for helpless victims. Even their most ardent admirers acknowledged their rough, volatile ways. "We have never professed," Herbert Burrows told reporters, "that [the girls] have been brought up in West End drawing-rooms." Burrows knew only too well from experience that these "girls" bore no resemblance to Andersen's quietly suffering little match girl: they often took matters into their own hands and acted without consulting him. See Hebert Burrows, May 20 and 27, 1894 interview with *London Dispatch*, reprinted in "The Match Industry," and "The Match Girls," *Auckland Star*, August 14, 1894, 2.

68. Amelia, Mary, and Eliza to Mrs. [Thornton] Smith, undated (probably Jan. 1, 1894), TUC online archive. I am surmising that Amelia was Amelia Gifford. See explanation below (note 77) about committee member Amelia Gifford's subsequent arrest and imprisonment.

69. George Lansbury served as Macdonald's electoral agent and continued to ad-

mire him even after Lansbury left the Liberal Party and became a socialist. See Lansbury, *My Life* (London, 1928), 72–75.

70. *Parliamentary Debates*, 4th ser., vol. 21 (February 12, 1894), cols. 282–83. This exchange was widely reprinted in the London, national, and international press. See, for example, "The Democrat in Parliament. Labour Questions," *Reynolds's Newspaper* (hereafter cited as *Reynolds's*), Feb. 18, 1894, 3. Macdonald was a founding member of an influential extraparliamentary discussion group of New Liberals, the Rainbow Circle. Devoted to progressive causes, it included the famous critic of imperialism, J. A. Hobson, and Herbert Burrows among its members.

71. Asquith kept to himself whatever thoughts he may have had about this meeting and the Bell's match girls' strike; but it was probably no coincidence that the Home Office found that R. Bell had violated the Truck Act and other occupational health regulations governing the match industry. See letter from Asquith's secretary in Whitehall, E. Leigh Pemberton, to J. A. Murray Macdonald, March 9, 1894, in reference to Burrows's letter of January 13, detailing complaints about R. Bell. TUC online archive.

72. At the Quarterly Meeting of the Matchmakers Union on March 2, 1894 Burrows praised the girls for "sticking together," while gently chastising them for not first consulting the committee before going on strike. Minutes, TUC online archive. One indication of Burrows's anxiety about maintaining order is his decision to conclude his speech at the union's quarterly meeting by urging the "girls not to make any hostile demonstration outside the works when they went to draw their pay." See "Strike of the Match Factory Girls at Bromley-by-Bow," *Reynolds's*, March 11, 1894, 3.

73. Hubbard lived on Streatfield Road in the 1890s as a married but single mother of two daughters. She was still employed as a forewoman at Bell's in 1901, but she had moved to West Ham. I reconstruct Hubbard's addresses and occupations from census data for 1891 and 1901, Ancestry.com. Conway's parents, James and Ann, were both born in Ireland. Conway was nineteen at the time of her arrest.

74. The cashier of the Docker's Union, Henry Kay, offered surety for Conway during the appeal process—proof of the close ongoing links between match workers, dockers, and their trade unions in the 1880s and 1890s. See "The Match Girls' Strike," *Reynolds's*, March 25, 1894, 1. On Conway's appeal, see *Reynolds's*, March 18, 1894, 8.

75. See William Saunders, *History of the First London County Council, 1889–1890–1891* (London, 1892), 537. Saunders published verbatim the minutes of the London County Council meeting, October 20, 1891.

76. See "Match Girls' Strike.- The Appeal," *Reynolds's*, April 22, 1894, 8.

77. On Gifford, see "Political Notes," *Pall Mall Gazette*, April 10, 1894, 8. Bow and Bromley's Liberal MP J. A. Macdonald demanded on the floor of the House of Commons that the Home Secretary immediately release Gifford, but his request was met with laughter. See "Release from Prison Asked For," *Yorkshire Herald*, May 11, 1894, 5.

78. "The Match Girls' Strike," *Reynolds's*, April 8, 1894, 1. R. Bell and Company claimed that this sort of "intimidation" kept girls from returning to work and thus infringed on the girls' right to earn their living. See "Labour Notes, The Strike of Match Girls," London *Illustrated Police News*, March 1, 1894, 3. To curtail this sort of street violence, the metropolitan police denied Bell's match girls the right to picket in front of the factory. Many of East London's leading trade unionists saw the matter quite differently: they held a large rally in East London's great public park, Victoria Park, to denounce the

picketing ban as part and parcel of a more general assault on their right to engage in peaceful protest. On the rally in Victoria Park to raise money for Ellen Conway, see *Reynolds's*, April 8, 1894, 1.

79. Burrows detailed holdings by clergymen in R. Bell and Company as well. See "The Match Girls' Strike," *Reynolds's*, May 20, 1894, 1.

80. See Gracchus, "The Last of the Mahatmas," *Reynolds's*, November 18, 1894, 2; and "Mrs. Besant's Astral Body Makes a Call," *Aberdeen Evening Express*, November 14, 1894, 2.

81. "Labour Day in London," *Illustrated Police News*, May 12, 1894, 4.

82. "The Celebration of May Day. On the Embankment and in the Park," *Pall Mall Gazette*, May 2, 1894, 8. For a brilliant analysis of the cultural meanings and history of Ally Sloper, see Peter Bailey, "Ally Sloper's Half-Holiday: Comic Art in the 1880s," *History Workshop Journal* 16, no. 1 (1983): 4–32.

83. By the mid-1890s, he and his wife were the most visible supporters of the Clifden Institute's match girls' club and he readily praised its matron, Miss Nash, whose "marvelous" influence over the "girls" led many to embrace temperance as well as regularity in their work and private lives. See "Interview with Mr Gilbert Bartholomew, managing director of Bryant and May's match factory," June 8, 1897, B178, pp. 133–45, Charles Booth Papers, BLPES. Bartholomew complained to Booth that he and his firm had been calumnied by outsiders and that the firm had virtually eliminated phossy jaw. Revelations by the *Star* less than a year later contradicted nearly all of his claims.

84. See Lloyd Lester, "The Cinderellas of the National Household. The Match-Makers of East London. A Visit to Bryant and May's," *Girl's Own Paper*, December 7, 1895, 148. Lester was not the first to use the phrase "Cinderellas of the national household" to describe match girls. It appeared in W. P. Byles's contribution, "Ideals: Imperial and Social," in a book of idealistic and fervent essays describing the birth of the so-called New Party. Herbert Burrows contributed a manifesto outlining the group's "Principles, Hopes, Ideals." Other contributors included ILP socialists Keir Hardie and Margaret McMillan and the women's trade unionist Frances Hicks. See Andrew Reid, ed., *The New Party, described by some of its members* (London, 1895), 31.

85. The error of assuming that match girls retained strong links with radical working-class politics based on the 1888 strike is underscored by the apparent decision of Bell's match girls to campaign as a unanimous bloc *against* George Lansbury in the 1912 election, on which he staked his own political fortunes by backing women's suffrage along with efforts to abolish the Poor Law. See the *Daily Graphic*, Nov. 26, 1912, Clipping Notebook, 670.1 Tower Hamlets Local History Library.

86. See St. Andrews Poor Law Infirmary, Hospital admissions records, 1890. See SA/M/1/17, Royal London Hospital Archives.

87. Miss Jean Price, *Life among Factory Girls and Lads* (London, 1897), published for the Welcome Institute, Millwall, East, 11. This booklet is located within "Interview with Miss Price, The Welcome Institute, coffee Tavern for Factory Girls, 333 West Ferry Road," May 21, 1897, B173, pp. 102–115, Charles Booth Papers, BLPES.

88. Bell discussed the pressures of cheap European imports on English trade and their impact on his decision to establish a company in New Zealand. See "Wax Matches," *Bay of Plenty Times*, August 13, 1894, 4.

89. See "Wax Matches," *Canterbury Press*, July 28, 1894, 6.

90. Many notices appeared in New Zealand newspapers about Bell's visit and the assistance the government offered him. See "Match Factory Project," *Poverty Bay Herald*, July 20, 1894, 2; "A Bell and Black Match Factory," *Grey River Argus*, July 21, 1894, 4; *Marlborough Express*, July 20, 1894, 2.

91. On Seddon's use of protective trade policies and his views of Bell's match factory, see "An Object Lesson in Protection," *Hawkes's Bay Herald*, September 5, 1895, 2. New Zealand Liberals felt much freer than their namesakes in Britain to modify the party's founding free trade doctrines. Of course, issues of empire and protective tariffs had already done much to rip apart and reconfigure Gladstone's Liberal Party in 1886, when the charismatic imperialist Joseph Chamberlain led opponents of Irish Home Rule to form the Liberal Unionist Party, which in turn allied with the Conservatives.

92. For Seddon's elaboration of "fair trade" in relation to R. Bell and Company, see "Financial Statement," in *New Zealand Parliamentary Debates, First Session of the Fourteenth Parliament, Legislative Council and House of Representatives*, vol. 113, August 28, 1900, 288–291.

93. See "Passing Notes," *Otago Witness*, July 26, 1894. Apparently, Bell had actually imported the plant for the factory to Auckland; he then had to take it down to Wellington.

94. On R. Bell's temporary location on Cornhill Street, see *Nelson Evening Mail*, August 9, 1894. By November, neighbors lodged complaints about smoke from the factory.

95. McLay was the middle-class son of a Scottish soap manufacturer in Wandsworth, where the Bell family and its match company originated. He remained in New Zealand for the rest of his long career as a match manufacturer.

96. For a brilliantly vituperative critique of Seddon's support for R. Bell and Charles Bell's testimony before the tariff commission, see "An Object Lesson in Protection," *Tuapeka Times*, September 18, 1895, 4.

97. During the protracted debate over Seddon's global trade policy in relation to R. Bell's match factory, MPs introduced evidence to document the government's dealings with C.R.E. Bell, including letters and testimony from previous Tariff Commission hearings. See the debates over Customs and Excise, September 18, 1895, in *New Zealand Parliamentary Debates, Second Session of the Twelfth Parliament, Legislative Council and House of Representatives*, vol. 19, September 3 to October 1, 1895 (Wellington, 1895), 343–345.

98. It is possible to track R. Bell's slight retail sale price advantage over imported Bryant and May matches through the *New Zealand Trade Review and Wellington Price Current*, which quoted figures for wholesale and retail costs as well as number of imported wax vestas. For example, on November 26, 1896, it reported that Bryant and May's "plaids" sold for 3/8 to 3/10, compared to Bell's "plaids," which sold for 3/6 to 3/8. *New Zealand Trade Review and Wellington Price Current*, November 26, 1896, 7.

99. For a summary of Bell's speech, extracted from the *New Zealand Times*, see *Hawkes's Bay Herald*, July 17, 1895, 2. The *Manawatu Herald* snidely lampooned Bell's speech a few days later and implicitly asked readers to consider the high price they had been asked to pay to subsidize this new industry: "In the Messrs. Bell's match factory all that this colony supplies to make a match is the fat, which sounds true in other meanings. *Manawatu Herald*, July 23, 1895, 2.

100. Seddon preferred the title prime minister to that of premier. The official name

for his office changed during his tenure from premier to prime minister. Newspapers offered different although not contradictory accounts of Bell's and Seddon's remarks at the opening of the new factory. See "A New Industry. Opening of a Match Factory in Wellington," *Wanganui Herald*, July 16, 1895, 2; *Timaru Herald*, July 16, 1895, 3; *Hawkes's Bay Herald*, July 17, 1895, 2; "Local and General News," *Inangahua Times*, July 19, 1895, 2.

101. See "The Match Factory," *Observer*, August 4, 1894, 2, for a highly critical account of the health hazards of match making and the undesirability of establishing match manufacture in New Zealand.

102. These clippings are part of the digitized archive of the Match Makers Union available online at the Trade Union Congress history website, TUC online archive, http://www.unionhistory.info/matchworkers/links.php.

103. *Star* (Canterbury, NZ), August 22, 1894, 2.

104. James Drummond, *The Life and Work of Richard John Seddon. Premier of New Zealand 1893–1906 with a history of the Liberal Party in New Zealand* (Christchurch, Wellington, and Dunedin, NZ, Melbourne, and London, 1907), 223.

105. My thanks to Nellie's distant relative, Lorraine Sloan Lee, for explaining her great-grandfather's complicated household arrangements.

106. The Endersbee family lived on Marner Street for several decades. Harry's father, Thomas, was a gas worker. They occupied 101 Marner in 1881; in 1891 and 1901, they occupied 4 Marner.

107. The circumscribed local geographies of people in Bow are captured well in a Booth interview conducted by George Arkwright with Sister Nellie, a Wesleyan sister of the people born in Bow and associated with the Wesleyan Church in Old Ford Road. She informed the interviewer that she "seldom passes south of this line [formed by the Great Eastern Railway] which is a very distinct barrier." See "Interview with Sister Nellie, Old Ford Wesleyan Church," June 28, 1897, B176, pp. 179, Charles Booth Papers, BLPES.

108. There were at least some precedents within Nellie's family for such far-flung travel. The Dowells' fortunes—and misfortunes—had once been intimately bound to overseas trade. Nellie's father William and maternal grandfather Hugh Sloan were mariners. Hugh had also been a sometime customs and revenue officer; William was en route to Australia when he died in 1881. Hugh died long before Nellie was born and her memories of her father must have been faint at best. No doubt she grew up hearing stories about them and their seafaring adventures. As pensioners of Trinity House, Harriet Sloan and her daughter Harriet Dowell necessarily remained closely connected to the maritime networks of their long-dead husbands.

109. Poverty on Marner Street, where the Dowell-Endersbee-Dellar clan lived for several decades, may have been endemic, but according to the investigator sent by the great social surveyor Charles Booth, it was neither "dangerous" nor "vicious" like that notorious hotbed of Irish unruliness, the "Fenian Barracks." See "Walk with Mr Carter, District Inspector of Police, District 12 [Bow and Bromley]," May 31, 1897, B346, pp. 48–49, Charles Booth Papers, BLPES. The Fenian Barracks, only a short distance to the west of Nellie's home across Devons Road, were widely reputed to be among "the worst streets in any district. . . . Men are not human they are wild beasts. . . . All are Irish Cockney. Not an Englishman or a Scotchman wd live among them."

110. On the Chinese in East London, see Ross Forman, "A Cockney Chinatown: the

Literature of Limehouse, London," in *China and the Victorian Imagination: Empires Entwined* (Cambridge, 2013).

111. Opponents of Jewish immigration and white female emigration included the reactionary conservative Arnold White as well as some progressive socialists, such as Margaret Harkness, who had contributed money to support the Bryant and May girls. On White and Harkness, see Seth Koven, "The Jewish Question and the Social Question in late-Victorian London: The Fictions and Investigative Journalism of Margaret Harkness," in *Imagination and Commitment: The Representations of the Social Question*, ed. Ilja van den Broek, Christianne Smit, and Dirk Jan Wolffram (Groeningen, 2010),37–48.

112. See Nigel Murphy, "Joe Lum v. Attorney General: The Politics of Exclusion," in Manying Ip, ed., *Unfolding History, Evolving Identity: The Chinese in New Zealand* (Auckland, 2003).

113. I've drawn these census statistics from John Stone, ed., *Stone's Wellington, Hawkes's Bay and Taranaki Directory and New Zealand Annual*, appendix "Birthplaces of People in N.Z. from 1901 Census" (Tawa, NZ, 1901), 59a.

114. Lester, "From Birth to Death, 1, Bishopsgate.

115. "Conciliation Board. The Match Factory Case," *Evening Post* (Wellington, NZ), June 26, 1900, 6.

116. Ibid.

117. "The Match Industry," *Observer*, November 7, 1896, 2.

118. The MP reproduced the arguments detailed as early as 1895 by the anonymous author of "An Object Lesson in Protection," *Tuapeka Times*, September 18, 1895, 4. The author calculated that the colony was paying £146 per worker to "protect" the factory while enriching the manufacturers.

119. See speech by Thomas Noble Mackenzie, Scottish émigré marketing agent and opposition political leader, during debate over tariff bill on August 30, 1900, as quoted in "New Zealand Parliament," *Otago Witness*, September 5, 1900, 30.

120. See speech by David Buddo in *New Zealand, Parliamentary Debates, First Session, 14th Parliament, Legislative Council and House of Representations*, August 16 to September 13, 1900 (Wellington, 1900), 355. A Scottish émigré to New Zealand in 1874, Buddo was a member of the reformist wing of the Liberal Party, He remained an inveterate foe of the match industry. In 1909, he had the satisfaction of successfully shepherding through Parliament legislation banning all industrial uses of white phosphorous in New Zealand.

121. Speech by R. Mackenzie, August 30, 1900, in New Zealand, Parliamentary Debates, First Session, 14th Parliament, Legislative Council and House of Representations, August 16 to September 13, 1900 (Wellington, 1900), 358.

122. See Carolyn Malone, "Sensational Stories, Endangered Bodies: Women's Work and the New Journalism in England in the 1890s," on the *Star*'s 1898 campaign against Bryant and May. See also "Match Factory Horrors. Bryant and May Fined," *Evening Post* (Wellington, NZ) June 3, 1898, 5; and "Health," letter to the editor, *Evening Post* (Wellington, NZ), September 28, 1898, 6.

123. "Phosphorus-Poisoning in Match-Factories," *New Zealand Journal of the Department of Labour* (Wellington, NZ, 1898), 676–77. Reeves was no admirer of Seddon. On their rivalry for office, see Keith Sinclair, *William Pember Reeves: New Zealand Fabian* (Oxford, 1965), chap. 11.

124. See Register of Industrial Unions of Workers, The Wellington Match Factory Employees' and Union of Workers, no. 187, Register of Unions and Employer Organisations, ABLC W4234 18111 Box 1, Archives New Zealand, Wellington.

125. For the terms of the act, see David McIntyre and W. J. Gardner, ed., *Speeches and Documents on New Zealand History* (Oxford, 1971), 209–12.

126. In 1900, there were approximately 18,000 registered members of trade unions, with the largest concentration in the transport and building industries. At the outset, Reeves hoped that most cases would be settled through Conciliation, but by Nellie's arrival in 1900 Arbitration courts invariably resolved industrial disputes. The next year, Conciliation Boards were effectively abolished as a costly and ineffective prelude to Arbitration. See National Industrial Conference Board, *Conciliation and Arbitration in New Zealand: Research Report 23* (Boston, 1919).

127. This was, ironically, an exact reversal of the policy that had first triggered worker protest in London in 1893. R. Bell had refused to pay by the gross because its matchbox fillers had packed and shipped off so many empty boxes.

128. See "Conciliation Board. Match Factory Case," *Evening Post* (Wellington, NZ), June 26, 1900, 5.

129. See "The Match Factory Case," *Evening Post* (Wellington, NZ), June 25, 1900, 6.

130. See *Hawkes's Bay Herald*, July 17, 1895, for a reprint of article about R. Bell and Company from the *New Zealand Times*.

131. "Match-Making Industry," *Evening Post* (Wellington, NZ), July 25, 1906, 2.

132. John Stone, ed., *Stone's Wellington, Hawkes's Bay and Taranaki Directory and New Zealand Annual*, appendix "Birthplaces of People in N.Z. from 1901 Census" (Tawa, NZ, 1901), 59a.

133. Stone's directory listed Lacey's occupation as a laborer for 1900. My survey of tax records indicates that Lacey owned no property in Wellington, so he must have either managed the boardinghouse for the property owner or rented and managed the property for his own profit. See Rate Books, Wellington City Council, Te Aro Ward and Cook Ward, for 1900–1902, 00163: 0:142, Wellington City Archives, Wellington, New Zealand.

134. *Evening Post* (Wellington, NZ), June 26, 1900, 5.

135. Testimony of G. W. Lacey before Arbitration Court, as reported in *Evening Post* (Wellington, NZ),, July 24, 1900, 6.

136. R. Bell successfully sued the commissioner to recover damages for lost goods and legal costs on a technical loophole in the law that required the commission to prove that the offending firm had "intended" to deceive. See "The Commissioner of Trade and Customs v. R. Bell and Co. (Limited)," in Martin Chapman, ed., *The New Zealand Law Reports: Cases Determined by the Supreme Court and the Court of Appeal of New Zealand* (Wellington, 1901), 19: 813–39.

137. For Seddon's views on the paramount importance of Imperial Unity, see Richard Seddon to Lord Ranfurly, May 10, 1900, Seddon Family Papers, Folder 10, 1619, Archives New Zealand.

138. "New Zealand Match Factories," *Otago Witness*, July 19, 1900, 32.

139. R. Seddon, speech in reply to question by Mr. Wilford (Member, Wellington Suburbs), on "Match Making Industry," vol. 111, New Zealand, Parliamentary Debates

First Session, Fourteenth Parliament, Legislative Council and House of Representatives (Wellington, 1900), July 13, 1900, 546.

140. For details of the transaction, see report in the *Financial Half-Year* vol. 2, April 1 to Sept 30, 1901 (London, 1901), 244–45. This was a semiannual yearbook about business and finance issued by the *Times*.

141. New Zealand newspapers covered technological developments in the match industry. For an admiring description of the Diamond Match Company's remarkable new machinery, see "A Marvelous Machine," *Grey River Argus*, August 10, 1896, 4.

142. Henry Macrosty and S. G. Hobson, "The Billion Dollar Trust. II." *Contemporary Review* 80 (September, 1901): 333–54; "John Bull and Brother Jonathan. The Buying up of Bryant and May," *Supplement to the Review of Reviews,* August 15, 1901, 212.

143. Bryant and May's "Buy British" campaign began soon after the strike of 1888 and continued well into the 20th century. See its advertisement proclaiming that purchasing its products was a way to "Buy British" and support the unemployed by increasing their wages in *Funny Folks* (London), December 1, 1889, 415; see also *Girl's Own Paper*, December 1, 1900. On the "skillful absorption" of Bryant and May by American Match to deceive British consumers, see "Match Makers' Denial," *The Star* (London), April 10, 1916.

144. Rabindranath Tagore, *My Reminiscences*, chap. 22 (New York, 1917), 53.

145. "The Growth of Newtown," *Evening Post* (Wellington, NZ), April 2, 1898, 2.

146. See "Bell, R. and Co.," *The Cyclopedia New Zealand* [Wellington Provincial District] (Wellington, 1897), 748.

147. I have reconstructed Swiney's career as builder and landlord in Berhampore from the Wellington City Council Rate Books for 1900–1903, Series 00163.

148. John Stone, ed., *Stone's Wellington, Hawkes's Bay and Taranaki Directory and New Zealand Annual* (Tawa, NZ, 1903), 41.

149. William Pember Reeves, *State Experiments in Australia and New Zealand*, vol. 1 (Cambridge, 1902, 2011) 68.

150. See Patricia Grimshaw, *Women's Suffrage in New Zealand* (Auckland, 1972); on Women's Christian Temperance Union in global perspective, see Ian Tyrrell, *Woman's World, Woman's Empire: The Women's Christian Temperance Union in International Perspective* (London, 1991); see also Charlotte Macdonald, *The Vote, the Pill, and the Demon Drink: A History of Feminist Writing in New Zealand* (Wellington, 1993), chap.2.

151. Lester, *Salt of the Earth*, 16. Muriel's chronology is often confused. This would date Nellie's time in New Zealand to 1904–5. Muriel also betrays her preference for the nonviolent constitutional arguments of the suffragists over the militancy of the suffragettes. Given the close alliance between the leading suffragettes and the pursuit of war during World War I, this is hardly surprising.

152. Newtown Electoral Rolls, New Zealand, 1902.

153. In *From Birth to Death*, Muriel indicates that the man for whom Nellie voted was called Fraser. A Fraser sat on Wellington Town Council for the Cook district of Wellington in 1900.

154. For a contemporary assessment of the Swedish match industry, see Gustav Sunbarg, ed., *Sweden, Its People and Its Industry* (Stockholm, 1904), 822–27.

155. See "Building Application, Match Factory," April, 1910, 00053:157:8663, Wellington City Archives.

156. See "Report of an Inquiry into the Price of Matches," Cmd. 924, Reports from Commissioners, Inspectors and Others, Vol. XXIII (London, 1920), 5, prepared by the Sub-Committee appointed by the Standing Committee on the Investigation of Prices. The Swedish match industry has received considerable scholarly attention. See K. G. Hildebrand, *The Swedish Match Company, 1917–1939* (Stockholm, 1985); H. Lindgren, *Corporate Growth: The Swedish Match Industry in Its Global Setting* (Stockholm, 1979); and L. Hassbring, *The International Development of the Swedish Match Company, 1917–1924* (Stockholm, 1979).

157. Lester, "From Birth to Death, 1," Bishopsgate.

158. A lifelong bachelor, Snell said nothing about his private life in his autobiography, *Men, Movements and Myself* (London, 1936).

159. The East London branch of the Ethical Society, founded in 1889, numbered fewer than one hundred regular members at the turn of the century according to Charles Booth, who met with the society's Hon. Sec. Miss Z. Vallance in May 1897. Vallance characterized members as "the better class of working-men and women, clerks, teachers," whose willingness to endure minor persecutions for the views implied a "certain seriousness." See "Interview with Miss Vallance, The Deanery Stratford, honorary secretary of East London Ethical Society," May 20, 1897, B178, pp. 70–87, Booth Papers, BLPES.

160. Fifty-nine people attended services at the Bow Road Ethical Society on the evening of the *Daily News* religious census of 1902–3. See Richard Mudie-Smith, ed., *The Religious Life of London* (London, 1904), 48.

161. Horace Bridges, Stanton Coit, G. E. O'Dell, and Harry Snell, *The Ethical Movement, Its Principles and Aims* (London, 1911), 1–2.

162. See G. Spiller, ed. *Papers on Inter-Racial Problems, Communicated to the First Universal Races Congress* (London, 1911), xix. On the diverse people involved in this remarkable gathering, see Susan Pennybacker, "The Universal Races Congress, London Political Culture, and Imperial Dissent," *Radical History Review* (Spring 2005): 103–17.

163. H. Snell, *The Foreigner in England—an Examination of the Problems of Alien Immigration*. Tracts for the Times Series, no. 4, n.s. (Keighley, 1904), 3–7.

164. The 1911 census lists William Dellar as an inmate of the Forest Gate poorhouse run by Poplar Guardians. He was admitted to the Poplar and Stepney Poor Law Infirmary on March 1, 1906, Admission and Discharge Register, SA/ M/1/32, Royal London Hospital Archives. There is some ambiguity in the surviving records about his discharge in August 1906.

165. Lester, "From Birth to Death,1," Bishopsgate.

166. See Register of Enquiries and Complaints relating to the employment of girls and women (and some males), Industrial Law Committee, YWCA Archives, MSS.243/142/2, Modern Record Centre, University of Warwick, Coventry, UK. The complaint was handled by Miss [Adelaide] Anderson.

167. A. G. Hopkins, "The History of Globalization—and the Globalization of History?" in A. G. Hopkins, ed., *Globalization in World History* (London, 2002), 28.

168. W. T. Stead, "To All English-Speaking Folk," *Review of Reviews* (January, 1890): 15–20.

169. The metropolitan and colonial press offered extensive coverage of the *Waiwera's* departure with New Zealand soldiers contributing to Britain's efforts during the Boer

War. See "The Boer War, The New Zealand Contingent," *Illustrated London News*, December 9, 1899, 837.

170. See "Imperialism as an Outlet for Population," in J. A. Hobson, *Imperialism: A Study* (London, 1902), 49.

171. Lester, "From Birth to Death, 1," Lester Papers, Bishopsgate.

172. W. E. Burghardt Du Bois, *The Souls of Black Folk: Essays and Sketches* (Chicago, 1903), 1.

173. Ranajit Guha, "Chandra's Death," in Guha, ed., *Subaltern Studies V, Writings on South Asian History* (Delhi, 1987), 138–39.

Chapter Three. "Being a Christian in Edwardian Britain

1. On Mafeking night and the impact of popular journalism in its choreography, see Paula Krebs, *Gender, Race, and the Writing of Empire: Public Discourse and the Boer War* (Cambridge, 1999). Krebs argues that journalists allied with state power to blur distinctions between working-class jingoism and middle-class patriotism. Muriel's responses fully support this interpretation. See also Richard Price's groundbreaking study, *An Imperial War and the British Working Class: Working–Class Attitudes and Reactions to the Boer War, 1899–1902* (London, 1972) which debunked the myth of unthinking working-class jingoism.

2. Closer to home, Muriel's older half-sister Jen and her husband (Sir) George Hardy had "tainted" themselves with pro-Boer sentiments. See Muriel Lester, *It Occurred to Me* (New York, 1937), 11. On the pro-Boers, see Stephen Koss, *The Pro-Boers: Anatomy of an Antiwar Movement* (Chicago, 1973). See also Emily Hobhouse, *The Brunt of the War and Where It Fell* (London, 1902), and her explosive exposé of British inhumanity to Boer women and children, "Concentration Camps," *Contemporary Review* 80 (October 1901): 528–37. On Hobhouse's tactics within the framework of women's pacifist "internationalism," see Heloise Brown, *'The Truest Form of Patriotism:' Pacifist Feminism in Britain, 1870–1902* (Manchester, 2003), chap. 10.

3. In her diary, she quoted Tennyson's narrator in the poem "Maud" (1855), who felt impatient with those who "prated" of the "blessings of peace." Muriel Lester Diary, 1897–1906, 1/1/2 Lester Papers, Bishopsgate.

4. Ibid. See also Lester, *It Occurred to Me*, 7, 11.

5. Muriel had extensive knowledge of and contact with the Brotherhood Church during World War I because she was part of the radical "Crusader" group of pacifists who wrote about and defended the Brotherhood Church after it was raided and sacked in 1917. See chapter 4.

6. For a hugely influential formulation of the transatlantic quest for personal "authenticity," and a crisis of "self" within the dialectical framework of "antimodernism" and modernism, see T. J. Jackson Lears, *No Place of Grace: Antimodernism and the Transformation of American Culture, 1880–1920* (Chicago, 1981). My account offers a more optimistic trajectory about the prospect of such spiritual and ethical values in animating projects to change the world while acknowledging, as Lears does, their potential for therapeutic self-absorption.

7. J. R. Seeley, *Ecce Homo* (London, 1865, 1916), v; see also Seeley's essay that gave

the title to an edited collection published by the Ethical Society, *Ethics and Religion* (London, 1900), 7, 11, 14.

8. See Julie Melnyk, ed., *Women's Theology in the Nineteenth Century: Transfiguring the Faith of Their Fathers* (1998). Let me underscore that God's love figured crucially in most Christian theology. What is so distinctive about the tradition that I consider here is that God's love was not bound up in sin and fallenness.

9. In simplest terms, the Atonement refers to Jesus's death and resurrection as the necessary means by which sinful humanity is reconciled to God. On the centrality of the Atonement to evangelical political culture and social argument, see Boyd Hilton's superb *Age of Atonement: The Influence of Evangelicalism on Social and Economic Thought, 1785–1895* (Oxford, 1986).

10. This conception of God is captured well by R. G. Burnett's account of Methodist missionary work in East London from the 1880s to 1920s. He describes God in this way: "He is the Unseen Comrade, the Unfailing Friend." See R. G. Burnett, *Christ Down East* (London, 1931), 106.

11. Henry Lester, "Learning of Christ," Presidential Address, *Report of the Essex Baptist Union for the year 1903–1904*, (1904), 16–17 in D/NB 2/26, Annual Reports of the Essex Baptist Union, Essex Record Office.

12. See Kate Flint's analysis of women's reading in relationship to their construction of an autobiographical self, *The Woman Reader, 1837 to 1914* (Oxford, 1993), 15.

13. Arthur James Balfour, *Foundations of Belief* (London, 1895), 17.

14. Theodore Roosevelt was so enamored by Wagner that he delivered a major speech about his anti-materialist doctrine and invited him to the United States. For a copy of Roosevelt's speech, see the digitized typescript held at Houghton Library, Harvard University.

15. Charles Wagner, *The Simple Life*, trans. Mary Louise Hendee (New York, 1901), 8, 23–24, 35.

16. According to Gilbert Murray, the great classicist and liberal public intellectual, "Tolstoi's doctrines were so extreme that actual Tolstoians were rare [before World War I]; but almost every young man and woman in Europe who possessed any free religious life at all had been to some extent influenced by Tolstoi. And his influence was probably at its greatest in Russia and England." Gilbert Murray, "Introduction," to Mrs. Henry Hobhouse, *"I Appeal unto Caesar": The Case of the Conscientious Objector*, 2nd ed. (London, 1917), v–vi. For a copy of Tolstoy's open letter and the historical context of its writing and reception, see Kenneth Wenzer, ed., *An Anthology of Tolstoi's Spiritual Economics* (Rochester, NY, 1997).

17. For a viciously witty account of free love and chaotic disputes over property rights in the Tolstoyan colony in Purleigh, see Gracchus, "Collapse of a Communist Colony," *Reynolds's Newspaper*, October 15, 1899, 2.

18. For a wonderful evocation of Tolstoyan and Simple Life communities and the mingling of aesthetics and ethical concerns, see Diana Maltz, "Living by Design: C.R. Ashbee's Guild of Handicraft and Two English Tolstoyan Communities, 1897–1907," *Victorian Literature and Culture* 39:2 (September 2011): 409–26. See also Charlotte Alston, *Tolstoy and His Disciples: The History of an International Movement* (London, 2014), esp. chapters 3 and 4; James Hunt, "Gandhi, Tolstoy, and the Tolstoyans," in Harvey Dyck, ed., *The Pacifist Impulse in Historical Perspective* (Toronto, 1996).

19. G. K. Chesterton, *Heretics* (London, 1905), chap. 10.

20. His disciple-in-exile in Britain, V. G. Chertkov, churned out tens of thousands of copies of his books from the Free Age Press. On Chertkov and his Free Age Press, see Michael Holman, "Translating Tolstoy for the Free Age Press: Vladimir Chertkov and his English Manager Arthur Fifield," *Slavonic and Eastern Europe Review* 66:2 (April 1988): 125–38. On the dissemination of Tolstoy at the turn of the twentieth century, see Stephen Hobhouse, "Our Debt to Leo Tolstoi," *Reconciliation* (June 1949): 596.

21. On Stephen Hobhouse's response to Tolstoy, see Stephen Hobhouse to Kate Courtney, August 7, 1902, Courtney 15/19, Leonard and Kate Courtney Papers, BLPES; see also, Stephen Hobhouse, *The Autobiography of Stephen Hobhouse: Reformer, Pacifist, Christian* (Boston, 1951), 67.

22. Stephen Hobhouse to Henry Hobhouse, August 8, n.d. from Stepney Craft Camp in Rosa Waugh Hobhouse, ed., "Towards Harmony. A Century of Letters by Stephen Hobhouse," typescript, pp. 88–89, Library of the Society of Friends, London.

23. Stephen Hobhouse to Kate Courtney, August 7, 1902, Courtney 15/19, Leonard and Kate Courtney Papers, BLPES.

24. Lester, *It Occurred to Me*, 12–13. Her response to Tolstoy precipitated an "epiphanic moment" of modernity, to use Thomas Linehan's framework. See Thomas Linehan, *Modernism and British Socialism* (Basingstoke, 2012)

25. See Leo Tolstoy, "How I Came to Believe," in *Christ's Christianity* (1885), 51.

26. See Leo Tolstoy, *On the Personal Christian Life, Letters to Friends*, threepence edition (London, n.d.). This short set of letters reflected on how a Christian ought rightly to respond to a robber threatening to murder an innocent child; Tolstoy concluded that to kill the would-be murderer was ethically unacceptable, even if it meant not rescuing the child.

27. Shaw published his review of Maude's biography in the *Fabian News*, but my quotations of Shaw come from a lengthy essay, "Bernard Shaw's Criticism of Tolstoy," *Current Literature* LI (July 1911): 71–72. No doubt Shaw's irritation with Tolstoy was exacerbated by their private correspondence in which Tolstoy upbraided Shaw for daring to use humor in tackling fundamental questions of good and evil. See "Tolstoy Rebuked Shaw for Levity," *New York Times*, April 7, 1912.

28. On Kenworthy and Tolstoy, see John Kenworthy, "A Visit to Tolstoy," *Humane Review* (October, 1900): 262–326; John Coleman Kenworthy, *Tolstoi: His Life and Works* (London, 1902); see also Stephen Marks, *How Russia Shaped the Modern World: From Art to Antisemitism, Ballet to Bolshevism* (Princeton, 2003), 121–22.

29. On the economic and social program of the Church, see J. Bruce Wallace, *Preparing for the Twentieth Century*, 2nd ed. (London, 1897), 4, 5, 16.

30. See John Coleman Kenworthy, *From Bondage to Brotherhood* (London, 1894).

31. See Warren Sylvester Smith, *The London Heretics, 1870–1914* (London, 1967), 139. See also Mark Bevir, *The Making of British Socialism* (Princeton, 2011), chap. 12. On the Fellowship from the perspective of Edith Lees Ellis, see Jo Ann Wallace, "The Case of Edith Ellis," in Hugh Stevens and Caroline Howlett, eds., *Modernist Sexualities* (Manchester, 2000), 13–40.

32. William Jupp, *The Forgiveness of Sins and the Law of Reconciliation* (London, 1903).

33. Lily Dougall, *The Practice of Christianity* (London, 1913), 123. For a detailed

examination of Dougall's "experiential faith" (rather than her "spirituality"), see Joanne Dean, *Religious Experience and the New Woman* (Bloomington, IN, 2007).

34. See chapter 2 for a short discussion of its founding and aims. It is possible, though I think unlikely, that Nellie had once been a member of this club. The only other scholarly study of Lester argues, I think incorrectly, that this was the club that Muriel visited when she went slumming.

35. See "Theosophical Activities," *Lucifer* (October 15, 1893): 165.

36. For a report on the Brotherhood Club in Bow, see *Universal Brotherhood Path* (July 1902): 299.

37. My account of Theosophy is heavily indebted to Joy Dixon, *Divine Feminine: Theosophy and Feminism in England* (Baltimore, 2001).

38. On Theosophy in relation to Tolstoy, see "Leo Tolstoi and His Unecclesiastical Christianity," *Lucifer* 7, (September 1890): 9–14.

39. Doris's most influential teacher, the Sunday School pedagogue Emily Huntley, spoke for many Protestants committed to building international networks when she declared "Hinduism has no message of salvation for the child. It poisons his life at the spring through unholy rites, false ideals, corrupt stories." Racism all too often was embedded in "progressive" social and religious politics like Huntley's. See Emily Huntley, "India's Needs through the Sunday-School," in Charles Gallaudet Trumbull, ed., *World Wide Sunday-School Work, The Official Report of the World's Seventh Sunday-School Convention* (London, 1913), 247. If Doris critiqued her mentor's racism, I have found no record of it.

40. See Evelyn Underhill, *Mysticism* (London, 1911). Underhill exerted a powerful influence over Muriel's ideas about prayer and the body in the aftermath of World War I.

41. See Muriel Lester, *Entertaining Gandhi* (London, 1932), 116–17.

42. On Headlam, see F. G. Bettany, *Stewart Headlam: A Biography* (London, 1926); and John Orens, *Stewart Headlam's Radical Anglicanism: The Mass, the Masses, and the Music Hall* (Urbana, IL, 2003). See also Peter D'Alroy Jones, *The Christian Socialist Revival 1877–1914: Religion, Class and Social Conscience in Late-Victorian England* (Princeton, 1968).

43. Charles Gore, "The Holy Spirit and Inspiration," in *Lux Mundi: A Series of Studies in the Religion of the Incarnation* (1889), 230, 264.

44. Charles Gore, *The Incarnation of the Son of God* (London, 1891), 162, 160, 111.

45. Doris Lester, typescript autobiography, Lester/3/1, Lester Papers, Bishopsgate.

46. Spurred by the godless mischief of socialists, even the Holy Father Leo XIII awakened to the "utter poverty of the masses" and expounded the "rights and duties" of the rich and poor in his 1891 encyclical, *Rerum Novarum*. He enjoined "brotherly love and friendship" as an antidote to class conflict.

47. This was how Alfred Garvie characterized the religious and theological mood of the turn of the century in his lectures delivered at Mansfield College, Oxford in 1901. See Alfred Garvie, *Ritschlian Theology: Critical and Constructive* (Edinburgh, 1902), 18.

48. For a sympathetic account of the army's many outreach activities and its religious services, see H. Rider Haggard, *Regeneration* (London, 1910). See Pamela Walker, *Pulling the Devil's Kingdom Down: The Salvation Army in Victorian Britain* (Berkeley, CA, 2001).

49. See chapter 1.

50. See Paul Dekar, "Muriel Lester, 1883–1968, Baptist Saint?" *Baptist Quarterly* 34 (1992): 337. East London and Essex newspapers regularly reported on Henry Lester's church-related civic contributions. On his work with the Band of Hope, see "Stratford," *East London Observer*, March 22, 1879, 7; on his opening a new mission hall, see "Leytonstone," *Essex County Chronicle*, June 12, 1896, 7.

51. Stanley B. James, *The Adventures of a Spiritual Tramp*, (London, 1925), 76–77. See also Doris Lester, typescript autobiography, chap.2, 3/1, Lester Papers, Bishopsgate; Muriel Lester, *It Occurred to Me*, 41.

52. For a respectful albeit sharply critical assessment of Campbell's "theology," see Frank Thilly, "Can Christianity Ally Itself With Monistic Ethics?" *American Journal of Theology* 12 (October 1908): 447–564.

53. Lester, *It Occurred to Me*, 41; Doris Lester, "The Pattern Changes," chap. 2, Typescript autobiography, Lester/3/1, Lester Papers, Bishopsgate.

54. "If Christ Came to London. Rev. R. J. Campbell preaches remarkable sermon in City Temple," *New York Times*, December 16, 1907. There was a rich tradition of imagining how Christ would respond to the sordid conditions of modern urban life. See W. T. Stead, *If Christ Came to Chicago* (Chicago, 1894).

55. W[illiam]. E. Orchard, *From Faith to Faith: An Autobiography of Religious Development* (New York, 1933), 85. The Lesters remained closely connected to Orchard well after the demise of New Theology.

56. Many of Muriel's diary entries are undated, including this one. In most cases, it is possible to offer a range of likely dates based on dated entries. This entry probably dates from 1902 to 1905. It is not possible to be certain that the scene Muriel narrates in her diary actually took place; it may have been an inner conversation she had with herself about her fellow congregants and her relationship to them.

57. On women's religious authority—its constraints and possibilities, see the stimulating essays in Sue Morgan and Jaqueline Devries, eds., *Women, Gender and Religious Cultures in Britain, 1800–1940* (London, 2010).

58. Muriel Lester Diary, 1897–1906, Lester/1/1/2, Lester Papers, Bishopsgate.

59. The great Congregationalist preacher, Dr. G. Campbell Morgan, outlined what it meant to crucify oneself with Christ at the time Muriel penned these words. His meaning probably comes close to her thinking. "If I am crucified with Christ, then I am abandoned for evermore to the will of God. If I am crucified with Christ, I accept Christ's attitude toward my fellow-men. If I am crucified with Christ, I choose Christ's way of reaching the ultimate victory." For Morgan, being crucified with Christ was indivisible from rebirth in and with Christ. See Dr. G. Campbell Morgan, "Crucified with Christ," in *Westminster Bible Conference, Mundesley, 1910, Verbatim Reports of Sermons and Lectures* (London, 1910), 360.

60. Muriel Lester Diary, 1897–1906, Lester/1/1/2 Lester Papers, Bishopsgate.

61. Ibid.

62. Each of these agencies had many smaller mission organizations and clubs. Thompson's Paddy Goose missionary centre sponsored "Girls' Guilds and Nursing Corps, Boys' Brigade and Boy Scouts, Mothers' Meetings and Dockers' Unions" which "jostle[d] one another in their effort to get the space they require." See Rosalie Budgett Thompson, *Peter Thompson*, Foreword by Rev. Canon Barnett (London, 1910), 63. For

an overview of British Nonconformity's contribution to slum work and social welfare, see Lesley Husselbee and Paul Ballard, eds., *Free Churches and Society: The Nonconformist Contribution to Social Welfare 1800–2010* (London, 2012), especially contributions by David Bebbington, "Conscience and Politics," and Peter Catterall, "Slums and Salvation."

63. Peter Thompson, "Obligations of the Church in Relation to the Social Condition of the People," in Rev. William Archer, introduction to *Proceedings of the Second Ecumenical Methodist Conference* (New York, 1892), 459, 461, 463. On Thompson, see also H [enry] M[urray, *'Twixt Aldgate Pump and Poplar, The Story of Fifty Years Adventure in East London* (London, 1935), 30, 50. Thompson along with fellow evangelical Frederick Charrington served as Treasurers for the Dockers' Union during the Great Dock Strike of 1889—an indication of evangelical Nonconformity's alliance with East London trade unionism. See Rosalie Thompson, *Peter Thompson*, 71–82.

64. Muriel Lester Diary, 1897–1906, Lester/1/1/2 Lester Papers, Bishopsgate.

65. My thanks to Yvette Lane for conversations that have helped clarify this argument.

66. Lester, *It Occurred to Me*, 20.

67. Ibid., 5.

68. For a lively account of domestic service from servants' own perspectives, see Lucy Lethbridge, *Servants: A Downstairs View of Twentieth-century Britain* (London, 2013). See also Lucy Delap, *Knowing Their Place: Domestic Service in Twentieth-Century Britain* (Oxford, 2011).

69. See, for example, the depiction of the ladies' maid Dixon in Elizabeth Gaskell's *North and South* and the effeminate nurse-turned-manservant Job in Rider Haggard's *She.*

70. Robert Tressell's *Ragged Trousered Philanthropists* (written 1911, posthumously published 1914) laments such divisions among the working class that hinder the growth of a socialist class consciousness.

71. My thanks to Katie Trumpenauer for sharing her work in progress on modernist women writers and the children's nursery.

72. Arthur Morrison, "A Street," *Macmillan's Magazine* 64 (October 1891): 460–61.

73. See excerpts from Arthur Morrison's *Daily Chronicle* appeal as reported in "Free-Trade England. Winter and Want." *The Age*, February 18, 1903. The Lesters would certainly have read and discussed Morrison's appeal, given its prominence and their proximity to the famous writer.

74. "An East End Parish," *All the Year Round*, July 10, 1880, 206, 209.

75. Lester, *It Occurred to Me*, 20.

76. See Ella Hepworth Dixon, *The Story of a Modern Woman* (London, 1894), 38–40, in which the "handsome clever" aristocratic Alison Ives runs a club and home for "my East End girls."

77. Muriel Lester, "Autobiographical Notes," "Beginnings in Bow," 2/1, Lester Papers, Bishopsgate. In one draft typescript, Muriel noted that she and her mother had gone to South London to speak with this woman about volunteer opportunities for Muriel. She had encouraged Muriel to give an afternoon each week to playing games with slum girls.

78. Most public schools, male and female, sponsored their own philanthropic proj-

ects, many in the slums of London. St. Leonard's funded and managed a seaside convalescent home for poor sick children.

79. Hon. S. Lyttleton, "Girl's Clubs," in Emily Janes, ed., *Englishwoman's Year Book*, (London, 1900), 228.

80. Lester, *It Occurred to Me*, 20–23.

81. Muriel's homage to Mrs. Pryke's domestic genius had several precedents in the writings of Edwardian female social investigators such as the Bermondsey settlement worker Anna Martin. See Anna Martin, "The Mother and Social Reform," *The Nineteenth Century and After* (May 1913); and "The Mother and Social Reform, Part II," *The Nineteenth Century and After* (June 1913). See also Ross McKibbon, *Ideologies of Class: Social Relations in Britain 1880–1950* (Oxford, 1990), chap. 6; Ellen Ross, *Love and Toil: Motherhood in Outcast London, 1970–1918* (Oxford, 1993).

82. On female gift economies and aggression in Victorian culture, see Jill Rappoport, *Giving Women: Alliance and Exchange in Victorian Culture* (Oxford, 2012), esp. intro.

83. Terry Carter, "Down the Lane-with thanks to Will Francies," *Loughton and District Historical Society Newsletter* 184 (January/February 2010): 10. The description is drawn from an article written by a resident of Smarts Lane at the turn of the century.

84. See November 13, 1911, Minutes of Loughton Chapel Sunday School, D/NB 3/87, Essex Record Office.

85. Doris and Muriel reorganized the Loughton Union Chapel Sunday School along graded school lines in 1908; Doris taught the primary division, Muriel the junior. See Rev. Vivian Lewis, *Come with Us, The Story of the Loughton Union Church 1817–1973* (Loughton, 1974), 22–23. See George Bowtle to Muriel Lester, July 29, 1914, Lester/2/5, Bishopsgate.

86. See "Interview with Reverend W. Knight, Baptist chaplain of the Poplar and Bromley Tabernacle, Brunswick Road, 16 New Fillebrook Road, Leytonstone," May 31, 1897, B176, pp. 48–61, Charles Booth Papers, BLPES.

87. He must have found his calling to enter the ministry between 1901 and 1907. I have reconstructed Morrell's trajectory using the 1871, 1881, 1891, 1901, and 1911 census data; digitized registers of voters in London document his move to Marylebone; along with his probate record after his death. He retired from active ministry at Bruce Road in 1929. See *The Congregational Quarterly,* vol. 7 (1929): 280, published by the Congregational Union of England and Wales.

88. Lester, *It Occurred to Me*, 28. Muriel mentioned neither Morrell's name nor the name of the Church, but Doris did in a correction to her typescript autobiography.

89. Charles Booth, "Walk among the Following Churches," January 22, 1899, B385, pp. 85–91, Charles Booth Papers, BLPES.

90. "Interview with Mr. French" in Geoff Richman, *Fly A Flag for Poplar* (London, 1974), 105.

91. See *Boys' Brigade Gazette*, June 1, 1897, 159.

92. William Walsham How, "Introduction," in Mrs. Donaldson, *Home Duties for Wives and Mothers, Illustrated by Women of Scripture* (London, 1882), v.

93. W. E. Clapham, *The Good Fight At Bow* (London, 1938), 96.

94. Richard Mudie-Smith, ed., *Religious Life in London* (London, 1904), 27, 9.

95. See Lena Orman Cooper, "My Mother's Meeting," *The Quiver* (January 1900): 767–68.

96. Violet Myers, "A 'Mothers' Meeting' in the East End," *The Idler* 17 (July 1900): 569–74

97. Lester, *It Occurred to Me*, 29.

98. Ibid., 44.

99. Doris Lester, typescript autobiography, Lester/3/1, Lester Papers, Bishopsgate.

100. Cox and Box refers to the 1866 comic operetta of that name by Arthur Sullivan and Francis Burnand, in which two men, one who works a day shift and the other a night shift, unknowingly rent a single room from a greedy landlord.

101. Emmeline Pethick-Lawrence, *My Part in a Changing World* (London, 1938), 72.

102. Doris Lester, typescript autobiography, Lester/3/1, Lester Papers, Bishopsgate.

103. Lester, *It Occurred to Me*, 34–35. In this vignette, Muriel described the club as well established and respected with the manager of the match factory as a major benefactor. Both are true of Clifden Institute's Factory Girls' Club for match girls. The managing partner of Bryant and May, Gilbert Bartholomew was one of the club's most generous donors.

104. On its founding, see Mrs. H. Grattan Guinness, *The Wide World and Our Work In It: The Story of the East London Institute for Home and Foreign Missions* (London, 1886), 118–21.

105. See Lester, *It Occurred to Me*, 44. Muriel was more generous in her assessment in an unpublished draft chapter. She thanked Doric Lodge for its hospitality to her and Doris. See Muriel Lester, Draft Autobiographical Accounts of *It Occurred to Me*, Lester/2/1, Lester Papers, Bishopsgate.

106. For an assessment of its place in global evangelicalism, see "A New Global Spiritual Unity" in Mark Hutchinson and John Wolffe, *A Short History of Global Evangelicalism* (Cambridge, 2012), chap.5. Hutchinson and Wolffe helpfully illuminate the widely varied responses of evangelicalism to modern life, from a corporate commitment to activist engagement with social problems to quietist withdrawal.

107. Militant suffragette Christabel Pankhurst was deeply influenced by Grattan Guinness's "scientific" predictions and theology. See Timothy Larsen, *Christabel Pankhurst: Fundamentalism and Feminism in Coalition* (Woodbridge, 2002), 36–40.

108. Harry Grattan Guinness, *The Approaching End of the Age* (London, 1878) and Mr. and Mrs. Harry Grattan Guinness, *Light for the Last Days* (London, 1887).

109. See Harry Grattan Guinness, *The Heresy Taught by the Rev. G. O. Barnes Exposed and Answered* (London, 1884).

110. Leaders of Doric Lodge characterized it as a "cosmopolitan gathering" with a "great diversity of character and temperament." In 1907–8, students at Harley College hailed from Norway and Armenia, Italy and Patagonia, Palestine and Australia; they were Baptists and Episcopalians, Wesleyans and Presbyterians. They mastered Greek, Hebrew, French, and Spanish. See Harry Guinness, *These Thirty Years* (London, 1903), 19. On Regions Beyond, see Joseph Conley, *Drumbeats that Changed the World* (Pasadena, CA, 2000).

111. Dr. Harry Guinness, *Not Unto Us, A Record of 21 Years Missionary Service* (London, 1908), 39–41. Muriel acknowledged the insufficiency of her education in geogra-

phy and nonwestern cultures. "When I arrived in India . . . my mental equipment was very meagre." See Muriel Lester, *My Host the Hindu* (London, 1931), 15.

112. For example, see Monday, October 8, 1900, Deacons' Minute Books, Loughton Union Church, 1900–1904, D/NB/3/4, Essex Record Office.

113. See Chapter 4.

114. A large literature charts Leopold's regime in Congo, none more riveting and moving than Adam Hochschild, *King Leopold's Ghost: A Story of Greed, Terror and Heroism in Colonial Africa* (New York, 1998). Hochschild's account brilliantly integrates American, British, African, and Belgian actors but surprisingly never mentions Grattan Guinness.

115. See Sharon Sliwinski, "The Childhood of Human Rights: the Kodak on the Congo," *Journal of Visual Culture* 5: 3 (2006): 333–63.

116. This was the case put forward anonymously in *Dr. Grattan Guinness Self-Refuted* (Edinburgh, 1905).

117. Henry Jr. presented himself as a victim of Leopold's duplicity. He attributed his personal observation of abuses during his time in Congo in 1890–91 as examples of corrupt local officials rather than systematic exploitation. See Dr. Henry Grattan Guinness, "The Story of a Disillusionment," *Regions Beyond* (January–February1908): 12–14.

118. Kevin Grant argues "evangelical Christianity, rather than [secular] radicalism, remained the predominant force in the humanitarian politics of empire in Britain in the early twentieth century." Kevin Grant, "Christian Critics of Empire: Missionaries, Lantern Lectures, and the Congo Reform Campaign in Britain," *Journal of Imperial and Commonwealth History* 29:1 (2001): 29. My account of the role of Regions Beyond in the Congo Reform Association draws heavily on Grant's article.

119. In the aftermath of World War I, Morel fanned the flames of racism with his sensationalized account of African soldiers putative sexual violation of white women in Germany. Muriel accepted Morel's judgments and likewise condemned the conduct of African troops.

120. On Du Bois's proclamation, see C. G. Contee, "The Emergence of Du Bois as an African Nationalist," *The Journal of Negro History*, 54: 1 (January 1969): 48–63. For the text of the proclamation, see W.E.B. Du Bois, "An Address to the Nations of the World," in *W.E.B. Du Bois: A Reader*, ed. David Levering Lewis (New York, 1995), 639.

121. See "Women's Branch of the Congo Reform Association," *London Times*, April 24, 1909, 8. Muriel was the only unmarried woman at the meeting. The women's branch focused on the conditions of women and children in the Congo.

122. See *Loughton Chapel Magazine* (July 1908), D/NB 3/155, Essex Record Office.

123. Forbes Jackson, "Daniel Hayes, An Appreciation," in Harry Guinness, *Not Unto Us: A Record of Twenty-One Years' Missionary Service* (London, 1908), 64. The Lesters had many ties to Berger Hall. It was widely hailed as the Baptists' most outstanding outpost of slum work and was supported by many of the Lesters' close friends including the Marnham family. The Marnhams provided generous donations to Muriel and Doris throughout their careers and also volunteered their services to Kingsley Hall. See "Bromley's Stronghold, A Notable Anniversary," *East End News*, October 22, 1909, about Pastor Hayes's ninth anniversary at Berger Hall. Tower Hamlets Local History Library Clippings Collection.

124. Lester, *It Occurred to Me*, 41. Hayes's public lectures had not always emphasized

the barbarism of Belgian rule. In a 1902 lecture at the Falkirk YMCA, he played upon the barbarism of natives, cannibals in the Horse Shoe Bend district, among whom he had toiled in Christ's name. See "Missionary Lecture," *Falkirk Herald and Midland Counties Journal* (February 19, 1902): 3.

125. In January 1909, Campbell suggested the value of strong British intervention in the Congo. See "The Congo Question. Rev. R. J. Campbell and Possible Intervention," *Western Times*, January 29, 1909, 13.

126. George Haw, *From Workhouse to Westminster: The Life Story of Will Crooks, MP* (London, 1907), chaps. 1–2.

127. Opposition to the New Poor Law politicized laboring men and women in the 1830s. On Anti-Poor Law Associations and political protest, see Anna Clark, *The Struggle for the Breeches: Gender and the Making of the British Working Class* (Los Angeles, 1995).

128. "Separate Report by H. Russell Wakefield, Francis Chandler, George Lansbury, and Mrs. Sidney Webb," Royal Commission on the Poor Law, PP 1909. On Beatrice and Sidney Webb's contributions to this report, see A. M. McBriar, *An Edwardian Mixed Doubles, The Bosanquets versus the Webbs: A Study in British Social Policy, 1890–1929* (Oxford, 1987).

129. On membership numbers, see Michael Ward, *Beatrice Webb: Her Quest for a Fairer Society; A Hundred Years of the Minority Report* (The Smith Institute, 2011), 32.

130. George Lansbury, *My Life* (London, 1928), 2.

131. Ibid., 81.

132. George Lansbury, "A Socialist View of Government," *National Review* (June 1895): 567.

133. On socialism, Labour, and religion, see Stephen Yeo, "A New Life: The Religion of Socialism in Britain, 1883–1896," *History Workshop* 4 (Autumn 1977): 5–56.

134. See David M. Young, "People, Place and Party: The Social Democratic Federation 1884–1911," PhD diss., University of Durham, 2003, 124.

135. Lansbury's spiritual journey had been circuitous and tortured. Educated by Primitive Methodists, Welsh Nonconformists, and Anglicans, Lansbury had even joined a Salvation Army temperance organization in his youth.

136. For a passionate articulation of the links between Christianity and Labour, see *Labour and Religion by Ten Labour Members of Parliament and of Other Bodies* (St. Albans, 1910). Contributors included Keir Hardie, Will Crooks, Philip Snowden, Arthur Henderson, and George Lansbury.

137. Claude McKay, *A Long Way From Home* (New York, 1937). McKay encountered Lansbury right after World War I when he came to London in 1919.

138. On these pre–World War I campaigns, see George Haw, *From Workhouse to Westminster: The Life Story of Will Crooks, M.P.* (London, 1907); George Lansbury, *My Life* (1928); on Crooks and Lansbury's localist and "organic" political idiom as defenders of popular rights, see Jon Lawrence, *Speaking for the People: Party, Language and Popular Politics in England, 1867–1914* (Cambridge, 2002), 237–39.

139. For a summary of the findings and debate over this particular charge, see Gordon Crosse, "The Poplar Workhouse Inquiry," *Economic Review* 17:1 (January 1907): 46.

140. See testimony of George Lansbury and Will Crooks on 8 June 1906 in *Poplar Union. Transcript of Shorthand Notes Taken at the Public Inquiry Held by J.S. Davy, C.B. into the General Conditions of the Poplar Union, Its Pauperism, and the Administration of the Guardians and Their Officers* Cd.3274 (London, 1906), 24.

141. George Eliot, ed., Thomas Noble, "Janet's Repentance," *Scenes of Clerical Life* (Oxford, 2000), 260.

142. The phrase is John Trevor's, founder of the Labour Church, which sought to "occupy the ground that Secularism has cleared and build a new Temple upon it." See John Trevor, "Labour Church," in Joseph Edwards, ed., *Labour Annual* (London, 1906), 41.

143. On the Baptist Zenana Mission, see Karen Smith, "Cultural Captivity: British Women and the Zenana Mission" *Baptist History and Heritage* 40:1 (Winter, 2006): 30–41. On British women's discursive and political use of the zenana in shaping the professional fortunes of British women medical doctors, see Antoinette Burton, "Contesting the Zenana: The Mission to Make 'Lady Doctors' for India, 1874–1885," *Journal of British Studies* (July 1996): 368–97.

144. For a typical account of the zenana as a site of oppression from which British missionaries would rescue Indian women, see "India's Daughters and England's Daughters," *Illustrated Missionary News* (Feb. 1, 1877): 19. As late as 1917, the Baptist Zenana Mission insisted the Indian women were "unwelcomed at birth, untaught in childhood, enslaved in marriage, degraded in widowhood and unlamented at death." See *Jubilee, 1867–1917, Fifty Years' Work Among Women in the Far East. Women's Missionary Association of the Baptist Missionary Society* (London, 1917), 3. Geraldine Forbes concludes that women missionaries to India in were "not only the helpmates of the imperialists, they were themselves cultural imperialists providing an education based entirely on English values." See Geraldine Forbes, " 'Pure Heathen': Missionary Women in Nineteenth Century India," *Economic and Political Weekly* (April 26, 1986): 8.

145. On the internal tensions within Baptist ideas about the brotherhood of mankind and spiritual equality across racial divides, see Catherine Hall, *Civilising Subjects: Metropole and Colony in the English Imagination* (Chicago, 2002).

146. For a panoramic overview of evangelicalism, see David Bebbington, *Evangelicalism in Modern Britain: A History from the 1730s to 1980s* (London, 1989), especially chapter Six, "Walking Apart: Conservative and Liberal Evangelicals in the Early Twentieth Century." My interpretation emphasizes how rank-and-file Christians like Muriel founds ways to combine competing understandings of Christianity.

Chapter Four. Body Biographies in War and Peace

1. Muriel Lester, "Salt of the Earth," 17.

2. Nancy Scheper-Hughes and Margaret Lock, "The Mindful Body: A Prolegomenon to Future Work in Medical Anthropology," *Medical Anthropology Quarterly* 1:1 (March 1987): 7–8. For an example of using the history of a body as a form of biographical-historical analysis, see Stephen Brooke, "The Body and Socialism: Dora Russell in the 1920s," *Past and Present* (November 2005). Like Brooke, I am interested in my subjects' bodies and in their thinking about the body in relation to a range of social, cultural and political debates. On working-class attitudes toward health and medical services in Preston, Lancaster, and Barrow, see Lucinda McCray Beier, *For Their Own Good: the Transformation of English Working-class Health Culture, 1880–1970* (Columbus, 2008).

3. I borrow this formulation from Julie Livingston, *Debility and the Moral Imagination in Botswana* (Bloomington, IN, 2005), 27.

4. My thinking about "interiority" has been shaped in conversation with Carolyn Steedman's beautiful analysis in *Strange Dislocations: Childhood and the Idea of Human Interiority, 1780–1930* (Cambridge, 1995).

5. See W.H.R. Rivers, "The Repression of War Experience," a paper delivered before the Section of the Psychiatry, Royal Society of Medicine on December 4, 1917, *Lancet* (February 2, 1918). On non-white soldiers' relationship to rehabilitative regimens and the trauma industry, see Hilary Buxton, "Disabled Empire: Race, Rehabilitation, and the Politics of Healing Nonwhite Colonial Soldiers, 1900–1945," dissertation in progress, Rutgers University.

6. The literature on shell shock is vast. For a recent assessment of it in relation to pre–war and wartime developments, see Tracey Loughran, "Shell-Shock and Psychological Medicine in First World War Britain," *Social History of Medicine* 22:1 (2009): 79–95. Loughran summarizes the debate about the relative permeability between physiological and psychological explanatory categories. On shell shock as the "body language of masculine complaint," see Elaine Showalter, *The Female Malady: Women, Madness and English Culture 1830–1980* (London, 1987), 172. On World War I shell shock and modernity, see Martin Stone, "Shellshock and the Psychologists," in W. F. Bynum, Roy Porter, and Michael Shepherd, eds., *The Anatomy of Madness: Essays on the History of Psychiatry*, vol. 2 (London, 1985).

7. See Poplar and Stepney Poor Law Asylum Hospital Discharge and Admission Register, admitted February 9, 1890, discharged March 12, 1890, SA/M/2/1, Records of St. Andrew's Hospital, Royal London Hospital Archives. See also Religious Creed Register, July 1889-July 1891, SA/M/4/6, Royal London Hospital Archives. The case notes of her admitting physician at London Hospital, Dr. F. J. Smith, indicate that the first phase of her illness began in December, 1909. See RLHLH/M/14/65—Dr F. J. Smith, Medical female patients case notes, 1910.

8. Thomas Barlow, "Notes on Rheumatism and its Allies in Childhood," *British Medical Journal* 2 (September 15, 1883): 509–19.

9. See B. N. Dalton, MD, "The Etiology of Rheumatic Fever, and an Explanation of its Relations to Other Diseases," *The British Medical Journal* (March 1, 1890): 472–74. See also Peter English, *History of Rheumatic Fever* (New Brunswick, NJ, 1999).

10. See Case Notes for Eleanor Dowell, March 1910, Dr. F.J. Smith, Medical female patients case notes, RLHLH/M/14/65 London Hospital, Royal London Hospital Archives; see also Lester, "From Birth to Death, 1" Lester Papers, Bishopsgate.

11. See Whitechapel Infirmary, Admission and Discharge Register, March 11, 1910: admitted at 5:40 pm, p. 97, STBG/WH/123/45, Stepney Board of Guardians, London Metropolitan Archives.

12. This was standard hospital procedure from the 1870s onwards following widespread acceptance of the finding of Carl Wunderlich's *Medical Thermometry and Human Temperature* (first published in German in 1868; English trans. 1871).

13. Obituary, F. J. Smith, MD, FRCP, Consulting Physician, *British Medical Journal* 3045 (May 10, 1919): 593–94.

14. See Lauren Berlant, "On the Case," *Critical Inquiry* 33 (Summer 2007): 663–72.

15. The notes by various specialist doctors about Nellie are recorded in the Medical Index, 1910, LH/M/58, London Hospital, Royal London Hospital Archives. The nurses' notes about Nellie are included in Dr. F. J. Smith's case report on Nellie, which also in-

corporates observations from each of the specialist doctors. In the case file, doctors' observations are marked, "DS," and nurses', "NS." Nellie's medical case file is contained in Dr. F. J. Smith, Medical Female Patients Case Notes, 1910, LH/M/14/65, London Hospital, Royal London Hospital Archives. I thank Kate Richardson for her invaluable assistance in locating these records and Dr. Fredric Mintz for interpreting them with me.

16. Participants in the Poplar rate strike of 1921 and historians have written voluminously about it. See John Scurr, *The Rate Protest of Poplar* (London 1922) and Noreen Branson, *Poplarism, 1919–1925: George Lansbury and the Councillors' Revolt* (London, 1979); on Minnie Lansbury's death, see Janine Booth, *Guilty and Proud of it! Poplar's Rebel Councillors and Guardians 1919–25* (2010), 89.

17. See Muriel Lester, typescript, 2/3, Lester Papers, Bishopsgate.

18. Muriel Lester, "An East End Problem. Ought One to Speak the Truth?" *Christian World* (August, 22 1918).

19. Muriel Lester, "From Birth to Death, 1," Lester Papers, Bishopsgate.

20. Ibid.

21. Eva C. E. Luckes, *Hospital Sisters and Their Duties* (London, 1886), 66.

22. Entry by Eva Luckes, Head Matron, March 12, 1910, Official Ward Book, No. 2 (mislabeled 1909), LH/N/6/13, London Hospital, Royal London Hospital Archives.

23. See Admission and Discharge Register, London Hospital, 1910, Reg. No . 624, Eleanor Dowell, March 4–11, 1910, LH/M/2/58, Royal London Hospital Archives.

24. Muriel Lester, "From Birth to Death, 1." See also Graham Mooney and Jonathan Reinarz, "Hospital and Asylum Visiting in Historical Perspective," in Mooney and Reinarz, eds. *Permeable Walls: Historical Perspectives on Hospital and Asylum Visiting* (New York, 2009), 9. For an analysis of hospital attitudes toward patients' family member in the US, see Charles Rosenberg, *The Care of Strangers* (Baltimore, 1987), esp. 286–87.

25. See Whitechapel Infirmary, Admission and Discharge Register, March 14, 1910, STBG/WH/123/45, Stepney Board of Guardians, London Metropolitan Archives..

26. Muriel Lester, "From Birth to Death, 1."

27. E. W. Morris, *History of London Hospital* (London, 1910), 225.

28. Dr. F. J. Smith Case Notes.

29. Ibid.

30. On Smith's career, see Obituary, F. J. Smith, MD, FRCP, Consulting Physician, *British Medical Journal* 3045 (May 10, 1919): 593–94.

31. See entry dated March 8, 1910, Official Ward Book, No. 2 (mislabeled 1909), LH/N/6/13, London Hospital, Royal London Hospital Archives. There was clearly some sort of error here since March 8, 1910 was a Tuesday, not Saturday as indicated in the record.

32. For her admission, see Porters Admission and Discharge Registers, March 11, 1910, Whitechapel Infirmary, STBG/WH/123/45, London Metropolitan Archives.

33. Ernest Hart, *Report of the Lancet Sanitary Commission for Investigating the State of the Infirmaries of Workhouses, 1866*; "The Condition of Our State Hospitals," *Fortnightly Review* 3 (December 1865): 218–21; "Metropolitan Infirmaries for the Pauper Sick," *Fortnightly Review* 4 (April 1866): 460–62.

34. See Certification of Lunacy of A.A., April 28, 1904, Whitechapel Infirmary,

STBG/WH/115/2 and Certification of Lunacy for R.K.S., October 31, 1905, STBG/L/118/2, Bromley-by-Bow Infirmary, 1904, London Metropolitan Archives.

35. This detail comes from corrected typescript that Muriel labeled, "1916- Very Early Account of Finding the Prayer of Relaxation," 2/1a, Lester Papers, Bishopsgate Institute.

36. Muriel Lester, *Ways of Praying* (London, 1932), 22.

37. Muriel Lester, *It Occurred to Me* (London, 1937), 63–67.

38. Lester republished this article as a separate chapter of her book, *Ways of Praying*, 20–23.

39. Medical anthropologists have explored deeply the relationships between curing and healing the body. See Thomas J. Csordas, *Body/Meaning/Healing* (Basingstoke, 2002)

40. I am certain that she did not write this document in 1916: the date refers to the time that she suffered her collapse.

41. These dates don't quite square. Born in December 1883, Muriel turned 33 in December 1916; eighteen months after Kingsley Hall's founding was mid-August 1916. Surviving files from the LCC suggest the new kinds of challenges Muriel faced as she sought to negotiate bureaucracies to pass inspections and get official approval for the new Kingsley Hall. See "Report to the Theatres Committee made on Kingsley Hall, Botolphs Road, Bow," and associated correspondence, GLC/AR/BR/07/2946, London Metropolitan Archives. Apparently, Muriel withdrew her application for a music license.

42. On Bright, See Patrick Joyce, *Democratic Subjects: The Self and the Social* (Cambridge, 1994); on overwork as explanation for men's breakdowns, see Janet Oppenheim, *Shattered Nerves: Doctors, Patients, and Depression in Victorian England* (New York, 1991).

43. Nellie Dowell to Muriel Lester, February 14, 1912, Nellie Dowell Letters, Bishopsgate.

44. Nellie Dowell to Muriel Lester, August 1912, Nellie Dowell Letters, Bishopsgate.

45. Nellie Dowell to Muriel Lester, n.d. [December 1912], Nellie Dowell Letters, Bishopsgate.

46. On political debates and discursive pathologies surrounding spinsters written in the context of early 1980s feminist debates about violence, pornography, and sexual pleasure, see Sheila Jeffreys, *The Spinster and Her Enemies: Feminism and Sexuality, 1880-1930* (London, 1985). On women and mental illness, see Elaine Showalter, *The Female Malady: Women, Madness and English Culture, 1830-1980* (NY, 1987).

47. There is a substantial scholarly literature on the bodies of female hysterics, New Women, feminists, and suffragettes—as well as their representation. See Lisa Tickner, *The Spectacle of Suffrage: Imagery of the Suffrage Campaign, 1904-1914* (Chicago, 1988); on spinsters' and suffragettes' body politics, see Martha Vicinus, *Independent Women, Work and Community for Single Women 1850-1920* (Chicago, 1985), chap.7; on hunger strikes, see James Vernon, *Hunger: A Modern History* (Cambridge, MA, 2007), chap. 3. For a vivid, political analysis of forced feeding, see Constance Lytton, *Prisons and Prisoners, Some Personal Experiences* (London, 1914).

48. Lester, *It Occurred to Me*, 64–65.

49. Ibid., 38.

50. Muriel Lester, Typsescript autobiographical draft with corrections, 2/1(a), Lester Papers, Bishopsgate.

51. Lester, *It Occurred to Me*, 40.

52. Mary Baker G. Eddy, *Science and Health with Key to The Scriptures* (Boston, 1906), 16.

53. See Thomson Jay Hudson, "The Truth About 'Christian Science.' A Psychopathic Study," *Everybody's Magazine* 4:22 (June 1901): 672.

54. Mary Baker G. Eddy, *Science and Health with Key to The Scriptures* (Boston, 1906), 19.

55. See Mary Baker Eddy, *Unity of Good* (Boston, 1887), 9–10.

56. See William Arthur Purrington, *Christian Science: An Exposition of Mrs. Eddy's Wonderful Discovery* (New York, 1900), 6.

57. See "The Origin of 'Christian Science,'" *Blackwoods* (May 1899): 847. On excess stimulation as symptom of modern urban life, see Georg Simmel's account of "The Metropolis and Mental Life" (1903) in Gary Bridge and Sophie Watson, eds., *The Blackwell City Reader* (Oxford, 2002).

58. Sir William Osler, "The Faith That Heals," *The British Medical Journal* (June 18, 1910): 1471–72

59. See "Harvest News," *Master Mind Magazine* (January 1912): 112.

60. See Thomas Troward, "What is Higher Thought?," *The Hidden Power and Other Papers Upon Mental Science* (New York, 1921; 1936), 213–14.

61. On the commodity culture of early twentieth-century British medicine, see Takahiro Ueyama, *Health in the Market Place: Professionalism, Therapeutic Desires, and Medical Commodification in Late-Victorian London* (Seattle, WA, 2010).

62. Lester, *It Occurred to Me*, 41.

63. Ibid., 32.

64. See *Biographical History of Gonville and Caius College*, vol. 4 (Cambridge, 1912). For his matriculation record (he joined Caius in October 1906) see TUT/01/01/06; for his examination results, see Praelectors's Book, 1899–1920. He was involved in the college Musical Society and performed in various concerts. See the *Caian*, editions XVIII and XIX. I thank the archivists at Gonville and Caius for their help.

65. Nellie Dowell to Muriel Lester, late 1912, Nellie Dowell Letters, Bishopsgate. On the culture of bourgeois invalidism, see Maria Frawley, *Invalidism and Identity in Nineteenth-Century Britain* (Chicago, 2004).

66. Ben Platten, writing on behalf of Muriel's men's night school members, was glad to "see you disregarded the usual custom of (supposed) mourning"; but the eulogies praising Kingsley's good life made him feel "envious" and discontented with his own "little good work." Ben Platten to Muriel Lester, September 13, 1914, 2/5, Lester Papers, Bishopsgate.

67. Muriel Lester, "K.H.," Typescript Autobiography, 2/1a, Lester Papers, Bishopsgate.

68. "Notes and Jottings," *Mill Hill Magazine* 13, no. 4 (December 1914): 130–31. I thank the school's archivist, Marion Taylor, for her help.

69. Charles Carpenter, a leader in the Band of Hope temperance movement in Devon, founded Huntley in 1878. It attracted prominent Congregationalists including Hugh Price Hughes.

70. For local press reports about her charitable activities, see "Teignmouth," *Devon and Exeter Gazette*, December 6, 1912, 5 on opening Wesleyan school work rooms; for her work with the local Pleasant Sunday Afternoon, see "Teignmouth," *Devon and Ex-*

eter Gazette, January 31, 1913, 5; for her involvement with the branch of the Wesleyan Foreign Missions Society, see "Teignmouth," *Western Times*, March 4, 1913, 2.

71. See Black's *Guide to Devonshire*, ed. A. R. Hope Moncrieff, 17th edition (London, 1902), 60. For a comprehensive guide to hydropathic establishments in Britain and Europe with an account of their various restorative treatments, see B. Bradshaw's *Dictionary of Mineral Waters, Climatic Health Resorts, Sea Baths, and Hydropathic Establishments, 1903* (London, 1903). On Huntley, see p. 43.

72. Entire books praised Torquay's curative powers such as Dr. Charles Radclyffe Hall, *Torquay, In Its Medical Aspect as a Resort for Pulmonary Invalids* (London, 1857).

73. See James Orr, "Faith-healing and Mind Cure in America," *London Quarterly Review* (January 1904): 100–127.

74. There is a burgeoning and brilliant scholarship about the "reenchantment" of modernity that pushes back against Max Weber's hugely influential account of the rise of disenchanted, bureaucratic rationality. On the "reenchantment" of modernity, see Michael Saler, *As If: The Literary Prehistory of Virtual Reality* (New York, 2012); and Alex Owen, *British Occultism and the Place of the Modern* (Chicago, 2004); Simon During, *Modern Enchantment: The Cultural Power of Secular Magic* (Cambridge, MA, 2002). My thinking about body disciplines across East-West divides has benefited from ongoing conversations with Kate Imy. See Kate Imy, "Spiritual Soldiers: Masculinity and the Body in the British Indian Army, 1900–1940," PhD in progress, Rutgers University.

75. She borrowed the phrase "The Renascence of Wonder," from a celebrated essay by the renowned literary critic Theodore Watts-Dunton, who traced this revival of wonder to the early Romantics and their capacity to challenge accepted conventions with "eyes of inquiry and wonder." Watts-Dunton explicitly connected "wonder" to the modern world's recuperation of the life-giving force of the "primitive." See Theodore Watts-Dunton, "The Renascence of Wonder in English Poetry," in D. Patrick, ed., *Chambers Cyclopedia of English Literature*, vol. 3 (London, 1903). For Muriel's use of this phrase, see Muriel Lester, *Why Worship* (Nashville, 1937), 13.

76. See Jay Winter on the dialectic of World War I as the "modern" war that unleashed an avalanche of the "unmodern." Jay Winter, *Sites of Memory, Sites of Mourning: The Great War in European Cultural History* (Cambridge, 1995), 54. For a contemporary example, see Arthur Machen's wonderful novel *The Great Return* (London, 1915). It opens with an Eastern "spiritual" mystery, compactly transformed into a Reuters press announcement, which the narrator then uses to consider the impact of war on the religious and psychic lives of Britons living in the Welsh countryside.

77. On Conan Doyle and his creation Sherlock Holmes as examples of the ironic imagination of "enchanted disenchantment," see Michael Saler, *As If: Modern Enchantment and the Literary Prehistory of Virtual Reality* (New York, 1912), chap. 3. On spiritualism and scientific research, see Janet Oppenheim, *Shattered Nerves: Doctors, Patients, and Depression in Victorian England* (New York, 1991); and Alex Owen, *Darkened Room: Women, Power, and Spiritualism in Late Victorian England* (Chicago, 2004). See also Rene Kollar, *Searching for Raymond: Anglicanism, Spiritualism and Bereavement between the Two World Wars* (Lanham, MD, 2000), esp. pp. 11–15 on Conan Doyle.

78. The bachelor son of Britain's queerest clerical family, Robert Hugh Benson had

been ordained as an Anglican clergyman by his father, the erudite Archbishop of Canterbury. See A. C. Benson, *Hugh, Memoirs of a Brother* (London, 1915), 134.

79. She later paid homage to Lawrence's influence on her during her lecture tour in the United States in 1930 that provided the core of her book, *Ways of Praying*. See also Patricia Faith Appelbaum, *Kingdom to Commune: Protestant Pacifist Culture Between World War 1 and the Vietnam Era* (Chapel Hill, NC, 2009), 115–16.

80. *The Practice of the Presence of God, Being Conversations and Letters of Brother Lawrence (Nicholas Herman of Lorraine), New and Revised Edition* (London, 1906), 59, 62.

81. Evelyn Underhill, *Practical Mysticism* (London, 1914, 1991). Foreword by Canon John Tyers, xiii, xv, 2, 24. See also chap. 6 on "Love and Will."

82. In her last unpublished autobiographical writings written when she was 81, she recalled her prewar rambles with Doris in the Cornish countryside with Doris reading "Evelyn Underhill's book on Christian mystics" as she read histories. See Muriel Lester, "Prologue," 2/1a. Bishopsgate. An excerpt from Underhill's poem, "The Liberated Hosts," graced the inside cover of Kingsley Hall's Second Year Report for 1916, about the "friendship of the happy dead" with the living.

83. See the vitriolic exchanges in the *British Medical Journal* during the summer of 1910 between various medical doctors and Rev. Boyd about the Guild's dangerous interference in the domain of allopathic doctors' medical expertise. For the opening exchange, see Rev. Francis Boyd, "On Faith and Healing," and Stanley Bousfield, "Spiritual Healing and the 'Guild of Health,'" *British Medical Journal* (Aug 20, 1910): 464–65.

84. The replacement of the priest-confessor by the psychoanalyst is one of Foucault's influential metanarratives about madness, mental health, and modernity. See Michel Foucault, *Madness and Civilization: A History of Insanity in the Age of Reason* (New York, 1965). It was this long-term "secular" tendency against which Guild members like Gladys Edge and Muriel Lester battled. Edge worried that people were "turning to professional psychologists for inspiration and healing" rather than to Jesus. See G. N. Edge, "Vital Thought and Health," *Guild of Health Monthly For the Study and Practice of Spiritual Healing* 1:2 (May 1924): 7–8.

85. "Guild Notes," *Guild of Health Monthly For the Study and Practice of Spiritual Healing* 1:1 (April 1924): 3.

86. One of the Guild's leaders, the Bishop of Kensington, John Primatt Maud, connected the Guild's interest in mind concentration to the extraordinary powers wielded by Yogis. See his "Healing by Spiritual Means," *Guild of Health Monthly* 1:2 (May 1924): 6.

87. Conrad Noel and Percy Dearmer were two of the Guild's best-known leaders. Dearmer surveyed faith healing across several millennia in *Body and Soul: An Enquiry into the Effect of Religion Upon Health* (New York, 1909). On his contributions to the Guild, see Nan Dearmer, *The Life of Percy Dearmer* (London, 1940). On the Guild's critique of Christian Science and its stance on the Incarnation, see Harold Anson, "The Incarnation and Christian Science," *God in Relation to the Material World, Papers Read at the Guild of Health Conference held at Girton College, Cambridge, 1922* (Croydon, 1922), esp. 17.

88. On the links between religion and queer sexuality in the late nineteenth century,

see Harry Cocks, "Religion and Spirituality," in H. G. Cocks and Matt Houlbrook, eds., *The Modern History of Sexuality* (New York, 2006), 157–79.

89. For a subtle and convincing analysis of this, see Joy Dixon, "'Dark Ecstasies': Sex, Mysticism, and Psychology in Early Twentieth Century England," *Gender and History*, 25: 3 (November 2013).

90. See Eustace Miles, *Avenues to Health* (London, 1902); see also Ina Zweiniger-Bargielowka, *Managing the Body, Beauty, Health and Fitness in Britain, 1880–1939* (Oxford, 2010). Miles was notably nondoctrinaire and offered readers a wide array of healthy life choices from which he invited them to select the ones that worked best for each person.

91. Underhill does not specify to whom "psychoanalysis" refers. After World War I, her published work refers explicitly to Freud.

92. The texts from which Tagore and Underhill worked had faint similarities with the originals. Scholars agree that the "poems" or "songs" are less "translations" of Kabîr than works inspired by him. See Sisir Kumar Das, ed., *English Writings of Rabindranath Tagore*, vol. 1 (New Delhi, 1994), 622.

93. Kipling's "Ballad of East and West" (1895) dramatically contradicted its bold opening lines by showing that such borders collapse when "two strong men stand face to face." Kipling emphasized exchange, connection and dialogue—not separation—between East and West.

94. See Mrinilina Sinha, *Colonial Masculinity: The "Manly Englishman" and the "Effeminate" Bengali in the Late Nineteenth Century* (Manchester, 1995), 21. See also Narasingha Prosad Sil, *Vivikananda, A Reassessment* (Selinsgrove, PA, 1997), especially chap. 11 on his Western audience.

95. See "Swami Vivekananda in England," *Friend of India and Statesman* (November 20, 1895): 21.

96. See Peter Van Der Veer, "Spirituality in Modern Society," *Social Research* 76:4 (Winter 2009): 1106. My thinking about the global circulation of knowledge about body practices is indebted to Joseph Alter's *Gandhi's Body: Sex, Diet, and the Politics of Nationalism* (Philadelphia, 2000).

97. Muriel Lester, "Brethren of the Common Table," *London Evening Standard*, April 2, 1921.

98. Muriel Lester, *What IS Kingsley Hall?* n.d., printed circular, Lester/7/2/12, Lester Papers, Bishopsgate.

99. Kuhne and Just sought to reconnect humanity with the primitive healing force of water, light, air, and earth. "The more animal heat one has," Just declared, "the healthier one is." Kuhne and Just both drew upon Hindu and Buddhist conceptions of the body and health in their writings even as Mohandas Gandhi gratefully acknowledged his debts to them in his biomoral vision of public health, *The Nature Cure*. See Adolf Just, *Return to Nature, The True Natural Method of Healing and Living and the True Salvation of the Soul*, trans. Benedict Lust (New York: 1896; 2nd ed., 1904), 11. For a powerful analysis of the place of "stories" in the history of mind–body healing see Anne Harrington, *The Cure Within: A History of Mind–Body Medicine* (New York, 2008).

100. See Hervé Guillemain, *La Méthode Coué. Histoire d'une pratique de guérison au XXe siècle* (Paris, 2010).

101. Henry Lindlahr, *Practice of the Natural Therapeutics* (Chicago, 1922, 5th ed.), Part One, Section One.

102. Muriel and her close friend Rosa Waugh Hobhouse viewed allopathic medicine as a form of violence against the body in its use of drugs and surgical interventions. See Rosa Waugh Hobhouse, "Fearfully and Wonderfully Made: A Brief Comparison of Two Schools of Medicine," unpublished typescript, Box 1, Rosa Waugh Hobhouse Papers, Hadspen.

103. The pioneering French psychologist, J. M. Charcot, had famously argued in 1892 that faith cures had remarkable curative powers for diseases rooted in hysterical origins, but none at all for bodily disfigurement such as amputation. See J. M. Charcot, "The Faith-Cure," *New Review* 8:44 (January 1893): 19.

104. See Gladys Mary Wauchope, *The Story of a Woman Physician* (Baltimore, 1963), 26. Wauchope, six years younger than Lester, also attended St. Leonard's in Scotland and lived in Loughton. She worked as a Voluntary Aid Detachment member in Braeside Hospital during the war.

105. On the care, treatment and rehabilitation of wounded soldiers, see Seth Koven, "Remembering and Dismemberment: Crippled Children, Wounded Soldiers, and the Great War in Great Britain," *The American Historical Review* 99:4 (October 1994): 1167–1202; Joanna Bourke, *Dismembering the Male: Men's Bodies, Britain, and the Great War* (Chicago, 1996); Jeffrey Reznick, *Healing the Nation: Soldiers and the Culture of Caregiving in Britain during the Great War* (Manchester, 2005); Deborah Cohen, *The War Come Home: Disabled Veterans in Britain and Germany, 1914–1939* (Berkeley, 2001).

106. In a typescript autobiographical fragment, Muriel wrote that "our deep sorrow was shot through and through with joy. He would not be harried either into killing human beings, God's German children or having to face a public tribunal, a dread and paralyzing process, trying to prove that one's conscience fitted in to a category." Muriel Lester, "K.H.", Typescript Autobiography, 2/1a, Lester Papers, Bishopsgate.

107. See Nadja Durbach, "Class, Gender and the Conscientious Objector to Vaccination, 1898–1907," *Journal of British Studies* 41:1 (January 2002): 58–83.

108. See D. R. Pugh, "English Nonconformity, Education and Passive Resistance 1903–6," *History of Education* 19:4 (1990): 355–70. On Lester, see "Petty Session, March 9th," *Essex County Chronicle*, March 16, 1906, 7.

109. Muriel appears not to have published anything about either Platten or Hobhouse's imprisonment. She did, however, offer a poignant portrait of an East London barber and Christian missionary who was imprisoned as a conscientious objector. Muriel noted that confinement in prison led conscientious objectors to be "unable to marshal their thoughts properly; through enforced silence they lose the power of expressing themselves. . . ." See Muriel Lester, *Kill or Cure* (Nashville, 1937), 54.

110. Lester, *It Occurred to Me*, 72.

111. "What Parents Think," undated newspaper clipping, Notebook of news clippings about Platten and conscientious objectors in Loughton, Benjamin Platten Papers, Loughton Library, Loughton; hereafter cited as Platten News Clippings.

112. Handwritten copy of application for complete exemption, Local Tribunal, Loughton, February 26, 1916. All of Platten's correspondence with military officials and tribunals are preserved in the Benjamin Platten Papers, Loughton Library, Loughton.

113. See "Conscience and Objectors, By a Loughton Fighter," undated newspaper clipping, Platten News Clippings. The Plattens created a scrapbook of news articles about his case as well as discussions of conscientious objectors in the local Essex press.

114. See Rosa Hobhouse, ed., *Towards Harmony: A Century of Letters by Stephen*

Hobhouse, Fifth Series, To His Wife (From Prison), unpublished typescript, Library of the Society of Friends.

115. Mrs. Hobhouse retained copies of these letters and responses to them. See Papers of Margaret Potter Hobhouse, ALH/27, Hobhouse Papers, Hadspen, Somerset. I thank Niall Hobhouse and staff at Hadspen for their hospitality in allowing me to stay there while consulting the papers of Margaret Potter Hobhouse, Stephen Hobhouse, and Rosa Waugh Hobhouse.

116. On the history of conscientious objection and the Hobhouses, see Seth Koven, "Mrs. Henry Hobhouse Goes to War: Conscience and Christian Radicalism in WWI Britain," *R K Webb Lecture*, November 6, 2008, University of Maryland, Baltimore County, access via YouTube. For a powerful account of the way the war divided families including the Hobhouses, see Adam Hochschild, *To End All Wars: A Story of Loyalty and Rebellion, 1914–1918* (Boston, 2011). See also Peter Brock, *Against the Draft: Essays on Conscientious Objection from the Radical Transformation to the Second World War* (Toronto, 2006), chap. 17. For most contemporaries, conscientious objectors had nothing in common with the soldier hero. On the soldier hero in Victorian and early 20th century culture, see Graham Dawson, *Soldier Heroes: British Adventure, Empire and the Imagining of Masculinities* (London, 1994).

117. On the concept of "informal English" to describe the prose of working-class authors, see Carolyn Steedman, *The Radical Soldier's Tale, John Pearman, 1819–1908* (New York, 1988), esp. 20–24.

118. Gertrude Stein, "Do Let Us Go Away, A Play" (1918) reprinted in Gertrude Stein, *Geography and Plays*, introduction by Cyrena N. Pondrom (Madison, WI, 1993), 216, 218; Nellie Dowell Letters, c. 1916, Bishopsgate.

119. See Doris Cairns Watson, *Gertrude Stein and the Essence of What Happens* (Nashville, 2005), 32. Stein coined the phrase "auditory consciousness" to describe the relationship between her listening and writing in 1896.

120. Gertrude Stein, *Everybody's Autobiography* (New York, 1937), 91.

121. Nellie Dowell Letters, February 14, 1912, Bishopsgate.

122. Nellie Dowell Letters, July 1, 1912, Bishopsgate.

123. Nellie Dowell Letters, November 13, [1910], Bishopsgate.

124. Ibid.

125. On the role of aggression within women's benevolent gift economy and friendships, see Jill Rappoport, *Giving Women: Alliance and Exchange in Victorian England* (Oxford, 2012).

126. Nellie Dowell to Muriel Lester, c. 1916, Nellie Dowell Letters, Bishopsgate.

127. This phrase comes from Nellie's letter to Muriel, July 1, 1912, Nellie Dowell Letters, Bishopsgate.

128. On "overwork" as a sanctioned explanation for "shattered nerves," see Janet Oppenheim, *Shattered Nerves* (New York, 1991).

129. Nellie Dowell Letters, February 14, 1912, Bishopsgate.

130. On the female invalid as a figure of bourgeois culture, see Maria Frawley, *Invalidism and Identity in Nineteenth-Century Britain* (Chicago, 2004). Nellie's experience suggests that at least some laboring people experienced "invalidism" even if they could not afford to participate in the full consumer economy catering to afflicted middle- and upper-class men and women.

131. Nellie Dowell to Muriel Lester, n.d. [autumn 1916], Nellie Dowell Letters, Bishopsgate.

132. Nellie Dowell Letters, November 13, n.d. [1910], Bisphopsgate.

133. Nellie Dowell Letters, March 24, 1912, Bishopsgate.

134. Nellie Dowell Letters, n.d., Bishipsgate.

135. Nellie Dowell to Muriel Lester, n.d.[late 1922], Nellie Dowell Letters, Bishopsgate.

136. Nellie Dowell to Muriel Lester, November 13 [1910] and February 14, 1912, Nellie Dowell Letters, Bishopsgate.

137. Carroll Smith-Rosenberg argued that middle-class women's passionate "romantic friendships" often complemented their marriages to men while occupying a continuum from the non-sexual to the fully sexual. Carroll Smith-Rosenberg, "The Female World of Love and Ritual: Relations between Women in Nineteenth-Century America," *Signs* 1 (Autumn 1975): 1–29. See also Lillian Faderman, *Surpassing the Love of Men: Romantic Friendship and Love Between Women from the Renaissance to the Present* (New York, 1981), pts. 2 and 3.

138. Martha Vicinus, *Intimate Friends: Women Who Loved Women, 1778–1928* (Chicago, 2006), xxv–xxvii, 7, 88. "Intimate friends" often used familial metaphors to describe their relationship: mother/daughter, husband/wife and sisterly. Vicinus identifies "gifts, letters and long private conversations" as the repertoire of gestures and acts that led women from friendship into "intimate friendship."

139. See Sharon Marcus's persuasive critique of the continuum model in *Between Women, Friendship, Desire and Marriage in Victorian England* (Princeton, 2007), 10–12, 32, 54. See also Liz Stanley's insightful intervention about female friendship and the relationship of sexology to women's own understanding of their sexual selves. Liz Stanley, "Epistemological Issues in Researching Lesbian History: The Case of "Romantic Friendship," in Hilary Hinds, Ann Phoenix and Jackie Stacey, eds., *Working Out: New Directions for Women's Studies* (London, 2004), 161–72.

140. Nellie Dowell to Muriel Lester, n.d. [November 1910], Nellie Dowell Letters, Bishopsgate.

141. It seems very likely Muriel encountered such relationships in her exploration of Christian mystical traditions. See Cornelia Wilde, *Friendship, Love and Letters: Ideals and Practices of Seraphic Friendship in Seventeenth-Century England* (Heidelberg, Germany, 2012); See also Frances Harris's gorgeous and penetrating study of opposite sex "seraphic friendship," *Transformations of Love: The Friendship of John Evelyn and Margaret Godolphin* (Oxford, 2002).

142. Phyllis Mack, *Heart Religion in the British Enlightenment: Gender and Emotion in Early Methodism* (Cambridge, 2008), 154.

143. Nellie Dowell to Muriel Lester, n.d. Nellie Dowell Letters, Bishopsgate.

144. On this dynamic in a cross-age dynamic, see Martha Vicinus, "Distance and Desire: English Boarding School Friendships, 1870–1920," *Signs* 9:4 (Summer 1984): 600–622.

145. See Jeffrey Weeks's path-breaking work on homosexual community and identity in Britain that established the essential parameters of this debate, *Coming Out: Homosexual Politics in Britain from the Nineteenth Century to the Present* (London, 1977) and *Sex, Politics and Society: The Regulation of Sexuality since 1800* (London, 1981).

146. Inspired by Foucault's "knowledge is power" paradigm, scholars have generated a vast literature about what people know about sex and how they produce sexual knowledge about themselves and others. The timing of the invention of sexual categories such as homosexual and lesbian, along with their dissemination and meaning across class, gender, space, and place have been hotly debated. For some scholars, identities can't exist without the vocabulary and categories that go with them. Put simply, women who had sex with other women can't *be* lesbians until the category lesbian existed. Men who had sex with other men can't *be* homosexuals, until the category homosexual existed. This position is most closely connected to the work of David Halperin. See *One Hundred Years of Homosexuality and Other Essays on Greek Love* (New York, 1990).

147. See Laura Doan's essential *Fashioning Sapphism: The Origins of a Modern English Lesbian Culture* (New York, 2001). Richard Dellamora notes that Radclyffe Hall, *the* exemplary lesbian of British public culture in the twentieth century, nonetheless eschewed the word "lesbian" in favor of Sapphic culture, sexual inversion, and Christian-inspired language of "cross-gendered" female-female desire. Hall cultivated what Dellamora calls "vernacular Christian mysticism," which spiritualized her "cousinage" model of female friends, blood relatives, and sexual intimates. See Richard Dellamora, *Radclyffe Hall: A Life in the Writing* (Philadelphia, 2011), see esp. preface, and chaps.1, 3, and 8.

148. Such lexical tracking is now possible because of massive digitized databases of periodicals and newspapers. Built in 1874, *The Lesbian* was scrapped in 1903. A new *Lesbian* plied the seas from 1923–1940. By 1920, the word "Lesbian" appeared in British print in relation to female homosexuality on the Parisian stage. See "The Post-War Theatre in Paris," *Saturday Review*, September 25, 1920, 256. The heroine of a play was described as "coquettishly Lesbian in her proclivities."

149. Mateship among laboring women remains unexplored by historians, in part because extant sources are so scarce. I touch on it briefly in *Slumming*, 218

150. According to Lee Edelman, "queerness" rejects the "viability of the social" and the "substantiability of identity"—and thus the future orientation of liberal social politics. See Lee Edelman, *No Future: Queer Theory and the Death Drive* (Durham, 2004); see also Laura Doan's critique of gay and lesbian historiography, *Disturbing Practices: History, Sexuality, and Women's Experience of Modern War* (Chicago, 2013). Doan combines archival research into women's lives like that of visitor to Kingsley Hall in 1925, Violet Douglas-Pennant, with a searching methodological critique of the limits of "queerness" as an identity. She proposes queerness as a way of thinking about and doing history that "disturbs" and frustrates the desire to make claims about identity; such an approach embraces the fragmentary nature of queer archives as a methodological incitement.

151. For a strong statement of this position, see Scott Herring, *Queering the Underworld: Slumming, Literature and the Undoing of Lesbian and Gay History* (Chicago, 2007).

152. For a critique of gay and lesbian identity politics and "queerness as being," see Matt Houlbrook, "Thinking Queer: The Social and the Sexual in Interwar Britain," in Brian Lewis, ed., *British Queer History: New Approaches and Perspectives* (Manchester, 2013).

153. Hera Cook suggests that physical intimacy and proximity sometimes, but not

necessarily, led to genital contact and pleasure between women. She argues that physical affection between women—"embracing, kissing, sitting close together, and sharing the same bed at night"—was fairly common. Women "who identified as lesbians" "gradually moved to genital sexual activity with women . . . suggesting that they, like many heterosexual women, did not initially identify their genitals as sources of pleasure." See Hera Cook, *The Long Sexual Revolution: English Women, Sex and Contraception, 1800–1975* (Oxford, 2004), 177.

154. Lester, *It Occurred to Me*, 83.

155. She, like so many other members of the British Left, uncritically accepted E. B. Morel's racist attack on the sexual mores of black French African troops who purportedly engaged in mass rape of German women in the occupied Rhine at the end of World War I.

156. See Muriel Lester, "Draft Autobiographical Accounts," Lester/2/1, Lester Papers, Bishopsgate.

157. See Spencer Cecil Carpenter, *The Biography of Arthur Foley Winnington Ingram, Bishop of London, 1901–1939* (London, 1949), 77. See Vera Brittain, *Testament of Youth* (London, 1933), esp. chap. 6; on Flora Major's mourning of her fallen soldier, see Sybil Oldfield, *Spinsters of This Parish: The Life and Times of F.M. Mayor and Mary Sheepshanks* (London, 1984).

158. I develop this argument about celibacy in Seth Koven, *Slumming: Sexual and Social Politics in Victorian London* (Princeton, NJ, 2004), chap. 4.

159. William Cecil Dampier-Whetham and Catherine Durning Whetham, *The Family and the Nation, A Study in Natural Inheritance and Social Responsibility* (London, 1909), 195–99. See also Laura Doan, *Fashioning Sapphism: The Origins of a Modern English Lesbian Culture* (New York, 2001), 59.

160. See Alison Falby, "Maude Royden's Sacramental Theology of Sex and Love," *Anglican and Episcopal History*, 79: 2 (June 2010); see also Marcus Collins' insightful discussion of Royden and Christian sexual ethics in interwar Britain in *Modern Love: Personal Relationships in Twentieth-Century Britain* (Newark DE, 2003).

161. Agnes Maude Royden, *Sex and Common-Sense* (1921), 6, 25–27. On Royden, see Sue Morgan's excellent, "Sex and Common-Sense: Maude Royden, Religion and Modern Sexuality," *Journal of British Studies* 52 (2013): 153–78. Pacifist feminist Helena Swanwick critiqued sexual repression as unhealthy for women as part of her analysis of the costs and consequences of war on women's lives. See Helena Swanwick, *War in Its Effect on Women* (London, 1916), 21.

162. Sigmund Freud, *Civilization and Its Discontents*, trans. James Strachey (New York, 1961), 49.

163. In her unpublished memoir, Royden recalled being asked whether she thought "all talk of sublimation as a panacea for frustrated sex feeling was not 'all bunk.'" "No, I don't think it is" was her response. Few were able to entirely sublimate sexual feelings. For those who did sublimate sexual feelings, "life can be full and satisfying." See Maude Royden, "Bid Me Discourse," 7/AMR, Box 224, Agnes Maude Royden Papers, Women's Library (now transferred to BLPES).

164. On the interwar interpretations of the category "spinster" and feminist reworkings of "repression" by Stella Browne, Mary Scharlieb, Esther Harding, Maude Royden, Winifred Holtby and others, see Alison Oram, "Repressed and thwarted, or bearer of the

new world? The Spinster in Inter-war Feminist Discourses, *Women's History Review*, 1:3 (1992): 413–33. See also Lesley A. Hall, *Sex, Gender, and Social Change in Britain Since 1880* (New York, 2000), chap. 6.

165. Virginia Woolf, "Modern Fiction," reprinted in Andrew McNeille, ed., *The Essays of Virginia Woolf, Volume 4: 1925–1928* (London, 1984), 162

166. Nellie Dowell to Muriel Lester, n.d. (1916), Nellie Dowell Letters, Bishopsgate.

167. See "Monastic Life For Penny A Night," November 9, 1928, (London) *Evening News*; and "Social Centre Like a Monastery," September 13, 1928, (London) *Daily Chronicle*. My thanks to Kate Imy for suggesting this line of argument.

168. For a fascinating analysis of the rivalries among disciples of another charismatic, post–World War I, heterodox female religious leader, see Jane Shaw, *Octavia, Daughter of God* (London, 2011).

169. Nellie Dowell to Muriel Lester, November 1910, Nellie Dowell Letters, Bishopsgate.

170. This formulation is indebted to Martha Vicinus's foundational essay, "Distance and Desire: English Boarding-School Friendships, 1870–1920," *Signs* 9:4 (Summer 1984): 600–622.

171. On their relationship see Naomi Lloyd's fine study, "Evangelicalism and the Making of Same-Sex Desire: the Life and Writings of Constance Maynard," PhD diss., University of British Columbia, 2011. See also Pauline Phipps, "Faith, Desire and Sexual Identity: Constance Maynard's Atonement," *Journal of the History of Sexuality* 18:2 (2009): 265–86.

172. Constance Maynard, unpublished autobiography, pt. 5, chap. 35 (1879), 374, Constance Maynard Papers, Queen Mary, University.

173. Maynard, unpublished autobiography, pt. 4, chap. 31 (1877), 237. Constance Maynard Papers, Queen Mary University.

174. Vera Brittain to Rosa Waugh Hobhouse, July 30, 1963, Box 4, Orange Folder, Rosa Hobhouse Papers, Hadpsen, Somerset.

175. Elizabeth Barrett to Julia Martin, October 22, 1842 in Philip Kelley and Ronald Hudson, eds., *The Brownings' Correspondence*, vol. 6 (Winfield, KS, 1988), 117. My thanks to Beverly Taylor for alerting me to Barrett's letter.

176. Arthur Hugh Clough, *Amours de Voyage*, Canto II, X, line 14; Canto I, I, line 1.

177. Here, I borrow from Maria Tomboukou's use of Foucault in analyzing letters between women. See Maria Tamboukou, *Women, Education and the Self, A Foucauldian Perspective* (London, 2003), 166–73.

178. For accounts of psychological interiority, modernity, governance, and coercion, see Michael Foucault, *Discipline and Punish: The Birth of the Prison*, trans. Alan Sheridan (New York, 1979); See also Nikolas Rose *The Psychological Complex: Psychology, Politics and Society in England, 1869–1939* (London, 1984), and *Governing the Soul: The Shaping of the Private Self* (London, 1989). On the role of expertise in the domain of social science and the rise of interwar non-governmental organizations as a new kind of privatized political sphere, see Matthew Hilton, James McKay, Nicholas Crowon, and Jean-François Mouhot, *The Politics of Expertise, How NGOs Shaped Modern Britain* (Oxford, 2013).

179. For a fine overview of a wide range of approaches to and uses of psychology and

popular "regimes of self-improvement," see Matthew Thomson, *Psychological Subjects: Identity, Culture and Health in Twentieth-Century Britain* (Oxford, 2006).

Chapter Five. Love and Christian Revolution

1. H. G. Wells, *The War That Will End War* (New York, 1914). Wells insisted that Britons were fighting a war of "whole peoples" that demanded either total victory or complete defeat.

2. *What IS Kingsley Hall?* (London, 1933), Lester/7/2/12, Lester Papers, Bishopsgate.

3. Muriel Lester, "The Salt of the Earth," 15.

4. On the Fellowship, see Jill Wallis, *Valliant for Peace: History of the Fellowship of Reconciliation 1914–1989* (London, 1991), and Henry Hodgkin, *Lay Religion* (London, 1919), 218.

5. This phrase appeared in all of Kingsley Hall's promotional literature.

6. Muriel Lester to household members at Kingsley Hall, 60 Bruce Road and Children's House, undated circular letter (c.1929), Lester/2/3, Lester Papers, Bishopsgate. There were even more detailed rules about household and personal cleanliness and management for Children's House after it opened in 1923. Muriel and Doris lived in Children's House. See "The Rule," n.d. (c.1923), Lester/2/2, Lester Papers, Bishopsgate

7. On gossip as "secret diplomacy," see Muriel Lester to "Dear Comrades of Number Sixty," undated letter, Lester/2/2, Lester Papers, Bishopsgate. The argument that World War I was caused by "secret diplomacy" was widely accepted by the 1920s when revisionists assessed the war's causes and consequences. For its use during World War I, see Bertrand Russell, "Secret Diplomacy," *The Tribunal*, September 13, 1917, 2.

8. On the roots of left politicians' attraction to militarism before and at the outset of World War I, see Matthew Johnson, *Militarism and the British Left, 1902–1914* (Basingstoke, 2013).

9. Jo Guldi shows that disproportionate numbers of soldiers became Methodists, in part attracted by the mobile life and brotherly camaraderie of service. See Jo Guldi, *Roads to Power: Britain Invents the Infrastructure State* (Cambridge, MA, 2012), 157–67. The most conspicuous conflation and connection between religious zeal and military discipline and organization in Modern Britain is William and Mary Booth's Salvation Army.

10. Halévy first tested his thesis that Methodism explained modern England's immunity from revolutionary tumult in a 1906 article in *La Revue de Paris*. Halévy elaborated his argument in *England in 1815* (1913). For revisions of Halévy, see Bernard Semmel, *The Methodist Revolution* (New York, 1973) and E. P. Thompson, *The Making of the English Working Class* (New York, 1964).

11. For a cogent summary of the history anticlericalism and de-Christianization in revolutionary France, see Mona Ozouf, "De-Christianization," in François Furet and Mona Ozouf, eds., *A Critical Dictionary of the French Revolution* (Cambridge, MA, 1989), 21–32.

12. Ross McKibbin argues that religion "inhibited" the emergence of "continental politics" in Britain; "what religion gave with one hand" to Labour leaders, "it took away with the other." He argues that religion led Labour leaders to invest in the status quo

rather than demand its overthrow. See Ross McKibbin, "Why Was There No Marxism in Britain," *English Historical Review* (April 1984): 297–331.

13. "VIOLENCE UPHELD AS SOCIAL WEAPON: Its Banning Would Aid Privileged, Prof. Niebuhr Tells Reconciliation Parley. GANDHI TACTICS LAUDED but They Are Not Suited to America, Miss Lester Says—Rautenstrauch Speaks," *New York Times*, October 13, 1934, 11.

14. Niebuhr elaborated his case against pacifism as incompatible with the actual workings of power in society in *Moral Man and Immoral Society* (New York, 1932).

15. Lester acknowledged this criticism in an interview with an American reporter. "The young communists in the East End laugh at us . . . for believing the rich will part with their wealth voluntarily. They believe that only force will accomplish this, but we are more optimistic." See Hayden Church, "Millionaires and Paupers Join in Self Denial," *Deseret News* [Salt Lake City, Utah], July 2, 1921, sec. 3, 1.

16. Muriel Lester, *It Occurred to Me* (New York, 1973), 93–94.

17. On the rejuvenation and growth of internationalism in interwar Britain, especially connected to the League of Nations and World Council of Churches, see Daniel Gorman, *The Emergence of International Society* (Cambridge, 2012). On the growth of broadly based interwar movements against war, see Keith Robbins, *The Abolition of War: The "Peace Movement" in Britain, 1914–1918* (Cardiff, 1976); James Hinton, *Protests and Visions: Peace Politics in 20th Century Britain* (London, 1989); and Peter Brock, *Twentieth-Century Pacifism* (New York, 1970).

18. See Tony Judt, *Postwar: A History of Europe since 1945* (New York, 2005), 5.

19. Burnett H. Streeter, "God and the World's Pain," in Lily Dougall, Harold Anson, et al., *Concerning Prayer: Its Nature, Its Difficulties and Its Value* (London, 1921), 19.

20. See Richard Overy, *The Morbid Age: Britain between the Wars* (London, 2009), 2. Overy analyzes what he calls a "strong presentiment of impending disaster" widely shared in interwar Britain.

21. Muriel Lester, "Draft Autobiographical Accounts," Lester/2/1, Lester Papers, Bishopsgate.

22. See Muriel Lester, "Draft Autobiographical Accounts," and "K.H," Lester/2/1a, Lester Papers, Bishopsgate.

23. Strachey's *Eminent Victorians* (London, 1918) suggested that love of power and hypocritical neuroses fueled his subjects' religiously inspired zeal to better the world.

24. In 1915, this was certainly undeserved praise although from the 1930s onwards, American newspapers regularly called Muriel "London's Jane Addams." See Robert Tate Allan, "Muriel Lester, the Jane Addams of London, Forsook Life of Ease for Christian Service," *Washington Post*, December 21, 1940, 14.

25. Muriel Lester, untitled typescript (12 pages), "Account of the Early History of Kingsley Hall," Lester/2/3, Lester Papers, Bishopsgate.

26. Typescripts of speeches delivered at opening ceremony of Kingsley Hall, February 15, 1915, "Report of the Kingsley Hall Opening," Lester/2/2, Lester Papers, Bishopsgate.

27. George Mortimer's 1911 census data only indicates "dog biscuit manufacturer." This factory can only be Spratt's, which was located a short distance from their home on Blackthorn Street just along the canal, the Limehouse Cut, that literally "cut" through Poplar and Bow connecting the Thames to the River Lea. See Bridget Cherry, Charles O'Brien, and Nikolaus Pevsner, *The Buildings of England, London 5: East* (New Haven, 2005), 48.

28. See Nellie Dowell Letters, November 13, [1910], Bishopsgate; and Sarah C Williams, "The Problem of Belief: The Place of Oral History in the Study of Popular Religion," *Oral History* 24:2 (Autumn, 1996): 27. See also Sarah C. Williams, *Religious Belief and Popular Culture in Southwark, c. 1880–1939* (Oxford, 1999). Hugh McLeod's many books are the crucial starting point for any analysis of religious belief, secularization, and the urban poor in modern Britain. See his *Religion and the Working Class in Nineteenth-Century Britain* (London, 1984) and *Piety and Poverty: Working-Class Religion in Berlin, London, and New York, 1870–1914* (New York, 1996). For a reperiodization of the debate over secularization that places women at the center of the story, see Callum Brown, *The Death of Christian Britain* (London, 2001).

29. There is a well-established scholarly literature about elite women's "visiting" the poor in the nineteenth and early twentieth centuries including Frank Prochaska's pioneering *Women and Philanthropy in Nineteenth-Century England* (Oxford, 1980). For a reworking of "visiting" within the more egalitarian framework of Salvation Army slum sisters, see Jill Rappaport, *Giving Women: Alliance and Exchange in Victorian Culture* (New York, 2012), chap. 5. Frederick Engels had depended upon two poor laboring women and sisters, Mary and Lizzy Burns, each of whom became his mistress, to guide his explorations of the slums of Manchester in the 1840s. For an early account of his relationships, see Gustav Mayer, *Friedrich Engels: A Biography* (London, 1936), 226. See also Steven Marcus, *Engels, Manchester and the Working Class* (New York, 1974), 98–100. Marcus foregrounds what he calls the mingling of the "erotic, the social, and the intellectual passions."

30. See Muriel Lester, typescript, ~~"Remembered Moments on Receipt of a Radiogram,"~~ Lester/2/3, Lester Papers, Bishopsgate. There is a second single-spaced typescript of this early history in the same file and the discussion of Nellie is on p. 9.

31. In July 1912, she invited Alice Biscoe, a fellow matchbox filler, to join her at Muriel's Bible class the next Sunday.

32. Doris Lester, typescript autobiography, Lester/3/1, Lester Papers, Bishopsgate Institute.

33. "Report of the Kingsley Hall Opening," Lester/2/2, Lester Papers, Bishopsgate.

34. This was the expression she used in the 1931 Pathé film clip to characterize Kingsley Hall. The American socialist novelist Upton Sinclair included Elliott's People's Anthem in his 1915 edited anthology, *The Cry for Justice: An Anthology of the Literature of Social Protest* (Philadelphia, 1915). The transatlantic circulation and shifting contextual meanings of Elliott's poem have yet to receive scholarly attention. On its enduring power as a critique of socioeconomic injustice, see Francis Neilson, "The Corn Law Rhymes," *American Journal of Economics and Sociology* 10:4 (July 1951): 407–15. Alexis Easley emphasizes the conservative implications of Elliott's endorsement of working-class domesticity in "Ebenezer Elliott and the Reconstruction of Working-Class Masculinity," *Victorian Poetry* 39:2 (Summer 2001): 302–18.

35. The surviving typescript of the evening notes that Lansbury took over from Mr. LeMare as chair of the ceremony.

36. The extensive report of the opening ceremonies at Kingsley Hall in the *East London Observer* did mention Doris as well as Muriel. See "Kingsley Hall, Bow. A Club for Men and Women," *East London Observer*, February 20, 1915.

37. See Henrietta Barnett's 1881 essay, "'At Home' to the Poor," *Cornhill Magazine* (May 1881), in which she reminded readers that because "the minds of the poor being emptier" than their own, the poor needed more active entertainment. On the role of beauty in social uplift, see Diana Maltz, *British Aestheticism and the Urban Working Classes, 1870–1900: Beauty for the People* (New York, 2006). On High Victorian attribution of positive moral value to well-chosen objects in relation to the shift from a theological focus on the "atonement" to the "incarnation" after 1860, see Deborah Cohen, *Household Gods: The British and Their Possessions* (New Haven, 2006).

38. See Andrew Goldstone on the occluded labor of domestic servants in aestheticist and modernist literature in "Servants, Aestheticism, and 'The Dominance of Form,'" *ELH* 77:3 (Fall 2010): 615–43.

39. See Rosa Waugh Hobhouse, *Interplay of Life and Art* (unpublished typescript autobiography, 1958–59), 114, Library of the Society of Friends.

40. See Rosa Waugh Hobhouse to Stephen Hobhouse, 1917 in Rosa Waugh Hobhouse, ed. *The Letters of Stephen Hobhouse*, unpublished typescript, 377, Library of the Society of Friends.

41. Muriel Lester, autobiographical manuscript about Kingsley Hall's founding, Lester/2/1, Lester Papers, Bishopsgate.

42. Muriel Lester, "Kingsley Hall People," *First Year's Report* (London, 1916): 8. Sanitas Company's London factory was in Bethnal Green in East London. See the company's published guide by Charles Thomas Kingzett, *How to Disinfect: A Guide to Practical Disinfection in Everyday Life, and During Cases of Infectious Illness* (New York and London, 1895).

43. For a vivid account of these communities, see Ruth Brandon, *The New Women and the Old Men: Love, Sex, and the Woman Question* (New York, 1990); and on the leading figure within this countercultural configuration, see Sheila Rowbotham, *Edward Carpenter: A Life of Liberty and Love* (London, 2008).

44. Edith Lees Ellis, "The Masses and the Classes, A Plea, a lecture given in Ancoats for the Ancoats Brotherhood," (1893), 20–21.

45. The history of domestic service and servants has recently attracted substantial scholarly interest. Carolyn Steedman repositions servants at the very heart of the history of class formation in the eighteenth and early nineteenth centuries. See Carolyn Steedman, *Master and Servant: Love and Labour in the English Industrial Age* (Cambridge, 2007) and *Labours Lost: Domestic Service and the Making of Modern England* (Cambridge, 2009); see also Lucy Delap, *Knowing Their Place: Domestic Service in Twentieth Century Britain* (Oxford, 2011).

46. Honnor Morten, *Questions for Women (and Men)* (London, 1899), 92. The original settlers included Miss Rose Petty, the London School Board's first appointed nurse. See E.M.E., "Women's Settlements," *Hearth and Home* (September 14, 1899): 436. Morten told an interviewer, "My tendencies are Socialistic, because, perhaps, I have worked and lived so much in the East end and know Whitechapel down to its boots—when it has any." "Interview, Miss Honnor Morten," *The Women's Penny Paper*, November 29, 1890, 82–83. Morten had trained as a nurse under Eva Luckes in London Hospital, joined the School Board for London and established a settlement in workmen's flats (Bleyton Buildings) in Hoxton in the late 1890s. In 1905, she founded her settlement in Rotherfield, called the Tolstoi Settlement, on funds generated by sales of the English

translation of Tolstoi's *Resurrection*. See "Miss Honnor Morten," *Votes For Women*, July 18, 1913, 621. On Morten, see Ellen Ross, *Slum Travelers: Ladies and London Poverty, 1860–1920* (Berkeley, 2007), 161–63.

47. Elizabeth Sloan Chesser, M.D., "Practical Philanthropy and the Simple Life," *The Quiver* (June 1910): 771–72.

48. This capsule summary of daily life activities is based on the first two annual reports for 1915 and 1916.

49. On Craven, see Enid Huws Jones, *Margery Fry: The Essential Amateur* (London 1966), 135.

50. See "The Club," *Third Year's Report* (London, 1917): 3–4; "Kingsley Hall Club," *Fourth Year's Report* (London, 1918): 3–4; B. G. Platten, "The Evening Club," *Sixth Year's Report* (London, 1921): 11.

51. Jack Rollason, "The Adult School," *Adventures in Fellowship, Being the Eighth Annual Report of Kingsley Hall* (London, 1923), 17. In 1931, Jack's wife Martha famously asked a shy but pleased Gandhi to dance at one of Kingsley Hall's Joy Nights. See Rajmohan Gandhi, *The Good Boatman: A Portrait of Gandhi* (New Delhi, 1995), 115.

52. While nondenominational and nonsectarian, the Adult School movement was, according to Charles Booth, an outgrowth of Quakerism. See Charles Booth, "Interview with Mr. G.H. Wilding, Secretary of the Old Ford Adult School," May 29, 1897, B178, pp. 89–99, Booth Papers, BLPES.

53. See A.W.R., "Mutual Help Home Mission," *The Illustrated Missionary News*, October 1, 1895, on the Old Ford Adult School not far from Bromley-by-Bow.

54. In *It Occurred to Me*, Muriel noted that she saw no reason why she should not expand her work to men. In her letter to the female residents of Number 60, she pointed out their tendency to pout and backstab and identified it with the fact that they were a group of women living together. See Muriel Lester to "Dear Comrades of Number Sixty," n.d., internal evidence suggests 1923, Lester/2/2, Lester Papers, Bishopsgate.

55. Bruce Road Men's Adult School, Minutes, June 21, 1914, Minute Book, Lester/1/1/3, Lester Papers, Bishopsgate.

56. There is a substantial and contentious literature exploring "community" and "neighborhood" and the relationship between the two as historical, sociological, imagined, and discursive constructs. Gillian Rose briefly surveys these debates and applies them to the "community" and "neighborhood" of Kingsley Hall, though she does not mention Kingsley Hall. See Gillian Rose, "Imagining Poplar in the 1920s: Contested Concepts of Community," *Journal of Historical Geography* 16 (October 1990): 425–37.

57. Bruce Road Men's Adult School, Minute Book, June 1914, Lester/1/1/3, Lester Papers, Bishopsgate.

58. Muriel developed her arguments for women's rights to full religious citizenship as preachers and leaders in *Why Forbid Us?* (London, 1930), published by the Society for the Ministry of Women.

59. "Kingsley Hall, Bow," *East London Observer*, February 13, 1915.

60. The literature on women's suffrage is vast, but several outstanding guides to its intricacies include Laura Mayhall, *The Militant Suffrage Movement: Citizenship and Resistance in Britain, 1860–1930* (Oxford, 2003); Sandra Holton, *Feminism and Democracy: Women's Suffrage and Reform Politics in Britain, 1900–1918* (Cambridge, 1986); Andrew Rosen, *Rise Up, Women! The Militant Campaign of the Women's Social and Po-*

litical Union 1903–1914, (New York, 1974). The literature on women in wartime Britain is also extensive and rich in chronicling both well-to-do and working-class women's work. See Angela Woollacott, *On Her Their Lives Depend: Munitions Workers in the Great War* (Berkeley, 1994); Deborah Thom, *Nice Girls and Rude Girls: Women Workers and the First World War* (London, 1998); see also Gail Braybon and Penny Summerfield, eds., *Out of the Cage: Women's Experiences in Two World Wars* (London, 1987).

61. On this election and the legal struggles that ultimately kept Cobden from actually serving on the Council, see Jonathan Schneer, "Politics and Feminism in 'Outcast London': George Lansbury and Jane Cobden's Campaign for the First London County Council," *Journal of British Studies* 30:1 (January 1991): 63–82.

62. Kingsley Hall's Second Year's Report for 1916 listed Julia Scurr's husband, John Scurr, as a contributor. See Muriel Lester and Doris Lester, *Kingsley Hall, Bow, London. Second Year's Report*, (n.d., 1917), 28.

63. In the 1920s, Muriel worked closely with both of them as members of the Poplar Borough Council. Scurr even placed the brick of Labour at the foundation stone ceremony of Kingsley Hall's Children House in 1921.

64. See Patricia Romero, *E. Sylvia Pankhurst: Portrait of a Radical* (New Haven, 1987), chap. 10.

65. For a report on this meeting, see "Mr. Asquith Receives a Delegation," *Life and Labour: A Monthly Magazine* 4 (1914): 255. For a detailed account, see E. Sylvia Pankhurst, *The Suffragette Movement, An Intimate Account of Persons and Ideals* (London, 1931), 572–77.

66. Gilbert Bartholomew, the managing director of giant matchmaker Bryant and May, led the Conservative opposition. This opposition, called the Municipal Alliance, had already campaigned for several years against Lansbury's costly efforts to "humanize" poor relief. It remained eager to defeat him in 1912. See George Lansbury, *My Life* (London, 1928), 168.

67. Sylvia Pankhurst attributed the ferocity and imprudence of Lansbury's official stance to her sister Christabel's influence over him. See E. Sylvia Pankhurst, *The Suffragette Movement, An Intimate Account of Persons and Ideals* (London, 1931), 421.

68. The literature on relations between Liberals and Labour in the early twentieth century is vast, but reliable starting points include Michael Freeden, *The New Liberalism: An Ideology of Social Reform* (Oxford, 1978); see also Paul Thompson, *Socialists, Liberals and Labour: The Struggle for London 1885–1914* (London, 1967); and Susan Pennybacker, *A Vision for London 1889–1914: Labour, Everday Life and the LCC Experiment* (London, 1995).

69. On these tensions between local feminist and Labour organizers during Lansbury's by-election in Bow, see John Shepherd, *George Lansbury: At the Heart of Old Labour* (Oxford, 2002), chap. 7; see also George Dangerfield, *The Strange Death of Liberal England*, (New York, 1935), 187–88.

70. See "Notes of the Week," *The New Age, A Weekly Review of Politics, Literature, and Art* (December 5, 1912): 97.

71. *Daily Telegraph*, November 22, 1912, as quoted in John Shepherd, *George Lansbury: At the Heart of Old Labour* (Oxford, 2002), 124. For an extensive analysis of Lansbury's relationship to feminism, see Jonathan Schneer, *George Lansbury* (Manchester, 1990), chap. 2.

72. See *Votes for Women*, February 7, 1913, 273 as quoted by Brian Harrison, "Emmeline Pethick-Lawrence," *Oxford Dictionary of National Biography*, on-line, accessed June 20, 2013. This was a position that an earlier breakaway group from the WSPU had already adopted.

73. Such a break seemed inconceivable to the Pethick-Lawrences given their quasi-parental role with Christabel. For a detailed account of the split between the Pethick-Lawrences and the Pankhursts, see June Purvis, *Emmeline Pankhurst: A Biography* (London, 2002), chap. 14. Their disagreement over the character of militancy was apparent, Purvis shows, from their first meeting in July upon their release from jail.

74. See *Punch*, October 30, 1912, 349.

75. *It Occurred to Me* offers only vague generalities about how Muriel and members of her Women's Meeting on Bruce Road—to which Nellie was so devoted—came to see the necessity of women's suffrage as they confronted "women's" issues around food, housing, and education. 30.

76. On their marriage, see Brian Harrison, "The politics of a marriage: Emmeline and Fred Pethick-Lawrence,'" in *Prudent Revolutionaries: Portraits of British Feminists between the Wars* (Oxford, 1987), 242–72.

77. See Israel Zangwill, "The Militant Suffragists," in *The War for the World* (Baltimore, 1915, 1921), 305. Jacqueline DeVries's work has called particular attention to the links between feminism, suffrage, and religion. See "Transforming the Pulpit: Preaching and Prophesying in the British Women's Suffrage Movement," in Beverly Kienzle and Pamela Walker, eds., *Women Preachers and Prophets in Christian Traditions* (Berkeley, 1998); and "'Challenging Traditions': Denominational Feminism in Britain, 1900–1920" in Billie Melman, ed., *Borderlines: Gender Identities in Peace and War*, (London, 1998).

78. Emmeline Pethick-Lawrence, "What the Vote Means to Those Who are Fighting the Battles," *Votes for Women* (January 1908): 49 as quoted in Kabi Hartman, "'What Made me a Suffragette': The New Woman and the New (?) Conversion Narrative," *Women's History Review* 12:1 (2003): 35.

79. Emmeline Pethick-Lawrence, "Vote for Women," *The Speaker* (May 5, 1906): 119. See Madeline Doty, *Behind the Battle Line, Around the World in 1918* (New York, 1918), 187.

80. The Women's Freedom League broke with the Pankhursts over their disdain for democratic decision making in 1907. They used techniques such as tax resistance, championed by Nonconformists only a few years earlier. See Claire Eustance, "Meanings of Militancy: The Ideas and Practice of Political Resistance in the Women's Freedom League, 1907–14," in Maroula Joannou and June Purvis, eds., *The Women's Suffrage Movement: New Feminist Perspectives* (Manchester, 1998), chap. 3. On the Women's Freedom League's ideas about gender and power, see Carol McPhee and Ann Fitzgerald, eds., *The Non-Violent Militant: Selected Writings of Teresa Billington-Greig* (London, 1987).

81. See Krista Cowman, "'A Party Between Revolution and Peaceful Persuasion': A Fresh Look at the United Suffragists," in Maroula Joannou and June Purvis, eds., *The Women's Suffrage Movement: New Feminist Perspectives* (Manchester, 1998), chap. 5.

82. Laura Mayhall usefully analyzes these tensions as competing ethical strategies and shows the rich diversity of perspectives within the militant suffrage movement. On resistance versus service paradigms and programs during World War I, see Laura E.

Nym Mayhall, *The Militant Suffrage Movement: Citizenship and Resistance in Britain, 1860–1930* (Oxford, 2003), chaps. 6–7.

83. Christabel Pankhurst linked pacifism, pro-Germanism, and the radical shop stewards movement in 1917. See Christabel Pankhurst, "Shop Stewards," *Britannia* (December 7, 1917) as quoted in Angela K. Smith, *Suffrage Discourse in Britain during the First World War* (Aldershot, 2005), 30. On feminists' "misgivings" and confusion about the war in the context of transatlantic alliances, see Lucy Delap, *The Feminist Avant-Garde: Transatlantic Encounters of the Early Twentieth Century* (Cambridge, 2007), chap. 8.

84. The London Society, almost from the moment Britain entered the war, redefined itself as a women's service organization in support of the war effort. It served as a clearinghouse to match women's interests and skills with the needs of the war economy. Its provision of day nurseries and canteens for women workers probably first attracted Muriel's attention. See Leaflet, "Women's Service," S and P, 1.2/27, Women at Work Collection, Imperial War Museum; accessed via *Women, War and Society, 1914–1918*, Gage Cengage. For a summary of NUWSS war work, see Mrs. Henry Fawcett, *War Work of the National Union* (Birmingham, 1916). On the NUWSS's Women's Patriotic Service Fund, see "A Practical Scheme to Help Professional Women," *Westminster Gazette*, January 9, 1915.

85. On the impact of feminist politics on gender and social policy in World War I Britain, see Susan Pedersen, *Family, Dependence, and the Origins of the Welfare State: Britain and France, 1914–1945* (Cambridge, 1993), chap. 2.

86. This paragraph relies on Julia Bush's vivid account of the impact of World War I on the daily lives and political attitudes of East Londoners. See Julia Bush, *Behind the Lines: East London Labour 1914–1919* (London, 1984), chap. 2.

87. See *The Suffrage Annual and Women's Who's Who* (London, 1913).

88. See Barbara Caine, *From Bombay to Bloomsbury: A Biography of the Strachey Family* (Oxford, 2005), chap. 11. In 1911, Pippa Strachey asked Mrs. Fawcett to "loan" her two or three "pit brow girls'" for a suffrage "At Home." Presumably, Strachey had invited them as curiosities for lady guests to enjoy, not as sisters in the struggle for political and social justice for women. See Jo Vellacott's excellent and detailed account of this internal wrangling in *Pacifists, Patriots and the Vote: The Erosion of Democratic Suffragism in Britain During the First World War* (Basingstoke, 2007), 13.

89. See Jo Vellacott, *From Liberal to Labour with Women's Suffrage: The Story of Catherine Marshall* (Montreal, 1993) on Marshall's political and intellectual development up to World War I. Marshall, like Muriel, was a graduate of St. Leonard's and later served as chair of Kingsley Hall's Trustees.

90. On the backdrop to and proceedings of the conference, see Lela Costin, "Feminism, Pacifism, Internationalism and the 1915 International Congress of Women," *Women's Studies International Forum* 5 (1982): 301–15.

91. Jo Vellacott, *From Liberal to Labour with Women's Suffrage*, 92, 86.

92. Had she known that the Society was unwilling to assume responsibility for the accounts, she informed Strachey, she would have sought out the services of Sir William Plender, one of Edwardian Britain's most respected accounting wizards and husband of Nellie's longtime friend, Lady Plender. See Muriel Lester to Miss Strachey, January 9, 1915, Kingsley Hall, East End Working Women's Factory Club, 2LSW/E/06/01, London

Society for Women's Suffrage Wartime Correspondence, Women's Library (now transferred to BLPES), hereafter referred to as Kingsley Hall Factory Women's Club, Women's Library. The entire correspondence is in a single folder.

93. Unsigned letter to Muriel Lester, January 7, 1915, Kingsley Hall Factory Women's Club, Women's Library.

94. Muriel Lester to Miss Strachey, December 31, 1914, Kingsley Hall Factory Women's Club, Women's Library.

95. This is presumably the draft of Winifred Foulkes's letter to Muriel Lester, no date (early January 1915), Kingsley Hall Factory Women's Club, Women's Library.

96. Muriel Lester to Miss Strachey, January 24, 1915, Kingsley Hall Factory Women's Club, Women's Library.

97. A glowing account of the cost-price restaurant and club appeared in the August 21, 1915 number of the *East London Observer*. It made no mention of the Lester sisters and noted that the club was run under the auspices of the London Society at Kingsley Hall. May Hughes donated the bulk of the funds to run it.

98. Kingsley Hall, *Report for Second Year* (London, 1916).

99. See *Woman's Dreadnought,* August 12, 1916, 530. Muriel sponsored an essay prize through the pages of *Woman's Dreadnought* on the topic, "Who Suffers Most by the War?" The winner, E. L. Osmund, argued that mothers suffer the most. See *Woman's Dreadnought,* September 2, 1916, 539 and October 28, 1916. By the early 1930s, a Canadian visitor felt that Muriel had abandoned democratic principles to protect her religious commitments from "Communists." See Mildred Osterhout, "In Which the Heroine Arrives in Bow," University of British Columbia *Graduate Chronicle* (May 1932): 19–21.

100. Susan Pedersen, *Eleanor Rathbone and the Politics of Conscience* (London, 2004), 116.

101. See Muriel Lester, manuscript autobiographical notes about Kingsley Hall's founding, Lester 2/1, Lester Papers, Bishopsgate.

102. The indispensable guide to the history of pacifism and its entwining with religion remains Martin Ceadel's *Pacifism in Britain 1914–1945: The Defining of a Faith* (Oxford, 1980). See also Ceadel's *Thinking about Peace and War* (Oxford, 1987) and *Semi-Detached Idealists: The British Peace Movement and International Relations, 1854–1945* (Oxford, 2000).

103. Muriel Lester, *It Occurred to Me,* 52.

104. Muriel Lester, *Kill or Cure* (Nashville, 1937), 34.

105. John Kenworthy and the Brotherhood Church in Croydon (discussed in chapter 3) founded the Brotherhood Publishing Company to publish work that aimed to "fully and directly apply the principles of The Sermon on the Mount to individual and social life." See Leo Tolstoy, *The Four Gospels Harmonised and Translated* (London, 1896), 377.

106. In his autobiography, Ruskin claimed that he knew by heart the Sermon on the Mount. *Praeterita,* vol. 1 (New York, 1894), 222. See John Ruskin, *Modern Painters,* vol. 3, pt. 4, pars. 33–34 in E. T. Cook and Wedderburn, eds., *Collected Works of John Ruskin,* vol. 5 (London, 1903–12), 378–79.

107. G. K. Chesterton, *Twelves Types* (London, 1902), 152; Muriel Lester, *Kill or Cure,* 43.

108. See Charles Gore, *The Sermon on the Mount: A Practical Exposition* (London, 1896; reprinted in 1904), 26. Gore had sketched some of his ideas in "The Social Doctrine of the Sermon on the Mount," *Economic Review* 2 (April 1892): 145–60.

109. Charles William Stubbs, *Christ and Economics in the Light of the Sermon on the Mount* (London, 1894), 71.

110. Ibid., p .64.

111. See Minutes, October 11–12, 1915, Education Subcommittee, Fellowship of Reconciliation, Coll. Misc. 456, FOR 5/4, Fellowship of Reconciliation (England), Papers, BLPES; see also Council Minutes, October 11–12, 1915, Coll.Misc 456, FOR 1/2, hereafter cited as FOR Papers, BLPES.

112. See Minutes of General Committee, November 12 and 13, 1917, Coll Misc. 456, FOR 1/2, FOR Papers, BLPES. From 1920 to 1924, Muriel chaired the London Fellowship of Reconciliation. See April 15, 1924, Minutes of General Committee, The London Union of the Fellowship of Reconciliation, "Report of Annual Meeting." In April 1917, Kingsley Hall hosted the FoR's study school. See Minutes of General Committee, April 16–17, 1917, CollMisc. 456, FOR 1/2, FOR Papers, BLPES.

113. For meeting held at Kingsley Hall, see October 16, 1922, Minutes of General Committee, London Union, Coll. Misc.456, FOR 1/2, FOR Papers, BLPES.

114. Vera Brittain, *The Rebel Passion: A Short History of Some Pioneer Peacemakers* (London, 1964)

115. By 1917, it had approximately 7,000 members nationwide.

116. Jill Wallis recounts this story in *Valiant for Peace: A History of the Fellowship of Reconciliation, 1914–1989 (London, 1991)*, 3–4. See Herbert George Wood, *Henry T. Hodgkin, A Memoir* (London, 1937), 145–46; see also Vera Brittain, *The Rebel Passion: A Short History of Some Pioneer Peace-makers* (London, 1964), 30. From its first meetings, the FoR cemented alliances with Indian and Chinese students in London. Hodgkin spent many years in China under the Friends Foreign Mission Association, so this was a logical connection for the group. See Record of Second Committee Meeting, January 21, 1915, Coll. Misc.456, FOR 1/1, FOR Papers, BLPES.

117. This is taken from printed pamphlet glued into the opening pages of the first FOR Minute Book. Coll. Misc.456, FOR/1/1, BLPES.

118. *First Annual Report of the Fellowship of Reconciliation* (London, 1916), 4.

119. For concise and excellent critical summaries of these arguments, see Wolfgang Mommsen, *Theories of Imperialism* (New York, 1980).

120. Henry T. Hodgkin, *The Christian Revolution* (Shanghai, 1922), 23, 67–68.

121. See chapter 4.

122. Muriel Lester, *My Host the Hindu* (London, 1931), 120.

123. Muriel Lester, typescript Indian circular, letters, Letter 8, c.1926, Lester 2/7, Lester Papers, Bishopsgate.

124. Henry Hodgkin, *Lay Religion* (New York, 1919), 138–40; and Hodgkin, *The Christian Revolution*, 10.

125. See Richard Roberts, "How the Fellowship Began," *The Friend* 9:1 (January 1943): 5. On Roberts, see Bert den Boggende, "Richard Roberts' Vision and the Founding of the Fellowship of Reconciliation," *Albion* (Winter 2004): 608–35. Roberts focused less on the Sermon on the Mount than on the atonement and 2 Corinthians 5:17–19 with Christ's "reconciling the world unto Himself" and with God.

126. See Minute Book for the General Committee, January 21–22, 1918, Coll. Misc. 456, FOR 1/1, BLPES.

127. Record of Seventh Committee Meeting, March 11, 1915 Coll. Misc. 456, FOR 1/1, BLPES.

128. Stanley James, *The Adventures of a Spiritual Tramp* (London, 1925), 108.

129. Hodgkin, *The Lay Religion*, 153, 160.

130. See Martin Ceadel, *Pacifism in Britain 1914–1945: The Defining of a Faith* (Oxford, 1980). See also, Thomas C. Kennedy, *The Hound of Conscience: The History of the No-Conscription Fellowship, 1914–1919* (Arkansas, 1981)

131. Stanley James, *The Adventures of a Spiritual Tramp* (London, 1925); he published prolifically under a variety of "radical" pen names including Piers Plowman and the Tramp.

132. See Martin Ceadel, *Pacifism in Britain 1914–1945*, 50.

133. Wilfred Wellock, *Off the Beaten Track: Adventures in the Art of Living* (Tanjore, India, 1961), 60–61. Muriel later introduced Wellock to Gandhi during his stay at Kingsley Hall in 1931. On Wellock's life based on his published writings, see Andrew Rigby, *A Life in Peace: A Biography of Wilfrid [sic] Wellock* (Bridport, Dorset, 1988). Rigby lists Muriel Lester as among the eight members of the informal "Crusader" group on p. 25.

134. Wilfred Wellock: "The Next Phase: World Citizenship," *The New Crusader*, December 12, 1919, 8.

135. Wilson joined the FOR's General Committee on February 17, 1915. Stanley James, who edited the Crusader for Wilson and worked closely with Muriel, admired Wilson's "high spirits, big-heartedness and sheer anarchism." See Stanley James, *The Adventures of a Spiritual Tramp* (London, 1925), 114.

136. She signed Kingsley Hall's Visitors' Book on February 25, 1917. See Visitors Book, Kingsley Hall, Lester/1/1/4, Lester Papers, Bishopsgate. Wilson, author of numerous children's books, also financed and edited an offshoot pacifist journal for boys and girls called *The Venturer*. The first number appeared in April 1917 as a supplement to the *New Crusader*.

137. See Roger Smalley, "Theodora Wilson Wilson, Westmoreland's Forgotten Rebel," *CeNtre WoRdS*, Centre for Northwest Regional Studies 9 (2010): 30–40.

138. See "The Shareholders' Statement," *The New Crusader*, November 7, 1919, 8. There were precedents for Wilson's campaigns. From the mid-1880s onwards, Mrs. G. S. Reaney owned shares in the London Bus and Tramway Companies and used semi-annual meetings to plead for fair wages and hours of labor. She described her tactics as "peaceful agitation." See Mrs. [Isabel] G. S. Reaney, "Slave Driving by Public Companies," *Contemporary Review* (November 1889): 649–658

139. Wilfred Wellock, "The Only Way," *The New Crusader*, August 5, 1916, 2–3.

140. Maude Royden, *The Great Adventure—The Way to Peace* (London, 1915) as reprinted in *Messenger of Peace* (June 1923), 90. Bertrand Russell famously rejected absolutist pacifism and the complete disavowal of the threat of force as a hindrance to achieving revolution. Some hint of his position was already evident in one of his early responses to the Russian Revolution in which he said he "hoped" revolution could be achieved with passive resistance alone. See Bertrand Russell, "A Pacifist Revolution?" *The Tribunal*, July 19, 1917, 2.

141. Wilfred Wellock, *Off the Beaten Track, Adventures in the Art of Living* (Tanjore, India, 1961), 22.

142. See *The New Crusader*, April 19, 1917, 3.

143. See The Council of Workers and Soldiers Delegates, *What Happened at Leeds* (London, 1917).

144. Rev. William Orchard debated this point with Hodgkin on March 23, 1915. See Coll. Misc. 456, FOR 1/1, BLPES.

145. Following Martin Ceadel's nomenclature, "pacifists" referred only to absolutists who rejected all forms of war and violence. "Pacificists" comprised a much more general and looser group of opponents to war, some of whom accepted violence as an unavoidable part of conflict resolution. Lenin's views were not well known in Britain. His critique of imperialism as the highest stage of capitalism was not translated into French and German until 1920, though published in Russian in 1916. On May 15, 1920, Sylvia Pankhurst published Lenin's banned "Appeal to the Toiling Masses" (first issued in English in 1918) in the *Workers' Dreadnought*. Pankhurst's publications regularly translated into English polemical tracts by Bolsheviks.

146. "Coup D´État in Petrograd," *The London Times*, November 9, 1917, 7.

147. FoR members began to grasp the incompatibility of Bolshevism with their own views between February and April 1918. See "International Notes," *The Venturer* (February 1915): 121. In March 1918 the *Venturer* commented "The Bolsheviks are visionaries who believe in the majesty of ideals; but woe betide the men or the people who come between them and the realization of the things they desire!" The writer disapproved of the Bolsheviks' use of violence and coercion in Finland, Ukraine, and the Constituent Assembly in Petrograd. See "International Notes," *The Venturer* 3:6 (March 1918): 150.

148. This was not only a product of their naïveté but also the skillful work of the Bolsheviks' chief propagandist in Britain in 1917–1919, Maxim Litvinov. The radical son of Russian Jewish bankers, Litvinov married the daughter of a wealthy and prominent Anglo-Jewish family, Ivy Lowe, during one of his many long exiles from pre–Revolutionary Russia. He skillfully presented the Bolsheviks in a way calculated to appeal to British socialists and Labour leaders by stressing the "astonishingly mild" use of force by Bolsheviks. See Maxim Litvinoff, *The Bolshevik Revolution: Its Rise and Meaning* (London, 1919), 32.

149. See Minutes of Social Service Committee, Fellowship of Reconciliation, December 13, 1915, and January 17, 1916, Coll Misc. 456, FOR 5/7, BLPES.

150. Walke first joined the FoR some time in 1917 according to his autobiography. See Bernard Walke, *Twenty Years at St. Hilary* (London, 1935), 110.

151. For example, see "Nativity Play in Cornwall," *Western Morning News*, December 24, 1929, 3. On the controversies that led to violence against the church, see "Choir Voices Drowned," *Western Morning News*, November 28, 1932, 3.

152. See Bernard Walke, *Twenty Years at St. Hilary* (London, 1935), 147.

153. Bernard Walke to Rosa Waugh Hobhouse, n.d. (c.1918); see also "The Brethren of the Common Table," four-page printed manifesto (n.d.), outlining principles and directions for forming chapters Box 1, Rosa Waugh Hobhouse Papers, Hadspen, Somerset.

154. See James Hinton, *Protests & Visions: Peace Politics in 20th Century Britain* (London, 1989), chap. 5.

155. On the riot and press coverage of it, see "Another Riot at the Brotherhood Church," *The Tribunal*, October 11, 1917, 3.

156. A year after leaving Kingsley Hall, Rosa herself was briefly jailed under the terms of DORA for distributing pacifist literature in the English countryside and hindering recruitment efforts.

157. See "Revolution and Non-Resistance, an Appeal for an Unarmed Revolution," supplement to the *Tribunal*, July 19, 1917. These statements were the result of a joint meeting of the Friends' Service Committee, the No-Conscription Fellowship and the Fellowship of Reconciliation from July 14–16, 1917.

158. See Clifford Allen, "Our Point of View," *The Tribunal*, March 8, 1916, 1. Allen here was referring specifically to how Tribunals treated conscientious objectors who came before them seeking exemption from military service.

159. Muriel Lester, "The Salt of the Earth," *Adventures in Fellowship, Being the Eight Annual Report of Kingsley Hall* (London, 1923), 16.

160. For a brilliant and vivid account of such divided families, including the Despards and the Hobhouses, see Adam Hochschild, *To End All Wars: A Story of Loyalty and Rebellion, 1914–1918* (Boston, 2011). See also Charlotte Despard to Muriel Lester, n.d. [March 1918?], Lester/2/3/4, Lester Papers, Bishopsgate. Despard consoled Muriel about her "hard times" in Bow and sent her best wishes for Kingsley Hall.

161. I cannot identify the precise date that Caroline moved to Bruce Road. Voting records indicate that she lived at 64 Bruce Road immediately after the war.

162. Nellie Dowell to Muriel Lester, February 14, 1912, Nellie Dowell Letters, Bishopsgate.

163. Nellie Dowell to Muriel Lester, n.d. (c.1916), Nellie Dowell Letters, Bishopsgate.

164. I have reconstructed William Joseph Dellar's movements using census data and voting registration, and army enlistment records. Apparently, Dellar's skills were sufficiently important that he was able to leave Forest Gate workhouse and enlist in the army himself in April 1915. After the war, he was reunited with Nellie's sister Florence. They lived not far from Bruce Road on Donald Road.

165. Lester, *Kill or Cure*, 25–26.

166. Age seems to have been a flexible concept for many laboring people. His birth certificate indicates that he was born in April 1898. However, for purposes of enrolling him in the infants' room at Marner Street School in October 1901, his parents Florence and William told school officials that he had been born in September 1897. See Admissions Log Book, Marner Street School, London Metropolitan Archives; Birth and census data all accessed via Ancestry.com.

167. Electoral registers indicate that he lived at 60 Bruce Road well into the 1930s.

168. See Anna Braithwaite Thomas, *St. Stephens House: Friends Emergency Work in England 1914–1920* (London, 1920).

169. "The Anti-German Riots," *First Year's Report*, Kingsley Hall, Bow (London, n.d.), 22.

170. The press described East Londoners' violence as "fierce reprisals" and "righteous anger" against "German atrocities." See "The German Atrocities," *East End News*, May 14, 1915.

171. "The Air Raid in Norfolk," *The London Times*, January 21, 1915, as quoted in

Susan Grayzel, *At Home and Under Fire: Air Raids and Culture in Britain from the Great War to the Blitz* (Cambridge, 2012), 26.

172. "Take Up the Sword of Justice," Sir Bernard Partridge, 1861–1945, Harrow: David Allen & Sons, Ltd., June 1915, 39 3/4 x 24 1/2, Parliamentary Recruiting Committee, London, Reference: Hardie & Sabin, 2. Library of Congress.

173. Nicoletta Gullace argues "in Britain during the great War notions of fictive kinship, based on an imagined community of blood ties and racial stock, began to undercut the living bonds of neighbourliness, familial affection. . . . In this process a liberal notion of inclusion, based on law and individual rights, came under pressure from more popular and emotive concepts of belonging." See "Friends, Aliens and Enemies: Fictive Communities and the Lusitania Riots of 1915," *Journal of Social History* 39 (Winter 2005): 345–46. On anti-German rioting in relation to xenophobia, racism, and anti-immigrant attitudes, see Panikos Panayi, "Anti-German Riots in London during the First World War," *German History* 7:2 (April 1989): 184–203, and his edited volume *Germans in Britain since 1500* (London, 1996), chap. 7. My formulation of the local as a way of knowing is indebted to Shannon Jackson's *Lines of Activity: Performance, Historiography, Hull-House Domesticity* (Ann Arbor, MI, 2000).

174. Sylvia Pankhurst, "Let Us Not Be Cowards," *Woman's Dreadnought*, May 15, 1915, 246.

175. Lester, *It Occurred to Me*, 68.

176. "The Salt of the Earth," 17. Somewhat surprisingly, Sylvia Pankhurst claimed that Doris Lester, not Muriel, was hurt during the Lusitania Riots. I suspect that she mixed up the two sisters since no other evidence places Doris in Bow during the riots. See Pankhurst, *Home Front* (London, 1932), 171.

177. Here, I follow Ann Stoler on the relationship between affective and political registers. See Ann Laura Stoler, *Carnal Knowledge and Imperial Power* (Los Angeles, 2002).

178. A Club Member.-N[ellie].D[owell]."Stolen Goods" *Second Year's Report* (London, 1917), 24–26. In "The Salt of the Earth," Muriel explicitly alludes to Nellie's part in recovering the "stolen goods."

179. Captain Arthur St. John to Muriel Lester, January 2, 1916, printed in *First Year's Report*, Kingsley Hall (London, 1916), 44.

180. Muriel Florie Archer remained a lifelong friend of Muriel's and supporter of Kingsley Hall. Daughter of a Baptist minister in Yorkshire, Archer was born in 1897, thus a very young woman at the time of the Lusitania riots.

181. Nellie Dowell to Muriel Lester, n.d. (1916–7), Nellie Dowell Letters, Bishopsgate.

182. See Gabrielle Bell, "The Raid," *Second Year's Report* (London, 1917), 12.

183. Nellie Dowell to Muriel Lester, n.d. [1916], Nellie Dowell Letters, Bishopsgate. In this letter, Nellie explains how she teaches "true fellowship" even to those she does not like. Leela Gandhi eloquently theorizes such "small gestures" as "countercultural revolutionary practices for which I claim the name 'politics of friendship.'" See Leela Gandhi, *Affective Communities: Anticolonial Thought, Fin-de-Siècle Radicalism, and the Politics of Friendship* (Durham, NC, 2006), 9.

184. A Club Member.-N[ellie].D[owell]."Stolen Goods" *Second Year's Report* (London, 1917), 25.

185. Ibid., 26.

186. See Keith Robbins, *The Abolition of War: The "Peace Movement" in Britain, 1914–1919* (Cardiff, 1976), chap. 7. Robbins offers a balanced assessment of those who abhorred Lansdowne's letter as well as his supporters. See also Lord Newton, *Lord Lansdowne, A Biography* (London, 1929), chap. 20.

187. Lord Lansdowne, *Daily Telegraph*, November 29, 1916 as quoted in Newton, *Lord Lansdowne*, 467.

188. *Mr. Punch's History of the Great War* (London, 1919), 192.

189. Vera Brittain, *Rebel Passion*, 42.

190. Frank Hancock, *Reconciliation, A Monthly Review of the Things of Peace* (January 1962): 9–10

191. Maude Royden, "Bid Me Discourse," chapter 8, 7/AMR, Box 224, Agnes Maude Royden Papers, Women's Library (transferred to BLPES).

192. Muriel Lester, Typescript History of Kingsley Hall, "~~Remembered Moments on Receipt of a Radiogram~~," Lester/2/3, pp. 11–12, Lester Papers, Bishopsgate. There is a later corrected single-spaced typescript version of this early history as well in the same file.

193. Sylvia Pankhurst, April 21, 1917, *Woman's Dreadnought* as quoted in Julia Bush, *Behind the Lines* (London, 1984), 73.

194. See Stephen Hobhouse, *The Autobiography of Stephen Hobhouse: Reformer, Pacifist, Christian* (Boston, 1952), 165.

195. Muriel Lester, "An East-End Problem. 'Ought One to Speak the Truth?'" *Christian World* (August 22, 1918).

196. Muriel Lester to "Dear Comrades of Number Sixty," n.d., internal evidence suggests 1923, Lester/2/2, Lester Papers, Bishopsgate.

197. Nellie Dowell to Muriel Lester, n.d. (c.1916), Nellie Dowell Letters, Bishopsgate. Internal evidence suggests it was written in the last months of 1915, after Nellie's nephew Willie Dellar, who lived with her and Muriel at 60 Bruce Road, enlisted in the army in July 1915.

198. The phrase "prickly barriers" comes from Muriel Lester's speech at the opening of Kingsley Hall. "Report of the Kingsley Hall Opening," Lester/2/2, Lester Papers, Bishopsgate.

199. See Muriel Lester, typescript notes on Kingsley Hall, Lester/2/1, Lester Papers, Bishopsgate.

200. Arthur Ransome published his firsthand account of events in Russia including the Third International of March 1919 in June 1919 under the title, *Six Weeks in Russia* (London, 1919). On the shop stewards, see James Hinton's *The First Shop Stewards' Movement* (London, 1973).

201. See Muriel Lester, "An Indictment," *The New Crusader*, January 23, 1920, 11. The original letter appeared in Kingsley Hall's periodical *The Gleam*.

202. For a grim description of the economic and social mood in Britain in spring 1921, see "SCENE SETTING: LONDON 1921," *Pearson's Magazine* 46 (May 1921): 403–4.

203. On the British public's starkly divided responses to the Amritsar massacre, see Derek Sayer, "British Reaction to the Amritsar Massacre, 1919–1920," *Past and Present* 131 (1991): 130–64. On the "dirty war" against Irish nationalists, see Peter Hart, *The I.R.A. and Its Enemies: Violence and Community in Cork, 1916–1923* (Oxford, 1998).

204. Lester, *It Occurred to Me*, 82.

205. See Linda Mahood, *Feminism and Voluntary Action: Eglantyne Jebb and Save the Children, 1876–1928* (London, 2009); Clare Mulley, *The Woman Who Saved the Children: A Biography of Eglantyne Jebb, Founder of Save the Children* (Oxford, 2009).

206. On Marie, see Doris Lester, Typescript autobiography, "Our First Refugee," Lester/3/1, Lester Papers, Bishopsgate.

207. See Andrew Rigby, *A Life in Peace: A Biography of Wilfrid [sic] Wellock* (Bridport, Dorset, 1988), 49–51.

208. Jon Lawrence, "Forging a Peaceable Kingdom: War, Violence, and Fear of Brutalization in Post–First World War Britain," *Journal of Modern History* 75 (September 2003): 558. See also Adrian Gregory, "Peculiarities of the English? War, Violence and Politics: 1900–1939," *Journal of Modern European History* 1:1 (March 2003): 44–59.

209. See "Voluntary Poverty, East End Invitation to the Wealthy West," *Daily News*, March 15, 1921, reprinted in Muriel Lester, *Entertaining Gandhi* (London, 1932), 195–197; see also "Invitation to Life of Poverty. East End Call to the Wealthy West," *Star* (March 15, 1921); "Disciples of St. Francis, A Voluntary Poverty Movement," *Christian World*, March 24, 1921, and "Brethren of the Common Table. People Without Possessions and No Desire for Riches," *Evening Standard*, April 2, 1921.

210. "Brethren of the Common Table. People Without Possessions and No Desire for Riches," *Evening Standard*, April 2, 1921.

211. Ibid.

212. See Hayden Church, "Millionaires and Paupers Join in Self Denial," *Deseret News* [Salt Lake City, Utah], July 2, 1921, sec. 3, 1.

213. See Rosa Waugh Hobhouse, *Interplay of Life and Art* (unpublished typescript autobiography, 1958–59), 138, 173, Library of the Society of Friends. Rosa had worked out the core concepts of voluntary poverty in 1914 in responses to George Lansbury's campaign to teach workers to "hate their poverty" through articles in the *Daily Mail* in July 1914. See Rosa Waugh Hobhouse, "One Standard of Values," typescript, 1914, Rosa Waugh Hobhouse Papers, RWH, Box 1, Hadspen.

214. See Muriel Lester, *It Occurred to Me*, 88.

215. This story of May Hughes' attempts to find ethical ways to dispose of her wealth while micromanaging the behavior of its recipients is detailed in the May Hughes Papers, in private hands, Longcot. My thanks to Robert Baker for granting me access to these papers.

216. See Tierl Thompson, ed., *Dear Girl: The Diaries and Letters of Two Working Women 1897–1917* (London, 1987), 272, 304–5.

217. "Brethren of the Common Table. People Without Possessions and No Desire for Riches," *Evening Standard*, April 2, 1921.

218. "HOW TO SPEND £400 A YEAR. Novel Suggestions at Women's Meeting. REJECTED LEGACY," *Daily Chronicle*, October 18, 1927. Lester's use of her legacy invites comparison with Virginia Woolf's much more famous—and self-centered—imagining of how best to use a legacy of £500 p.a. in *A Room of One's Own* (1928). For a sensitive reading of Woolf set against a range of feminist aspirations in the 1920s, see Sally Alexander, "Room of One's Own: 1920s Feminist Utopias," *Women: A Cultural Review* 11:3 (2000): 273–288.

219. On Tawney's moral and spiritual politics at this time, see Lawrence Goldman, *The Life of R. H Tawney: Socialism and History* (London, 2013), chaps. 6 and 7.

220. On the role of "home helps" in reducing maternal and infant mortality in early

twentieth-century London, see Lara Marks, *Metropolitan Maternity* (Amsterdam, 1996). This choice reflected Muriel's priorities as chair of Poplar Borough Council's Maternity and Child Welfare Committee.

221. "Refused £400 a year legacy and now scrubs floors." *Daily Chronicle*, September 13, 1928.

222. Miscarriages of colonial justice such as the brutal assaults on Black Jamaicans during the so-called Morant Bay Mutiny in October 1865 prompted early attempts to use Restitution Funds as tools of humanitarian relief for victims. See Edinburgh Ladies' Emancipation Society, *Annual Report* (1867), as reprinted in Esther Breitenbach, Linda Fleming, S. Karly Kehoe, and Lesley Orr, eds., *Scottish Women: A Documentary History, 1780–1914* (Edinburgh, 2013), 316. See also "Restitution," *The Freed-Man*, November 1, 1866, 45–47.

223. Alma Whitaker, "Poverty is Your Salvation," *Los Angeles Times*, March 3, 1935, J7.

224. James Warnack, "The Greatest of These," *Los Angeles Times*, April 19, 1936, A4.

225. Muriel Lester, "The Salt of the Earth," 16.

226. Nellie Dowell letters, n.d., Bishopsgate Institute.

227. Muriel wrote this phrase next to the date of Nellie's death beneath the title of her homage to her. See "The Salt of the Earth," 14.

228. See admission entry, January 18, 1923, Dowell, Ellen, discharged, January 26, 1923, Creed Register, St. Andrews Hospital, Bow, SA/M/4/29. Royal London Hospital Archives.

229. See Richard Roberts, "The Task of the Church," *The Venturer*, (November 1916): 35.

230. For a contemporary definition of this genre, see Thomas Frederick Crane, *The Exempla or Illustrative Stories from the Sermones Vulgares of Jacques de Vitry* (London, 1890), xvii-xxi.

231. Virginia Woolf, "Mr. Bennett and Mrs. Brown," in Leonard Woolf, ed., *Collected Essays*, vol. 1 (London, 1966), 334, 320. George Dangerfield, like Woolf, emphasizes the pre–World War I demise of Victorian values enacted through politically motivated violence in his brilliant, much criticized but still influential 1935 study, *The Strange Death of Liberal England*.

232. Susan Kent argues that this culture of violence led Britons to seek solace in "an English version of what might be called a fascistic sensibility" (193) that paradoxically limited the appeal of formal membership in fascist organizations. She cites George Lansbury's 1931 critique of the National government as "the essence of Fascism." See Kent, *Aftershocks, Politics and Trauma in Britain, 1918–1931* (Basingstoke, 2009), 192–93. On shifting postwar narratives about the war as rupture, see Janet Watson, *Fighting Different Wars: Experience, Memory and the First World War in Britain* (Cambridge, 2004). See Robert Graves and Alan Hodge, *The Long Week-End, A Social History of Great Britain 1918–1939* (London, 1940).

233. While using very different materials and stressing radical rather than conservative cultural-political strands, my approach resembles Alison Light's to interwar Britain as a period of particularly intense dialectical tensions between "old and new . . . between holding on and letting go, conserving and moving on." Light does preserve the concept of the "modern" as necessarily a "revolt against Victorianism." See Alison Light, *Forever England: Femininity, Literature and Conservatism Between the Wars* (London 1991), 11, 19, and chap. 1.

234. This chapter adds to the growing body of scholarship that highlights "the resilience of pre–war social structures and attitudes" and their adaption to war and postwar; see Gerard J. DeGroot, *Blighty: British Society in an Era of Great War* (London, 1996).

235. See Muriel Lester to "Dear Comrades of Number Sixty," n.d., internal evidence suggests 1923, Lester/2/2, Lester Papers, Bishopsgate.

Afterlives

1. Muriel wrote two popular books about her time in India and Gandhi's visit to London. See Muriel Lester, *My Host the Hindu* (London, 1931) and *Entertaining Gandhi* (London, 1932). See also Muriel Lester, *Gandhi: World Citizen* (Allahabad, 1945); *Gandhi's Signature* (New York, 1949); and "Gandhiji, 1926–1949," in C. Shukla, ed., *Incidents of Gandhiji's Life* (Bombay, 1949).

2. Krishna Dutta and Andrew Robinson, eds., *Selected Letters of Rabindranath Tagore* (Cambridge, 1997), 440.

3. Voysey, son of the eminent Arts and Crafts architect, had previously designed Children's House for the Lesters, which opened in 1923, as a combined Montessori-inspired school and residence for workers. It too had a flat roof, used extensively as a playground and sleeping space for the children.

4. For descriptions of the building, see "Kingsley Hall, Bow, Designed by C. Cowles Voysey," *The Architects' Journal* (July 16, 1930): 79; and Muriel Lester, *It Occurred to Me* (London, 1937), 152.

5. See Rosa Hobhouse, *Mary Hughes: Her Life for the Dispossessed* (London, 1949), 62.

6. Lord Knebworth apparently stood in for his father, Lord Lytton, the Viceroy of India with whom Muriel had met before leaving India in late-December 1926. See draft letter, Muriel Lester to Lord Lytton, December 31, 1926, Lester/2/7, Lester Papers, Bishopsgate.

7. "The New Kingsley Hall. Opened By Lord Knebworth. Beautiful Home of Social Work," *East London Advertiser*, September 22, 1928.

8. Ida Dellar lived with Willie at 58 Bruce Road and was Treasurer of the Kingsley Hall Club in the 1930s and headed the Young People's Fellowship. I don't know what her relationship to Willie was since he later married Isabelle Dellar. For Ida Dellar's work at Kingsley Hall, See Minutes for April 12, 1932 and July 12, 1932, Kingsley Hall Sunday Evening Fellowship, Lester/1/1/5, Lester Papers, Bishopsgate.

9. Lester, *It Occurred to Me*, 107.

10. See "Mr. Chaplin Meets Mr. Gandhi," *Daily Telegraph*, September 23, 1931; and "Mr. Chaplin and Mr. Gandhi," *Daily Mail*, September 23, 1931.

11. Lester, *It Occurred to Me*, 75.

12. On maternalist politics, see Seth Koven and Sonya Michel, "Womanly Duties: Maternalist Politics and the Origins of Welfare States in Britain, France, Germany and the United States," *American Historical Review* 95:4 (October 1990): 1076–1108. See also Seth Koven, "Borderlands: Women, Voluntary Action, and Child Welfare in Britain," in Seth Koven and Sonya Michel, eds., *Mothers of a New World: Maternalist Politics and the Origins of Welfare States* (New York, 1993).

13. For Lester's version of events, see *It Occurred to Me*, 98–100. See also Poplar

Borough Council Minutes, Report of Maternity and Child Welfare Committee, January 22, 1923, Tower Hamlets Local History Library.

14. Lester, *It Occurred to Me*, 155.

15. "Open House," *Kingsley Hall, Annual Report* (London, 1930), 4.

16. Lester, *It Occurred to Me*, 155.

17. Grace Neary, interview by Louise Joly, 2009, Oral History Project, Kingsley Hall, audio recording in author's possession.

18. Transcripts and tapes from the Oral History Project associated with the National Heritage Lottery Grant, Kingsley Hall, and the Legacy of Muriel Lester. Louise Joly interviewing Sylvia Parrott Bishopp (born 1925) on April 2, 2009 in Mayfield Road, Sanderstead, Croyden.

19. Edgar Lansbury, *Poplarism: The Truth about the Poplar Scale of Relief and the Action of the Ministry of Health* (London, 1924), 1.

20. The Parrotts' involvement with Kingsley Hall seems to confirm Edwin Pugh's observation in 1913: "There are socialistic Countesses, but never a flower-girl, that is not an individualist." Pugh as quoted in Gareth Stedman Jones, "The 'Cockney' and the 'Nation,' 1780–1988," in David Feldman and Gareth Stedman Jones, eds., *Metropolis, London: Histories and Representations since 1800* (London, 1989), 304.

21. She chronicled this work in *It So Happened* (New York, 1947).

22. Lester and the household members asked themselves, "Are our ideals wrong after all?" but remained optimistic even as they "stare[d] at our own failure." See Lester, *It Occurred to Me*, 149–56.

23. My interpretation is indebted to Isaiah Berlin's critique of the utopian pursuit of perfection and the impossibility—and undesirability—of producing a single set of rules to resolve moral conflicts. See his "On the Pursuit of the Ideal," *New York Review of Books* 35:4 (March 17, 1988).

24. Muriel Lester to Dear Child [Doris Lester], n.d., "Saturday 8 pm [1934]," Lester/2/7, Lester Papers, Bishopsgate.

25. Doris Lester, unpublished typescript and manuscript autobiography, Lester/3/1, Lester Papers, Bishopsgate.

26. Muriel Lester to Darlingest Precious [Doris Lester], no date, 1934, Lester/2/7, Lester Papers, Bishopsgate.

27. Muriel Lester to Alan and Elizabeth Hunter, March 4, 1934, Lester/2/7, Lester Papers, Bishopsgate.

28. Muriel Lester to Darlingest Precious (Doris Lester), n.d. [1934], Lester/2/7, Lester Papers, Bishopsgate.

29. Doris Lester, "The Pattern Changes," Typescript and manuscript autobiography, Lester/3/1, Lester Papers, Bishopsgate.

30. See Tara Booth, "Heritage Lottery Fund Grant of £49,900 Aids Muriel Lester Legacy," *Culture24*, (September 26, 2008), accessed on September 26, 2013.

31. On the history of blue plaques in London, see *Blue Plaques on Houses of Historical Interest* (reprint of *Commemorative Tablets*, London, 1960), Forward by the Countess of Dartmouth. For the administrative rules governing blue plaques as well as extant nomination forms and correspondence controlled by the Historic Buildings Board, see "Commemorative Plaques, The Twenty Year Rule," Report, July 8, 1974, GLC/DG/PT1/H/2/113, London Metropolitan Archives.

32. Lyn Olley, "Cash Squeeze Hampers Plans for Flats and Centre," *Essex and East London Newspapers*, January 30, 1978.

33. Muriel Lester to Victor Gollancz, June 9, 1963, MSS 151/3/P/ME/2, Gollancz Papers, Modern Records Centre, University of Warwick.

34. Electoral registers for Bromley North-East Ward for 1933 indicate that Alice Whipps lived at Kingsley Hall with Muriel and seven other residents. Her father was a general laborer. Alice appeared regularly in the early 1930s in the Minutes of the mixed-sex Fellowship that emerged out of the Bruce Road Men's Adult School.

35. Muriel Lester, "Our Al," Lester/5/1, Lester Papers, Bishopsgate.

36. Alice Whipps to Victor Gollancz, November 10, 1963, MSS 151/3/P/ME/2, Gollancz Papers, Modern Record Office, Warwick.

37. "Notebook with advice to her executors, January 29, 1968," p. 102, Lester/1/2/12, Lester Papers, Bishopsgate.

38. See Gertrude Himmelfarb's eloquent and influential analysis of these so-called virtuous Victorian understandings of charity and philanthropic action and their withering in the twentieth century in *Poverty and Compassion: The moral imagination of the late Victorians* (New York, 1991) and *The Demoralization of Society: From Victorian Virtues to Modern Values* (New York, 1995). On Lester's partnership with Gandhi, see Thomas Weber, *Going Native: Gandhi's Relationship with Western Women* (New Delhi, 2011).

Index